# Colorado Revised Statutes

## TITLE 18

## CRIMINAL CODE

**Table of Contents**

**ARTICLE 1**

Provisions Applicable to Offenses Generally

PART 1

PURPOSE AND SCOPE OF CODE - CLASSIFICATION OF OFFENSES

**18-1-101. Citation of title 18.** (1) This title shall be known and may be cited as the "Colorado Criminal Code"; within this title, the "Colorado Criminal Code" is sometimes referred to as "this code".

The portion of any section, subsection, paragraph, or subparagraph contained in this code which precedes a list of examples, requirements, conditions, or other items may be referred to and cited as the "introductory portion" of the section, subsection, paragraph, or subparagraph.

**18-1-102. Purpose of code, statutory construction.** (1) This code shall be construed in such manner as to promote maximum fulfillment of its general purposes, namely:

To define offenses, to define adequately the act and mental state which constitute each offense, to place limitations upon the condemnation of conduct as criminal when it is without fault, and to give fair warning to all persons concerning the nature of the conduct prohibited and the penalties authorized upon conviction;

To forbid the commission of offenses and to prevent their occurrence through the deterrent influence of the sentences authorized; to provide for the rehabilitation of those convicted and their punishment when required in the interests of public protection;

To differentiate on reasonable grounds between serious and minor offenses, and prescribe penalties which are proportionate to the seriousness of offenses and which permit recognition of differences in rehabilitation possibilities as between individual offenders;

To prevent arbitrary or oppressive treatment of persons accused or convicted of offenses

and to identify certain minimum standards for criminal justice which, within the concept of due process of law, have the stature of substantive rights of persons accused of crime;

To promote acceptance of responsibility and accountability by offenders and to provide restoration and healing for victims and the community while attempting to reduce recidivism and the costs to society by the use of restorative justice practices.

**18-1-102.5. Purposes of code with respect to sentencing.** (1) The purposes of this code with respect to sentencing are:

To punish a convicted offender by assuring the imposition of a sentence he deserves in relation to the seriousness of his offense;

To assure the fair and consistent treatment of all convicted offenders by eliminating unjustified disparity in sentences, providing fair warning of the nature of the sentence to be imposed, and establishing fair procedures for the imposition of sentences;

To prevent crime and promote respect for the law by providing an effective deterrent to others likely to commit similar offenses;

To promote rehabilitation by encouraging correctional programs that elicit the voluntary cooperation and participation of convicted offenders;

To select a sentence, a sentence length, and a level of supervision that addresses the offender's individual characteristics and reduces the potential that the offender will engage in criminal conduct after completing his or her sentence; and

To promote acceptance of responsibility and accountability by offenders and to provide restoration and healing for victims and the community while attempting to reduce recidivism and the costs to society by the use of restorative justice practices.

**18-1-103. Scope and application of code.** (1) Except as otherwise expressly provided by sections 18-1.3-402 and 18-1.3-504, or unless the context otherwise requires, the provisions of this code govern the construction of and punishment for any offense defined in any statute of this state, whether in this title or elsewhere, and which is committed on or after July 1, 1972, as well as the construction and application of any defense to a prosecution for such an offense.

Except as otherwise provided by section 18-1-410, the provisions of this code do not apply to or govern the construction of, prosecution for, and punishment for any offense committed prior to July 1, 1972, or the construction and application of any defense to a prosecution for such an offense. Such an offense shall be tried and disposed of according to the provisions of law existing at the time of the commission thereof in the same manner as if this code had not been enacted. All pending actions shall proceed to final disposition in the same manner as if this code had not been enacted.

The provisions of this code do not bar, suspend, or otherwise affect any right or liability to damages, penalty, forfeiture, or other remedy authorized by law to be recovered or enforced in a civil action for any conduct which this code makes punishable; and the civil injury is not merged in the offense.

**18-1-104. "Offense" defined - offenses classified - common-law crimes abolished.** (1) The terms "offense" and "crime" are synonymous and mean a violation of, or conduct defined by, any state statute for which a fine or imprisonment may be imposed.

Each offense falls into one of eleven classes, one of six drug offense levels, or one unclassified category. There are six classes of felonies as described in section 18-1.3-401 and four levels of drug felonies as described in section 18-1.3-401.5, three classes of misdemeanors as described in section 18-1.3-501 and two levels of drug misdemeanors as described in section 18-1.3- 501, two classes of petty offenses as described in section 18-1.3-503, and the category of drug petty offense as described in section 18-1.3-501 (1) (e).

Common-law crimes are abolished and no conduct shall constitute an offense unless it is described as an offense in this code or in another statute of this state, but this provision does not affect the power of a court to punish for contempt, or to employ any sanction authorized by law for the enforcement of an order lawfully entered, or a civil judgment or decree; nor does it affect the use of case law as an interpretive aid in the construction of the provisions of this code.

**18-1-105. Felonies classified - presumptive penalties.** (Repealed)

**18-1-106. Misdemeanors classified - penalties.** (Repealed)

18-1-107. Petty offenses classified - penalties. (Repealed)

18-1-108. Offenses not classified. (Repealed)

18-1-109. Penalty not fixed by statute - punishment. (Repealed)

18-1-110. Payment and collection of fines for class 1, 2, or 3 misdemeanors and class 1 or 2 petty offenses - release from incarceration. (Repealed)

## PART 2 JURISDICTION AND PLACE OF TRIAL

18-1-201. State jurisdiction. (1) A person is subject to prosecution in this state for an offense which he commits, by his own conduct or that of another for which he is legally accountable, if:

The conduct constitutes an offense and is committed either wholly or partly within the state; or

The conduct outside the state constitutes an attempt, as defined by this code, to commit an offense within the state; or

The conduct outside the state constitutes a conspiracy to commit an offense within the state, and an act in furtherance of the conspiracy occurs in the state; or

The conduct within the state constitutes an attempt, solicitation, or conspiracy to commit in another jurisdiction an offense prohibited under the laws of this state and such other jurisdiction.

An offense is committed partly within this state if conduct occurs in this state which is an element of an offense or if the result of conduct in this state is such an element. In homicide, the "result" is either the physical contact which causes death or the death itself; and if the body of a criminal homicide victim is found within the state, the death is presumed to have occurred within the state.

Whether an offender is in or outside of the state is immaterial to the commission of an offense based on an omission to perform a duty imposed by the law of this state.

18-1-202. Place of trial. (1) Except as otherwise provided by law, criminal actions shall be tried in the county where the offense was committed, or in any other county where an act in furtherance of the offense occurred.

If a person committing an offense upon the person of another is in one county and his victim is in another county at the time of the commission of an act constituting an element of the offense, the offense is committed and trial may be had in either of said counties.

In a case involving the death of a person, the offense is committed and the offender may be tried in any county in which the cause of death is inflicted, or in which death occurs, or in which the body of the deceased or any part of such body is found.

Theft of property is committed and the offender may be tried in any county in which he exercised control over the property.

If the commission of an offense commenced outside the state is consummated within this state, the offense is committed and the offender shall be tried in the county where the offense is consummated.

If an offense is committed in or upon any automobile, trailer, railroad car, aircraft, or other vehicle of transportation passing within or over this state, the offense is deemed to have been committed and the offender may be tried in any county through or over which the vehicle of transportation passed.

(a) When multiple crimes are based upon the same act or series of acts arising from the same criminal episode and are committed in several counties, the offender may be tried in any county in which any one of the individual crimes could have been tried, regardless of whether or not the counties are in the same judicial district.

(I) For purposes of this subsection (7), when a person commits one of the offenses listed in subparagraph (II) of this paragraph (b) on two or more occasions within a six-month period, it may be considered part of the same criminal episode. Nothing in this subsection (7) shall bar prosecution of an offense that could have been joined in another prosecution.

(II) The provisions of subparagraph (I) of this paragraph (b) shall apply to the following offenses:

Theft, as defined in section 18-4-401;

and (C) Repealed.

Criminal mischief, as defined in section 18-4-501;

Fraud by check, as defined in section 18-5-205;

Defrauding a secured creditor or debtor, as defined in section 18-5-206;

Failure to pay over assigned accounts, as defined in section 18-5-502;

Concealment or removal of secured property, as defined in section 18-5-504;

Failure to pay over proceeds, as defined in section 18-5-505;

Unauthorized use of a financial transaction device, as defined in section 18-5-702;

Computer crime, as defined in section 18-5.5-102;

Procuring food or accommodation with intent to defraud, as defined in section 12-44-102, C.R.S.;

Trafficking in food stamps, as defined in section 26-2-306, C.R.S.;

Unlawful use of a patient personal needs trust fund, as defined in section 25.5-6-206, C.R.S.;

Criminal tampering with a motor vehicle, as defined in section 42-5-103, C.R.S.;

Theft of motor vehicle parts, as defined in section 42-5-104, C.R.S.;

Theft in connection with assistive technology, as described in section 6-1-409, C.R.S.;

Theft of farm products, as defined in section 12-16-118, C.R.S.;

Fraud in connection with obtaining public assistance, as described in section 26-1-127,

Fraud in connection with obtaining food stamps, as described in section 26-2-305,

An offense described in part 1 of article 5 of this title;

Forgery, as defined in sections 18-5-102 and 18-5-104; and

Identity theft, as defined in section 18-5-902.

(I) For an indictment or information that includes an offense described in article 5 of this title, the offender may be tried in a county where the offense occurred, in a county where an act in furtherance of the offense occurred, or in a county where a bank, savings and loan, credit union, or government agency processed a document or transaction related to the offense.

(II) For the purpose of this section, "processed" means to physically handle a document or to make a written or electronic entry in a permanent or temporary record of the transaction, whether the entry is made manually or through automated means.

An inchoate offense is committed and the offender may be tried in any county in which any act which is an element of the offense, including formation of the agreement in conspiracy, is committed.

When a person in one county solicits, abets, agrees, aids, or attempts to aid another in the planning or commission of an offense in another county, the offense is committed and the offender may be tried for the offense in either county, or in any other county in which the principal offense could be tried.

When an offense is committed on the boundary line between two counties, or so close thereto as to be difficult to readily ascertain in which county the offense occurred, the offense is committed and the offender may be tried for the offense in either county.

Proof of the county in which the offense occurred or which county is the proper place for trial pursuant to this section shall not constitute an element of any offense and need not be proven by the prosecution at trial unless required by the statute defining the offense. Any challenge to the place of trial pursuant to this section shall be made by motion in writing no later than twenty-one days after arraignment, except for good cause shown. The court shall determine any such issue prior to the commencement of the trial and the selection of a jury. If the court finds that trial is not proper in the county in which the charges were filed, the court shall transfer the case to a court of appropriate jurisdiction in the proper county. Failure to challenge the place of trial as provided in this subsection (11) shall constitute a waiver of any objection to the place of trial. Pursuant to section 16- 12-102 (2), C.R.S., the prosecution may file an interlocutory appeal of a decision transferring the case to another county.

If a person commits the offense of failure to register as a sex offender as provided in section 18-3-412.5, the offense is committed and the offender may be tried in the county in which the offender was released from incarceration for commission of the offense requiring registration, in the county in which the offender resides, in the county in which the offender completed his or her last registration, or in the county in which the offender is apprehended.

If a person commits identity theft as described in section 18-5-902, identity theft is committed and the offender may be tried in any county where a prohibited act was committed, in any county where an act in furtherance of the offense was committed, or in any county where the victim resides during all or part of the offense. For purposes of this subsection (13), a business entity resides in any county in which it maintains a physical location.

PART 3

WHEN PROSECUTION BARRED BY FORMER PROCEEDINGS

18-1-301. Second trial barred by former prosecution for same offense. (1) If a prosecution is for a violation of the same provision of law and is based upon the same facts as a former prosecution, it is barred by the former prosecution under the following circumstances:

The former prosecution resulted in an acquittal. There is an acquittal if the prosecution resulted in a finding of not guilty by the trier of fact or in a determination that there was insufficient evidence to warrant a conviction. A finding of guilty of a lesser included offense is an acquittal of the greater inclusive offense even though the conviction is subsequently set aside.

The former prosecution was terminated by a final order or judgment for the defendant that has not been set aside, reversed, or vacated, and that necessarily required a determination inconsistent with a fact or a legal proposition that must be established for conviction of the offense.

The former prosecution resulted in a conviction. There is a conviction if the prosecution resulted in a judgment of conviction that has not been reversed or vacated, a verdict of guilty that has not been set aside and that is capable of supporting a judgment, or a plea of guilty accepted by the court. In the latter two instances, failure to enter judgment must be for a reason other than a motion of the defendant.

The former prosecution was improperly terminated. Except as otherwise provided in subsection (2) of this section, there is an improper termination of a prosecution if the termination is for reasons not amounting to an acquittal, and it takes place after the jury is sworn if the case is tried by a jury or after the first prosecution witness is sworn if trial is by court following waiver of jury trial.

Termination is not improper under any of the following circumstances:

The defendant consents to the termination or waives his right to object to the termination. The defendant is deemed to have waived all objections to a termination of the trial unless his objections to the order of termination are made of record at the time of the entry thereof.

The trial court finds that:

The termination is necessary because it is physically impossible to proceed with the trial in conformity with the law; or

There is a legal defect in the proceedings that would make any judgment entered upon a verdict reversible as a matter of law; or

Prejudicial conduct has occurred in or outside the courtroom making it unjust either to the defendant or to the state to proceed with the trial; or

The jury is unable to agree upon a verdict; or

False statements of a juror on voir dire prevent a fair trial.

18-1-302. Second trial barred by former prosecution for different offense. (1) Although a prosecution is for a violation of a different provision of law than a former prosecution or is based on different facts, it is barred by the former prosecution under the following circumstances:

The former prosecution resulted in an acquittal or a conviction as defined in section 18-1- 301 (1) (a) and (1) (c) and the subsequent prosecution is for:

Any offense of which the defendant could have been convicted under the allegation of the complaint, information, or indictment of the first

4

prosecution; or

The same conduct, unless the offense of which the defendant was formerly convicted or acquitted and the offense for which he is subsequently prosecuted each requires proof of a fact not required by the other and the law defining each of the offenses is intended to prevent a substantially different harm or evil or the second offense was not consummated when the former trial began.

The former prosecution was terminated by an acquittal or by a final order or judgment for the defendant that has not been set aside, reversed, or vacated and that necessarily required a determination inconsistent with a fact that must be established for conviction of the second offense.

The former prosecution was improperly terminated, as improper termination is defined in section 18-1-301 (1) (d) and (2), and the subsequent prosecution is for an offense of which the defendant could have been convicted had the former prosecution not been improperly terminated.

18-1-303. Second trial barred by prosecution in another jurisdiction. (1) If conduct constitutes an offense within the concurrent jurisdiction of this state and of the United States, or

another state, or of a municipality, a prosecution in any other of these jurisdictions is a bar to a subsequent prosecution in this state under either of the following circumstances:

The first prosecution resulted in a conviction or an acquittal as defined in section 18-1- 301 (1) (a) and (1) (c), and the subsequent prosecution is based on the same conduct, unless:

The offense for which the defendant was formerly convicted or acquitted requires proof of a fact not required by the offense for which he is subsequently prosecuted and the law defining each of the offenses is intended to prevent a substantially different harm or evil; or

The second offense was not consummated when the former trial began.

The former prosecution was terminated by an acquittal or by a final order or judgment for the defendant that has not been set aside, reversed, or vacated and that necessarily required a determination inconsistent with a fact that must be established for conviction of the offense for which the defendant is subsequently prosecuted.

18-1-304. Former prosecution not a bar. (1) A former prosecution is not a bar within the meaning of sections 18-1-301 to 18-1-303, if the former prosecution:

Was before a court that lacked jurisdiction over the defendant or the offense; or

Was procured by the defendant without the knowledge of the appropriate prosecuting official and with the intent to avoid the sentence that otherwise might be imposed; or

Resulted in a judgment of conviction that was set aside, reversed, or vacated upon appeal or in any other subsequent judicial proceeding.

PART 4

RIGHTS OF DEFENDANT

18-1-401. Purpose. It is the intent of this part 4 to confer upon every person accused of an offense the benefits arising from said part 4 as a matter of substantive right, in implementation of minimum standards of criminal justice within the concept of due process of law.

18-1-402. Presumption of innocence. Every person is presumed innocent until proved guilty. No person shall be convicted of any offense unless his guilt thereof is proved beyond a reasonable doubt.

18-1-403. Legal assistance and supporting services. All indigent persons who are charged with or held for the commission of a crime are entitled to legal representation and supporting services at state expense, to the extent and in the manner provided for in articles 1 and 2 of title 21, C.R.S.

18-1-404. Preliminary hearing or waiver - dispositional hearing. (1) Every person accused of a class 1, 2, or 3 felony or level 1 or level 2 drug felony by direct information or felony complaint has the right to demand and receive a preliminary hearing within a reasonable time to determine whether probable cause exists to believe that the offense charged in the information has been committed by the defendant. In addition, only those persons accused of a class 4, 5, or 6 felony by direct information or felony complaint which felony requires mandatory sentencing or is a crime of violence as defined in section 18-1.3-406, or is a sexual offense under part 4 of article 3 of this title, shall have the right to demand and receive a preliminary hearing within a reasonable time to determine whether probable cause exists to believe that the offense charged in the information or felony complaint was committed by the defendant. The procedure to be followed in asserting the right to a preliminary hearing, and the time within which demand therefor must be made, as well as the time within which the hearing, if demanded, shall be had, shall be as provided by rule of the supreme court of the state of Colorado. A failure to observe and substantially comply with such rule is a waiver of the right to a preliminary hearing.

(2) (a) No person accused of a class 4, 5, or 6 felony or level 3 or level 4 drug felony by direct information or felony complaint, except those which require mandatory sentencing or which are crimes of violence as defined in section 18-1.3-406, or which are sexual offenses under part 4 of article 3 of this title, shall have the right to demand or receive a preliminary hearing; except that such person shall participate in a dispositional hearing for the purposes of case evaluation and potential resolution.

(b) Any defendant accused of a class 4, 5, or 6 felony or level 3 or level 4 drug felony who is not otherwise entitled to a preliminary hearing pursuant to paragraph (a) of this subsection (2), may demand and shall receive a preliminary hearing within a reasonable time pursuant to subsection of this section, if the defendant is in custody; except that, upon motion of either party, the court shall vacate the preliminary hearing if there is a reasonable showing that the defendant has been released from custody prior to the preliminary hearing.

18-1-405. Speedy trial. (1) Except as otherwise provided in this section, if a defendant is not brought to trial on the issues raised by the complaint, information, or indictment within six months from the date of the entry of a plea of not guilty, he shall be discharged from custody if he has not been admitted to bail, and, whether in custody or on bail, the pending charges shall be dismissed, and the defendant shall not again be indicted, informed against, or committed for the same offense, or for another offense based upon the same act or series of acts arising out of the same criminal episode. If trial results in conviction which is reversed on appeal, any new trial must be commenced within six months after the date of the receipt by the trial court of the mandate from the appellate court.

If a trial date has been fixed by the court, and thereafter the defendant requests and is granted a continuance for trial, the period within which the trial shall be had is extended for an additional six-month period from the date upon which the continuance was granted.

(3.5) If a trial date has been fixed by the court and the defendant fails to make an appearance in person on the trial date, the period within which the trial shall be had is extended for an additional

six-month period from the date of the defendant's next appearance.

If a trial date has been fixed by the court, and thereafter the prosecuting attorney requests and is granted a continuance, the time is not thereby extended within which the trial shall be had, as is provided in subsection (1) of this section, unless the defendant in person or by his counsel in open court of record expressly agrees to the continuance or unless the defendant without making an appearance before the court in person or by his counsel files a dated written waiver of his rights to a speedy trial pursuant to this section and files an agreement to the continuance signed by the defendant. The time for trial, in the event of such agreement, is then extended by the number of days intervening between the granting of such continuance and the date to which trial is continued.

To be entitled to a dismissal under subsection (1) of this section, the defendant must move for dismissal prior to the commencement of his trial and prior to any pretrial motions which are set for hearing immediately before the trial or prior to the entry of a plea of guilty to the charge or an included offense. Failure to so move is a waiver of the defendant's rights under this section. (5.1) If a trial date is offered by the court to a defendant who is represented by counsel and neither the defendant nor his counsel expressly objects to the offered date as being beyond the time within which such trial shall be had pursuant to this section, then the period within which the trial shall be had is extended until such trial date and may be extended further pursuant to any other

applicable provisions of this section.

In computing the time within which a defendant shall be brought to trial as provided in subsection (1) of this section, the following periods of time shall be excluded:

Any period during which the defendant is incompetent to stand trial, or is unable to appear by reason of illness or physical disability, or is under observation or examination at any time after the issue of the defendant's mental condition, insanity, incompetency, or impaired mental condition is raised;

The period of delay caused by an interlocutory appeal whether commenced by the defendant or by the prosecution;

A reasonable period of delay when the defendant is joined for trial with a codefendant as to whom the time for trial has not run and there is good cause for not granting a severance;

The period of delay resulting from the voluntary absence or unavailability of the defendant; however, a defendant shall be considered unavailable whenever his whereabouts are known but his presence for trial cannot be obtained, or he resists being returned to the state for trial;

The period of delay caused by any mistrial, not to exceed three months for each mistrial;

The period of any delay caused at the instance of the defendant;

The period of delay not exceeding six months resulting from a continuance granted at the request of the prosecuting attorney, without the consent of the defendant, if:

The continuance is granted because of the unavailability of evidence material to the state's case, when the prosecuting attorney has exercised due diligence to obtain such evidence and there are reasonable grounds to believe that this evidence will be available at the later date; or

The continuance is granted to allow the prosecuting attorney additional time in felony cases to prepare the state's case and additional time is justified because of exceptional circumstances of the case and the court enters specific findings with respect to the justification;

The period of delay between the new date set for trial following the expiration of the time periods excluded by paragraphs (a), (b), (c), (d), and (f) of this subsection (6), not to exceed three

months;

The period of delay between the filing of a motion pursuant to section 18-1-202 (11) and any decision by the court regarding such motion, and if such decision by the court transfers the case to another county, the period of delay until the first appearance of all the parties in a court of appropriate jurisdiction in the county to which the case has been transferred, and in such event the provisions of subsection (7) of this section shall apply.

If a trial date has been fixed by the court and the case is subsequently transferred to a court in another county, the period within which trial must be had is extended for an additional three months from the date of the first appearance of all of the parties in a court of appropriate jurisdiction in the county to which the case has been transferred.

18-1-406. Right to jury trial. (1) Except as otherwise provided in subsection (7) of this section, every person accused of a felony has the right to be tried by a jury of twelve whose verdict shall be unanimous. In matters involving misdemeanors, the accused is entitled to be tried by a jury of six. In matters involving "petty offenses", the accused has the right to be tried by a jury under the terms and conditions of section 16-10-109, C.R.S.

Except as to class 1 felonies, the person accused of a felony or misdemeanor may waive a trial by jury by express written instrument filed of record or by announcement in open court appearing of record.

A defendant may not withdraw a voluntary and knowing waiver of trial by jury as a matter of right, but the court, in its discretion, may permit withdrawal of the waiver prior to the commencement of the trial.

Except as to class 1 felonies, the defendant in any felony or misdemeanor case may, with the approval of the court, elect, at any time before the swearing in of the jury, or after the swearing in of the jury and before verdict, with the agreement of the district attorney and the approval of the court, to be tried by a number of jurors less than the number to which he would otherwise be entitled.

Upon request of the defendant in advance of the commencement of the trial, the defendant shall be furnished with a list of prospective jurors who will be subject to call in the trial.

Either the district attorney or the defendant may challenge the array on the ground that there has been a material departure from the requirements of the law governing the selection of jurors, but such challenge shall be made in writing setting forth the particular grounds upon which it is based and shall be filed prior to the swearing in of the jury selected to try the case.

Except as to class 1 felonies, with respect to a twelve-person jury, if the court excuses a juror for just cause after the jury has retired to consider its verdict, the court in its discretion may allow the remaining eleven jurors to return the jury's verdict.

18-1-407. Affirmative defense. (1) "Affirmative defense" means that unless the state's evidence raises the issue involving the alleged defense, the defendant, to raise the issue, shall present some credible evidence on that issue.

If the issue involved in an affirmative defense is raised, then the guilt of the defendant must be established beyond a reasonable doubt as to that issue as well as all other elements of the

offense.

**18-1-408. Prosecution of multiple counts for same act.** (1) When any conduct of a defendant establishes the commission of more than one offense, the defendant may be prosecuted for each such offense. He may not be convicted of more than one offense if:

One offense is included in the other, as defined in subsection (5) of this section; or

One offense consists only of an attempt to commit the other; or

Inconsistent findings of fact are required to establish the commission of the offenses; or

The offenses differ only in that one is defined to prohibit a designated kind of conduct generally and the other to prohibit a specific instance of such conduct; or

The offense is defined as a continuing course of conduct and the defendant's course of conduct was uninterrupted, unless the law provides that specific periods or instances of such conduct constitute separate offenses.

If the several offenses are actually known to the district attorney at the time of commencing the prosecution and were committed within the district attorney's judicial district, all such offenses upon which the district attorney elects to proceed must be prosecuted by separate counts in a single prosecution if they are based on the same act or series of acts arising from the same criminal episode. Any offense not thus joined by separate count cannot thereafter be the basis of a subsequent prosecution; except that, if at the time jeopardy attaches with respect to the first prosecution against the defendant the defendant or counsel for the defendant actually knows of additional pending prosecutions that this subsection (2) requires the district attorney to charge and the defendant or counsel for the defendant fails to object to the prosecution's failure to join the charges, the defendant waives anyclaim pursuant to this subsection (2) that a subsequent prosecution is prohibited.

When two or more offenses are charged as required by subsection (2) of this section and they are supported by identical evidence, the court upon application of the defendant may require the state, at the conclusion of all the evidence, to elect the count upon which the issues shall be tried. If more than one guilty verdict is returned as to any defendant in a prosecution where multiple counts are tried as required by subsection (2) of this section, the sentences imposed shall run concurrently; except that, where multiple victims are involved, the court may, within its discretion, impose consecutive sentences.

When a defendant is charged with two or more offenses based on the same act or series of acts arising from the same criminal episode, the court, on application of either the defendant or the district attorney, may order any such charge to be tried separately, if it is satisfied that justice so requires.

A defendant may be convicted of an offense included in an offense charged in the indictment or the information. An offense is so included when:

It is established by proof of the same or less than all the facts required to establish the commission of the offense charged; or

It consists of an attempt or solicitation to commit the offense charged or to commit an offense otherwise included therein; or

It differs from the offense charged only in the respect that a less serious injury or risk of

injury to the same person, property, or public interest or a lesser kind of culpability suffices to establish its commission.

The court shall not be obligated to charge the jury with respect to an included offense unless there is a rational basis for a verdict acquitting the defendant of the offense charged and convicting him of the included offense.

If the same conduct is defined as criminal in different enactments or in different sections of this code, the offender may be prosecuted under any one or all of the sections or enactments subject to the limitations provided by this section. It is immaterial to the prosecution that one of the enactments or sections characterizes the crime as of lesser degree than another, or provides a lesser penalty than another, or was enacted by the general assembly at a later date than another unless the later section or enactment specifically repeals the earlier.

Without the consent of the prosecution, no jury shall be instructed to return a guilty verdict on a lesser offense if any juror remains convinced by the facts and law that the defendant is guilty of a greater offense submitted for the jury's consideration, the retrial of which would be barred by conviction of the lesser offense.

**18-1-409. Appellate review of sentence for a felony.** (1) When sentence is imposed upon any person following a conviction of any felony, other than a class 1 felony in which a death sentence is automatically reviewed pursuant to section 18-1.3-1201 (6), 18-1.3-1302 (6), or 18-1.4- 102 (6), the person convicted shall have the right to one appellate review of the propriety of the sentence, having regard to the nature of the offense, the character of the offender, and the public interest, and the manner in which the sentence was imposed, including the sufficiency and accuracy of the information on which it was based; except that, if the sentence is within a range agreed upon by the parties pursuant to a plea agreement, the defendant shall not have the right of appellate review of the propriety of the sentence. The procedures to be employed in the review shall be as provided by supreme court rule. No appellate court shall review any sentence which is imposed unless, within forty-nine days from the date of the imposition of sentence, a written notice is filed in the trial court to the effect that review of the sentence will be sought; said notice must state the grounds upon which it is based.

(2.1) and (2.2) Repealed.

The reviewing court shall have power to affirm the sentence under review, substitute for the sentence under review any penalty that was open to the sentencing court other than granting probation or other conditional release, or remand the case for any further proceedings that could have been conducted prior to the imposition of the sentence under review, and for resentencing on the basis of such further proceedings. No sentence in excess of the one originally imposed shall be given unless matters of aggravation in addition to those known to the court at the time of the original sentence are brought to the attention of the court during the hearing conducted under this section. If the court imposes a sentence in excess of the one first given, it shall specifically identify the additional aggravating facts considered by it in imposing the increased sentence.

**18-1-409.5. Appellate review of sentence not within the presumptive range. (Repealed)**

**18-1-410. Postconviction remedy.** (1) Notwithstanding the fact that no review of a conviction of crime was sought by appeal within the time prescribed therefor, or that a judgment of conviction was affirmed upon appeal, every person convicted of a crime is entitled as a matter of right to make applications for postconviction review. Except as otherwise required by subsection (1.5) of this section, an application for postconviction review must, in good faith, allege one or more of the following grounds to justify a hearing thereon:

That the conviction was obtained or sentence imposed in violation of the constitution or laws of the United States or the constitution or laws of this state;

That the applicant was convicted under a statute that is in violation of the constitution of the United States or the constitution of this state, or that the conduct for which the applicant was prosecuted is constitutionally protected;

That the court rendering judgment was without jurisdiction over the person of the applicant or the subject matter;

That the sentence imposed exceeded the maximum authorized by law, or is otherwise not in accordance with the sentence authorized by law;

That there exists evidence of material facts, not theretofore presented and heard, which, by the exercise of reasonable diligence, could not have been known to or learned of by the defendant or his attorney prior to the submission of the issues to the court or jury, and which requires vacation of the conviction or sentence in the interest of justice;

(I) That there has been significant change in the law, applied to the applicant's conviction or sentence, allowing in the interests of justice retroactive application of the changed legal standard.

(II) The ground set forth in this paragraph (f) may not be asserted if, prior to filing for relief pursuant to this paragraph (f), a person has not sought appeal of a conviction within the time prescribed therefor or if a judgment of conviction has been affirmed upon appeal.

Any grounds otherwise properly the basis for collateral attack upon a criminal judgment;

or

That the sentence imposed has been fully served or that there has been unlawful

revocation of parole, probation, or conditional release.

(1.5) An application for postconviction review in a class 1 felony case where a sentence of death has been imposed shall be limited to claims of newly discovered evidence and ineffective assistance of counsel; except that, for any sentence of death imposed on or after the date upon which the Colorado supreme court adopts rules implementing the unitary system of review established by part 2 of article 12 of title 16, C.R.S., any application for postconviction review in such case shall be governed by the provisions of part 2 of article 12 of title 16, C.R.S.

(a) Except as otherwise required by paragraph (b) of this subsection (2), procedures to be followed in implementation of the right to postconviction remedy shall be as prescribed by rule of the supreme court of the state of Colorado.

(b) In any class 1 felony case where a sentence of death has been imposed, the district court shall expeditiously consider an application for postconviction remedy. It is the general assembly's intent that the district court give priority to cases in which a sentence of death has been imposed.

(a) Except as otherwise provided in paragraph (b) of this subsection (3), an appeal of any order by the district court granting or denying postconviction relief in a case in which a sentence of death has been imposed shall be to the Colorado supreme court as provided by section 13-4-102 (1) (h), C.R.S. The procedures to be followed in the implementation of such review shall be in accordance with any rules adopted by the Colorado supreme court in response to the legislative intent expressed in section 16-12-101.5 (1), C.R.S.

In any class 1 felony case in which a sentence of death is imposed on or after the date upon which the Colorado supreme court adopts rules implementing the unitary system of review established under part 2 of article 12 of title 16, C.R.S., the procedures for appealing any order by the district court granting or denying postconviction relief and review by the Colorado supreme court of such order shall be governed by the provisions of part 2 of article 12 of title 16, C.R.S., and by such rules adopted by the supreme court.

18-1-411. Postconviction testing of DNA - definitions. As used in this section and in sections 18-1-412 to 18-1-416, unless the context otherwise requires:

"Actual innocence" means clear and convincing evidence such that no reasonable juror would have convicted the defendant.

"Actual or constructive possession" means the biological evidence is maintained or stored on the premises of the law enforcement agency or at another location or facility under the custody or control of the law enforcement agency, including pursuant to an agreement or contract with the law enforcement agency and a third-party service provider, in Colorado or elsewhere.

"DNA" means deoxyribonucleic acid.

"Incarcerated" means physically housed in a department of corrections facility, a private correctional facility under contract with the department of corrections, or a county jail following a felony conviction, or in a juvenile facility following adjudication for an offense that would have been a felony if committed by an adult, or under parole supervision.

18-1-412. Procedure for application for DNA testing - appointment of counsel. (1) An incarcerated person may apply to the district court in the district where the conviction was secured for DNA testing concerning the conviction and sentence the person is currently serving.

A motion filed pursuant to this section shall include specific facts sufficient to support a prima facie showing that post-conviction relief is warranted under the criteria set forth in section 18-1-413. The motion shall include the results of all prior DNA tests, regardless of whether a test was performed by the defense or the prosecution.

If the motion, files, and record of the case show to the satisfaction of the court that the petitioner is not entitled to relief based on the criteria specified in section 18-1-413, the court shall deny the motion without a hearing and without appointment of counsel. The court may deny a second or subsequent motion requesting relief pursuant to this section.

If the court does not deny the petitioner's motion for testing, the court shall appoint counsel if the court determines the petitioner is indigent and has requested counsel. The court shall forward a copy of the motion for DNA testing to the district attorney.

Counsel for the defendant may request the court to set the matter for a hearing, if, upon investigation of the petitioner's motion for testing, counsel believes sufficient grounds exist to support an order for DNA testing. If the petitioner represents himself or herself, the court may set the matter for a hearing upon his or her request.

Following a request for a hearing, the court shall allow the district attorney a reasonable amount of time, but not less than thirty-five days, to respond to the motion and any supplement filed by the petitioner's counsel and to prepare for the hearing.

A court shall not order DNA testing without a hearing, except upon written stipulation of the district attorney.

The court shall deny a motion for production of transcripts unless the petitioner makes a prima facie showing that a transcript will be necessary at a hearing conducted pursuant to this section.

Upon motion of the defendant or his or her counsel, the court shall order a database search by a law enforcement agency if the court determines that a reasonable probability exists that the database search will produce exculpatory or mitigating evidence relevant to a claim of wrongful conviction or sentencing. DNA profiles must meet current national DNA database index system eligibility standards and conform to current federal bureau of investigation quality assurance standards in order to be eligible for search against the state index system.

18-1-413. Content of application for DNA testing. (1) A court shall not order DNA testing unless the petitioner demonstrates by a preponderance of the evidence that:

Favorable results of the DNA testing will demonstrate the petitioner's actual innocence;

A law enforcement agency collected biological evidence pertaining to the offense and retains actual or constructive possession of the evidence that allows for reliable DNA testing;

(I) Conclusive DNA results were not available prior to the petitioner's conviction; and

(II) The petitioner did not secure DNA testing prior to his or her conviction because DNA testing was not reasonably available or for reasons that constitute justifiable excuse, ineffective assistance of counsel, or excusable neglect; and

The petitioner consents to provide a biological sample for DNA testing.

18-1-414. Preservation of evidence. (1) A petitioner shall not be entitled to relief based solely on an allegation that a law enforcement agency failed to preserve biological evidence.

(a) A court granting a motion for hearing pursuant to section 18-1-412 shall order the appropriate law enforcement agency to preserve existing biological evidence for DNA testing.

If a law enforcement agency, through negligence, destroys, loses, or otherwise disposes of biological evidence that is the subject of an order pursuant to this subsection (2) before the evidence may be tested, the court shall set a hearing to determine whether a remedy is warranted. If the court determines that a remedy is warranted, the court may order whatever remedy the court finds is just, equitable, and appropriate. Nothing in this subsection (2) shall be construed to limit or eliminate the court's authority to order any remedy otherwise available under law for the destruction, loss, or disposal of evidence.

For the purposes of this subsection (2), "negligence" means a departure from the ordinary standard of care.
Except as provided in subsection (2) of this section, this section does not create a duty to preserve biological evidence. Notwithstanding the provisions of subsection (2) of this section, this section does not create a liability on the part of a law enforcement agency for failing to preserve biological evidence.

18-1-415. Testing - payment. All testing shall be performed at a law enforcement facility, and the petitioner shall pay for the testing. If the petitioner is indigent and represented by either the public defender or alternate defense counsel, and with the approval of the public defender or the alternate defense counsel, the costs of the testing shall be paid from their budget.

18-1-416. Results of the DNA test. (1) Notwithstanding any law or rule of procedure that bars a motion for post-conviction review as untimely, a petitioner may use the results of a DNA test ordered pursuant to section 18-1-413 as the grounds for filing a motion for post-conviction review under section 18-1-410 and the Colorado rules of criminal procedure.

(2) The testing laboratory shall make the results of a DNA test ordered pursuant to section 18-1-413 available to the combined DNA index system and to any Colorado, federal, or other law enforcement DNA databases.

18-1-417. Ineffective assistance of counsel claims - waiver of confidentiality. (1) Notwithstanding any other provision of law, whenever a defendant alleges ineffective assistance of counsel, the defendant automatically waives any confidentiality, including attorney-client and work-product privileges, between counsel and defendant, and between the defendant or counsel and any expert witness retained or appointed in connection with the representation, but only with respect to the information that is related to the defendant's claim of ineffective assistance. After the defendant alleges ineffective assistance of counsel, the allegedly ineffective counsel and an expert witness may discuss with, may disclose any aspect of the representation that is related to the defendant's claim of ineffective assistance to, and may produce documents related to such representation that are related to the defendant's claim of ineffective assistance to the prosecution without the need for an order by the court that confidentiality has been waived.

(2) If the allegedly ineffective counsel or an expert witness has released his or her file or a portion thereof to defendant or defendant's current counsel, defendant or current counsel shall permit the prosecution to inspect and copy any or all portions of the file that are related to the defendant's claim of ineffective assistance upon request of the prosecution.

PART 5

PRINCIPLES OF CRIMINAL CULPABILITY

18-1-501. Definitions. The following definitions are applicable to the determination of culpability requirements for offenses defined in this code:
"Act" means a bodily movement, and includes words and possession of property.
"Conduct" means an act or omission and its accompanying state of mind or, where relevant, a series of acts or omissions.
"Criminal negligence". A person acts with criminal negligence when, through a gross deviation from the standard of care that a reasonable person would exercise, he fails to perceive a substantial and unjustifiable risk that a result will occur or that a circumstance exists.

"Culpable mental state" means intentionally, or with intent, or knowingly, or willfully, or recklessly, or with criminal negligence, as these terms are defined in this section.
"Intentionally" or "with intent". All offenses defined in this code in which the mental culpability requirement is expressed as "intentionally" or "with intent" are declared to be specific intent offenses. A person acts "intentionally" or "with intent" when his conscious objective is to cause the specific result proscribed by the statute defining the offense. It is immaterial to the issue of specific intent whether or not the result actually occurred.
"Knowingly" or "willfully". All offenses defined in this code in which the mental culpability requirement is expressed as "knowingly" or "willfully" are declared to be general intent crimes. A person acts "knowingly" or "willfully" with respect to conduct or to a circumstance described by a statute defining an offense when he is aware that his conduct is of such nature or that such circumstance exists. A person acts "knowingly" or "willfully", with respect to a result of his conduct, when he is aware that his conduct is practically certain to cause the result.
"Omission" means a failure to perform an act as to which a duty of performance is imposed by law.
"Recklessly". A person acts recklessly when he consciously disregards a substantial and unjustifiable risk that a result will occur or that a circumstance exists.
"Voluntary act" means an act performed consciously as a result of effort or determination, and includes the possession of property if the actor was aware of his physical possession or control thereof for a sufficient period to have been able to terminate it.

18-1-502. Requirements for criminal liability in general and for offenses of strict liability and of mental culpability. The minimum requirement for criminal liability is the performance by a person of conduct which includes a voluntary act or the omission to perform an act which he is physically capable of performing. If that conduct is all that is required for commission of a particular offense, or if an offense or some material element thereof does not require a culpable mental state on the part of the actor, the offense is one of "strict liability". If a culpable mental state on the part of the actor is required with respect to any material element of an offense, the offense is one of "mental culpability".

18-1-503. Construction of statutes with respect to culpability requirements. (1) When the commission of an offense, or some element of an offense, requires a particular culpable mental state, that mental state is ordinarily designated by use of the terms "intentionally", "with intent", "knowingly", "willfully", "recklessly", or "criminal negligence" or by use of the terms "with intent to defraud" and "knowing it to be false" describing a specific kind of intent or knowledge.

Although no culpable mental state is expressly designated in a statute defining an offense, a culpable mental state may nevertheless be required for the commission of that offense, or with respect to some or all of the material elements thereof, if the proscribed conduct necessarily involves such a culpable mental state.

If a statute provides that criminal negligence suffices to establish an element of an offense, that element also is established if a person acts recklessly, knowingly, or intentionally. If recklessness suffices to establish an element, that element also is established if a person acts knowingly or intentionally. If acting knowingly suffices to establish an element, that element also is established if a person acts intentionally.

When a statute defining an offense prescribes as an element thereof a specified culpable mental state, that mental state is deemed to apply to every element of the offense unless an intent to limit its application clearly appears.

18-1-503.5. Principles of criminal culpability. (1) If the criminality of conduct depends on a child being younger than eighteen years of age and the child was in fact at least fifteen years of age, it shall be an affirmative defense that the defendant reasonably believed the child to be eighteen years of age or older. This affirmative defense shall not be available if the criminality of conduct depends on the defendant being in a position of trust.

If the criminality of conduct depends on a child's being younger than eighteen years of age and the child was in fact younger than fifteen years of age, there shall be no defense that the defendant reasonably believed the child was eighteen years of age or older.

If the criminality of conduct depends on a child being younger than fifteen years of age, it shall be no defense that the defendant did not know the child's age or that the defendant reasonably believed the child to be fifteen years of age or older.

18-1-504. Effect of ignorance or mistake upon culpability. (1) A person is not relieved of criminal liability for conduct because he engaged in that conduct under a mistaken belief of fact, unless:

It negatives the existence of a particular mental state essential to commission of the offense; or

The statute defining the offense or a statute relating thereto expressly provides that a factual mistake or the mental state resulting therefrom constitutes a defense or exemption; or

The factual mistake or the mental state resulting therefrom is of a kind that supports a defense of justification as defined in sections 18-1-701 to 18-1-707.

A person is not relieved of criminal liability for conduct because he engages in that conduct under a mistaken belief that it does not, as a matter of law, constitute an offense, unless the

conduct is permitted by one or more of the following:

A statute or ordinance binding in this state;

An administrative regulation, order, or grant of permission by a body or official authorized and empowered to make such order or grant the permission under the laws of the state of Colorado;

An official written interpretation of the statute or law relating to the offense, made or issued by a public servant, agency, or body legally charged or empowered with the responsibility of administering, enforcing, or interpreting a statute, ordinance, regulation, order, or law. If such interpretation is by judicial decision, it must be binding in the state of Colorado.

Any defense authorized by this section is an affirmative defense.

18-1-505. Consent. (1) The consent of the victim to conduct charged to constitute an offense or to the result thereof is not a defense unless the consent negatives an element of the offense or precludes the infliction of the harm or evil sought to be prevented by the law defining the offense.

When conduct is charged to constitute an offense because it causes or threatens bodily injury, consent to that conduct or to the infliction of that injury is a defense only if the bodily injury consented to or threatened by the conduct consented to is not serious, or the conduct and the injury are reasonably foreseeable hazards of joint participation in a lawful athletic contest or competitive sport, or the consent establishes a justification under sections 18-1-701 to 18-1-707.

Unless otherwise provided by this code or by the law defining the offense, assent does not constitute consent if:

It is given by a person who is legally incompetent to authorize the conduct charged to constitute the offense; or

It is given by a person who, by reason of immaturity, mental disease or mental defect, or intoxication, is manifestly unable and is known or reasonably should be known by the defendant to be unable to make a reasonable judgment as to the nature or harmfulness of the conduct charged to constitute the offense; or

It is given by a person whose consent is sought to be prevented by the law defining the offense; or

It is induced by force, duress, or deception.

Any defense authorized by this section is an affirmative defense.

PART 6

PARTIES TO OFFENSES - ACCOUNTABILITY

18-1-601. Liability based upon behavior. A person is guilty of an offense if it is committed by the behavior of another person for which he is legally accountable as provided in sections 18-1- 602 to 18-1-607.

18-1-602. Behavior of another. (1) A person is legally accountable for the behavior of another person if:

He is made accountable for the conduct of that person by the statute defining the offense or by specific provision of this code; or

He acts with the culpable mental state sufficient for the commission of the offense in question and he causes an innocent person to engage in such behavior.

(2) As used in subsection (1) of this section, "innocent person" includes any person who is not guilty of the offense in question, despite his behavior, because of duress, legal incapacity or exemption, or unawareness of the criminal nature of the conduct in question or of the defendant's criminal

purpose, or any other factor precluding the mental state sufficient for the commission of the offense in question.

18-1-603. Complicity. A person is legally accountable as principal for the behavior of another constituting a criminal offense if, with the intent to promote or facilitate the commission of the offense, he or she aids, abets, advises, or encourages the other person in planning or committing the offense.

18-1-604. Exemptions from liability based upon behavior of another. (1) Unless otherwise provided by the statute defining the offense, a person shall not be legally accountable for behavior of another constituting an offense if he is a victim of that offense or the offense is so defined that his conduct is inevitably incidental to its commission.
It shall be an affirmative defense to a charge under section 18-1-603 if, prior to the commission of the offense, the defendant terminated his effort to promote or facilitate its commission and either gave timely warning to law enforcement authorities or gave timely warning to the intended victim.

18-1-605. Liability based on behavior of another - no defense. In any prosecution for an offense in which criminal liability is based upon the behavior of another pursuant to sections 18-1- 601 to 18-1-604, it is no defense that the other person has not been prosecuted for or convicted of any offense based upon the behavior in question or has been convicted of a different offense or degree of offense, or the defendant belongs to a class of persons who by definition of the offense are legally incapable of committing the offense in an individual capacity.

18-1-606. Criminal liability of business entities. (1) A business entity is guilty of an offense if:
The conduct constituting the offense consists of an omission to discharge a specific duty of affirmative performance imposed on the business entity by law; or
The conduct constituting the offense is engaged in, authorized, solicited, requested,

commanded, or knowingly tolerated by the governing body or individual authorized to manage the affairs of the business entity or by a high managerial agent acting within the scope of his or her employment or in behalf of the business entity.
As used in this section:
"Agent" means any director, officer, or employee of a business entity, or any other person who is authorized to act in behalf of the business entity, and "high managerial agent" means an officer of a business entity or any other agent in a position of comparable authority with respect to the formulation of the business entity's policy or the supervision in a managerial capacity of subordinate employees.
"Business entity" means a corporation or other entity that is subject to the provisions of title 7, C.R.S.; foreign corporations qualified to do business in this state pursuant to article 115 of title 7, C.R.S., specifically including federally chartered or authorized financial institutions; a corporation or other entity that is subject to the provisions of title 11, C.R.S.; or a sole proprietorship or other association or group of individuals doing business in the state.
Every offense committed by a corporation prior to July 1, 1985, which would be a felony if committed by an individual shall subject the corporation to the payment of a fine of not less than one thousand dollars nor more than fifteen thousand dollars. For such offenses committed on or after July 1, 1985, the corporation shall be subject to the payment of a fine within the presumptive ranges authorized by section 18-1.3-401 (1) (a) (III). Every offense committed by a corporation which would be a misdemeanor or petty offense if committed by an individual shall subject the corporation to the payment of a fine within the minimum and maximum fines authorized by sections 18-1.3-501 and 18-1.3-503 for the particular offense of which the corporation is convicted. For an offense committed on or after July 1, 2003, a business entity shall be subject to the payment of a fine within the presumptive ranges authorized by section 18-1.3-401 (1) (a) (III). An offense committed by a business entity that would be a misdemeanor or petty offense if committed by an individual shall subject the business entity to the payment of a fine within the minimum and maximum fines authorized by sections 18-1.3-501 and 18-1.3-503 for the particular offense of which the business entity is convicted.

18-1-607. Criminal liability of an individual for corporate conduct. A person is criminally liable for conduct constituting an offense which he performs or causes to occur in the name of or in behalf of a corporation to the same extent as if that conduct were performed or caused by him in his own name or behalf.

PART 7

JUSTIFICATION AND EXEMPTIONS FROM CRIMINAL RESPONSIBILITY

18-1-701. Execution of public duty. (1) Unless inconsistent with other provisions of sections 18-1-702 to 18-1-710, defining justifiable use of physical force, or with some other

provision of law, conduct which would otherwise constitute an offense is justifiable and not criminal when it is required or authorized by a provision of law or a judicial decree binding in Colorado.
A "provision of law" and a "judicial decree" in subsection (1) of this section mean:
Laws defining duties and functions of public servants;
Laws defining duties of private citizens to assist public servants in the performance of certain of their functions;
Laws governing the execution of legal process;
Laws governing the military service and conduct of war;
Judgments and orders of court.

18-1-702. Choice of evils. (1) Unless inconsistent with other provisions of sections 18-1- 703 to 18-1-707, defining justifiable use of physical force, or with some other provision of law, conduct which would otherwise constitute an offense is justifiable and not criminal when it is necessary as an emergency measure to avoid an imminent public or private injury which is about to occur by reason of a situation occasioned or developed through no conduct of the actor, and which is of sufficient gravity that, according to ordinary standards of intelligence and morality, the desirability and urgency of avoiding the injury clearly outweigh the desirability of avoiding the injury sought to be prevented by the statute defining the offense in issue.

The necessity and justifiability of conduct under subsection (1) of this section shall not rest upon considerations pertaining only to the morality and advisability of the statute, either in its general application or with respect to its application to a particular class of cases arising thereunder. When evidence relating to the defense of justification under this section is offered by the defendant, before it is submitted for the consideration of the jury, the court shall first rule as a matter of law whether the claimed facts and circumstances would, if established, constitute a justification.

18-1-703. Use of physical force - special relationships. (1) The use of physical force upon another person which would otherwise constitute an offense is justifiable and not criminal under any of the following circumstances:

A parent, guardian, or other person entrusted with the care and supervision of a minor or an incompetent person, and a teacher or other person entrusted with the care and supervision of a minor, may use reasonable and appropriate physical force upon the minor or incompetent person when and to the extent it is reasonably necessary and appropriate to maintain discipline or promote the welfare of the minor or incompetent person.

A superintendent or other authorized official of a jail, prison, or correctional institution may, in order to maintain order and discipline, use reasonable and appropriate physical force when and to the extent that he reasonably believes it necessary to maintain order and discipline, but he may use deadly physical force only when he reasonably believes it necessary to prevent death or serious bodily injury.

A person responsible for the maintenance of order in a common carrier of passengers, or a person acting under his direction, may use reasonable and appropriate physical force when and to the extent that it is necessary to maintain order and discipline, but he may use deadly physical

force only when it is reasonably necessary to prevent death or serious bodily injury.

A person acting under a reasonable belief that another person is about to commit suicide or to inflict serious bodily injury upon himself may use reasonable and appropriate physical force upon that person to the extent that it is reasonably necessary to thwart the result.

A duly licensed physician, advanced practice nurse, or a person acting under his or her direction, may use reasonable and appropriate physical force for the purpose of administering a recognized form of treatment that he or she reasonably believes to be adapted to promoting the physical or mental health of the patient if:

The treatment is administered with the consent of the patient, or if the patient is a minor or an incompetent person, with the consent of his parent, guardian, or other person entrusted with his care and supervision; or

The treatment is administered in an emergency when the physician or advanced practice nurse reasonably believes that no one competent to consent can be consulted and that a reasonable person, wishing to safeguard the welfare of the patient, would consent.

18-1-704. Use of physical force in defense of a person. (1) Except as provided in subsections (2) and (3) of this section, a person is justified in using physical force upon another person in order to defend himself or a third person from what he reasonably believes to be the use or imminent use of unlawful physical force by that other person, and he may use a degree of force which he reasonably believes to be necessary for that purpose.

Deadly physical force may be used only if a person reasonably believes a lesser degree of force is inadequate and:

The actor has reasonable ground to believe, and does believe, that he or another person is in imminent danger of being killed or of receiving great bodily injury; or

The other person is using or reasonably appears about to use physical force against an occupant of a dwelling or business establishment while committing or attempting to commit burglary as defined in sections 18-4-202 to 18-4-204; or

The other person is committing or reasonably appears about to commit kidnapping as defined in section 18-3-301 or 18-3-302, robbery as defined in section 18-4-301 or 18-4-302, sexual assault as set forth in section 18-3-402, or in section 18-3-403 as it existed prior to July 1, 2000, or assault as defined in sections 18-3-202 and 18-3-203.

Notwithstanding the provisions of subsection (1) of this section, a person is not justified in using physical force if:

With intent to cause bodily injury or death to another person, he provokes the use of unlawful physical force by that other person; or

He is the initial aggressor; except that his use of physical force upon another person under the circumstances is justifiable if he withdraws from the encounter and effectively communicates to the other person his intent to do so, but the latter nevertheless continues or threatens the use of unlawful physical force; or

The physical force involved is the product of a combat by agreement not specifically authorized by law.

In a case in which the defendant is not entitled to a jury instruction regarding self-defense

as an affirmative defense, the court shall allow the defendant to present evidence, when relevant, that he or she was acting in self-defense. If the defendant presents evidence of self-defense, the court shall instruct the jury with a self-defense law instruction. The court shall instruct the jury that it may consider the evidence of self-defense in determining whether the defendant acted recklessly, with extreme indifference, or in a criminally negligent manner. However, the self-defense law instruction shall not be an affirmative defense instruction and the prosecuting attorney shall not have the burden of disproving self-defense. This section shall not apply to strict liability crimes.

18-1-704.5. Use of deadly physical force against an intruder. (1) The general assembly hereby recognizes that the citizens of Colorado have a right to expect absolute safety within their own homes.

Notwithstanding the provisions of section 18-1-704, any occupant of a dwelling is justified in using any degree of physical force, including deadly physical force, against another person when that other person has made an unlawful entry into the dwelling, and when the occupant has a reasonable belief that such other person has committed a crime in the dwelling in addition to the uninvited entry, or is committing or intends to commit a crime against a person or property in addition to the uninvited entry, and when the occupant reasonably believes that such other person might use any physical force, no matter how slight, against any occupant.

Any occupant of a dwelling using physical force, including deadly physical force, in accordance with the provisions of subsection (2) of this section shall be immune from criminal prosecution for the use of such force.

Any occupant of a dwelling using physical force, including deadly physical force, in accordance with the provisions of subsection (2) of this section shall be immune from any civil liability for injuries or death resulting from the use of such force.

As used in this section, unless the context otherwise requires, "dwelling" does not include any place of habitation in a detention facility, as defined in section 18-8-211 (4).

18-1-705. Use of physical force in defense of premises. A person in possession or control of any building, realty, or other premises, or a person who is licensed or privileged to be thereon, is justified in using reasonable and appropriate physical force upon another person when and to the extent that it is reasonably necessary to prevent or terminate what he reasonably believes to be the commission or attempted commission of an unlawful trespass by the other person in or upon the building, realty, or premises. However, he may use deadly force only in defense of himself or another as described in section 18-1-704, or when he reasonably believes it necessary to prevent what he reasonably believes to be an attempt by the trespasser to commit first degree arson.

18-1-706. Use of physical force in defense of property. A person is justified in using reasonable and appropriate physical force upon another person when and to the extent that he reasonably believes it necessary to prevent what he reasonably believes to be an attempt by the other person to commit theft, criminal mischief, or criminal tampering involving property, but he may use

deadly physical force under these circumstances only in defense of himself or another as described in section 18-1-704.

18-1-707. Use of physical force in making an arrest or in preventing an escape - definitions. (1) Except as provided in subsections (2) and (2.5) of this section, a peace officer is justified in using reasonable and appropriate physical force upon another person when and to the extent that he reasonably believes it necessary:
To effect an arrest or to prevent the escape from custody of an arrested person unless he knows that the arrest is unauthorized; or
To defend himself or a third person from what he reasonably believes to be the use or imminent use of physical force while effecting or attempting to effect such an arrest or while preventing or attempting to prevent such an escape.
A peace officer is justified in using deadly physical force upon another person for a purpose specified in subsection (1) of this section only when he reasonably believes that it is necessary:
To defend himself or a third person from what he reasonably believes to be the use or imminent use of deadly physical force; or
To effect an arrest, or to prevent the escape from custody, of a person whom he reasonably believes:
Has committed or attempted to commit a felony involving the use or threatened use of a deadly weapon; or
Is attempting to escape by the use of a deadly weapon; or
Otherwise indicates, except through a motor vehicle violation, that he is likely to endanger human life or to inflict serious bodily injury to another unless apprehended without delay. (2.5) (a) A peace officer is justified in using a chokehold upon another person for the purposes specified in subsection (1) of this section only when he or she reasonably believes that it
is necessary:
To defend himself or herself or a third person from what he or she reasonably believes to be the use or imminent use of deadly physical force or infliction of bodily injury; or
To effect an arrest, or to prevent the escape from custody, of a person whom he or she reasonably believes:
Has committed or attempted to commit a felony involving or threatening the use of a deadly weapon; or
Is attempting to escape by the use of physical force; or
Indicates, except through a motor vehicle, that he or she is likely to endanger human life or to inflict serious bodily injury to another unless he or she is apprehended without delay.
(b) For the purposes of this subsection (2.5), "chokehold" means a method by which a person holds another person by putting his or her arm around the other person's neck with sufficient pressure to make breathing difficult or impossible and includes, but is not limited to, any pressure to the throat or windpipe, which may prevent or hinder breathing or reduce intake of air.
Nothing in subsection (2) (b) or subsection (2.5) of this section shall be deemed to constitute justification for reckless or criminally negligent conduct by a peace officer amounting to

an offense against or with respect to innocent persons whom he is not seeking to arrest or retain in custody.
For purposes of this section, a reasonable belief that a person has committed an offense means a reasonable belief in facts or circumstances that if true would in law constitute an offense. If the believed facts or circumstances would not in law constitute an offense, an erroneous though not unreasonable belief that the law is otherwise does not render justifiable the use of force to make an arrest or to prevent an escape from custody. A peace officer who is effecting an arrest pursuant to a warrant is justified in using the physical force prescribed in subsections (1), (2), and (2.5) of this section unless the warrant is invalid and is known by the officer to be invalid.
Except as provided in subsection (6) of this section, a person who has been directed by a peace officer to assist him to effect an arrest or to prevent an escape from custody is justified in using reasonable and appropriate physical force when and to the extent that he reasonably believes that force to be necessary to carry out the peace officer's direction, unless he knows that the arrest or prospective arrest is not authorized.
A person who has been directed to assist a peace officer under circumstances specified in subsection (5) of this section may use deadly physical force to effect an arrest or to prevent an escape only when:
He reasonably believes that force to be necessary to defend himself or a third person from what he reasonably believes to be the use or imminent use of deadly physical force; or
He is directed or authorized by the peace officer to use deadly physical force and does not know, if that happens to be the case, that the peace officer himself is not authorized to use deadly physical force under the circumstances.
A private person acting on his own account is justified in using reasonable and appropriate physical force upon another person when and to the extent that he reasonably believes it necessary to effect an arrest, or to prevent the escape from custody of an arrested person who has committed an offense in his presence; but he is justified in using deadly physical force for the purpose only when he reasonably believes it necessary to defend himself or a third person from what he reasonably believes to be the use or imminent use of deadly physical force.
A guard or peace officer employed in a detention facility is justified:
In using deadly physical force when he reasonably believes it necessary to prevent the escape of a prisoner convicted of, charged with, or held for a felony or confined under the maximum security rules of any detention facility as such facility is defined in subsection (9) of this section;
In using reasonable and appropriate physical force, but not deadly physical force, in all other circumstances when and to the extent that he reasonably believes it necessary to prevent what he reasonably believes to be the escape of a prisoner from a detention facility.
"Detention facility" as used in subsection (8) of this section means any place maintained for the confinement, pursuant to law, of persons charged with or convicted of an offense, held pursuant to the "Colorado Children's Code", held for extradition, or otherwise confined pursuant to an order of a court.

18-1-708. Duress. A person may not be convicted of an offense, other than a class 1 felony, based upon conduct in which he engaged at the direction of another person because of the use or

threatened use of unlawful force upon him or upon another person, which force or threatened use thereof a reasonable person in his situation would have been unable to resist. This defense is not available when a person intentionally or recklessly places himself in a situation in which it is foreseeable that he will be subjected to such force or threatened use thereof. The choice of evils defense, provided in section 18-1-702, shall not be available to a defendant in addition to the defense of duress provided under this section unless separate facts exist which warrant its application.

18-1-709. Entrapment. The commission of acts which would otherwise constitute an offense is not criminal if the defendant engaged in the proscribed conduct because he was induced to do so by a law enforcement official or other person acting under his direction, seeking to obtain evidence for the purpose of prosecution, and the methods used to obtain that evidence were such as to create a substantial risk that the acts would be committed by a person who, but for such inducement, would not have conceived of or engaged in conduct of the sort induced. Merely affording a person an opportunity to commit an offense is not entrapment even though representations or inducements calculated to overcome the offender's fear of detection are used.

18-1-710. Affirmative defense. The issues of justification or exemption from criminal liability under sections 18-1-701 to 18-1-709 are affirmative defenses.

18-1-711. Immunity for persons who suffer or report an emergency drug or alcohol overdose event - definitions. (1) A person is immune from arrest and prosecution for an offense described in subsection (3) of this section if:
The person reports in good faith an emergency drug or alcohol overdose event to a law enforcement officer, to the 911 system, or to a medical provider;
The person remains at the scene of the event until a law enforcement officer or an emergency medical responder arrives or the person remains at the facilities of the medical provider until a law enforcement officer arrives;
The person identifies himself or herself to, and cooperates with, the law enforcement officer, emergency medical responder, or medical provider; and
The offense arises from the same course of events from which the emergency drug or alcohol overdose event arose.
The immunity described in subsection (1) of this section also extends to the person who suffered the emergency drug or alcohol overdose event if all of the conditions of subsection (1) are satisfied.
The immunity described in subsection (1) of this section shall apply to the following criminal offenses:
Unlawful possession of a controlled substance, as described in section 18-18-403.5 (2) (a) (I), (2) (b) (I), or (2) (c);
Unlawful use of a controlled substance, as described in section 18-18-404;
Unlawful possession of two ounces or less of marijuana, as described in section 18-18-

406 (5) (a) (I); or more than two ounces of marijuana but no more than six ounces of marijuana, as described in section 18-18-406 (4) (c); or more than six ounces of marijuana but no more than twelve ounces of marijuana or three ounces or less of marijuana concentrate as described in section 18-18- 406 (4) (b);
Open and public display, consumption, or use of less than two ounces of marijuana as described in section 18-18-406 (5) (b) (I);
Transferring or dispensing two ounces or less of marijuana from one person to another for no consideration, as described in section 18-18-406 (5) (c);
Use or possession of synthetic cannabinoids or salvia divinorum, as described in section 18-18-406.1;
Possession of drug paraphernalia, as described in section 18-18-428; and
Illegal possession or consumption of ethyl alcohol or marijuana by an underage person or illegal possession of marijuana paraphernalia by an underage person, as described in section 18- 13-122.
Nothing in this section shall be interpreted to prohibit the prosecution of a person for an offense other than an offense listed in subsection (3) of this section or to limit the ability of a district attorney or a law enforcement officer to obtain or use evidence obtained from a report, recording, or anyother statement provided pursuant to subsection (1) of this section to investigate and prosecute an offense other than an offense listed in subsection (3) of this section.
As used in this section, unless the context otherwise requires, "emergencydrug or alcohol overdose event" means an acute condition including, but not limited to, physical illness, coma, mania, hysteria, or death resulting from the consumption or use of a controlled substance, or of alcohol, or another substance with which a controlled substance or alcohol was combined, and that a layperson would reasonably believe to be a drug or alcohol overdose that requires medical assistance.

18-1-712. Immunity for a person who administers an opiate antagonist during an opiate-related drug overdose event - definitions. (1) Legislative declaration. The general assembly hereby encourages the administration of opiate antagonists for the purpose of saving the lives of people who suffer opiate-related drug overdose events. A person who administers an opiate antagonist to another person is urged to call for emergency medical services immediately.
General immunity. A person, other than a health care provider or a health care facility, who acts in good faith to furnish or administer an opiate antagonist to an individual the person believes to be suffering an opiate-related drug overdose event or to an individual who is in a position to assist the individual at risk of experiencing an opiate-related overdose event is immune from criminal prosecution for the act. This subsection (2) also applies to a first responder or an employee or volunteer of a harm reduction organization acting in accordance with section 12-42.5-120 (3) (d), C.R.S.
(a) Licensed prescribers and dispensers. An individual who is licensed by the state under title 12, C.R.S., and is permitted by section 12-36-117.7, 12-38-125.5, or 12-42.5-120 (3), C.R.S., or by other applicable law to prescribe or dispense an opiate antagonist is immune from criminal prosecution for:

Prescribing or dispensing an opiate antagonist in accordance with the applicable law; or
Any outcomes resulting from the eventual administration of the opiate antagonist by a layperson.
(b) Repealed.
The provisions of this section shall not be interpreted to establish any duty or standard of care in the prescribing, dispensing, or administration of an opiate antagonist.
Definitions. As used in this section, unless the context otherwise requires:
"Health care facility" means a hospital, a hospice inpatient residence, a nursing facility, a dialysis treatment facility, an assisted living residence, an entity that provides home- and community-based services, a hospice or home health care agency, or another facility that provides or contracts to provide health care services, which facility is licensed, certified, or otherwise authorized or permitted by law to provide medical treatment.
(I) "Health care provider" means:
A licensed or certified physician, nurse practitioner, physician assistant, or pharmacist; or

A health maintenance organization licensed and conducting business in this state.
(II) "Health care provider" does not include a podiatrist, optometrist, dentist, or veterinarian.
"Opiate" has the same meaning as set forth in section 18-18-102 (21).
"Opiate antagonist" means naloxone hydrochloride or any similarly acting drug that is
not a controlled substance and that is approved by the federal food and drug administration for the treatment of a drug overdose.
"Opiate-related drug overdose event" means an acute condition, including a decreased level of consciousness or respiratory depression, that:
Results from the consumption or use of a controlled substance or another substance with which a controlled substance was combined;
A layperson would reasonably believe to be an opiate-related drug overdose event; and
Requires medical assistance.

## PART 8 RESPONSIBILITY

18-1-801. Insufficient age. The responsibility of a person for his conduct is the same for persons between the ages of ten and eighteen as it is for persons over eighteen except to the extent that responsibility is modified by the provisions of the "Colorado Children's Code", title 19, C.R.S. No child under ten years of age shall be found guilty of any offense.


18-1-802. Insanity. (1) (a) A person who is insane, as defined in section 16-8-101, C.R.S., is not responsible for his or her conduct defined as criminal. Insanity as a defense shall not be an issue in any prosecution unless it is raised by a plea of not guilty by reason of insanity as provided in section 16-8-103, C.R.S.

(b) This subsection (1) applies to offenses committed before July 1, 1995.
(2) (a) A person who is insane, as defined in section 16-8-101.5, C.R.S., is not responsible for his or her conduct defined as criminal. Insanity as a defense shall not be an issue in any prosecution unless it is raised by a plea of not guilty by reason of insanity as provided in section 16- 8-103, C.R.S.
(b) This subsection (2) shall apply to offenses occurring on or after July 1, 1995.


18-1-803. Impaired mental condition. (1) Evidence of an impaired mental condition, as defined in section 16-8-102 (2.7), C.R.S., though not legal insanity may be offered in a proper case as bearing upon the capacity of the accused to form the culpable mental state which is an element of the offense charged.
An intention to assert the affirmative defense of impaired mental condition shall be made pursuant to section 16-8-103.5, C.R.S.
When the affirmative defense of impaired mental condition has been raised, the jury will be given special verdict forms containing interrogatories. The trier of fact shall decide first the question of guilt as to felony charges which are before the court. If the trier of fact concludes that guilt has been proven beyond a reasonable doubt as to one or more of the felony charges submitted for consideration, the special interrogatories shall not be answered. Upon completion of its deliberations on the felony charges as previously set forth in this subsection (3), the trier of fact shall consider any other charges before the court in a similar manner; except that it shall not answer the special interrogatories regarding such charges if it has previously found guilt beyond a reasonable doubt with respect to one or more felony charges. The interrogatories shall provide for specific findings of the jury with respect to the affirmative defense of impaired mental condition in accordance with the Colorado rules of criminal procedure. When the court sits as the trier of fact, it shall enter appropriate specific findings with respect to the affirmative defense of impaired mental condition. If the trier of fact finds that the defendant is not guilty by reason of the affirmative defense of impaired mental condition, the court shall commit the defendant to the department of human services pursuant to section 16-8-103.5 (5), C.R.S.
This section shall apply to offenses committed before July 1, 1995.


18-1-804. Intoxication. (1) Intoxication of the accused is not a defense to a criminal charge, except as provided in subsection (3) of this section, but in any prosecution for an offense, evidence of intoxication of the defendant may be offered by the defendant when it is relevant to negative the existence of a specific intent if such intent is an element of the crime charged.
Intoxication does not, in itself, constitute mental disease or defect within the meaning of section 18-1-802.
A person is not criminally responsible for his conduct if, by reason of intoxication that is not self-induced at the time he acts, he lacks capacity to conform his conduct to the requirements of the law.
"Intoxication", as used in this section means a disturbance of mental or physical capacities resulting from the introduction of any substance into the body.

"Self-induced intoxication" means intoxication caused by substances which the defendant knows or ought to know have the tendency to cause intoxication and which he knowingly introduced or allowed to be introduced into his body, unless they were introduced pursuant to medical advice or under circumstances that would afford a defense to a charge of crime.


18-1-805. Responsibility - affirmative defense. The issue of responsibility under sections 18-1-801 to 18-1-804 is an affirmative defense.

## PART 9 DEFINITIONS

18-1-901. Definitions. (1) Definitions set forth in any section of this title apply wherever the same term is used in the same sense in another section of this title unless the definition is specifically limited or the context indicates that it is inapplicable.
The terms defined in section 18-1-104 and in section 18-1-501, as well as the terms defined in subsection (3) of this section, are terms which appear in various articles of this code. Other terms which need definition but which are used only in a limited number of sections of this code are defined in the particular section or article in which the terms appear.
(a) "To aid" or "to assist" includes knowingly to give or lend money or extend credit to be used for, or to make possible or available, or to further the activity thus aided or assisted.
"Benefit" means any gain or advantage to the beneficiary including any gain or advantage to another person pursuant to the desire or consent of the beneficiary.
"Bodily injury" means physical pain, illness, or any impairment of physical or mental condition.
"Deadly physical force" means force, the intended, natural, and probable consequence of which is to produce death, and which does, in fact, produce death.

"Deadly weapon" means:

A firearm, whether loaded or unloaded; or

A knife, bludgeon, or any other weapon, device, instrument, material, or substance, whether animate or inanimate, that, in the manner it is used or intended to be used, is capable of producing death or serious bodily injury.

and (IV) (Deleted by amendment, L. 2013.)

"Deface" means to alter the appearance of something by removing, distorting, adding to, or covering all or a part of the thing.

"Dwelling" means a building which is used, intended to be used, or usually used by a person for habitation.

"Firearm" means any handgun, automatic, revolver, pistol, rifle, shotgun, or other instrument or device capable or intended to be capable of discharging bullets, cartridges, or other explosive charges.

"Government" includes the United States, any state, county, municipality, or other

political unit, any branch, department, agency, or subdivision of any of the foregoing, and any corporation or other entity established by law to carry out any governmental function.

"Governmental function" includes any activity which a public servant is legally authorized to undertake on behalf of government.

"Motor vehicle" includes any self-propelled device by which persons or property may be moved, carried, or transported from one place to another by land, water, or air, except devices operated on rails, tracks, or cables fixed to the ground or supported by pylons, towers, or other structures. Repealed.

"Pecuniary benefit" means benefit in the form of money, property, commercial interests, or anything else, the primary significance of which is economic gain.

"Public place" means a place to which the public or a substantial number of the public has access, and includes but is not limited to highways, transportation facilities, schools, places of amusement, parks, playgrounds, and the common areas of public and private buildings and facilities.

"Public servant" means any officer or employee of government, whether elected or appointed, and any person participating as an advisor, consultant, process server, or otherwise in performing a governmental function, but the term does not include witnesses.

(o.5) "Restorative justice practices" means practices that emphasize repairing the harm caused to victims and the community by offenses. Restorative justice practices include victim- offender conferences, family group conferences, circles, community conferences, and other similar victim-centered practices. Restorative justice practices are facilitated meetings attended voluntarily by the victim or victim's representatives, the victim's supporters, the offender, and the offender's supporters and mayinclude community members. By engaging the parties to the offense in voluntary dialogue, restorative justice practices provide an opportunityfor the offender to accept responsibility for the harm caused to the victim and community, promote victim healing, and enable the participants to agree on consequences to repair the harm, to the extent possible, including but not limited to apologies, community service, reparation, restoration, and counseling. Restorative justice practices may be used in addition to any other conditions, consequences, or sentence imposed by the court.

"Serious bodily injury" means bodily injury which, either at the time of the actual injury or at a later time, involves a substantial risk of death, a substantial risk of serious permanent disfigurement, a substantial risk of protracted loss or impairment of the function of any part or organ of the body, or breaks, fractures, or burns of the second or third degree.

"Tamper" means to interfere with something improperly, to meddle with it, or to make unwarranted alterations in its condition.

"Thing of value" includes real property, tangible and intangible personal property, contract rights, choses in action, services, confidential information, medical records information, and any rights of use or enjoyment connected therewith.

"Utility" means an enterprise which provides gas, sewer, electric, steam, water, transportation, or communication services, and includes any carrier, pipeline, transmitter, or source, whether publicly or privately owned or operated.

PART 10

ORDERS AND PROCEEDINGS AGAINST DEFENDANT

18-1-1001. Protection order against defendant - definitions. (1) There is hereby created a mandatory protection order against any person charged with a violation of any of the provisions of this title, which order shall remain in effect from the time that the person is advised of his or her rights at arraignment or the person's first appearance before the court and informed of such order until final disposition of the action. Such order shall restrain the person charged from harassing, molesting, intimidating, retaliating against, or tampering with any witness to or victim of the acts charged. The protection order issued pursuant to this section shall be on a standardized form prescribed by the judicial department and a copy shall be provided to the protected parties.

At the time of arraignment or the person's first appearance before the court, the court shall inform the defendant of the protection order effective pursuant to this section and shall inform the defendant that a violation of such order is punishable by contempt.

Nothing in this section shall preclude the defendant from applying to the court at any time for modification or dismissal of the protection order issued pursuant to this section or the district attorney from applying to the court at any time for further orders, additional provisions under the protection order, or modification or dismissal of the same. The trial court shall retain jurisdiction to enforce, modify, or dismiss the protection order until final disposition of the action. Upon motion of the district attorney or on the court's own motion for the protection of the alleged victim or witness, the court may, in cases involving domestic violence as defined in section 18-6-800.3 (1) and cases involving crimes listed in section 24-4.1-302, C.R.S., except those listed in paragraphs (cc.5) and (cc.6) of subsection (1) of that section, enter any of the following further orders against the defendant:

An order to vacate or stay away from the home of the alleged victim or witness and to stay away from any other location where the victim or witness is likely to be found;

An order to refrain from contact or direct or indirect communication with the alleged victim or witness;

An order prohibiting possession or control of firearms or other weapons;

An order prohibiting possession or consumption of alcohol or controlled substances; and

Any other order the court deems appropriate to protect the safety of the alleged victim or witness.

Any person failing to comply with a protection order issued pursuant to this section commits the crime of violation of a protection order and may be punished as provided in section 18- 6-803.5.

Before a defendant is released on bail pursuant to article 4 of title 16, C.R.S., the court shall, in cases involving domestic violence as defined in section 18-6-800.3 (1), in cases of stalking pursuant to section 18-3-602, or in cases involving unlawful sexual behavior as defined in section 16-22-102 (9), C.R.S., state the terms of the protection order issued pursuant to this section, including any additional provisions added pursuant to subsection (3) of this section, to the defendant on the record, and the court shall further require the defendant to acknowledge the protection order in court and in writing prior to release as a condition of any bond for the release of the defendant.

16

The prosecuting attorney shall, in such domestic violence cases, stalking cases, or in cases involving unlawful sexual behavior as defined in section 16-22-102 (9), C.R.S., notify the alleged victim, the complainant, and the protected person of the order if such persons are not present at the time the protection order is issued.

The defendant or, in cases involving domestic violence as defined in section 18-6-800.3 (1), in cases of stalking pursuant to section 18-3-602, or in cases involving unlawful sexual behavior as defined in section 16-22-102 (9), C.R.S., the prosecuting attorney may request a hearing before the court to modify the terms of a protection order issued pursuant to this section. Upon such a request, the court shall set a hearing and the prosecuting attorney shall send notice of the hearing to the defendant and the alleged victim. At the hearing the court shall review the terms of the protection order and any further orders entered and shall consider the modifications, if any, requested by the defendant or the prosecuting attorney.

The duties of peace officers enforcing orders issued pursuant to this section shall be in accordance with section 18-6-803.5 and any rules adopted by the Colorado supreme court pursuant to said section.

For purposes of this section:

"Court" means the trial court or a designee of the trial court.

(a.5) "Protection order" shall include a restraining order entered pursuant to this section prior to July 1, 2003.

"Until final disposition of the action" means until the case is dismissed, until the defendant is acquitted, or until the defendant completes his or her sentence. Any defendant sentenced to probation is deemed to have completed his or her sentence upon discharge from probation. A defendant sentenced to incarceration is deemed to have completed his or her sentence upon release from incarceration and discharge from parole supervision.

(a) When the court subjects a defendant to a mandatory protection order that qualifies as an order described in 18 U.S.C. sec. 922 (g) (8), the court, as part of such order:

Shall order the defendant to:

Refrain from possessing or purchasing any firearm or ammunition for the duration of the order; and

Relinquish, for the duration of the order, any firearm or ammunition in the defendant's immediate possession or control or subject to the defendant's immediate possession or control; and

May require that before the defendant is released from custody on bond, the defendant shall relinquish, for the duration of the order, any firearm or ammunition in the defendant's immediate possession or control or subject to the defendant's immediate possession or control.

Upon issuance of an order pursuant to paragraph (a) of this subsection (9), the defendant shall relinquish any firearm or ammunition not more than twenty-four hours after being served with the order; except that a court may allow a defendant up to seventy-two hours to relinquish a firearm or up to five days to relinquish ammunition pursuant to this paragraph (b) if the defendant demonstrates to the satisfaction of the court that he or she is unable to comply within twenty-four hours. To satisfy this requirement, the defendant may:

Sell or transfer possession of the firearm or ammunition to a federally licensed firearms dealer described in 18 U.S.C. sec. 923, as amended; except that this provision shall not be interpreted to require any federally licensed firearms dealer to purchase or accept possession of any firearm or

ammunition;

Arrange for the storage of the firearm or ammunition by a law enforcement agency; except that this provision shall not be interpreted to require any law enforcement agency to provide storage of firearms or ammunition for any person; or

Sell or otherwise transfer the firearm or ammunition to a private party who may legally possess the firearm or ammunition; except that a defendant who sells or transfers a firearm pursuant to this subparagraph (III) shall satisfy all of the provisions of section 18-12-112, concerning private firearms transfers, including but not limited to the performance of a criminal background check of the transferee.

If a defendant is unable to satisfy the provisions of paragraph (b) of this subsection (9) because he or she is incarcerated or otherwise held in the custody of a law enforcement agency, the court shall require the defendant to satisfy such provisions not more than twenty-four hours after his or her release from incarceration or custody or be held in contempt of court. Notwithstanding any provision of this paragraph (c), the court may, in its discretion, require the defendant to relinquish any firearm or ammunition in the defendant's immediate possession or control or subject to the defendant's immediate possession or control before the end of the defendant's incarceration. In such a case, a defendant's failure to relinquish a firearm or ammunition as required shall constitute contempt of court.

A federally licensed firearms dealer who takes possession of a firearm or ammunition pursuant to this section shall issue a receipt to the defendant at the time of relinquishment. The federally licensed firearms dealer shall not return the firearm or ammunition to the defendant unless the dealer:

Contacts the bureau to request that a background check of the defendant be performed;

and check.

Obtains approval of the transfer from the bureau after the performance of the background

A local law enforcement agency may elect to store firearms or ammunition for persons pursuant to this subsection (9). If an agency so elects:

The agency may charge a fee for such storage, the amount of which shall not exceed the direct and indirect costs incurred by the agency in providing such storage;

The agency may establish policies for disposal of abandoned or stolen firearms or ammunition; and

The agency shall issue a receipt to each defendant at the time the defendant relinquishes possession of a firearm or ammunition.

If a local law enforcement agency elects to store firearms or ammunition for a defendant pursuant to this subsection (9), the law enforcement agency shall not return the firearm or ammunition to the defendant unless the agency:

Contacts the bureau to request that a background check of the defendant be performed; and check.

Obtains approval of the transfer from the bureau after the performance of the background

(I) A law enforcement agency that elects to store a firearm or ammunition for a defendant
pursuant to this subsection (9) may elect to cease storing the firearm or ammunition. A law

enforcement agency that elects to cease storing a firearm or ammunition for a defendant shall notify the defendant of such decision and request that the defendant immediately make arrangements for the transfer of the possession of the firearm or ammunition to the defendant or, if the defendant is prohibited from possessing a firearm, to another person who is legally permitted to possess a firearm.

(II) If a law enforcement agency elects to cease storing a firearm or ammunition for a person and notifies the defendant as described in subparagraph (I) of this paragraph (g), the law enforcement agency may dispose of the firearm or ammunition if the defendant fails to make arrangements for the transfer of the firearm or ammunition and complete said transfer within ninety days of receiving such notification.

If a defendant sells or otherwise transfers a firearm or ammunition to a private party who may legally possess the firearm or ammunition, as described in subparagraph (III) of paragraph (b) of this subsection (9), the defendant shall acquire:

From the transferee, a written receipt acknowledging the transfer, which receipt shall be dated and signed by the defendant and the transferee; and

From the licensed gun dealer who requests from the bureau a background check of the transferee, as described in section 18-12-112, a written statement of the results of the background check.

(I) Not more than three business days after the relinquishment, the defendant shall file a copy of the receipt issued pursuant to paragraph (d), (e), or (h) of this subsection (9) and, if applicable, the written statement of the results of a background check performed on the defendant as described in subparagraph (II) of paragraph (h) of this subsection (9), with the court as proof of the relinquishment. If a defendant fails to timely file a receipt or written statement as described in this paragraph (i):

The failure constitutes a violation of the protection order pursuant to section 18-6-803.5

(1) (c); and

The court shall issue a warrant for the defendant's arrest.

(II) In any subsequent prosecution for a violation of a protection order described in this paragraph (i), the court shall take judicial notice of the defendant's failure to file a receipt or written statement, which will constitute prima facie evidence of a violation of the protection order pursuant to section 18-6-803.5 (1) (c), C.R.S., and testimony of the clerk of the court or his or her deputy is not required.

Nothing in this subsection (9) shall be construed to limit a defendant's right to petition the court for dismissal of a protection order.

A person subject to a mandatory protection order issued pursuant to this subsection (9) who possesses or attempts to purchase or receive a firearm or ammunition while the protection order is in effect violates the order pursuant to section 18-6-803.5 (1) (c).

(I) A law enforcement agency that elects in good faith to not store a firearm or ammunition for a defendant pursuant to sub-subparagraph (B) of subparagraph (III) of paragraph (b) of this subsection (9) shall not be held criminally or civilly liable for such election not to act.

(II) A law enforcement agency that returns possession of a firearm or ammunition to a defendant in good faith as permitted by paragraph (f) of this subsection (9) shall not be held criminally or civilly liable for such action.


18-1-1002. Criminal contempt proceedings - notice to district attorney. Before a criminal contempt proceeding is heard before the court, notice of the proceedings shall be provided to the district attorney for the district of the court where the proceedings are to be heard and the district attorney for the district of the court where the alleged act of criminal contempt occurred. The district attorney for either district shall be allowed to appear and argue for the imposition of contempt sanctions.

PART 11 PRESERVATION OF DNA EVIDENCE

18-1-1101. Definitions. As used in this part 11, unless the context otherwise requires:

"Disposed of" means evidence is destroyed, thrown away, or returned to the owner or his or her designee.

"DNA" means deoxyribonucleic acid.

"DNA evidence" means all evidence collected by law enforcement in a criminal investigation, which evidence may be reasonably believed to contain DNA that is relevant to a disputed issue in the investigation and prosecution of the case.

"DNA profile" means an identifier obtained as a result of a specific DNA analysis.


18-1-1102. Scope. (1) The provisions of this part 11 shall apply to the preservation of DNA evidence only when:

The investigation of a felony does not result in or has not resulted in charges being filed;

or

The filed charges resulted in a conviction for a class 1 felony or for a sex offense that
carries an indeterminate sentence pursuant to section 18-1.3-1004; or

The filed charges resulted in a conviction for a felony not covered by paragraph (b) of this subsection (1); or

The filed charges resulted in a conviction for any offense not covered by paragraphs (b) and (c) of this subsection (1), and at least one of the charges filed involved a sex offense as defined in section 18-1.3-1003 (5).

For purposes of subsection (1) of this section, conviction shall include a verdict of guilty by a judge or jury, a plea of guilty or nolo contendere, or a deferred judgment and sentence. For purposes of paragraph (d) of subsection (1) of this section, conviction shall also include a juvenile delinquent adjudication or deferred adjudication.

This part 11 does not impose a statutory duty to retain or store evidence other than in the situations described in this section.


18-1-1103. Duty to preserve DNA evidence. (1) A law enforcement agency that collects DNA evidence in conducting a criminal investigation of a felony that does not result in or has not resulted in charges being filed shall preserve the DNA evidence for the length of the statute of limitations for the felony crime that was investigated.

(2) Except as provided in sections 18-1-1105 to 18-1-1107, a law enforcement agency that collects DNA evidence in conducting a criminal investigation that results in a conviction listed in section 18-1-1102 (1) shall preserve the DNA evidence for the life of the defendant who is convicted.

18-1-1104. Manner and location of preservation of DNA evidence. (1) When DNA evidence that is subject to preservation pursuant to section 18-1-1103 is processed for the development of a DNA profile, the DNA profile shall be preserved by the accredited laboratory in Colorado that develops the DNA profile. If the DNA profile is not developed by an accredited laboratory in Colorado, the laboratory that processes the DNA profile shall send the DNA profile to an accredited laboratory in Colorado for preservation.

A law enforcement agency that has custody of DNA evidence that is subject to preservation pursuant to section 18-1-1103 shall preserve the evidence in an amount and manner sufficient to develop a DNA profile, based on the best scientific practices at the time of collection, from the biological material contained in or included on the evidence. If DNA evidence is of such a size, bulk, or physical character as to render retention impracticable, the law enforcement agency shall remove and preserve portions of the evidence likely to contain DNA related to the offense in a quantity sufficient, based on the best scientific practices at the time of collection, to permit future DNA testing. The preserved DNA evidence shall, whenever possible, include a sample sufficient to allow for independent testing by the defendant. After preserving the necessary amount of the DNA evidence, the law enforcement agency may dispose of the remainder of the evidence.

If a law enforcement agency is asked to produce DNA evidence that is subject to preservation pursuant to section 18-1-1103 and cannot produce the evidence, the chief evidence custodian for the law enforcement agency shall provide an affidavit in which he or she describes, under penalty of perjury, the efforts taken to locate the DNA evidence and affirms that the DNA evidence could not be located.

If upon request a law enforcement agency cannot produce DNA evidence that is subject to preservation pursuant to section 18-1-1103, the court shall determine whether the disposal of the DNA evidence violated the defendant's due process rights, and, if so, the court shall order an appropriate remedy.

18-1-1105. Law enforcement agency request for permission to dispose of evidence - procedures. (1) A law enforcement agency may not request permission to dispose of DNA evidence in cases described in section 18-1-1102 (1) (a) and (1) (b).

In cases described in section 18-1-1102 (1) (c) and (1) (d), a law enforcement agency may seek to dispose of DNA evidence by providing notice, in the form developed pursuant to section 18-

1-1108, to the district attorney that prosecuted the charges arising out of the investigation.

Upon receipt of the notice described in subsection (2) of this section, the district attorney shall determine whether to object to the disposal of the DNA evidence. The district attorney may determine that a portion of the DNA evidence may be disposed of and a portion of the DNA evidence shall be preserved.

(a) If the district attorney determines that the DNA evidence should not be disposed of, the district attorney shall provide notice to the law enforcement agency that the DNA evidence shall be preserved. Upon the receipt of the notice from the district attorney to preserve the DNA evidence, the law enforcement agency shall preserve the DNA evidence until such time as the law enforcement agency is permitted by a court order to dispose of the DNA evidence.

(I) If the district attorney determines that all or a portion of the DNA evidence may be disposed of, he or she shall send notice to the defendant and the law enforcement agency specifying which DNA evidence may be disposed of. Notice to the defendant shall include a copy of the notice form prepared by the law enforcement agency pursuant to subsection (2) of this section.

The defendant shall have ninety-eight days from the date the notice was sent by the district attorney to file a motion to preserve DNA evidence in the court in which the defendant was convicted. The motion shall state specific grounds supporting the preservation of the DNA evidence, and the defendant shall provide copies of the motion to the district attorney and the law enforcement agency.

If no motion is filed within the ninety-eight-day period, the district attorney or the law enforcement agency requesting disposal of the evidence shall file with the court a copy of the notice sent to the defendant pursuant to subparagraph (I) of this paragraph (b), and the court shall forthwith, without hearing, enter an order authorizing disposal of the DNA evidence and provide copies of the order to the defendant, district attorney, and law enforcement agency.

If the defendant files a motion, the court shall follow the procedure set forth in subsection (6) of this section.

(I) If the law enforcement agency does not receive notice from the district attorney as described in paragraph (a) or (b) of this subsection (4) within a reasonable amount of time or does receive timely notice from the district attorney pursuant to paragraph (a) of this subsection (4), the law enforcement agency may file a motion with the court that entered the conviction in the case in which the evidence was collected, asking for a court order to dispose of the DNA evidence. The motion shall include a copy of the notice the law enforcement agency provided to the district attorney. The law enforcement agency shall provide a copy of the disposal motion to the district attorney and the defendant contemporaneously with the filing of the motion. The law enforcement agency shall specify the DNA evidence for which disposal is requested in the motion.

(II) The defendant or the district attorney shall have ninety-eight days after the disposal motion is sent to file an objection in the court in which the disposal motion was filed. The objection shall state specific grounds supporting the preservation of the DNA evidence. If the district attorney files an objection, the district attorney shall provide copies of the objection to the defendant and the law enforcement agency. If the defendant files an objection, the defendant shall provide copies of the objection to the district attorney and the law enforcement agency.

The defendant, through legal counsel, shall have a reasonable right to review the DNA evidence to prepare the filing of a timely objection to the disposal motion or the district attorney's

notice received pursuant to paragraph (b) of subsection (4) of this section.

(a) Upon receipt pursuant to subparagraph (II) of paragraph (c) of subsection (4) of this section of a timely filed objection, the court may deny the objection without a hearing if it finds on the face of the objection no grounds supporting the request to preserve the DNA evidence. The court shall then enter an order authorizing disposal of the DNA evidence and provide copies of the order to the defendant, district attorney, and law enforcement agency.

If the court determines that a timely filed objection or motion to preserve states adequate grounds to require preservation of the DNA evidence, the court may set a hearing on the objection or motion to preserve, with notice to the district attorney, the law enforcement agency, and the defendant, or the court may deny the disposal motion without a hearing.

In considering an objection or motion to preserve pursuant to this subsection (6), the court shall consider the following factors in determining whether to order preservation of the DNA evidence:

Whether identification was a disputed issue;

Whether the evidence contains known DNA;

Whether it is possible to perform DNA testing on the evidence that has not previously been performed;

Whether the defendant has served all of his or her sentence; and

Whether the defendant has state appellate or collateral attack rights that have not been exhausted, in which case there shall be a presumption that the DNA evidence should be preserved.

Following a hearing on a disposal motion or motion to preserve, the court shall enter an order either authorizing disposal of the DNA evidence or ordering the DNA evidence to be preserved. If the court orders preservation, the order may state the length of time the DNA evidence shall be preserved or establish a condition precedent for the disposition of the DNA evidence.

18-1-1106. Defendant request for disposition of or waiver of preservation of DNA evidence - procedures. (1) In a case described in section 18-1-1102 (1), a defendant may petition the court on his or her own behalf for the disposal of DNA evidence in his or her case. The defendant shall provide a copy of the petition to the district attorney, who may join with or object to the defendant's petition. Upon the filing of the petition, the timing and procedures of section 18-1-1105 shall apply. By filing a petition for disposition of DNA evidence, the defendant waives any right to preservation of that evidence under this part 11. However, a defendant may not be compelled to file a motion under this section in order to obtain a plea or sentence agreement.
(2) In a case described in section 18-1-1102 (1), a defendant may waive his or her right to preservation of DNA evidence under this part 11 at any stage of the proceeding by making a knowing and voluntary waiver. A waiver executed as a part of a plea bargain or sentencing agreement shall be voluntarily agreed to by all parties and shall include a written list describing all evidence to be disposed of.

18-1-1107. Victim request for disposition of DNA evidence - procedures. In a case described in section 18-1-1102 (1), if DNA evidence is being held that is the property of the victim,

as defined in section 24-4.1-302 (5), C.R.S., of the crime, the victim may request the district attorney to review whether the DNA evidence may be returned. If the district attorney determines the DNA evidence may be returned, the district attorney may file a petition with the court for the return of the DNA evidence. The district attorney shall provide notice to the defendant of the petition. Upon the filing of the petition, the timing and procedures of section 18-1-1105 shall apply.

18-1-1108. Notice - form and sufficiency. (1) Notice to the defendant as required by this part 11 shall be proper if it is sent by United States mail or hand-delivered to the attorney of record for the defendant as defined in rule 44 of the Colorado rules of criminal procedure. If there is no attorney of record, notice to the defendant shall be proper if it is sent by United States mail to the last-known address of the defendant as reflected in the current motor vehicle records or, if no such record exists, the last-known address in the court file. Prior to sending notice by United States mail, however, the district attorney shall first review the department of corrections records to determine whether the defendant is in the physical custody of the department of corrections or on parole. If the defendant is in the physical custody of the department of corrections or on parole, the district attorney shall send notice by United States mail to the correctional facility in which, according to the department's records, the defendant is housed or to the address to which the defendant has been paroled. If the letter is returned because the defendant has been transferred to a different correctional facility, the district attorney shall send notice to the new facility in which the defendant is housed.
(2) The department of public safety, in consultation with state and local law enforcement agencies, shall develop a form to be used by all law enforcement agencies for providing notice to the district attorney and the defendant as described in section 18-1-1105 (2).

18-1-1109. Court data collection - DNA evidence cases - repeal. (Repealed)

ARTICLE 1.3

Sentencing in Criminal Cases

PART 1 ALTERNATIVES IN SENTENCING

18-1.3-101. Pretrial diversion. (1) Legislative intent. The intent of this section is to facilitate and encourage diversion of defendants from the criminal justice system when diversion mayprevent defendants from committing additional criminal acts, restore victims of crime, facilitate the defendant's ability to pay restitution to victims of crime, and reduce the number of cases in the

criminal justice system. Diversion should ensure defendant accountabilitywhile allowing defendants to avoid the collateral consequences associated with criminal charges and convictions. A district attorney's office may develop or continue to operate its own diversion program that is not subject to the provisions of this section. If a district attorney's office accepts state moneys to create or operate a diversion program pursuant to this section, the district attorney's office must comply with the provisions of this section.
Period of diversion. In any case, either before or after charges are filed, the district attorney may suspend prosecution of the offense for a period not to exceed two years. The period of diversion may be extended for an additional time up to one year if the failure to pay restitution is the sole condition of diversion that has not been fulfilled, because of inability to pay, and the defendant has a future ability to pay. During the period of diversion the defendant may be placed under the supervision of the probation department or a diversion program approved by the district attorney.
Guidelines for eligibility. Each district attorney that uses state moneys for a diversion program pursuant to this section shall adopt policies and guidelines delineating eligibility criteria for pretrial diversion and may agree to diversion in any case in which there exists sufficient admissible evidence to support a conviction. In determining whether an individual is appropriate for diversion, the district attorney shall consider:
The nature of the crime charged and the circumstances surrounding it;
Any special characteristics or circumstances of the defendant;
Whether diversion is consistent with the defendant's rehabilitation and reintegration; and
Whether the public interest will be best served by diverting the individual from prosecution.
Before entering into a pretrial diversion agreement, the district attorney may require a defendant to provide information regarding prior criminal charges, education and work experience, family, residence in the community, and other information relating to the diversion program. The defendant shall not be denied the opportunity to consult with legal counsel before consenting to diversion. Legal counsel may be appointed as provided under article 1 of title 21, C.R.S.
In a jurisdiction that receives state moneys for the creation or operation of diversion programs pursuant to this section, an individual accused of an offense, the underlying factual basis of which involves domestic violence as defined in section 18-6-800.3 (1), is not eligible for pretrial diversion unless charges have been filed, the individual has had an opportunity to consult with counsel, and the individual has completed a domestic violence treatment evaluation, which includes the use of a domestic violence risk assessment instrument, conducted by a domestic violence treatment provider

approved by the domestic violence offender management board as required by section 16-11.8-103 (4), C.R.S. The district attorney may agree to place the individual in the diversion program established by the district attorney pursuant to this section if he or she finds that, based on the results of that evaluation and the other factors in subsection (3) of this section, that the individual is appropriate for the program.

In a jurisdiction that receives state moneys for the creation or operation of diversion programs pursuant to this section, an individual accused of a sex offense as defined in section 18- 1.3-1003 (5) is not eligible for pretrial diversion unless charges have been filed and, after the individual has had an opportunity to consult with counsel, the individual has completed a sex- offense-specific evaluation, which includes the use of a sex-offense-specific risk  assessment

instrument, conducted by an evaluator approved by the sex offender management board as required by section 16-11.7-103 (4), C.R.S. The district attorney may agree to place the individual in the diversion program established by the district attorney pursuant to this section if he or she finds that, based on the results of that evaluation and the other factors in subsection (3) of this section, that the individual is appropriate for the program.

Notwithstanding that a successfully completed diversion agreement does not constitute a history of sex offenses for purposes of sections 16-11.7-102 (2) (a)

(II) and 16-22-103 (2) (d), C.R.S., the information constituting the crimes charged and facts alleged shall be available for use by a court, district attorney, any law enforcement agency, or agency of the state judicial department, if otherwise permitted by law, in any subsequent criminal investigation, prosecution, risk or needs assessment evaluation, sentencing hearing, or during a probation or parole supervision period.

Notwithstanding any other provision of this section, an individual accused of any of the following sexual offenses is not eligible for participation in a diversion program established in a jurisdiction that receives state moneys for the creation or operation of diversion programs pursuant to this section:

Sexual assault as described in section 18-3-402;

Sexual assault on a child as described in section 18-3-405;

Any sexual offense committed against an at-risk adult or an at-risk juvenile, as defined in section 18-6.5-102 (2) and (4);

Any sexual offense committed with the use of a deadly weapon as described in section 18-1-901 (3) (e);

Enticement of a child, as described in section 18-3-305;

Sexual exploitation of a child as described in section 18-6-403;

Procurement of a child for exploitation, as described in section 18-6-404;

Sexual assault on a child by one in a position of trust, as described in section 18-3-405.3;

or

Any child prostitution offense in part 4 of article 7 of this title.

Diversion programs may include, but are not limited to, programs operated by law

enforcement upon agreement with a district attorney, district attorney internally operated programs, programs operated by other approved agencies, restorative justice programs, or supervision by the probation department. Referencesto "deferred prosecution" in Colorado statutes and court rules shall apply to pretrial diversion as authorized by this section.

Diversion agreements. (a) All pretrial diversions shall be governed by the terms of an individualized diversion agreement signed bythe defendant, the defendant's attorneyif the defendant is represented by an attorney, and the district attorney.

The diversion agreement shall include a written waiver of the right to a speedy trial for the period of the diversion. All diversion agreements shall include a condition that the defendant not commit any criminal offense during the period of the agreement. Diversion agreements may also include provisions, agreed to by the defendant, concerning payment of restitution and court costs, payment of a supervision fee not to exceed that provided for in section 18-1.3-204 (2) (a) (V), or participation in restorative justice practices as defined in section 18-1-901 (3) (o.5). Any pretrial diversion supervision fees collected may be retained by the district attorney for purposes of funding its adult pretrial diversion program. The conditions of diversion shall be limited to those specific to

the individual defendant or necessaryfor proper supervision of the individual defendant. A diversion agreement shall provide that if the defendant fulfills the obligations described therein, the court shall order all criminal charges filed against the defendant dismissed with prejudice.

The diversion agreement may require an assessment of the defendant's criminogenic needs, to be performed after the period of diversion has begun by either the probation department or a diversion program approved by the district attorney. Based on the results of that assessment, the probation department or approved diversion program may direct the defendant to participate in programs offering medical, therapeutic, educational, vocational, corrective, preventive, or other rehabilitative services. Defendants with the ability to pay may be required to pay for such programs or services.

The diversion agreement may include a statement of the facts the charge is based upon authored by the defendant and agreed to by the defendant's attorney if the defendant is represented byan attorneyand the district attorney. The statement is admissible as impeachment evidence against the defendant in the criminal proceedings if the defendant fails to fulfill the terms of the diversion agreement and criminal proceedings are resumed.

A defendant shall not be required to enter any plea to a criminal charge as a condition of pretrial diversion. A defendant's or counsel's statement in a diversion conference or in any other discussion of a proposed diversion agreement, including an evaluation performed pursuant to subsections (5) and (6) of this section, other than a statement provided for in paragraph (d) of this subsection (9), shall not be admissible as evidence in criminal proceedings on the crimes charged or facts alleged.

If the district attorney agrees to offer diversion in lieu of further criminal proceedings and the defendant agrees to all of the terms of the proposed agreement, the diversion agreement may be either filed with the court or held by the parties. A court filing shall be required only if the probation department supervises the defendant. When a diversion agreement is reached, the court shall stay further proceedings.

Diversion outcomes. (a) During the period of diversion, the supervising program or agency designated in the diversion agreement shall provide the level of supervision necessary to facilitate rehabilitation and ensure the defendant is completing the terms of the diversion agreement.

Upon the defendant's satisfactory completion of and discharge from supervision, the court shall dismiss with prejudice all charges against the defendant. The effect of the dismissal is to restore the defendant to the status he or she occupied before the arrest, citation, or summons. A successfully completed diversion agreement shall not be considered a conviction for any purpose. A person with an order of dismissal entered pursuant to this article may not be subject to charge, prosecution, or liability under Colorado law of perjury or otherwise giving a false statement by reason of his or her failure to recite or acknowledge the arrest, citation, or summons in response to any inquiry made for any purpose.

At any point after a diversion agreement is completed, a defendant may petition the court to seal all arrest and other criminal records pertaining to the offense using the procedure described in section 24-72-702, C.R.S. Unless otherwise prohibited under section 24-72-702 (4) (a), C.R.S., the court shall issue a sealing order if requested by the defendant following successful completion of a diversion agreement.

If the defendant violates the conditions of the diversion agreement, the supervising entity

shall provide written notice of the violation to the defendant, the district attorney, and the court. The district attorney, in his or her sole discretion, may initiate revocation of a diversion agreement by the filing of a criminal complaint, information, or indictment, or if charges have already been filed, by giving the court notice of intent to proceed with the prosecution. The defendant may, within fourteen days after the first court appearance following such a filing, request a hearing to contest whether a violation occurred. The district attorney has the burden by a preponderance of the evidence to show that a violation has in fact occurred, and the procedural safeguards required in a revocation of probation hearing pursuant to section 16-11-206,

C.R.S., shall apply. The court may, when it appears that the alleged violation of the diversion agreement is a pending criminal offense against the defendant, continue the diversion revocation hearing until the completion of the criminal proceeding. If the court finds a violation has occurred, or a hearing is not requested, the prosecution may continue. If the court finds the district attorney has not proven a violation, the court shall dismiss the criminal case without prejudice and return the defendant to the supervision of the diversion program to complete the terms of the agreement.

If a defendant is prosecuted following a violation of a diversion agreement, a factual statement entered pursuant to paragraph (d) of subsection (9) of this section is admissible as impeachment evidence. Any other information concerning diversion, including participation in a diversion program, including an evaluation performed pursuant to subsections (5) and (6) of this section, the terms of a diversion agreement, or statements made to treatment providers during a diversion program, shall not be admitted into evidence at trial for any purpose.


18-1.3-102. Deferred sentencing of defendant. (1) (a) In any case in which the defendant has entered a plea of guilty, the court accepting the plea has the power, with the written consent of the defendant and his or her attorney of record and the district attorney, to continue the case for the purpose of entering judgment and sentence upon the plea of guilty for a period not to exceed four years for a felony or two years for a misdemeanor or petty offense or traffic offense. The period shall begin to run from the date that the court continues the case.

The period may be extended for an additional time:

Up to one hundred eighty-two days if the failure to pay restitution is the sole condition of supervision which has not been fulfilled, because of inability to pay, and the defendant has shown a future ability to pay. During such time, the court may place the defendant under the supervision of the probation department; or

Up to two years if the deferred judgment is for an offense listed in section 16-11.7-102 (3), C.R.S., good cause is shown, and the district attorney and defendant consent to the extension.

Prior to entry of a plea of guilty to be followed by deferred judgment and sentence, the district attorney, in the course of plea discussion as provided in sections 16-7-301 and 16-7-302, C.R.S., is authorized to enter into a written stipulation, to be signed by the defendant, the defendant's attorney of record, and the district attorney, under which the defendant is obligated to adhere to such stipulation. The conditions imposed in the stipulation shall be similar in all respects to conditions permitted as part of probation. A person convicted of a crime, the underlying factual basis of which included an act of domestic violence, as defined in section 18-6-800.3 (1), shall stipulate to the conditions specified in section 18-1.3-204 (2) (b). In addition, the stipulation may require the

defendant to perform community or charitable work service projects or make donations thereto. Upon full compliance with such conditions by the defendant, the plea of guilty previously entered shall be withdrawn and the charge upon which the judgment and sentence of the court was deferred shall be dismissed with prejudice. The stipulation shall specifically provide that, upon a breach by the defendant of anycondition regulating the conduct of the defendant, the court shall enter judgment and impose sentence upon the guilty plea; except that, if the offense is a violation of article 18 of this title, the court may accept an admission or find a violation of the stipulation without entering judgment and imposing sentence if the court first makes findings of fact on the record stating the entry of judgment and sentencing would not be consistent with the purposes of sentencing, that the defendant would be better served by continuing the deferred judgment period, and that public safety

\pard softlinewould not be jeopardized by the continuation of the deferred judgment. If the court makes those findings and continues the deferred judgment over the objection of the prosecution, the court shall also impose additional and immediate sanctions upon the defendant to address the violation, to include, but not be limited to, the imposition of further terms and conditions that will enhance the likelihood of the defendant's success, respond to the defendant's noncompliance, and promote further individual accountability, including extending the time period of the deferred judgment for up to two additional years or incarceration in the county jail for a period not to exceed ninety days consistent with the provisions of section 18-1.3-202 (1), or both. When, as a condition of the deferred sentence, the court orders the defendant to make restitution, evidence of failure to pay the restitution shall constitute prima facie evidence of a violation. Whether a breach of condition has occurred shall be determined by the court without a jury upon application of the district attorney or a probation officer and upon notice of hearing thereon of not less than seven days to the defendant or the defendant's attorney of record. Application for entry of judgment and imposition of sentence may be made by the district attorney or a probation officer at any time within the term of the deferred judgment or within thirty-five days thereafter. The burden of proof at the hearing shall be by a preponderance of the evidence, and the procedural safeguards required in a revocation of probation hearing shall apply.

When a defendant signs a stipulation by which it is provided that judgment and sentence shall be deferred for a time certain, he or she thereby waives all rights to a speedy trial, as provided in section 18-1-405.

A warrant for the arrest of any defendant for breach of a condition of a deferred sentence may be issued by any judge of a court of record upon the report of a probation officer, or upon the verified complaint of any person, establishing to the satisfaction of the judge probable cause to believe that a condition of the deferred sentence has been violated and that the arrest of the defendant is reasonably necessary. The warrant may be executed by any probation officer or by a peace officer authorized to execute warrants in the county in which the defendant is found.


18-1.3-103. Deferred sentencing - drug offenders - legislative declaration - demonstration program - repeal. (Repealed)


18-1.3-103.4. Senate Bill 13-250 - legislative intent - clarification of internal reference

to level 4 drug felonies. The intent of the general assembly in enacting Senate Bill 13-250 was to allow courts, for offenses committed on and after October 1, 2013, to vacate certain level 4 drug felony convictions and enter misdemeanor convictions if the offender completes community-based sentencing. While the term "level 4 drug felony" to which section 18-1.3-103.5 (3) (b) refers was described in section 18-8-405 (2) (c) (II) of the introduced version of Senate Bill 13-250, an amendment to the bill during the legislative process moved the level 4 drug felony description to section 18-8-405 (2) (d). The conforming change was not made to the internal reference in section 18-1.3-103.5 (3) (b), resulting in an incorrect internal reference being published in the 2013 version of the Colorado Revised Statutes. When enacting Senate Bill 13-250, it was the intent of the general assembly that the level 4 drug felonies to which section 18-1.3-103.5 (3) (b) refers be those described in section 18-8-405 (2) (d). Accordingly, by the passage of Senate Bill 14-163, enacted in 2014, the general assembly corrects the internal reference found in section 18-1.3-103.5 (3) (b). The correction to the internal reference is effective as of the effective date of Senate Bill 13-250, October 1, 2013, and applies to offenses committed on or after October 1, 2013.


18-1.3-103.5. Felony convictions - vacate and enter conviction on misdemeanor after successful completion. (1) In order to expand opportunities for offenders to avoid a drug felony conviction, to reduce the significant negative consequences of that felony conviction, and to provide positive reinforcement for drug offenders who work to successfully complete any community-based sentence imposed by the court, the legislature herebycreates an additional opportunity for those drug offenders who may not otherwise have been eligible for or successful in other statutorily created programs that allow the drug offender to avoid a felony conviction, such as diversion or deferred judgment.

(a) In a case in which the defendant enters a plea of guilty or is found guilty by the court or a jury for a crime listed in subsection (3) of this section, the court shall order, upon successful completion of any community-based sentence to probation or to a community corrections program, the drug felony conviction vacated and shall enter a conviction for a level 1 drug misdemeanor offense of possession of a controlled substance pursuant to section 18-18-403.5. Upon entry of the judgment of conviction pursuant to section 18-18-403.5, the court shall indicate in its order that the judgment of conviction is entered pursuant to the provisions of this section.

(b) Whether a sentence is successfully completed shall be determined by the court without a jury with notice to the district attorney and the defendant or the defendant's attorney of record. A community-based sentence is not successfully completed if the defendant has not successfully completed the treatment as ordered by the court and determined appropriate to address the defendant's treatment needs.

This section applies to convictions for the following offenses:

Possession of a controlled substance; but only when the quantity of the controlled substance is not more than four grams of a schedule I or schedule II controlled substance, not more than two grams of methamphetamine, heroin, ketamine, or cathinones, or not more than four milligrams of flunitrazepam. The district attorney and defendant may stipulate to the amount of the controlled substance possessed by the defendant at the time of sentencing, or the court shall determine the amount at the time of sentencing.

(II);

A level 4 drug felony for distribution pursuant to the provisions of section 18-18-405 (2)

Possession of more than twelve ounces of marijuana or more than three ounces of marijuana concentrate; or
A violation of section 18-18-415.
Notwithstanding any provision of this section to the contrary, a defendant is not eligible for relief under this section if:
The defendant has a prior conviction for a crime of violence as described in section 18- 1.3-406 or a prior conviction for an offense that is required to be sentenced pursuant to the provisions of section 18-1.3-406 in this state, or a crime in another state, the United States, or any territory subject to the jurisdiction of the United States that would be a crime of violence or an offense required to be sentenced pursuant to the provisions of section 18-1.3-406 in this state;
The defendant is ineligible for probation pursuant to section 18-1.3-201; or
(I) The defendant has two or more prior felony convictions for a drug offense pursuant to this title, or a crime in another state, the United States, or any territory subject to the jurisdiction of the United States that would be a drug offense violation of this title.
For purposes of this paragraph (c), a felony conviction includes any diversion, deferred prosecution, or deferred judgment and sentence, whether or not completed, for a felony, and any conviction entered as a result of relief previously granted pursuant to this section or as a result of a guilty plea to a misdemeanor offense, as described in article 18 of this title, originally charged as a felony drug offense, as described in article 18 of this title.


18-1.3-104. Alternatives in imposition of sentence. (1) Within the limitations of the applicable statute pertaining to sentencing and subject to the provisions of this title, the trial court has the following alternatives in entering judgment imposing a sentence:
The defendant may be granted probation unless any provision of law makes him or her ineligible for probation. The granting or denial of probation and the conditions of probation including the length of probation shall not be subject to appellate review unless probation is granted contrary to the provisions of this title.
Subject to the provisions of sections 18-1.3-401 and 18-1.3-401.5, in class 2, class 3, class 4, class 5, and class 6 felonies and level 1, level 2, level 3, and level 4 drug felonies, the defendant may be sentenced to imprisonment for a definite period of time.
(b.5) (I) Except as otherwise provided by subparagraph (II) of this paragraph (b.5), any defendant who, in the determination of the court, is a candidate for an alternative sentencing option and who would otherwise be sentenced to imprisonment pursuant to paragraph (b) of this subsection may, as an alternative, be sentenced to a specialized restitution and community service program pursuant to section 18-1.3-302, which may include restorative justice practices, as defined in section 18-1-901 (3) (o.5), if such defendant is determined eligible and is accepted into such program. To be eligible for restorative justice practices, the defendant shall not have been convicted of unlawful sexual behavior as defined in section 16-22-102 (9), C.R.S., a crime in which the underlying factual basis involves domestic violence, as defined in section 18-6-800.3 (1), stalking as defined in section 18-3-602, or violation of a protection order as defined in section 18-6-803.5. If the court orders the

defendant to attend a restorative justice practices victim-offender conference, the facilitator of the conference shall provide his or her services for a fee of no more than one hundred twenty-five dollars, based on a sliding scale; however, the fee may be waived by the court. Any statements made during the conference shall be confidential and shall not be used as a basis for charging or prosecuting the defendant unless the defendant commits a chargeable offense during the conference.
(II) (A) The court shall consider and may sentence any defendant who is a nonviolent offender as defined in sub-subparagraph (B) of this subparagraph (II) pursuant to subsection (2) of this section.
(B) As used in this section, "nonviolent offender" means a person convicted of a felony other than a crime of violence as defined in section 18-1.3-406 (2), one of the felonies set forth in section 18-3-104, 18-4-203, 18-4-301, or 18-4-401 (2) (c), (2) (d), or (5), or a felony offense committed against a child as set forth in articles 3, 6, and 7 of this title, and who is not subject to the provisions of section 18-1.3-801.
The defendant shall be sentenced to death in those cases in which a death sentence is required under section 18-1.3-1201, 18-1.3-1302, or 18-1.4-102.
The defendant may be sentenced to the payment of a fine or to a term of imprisonment or to both a term of imprisonment and the payment of a fine; except that a person who has been twice convicted of a felony under the laws of this state, any other state, or the United States prior to the conviction for which he or she is being sentenced is not eligible to receive a fine in lieu of imprisonment. No fine shall be imposed for conviction of a felony except as provided in sections 18- 1.3-401 and 25-15-310, articles 22 to 29 of title 39, or article 3 of title 42, C.R.S.
The defendant may be sentenced to comply with any other court order authorized by law.
The defendant may be sentenced to payment of costs.
The defendant may be sentenced pursuant to part 4 or 5 of this article.
(I) If the defendant is eligible pursuant to section 18-1.3-407.5 or section 19-2-517 (6), C.R.S., the defendant may be sentenced to the youthful offender system in accordance with section 18-1.3-407.
Repealed.
Notwithstanding any provision of this subsection (1) to the contrary, the court shall sentence any person convicted of a sex offense, as defined in section 18-1.3-1003 (5), committed on or after November 1, 1998, pursuant to the provisions of part 10 of this article.
(a) The sentencing court shall consider the following factors in sentencing nonviolent offenders:
The nature and character of the offense;
The character and record of the nonviolent offender, including whether the offender is a first-time offender;
The offender's employment history;
The potential rehabilitative value of the sentencing alternatives available to the court;
Any potential impact on the safety of the victim, the victim's family, and the general public based upon sentencing alternatives available to the court; and
The offender's ability to pay restitution to the victim or the victim's family based upon the sentencing alternatives available to the court.
Repealed.

The court shall consider and may sentence a nonviolent offender to any one or any combination of the sentences described in this paragraph (c) if, upon consideration of the factors described in paragraph (a) of this subsection (2), the court does not grant probation pursuant to paragraph (b) of this subsection (2) or does not sentence the offender to the department of corrections as provided under paragraph (d) of this subsection (2):
A community corrections program pursuant to section 18-1.3-301;
A home detention program pursuant to section 18-1.3-105; or
A specialized restitution and community service program pursuant to section 18-1.3-302.
Nothing in this subsection (2) shall be construed as prohibiting a court from exercising
its discretion in sentencing a nonviolent offender to the department of corrections based upon, but not limited to, any one or more factors described in

paragraph (a) of this subsection (2).

(a) In determining the appropriate sentencing alternative for a defendant who has been convicted of unlawful sexual behavior as defined in section 16-22-102 (9), the sentencing court shall consider the defendant's previous criminal and juvenile delinquency records, if any, set forth in the presentence investigation report prepared pursuant to section 16-11-102 (1) (a), C.R.S.

(b) For purposes of this subsection (3), "convicted" means a conviction by a jury or by a court and shall also include a deferred judgment and sentence, a deferred adjudication, an adjudication, and a plea of guilty or nolo contendere.

18-1.3-104.5. Alternatives in imposition of sentence in drug felony cases - exhaustion of remedies. (1) The general assembly finds that it is essential in certain level 4 drug felony cases that the court consider all sentencing options to ensure that the state's costly prison resources are used for those offenders for whom another sentence is not appropriate or will not properly meet the goals of community safety and rehabilitation of the offender.

(2) (a) Prior to the imposition of any sentence to the department of corrections for a level 4 drug felony offense at sentencing or at resentencing after a revocation of probation or community corrections sentence, the court shall exhaust all reasonable and appropriate alternative sentences for the offense considering all factors outlined in paragraph (b) of this subsection (2).

If the court sentences the defendant to the department of corrections for a level 4 drug felony offense, it must determine that incarceration is the most suitable option given the facts and circumstances of the case, including the defendant's willingness to participate in treatment. Further, the court must also determine that all other reasonable and appropriate sanctions and responses to the violation that are available to the court have been tried and failed, do not appear likely to be successful if tried, or present an unacceptable risk to public safety.

In making the determination in paragraph (b) of this subsection (2), the court shall review, to the extent available, the information provided by the supervising agency, which includes, but is not limited to, a complete statement as to what treatment and sentencing options have been tried and have failed, what other community options are available and the reasons why any other available community options appear to be unlikely to be successful. The supervising agency shall provide to the court the risk level of the offender as determined by an evidence-based risk assessment

tool employed by the supervising agency and any other information relevant to the defendant's risk to public safety.

18-1.3-105. Authority of sentencing courts to utilize home detention programs. (1) (a) A sentencing judge is authorized to sentence any offender, as defined in subsection (5) of this section, to a home detention program operated pursuant to a contractual agreement with the department of public safety pursuant to this article for all or part of such offender's sentence.

Prior to sentencing any offender directly to a home detention program, the sentencing judge shall consider the following factors:

The safety of victims and witnesses of the offender's criminal acts;

The safety of the public at large;

The seriousness of any offense committed by the offender together with any information relating to the original charge against the offender;

The offender's prior criminal record; and

The ability of the offender to pay for the costs of home detention and any restitution to victims of his or her criminal acts.

The sentencing judge shall make every reasonable effort to notify the victims of crime that the offender has been sentenced to a home detention program. Such notice shall be sent to the last address in the possession of the court, and the victim of the crime has the duty to keep the court informed of his or her most current address.

An offender who has been convicted of a crime, the underlying factual basis of which was found by the court to include an act of domestic violence, as defined in section 18-6-800.3 (1), shall not be eligible for home detention in the home of the victim pursuant to this article.

Any offender who is directly sentenced to a home detention program pursuant to subsection (1) of this section and fails to carry out the terms and conditions prescribed by the sentencing court in his or her sentence to a home detention program shall be returned to the court and resentenced as soon as possible.

A sentencing judge is authorized to require any offender, as defined in subsection (5) of this section, as a condition of probation, to serve an appropriate period of time extending from ninety days to one year in a home detention program operated directly by the judicial department, or in a home detention program operated pursuant to a contractual agreement with the department of public safety.

The general assembly hereby declares that this section shall be effective July 1, 1990, only in the counties of Boulder, Larimer, and Pueblo in order to facilitate a pilot program in Boulder, Larimer, and Pueblo counties which shall extend from July 1, 1990, until July 1, 1992.

As used in this section, unless the context otherwise requires:

"Home detention" means an alternative correctional sentence or term of probation supervision wherein a defendant convicted of any felony, other than a class 1 or violent felony, is allowed to serve his or her sentence or term of probation, or a portion thereof, within his or her home or other approved residence. Such sentence or term of probation shall require the offender to remain within his or her approved residence at all times except for approved employment, court-ordered

activities, and medical needs.

"Offender" means any person who has been convicted of or who has received a deferred sentence for a felony, other than a class 1 or violent felony.

18-1.3-106. County jail sentencing alternatives - work, educational, and medical release
- home detention - day reporting. (1) (a) Any county may provide a program whereby any person sentenced to the county jail upon conviction for a crime, nonpayment of any fine or forfeiture, or contempt of court may be granted by the court the privilege of leaving the jail during necessary and reasonable hours for any of the following purposes:

Seeking employment;

Working at his or her employment;

Conducting his or her own business or other self-employed occupation including housekeeping and attending to the needs of the family;

Attendance at an educational institution;

Medical treatment;

Home detention; or

Day reporting.

(b) A court may order a person who would otherwise be sentenced to the county jail upon conviction of a crime to be sentenced directly to an available day reporting program if the court deems such a sentence to be appropriate for the offender.

(1.1) For purposes of this section, "home detention" means an alternative correctional sentence or term of legal supervision wherein a defendant charged or convicted of a misdemeanor, felony, nonpayment of any fine, or contempt of court is allowed to serve his or her sentence or term of supervision, or a portion thereof, within his or her home or other approved residence. Such sentence or term of supervision shall cause the defendant to remain within such defendant's approved residence at all times except for approved employment, court-ordered activities, and medical needs. Supervision of the defendant shall include personal monitoring by an agent or designee of the referring unit of government and monitoring by electronic or global positioning devices that are capable of detecting and reporting the defendant's absence or presence within the approved residence.

(1.3) Before a court may grant a person sentenced to the county jail the privilege of leaving the jail to attend a postsecondary educational institution, the court shall first notify the prosecuting attorney and the postsecondary educational institution of its intention to grant the privilege and request their comments thereon. The notice shall include all relevant information pertaining to the person and the crime for which he or she was convicted. Both the prosecuting attorney and the postsecondary institution shall reply to the court in writing within fourteen days after receipt of the notification or within such other reasonable time in excess of fourteen days as specified by the court. The postsecondary educational institution's reply shall include a statement of whether or not it will accept the person as a student. Acceptance by a state postsecondary educational institution shall be pursuant to section 23-5-106, C.R.S.

Unless directly sentenced to a day reporting program pursuant to paragraph (b) of subsection (1) of this section or unless such privilege is otherwise expressly granted by the

sentencing court, the prisoner shall be confined as sentenced. The prisoner may petition the court for such privilege at the time of sentencing or thereafter and, in the discretion of the court, may renew his or her petition. The court may withdraw the privilege at any time by order entered with or without notice.

The sheriff may endeavor to secure employment for unemployed prisoners under this section. If a prisoner is employed for wages or salary, the sheriff may collect the same or require the prisoner to turn over his or her wages or salary in full when received, and the sheriff shall deposit the same in a trust checking account and shall keep a ledger showing the status of the account of each prisoner.

Every prisoner gainfully employed shall be liable for the cost of his or her board in the jail or the cost of the supervision and administrative services if he or she is home-detained, as fixed by the board of county commissioners. If necessarily absent from jail at mealtime, he or she shall, at his or her request, be furnished with an adequate nourishing lunch to carry to work. The sheriff shall charge his or her account, if he or she has one, for such board. If the prisoner is gainfully self- employed, he or she shall pay the sheriff for such board, in default of which his or her privilege under this section shall be automatically forfeited. If the jail food is furnished directly by the county, the sheriff shall account for and pay over such board payments to the county treasurer. The board of county commissioners may, by resolution, provide that the county furnish or pay for the transportation of prisoners employed under this section to and from the place of employment. The sheriff shall reimburse the county or other disbursing agent for all such expenses incurred in accordance with this section and article 26 of title 17, C.R.S., as soon as adequate funds are available in the prisoner's account and in accordance with paragraph (b) of subsection (5) of this section.

By order of the court, the wages or salaries of employed prisoners shall be disbursed by the sheriff for the following purposes, in the order stated:

Payment of any current child support order;

Payment of any child support arrearage; (b.3) Payment of any child support debt order;

Payment of any spousal maintenance;

Payment of costs for the crime victim compensation fund, pursuant to section 24-4.1-119, C.R.S.;

Payment of surcharges for the victims and witnesses assistance and law enforcement fund, pursuant to section 24-4.2-104, C.R.S.;

Payment of restitution;

Payment of a time payment fee;

Payment of late fees;

Payment of any other fines, fees, or surcharges;

Payment of the board of the prisoner;

Payment of the supervision and administrative services provided to the prisoner during his or her home detention;

Payment of necessary travel expense to and from work and other incidental expenses of the prisoner;

Payment, either in full or ratably, of the prisoner's obligations acknowledged by him or her in writing or which have been reduced to judgment; and

The balance, if any, to the prisoner upon his or her discharge.

The court may by order authorize the sheriff to whom the prisoner is committed to arrange with another sheriff for the employment or home detention of the prisoner in the other's county and, while so employed or so detained, for the prisoner to be in the other's custody but in other respects to be and continue subject to the commitment.

If the prisoner was convicted in a court in another county, the court of record having criminal jurisdiction may, at the request or with the concurrence of the committing court, make all determinations and orders under this section which might otherwise be made by the sentencing court after the prisoner is received at the jail.

The board of county commissioners may, by resolution, direct that functions of the sheriff under either subsection (3) or (5) of this section, or both, be performed by the county department of social services; or, if the board of county commissioners has not so directed, a court of record may order that the prisoner's earnings be collected and disbursed by the clerk of the court. Such order shall remain in force until rescinded by the board or the court, whichever made it.

The county department of social services shall at the request of the court investigate and report to the court the amount necessary for the support of the prisoner's dependents.

The sheriff may refuse to permit the prisoner to exercise his or her privilege to leave the jail as provided in subsection (1) of this section for any breach of discipline or other violation of jail regulations. Any such breach of discipline or other violation of jail regulations shall be reported to the sentencing court.

A prisoner who has been convicted of one of the crimes of violence as defined in section 18-1.3-406 (2), who has been convicted of a sex offense as defined in sections 18-1.3-903 (5) and 18-3-411, who has been convicted of a crime, the underlying factual basis of which was found by the court to include an act of domestic violence, as defined in section 18-6-800.3 (1), or who has been convicted of a class 1 misdemeanor in which a deadly weapon is used shall not be eligible for home detention pursuant to this section.

(12) Persons sentenced to the county jail as a direct sentence or sentenced to the county jail as a condition of probation who are permitted to participate in work, educational, medical release, home detention, or day reporting programs pursuant to subsection (1) of this section shall receive one day credit against their sentences for each day spent in such programs. As used in this section, "day reporting program" means an alternative correctional sentence wherein a defendant is allowed to serve his or her sentence by reporting daily to a central location wherein the defendant is supervised in court-ordered activities.

18-1.3-107. Sentencing order - collateral relief - definitions. (1) At the time a defendant enters into an alternative to sentencing in this part 1, upon the request of the defendant or upon the court's own motion, a court may enter an order of collateral relief for the purpose of preserving or enhancing the defendant's employment or employment prospects and to improve the defendant's likelihood of success in the alternative to sentencing program. Application contents. (a) An application for an order of collateral relief must cite the grounds for granting the relief, the type of relief sought, and the specific collateral consequence from which the applicant is seeking relief and must include a copy of a recent Colorado bureau of

investigation fingerprint-based criminal history records check. The state court administrator may produce an application form that an applicant may submit in application.

(b) The applicant shall provide a copy of the application to the district attorney and to the regulatory or licensing body that has jurisdiction over the collateral consequence from which the applicant is seeking relief, if any, by certified mail or personal service within ten days after filing the application with the court.

An order of collateral relief may relieve a defendant of any collateral consequences of the conviction, whether in housing or employment barriers or any other sanction or disqualification that the court shall specify, including but not limited to statutory, regulatory, or other collateral consequences that the court may see fit to relieve that will assist the defendant in successfully completing probation or a community corrections sentence.

(a) Notwithstanding anyother provision of law, an order of collateral relief cannot relieve any collateral consequences imposed by law for licensure by the department of education or any collateral consequences imposed by law for employment with the judicial branch, the department of corrections, division of youth corrections in the department of human services, or any other law enforcement agency in the state of Colorado.

A court shall not issue an order of collateral relief if the defendant:

Has been convicted of a felony that included an element that requires a victim to suffer permanent disability;

Has been convicted of a crime of violence as described in section 18-1.3-406; or

Is required to register as a sex offender pursuant to section 16-22-103, C.R.S.

Hearing. (a) The court may conduct a hearing or include a hearing on the matter at the defendant's sentencing hearing on the application or on anymatter relevant to the granting or denying of the application and may take testimony under oath.

(b) The court may hear testimony from victims or any proponent or opponent of the application and may hear argument from the petitioner and the district attorney.

Standard for granting relief. (a) A court may issue an order of collateral relief if the court finds that:

The order of collateral relief is consistent with the applicant's rehabilitation; and

Granting the application would improve the applicant's likelihood of success in reintegrating into society and is in the public's interest.

The court that previously issued an order of collateral relief, on its own motion or either by cause shown by the district attorney or on grounds offered by the applicant, may at any time issue a subsequent judgment to enlarge, limit, or circumscribe the relief previously granted.

Upon the motion of the district attorney or probation officer or upon the court's own motion, a court may revoke an order of collateral relief upon evidence of a subsequent criminal conviction or proof that the defendant is no longer entitled to relief. Any bars, prohibitions, sanctions, and disqualifications thereby relieved shall be reinstated as of the date of the written order of revocation. The court shall provide a copy of the order of revocation to the holder and to any regulatory or licensing entity that the defendant noticed in his or her motion for relief.

If the court issues an order of collateral relief, it shall send a copy of the order of collateral relief through the Colorado integrated criminal justice information system to the Colorado

bureau of investigation, and the Colorado bureau of investigation shall note in the applicant's record in the Colorado crime information center that the order of collateral relief was issued.

Definitions. As used in this section, unless the context otherwise requires:

"Collateral consequence" means a collateral sanction or a disqualification.

"Collateral sanction" means a penalty, prohibition, bar, or disadvantage, however denominated, imposed on an individual as a result of the individual's conviction of an offense, which penalty, prohibition, bar, or disadvantage applies by operation of law regardless of whether the penalty, prohibition, bar, or disadvantage is included in the judgment or sentence. "Collateral sanction" does not include imprisonment, probation, parole, supervised release, forfeiture, restitution, fine, assessment, costs of prosecution, or a restraint or sanction on an individual's driving privilege.

"Conviction" or "convicted" means a verdict of guilty by a judge or jury or a plea of guilty or nolo contendere that is accepted by the court or a conviction of a crime under the laws of any other state, the United States, or any territory subject to the jurisdiction of the United States, which, if committed within this state, would be a felony or misdemeanor. "Conviction" or "convicted" also includes having received a deferred judgment and sentence; except that a person shall not be deemed to have been convicted if the person has successfully completed a deferred sentence.

"Disqualification" means a penalty, prohibition, bar, or disadvantage, however denominated, that an administrative agency, governmental official, or court in a civil proceeding is authorized, but not required, to impose on an individual on grounds relating to the individual's conviction of an offense.

## PART 2 PROBATION

18-1.3-201. Application for probation. (1) (a) A person who has been convicted of an offense, other than a class 1 felony or a class 2 petty offense, is eligible to apply to the court for probation.

(b) Repealed.

(2) (a) The provisions of this subsection (2) shall apply to any person whose application for probation is based on a conviction for a felony, which conviction occurred before May 25, 2010.

(a.5) A person who has been twice or more convicted of a felony under the laws of this state, any other state, or the United States prior to the conviction on which his or her application is based shall not be eligible for probation.

Notwithstanding any other provision of law except the provisions of paragraph (c) of this subsection (2), a person who has been convicted of one or more felonies under the laws of this state, any other state, or the United States within ten years prior to a class 1, 2, or 3 felony conviction on which his or her application is based shall not be eligible for probation.

Notwithstanding the provisions of paragraph (a.5) of this subsection (2) and subsection

of this section, an offender convicted of a violation of section 18-18-403.5 may be eligible for probation upon recommendation of the district attorney.

Repealed. (2.1) Repealed.

(2.5) (a) The provisions of this subsection (2.5) shall apply to any person whose application for probation is based on a conviction for a felony, which conviction occurred on or after May 25, 2010.

Except as described in paragraph (a) of subsection (4) of this section, a person who has been twice or more convicted of a felony upon charges separately brought and tried and arising out of separate and distinct criminal episodes under the laws of this state, any other state, or the United States prior to the conviction on which his or her application is based shall not be eligible for probation if the current conviction or a prior conviction is for:

First or second degree murder, as described in section 18-3-102 or 18-3-103;

Manslaughter, as described in section 18-3-104;

First or second degree assault, as described in section 18-3-202 or 18-3-203;

title; or

First or second degree kidnapping, as described in section 18-3-301 or 18-3-302;

A sexual offense as described in part 4 of article 3 of this title;

First degree arson, as described in section 18-4-102;

First or second degree burglary, as described in section 18-4-202 or 18-4-203;

Robbery, as described in section 18-4-301;

Aggravated robbery, as described in section 18-4-302 or 18-4-303;

Theft from the person of another, as described in section 18-4-401 (5);

Any felony offense committed against a child, as described in article 3, 6, or 7 of this

Any criminal attempt or conspiracy to commit any of the offenses specified in this paragraph (b).

Failure to register as a sex offender, as described in section 18-3-412.5, shall not constitute a sexual offense for the purposes of subparagraph (V) of paragraph (b) of this subsection (2.5).

An application for probation shall be in writing upon forms furnished by the court, but, when the defendant has been convicted of a misdemeanor or any petty offense, the court, in its discretion, may waive the written application for probation.

(a) (I) The restrictions upon eligibility for probation in subsections (2) and (2.5) of this section may be waived by the sentencing court regarding a particular defendant upon recommendation of the district attorney approved by an order of the sentencing court.

(II) Repealed.

(b) Upon entry of an order pursuant to this subsection (4) regarding a particular defendant, such defendant shall be deemed to be eligible to apply to the court for probation pursuant to this section.

For purposes of paragraph (a.5) of subsection (2) of this section and paragraph (a) of subsection (2.5) of this section, "conviction" means a verdict of guilty or the entry of a plea of guilty or nolo contendere. "Conviction" does not include a plea to a deferred judgment and sentence pursuant to section 18-1.3-102 until the deferred judgment and sentence is revoked.


18-1.3-202. Probationary power of court. (1) When it appears to the satisfaction of the court that the ends of justice and the best interest of the public, as well as the defendant, will be served thereby, the court may grant the defendant probation for such period and upon such terms and conditions as it deems best. The length of probation shall be subject to the discretion of the court and may exceed the maximum period of incarceration authorized for the classification of the offense of which the defendant is convicted but shall not exceed five years for any misdemeanor or petty offense. If the court chooses to grant the defendant probation, the order placing the defendant on probation shall take effect upon entry and, if any appeal is brought, shall remain in effect pending review by an appellate court unless the court grants a stay of probation pursuant to section 16-4-201, C.R.S. Unless an appeal is filed that raises a claim that probation was granted contrary to the provisions of this title, the trial court shall retain jurisdiction of the case for the purpose of adjudicating complaints filed against the defendant that allege a violation of the terms and conditions of probation. In addition to imposing other conditions, the court has the power to commit the defendant to any jail operated by the county or city and county in which the offense was committed during such time or for such intervals within the period of probation as the court determines. The aggregate length of any such commitment whether continuous or at designated intervals shall not exceed ninety days for a felony, sixty days for a misdemeanor, or ten days for a petty offense unless it is a part of a work release program pursuant to section 18-1.3-207. That the defendant submit to commitment imposed under this section shall be deemed a condition of probation.

The probation department in each judicial district may enter into agreements with any state agency or other public agency, any corporation, and any private agency or person to provide supervision or other services for defendants placed on probation by the court. The agreements shall not include management of any intensive supervision probation programs created pursuant to section 18-1.3-208.


18-1.3-203. Criteria for granting probation. (1) The court, subject to the provisions of this title and title 16, C.R.S., and having considered the purposes of sentencing described in section 18-1-102.5, in its discretion may grant probation to a defendant unless, having regard to the nature and circumstances of the offense and to the history and character of the defendant, it is satisfied that imprisonment is the more appropriate sentence for the protection of the public because:

There is undue risk that during a period of probation the defendant will commit another crime; or

The defendant is in need of correctional treatment that can most effectively be provided by a sentence to imprisonment as authorized by section 18-1.3-104; or

A sentence to probation will unduly depreciate the seriousness of the defendant's crime or undermine respect for law; or

His or her past criminal record indicates that probation would fail to accomplish its intended purposes; or

The crime, the facts surrounding it, or the defendant's history and character when considered in relation to statewide sentencing practices relating to persons in circumstances substantially similar to those of the defendant do not justify the granting of probation.

The following factors, or the converse thereof where appropriate, while not controlling the discretion of the court, shall be accorded weight in making determinations called for by subsection (1) of this section:

The defendant's criminal conduct neither caused nor threatened serious harm to another person or his or her property;

The defendant did not plan or expect that his or her criminal conduct would cause or threaten serious harm to another person or his or her property;

The defendant acted under strong provocation;

There were substantial grounds which, though insufficient to establish a legal defense, tend to excuse or justify the defendant's conduct;

The victim of the defendant's conduct induced or facilitated its commission;

The defendant has made or will make restitution or reparation to the victim of his or her conduct for the damage or injury which was sustained;

The defendant has no history of prior criminal activity or has led a law-abiding life for a substantial period of time before the commission of the present offense;

The defendant's conduct was the result of circumstances unlikely to recur;

The character, history, and attitudes of the defendant indicate that he or she is unlikely to commit another crime;

The defendant is particularly likely to respond affirmatively to probationary treatment;

The imprisonment of the defendant would entail undue hardship to himself or herself or his or her dependents;

The defendant is elderly or in poor health;

The defendant did not abuse a public position of responsibility or trust;

The defendant cooperated with law enforcement authorities by bringing other offenders to justice, or otherwise.

Nothing in this section shall be deemed to require explicit reference to these factors in a presentence report or by the court at sentencing.

18-1.3-204. Conditions of probation - interstate compact probation transfer cash fund - creation. (1) (a) The conditions of probation shall be such as the court in its discretion deems reasonably necessary to ensure that the defendant will lead a law-abiding life and to assist the defendant in doing so. The court shall provide as explicit conditions of every sentence to probation that the defendant not commit another offense during the period for which the sentence remains subject to revocation, that the defendant make restitution pursuant to part 6 of this article and article 18.5 of title 16, C.R.S., that the defendant comply with any court orders regarding substance abuse testing and treatment issued pursuant to sections 18-1.3-209 and 18-1.3-211 and article 11.5 of title 16, C.R.S., and that the defendant comply with any court orders regarding the treatment of sex offenders issued pursuant to article 11.7 of title 16, C.R.S. The court shall provide as an explicit condition of every sentence to probation that the defendant not harass, molest, intimidate, retaliate against, or tamper with the victim of or any prosecution witnesses to the crime, unless the court makes written findings that such condition is not necessary.

(b) Notwithstanding the provisions of paragraph (a) of this subsection (1), unless the

defendant is sentenced to probation for a conviction of a crime under article 43.3 of title 12, C.R.S., the possession or use of medical marijuana, as authorized pursuant to section 14 of article XVIII of the state constitution, shall not be considered another offense such that its use constitutes a violation of the terms of probation.

(1.5) If the defendant is being sentenced to probation as a result of a conviction of a felony offense or a qualifying misdemeanor offense pursuant to the "Interstate Compact for Adult Offender Supervision", part 28 of article 60 of title 24, C.R.S., a condition of probation shall be that the court shall require the defendant to execute or subscribe a written prior waiver of extradition stating that the defendant consents to extradition to this state and waives all formal proceedings in the event that he or she is arrested in another state while at liberty on such bail bond and acknowledging that he or she shall not be admitted to bail in any other state pending extradition to this state. If the offender is returned to the state pursuant to the "Interstate Compact for Adult Offender Supervision", part 28 of article 60 of title 24, C.R.S., a court may not impose the cost of the offender's return on the offender.

(a) When granting probation, the court may, as a condition of probation, require that the defendant:

Work faithfully at a suitable employment or faithfully pursue a course of study or of vocational training that will equip the defendant for suitable employment;

Undergo available medical or psychiatric treatment and remain in a specified institution if required for that purpose. In any case where inpatient psychiatric treatment is indicated, the court shall proceed in accordance with article 65 of title 27, C.R.S., and require the defendant to comply with the recommendation of the professional person in charge of the evaluation required pursuant to section 27-65-105 or 27-65-106, C.R.S.

Attend or reside in a facility established for the instruction, recreation, or residence of persons on probation;

(III.5) Participate in restorative justice practices, as defined in section 18-1-901 (3) (o.5), if available in the jurisdiction, and the defendant is determined suitable by a designated restorative justice practices facilitator. If a defendant wants to participate in restorative justice practices, the defendant must make the request to the district attorney or the law enforcement agency administering the program and may not make the request to the victim. If requested by the defendant, district attorney, or law enforcement agency, a victim-offender conference may only be conducted after the victim is consulted by the district attorney and offered the opportunity to participate or submit a victim impact statement. If a victim elects not to attend, a victim offender conference may be held with a suitable victim surrogate or victim advocate, and the victim may submit a victim-impact statement. To be eligible for restorative justice practices, the defendant shall not have been convicted of unlawful sexual behavior as defined in section 16-22-102 (9), C.R.S., a crime in which the underlying factual basis involves domestic violence, as defined in section 18-6-800.3 (1), stalking as defined in section 18-3-602, or violation of a protection order as defined in section 18-6-803.5. Any statements made during a restorative justice conference shall be confidential and shall not be used as a basis for charging or prosecuting the defendant unless the defendant commits a chargeable offense during the conference. Failure to complete the requirements arising from a restorative justice conference may be considered a violation of probation. Nothing in this subparagraph (III.5) shall be construed to require a victim to participate in restorative justice practices or a restorative justice

victim-offender conference.

Support the defendant's dependents and meet other family responsibilities, including arranging and fulfilling a payment plan for current child support, child support arrearages, and child support debt due under a court or administrative order through any delegate child support enforcement unit that may have a child support case with the defendant;

Pay reasonable costs of the court proceedings or costs of supervision of probation, or both. The probation supervision fee shall be fifty dollars per month for the length of ordered probation. Notwithstanding the amount specified in this subparagraph (V), the court may lower the costs of supervision of probation to an amount the defendant will be able to pay. The court shall fix the manner of performance for payment of the fee. If the defendant receives probation services from a private provider, the court shall order the defendant to pay the probation supervision fee directly to the provider. The fee shall be imposed for the length of ordered probation.

Pay any fines or fees imposed by the court;

(VI.5) Repay all or part of any reward paid by a crime stopper organization that led to the defendant's arrest and conviction in accordance with article 15.7 of title 16, C.R.S.;

Refrain from possessing a firearm, destructive device, or other dangerous weapon unless granted written permission by the court or probation officer;

Refrain from excessive use of alcohol or any unlawful use of controlled substances, as defined in section 18-18-102 (5), or of any other dangerous or abusable drug without a prescription; except that the court shall not, as a condition of probation, prohibit the possession or use of medical marijuana, as authorized pursuant to section 14 of article XVIII of the state constitution, unless:

The defendant is sentenced to probation for conviction of a crime under article 43.3 of title 12, C.R.S.; or

The court determines, based on any material evidence, that a prohibition against the possession or use of medical marijuana is necessary and appropriate to accomplish the goals of sentencing as stated in section 18-1-102.5;

Report to a probation officer at reasonable times as directed by the court or the probation officer;

Permit the probation officer to visit the defendant at reasonable times at the defendant's home and elsewhere;

Remain within the jurisdiction of the court, unless granted permission to leave by the court or the probation officer;

Answer all reasonable inquiries by the probation officer and promptly notify the probation officer of any change in address or employment;

Be subject to home detention as defined in section 18-1.3-106 (1.1);

Be restrained from contact with the victim or the victim's family members in cases in which the defendant was convicted of a crime, the underlying factual basis of which included an act of domestic violence, as defined in section 18-6-800.3 (1);

(XIV.5) Be subject to electronic or global position monitoring;

Satisfy any other conditions reasonably related to the defendant's rehabilitation and the purposes of probation.

When granting probation, in addition to the consideration of the provisions set forth in

paragraph (a) of this subsection (2), the court shall order as a condition of probation in cases in which the defendant was convicted of a crime, the underlying factual basis of which included an act of domestic violence, as defined in section 18-6-800.3 (1), that the defendant:

Comply with existing court orders regarding family support;

Comply with any existing court orders concerning a proceeding to determine paternity, custody, the allocation of decision-making responsibility, parenting time, or support;

Comply with the terms of any protection order in effect against the defendant during the probation period;

Refrain from possessing a firearm, destructive device, or other dangerous weapon, unless granted written permission by the court or probation officer which shall not be granted in such domestic violence cases unless:

It is required by the defendant's employment; and

The court finds that the defendant's possession of the weapon does not endanger the victim or the victim's children; and

The weapon is stored away from the home and the yard surrounding the home.

If the court orders counseling or treatment as a condition of probation, unless the court makes a specific finding that treatment in another facility or with another person is warranted, the court shall order that such treatment or counseling be at a facility or with a person:

Approved by the unit in the department of human services that administers behavioral health programs and services, including those related to mental health and substance abuse, established in article 80 of title 27, C.R.S., if the treatment is for alcohol or drug abuse;

Certified or approved by the sex offender management board, established in section 16- 11.7-103, C.R.S., if the offender is a sex offender;

Certified or approved by the domestic violence offender management board created in section 16-11.8-103, C.R.S., if the offender was convicted of or the underlying factual basis of the offense included an act of domestic violence as defined in section 18-6-800.3; or

Licensed or certified by the division of adult parole in the department of corrections, the department of regulatory agencies, the unit in the department of human services that administers behavioral health programs and services, including those related to mental health and substance abuse, the state board of nursing, or the Colorado medical board, whichever is appropriate for the required treatment or counseling.

Notwithstanding the provisions of paragraph (c) of this subsection (2), if the court orders counseling or treatment as a condition of probation for an offender convicted of an offense involving unlawful sexual behavior, as defined in section 16-22-102 (9), C.R.S., the court shall order such treatment or counseling be at a facility or with a person listed in paragraph (c) of this subsection (2), and the court may not make a specific finding that treatment in another facility or with another person is warranted.

If the defendant is convicted of an offense that subjects the defendant to genetic testing pursuant to section 16-11-102.4, C.R.S., the court shall assess to the defendant the cost of collecting and testing a biological substance sample from the defendant as required in section 16-11-102.4, C.R.S.

(2.2)        When granting probation, the court may include as a condition of probation a requirement that the defendant participate in drug treatment. If the defendant's assessed treatment

need is for residential treatment, the court may make residential drug treatment a condition of probation and may place the offender in a community corrections program that can provide the appropriate level of treatment subject to the provision of section 18-1.3-301 (4).

(2.3) (a) When granting probation, the court may, as a condition of probation, require any defendant who is less than eighteen years of age at the time of sentencing to attend school or an educational program or to work toward the attainment of a high school diploma or the successful completion of a high school equivalency examination, as that term is defined in section 22-33-102 (8.5), C.R.S.; except that the court shall not require any such juvenile to attend a school from which he or she has been expelled without the prior approval of that school's local board of education.

(b) Following specification of the terms and conditions of probation for a defendant who is less than eighteen years of age at the time of sentencing, where the conditions of probation include the requirement that the defendant attend school, the court shall notify the school district in which the defendant will be enrolled of such requirement.

(2.5) The order of priority for any payments required of a defendant pursuant to subparagraph (IV), (V), (VI), or (VI.5) of paragraph (a) of subsection (2) of this section shall be as follows:

Payment of a current child support order;

Payment of child support arrearage;

Payment of child support debt order;

Payment of spousal maintenance;

Payment of costs for the crime victim compensation fund, pursuant to section 24-4.1-119, C.R.S.;

Payment of surcharges for the victims and witnesses assistance and law enforcement fund, pursuant to section 24-4.2-104, C.R.S.;

Payment of restitution;

Payment of a time payment fee;

Payment of late fees;

(i.2)  Payment of probation supervision fees;

(i.4) Payment of a drug offender surcharge pursuant to article 19 of this title; (i.6)  Payment of a sex offender surcharge pursuant to article 21 of this title;

(i.7) Payment of a surcharge for a crime against an at-risk person pursuant to section 18-6.5-107;

(i.8) Payment of collection and chemical testing of a biological substance to determine the genetic markers thereof;

(i.9) Payment of a surcharge related to the address confidentiality program pursuant to section 24-30-2114, C.R.S.;

Payment of any other fines, fees, or surcharges; and

Repayment of all or part of any reward paid by a crime stopper organization that led to the defendant's arrest and conviction.

When a defendant is granted probation, he or she shall be given a written statement explicitly setting forth the conditions on which he or she is being released.

(a) For good cause shown and after notice to the defendant, the district attorney, and the probation officer, and after a hearing if the defendant or the district attorney requests it, the judge

may reduce or increase the term of probation or alter the conditions or impose new conditions.

(b) (I) If an offender applies to transfer his or her probation to another state, the offender shall pay a filing fee of one hundred dollars, unless the offender is indigent.

(II) (A) The clerk of the court shall transmit all moneys collected pursuant to this paragraph

(b) to the state treasurer, who shall credit the same to the interstate compact probation transfer cash fund, which fund is hereby created and referred to in this paragraph (b) as the "fund". Beginning January 1, 2013, the moneys in the fund are subject to annual appropriation by the general assembly to the judicial department for the direct and indirect costs associated with returning probationers to Colorado. The state treasurer may invest any moneys in the fund not expended for the purpose of this paragraph (b) as provided by law. The state treasurer shall credit all interest and income derived from the investment and deposit of moneys in the fund to the fund. Any unexpended and unencumbered moneys remaining in the fund at the end of a fiscal year remain in the fund and shall not be credited or transferred to the general fund or another fund.

(B) On or after January 1, 2013, a law enforcement agency may submit to the state court administrator a request to be reimbursed for the costs of returning a probationer pursuant to the "Interstate Compact for Adult Offender Supervision", part 28 of article 60 of title 24, C.R.S., incurred on or after January 1, 2013. The state court administrator shall, to the extent that funds are available, reimburse reasonable costs incurred by a law enforcement agency for the return of the probationer.

18-1.3-205. Restitution as a condition of probation. As a condition of every sentence to probation, the court shall order that the defendant make full restitution pursuant to the provisions of part 6 of this article and article 18.5 of title 16, C.R.S. Such order shall require the defendant to make restitution within a period of time specified by the court. Such restitution shall be ordered by the court as a condition of probation.

18-1.3-206. Repayment of crime stopper reward as a condition of probation. (1) As a condition of every sentence to probation where information received through a crime stopper organization led to the arrest and felony conviction of a defendant, the court may require such defendant, as a condition of probation, to repay all or part of any reward paid by such organization. The amount of such repayment shall not exceed the actual reward paid by any crime stopper organization and shall be used solely for paying rewards. The court shall fix the manner and time of repayment.

In the event the defendant fails to repay the crime stopper reward in accordance with an order of the court, the defendant shall be returned to the sentencing court and the court, upon proof of failure to pay, may:

Modify the amount of the repayment;

Extend the period of probation;

Order the defendant committed to jail with work release privileges; or

Revoke probation and impose the sentence otherwise required by law.

When, as a result of a plea bargain agreement, a defendant is ordered to repay a reward

pursuant to subsection (1) of this section, the department or agencysupervising the collection of such repayment may assess a charge of fifteen dollars to the defendant for collection of each bad check or each bad check received as a repayment.

Any order for the repayment of all or part of a crime stopper reward as a condition of probation shall be prioritized in accordance with section 18-1.3-204 (2.5).

As used in this section, unless the context otherwise requires:

"Bad check" has the same meaning provided in section 16-7-404.

"Crime stopper organization" has the same meaning provided in section 16-15.7-102 (1), C.R.S.

18-1.3-207. Work and education release programs. (1) As a specific condition of probation for a person convicted of a felony or misdemeanor, the court may require the probationer to participate for a period not to exceed two years or the term to which he or she might be sentenced for the offense committed, whichever is less, in a supervised work release or education release program. Utilization of the county jail, a municipal jail, or any other facility may be used for the probationer's full-time confinement, care, and maintenance, except for the time he or she is released for scheduled work or education.

(1.1) Before a final ruling by the court authorizing a probationer to participate in a supervised education release program, the court shall notify the prosecuting attorney and the postsecondary educational institution requesting their comments on the pending release. The notice shall include all relevant information pertaining to the probationer and to the nature of the crime for which he or she was convicted. Both the prosecuting attorney and the postsecondary educational institution shall reply to the court in writing within fourteen days after receipt of the notification or within such other reasonable time in excess of fourteen days as specified by the court. The postsecondaryeducational institution's reply shall include a statement of whether or not it will accept the probationer as a student. Acceptance by a state postsecondary educational institution shall be pursuant to section 23-5-106, C.R.S.

All employment income of a probationer participating in a work release program shall be received and deposited by the probation officer in the registry of the court. The court shall order disbursement of the funds so deposited in payment of the following items which are listed in the order of their priority:

Any current child support order;

Any child support arrearage;

Any child support debt order;

Any spousal maintenance;

Costs for the crime victim compensation fund, pursuant to section 24-4.1-119, C.R.S.;

Surcharges for the victims and witnesses assistance and law enforcement fund, pursuant to section 24-4.2-104, C.R.S.;

Restitution;

A time payment fee;

Late fees;

Any other fines, fees, or surcharges;

and

33

Room, board, and work supervision inside and outside the county jail or other facility;

The probationer.
Any acts by the probationer in violation of the conditions of probation under subsection
of this section may be asserted as a basis for revocation of probation as provided in sections 16- 11-205 and 16-11-206, C.R.S., and any willful failure to return to the jail or other facility may be punishable as an escape under section 18-8-208.


18-1.3-208. Intensive supervision probation programs - legislative declaration. (1) The general assembly finds and declares that intensive supervision probation programs are an effective and desirable alternative to sentences to imprisonment, community corrections, or jail. It is the purpose of this section to encourage the judicial department to establish programs for the intensive supervision of selected probationers. It is the intent of the general assembly that such programs be formulated so that they protect the safety and welfare of the public in the community where the programs are operating and throughout the state of Colorado.
The judicial department mayestablish an intensive supervision probation program in any judicial district or combination of judicial districts in order to provide supervision tailored to the specific characteristics that produce a risk classification requiring intensive services for the offender and to facilitate the offender's participation in rehabilitative programs intended to address those characteristics. When establishing such programs, the judicial department shall seek the counsel of the chief judge of the district court, the office of the district attorney, the state public defender or his or her designee, the county sheriff, the chief probation officer in the judicial district, the department of corrections, the local community corrections board, and members of the public at-large.
The judicial department shall require that offenders in the program receive the highest level of supervision that is provided to probationers.
When the court sentences any offender to probation, the probation department shall complete an initial assessment of the offender's risk and needs, using valid assessment tools approved bythe state court administrator's office. Offenders who are determined through assessment to be high risk and who meet the acceptance criteria may be placed in an intensive supervision probation program by probation. Furthermore, intensive supervision probation may be used for an offender who has been under the supervision of probation for a period of time and a reassessment indicates the offender's risk of reoffense has increased to high and the offender meets the acceptance criteria of the intensive program. For purposes of this section, "offender" shall have the same meaning as that set forth in section 17-27-102 (6), C.R.S.
The judicial department shall have the power to establish and enforce standards and criteria for the administration of intensive supervision probation programs.
(a) It is the intent of the general assembly in enacting this subsection (6) to recognize that high-risk offenders can be managed in the community with the appropriate supervision and the use of evidence-based treatment programs and practices.
(b) The judicial department is directed to create and implement intensive supervision probation programs based on the current evidence for reducing recidivism by October 1, 2013. Intensive supervision probation programs must require the use of validated assessments to determine

the offender's risk of reoffending. The judicial department shall develop acceptance criteria for placement in all intensive supervision probation programs. The judicial department shall develop criteria for offenders to transition from intensive supervision probation programs to regular probation, based on assessment of risk and need and program compliance. An offender may not be placed in or transferred out of an intensive supervision probation program without meeting established criteria.


18-1.3-209. Substance abuse assessment required. (1) Each person convicted of a felony committed on or after July 1, 1992, and each person convicted of a misdemeanor or petty offense on or after July 1, 2008, who is to be considered for probation or a deferred judgment and sentence that includes supervision by the probation department, shall be required to submit to an assessment for the use of controlled substances or alcohol developed pursuant to section 16-11.5-102 (1) (a), C.R.S., as part of the presentence or probation investigation required pursuant to section 16-11-102, C.R.S., or, if the investigation is waived pursuant to section 16-11-102 (4), C.R.S., and the person is sentenced to probation or supervised by a probation officer, then as a part of intake.
The court shall order each person required to submit to an assessment pursuant to subsection (1) of this section to comply with the recommendations of the alcohol and drug assessment. If the person is sentenced to probation, a deferred judgment and sentence that includes supervision by the probation department, or any other sentence except a sentence only to jail, the person shall be ordered to comply with the recommendations as a condition or as part of the sentence imposed, at the person's own expense, unless the person is indigent.
The assessment required by subsection (1) of this section shall be at the expense of the person assessed, unless the person is indigent.


18-1.3-210. Counseling or treatment for alcohol or drug abuse. (1) In any case in which treatment or counseling for alcohol or drug abuse is authorized in connection with a deferred prosecution, deferred judgment and sentence, or probation, the court may require the defendant to obtain counseling or treatment for the condition. If the court orders the counseling or treatment, the court shall order that the counseling or treatment be obtained from a treatment facility or person approved by the unit in the department of human services that administers behavioral health programs and services, including those related to mental health and substance abuse, established in article 80 of title 27, C.R.S., unless the court makes a finding that counseling or treatment in another facility or with another person is warranted. If the defendant voluntarily submits himself or herself for such treatment or counseling, the district attorney and the court may consider his or her willingness to correct his or her condition as a basis for granting deferred prosecution or deferred judgment and sentence.
(2) Notwithstanding the provisions of subsection (1) of this section, in any case in which treatment or counseling for alcohol or drug abuse is authorized and ordered by the court in connection with a deferred prosecution, deferred judgment and sentence, or probation for an offense involving unlawful sexual behavior, as defined in section 16-22-102 (9), C.R.S., the court shall order

that the counseling or treatment be obtained from a treatment facility or person approved by the unit in the department of human services that administers behavioral health programs and services, including those related to mental health and substance abuse, established in article 80 of title 27, C.R.S.


18-1.3-211. Sentencing of felons - parole of felons - treatment and testing based upon assessment required. (1) Each person sentenced by the court for a felony committed on or after July 1, 1992, shall be required, as a part of any sentence to probation, community corrections, or incarceration with the department of corrections, to undergo periodic testing and treatment for substance abuse that is appropriate to such felon based upon the recommendations of the assessment made pursuant to section 18-1.3-209, or based upon any subsequent recommendations by the department of corrections, the judicial department, or the division of criminal justice of the department of public safety, whichever is appropriate. Any such testing or treatment shall be at a facility or with a person approved by the unit in the department of human services that administers behavioral health programs and services, including those related to mental health and substance abuse, established in article 80 of title 27, C.R.S., and at such felon's own expense, unless such felon is indigent.

(2) Each person placed on parole by the state board of parole on or after July 1, 1992, shall be required, as a condition of such parole, to undergo periodic testing and treatment for substance abuse that is appropriate to such parolee based upon the recommendations of the assessment made pursuant to section 18-1.3-209 or any assessment or subsequent reassessment made regarding such parolee during his or her incarceration or any period of parole. Any such testing or treatment shall be at a facility or with a person approved by the unit in the department of human services that administers behavioral health programs and services, including those related to mental health and substance abuse, established in article 80 of title 27, C.R.S., and at such parolee's own expense, unless such parolee is indigent.

18-1.3-212. Drug testing of offenders by judicial department - pilot program. The judicial department is hereby authorized and directed to develop as soon as possible a pilot program for the drug testing of persons during presentence investigation and on probation. Such program shall include testing of persons during presentence investigation and may include random drug testing when an offender is assigned to specialized treatment and rehabilitation programs.

18-1.3-213. Sentencing order - collateral relief - definitions. (1) At the time of sentencing, upon the request of the defendant or upon the court's own motion, a court that sentences the defendant to probation may enter an order of collateral relief for the purpose of preserving or enhancing the defendant's employment or employment prospects and to improve the defendant's likelihood of success on probation or in the community corrections program.

Application contents. (a) An application for an order of collateral relief must cite the

grounds for granting the relief, the type of relief sought, and the specific collateral consequence from which the applicant is seeking relief and must include a copy of a recent Colorado bureau of investigation fingerprint-based criminal history records check. The state court administrator may produce an application form that an applicant may submit in application.

(b) The applicant shall provide a copy of the application to the district attorney and to the regulatory or licensing body that has jurisdiction over the collateral consequence from which the applicant is seeking relief, if any, by certified mail or personal service within ten days after filing the application with the court.

An order of collateral relief may relieve a defendant of any collateral consequences of the conviction, whether in housing or employment barriers or any other sanction or disqualification that the court shall specify, including but not limited to statutory, regulatory, or other collateral consequences that the court may see fit to relieve that will assist the defendant in successfully completing probation or a community corrections sentence.

(a) Notwithstanding anyother provision of law, an order of collateral relief cannot relieve any collateral consequences imposed by law for licensure by the department of education or any collateral consequences imposed by law for employment with the judicial branch, the department of corrections, division of youth corrections in the department of human services, or any other law enforcement agency in the state of Colorado.

A court shall not issue an order of collateral relief if the defendant:

Has been convicted of a felony that included an element that requires a victim to suffer permanent disability;

Has been convicted of a crime of violence as described in section 18-1.3-406; or

Is required to register as a sex offender pursuant to section 16-22-103, C.R.S.

Hearing. (a) The court may conduct a hearing or include a hearing on the matter at the defendant's sentencing hearing on the application or on anymatter relevant to the granting or denying of the application and may take testimony under oath.

(b) The court may hear testimony from victims or any proponent or opponent of the application and may hear argument from the petitioner and the district attorney.

Standard for granting relief. (a) A court may issue an order of collateral relief if the court finds that:

The order of collateral relief is consistent with the applicant's rehabilitation; and

Granting the application would improve the applicant's likelihood of success in reintegrating into society and is in the public's interest.

The court that previously issued an order of collateral relief, on its own motion or either by cause shown by the district attorney or on grounds offered by the applicant, may at any time issue a subsequent judgment to enlarge, limit, or circumscribe the relief previously granted.

Upon the motion of the district attorney or probation officer or upon the court's own motion, a court may revoke an order of collateral relief upon evidence of a subsequent criminal conviction or proof that the defendant is no longer entitled to relief. Any bars, prohibitions, sanctions, and disqualifications thereby relieved shall be reinstated as of the date of the written order of revocation. The court shall provide a copy of the order of revocation to the holder and to any regulatory or licensing entity that the defendant noticed in his or her motion for relief.

If the court issues an order of collateral relief, it shall send a copy of the order of collateral relief through the Colorado integrated criminal justice information system to the Colorado bureau of investigation, and the Colorado bureau of investigation shall note in the applicant's record in the Colorado crime information center that the order of collateral relief was issued.

Definitions. As used in this section, unless the context otherwise requires:

"Collateral consequence" means a collateral sanction or a disqualification.

"Collateral sanction" means a penalty, prohibition, bar, or disadvantage, however denominated, imposed on an individual as a result of the individual's conviction of an offense, which penalty, prohibition, bar, or disadvantage applies by operation of law regardless of whether the penalty, prohibition, bar, or disadvantage is included in the judgment or sentence. "Collateral sanction" does not include imprisonment, probation, parole, supervised release, forfeiture, restitution, fine, assessment, costs of prosecution, or a restraint or sanction on an individual's driving privilege.

"Conviction" or "convicted" means a verdict of guilty by a judge or jury or a plea of guilty or nolo contendere that is accepted by the court or a conviction of a crime under the laws of any other state, the United States, or any territory subject to the jurisdiction of the United States, which, if committed within this state, would be a felony or misdemeanor. "Conviction" or "convicted" also includes having received a deferred judgment and sentence; except that a person shall not be deemed to have been convicted if the person has successfully completed a deferred sentence.

"Disqualification" means a penalty, prohibition, bar, or disadvantage, however denominated, that an administrative agency, governmental official, or court in a civil proceeding is authorized, but not required, to impose on an individual on grounds relating to the individual's conviction of an offense.

PART 3

18-1.3-301. Authority to place offenders in community corrections programs. (1) (a) Any judge of a district court may refer any offender convicted of a felony to a community corrections program unless such offender is required to be sentenced pursuant to section 18-1.3-406 (1) or a sentencing provision that requires a sentence to the department of corrections. If an offender who is sentenced pursuant to section 18-1.3-406 (1) has such sentence modified upon the finding of unusual and extenuating circumstances pursuant to such section, such offender may be referred to a community corrections program if such offender is otherwise eligible for such program and is approved for placement pursuant to section 17-27-103 (5), C.R.S., and section 17-27- 104 (3), C.R.S. For the purposes of this article, persons sentenced pursuant to the provisions of sections 19-2-908 (1) (a) (I) and (1) (c) (I) (B) and 19-2-910 (2), C.R.S., shall be deemed to be offenders.

In making a direct sentence to a community corrections program, the sentencing court

may impose a sentence to community corrections which includes terms, lengths, and conditions pursuant to section 18-1.3-401. The sentencing court may also refer any offender to a community corrections program as a condition of probation pursuant to section 18-1.3-202. Any placement of offenders referred as a direct sentence or as a condition of probation shall be subject to approval pursuant to section 17-27-103 (5), C.R.S., and section 17-27-104 (3), C.R.S.

(b.5) As a condition of every placement in a community corrections program, the court shall require the offender, as a condition of placement, to execute or subscribe a written prior waiver of extradition stating that the offender consents to extradition to this state and waives all formal procedures incidental to extradition proceedings in the event that the offender is arrested in another state upon an allegation that the offender has violated the terms of his or her community corrections placement, and acknowledging that the offender shall not be admitted to bail in any other state pending extradition to this state.

A probation officer, in making a presentence report to the court pursuant to section 16- 11-102, C.R.S., or in making a report to the court after a probation violation, may recommend the utilization of a community corrections program in sentencing or resentencing an offender.

If an offender is rejected by a community corrections board or a community corrections program before placement in a program, the court shall promptly resentence the offender. If a sentence to the department of corrections was imposed upon the offender prior to the referral of the offender to communitycorrections, the resentence shall not exceed the sentence which was originally imposed upon the offender.

If an offender is rejected after acceptance by a community corrections board or a community corrections program, the court may resentence the offender without any further hearing so long as the offender's sentence does not exceed the sentence which was originally imposed upon the offender.

The probation department of the judicial district in which a community corrections program is located shall have jurisdiction over all offenders sentenced directly to a community corrections program. Such probation department shall initiate arrest warrants, process reports or other official documents regarding offenders at the direction of the court, coordinate with community corrections boards and communitycorrections programs, review offender supervision and treatment, authorize offender transfers between residential and nonresidential phases of placement, and carry out such other duties as the court directs.

The sentencing court may make appropriate orders for the detention, transfer, or resentencing of any offender whose placement in a community corrections program is terminated pursuant to section 17-27-103 (7), C.R.S., or section 17-27-104 (5), C.R.S. As to any offender held pursuant to section 17-27-104 (6), C.R.S., in a jail operated by a unit of local government in a county other than where the offender's original conviction occurred, the sentencing court shall order the transfer of the offender to the jail of the county where the original conviction occurred as soon as possible. The sentencing court is not required to provide the offender with an evidentiary hearing pertaining to the rejection of placement in a community corrections program prior to resentencing. (g.5) Notwithstanding any other provision of law to the contrary, if an offender is terminated or rejected from a community corrections program after having been sentenced to the program for a level 4 drug felony, the court shall conduct a resentencing hearing in order to comply with each exhaustion of remedy provision in section 18-1.3-405.5 or shall make written findings regarding

resentencing after consideration of all the information provided to the court pursuant to section 18- 1.3-104.5 (2) (c). Nothing in this section requires that a community corrections program accept or maintain an offender who has been terminated from a community corrections program.

(I) The sentencing court shall have the authority to modify the sentence of an offender who has been directly sentenced to a community corrections program in the same manner as if the offender had been placed on probation.

A defendant who successfully completes the residential phase of a community corrections sentence, has paid the costs of the residential program in full, and is being supervised on nonresidential status at either a minimum or administrative level is eligible for consideration for early termination of his or her community corrections sentence by the court.

When the defendant has met the eligibility criteria enumerated in subparagraph (II) of this paragraph (h), the defendant's probation officer shall submit a petition for early termination of sentence to the court and notify the district attorney and the defendant.

If victim notification is required, the probation officer shall provide victim notification pursuant to part 3 of article 4.1 of title 24, C.R.S.

In determining whether to grant or deny the petition, the court may consider the following factors:

The defendant's assessed risk of reoffense;

Victim input, if any;

The defendant's compliance with the terms and conditions of the sentence or community corrections program;

Completion of any treatment required by the court or community corrections program; and

Other factors deemed relevant by the court.

The fact that the defendant owes restitution, costs, fees, fines, or surcharges shall not

prohibit the court from granting the motion for early termination if the court finds the motion otherwise appropriate.

(I) An offender sentenced directly to a community corrections program by the sentencing court pursuant to this subsection (1) shall be eligible for time credit deductions from the offender's sentence not to exceed ten days for each month of placement upon a demonstration to the program administrator by the offender that the offender has made consistent progress in the following categories:

Maintenance of employment, education, or training, including attendance, promptness, performance, cooperation, care of materials, and safety;

Development and maintenance of positive social and domestic relations;

Compliance with rules, regulations, and requirements of residential or nonresidential program placement;

Completion and compliance with components of the individualized program plan; and

Demonstration of financial responsibility and accountability.

The administrator of each community corrections program shall develop objective standards for measuring progress in the categories listed in subparagraph (I) of this paragraph (i), shall apply such standards consistently to evaluations of all such offenders, and shall develop

procedures for recommending the award of time credits to such offenders.

The administrator of each community corrections program shall review the performance record of each offender directly sentenced to such program. Such review shall be conducted at intervals to be determined by each program administrator. Such reviews shall be conducted at least once every six months, but may be conducted at more frequent intervals as determined by the program administrator. If the program administrator determines that the offender engaged in criminal activity during the time period for which the time credits were granted, the program administrator may withdraw the time credits granted during such period. Prior to the time of the offender's release, the program administrator shall submit to the sentencing court the time credit deductions granted, withdrawn, or restored consistent with the provisions of this paragraph (i). Such time credit deductions shall be submitted on standardized forms prepared by the division of criminal justice of the department of public safety that include verification by the program administrator that the time credit deductions are true and accurate. The sentencing court shall certify such time credit deductions as part of the offender's permanent record. Any time credits authorized under this paragraph (i) shall vest upon certification of time credit deductions by the sentencing court at the time of the offender's release from the program.

An offender shall not be credited with more than one-half the allowable time credits for any month or portion thereof unless the offender was employed, was unable to be employed due to a disability waiver, or was participating in training, education, or treatment programs which precluded the ability to remain employed. This subparagraph (IV) shall not apply to those offenders excused from such employment or training by the program administrator or for medical reasons.

No time credit deductions shall be granted to any offender for time spent in jail, whether awaiting sentencing, placement in the program, disciplinary action, or as a result of a subsequent arrest, unless such time spent in jail was a prearranged component of the offender's individualized program plan and the offender has made consistent progress in the categories listed in subparagraph

(I) of this paragraph (i).

(VI) (Deleted by amendment, L. 2011, (SB 11-254), ch. 274, p. 1236, § 1, effective June 2,

2011.)

Except as otherwise provided in paragraph (k) of this subsection (1), any offender

sentenced to the department of corrections subsequent to placement in a community corrections program is entitled to credit against the term of confinement as described in section 17-27-104 (9),

C.R.S. The court shall make a finding of the amount of such time credits and include such finding in the mittimus that orders the offender to be placed in the custody of the department of corrections. The department of corrections shall apply credits for residential and nonresidential time completed in a community corrections program in the same manner as credits for time served in a department of corrections facility.

Any offender who escapes from a residential community corrections program or who absconds from a nonresidential community corrections program shall forfeit any time credit deductions earned pursuant to paragraph (i) of this subsection (1) and shall not be credited with any time on escape or absconder status. Within thirty-five days after an offender's escape or abscondment, the program administrator shall submit to the sentencing court a statement on the form described in subparagraph (III) of paragraph (i) of this subsection (1) of the time credit deductions that would have been earned by the offender.

(a) Initial referral. The executive director of the department of corrections may transfer any offender who is eligible pursuant to this subsection (2) to a community corrections program if such offender is accepted for placement by a community corrections board pursuant to section 17-27- 103, C.R.S., and a community corrections program pursuant to section 17-27-104, C.R.S.

Unless the offender has an active felony warrant or detainer or has refused community placement, the executive director of the department of corrections shall refer an offender who has displayed acceptable institutional behavior for placement in a community corrections program according to the following timeline:

No more than twenty-eight months prior to the offender's parole eligibility date for any offender who successfully completes a regimented inmate discipline program pursuant to article 27.7 of title 17, C.R.S.;

No more than sixteen months prior to the offender's parole eligibility date for any offender who is not serving a sentence for an offense referred to in section 18-1.3-406; and

No more than one hundred eighty days prior to the parole eligibility date for any other offender not described in subparagraph (I) or (II) of this paragraph (b).

Prior to placement of an offender in any community corrections program, the executive director of the department of corrections shall give the first right to refuse placement of such offender to the community corrections board and community corrections programs in the community where the offender intends to reside after release from custody of the department of corrections or parole by the state board of parole.

As to any offender held in a county jail pursuant to section 17-27-104 (6), C.R.S., the executive director of the department of corrections shall order transfer of such offender to a facility of the department of corrections as soon as possible.

Subsequent referrals. For an offender who is serving a sentence for a class 1 or 2 felony that constitutes a crime of violence under section 18-1.3-406, excluding escape, and whose parole hearing has been deferred for at least thirty-six months, the executive director of the department of corrections shall not refer the offender for placement in community corrections earlier than six months prior to the date of the offender's second or any subsequent parole hearing.

The state board of parole may refer any parolee for placement in a community corrections program. Such placement, if approved by the community corrections board pursuant to section 17- 27-103, C.R.S., and the community corrections program pursuant to section 17-27-104, C.R.S., may be made a condition of release on parole or as a modification of the conditions of an offender's parole after release or upon temporary revocation of parole pursuant to section 17-2-103 (11), C.R.S.

(a) District courts, county courts, and other local criminal justice officials may enter into agreements with community corrections programs which include the use of such programs to supervise offenders awaiting trial for felony or misdemeanor offenses, offenders convicted of misdemeanors, or offenders under deferred judgments. Such agreements are subject to review and approval by the community corrections board of the jurisdiction in which any community corrections program making such agreement is located. Any such use of a community corrections program may be supported with funding from local governments, public or private grants, offender fees, and other sources other than the state general fund.

(b) A district court, county court, and any other criminal justice official may enter into agreements with community corrections programs that provide residential drug treatment, for the

placement and supervision of offenders as a term and condition of probation when assessed treatment need levels indicate that residential drug treatment is necessary and appropriate. The agreement is subject to review and approval by the community corrections board in the jurisdiction where a community corrections program is located. A community corrections program used pursuant to this paragraph (b) may receive funds from the correctional treatment cash fund, as well as local funding, public or private grants, or offender fees.

18-1.3-302. Legislative declaration - offenders who may be sentenced to the specialized restitution and community service program. (1) The general assembly hereby finds that:

The taxpayer costs to incarcerate nonviolent offenders, most of whom have committed property-related offenses, usually outbalances the need to incarcerate such persons to protect the public's safety and that imprisonment generally renders offenders less able to compensate their victims. Therefore, the general assembly declares that the purpose for enacting this article regarding specialized restitution and community service programs is to increase the cost-efficiency and the effectiveness of Colorado corrections. This article authorizes the establishment of an intermediate sanction whereby nonviolent offenders, at less taxpayer cost than imprisonment, would be required to work under strict supervision in a highly structured program in order to compensate their victims and society for the damage they have caused; and

Using incarceration as a routine punishment for nonviolent offenders, either upon sentencing or upon the revocation of parole or probation, punishes Colorado's taxpayers. The general assembly finds that limiting the pool of offenders eligible for the specialized restitution and community service program to first-time offenders unreasonably restricts entrance into the program and that the level of supervision mandated for repeat offenders by this article is adequate to ensure public safety from such offenders. The general assembly further finds that the vast majority of repeat offenders do not possess the requisite skills to obtain legitimate employment and that the specialized restitution and community service program will train such repeat offenders for legitimate employment. Therefore, it is in the best interests of the people of the state of Colorado to allow nonviolent repeat offenders and offenders with technical violations of parole or probation into such program.

Any offender shall be eligible to be placed in a specialized restitution and community service program if:

The offender is not eligible for probation pursuant to section 18-1.3-201, and has been convicted of an offense other than a crime of violence, as described in section 18-1.3-406 (2) (a), or any felony offense committed against a child set forth in articles 3, 6, and 7 of this title, or an offense that requires incarceration or imprisonment in the department of corrections or community corrections, or any sexual offense as defined in section 18-1.3-1003; and

(I) A determination is made by the court that the offender would be incarcerated, either pursuant to section 18-1.3-104 (1) (b) or pursuant to a probation revocation, if such offender is not placed in the specialized restitution and community service program; or

(II) A determination is made by the parole board that the offender would be incarcerated pursuant to a parole violation.

Prior to sentencing an eligible offender to a specialized restitution and community service

program pursuant to this section, the court shall make the determinations required in subsection (2) of this section and such offender must have been accepted by both of the following:

The provider of the specialized restitution and community service program in which it is proposed that the offender be placed; and

The community corrections board, as defined in section 17-27-102 (2), C.R.S., of the community in which the program is located.

If an eligible offender is accepted by a provider pursuant to subsection (3) of this section, the court may sentence an offender to pay restitution or perform community service, or both, in an amount commensurate with the seriousness of the crime and to the custody of any specialized restitution and community service program adopted pursuant to this section or article 27.9 of title 17, C.R.S. Notwithstanding any other provision of law to the contrary, a minimum of full restitution may be imposed in an amount that exceeds any actual losses or damages suffered by a victim of the crime. An offender shall be supervised in accordance with and subject to the provisions of article 27 of title 17, C.R.S.

The parole board may place parole violators who meet the eligibility criteria of subsection (2) of this section and who have been accepted pursuant to paragraphs (a) and (b) of subsection (3) of this section in specialized restitution and community service programs. Such parole violators shall be supervised in accordance with and subject to the provisions of article 27 of title 17, C.R.S.

18-1.3-303. Sentencing order - collateral relief - definitions. (1) At the time of sentencing, upon the request of the defendant or upon the court's own motion, a court may enter an order of collateral relief if the court sentences the defendant to a community corrections program for the purpose of preserving or enhancing the defendant's employment or employment prospects and to improve the defendant's likelihood of success on probation or in the community corrections program.

Application contents. (a) An application for an order of collateral relief must cite the grounds for granting the relief, the type of relief sought, and the specific collateral consequence from which the applicant is seeking relief and must include a copy of a recent Colorado bureau of investigation fingerprint-based criminal history records check. The state court administrator may produce an application form that an applicant may submit in application.

(b) The applicant shall provide a copy of the application to the district attorney and to the regulatory or licensing body that has jurisdiction over the collateral consequence from which the applicant is seeking relief, if any, by certified mail or personal service within ten days after filing the application with the court.

An order of collateral relief may relieve a defendant of any collateral consequences of the conviction, whether in housing or employment barriers or any other sanction or disqualification that the court shall specify, including but not limited to statutory, regulatory, or other collateral consequences that the court may see fit to relieve that will assist the defendant in successfully completing probation or a community corrections sentence.

(a) Notwithstanding any other provision of law, an order of collateral relief cannot relieve any collateral consequences imposed by law for licensure by the department of education or any

collateral consequences imposed by law for employment with the judicial branch, the department of corrections, division of youth corrections in the department of human services, or any other law enforcement agency in the state of Colorado.

A court shall not issue an order of collateral relief if the defendant:

Has been convicted of a felony that included an element that requires a victim to suffer permanent disability;

Has been convicted of a crime of violence as described in section 18-1.3-406; or

Is required to register as a sex offender pursuant to section 16-22-103, C.R.S.

Hearing. (a) The court may conduct a hearing or include a hearing on the matter at the defendant's sentencing hearing on the application or on anymatter relevant to the granting or denying of the application and may take testimony under oath.

(b) The court may hear testimony from victims or any proponent or opponent of the application and may hear argument from the petitioner and the district attorney.

Standard for granting relief. (a) A court may issue an order of collateral relief if the court finds that:

The order of collateral relief is consistent with the applicant's rehabilitation; and

Granting the application would improve the applicant's likelihood of success in reintegrating into society and is in the public's interest.

The court that previously issued an order of collateral relief, on its own motion or either by cause shown by the district attorney or on grounds offered by the applicant, may at any time issue a subsequent judgment to enlarge, limit, or circumscribe the relief previously granted.

Upon the motion of the district attorney or probation officer or upon the court's own motion, a court may revoke an order of collateral relief upon evidence of a subsequent criminal conviction or proof that the defendant is no longer entitled to relief. Any bars, prohibitions, sanctions, and disqualifications thereby relieved shall be reinstated as of the date of the written order of revocation. The court shall provide a copy of the order of revocation to the holder and to any regulatory or licensing entity that the defendant noticed in his or her motion for relief.

If the court issues an order of collateral relief, it shall send a copy of the order of collateral relief through the Colorado integrated criminal justice information system to the Colorado bureau of investigation, and the Colorado bureau of investigation shall note in the applicant's record in the Colorado crime information center that the order of collateral relief was issued.

Definitions. As used in this section, unless the context otherwise requires:

"Collateral consequence" means a collateral sanction or a disqualification.

"Collateral sanction" means a penalty, prohibition, bar, or disadvantage, however denominated, imposed on an individual as a result of the individual's conviction of an offense, which penalty, prohibition, bar, or disadvantage applies by operation of law regardless of whether the penalty, prohibition, bar, or disadvantage is included in the judgment or sentence. "Collateral sanction" does not include imprisonment, probation, parole, supervised release, forfeiture, restitution, fine, assessment, costs of prosecution, or a restraint or sanction on an individual's driving privilege.

"Conviction" or "convicted" means a verdict of guilty by a judge or jury or a plea of guilty or nolo contendere that is accepted by the court or a conviction of a crime under the laws of any other state, the United States, or any territory subject to the jurisdiction of the United States,

which, if committed within this state, would be a felony or misdemeanor. "Conviction" or "convicted" also includes having received a deferred judgment and sentence; except that a person shall not be deemed to have been convicted if the person has successfully completed a deferred sentence. "Disqualification" means a penalty, prohibition, bar, or disadvantage, however denominated, that an administrative agency, governmental official, or court in a civil proceeding is authorized, but not required, to impose on an individual on grounds relating to the individual's conviction of an offense.

PART 4 SENTENCES TO IMPRISONMENT

18-1.3-401. Felonies classified - presumptive penalties. (1) (a) (I) As to any person sentenced for a felony committed after July 1, 1979, and before July 1, 1984, felonies are divided into five classes which are distinguished from one another by the following presumptive ranges of penalties which are authorized upon conviction:

Class        Presumptive Range

Life imprisonment or death
Eight to twelve years plus one year of parole
Four to eight years plus one year of parole
Two to four years plus one year of parole
One to two years plus one year of parole

As to any person sentenced for a felony committed on or after July 1, 1984, and before July 1, 1985, felonies are divided into five classes which are distinguished from one another by the following presumptive ranges of penalties which are authorized upon conviction:

Class        Presumptive Range

Life imprisonment or death
Eight to twelve years
Four to eight years
Two to four years
One to two years

(A) As to any person sentenced for a felony committed on or after July 1, 1985, except as otherwise provided in sub-subparagraph (E) of this subparagraph (III), in addition to, or in lieu of, any sentence to imprisonment, probation, community corrections, or work release, a fine within the following presumptive ranges may be imposed for the specified classes of felonies:

| Class | Minimum Sentence | Maximum Sentence |
|---|---|---|
| 1 | No fine | No fine |
| 2 | Five thousand dollars | One million dollars |
| 3 | Three thousand dollars | Seven hundred fifty thousand dollars |
| 4 | Two thousand dollars | Five hundred thousand dollars |
| 5 | One thousand dollars | One hundred thousand dollars |
| 6 | One thousand dollars | One hundred thousand dollars |

39

(A.5) Notwithstanding any provision of law to the contrary, any person who attempts to commit, conspires to commit, or commits against an elderly person any felony set forth in part 4 of article 4 of this title, part 1, 2, 3, or 5 of article 5 of this title, article 5.5 of this title, or section 11-51- 603, C.R.S., shall be required to pay a mandatory and substantial fine within the limits permitted by law. However, all moneys collected from the offender shall be applied in the following order: Costs for crime victim compensation fund pursuant to section 24-4.1-119, C.R.S.; surcharges for victims and witnesses assistance and law enforcement fund pursuant to section 24-4.2-104, C.R.S.; restitution; time payment fee; late fees; and any other fines, fees, or surcharges. For purposes of this sub-subparagraph (A.5), an "elderly person" or "elderly victim" means a person sixty years of age or older. Failure to pay a fine imposed pursuant to this subparagraph (III) is grounds for revocation of probation or revocation of a sentence to community corrections, assuming the defendant's ability to pay. If such a revocation occurs, the court may impose the maximum sentence allowable in the given sentencing ranges.

Each judicial district shall have at least one clerk who shall collect and administer the fines imposed under this subparagraph (III) and under section 18-1.3-501 in accordance with the provisions of sub-subparagraph (D) of this subparagraph (III).

All fines collected pursuant to this subparagraph (III) shall be deposited in the fines collection cash fund, which fund is hereby created. The general assembly shall make annual appropriations out of such fund for administrative and personnel costs incurred in the collection and administration of said fines. All unexpended balances shall revert to the general fund at the end of each fiscal year.

Notwithstanding the provisions of sub-subparagraph (A) of this subparagraph (III), a person who has been twice convicted of a felony under the laws of this state, any other state, or the United States prior to the conviction for which he or she is being sentenced shall not be eligible to receive a fine in lieu of any sentence to imprisonment, community corrections, or work release but shall be sentenced to at least the minimum sentence specified in subparagraph (V) of this paragraph

and may receive a fine in addition to said sentence.

As to any person sentenced for a felony committed on or after July 1, 1985, but prior to July 1, 1993, felonies are divided into six classes which are distinguished from one another by the following presumptive ranges of penalties which are authorized upon conviction:

| Class | Minimum Sentence | Maximum Sentence |
|---|---|---|
| 1 | Life imprisonment | Death |
| 2 | Eight years imprisonment | Twenty-four years imprisonment |
| 3 | Four years imprisonment | Sixteen years imprisonment |
| 4 | Two years imprisonment | Eight years imprisonment |
| 5 | One year imprisonment | Four years imprisonment |
| 6 | One year imprisonment | Two years imprisonment |

(A) Except as otherwise provided in section 18-1.3-401.5 for offenses contained in article 18 of this title committed on or after October 1, 2013, as to any person sentenced for a felony committed on or after July 1, 1993, felonies are divided into six classes that are distinguished from one another by the following presumptive ranges of penalties that are authorized upon conviction:

| Class | Minimum Sentence | Maximum Sentence | Mandatory Period of Parole |
|---|---|---|---|
| 1 | Life imprisonment | Death | None |
| 2 | Eight years imprisonment | Twenty-four years imprisonment | Five years |
| 3 | Four years imprisonment | Twelve years imprisonment | Five years |
| 4 | Two years imprisonment | Six years imprisonment | Three years |
| 5 | One year imprisonment | Three years imprisonment | Two years |
| 6 | One year imprisonment | Eighteen months imprisonment | One year |

Any person who is paroled pursuant to section 17-22.5-403, C.R.S., or any person who is not paroled and is discharged pursuant to law, shall be subject to the mandatory period of parole established pursuant to sub-subparagraph (A) of this subparagraph (V). Such mandatory period of parole may not be waived by the offender or waived or suspended by the court and shall be subject to the provisions of section 17-22.5-403 (6), C.R.S., which permits the state board of parole to discharge the offender at any time during the term of parole upon a determination that the offender has been sufficiently rehabilitated and reintegrated into societyand can no longer benefit from parole supervision.

Notwithstanding sub-subparagraph (A) of this subparagraph (V), the mandatory period of parole for a person convicted of a felony offense committed prior to July 1, 1996, pursuant to part 4 of article 3 of this title, or part 3 of article 6 of this title, shall be five years. Notwithstanding sub-subparagraph (A) of this subparagraph (V), and except as otherwise provided in sub-subparagraph (C.5) of this subparagraph (V), the period of parole for a person convicted of a felony offense committed on or after July 1, 1996, but prior to July 1, 2002, pursuant to part 4 of article 3 of this title, or part 3 of article 6 of this title, shall be set by the state board of parole pursuant to section 17- 2-201 (5) (a.5), C.R.S., but in no event shall the term of parole exceed the maximum sentence imposed upon the inmate by the court.

(C.3) (Deleted by amendment, L. 2002, p. 124, § 1, effective March 26, 2002.)

(C.5) Notwithstanding the provisions of sub-subparagraph (A) of this subparagraph (V), any

person sentenced for a sex offense, as defined in section 18-1.3-1003 (5), committed on or after November 1, 1998, shall be sentenced pursuant to the provisions of part 10 of this article.

(C.7) Any person sentenced for a felony committed on or after July 1, 2002, involving unlawful sexual behavior, as defined in section 16-22-102 (9), C.R.S., or for a felony, committed on or after July 1, 2002, the underlying factual basis of which involved unlawful sexual behavior, and who is not subject to the provisions of part 10 of this article, shall be subject to the mandatory period of parole specified in sub-subparagraph (A) of this subparagraph (V).

The mandatory period of parole imposed pursuant to sub-subparagraph (A) of this subparagraph (V) shall commence immediately upon the discharge of an offender from imprisonment in the custody of the department of corrections. If the offender has been granted release to parole supervision by the state board of parole, the offender shall be deemed to have discharged the offender's sentence to imprisonment provided for in sub-subparagraph (A) of this subparagraph (V) in the same manner as if such sentence were discharged pursuant to law; except that the sentence to imprisonment for any person sentenced as a sex offender pursuant to part 10 of this article shall not be deemed discharged on release of said person on parole. When an offender is released by the state board of parole or released because the offender's sentence was discharged pursuant to law, the mandatory period of parole shall be served by such offender. An offender sentenced for nonviolent felony offenses, as defined in section 17-22.5-405 (5), C.R.S., may receive earned time pursuant to section 17-22.5-405, C.R.S., while serving a mandatory parole period in accordance with this section, but not while such offender is reincarcerated after a revocation of the mandatory period of parole. An offender who is sentenced for a felony committed on or after July 1, 1993, and paroled on or after January 1, 2009, shall be eligible to receive any earned time while on parole or after reparole following a parole revocation. The offender shall not be eligible for earned time while the offender is reincarcerated after revocation of the mandatory period of parole pursuant to this subparagraph (V).

If an offender is sentenced consecutively for the commission of two or more felony offenses pursuant to sub-subparagraph (A) of this subparagraph (V), the mandatory period of parole for such offender shall be the mandatory period of parole established for the highest class felony of which such offender has been convicted.

Any person sentenced for a class 2, 3, 4, or 5 felony, or a class 6 felony that is the offender's second or subsequent felony offense, committed on or after July 1, 1998, regardless of the length of the person's sentence to incarceration and the mandatory period of parole, shall not be deemed to have fully discharged his or her sentence until said person has either completed or been discharged by the state board of parole from the mandatory period of parole imposed pursuant to subparagraph (V) of this paragraph (a).

(I) Except as provided in subsection (6) and subsection (8) of this section and in section 18-1.3-804, a person who has been convicted of a class 2, class 3, class 4, class 5, or class 6 felony shall be punished by the imposition of a definite sentence which is within the presumptive ranges set forth in paragraph (a) of this subsection (1). In imposing the sentence within the presumptive range, the court shall consider the nature and elements of the offense, the character and record of the offender, and all aggravating or mitigating circumstances surrounding the offense and the offender. The prediction of the potential for future criminality by a particular defendant, unless based on prior criminal conduct, shall not be considered in determining the length of sentence to be imposed.

As to any person sentenced for a felony committed on or after July 1, 1985, a person may be sentenced to imprisonment as described in subparagraph (I) of this paragraph (b) or to pay a fine that is within the presumptive ranges set forth in subparagraph (III) of paragraph (a) of this subsection (1) or to both such fine and imprisonment; except that any person who has been twice convicted of a felony under the laws of this state, any other state, or the United States prior to the conviction for which he or she is being sentenced shall not be eligible to receive a fine in lieu of any sentence to imprisonment as described in subparagraph (I) of this paragraph (b) but shall be sentenced to at least the minimum sentence specified in subparagraph (V) of paragraph (a) of this subsection (1) and may receive a fine in addition to said sentence.

(II.5) Notwithstanding anything in this section to the contrary, any person sentenced for a sex offense, as defined in section 18-1.3-1003 (5), committed on or after November 1, 1998, may be sentenced to pay a fine in addition to, but not instead of, a sentence for imprisonment or probation pursuant to section 18-1.3-1004.

Notwithstanding anything in this section to the contrary, as to any person sentenced for a crime of violence, as defined in section 18-1.3-406, committed on or after July 1, 1985, a person may be sentenced to pay a fine in addition to, but not instead of, a sentence for imprisonment.

If a person is convicted of assault in the first degree pursuant to section 18-3-202 or assault in the second degree pursuant to section 18-3-203 (1) (c.5), and the victim is a peace officer, firefighter, or emergency medical service provider engaged in the performance of his or her duties, as defined in section 18-1.3-501 (1.5) (b), notwithstanding the provisions of subparagraph (III) of paragraph (a) of this subsection (1) and subparagraph (II) of this paragraph (b), the court shall sentence the person to the department of corrections. In addition to a term of imprisonment, the court may impose a fine on the person pursuant to subparagraph (III) of paragraph (a) of this subsection (1).

Except as otherwise provided by statute, felonies are punishable by imprisonment in any correctional facility under the supervision of the executive director of the department of corrections. Nothing in this section shall limit the authority granted in part 8 of this article to increase sentences for habitual criminals. Nothing in this section shall limit the authority granted in parts 9 and 10 of this article to sentence sex offenders to the department of corrections or to sentence sex offenders to probation for an indeterminate term. Nothing in this section shall limit the authority granted in section 18-1.3-804 for increased sentences for habitual burglary offenders.

(a) A corporation which has been found guilty of a class 2 or class 3 felony shall be subject to imposition of a fine of not less than five thousand dollars nor more than fifty thousand dollars. A corporation which has been found guilty of a class 4, class 5, or class 6 felony shall be subject to imposition of a fine of not less than one thousand dollars nor more than thirty thousand dollars.

(b) A corporation which has been found guilty of a class 2, class 3, class 4, class 5, or class 6 felony, for an act committed on or after July 1, 1985, shall be subject to imposition of a fine which is within the presumptive ranges set forth in subparagraph (III) of paragraph (a) of subsection (1) of this section.

Every person convicted of a felony, whether defined as such within or outside this code, shall be disqualified from holding any office of honor, trust, or profit under the laws of this state or from practicing as an attorney in any of the courts of this state during the actual time of confinement

or commitment to imprisonment or release from actual confinement on conditions of probation. Upon his or her discharge after completion of service of his or her sentence or after service under probation, the right to hold any office of honor, trust, or profit shall be restored, except as provided in section 4 of article XII of the state constitution.

(a) A person who has been convicted of a class 1 felony shall be punished by life imprisonment in the department of corrections unless a proceeding held to determine sentence according to the procedure set forth in section 18-1.3-1201, 18-1.3-1302, or 18-1.4-102, results in a verdict that requires imposition of the death penalty, in which event such person shall be sentenced to death. As to any person sentenced for a class 1 felony, for an act committed on or after July 1, 1985, and before July 1, 1990, life imprisonment shall mean imprisonment without the possibility of parole for forty calendar years. As to any person sentenced for a class 1 felony, for an act committed on or after July 1, 1990, life imprisonment shall mean imprisonment without the possibility of parole.

(I) Notwithstanding the provisions of sub-subparagraph (A) of subparagraph (V) of paragraph (a) of subsection (1) of this section and notwithstanding the provisions of paragraph (a) of this subsection (4), as to a person who is convicted as an adult of a class 1 felony following direct filing of an information or indictment in the district court pursuant to section 19-2-517, C.R.S., or transfer of proceedings to the district court pursuant to section 19-2-518, C.R.S., the district court judge shall sentence the person to a term of life imprisonment with the possibility of parole after serving a period of forty years, less any earned time granted pursuant to section 17-22.5-405, C.R.S. Regardless of whether the state board of parole releases the person on parole, the person shall remain in the legal custody of the department of corrections for the remainder of the person's life and shall not be discharged.

(II) The provisions of this paragraph (b) shall apply to persons sentenced for offenses committed on or after July 1, 2006.

(I) Notwithstanding the provisions of sub-subparagraph (A) of subparagraph (V) of paragraph (a) of subsection (1) of this section and notwithstanding

41

the provisions of paragraphs (a) and (b) of this subsection (4), as to a person who is convicted as an adult of a class 1 felony following a direct filing of an information or indictment in the district court pursuant to section 19-2- 517, C.R.S., or transfer of proceedings to the district court pursuant to section 19-2-518, C.R.S., or pursuant to either of these sections as they existed prior to their repeal and reenactment, with amendments, by House Bill 96-1005, which felony was committed on or after July 1, 1990, and before July 1, 2006, and who received a sentence to life imprisonment without the possibility of parole:

If the felony for which the person was convicted is murder in the first degree, as described in section 18-3-102 (1) (b), then the district court, after holding a hearing, may sentence the person to a determinate sentence within the range of thirty to fifty years in prison, less any earned time granted pursuant to section 17-22.5-405, C.R.S., if, after considering the factors described in subparagraph (II) of this paragraph (c), the district court finds extraordinary mitigating circumstances. Alternatively, the court may sentence the person to a term of life imprisonment with the possibility of parole after serving forty years, less any earned time granted pursuant to section 17-22.5-405, C.R.S.

If the felony for which the person was convicted is not murder in the first degree, as

described in section 18-3-102 (1) (b), then the district court shall sentence the person to a term of life imprisonment with the possibility of parole after serving forty years, less any earned time granted pursuant to section 17-22.5-405, C.R.S.

In determining whether extraordinary mitigating circumstances exist, the court shall conduct a sentencing hearing, make factual findings to support its decision, and consider relevant evidence presented by either party regarding the following factors:

The diminished culpability and heightened capacity for change associated with youth;

The offender's developmental maturity and chronological age at the time of the offense and the hallmark features of such age, including but not limited to immaturity, impetuosity, and inability to appreciate risks and consequences;

The offender's capacity for change and potential for rehabilitation, including any evidence of the offender's efforts toward, or amenability to, rehabilitation;

The impact of the offense upon any victim or victim's immediate family; and

Any other factors that the court deems relevant to its decision, so long as the court identifies such factors on the record.

If a person is sentenced to a determinate range of thirty to fifty years in prison pursuant to this paragraph (c), the court shall impose a mandatory period of ten years parole.

If a person is sentenced to a term of life imprisonment with the possibility of parole after serving forty years, less any earned time granted pursuant to section 17-22.5-405, C.R.S., regardless of whether the state board of parole releases the person on parole, the person shall remain in the legal custody of the department of corrections for the remainder of his or her life and shall not be discharged.

In the event the death penalty as provided for in this section is held to be unconstitutional by the Colorado supreme court or the United States supreme court, a person convicted of a crime punishable by death under the laws of this state shall be punished by life imprisonment. In such circumstance, the court which previously sentenced a person to death shall cause such person to be brought before the court, and the court shall sentence such person to life imprisonment.

In imposing a sentence to incarceration, the court shall impose a definite sentence which is within the presumptive ranges set forth in subsection (1) of this section unless it concludes that extraordinary mitigating or aggravating circumstances are present, are based on evidence in the record of the sentencing hearing and the presentence report, and support a different sentence which better serves the purposes of this code with respect to sentencing, as set forth in section 18-1-102.5. If the court finds such extraordinary mitigating or aggravating circumstances, it may impose a sentence which is lesser or greater than the presumptive range; except that in no case shall the term of sentence be greater than twice the maximum nor less than one-half the minimum term authorized in the presumptive range for the punishment of the offense.

In all cases, except as provided in subsection (8) of this section, in which a sentence which is not within the presumptive range is imposed, the court shall make specific findings on the record of the case, detailing the specific extraordinary circumstances which constitute the reasons for varying from the presumptive sentence.

(a) The presence of any one or more of the following extraordinary aggravating circumstances shall require the court, if it sentences the defendant to incarceration, to sentence the

defendant to a term of at least the midpoint in the presumptive range but not more than twice the maximum term authorized in the presumptive range for the punishment of a felony:

The defendant is convicted of a crime of violence under section 18-1.3-406;

The defendant was on parole for another felony at the time of commission of the felony;

The defendant was on probation or was on bond while awaiting sentencing following revocation of probation for another felony at the time of the commission of the felony;

The defendant was under confinement, in prison, or in any correctional institution as a convicted felon, or an escapee from any correctional institution for another felony at the time of the commission of a felony;

At the time of the commission of the felony, the defendant was on appeal bond following his or her conviction for a previous felony;

At the time of the commission of a felony, the defendant was on probation for or on bond while awaiting sentencing following revocation of probation for a delinquent act that would have constituted a felony if committed by an adult.

In any case in which one or more of the extraordinary aggravating circumstances provided for in paragraph (a) of this subsection (8) exist, the provisions of subsection (7) of this section shall not apply.

Nothing in this subsection (8) shall preclude the court from considering aggravating circumstances other than those stated in paragraph (a) of this subsection (8) as the basis for sentencing the defendant to a term greater than the presumptive range for the felony.

(I) If the defendant is convicted of the class 2 or the class 3 felony of child abuse under section 18-6-401 (7) (a) (I) or (7) (a) (III), the court shall be required to sentence the defendant to the department of corrections for a term of at least the midpoint in the presumptive range but not more than twice the maximum term authorized in the presumptive range for the punishment of that class felony.

(II) In no case shall any defendant sentenced pursuant to subparagraph (I) of this paragraph

be eligible for suspension of sentence or for probation or deferred prosecution.

(I) If the defendant is convicted of the class 2 felony of sexual assault in the first degree under section 18-3-402 (3), commission of which offense occurs prior to November 1, 1998, the court shall be required to sentence the defendant to a term of at least the midpoint in the presumptive range but not more than twice the maximum term authorized in the presumptive range for the punishment of that class of felony.

In no case shall any defendant sentenced pursuant to subparagraph (I) of this paragraph

be eligible for suspension of sentence or probation.

As a condition of parole under section 17-2-201 (5) (e), C.R.S., a defendant sentenced pursuant to this paragraph (e) shall be required to participate in a program of mental health counseling or receive appropriate treatment to the extent that the state board of parole deems appropriate to effectuate the successful reintegration of the defendant into the community while recognizing the need for public safety.

(e.5) If the defendant is convicted of the class 2 felony of sexual assault under section 18-3-402 (5) or the class 2 felony of sexual assault in the first degree under section 18-3-402 (3) as it existed prior to July 1, 2000, commission of which offense occurs on or after November 1, 1998, the

court shall be required to sentence the defendant to the department of corrections for an indeterminate sentence of at least the midpoint in the presumptive range for the punishment of that class of felony up to the defendant's natural life.

The court may consider aggravating circumstances such as serious bodily injury caused to the victim or the use of a weapon in the commission of a crime, notwithstanding the fact that such factors constitute elements of the offense.

If the defendant is convicted of class 4 or class 3 felony vehicular homicide under section 18-3-106 (1) (a) or (1) (b), and while committing vehicular homicide the defendant was in immediate flight from the commission of another felony, the court shall be required to sentence the defendant to the department of corrections for a term of at least the midpoint in the presumptive range but not more than twice the maximum term authorized in the presumptive range for the punishment of the class of felony vehicular homicide of which the defendant is convicted.

The presence of any one or more of the following sentence-enhancing circumstances shall require the court, if it sentences the defendant to incarceration, to sentence the defendant to a term of at least the minimum in the presumptive range but not more than twice the maximum term authorized in the presumptive range for the punishment of a felony:

At the time of the commission of the felony, the defendant was charged with or was on bond for a felony in a previous case and the defendant was convicted of any felony in the previous case;

(a.5) At the time of the commission of the felony, the defendant was charged with or was on bond for a delinquent act that would have constituted a felony if committed by an adult;

At the time of the commission of the felony, the defendant was on bond for having pled guilty to a lesser offense when the original offense charged was a felony;

The defendant was under a deferred judgment and sentence for another felony at the time of the commission of the felony;

(c.5) At the time of the commission of the felony, the defendant was on bond in a juvenile prosecution under title 19, C.R.S., for having pled guilty to a lesser delinquent act when the original delinquent act charged would have constituted a felony if committed by an adult;

(c.7) At the time of the commission of the felony, the defendant was under a deferred judgment and sentence for a delinquent act that would have constituted a felony if committed by an adult;

At the time of the commission of the felony, the defendant was on parole for having been adjudicated a delinquent child for an offense which would constitute a felony if committed by an adult.

(a) The general assembly hereby finds that certain crimes which are listed in paragraph

of this subsection (10) present an extraordinary risk of harm to society and therefore, in the interest of public safety, for such crimes which constitute class 3 felonies, the maximum sentence in the presumptive range shall be increased by four years; for such crimes which constitute class 4 felonies, the maximum sentence in the presumptive range shall be increased by two years; for such crimes which constitute class 5 felonies, the maximum sentence in the presumptive range shall be increased by one year; for such crimes which constitute class 6 felonies, the maximum sentence in the presumptive range shall be increased by six months.

Crimes that present an extraordinary risk of harm to society shall include the following:

(I) to (VIII) Repealed.

Aggravated robbery, as defined in section 18-4-302;

Child abuse, as defined in section 18-6-401;

Unlawful distribution, manufacturing, dispensing, sale, or possession of a controlled substance with the intent to sell, distribute, manufacture, or dispense, as defined in section 18-18- 405;

Any crime of violence, as defined in section 18-1.3-406;

Stalking, as described in section 18-9-111 (4), as it existed prior to August 11, 2010, or section 18-3-602;

Sale or distribution of materials to manufacture controlled substances, as described in section 18-18-412.7;

Felony invasion of privacy for sexual gratification, as described in section 18-3-405.6;

A class 3 felony offense of human trafficking for involuntary servitude, as described in section 18-3-503;

A class 3 felony offense of human trafficking for sexual servitude, as described in section 18-3-504; and

Assault in the second degree, as described in section 18-3-203 (1) (i).

Repealed.

When it shall appear to the satisfaction of the court that the ends of justice and the best interest of the public, as well as the defendant, will be best served thereby, the court shall have the power to suspend the imposition or execution of sentence for such period and upon such terms and conditions as it may deem best; except that in no instance shall the court have the power to suspend a sentence to a term of incarceration when the defendant is sentenced pursuant to a sentencing provision that requires incarceration or imprisonment in the department of corrections, community corrections, or jail. In no instance shall a sentence be suspended if the defendant is ineligible for probation pursuant to section 18-1.3-201, except upon an express waiver being made by the sentencing court regarding a particular defendant upon recommendation of the district attorney and approval of such recommendation by an order of the sentencing court pursuant to section 18-1.3-201 (4).

Every sentence entered under this section shall include consideration of restitution as required by part 6 of this article and by article 18.5 of title 16, C.R.S.

(a) The court, if it sentences a defendant who is convicted of any one or more of the offenses specified in paragraph (b) of this subsection (13) to incarceration, shall sentence the defendant to a term of at least the midpoint, but not more than twice the maximum, of the presumptive range authorized for the punishment of the offense of which the defendant is convicted if the court makes the following findings on the record:

The victim of the offense was pregnant at the time of commission of the offense; and

The defendant knew or reasonably should have known that the victim of the offense was pregnant.

(Deleted by amendment, L. 2003, p. 2163, § 3, effective July 1, 2003.)

The provisions of this subsection (13) shall apply to the following offenses:

Murder in the second degree, as described in section 18-3-103;

Manslaughter, as described in section 18-3-104;

Criminally negligent homicide, as described in section 18-3-105;

Vehicular homicide, as described in section 18-3-106;

Assault in the first degree, as described in section 18-3-202;

Assault in the second degree, as described in section 18-3-203;

Vehicular assault, as described in section 18-3-205.

Notwithstanding any provision of this subsection (13) to the contrary, for any of the offenses specified in paragraph (b) of this subsection (13) that

constitute crimes of violence, the court shall sentence the defendant in accordance with the provisions of section 18-1.3-406.
The court may sentence a defendant to the youthful offender system created in section 18-1.3-407 if the defendant is an eligible young adult offender pursuant to section 18-1.3-407.5.


18-1.3-401.5. Drug felonies classified - presumptive and aggravated penalties. (1) The provisions of this section only apply to a conviction for a drug felony offense described in article 18 of this title committed on or after October 1, 2013. For purposes of this section, "felony" means any felony or drug felony defined in the state statutes.
(a) For offenses committed on or after October 1, 2013, drug felonies are divided into four levels that are distinguished from one another by the ranges of penalties, which are authorized upon conviction of a drug felony:

| Level | Presumptive Range | Period of Parole | |
|---|---|---|---|
| DF1 | Eight years | Thirty-two years | Three years |
| DF2 | Four years | Eight years | Two years |
| DF3 | Two years | Four years | One year |
| DF4 | Six months | One year | One year |

| Level | Aggravated Range | | |
|---|---|---|---|
| DF2 | Eight years | Sixteen years | Two years |
| DF3 | Four years | Six years | One year |
| DF4 | One year | Two years | One year |

(b) (I) As to any person sentenced for a drug felony committed on or after October 1, 2013, except as otherwise provided in subparagraph (V) of this paragraph (b) and in subsection (7) of this section, in addition to, or in lieu of, any sentence to imprisonment, probation, community corrections, or work release, a fine within the following ranges may be imposed for the specified level of drug felonies:

| Level | Minimum Sentence | Maximum Sentence |
|---|---|---|
| DF1 | Five thousand dollars | One million dollars |
| DF2 | Three thousand dollars | Seven hundred fifty thousand dollars |
| DF3 | Two thousand dollars | Five hundred thousand dollars |
| DF4 | One thousand dollars | One hundred thousand dollars |

Failure to pay a fine imposed pursuant to this paragraph (b) is grounds for revocation of probation, community corrections, or a suspended sentence, if the defendant has the ability to pay the fine.
If a revocation occurs pursuant to subparagraph (II) of this paragraph (b), the court may impose any sentence legally available, subject to the provisions of section 18-1.3-104.5 (2).
All fines collected pursuant to this paragraph (b) must be deposited in the fines collection fund created in section 18-1.3-401 (1) (a) (III) (D) and are subject to the provisions of that section.
Notwithstanding the provisions of subparagraph (I) of this paragraph (b), a person who has been twice convicted of a felony under the laws of this state, any other state, or the United States prior to the conviction for which he or she is being sentenced shall not be eligible to receive a fine in lieu of any sentence to imprisonment, community corrections, or work release but shall be sentenced to at least the minimum sentence specified in paragraph (a) of this subsection (2) and may receive a fine in addition to said sentence.
A person who is paroled pursuant to section 17-22.5-403, C.R.S., or any person who is not paroled and is discharged pursuant to law, shall be subject to the mandatory period of parole established pursuant to paragraph (a) of subsection (2) of this section. The mandatory period of parole may not be waived by the offender or waived or suspended by the court and is subject to the provisions of section 17-22.5-403 (6), C.R.S., which permits the state board of parole to discharge the offender at any time during the term of parole upon a determination that the offender has been sufficiently rehabilitated and reintegrated into society and can no longer benefit from parole supervision.
The mandatory period of parole imposed pursuant to paragraph (a) of subsection (2) of this section commences immediately upon the discharge of an offender from imprisonment in the custody of the department of corrections. If the offender has been granted release to parole supervision by the state board of parole, the offender is deemed to have discharged the offender's sentence to imprisonment provided for in subsection (2) of this section in the same manner as if such sentence were discharged pursuant to law. When an offender is released by the state board of parole or released because the offender's sentence was discharged pursuant to law, the mandatory period of parole must be served by the offender. An offender sentenced for a drug felony may receive earned time pursuant to section 17-22.5-405, C.R.S., while serving a mandatory parole period in accordance with this section.
If an offender is sentenced consecutively for the commission of two or more felony offenses pursuant to sentencing provisions in this section or section 18-1.3-401, the mandatory period of parole for the offender must be the longest mandatory period of parole established for a felony for which the offender was convicted.
Any person sentenced for a level 1, 2, 3, or 4 drug felony that is the offender's second or subsequent felony or drug felony offense, regardless of the length of the person's sentence to

incarceration and the mandatory period of parole, is not deemed to have fully discharged his or her sentence until the person either completes, or is discharged by the state board of parole from, the mandatory period of parole imposed pursuant to paragraph (a) of subsection (2) of this section.
Notwithstanding any provision of this section to the contrary, if the defendant is convicted of a level 1 drug felony, the court shall sentence the defendant to a term of incarceration in the department of corrections of at least eight years but not more than thirty-two years. The presence of one or more of the aggravating circumstances provided in paragraph (a) of subsection
of this section or in section 18-18-407 (1) requires the court to sentence a defendant convicted of a level 1 drug felony to a term of incarceration in the department of corrections of at least twelve years but no more than thirty-two years. The court may impose a fine in addition to imprisonment.

In imposing a sentence to incarceration, the court shall impose a definite sentence that is within the presumptive ranges set forth in subsection (2) of this section; except that, for level 2, level 3, and level 4 drug felonies, the court may sentence the defendant in the aggravated range if it concludes aggravating circumstances exist. The aggravating circumstances must be based on evidence in the record of the sentencing hearing, the presentence report, and any factors agreed to by the parties and must support a different sentence that better serves the purposes of this code with respect to sentencing, as set forth in section 18-1-102.5.

In all cases, except as provided in subsection (10) of this section, in which a sentence that is not within the presumptive range is imposed, the court shall make specific findings on the record, detailing the aggravating circumstances that constitute the reasons for varying from the presumptive sentence.

(a) Except for a level 1 drug felony, the presence of one or more of the following aggravating circumstances at the time of the commission of a drug felony offense requires the court, if it sentences the defendant to incarceration, to sentence the defendant to a term of at least the midpoint in the presumptive range but not more than the maximum term of the aggravated range:

The defendant was on parole for another felony;

The defendant was on probation or was on bond while awaiting sentencing following revocation of probation for another felony;

The defendant was under confinement, in prison, or in any correctional institution as a convicted felon, or an escapee from any correctional institution for another felony; or

(III.5) The defendant was on appeal bond following his or her conviction for a previous felony;

The defendant was on probation for or on bond while awaiting sentencing following revocation of probation for a delinquent act that would have constituted a felony if committed by an adult.

In any case in which one or more of the aggravating circumstances provided for in paragraph (a) of this subsection (10) exist, the provisions of subsection (9) of this section do not apply.

Nothing in this subsection (10) precludes the court from considering aggravating circumstances other than those stated in paragraph (a) of this subsection (10) as the basis for sentencing the defendant to a term greater than the presumptive range for the drug felony.

Except for a level 1 drug felony, the presence of any one or more of the following sentence-enhancing circumstances allows the court, if it sentences the defendant to incarceration, to

sentence the defendant to a term in the presumptive or aggravated range:

At the time of the commission of the drug felony, the defendant was charged with or was on bond for a felony in a previous case and the defendant was convicted of any felony in the previous case;

At the time of the commission of the drug felony, the defendant was charged with or was on bond for a delinquent act that would have constituted a felony if committed by an adult;

At the time of the commission of the drug felony, the defendant was on bond for having pled guilty to a lesser offense when the original offense charged was a felony;

(c.5) At the time of the commission of the drug felony, the defendant was under a deferred judgment and sentence for another felony;

At the time of the commission of the drug felony, the defendant was on bond in a juvenile prosecution under title 19, C.R.S., for having pled guilty to a lesser delinquent act when the original delinquent act charged would have constituted a felony if committed by an adult;

At the time of the commission of the drug felony, the defendant was under a deferred judgment and sentence for a delinquent act that would have constituted a felony if committed by an adult; or

At the time of the commission of the drug felony, the defendant was on parole for having been adjudicated a delinquent child for an offense that would constitute a felony if committed by an adult.

When it appears to the satisfaction of the court that the ends of justice and the best interest of the public, as well as the defendant, will be best served thereby, the court has the power to suspend the imposition or execution of sentence for such period and upon such terms and conditions as it may deem best; except that the court may not suspend a sentence when the defendant is convicted of a level 1 drug felony. In no instance may a sentence be suspended if the defendant is ineligible for probation pursuant to section 18-1.3-201, except upon an express waiver being made by the sentencing court regarding a particular defendant upon recommendation of the district attorney and approval of such recommendation by an order of the sentencing court pursuant to section 18-1.3- 201 (4).

Every sentence entered under this section must include consideration of restitution as required by part 6 of this article and by article 18.5 of title 16, C.R.S.

18-1.3-402. Felony offenses not classified. (1) Any felony defined by state statute without specification of its class shall be punishable as provided in the statute defining it. For felony offenses committed on or after July 1, 1993, if the sentencing court sentences an offender to incarceration pursuant to the provisions of this section, the sentencing court shall also impose a mandatory period of parole of two years.

(2) Every sentence entered under this section shall include consideration of restitution as required by part 6 of this article and by article 18.5 of title 16, C.R.S.

18-1.3-403. Penalty for felony not fixed by statute - punishment. (1) In all cases where

an offense is denominated by statute as being a felony and no penalty is fixed in the statute therefor, the punishment shall be imprisonment for not more than five years in a correctional facility, as defined in section 17-1-102, C.R.S., or a fine of not more than fifteen thousand dollars, or both such imprisonment and fine. For offenses committed on or after July 1, 1985, a fine of not more than one hundred thousand dollars may be levied. For offenses committed on or after July 1, 1993, if the sentencing court sentences an offender to incarceration pursuant to the provisions of this section, the sentencing court shall also impose a mandatory period of parole of two years.

(2) Every sentence entered under this section shall include consideration of restitution as required by part 6 of this article and by article 18.5 of title 16, C.R.S.

18-1.3-404. Duration of sentences for felonies. (1) Unless otherwise provided by law and except as otherwise provided in the "Colorado Children's Code", title 19, C.R.S., courts sentencing any person for the commission of a felony to the custody of the executive director of the department of corrections shall fix a definite term as provided by section 18-1.3-401. The persons so sentenced shall be imprisoned and discharged as provided by other applicable statutes. No person sentenced to a correctional facility for the commission of a felony shall be subjected to imprisonment for a term exceeding the term provided by the statute fixing the length of the sentence for the crime of which the person was convicted and for which the person was sentenced.

(a) If a court sentences a defendant to the custody of the department of corrections, the court shall, after fixing a definite term of imprisonment, read the following statement:

"The defendant mayspend less time incarcerated than the term announced here today. The actual time served will be influenced by a number of factors including, but not limited to, previous criminal activities, eligibility for earned time for good behavior, correctional education program earned time, credit for time served, or community corrections eligibility."

(b) By requiring the court to read the statement contained in paragraph (a) of this subsection (2), the general assembly does not intend to grant any additional rights to the defendant. Failure of a court to comply with the requirements of paragraph (a) of this subsection (2) shall not be grounds for a defendant to withdraw a guilty plea or in any way gain a reversal of a conviction or reduction in sentence.

(a) Nothing in subsection (2) of this section shall be construed to affect the duties otherwise imposed by law on the court or on the executive director of the department of corrections.

(b) Nothing in subsection (2) of this section shall be construed to limit, expand, or otherwise affect any provision of law concerning the availability, administration, entitlement, or award of good time credits and earned time credits.


18-1.3-405. Credit for presentence confinement. A person who is confined for an offense prior to the imposition of sentence for said offense is entitled to credit against the term of his or her sentence for the entire period of such confinement. At the time of sentencing, the court shall make

a finding of the amount of presentence confinement to which the offender is entitled and shall include such finding in the mittimus. The period of confinement shall be deducted from the sentence by the department of corrections. A person who is confined pending a parole revocation hearing is entitled to credit for the entire period of such confinement against any period of reincarceration imposed in the parole revocation proceeding. The period of confinement shall be deducted from the period of reincarceration by the department of corrections. If a defendant is serving a sentence or is on parole for a previous offense when he or she commits a new offense and he or she continues to serve the sentence for the previous offense while charges on the new offense are pending, the credit given for presentence confinement under this section shall be granted against the sentence the defendant is currently serving for the previous offense and shall not be granted against the sentence for the new offense.


18-1.3-406. Mandatory sentences for violent crimes - definitions. (1) (a) Any person convicted of a crime of violence shall be sentenced pursuant to the provisions of section 18-1.3-401

to the department of corrections for a term of incarceration of at least the midpoint in, but not more than twice the maximum of, the presumptive range provided for such offense in section 18-1.3- 401 (1) (a), as modified for an extraordinary risk crime pursuant to section 18-1.3-401 (10), without suspension; except that, within ninety-one days after he or she has been placed in the custody of the department of corrections, the department shall transmit to the sentencing court a report on the evaluation and diagnosis of the violent offender, and the court, in a case which it considers to be exceptional and to involve unusual and extenuating circumstances, may thereupon modify the sentence, effective not earlier than one hundred nineteen days after his or her placement in the custody of the department. Such modification may include probation if the person is otherwise eligible therefor. Whenever a court finds that modification of a sentence is justified, the judge shall notify the state court administrator of his or her decision and shall advise said administrator of the unusual and extenuating circumstances that justified such modification. The state court administrator shall maintain a record, which shall be open to the public, summarizing all modifications of sentences and the grounds therefor for each judge of each district court in the state. Except as described in paragraph (c) of this subsection (1), a court shall sentence a person convicted of two or more separate crimes of violence arising out of the same incident so that his or her sentences are served consecutively rather than concurrently.

Notwithstanding the provisions of paragraph (a) of this subsection (1), any person convicted of a sex offense, as defined in section 18-1.3-1003 (5), committed on or after November 1, 1998, that constitutes a crime of violence shall be sentenced to the department of corrections for an indeterminate term of incarceration of at least the midpoint in the presumptive range specified in section 18-1.3-401 (1) (a) (V) (A) up to a maximum of the person's natural life, as provided in section 18-1.3-1004 (1).

The court may require a defendant to serve his or her sentences concurrently rather than consecutively if the defendant is convicted of two or more separate crimes of violence arising out of the same incident and one of such crimes is:

Aggravated robbery, as described in section 18-4-302;

Assault in the second degree, as described in section 18-3-203; or

Escape, as described in section 18-8-208.

(a) (I) "Crime of violence" means any of the crimes specified in subparagraph (II) of this paragraph (a) committed, conspired to be committed, or attempted to be committed by a person during which, or in the immediate flight therefrom, the person:

Used, or possessed and threatened the use of, a deadly weapon; or

Caused serious bodily injury or death to any other person except another participant.

(II)  Subparagraph (I) of this paragraph (a) applies to the following crimes:

Any crime against an at-risk adult or at-risk juvenile;

Murder;

First or second degree assault;

Kidnapping;

A sexual offense pursuant to part 4 of article 3 of this title;

Aggravated robbery;

First degree arson;

First degree burglary;

Escape;

Criminal extortion; or

First or second degree unlawful termination of pregnancy.

(I) "Crime of violence" also means any unlawful sexual offense in which the defendant caused bodily injury to the victim or in which the defendant used threat, intimidation, or force against the victim. For purposes of this subparagraph (I), "unlawful sexual offense" shall have the same meaning as set forth in section 18-3-411 (1), and "bodily injury" shall have the same meaning as set forth in section 18-1-901 (3) (c).

(II) The provisions of subparagraph (I) of this paragraph (b) shall apply only to felony unlawful sexual offenses.

As used in this section, "at-risk adult" has the same meaning as set forth in section 18- 6.5-102 (2), and "at-risk juvenile" has the same meaning as set forth in section 18-6.5-102 (4).

In any case in which the accused is charged with a crime of violence as defined in subsection (2) (a) of this section, the indictment or information shall so allege in a separate count, even though the use or threatened use of such deadly weapon or infliction of such serious bodily injury or death is not an essential element of the crime charged.

The jury, or the court if no jury trial is had, in any case as provided in subsection (3) of this section shall make a specific finding as to whether the accused did or did not use, or possessed and threatened to use, a deadlyweapon during the commission of such crime or whether such serious bodily injury or death was caused by the accused. If the jury or court finds that the accused used, or possessed and threatened the use of, such deadly weapon or that such injury or death was caused by the accused, the penalty provisions of this section shall be applicable.

In any case in which the accused is charged with a crime of violence as defined in subsection (2) (b) (I) of this section, the indictment or information shall so allege in a separate count, even though the use of threat, intimidation, or force or the infliction of bodily injury is not an essential element of the crime charged.

The jury, or the court if no jury trial is had, in any case as provided in subsection (5) of this section shall make a specific finding as to whether the accused did or did not use threat,

intimidation, or force during the commission of such crime or whether such bodily injury was caused by the accused. If the jury or court finds that the accused used threat, intimidation, or force or that such bodily injury was caused by the accused, the penalty provisions of this section shall be applicable.

(a) In any case in which the accused is charged with a crime of violence as defined in this section and the indictment or information specifies the use of a dangerous weapon as defined in sections 18-12-101 and 18-12-102, or the use of a semiautomatic assault weapon as defined in paragraph (b) of this subsection (7), upon conviction for said crime of violence, the judge shall impose an additional sentence to the department of corrections of five years for the use of such weapon. The sentence of five years shall be in addition to the mandatory sentence imposed for the substantive offense and shall be served consecutively to any other sentence and shall not be subject to suspension or probation.

(b) For the purposes of this subsection (7), "semiautomatic assault weapon" means any semiautomatic center fire firearm that is equipped with a detachable magazine with a capacity of twenty or more rounds of ammunition.


18-1.3-407. Sentences - youthful offenders - legislative declaration - powers and duties of district court - authorization for youthful offender system - powers and duties of department of corrections - definitions. (1) (a) It is the intent of the general assembly that the youthful offender system established pursuant to this section shall benefit the state by providing as a sentencing option for certain youthful offenders a controlled and regimented environment that affirms dignity of self and others, promotes the value of work and self-discipline, and develops useful skills and abilities through enriched programming.

It is the further intent of the general assembly in enacting this section that female and male offenders who are eligible for sentencing to the youthful offender system pursuant to section 18-1.3-407.5 or section 19-2-517 (6) or 19-2-518 (1) (d) (II), C.R.S., receive equitable treatment in sentencing, particularly in regard to the option of being sentenced to the youthful offender system. Accordingly, it is the general assembly's intent that necessary measures be taken by the department of corrections to establish separate housing for female and male offenders who are sentenced to the youthful offender system without compromising the equitable treatment of either.

(I) It is the intent of the general assembly that offenders sentenced to the youthful offender system be housed and serve their sentences in a facility specifically designed and programmed for the youthful offender system and that offenders so sentenced be housed separate from and not brought into dailyphysical contact with inmates older than twenty-four years sentenced to the department of corrections who have not been sentenced to the youthful offender system, except as specifically provided under subsection (5) of this section.

For the purposes of public safety, academic achievement, rehabilitation, the development of pro-social behavior, or reentry planning for youthful offenders, the executive director or his or her designee may transfer any offender age twenty-four years or younger and sentenced to the department of corrections into and out of the youthful offender system at his or her discretion.

The facility that houses offenders sentenced to the youthful offender system shall be limited to two hundred fifty-six beds.


(A) The department of corrections shall develop policies and procedures for decision- making regarding the transfer of any offender not sentenced to the youthful offender system into the youthful offender system in order to ensure that the goals of the youthful offender system, as described in this section; the operations of the rehabilitative program within the youthful offender system; and the delivery of services to those offenders directly sentenced to the youthful offender system are not compromised in any way by the comingled population.

The department of corrections shall include in its annual report to the judiciary committees of the house of representatives and senate, or to any successor committees, pursuant to section 2-7-203, C.R.S., and in any annual youthful offender system report produced by the department, information regarding the policies and procedures developed bythe department pursuant to sub-subparagraph (A) of this subparagraph (IV), the characteristics of the population of youthful offenders transferred pursuant to this paragraph (c), and the impact, if any, of transferred inmates on any youthful offender system programming or department of corrections programming.

Notwithstanding any provisions of this section to the contrary, the department of corrections shall not initiate any transfers of inmates to the youthful offender system until the department has developed the policies and procedures described in sub-subparagraph (A) of this subparagraph (IV).

It is the intent of the general assembly that offenders sentenced to the youthful offender system be sentenced as adults and be subject to all laws and department of corrections rules, regulations, and standards pertaining to adult inmates, except as otherwise provided in this section.

(a) (I) A juvenile may be sentenced to the youthful offender system created pursuant to this section under the circumstances set forth in section 19-2-517 (6) (a) (II) or 19-2-518 (1) (d) (II),

C.R.S. A young adult offender may be sentenced to the youthful offender system created pursuant to this section under the circumstances set forth in section 18-1.3-407.5. In order to sentence a juvenile or young adult offender to the youthful offender system, the court shall first impose upon such person a sentence to the department of corrections in accordance with section 18-1.3-401. The court shall thereafter suspend such sentence conditioned on completion of a sentence to the youthful offender system, including a period of community supervision. The court shall impose any such sentence to the youthful offender system for a determinate period of not fewer than two years nor more than six years; except that a juvenile or young adult offender convicted of a class 2 felony may be sentenced for a determinate period of up to seven years. In imposing such sentence, the court shall grant authority to the department of corrections to place the offender under a period of community supervision for a period of not fewer than six months and up to twelve months any time after the date on which the offender has twelve months remaining to complete the determinate sentence. The court mayaward an offender sentenced to the youthful offender system credit for presentence confinement; except that such credit shall not reduce the offender's actual time served in the youthful offender system to fewer than two years. The court shall have a presentence investigation conducted before sentencing a juvenile or young adult offender pursuant to this section. Upon the request of either the prosecution or the defense, the presentence report shall include a determination by the warden of the youthful offender system whether the offender is acceptable for sentencing to the youthful offender system. When making a determination, the warden shall consider the nature and circumstances of the crime; the age, circumstances, and criminal history of the offender; the available bed space in the youthful offender system; and any other appropriate considerations.

Upon the successful completion of the determinate sentence to the youthful offender system, including the mandatory period of community supervision, the suspended sentence pursuant to section 18-1.3-401 shall have been completed. Whenever an offender is returned to the district court for revocation pursuant to subsection (5) of this section, the court shall impose the original sentence following the revocation of the sentence to the youthful offender system, except as otherwise provided in paragraph (b) of subsection (5) of this section.

For the purposes of this section, unless the context otherwise requires:

"Juvenile" means a person who is under eighteen years of age when the crime is committed and under twenty-one years of age at the time of sentencing pursuant to this section.

"Young adult offender" means a person who is at least eighteen years of age but under twenty years of age when the crime is committed and under twenty-one years of age at the time of sentencing pursuant to this section.

"Youthful offender" or "offender" means a juvenile or a young adult offender who has been sentenced to the youthful offender system or who is eligible for sentencing to the youthful offender system.

As used in this section, "community supervision" shall not be construed to mean a community corrections program, as defined in section 17-27-102, C.R.S.

(a.5) During any period of incarceration under the youthful offender system, privileges including, but not limited to, televisions, radios, and entertainment systems, shall not be available for an offender unless such privileges have been earned under a merit system.

Article 22.5 of title 17, C.R.S., concerning time credits, shall not apply to any person sentenced to the youthful offender system; except that an offender whose sentence to the youthful offender system is revoked pursuant to subsection (5) of this section may receive one day of credit against the suspended sentence imposed by the court following revocation of the sentence to the youthful offender system for each day the offender served in the youthful offender system, excluding any period of time during which the offender was under community supervision.

(2.1) (a) As originally enacted, this section applied only to offenses committed by juveniles on or after September 13, 1993. For purposes of extending the availability of sentencing options, a juvenile who meets the criteria set forth in section 19-2-517 (6) (a) (II), C.R.S., may be sentenced to the youthful offender system pursuant to this section, under the following circumstances:

The juvenile is sentenced on or after June 3, 1994, for an offense committed prior to, on, or after September 13, 1993;

The juvenile committed an offense prior to September 13, 1993, and was sentenced for the offense on or after September 13, 1993, but prior to June 3, 1994. Such a juvenile may only be resentenced to the youthful offender system if a court, in its discretion, so orders in response to a motion filed in accordance with rule 35 of the Colorado rules of criminal procedure.

A juvenile who committed an offense prior to September 13, 1993, and who was sentenced prior to September 13, 1993, shall not be eligible to be sentenced to the youthful offender system.

A juvenile described in paragraph (a) of this subsection (2.1) may be sentenced pursuant to this section only if the juvenile meets the age requirement set forth in subparagraph (III) of paragraph (a) of subsection (2) of this section.

The department of corrections shall develop and implement a youthful offender system

for offenders sentenced in accordance with subsection (2) of this section. The youthful offender system shall be under the direction and control of the executive director of the department of corrections. The youthful offender system shall be based on the following principles:

The system should provide for teaching offenders self-discipline by providing clear consequences for inappropriate behavior;

The system should include a daily regimen that involves offenders in physical training, self-discipline exercises, educational and work programs, and meaningful interaction, with a component for a tiered system for swift and strict discipline for noncompliance;

The system should use staff models and mentors to promote within an offender the development of socially accepted attitudes and behaviors;

The system should provide offenders with instruction on problem-solving skills and should incorporate methods to reinforce the use of cognitive behavior strategies that change offenders' orientation toward criminal thinking and behavior;

The system should promote among offenders the creation and development of new group cultures which result in a transition to prosocial behavior; and

The system should provide offenders the opportunity to gradually reenter the community while demonstrating the capacity for self-discipline and the attainment of respect for the community. (3.3) The youthful offender system consists of the following components, and the department of corrections has the authority described in paragraphs (a) to (d) of this subsection (3.3) in connection with the administration of the components:

An intake, diagnostic, and orientation phase;

Phase I, during which time a range of core programs, supplementary activities, and educational and prevocational programs and services are provided to offenders;

(I) Phase II, which may be administered during the last three months of the period of institutional confinement and during which time the department of corrections is authorized to transfer an offender to a twenty-four-hour custody residential program that serves youthful offenders.

(II) In connection with the component described in subparagraph (I) of this paragraph (c), the department of corrections is authorized to operate or to contract with a prerelease residential program for those sentenced as youthful offenders. The department of corrections or the contract provider shall provide for twenty-four-hour custody of offenders in phase II.

(I) Phase III, which is to be administered for the period of community supervision that remains after the completion of phase II and during which the offender is monitored during reintegration into society.

After the department determines appropriate phase III placement, the department shall notify, no later than thirty days prior to placement, the local law enforcement agency for the jurisdiction in which the offender shall be placed for phase III. The notice shall include the offender's name, the crime committed by the offender, the disposition of the offender's case, and the basis for the placement. The local law enforcement agency may appeal the placement, if the placement is in a jurisdiction other than the jurisdiction where the offender was convicted, it may appeal to the executive director of the department at least fifteen days prior to the placement. Except that the local law enforcement agency may not appeal if the placement is in the jurisdiction where the offender was residing at the time the offense was committed. If there is an appeal, after considering the department's basis for placement and the local law enforcement's basis for appeal, the executive

director shall make the final determination of the placement.

(3.4) In addition to the powers granted to the department of corrections in subsection (3.3) of this section, the department of corrections may:

Transfer a youthful offender to an appropriate facility for the purpose of accomplishing the offender's redirection goals, as long as the transfer does not jeopardize the safety and welfare of the offender;

Operate an emancipation program and provide other support or monitoring services and residential placement for offenders participating in phase II and phase III under the youthful offender system for whom family reintegration poses difficulties. The department of corrections shall provide reintegration support services to an offender placed in an emancipation house.

Contract with any public or private entity, including but not limited to a school district, for provision or certification of educational services. Offenders receiving educational services or diplomas from a school district under an agreement entered into pursuant to this paragraph (c) shall not be included in computing the school district's student performance on statewide assessments pursuant to section 22-7-1006.3, C.R.S., or the school district's levels of attainment of the performance indicators pursuant to article 11 of title 22, C.R.S.

(3.5) The executive director of the department of corrections shall have final approval on the hiring and transferring of staff for the youthful offender system. In staffing the youthful offender system, the executive director shall select persons who are trained in the treatment of youthful offenders or will be trained in the treatment of youthful offenders prior to working with such population, are trained to act as role models and mentors pursuant to paragraph (c) of subsection (3) of this section, and are best equipped to enable the youthful offender system to meet the principles specified in subsection (3) of this section. The executive director shall make a recommendation to the department of personnel regarding the classification of positions with the youthful offender system, taking into account the level of education and training required for such positions.

The youthful offender system shall provide for community supervision which shall consist of highly structured surveillance and monitoring and educational and treatment programs. Community supervision shall be administered by the department of corrections, and revocation of the inmate's supervision status shall be subject to the provisions of subsections (2) and (5) of this section.

(4.3) The youthful offender system shall provide sex offender treatment services for an offender who is sentenced to the youthful offender system and who has a history of committing a sex offense as defined in section 16-11.7-102 (3), C.R.S., or who has a history of committing any other offense, the underlying factual basis of which includes a sex offense. Prior to July 1, 2002, the sex offender treatment services provided pursuant to this subsection (4.3) shall comply with any existing national standards for juvenile sex offender treatment. On and after July 1, 2002, the sex offender treatment services provided pursuant to this subsection (4.3) shall comply with the sex offender treatment standards adopted by the sex offender management board pursuant to section 16-11.7-103, C.R.S.

(4.5) The consent of the parent, parents, or legal guardian of an offender under the age of eighteen years who has been sentenced to the youthful offender system pursuant to this section shall not be necessary in order to authorize hospital, medical, mental health, dental, emergency health, or emergency surgical care. In addition, neither the department nor any hospital, physician, surgeon,

mental health care provider, dentist, trained emergency health care provider, or agent or employee thereof who, in good faith, relies on such a minor offender's consent shall be liable for civil damages for failure to secure the consent of such an offender's parent, parents, or legal guardian prior to rendering such care. However, the parent, parents, or legal guardian of a minor offender described in this subsection (4.5) may be liable, as provided by law, to pay the charges for the care provided the minor on said minor's consent.

(a) Except as otherwise provided by paragraph (b) of this subsection (5), the department of corrections shall implement a procedure for the transfer of an offender to another facility when an offender in the system poses a danger to himself or herself or others. The executive director of the department of corrections shall review any transfer determination by the department prior to the actual transfer of an inmate, including a transfer back to the district court for revocation of the sentence to the youthful offender system. A transfer pursuant to this paragraph (a) shall be limited to a period not to exceed sixty days, at which time the offender shall be returned to the youthful offender facility to complete his or her sentence or returned to the district court for revocation of the sentence to the youthful offender system. In no case shall an offender initially sentenced to the youthful offender system be held in isolation or segregation or in an adult facility for longer than sixty consecutive days without action by the sentencing court.

(I) An offender who is thought to have a mental illness or developmental disability by a mental health clinician, as defined by regulation of the department of corrections, may be transferred to another facility for a period not to exceed sixty days for diagnostic validation of said illness or disability. At the conclusion of the sixty-day period, the psychiatrists or other appropriate professionals conducting the diagnosis shall forward to the executive director of the department of corrections their findings, which at a minimum shall include a statement of whether the offender has the ability to withstand the rigors of the youthful offender system. If the diagnosis determines that the offender is incapable of completing his or her sentence to the youthful offender system due to a mental illness or developmental disability, the executive director shall forward such determination to the sentencing court. Based on the determination, the sentencing court shall review the offender's sentence to the youthful offender system and may:

Impose the offender's original sentence to the department of corrections; or

Reconsider and reduce the offender's sentence to the department of corrections in consideration of the offender's mental illness or developmental disability.

Any offender who is resentenced pursuant to this paragraph (b) shall continue to be treated as an adult for purposes of sentencing and shall not be sentenced pursuant to article 2 of title 19, C.R.S.

In no event shall the sentencing court, after reviewing the offender's sentence to the youthful offender system pursuant to this paragraph (b), increase the offender's sentence to the department of corrections due to the offender's diagnosis of mental illness or determination of developmental disability. Any offender who is diagnosed as having mental illness or determined to have a developmental disability and is therefore incapable of completing his or her sentence to the youthful offender system may be housed in any department of corrections facility deemed appropriate by the executive director or transferred in accordance with procedures set forth in section 17-23-101, C.R.S., pending action by the sentencing court with regard to the offender's sentence.

The department of corrections shall implement a procedure for returning offenders who cannot successfully complete the sentence to the youthful offender system, or who fail to comply with the terms or conditions of the youthful offender system, to the district court. An offender returned to the district court pursuant to paragraph (a) of this subsection (5) or because he or she cannot successfully complete the sentence to the youthful offender system for reasons other than mental illness or a developmental disability, or because he or she fails to comply with the terms or conditions of the youthful offender system, shall receive imposition of the original sentence to the department of corrections. After the executive director of the department upholds the department's decision, the offender may be held in any correctional facility deemed appropriate by the executive director; except that an offender who cannot successfully complete the sentence to the youthful offender system for reasons other than mental illness or a developmental disability, or because he or she fails to comply with the terms or conditions of the youthful offender system, shall be transferred, within thirty-five days after the executive director upholds the department's decision, to a county jail for holding prior to resentencing. The department shall notify the district attorney of record, and the district attorney of record shall be responsible for seeking the revocation or review of the offender's sentence and the imposition of the original sentence or modification of the original sentence pursuant to sub-subparagraph (B) of subparagraph (I) of paragraph (b) of this subsection (5). The district court shall review the offender's sentence within one hundred twenty-six days after line notification to the district attorney of record by the department of corrections that the offender is not able to complete the sentence to the youthful offender system or fails to comply with the terms or conditions of the youthful offender system.

The department of corrections shall establish and enforce standards for the youthful offender system. Offenders in the youthful offender system, including those under community supervision, shall be considered inmates for the purposes of section 17-1-111, C.R.S.

The number of offenders in any program element under the youthful offender system shall be determined by the department within available appropriations.

The department of corrections may and is encouraged to contract with any private or public entity for the provision of services and facilities under the youthful offender system.

On or before November 1, 1993, the department, in conjunction with the division of criminal justice, shall develop and the department shall implement a process for monitoring and evaluating the youthful offender system. In implementing such system, the department may contract with a private agency for assistance.

(a) (Deleted by amendment, L. 2002, p. 881, § 19, effective August 7, 2002.)

(b) The division of criminal justice shall independently monitor and evaluate, or contract with a public or private entity to independently monitor and evaluate, the youthful offender system. On or before November 1, 2002, and on or before November 1 every two years thereafter, the division of criminal justice shall report its findings, or the findings of the contract entity, to the judiciary committees of the senate and the house of representatives. The department of corrections shall cooperate in providing the necessary data to the division of criminal justice or an entity designated by the division of criminal justice to complete the evaluation required in this section.

Any district attorney in the state shall maintain records regarding juveniles who are

sentenced to the youthful offender system and such records shall indicate which juveniles have been filed on as adults or are sentenced to the system and the offenses committed by such juveniles.

(11.5) (a) (I) An offender who is sentenced to the youthful offender system shall submit to and pay for collection and a chemical testing of a biological substance sample from the offender to determine the genetic markers thereof.

(II) Collection of the biological substance sample shall occur as soon as possible after being sentenced to the youthful offender system, and the results thereof shall be filed with and maintained by the Colorado bureau of investigation. The results of such tests shall be furnished to any law enforcement agency upon request.

The department of corrections or its designee or contractor may use reasonable force to obtain biological substance samples in accordance with paragraph (a) of this subsection (11.5).

Any moneys received from offenders pursuant to paragraph (a) of this subsection (11.5) shall be deposited in the offender identification fund created in section 24-33.5-415.6, C.R.S.

The Colorado bureau of investigation is directed to conduct the chemical testing of the biological substance samples obtained pursuant to this subsection (11.5).

The general assembly recognizes that the increased number of violent crimes committed by juveniles and young adults is a problem faced by all the states of this nation. By creating the youthful offender system, Colorado stands at the forefront of the states in creating a new approach to addressing this problem. The general assembly also declares that the cost of implementing and operating the youthful offender system will create a burden on the state's limited resources. Accordingly, the general assembly directs the department of corrections to seek out and accept available federal, state, and local public funds, including project demonstration funds, and private moneys and private systems for the purpose of conducting the youthful offender system.

Repealed.

18-1.3-407.5. Sentences - young adult offenders - youthful offender system - definitions. (1) (a) A young adult offender may be sentenced to the youthful offender system in the department of corrections in accordance with section 18-1.3-407, under the following circumstances:

The young adult offender is convicted of a felony enumerated as a crime of violence pursuant to section 18-1.3-406;

The young adult offender is convicted of a felony offense described in part 1 of article 12 of this title;

The young adult offender used, or possessed and threatened the use of, a deadly weapon during the commission of a felony offense against a person, as set forth in article 3 of this title;

The young adult offender is convicted of vehicular homicide, as described in section 18-3-106, vehicular assault, as described in section 18-3-205, or felonious arson, as described in part 1 of article 4 of this title;

The young adult offender is convicted of a felony offense described in section 18-1.3- 401 as a class 3 felony, other than the felonies described in section 18-3-402 (1) (d) and section 18-3- 403 (1) (e), as it existed prior to July 1, 2000, and has, within the two previous years, been adjudicated a juvenile delinquent for a delinquent act that would constitute a felony if committed by

an adult; or

The young adult offender is convicted of a felony offense, and is determined to have been an "habitual juvenile offender", as defined in section 19-1-103 (61), C.R.S.

(b) The offenses described in paragraph (a) of this subsection (1) shall include the attempt, conspiracy, or solicitation to commit such offenses.

(a) Notwithstanding the circumstances described in subsection (1) of this section, a young adult offender shall be ineligible for sentencing to the youthful offender system if the young adult offender is convicted of any of the following:

A class 1 or class 2 felony;

A sexual offense described in section 18-6-301, section 18-6-302, or part 4 of article 3 of this title; or

Any offense, if the young adult offender has received a sentence to the youthful offender system for any prior conviction.

(b) Notwithstanding the provisions of paragraph (a) of this subsection (2), a young adult offender who is charged with first degree murder as described in section 18-3-102 (1) (b) and pleads guilty to a class 2 felony as a result of a plea agreement is eligible for sentencing to the youthful offender system if the young adult offender would be eligible for sentencing to the youthful offender system for a conviction of the felony underlying the charge of first degree murder as described in section 18-3-102 (1) (b).

As used in this section, unless the context otherwise requires, a "young adult offender" means a person who is at least eighteen years of age but under twenty years of age at the time the crime is committed and under twenty-one years of age at the time of sentencing pursuant to this section.

18-1.3-408. Determinate sentence of imprisonment imposed by court. When a person has been convicted of a felony and a sentence of imprisonment imposed, the court imposing the sentence shall fix a definite term of imprisonment, which shall be not longer than the terms authorized in section 18-1.3-401; except that, for persons convicted on or after November 1, 1998, of a sex offense, as defined in section 18-1.3-1003 (5), the court shall impose an indeterminate sentence as provided in part 10 of this article.

18-1.3-409. Concurrent or consecutive sentences - court to clarify sentencing in mittimus. Before remitting any mittimus to the department of corrections sentencing a defendant to the custody of the department, a court shall confirm that the mittimus properly reflects the sentencing order of the court and includes all necessary information regarding the sentence and any information as to whether a sentence is to be served concurrent with, or consecutive to, the sentence for any other count or any other case.

PART 5 MISDEMEANOR AND PETTY

OFFENSE SENTENCING

50

18-1.3-501. Misdemeanors classified - drug misdemeanors and drug petty offenses classified - penalties - definitions. (1) (a) Except as otherwise provided in paragraph (d) of this subsection (1), misdemeanors are divided into three classes that are distinguished from one another by the following penalties that are authorized upon conviction except as provided in subsection (1.5) of this section:

<TBL.18-1.3-501> Class          Minimum Sentence    Maximum Sentence

Six months imprisonment, or five          Eighteen months imprisonment, hundred dollars fine, or both          or five thousand dollars fine, or both

Three months imprisonment, or two   Twelve months imprisonment,
hundred fifty dollars fine, or both or one thousand dollars fine, or both
Fifty dollars fine          Six months imprisonment, or seven hundred  fifty dollars fine, or both
</TBL.18-1.3-501>

A term of imprisonment for conviction of a misdemeanor shall not be served in a state correctional facility unless served concurrently with a term for conviction of a felony.

A term of imprisonment in a county jail for a conviction of a misdemeanor, petty, or traffic misdemeanor offense shall not be ordered to be served consecutively to a sentence to be served in a state correctional facility; except that if, at the time of sentencing, the court determines, after consideration of all the relevant facts and circumstances, that a concurrent sentence is not warranted, the court may order that the misdemeanor sentence be served prior to the sentence to be served in the state correctional facility and prior to the time the defendant is transported to the state correctional facility to serve all or the remainder of the defendant's state correctional facility sentence.

For purposes of sentencing a person convicted of a misdemeanor drug offense described in article 18 of this title, committed on or after October 1, 2013, drug misdemeanors are divided into two levels that are distinguished from one another by the following penalties that are authorized upon conviction:

| Level | Minimum Sentence | Maximum Sentence |
|---|---|---|
| DM1 | Six months imprisonment, five hundred dollars fine, or both | Eighteen months imprisonment, five thousand dollars fine, or both |
| DM2 | No imprisonment, fifty dollars fine | Twelve months imprisonment, seven hundred fifty dollars fine, or both |

For each drug petty offense, the sentencing range is stated in the offense statute.

(1.5) (a) If a defendant is convicted of assault in the third degree under section 18-3-204 and the victim is a peace officer, emergency medical service provider, emergency medical care provider, or firefighter engaged in the performance of his or her duties, notwithstanding subsection (1) of this section, the court shall sentence the defendant to a term of imprisonment greater than the maximum sentence but no more than twice the maximum sentence authorized for the same crime when the victim is not a peace officer, emergency medical service provider, emergency medical care provider, or firefighter engaged in the performance of his or her duties. In addition to the term of imprisonment, the court may impose a fine on the defendant under subsection (1) of this section. At any time after sentencing and before the discharge of the defendant's sentence, the victim may request that the defendant participate in restorative justice practices with the victim. If the defendant accepts responsibility for and expresses remorse for his or her actions and is willing to repair the harm caused by his or her actions, an individual responsible for the defendant's supervision shall make the necessary arrangements for the restorative justice practices requested by the victim.
(b) As used in this section, "peace officer, emergency medical service provider, emergency medical care provider, or firefighter engaged in the performance of his or her duties" means a peace officer as described in section 16-2.5-101, C.R.S., emergency medical service provider as defined in part 1 of article 3.5 of title 25, C.R.S., emergency medical care provider as defined by section 18- 3-201 (1), or a firefighter as defined in section 18-3-201 (1.5), who is engaged or acting in or who is present to engage or act in the performance of a duty, service, or function imposed, authorized, required, or permitted by law to be performed by a peace officer, emergency medical service provider, emergency medical care provider, or firefighter, whether or not the peace officer, emergency medical service provider, emergency medical care provider, or firefighter is within the territorial limits of his or her jurisdiction, if the peace officer, emergency medical service provider, emergency medical care provider, or firefighter is in uniform or the person committing an assault upon or offense against or otherwise acting toward the peace officer, emergency medical service provider, emergency medical care provider, or firefighter knows or reasonably should know that the victim is a peace officer, emergency medical service provider, emergency medical care provider, or firefighter or if the peace officer, emergency medical service provider, emergency medical care provider, or firefighter is intentionally assaulted in retaliation for the performance of his or her official duties.
(1.7) (a) If a defendant is convicted of assault in the third degree pursuant to section 18-3- 204 or reckless endangerment pursuant to section 18-3-208 and the victim is a mental health professional employed by or under contract with the department of human services engaged in the performance of his or her duties, notwithstanding the provisions of subsection (1) of this section, the court may sentence the defendant to a term of imprisonment greater than the maximum sentence but not more than twice the maximum sentence authorized for the crime when the victim is not a mental health professional employed by or under contract with the department of human services engaged in the performance of his or her duties. In addition to a term of imprisonment, the court may impose a fine on the defendant pursuant to subsection (1) of this section.
(b) "Mental health professional" means a mental health professional licensed to practice medicine pursuant to part 1 of article 36 of title 12, C.R.S., or a person licensed as a mental health professional pursuant to article 43 of title 12, C.R.S., a person licensed as a nurse pursuant to part 1 of article 38 of title 12, C.R.S., a nurse aide certified pursuant to part 1 of article 38.1 of title 12,

C.R.S., and a psychiatric technician licensed pursuant to part 1 of article 42 of title 12, C.R.S.
The defendant may be sentenced to perform a certain number of hours of community or useful public service in addition to any other sentence provided by subsection (1) of this section, subject to the conditions and restrictions of section 18-1.3-507. An inmate in county jail acting as a trustee shall not be given concurrent credit for community or useful public service when such service is performed in his or her capacity as trustee. For the purposes of this subsection (2), "community or useful public service" means any work which is beneficial to the public, any public entity, or any bona fide nonprofit private or public organization, which work involves a minimum of direct supervision or other public cost and which work would not, with the exercise of reasonable care, endanger the health or safety of the person required to work.

51

(a) The general assembly hereby finds that certain misdemeanors which are listed in paragraph (b) of this subsection (3) present an extraordinary risk of harm to society and therefore, in the interest of public safety, the maximum sentence for such misdemeanors shall be increased by six months.

(b) Misdemeanors that present an extraordinary risk of harm to society shall include the following:

Assault in the third degree, as defined in section 18-3-204; (I.5) (A) Sexual assault, as defined in section 18-3-402; or

(B) Sexual assault in the second degree, as defined in section 18-3-403, as it existed prior to July 1, 2000;

(A) Unlawful sexual contact, as defined in section 18-3-404; or

(B) Sexual assault in the third degree, as defined in section 18-3-404, as it existed prior to July 1, 2000;

Child abuse, as defined in section 18-6-401 (7) (a) (V);

Second and all subsequent violations of a protection order as defined in section 18-6- 803.5 (1.5) (a.5);

Misdemeanor failure to register as a sex offender, as described in section 18-3-412.5;

and 405.6.

Misdemeanor invasion of privacy for sexual gratification, as described in section 18-3-

Notwithstanding any provision of law to the contrary, any person who attempts to
commit, conspires to commit, or commits against an elderly person any misdemeanor set forth in part 4 of article 4 of this title, part 1, 2, 3, or 5 of article 5 of this title, or article 5.5 of this title shall be required to pay a mandatory and substantial fine within the limits permitted by law. However, all moneys collected from the offender shall be applied in the following order: Costs for crime victim compensation fund pursuant to section 24-4.1-119, C.R.S.; surcharges for victims and witnesses assistance and law enforcement fund pursuant to section 24-4.2-104, C.R.S.; restitution; time payment fee; late fees; and any other fines, fees, or surcharges. For purposes of this subsection (4), an "elderly person" or "elderly victim" means a person sixty years of age or older.
Every sentence entered under this section shall include consideration of restitution as required by part 6 of this article and by article 18.5 of title 16, C.R.S.
For a defendant who is convicted of assault in the third degree, as described in section 18-3-204, the court, in addition to any fine the court may impose, shall sentence the defendant to a

term of imprisonment of at least six months, but not longer than the maximum sentence authorized for the offense, as specified in this section, which sentence shall not be suspended in whole or in part, if the court makes the following findings on the record:
The victim of the offense was pregnant at the time of commission of the offense; and
The defendant knew or should have known that the victim of the offense was pregnant.
(Deleted by amendment, L. 2003, p. 2163, § 4, effective July 1, 2003.)


18-1.3-502. Duration of sentences for misdemeanors. Courts sentencing any person for the commission of a misdemeanor to the custody of the executive director of the department of corrections shall not fix a minimum term but may fix a maximum term less than the maximum provided by law for the offense. The persons so sentenced shall be imprisoned, released under parole, and discharged as provided by other applicable statutes. No person sentenced to a correctional facility for the commission of a misdemeanor shall be subjected to imprisonment for a term exceeding the maximum term provided by the statute fixing the maximum length of the sentence for the crime of which he or she was convicted and for which he or she was sentenced. A person sentenced to a term of imprisonment for the commission of a misdemeanor shall be entitled to the same time credits as if he or she were sentenced to a term of imprisonment for the commission of a felony. No person committed as a juvenile delinquent shall be imprisoned for a term exceeding two years, except as otherwise provided for aggravated juvenile offenders in section 19-2-601, C.R.S.


18-1.3-503. Petty offenses classified - penalties. (1) A violation of a statute of this state is a "petty offense" if specifically classified as a class 1 or class 2 petty offense. The penalty for commission of a class 1 petty offense, upon conviction, is a fine of not more than five hundred dollars, or imprisonment for not more than six months other than in state correctional facilities, or both. The penalty for commission of a class 2 petty offense is a fine specified in the section defining the offense. The penalty assessment procedure of section 16-2-201, C.R.S., is available for the payment of fines in class 2 petty offense cases.
(2) Every sentence entered under this section shall include consideration of restitution as required by part 6 of this article and by article 18.5 of title 16, C.R.S.


18-1.3-504. Misdemeanors and petty offenses not classified. (1) Any misdemeanor or pettyoffense defined bystate statute without specification of its class shall be punishable as provided in the statute defining it.
(2) Every sentence entered under this section shall include consideration of restitution as required by part 6 of this article and by article 18.5 of title 16, C.R.S.


18-1.3-505. Penalty for misdemeanor not fixed by statute - punishment. (1) In all cases where an offense is denominated a misdemeanor and no penalty is fixed in the statute therefor, the

punishment shall be imprisonment for not more than one year in the county jail, or a fine of not more than one thousand dollars, or both such imprisonment and fine.
Every sentence entered under this section shall include consideration of restitution as required by part 6 of this article and by article 18.5 of title 16, C.R.S.


18-1.3-506. Payment and collection of fines for class 1, 2, or 3 misdemeanors and class 1 or 2 petty offenses - release from incarceration. (1) Whenever the court imposes a fine for a nonviolent class 1, 2, or 3 misdemeanor or for a class 1 or 2 petty offense, if the person who committed the offense is unable to pay the fine at the time of the court hearing or if he or she fails to pay any fine imposed for the commission of such offense, in order to guarantee the payment of such fine, the court may:
Require the person to post sufficient bond or collateral; or
Enter a judgment in favor of the state or political subdivision to whom the fine is owed and enter an order based on such judgment for the garnishment of the person's earnings in accordance with the provisions of either article 54 or 54.5 of title 13, C.R.S., for the purpose of collecting said fine and the costs incurred in collecting said fine; or
Enter a judgment in favor of the state or political subdivision to whom the fine is owed and execute a lien based on such judgment on any chattels, lands, tenements, moneys, and real estate of the person in accordance with article 52 of title 13, C.R.S., for the purpose of collecting said fine and the costs incurred in collecting said fine.
The state or a political subdivision may appear before a court of record in this state and request that the court order the release from a county jail or a correctional facility of a person who has been incarcerated as a result of the failure to pay a fine or the failure to appear in court in connection with the commission of a nonviolent class 1, 2, or 3 misdemeanor or a class 1 or 2 petty offense upon the condition that the fine and any costs of collection are collected from the person incarcerated by the use of one of the methods set forth in subsection (1) of this section.
For the purposes of this section, "nonviolent class 1, 2, or 3 misdemeanor" means a class 1, 2, or 3 misdemeanor that does not involve cruelty to an animal, as described in section 18-9-202
(a), or the use or threat of physical force on or to a person in the commission of the misdemeanor.

18-1.3-507. Community or useful public service - misdemeanors. (1) Any sentence imposed pursuant to section 18-1.3-501 (2) shall be subject to the conditions and restrictions of this section.

(a) A probation department, sentencing court, county sheriff, board of county commissioners, or any other governmental entity, or a private nonprofit or for-profit entity that has a contract with a governmental entity, may establish a community or useful public service program. It is the purpose of the community or useful public service program: To identify and seek the cooperation of governmental entities and political subdivisions thereof, as well as corporations, associations, or charitable trusts, for the purpose of providing community or useful public service jobs; to interview persons who have been ordered by the court to perform community or useful public service and to assign such persons to suitable community or useful public service jobs; and

to monitor compliance or noncompliance of such persons in performing community or useful public service assignments within the time established by the court.

(b) Nothing in this subsection (2) shall limit the authority of an entity which is the recipient of community or useful public service to accept or reject such service, in its sole discretion.

(2.5) A charitable trust that is exempt from taxation under section 501 (c) (3) of the federal "Internal Revenue Code of 1986", as amended, shall be eligible to provide community or useful public service jobs established under this article or any other provision of law, so long as the charitable trust meets any other requirement related to the provision of such jobs.

Any general public liability insurance policy obtained pursuant to this section shall provide coverage for injuries caused by a person performing services under this section and shall be in a sum of not less than the current limit on government liability under the "Colorado Governmental Immunity Act", article 10 of title 24, C.R.S.

For the purposes of the "Colorado Governmental Immunity Act", article 10 of title 24, C.R.S., public employee, as defined in section 24-10-103, C.R.S., does not include any person who is sentenced to participate in any type of community or useful public service.

No governmental entity or private nonprofit or for-profit entity which has a contract with a governmental entity shall be liable under the "Workers' Compensation Act of Colorado", articles 40 to 47 of title 8, C.R.S., or under the "Colorado Employment Security Act", articles 70 to 82 of title 8, C.R.S., for any benefits on account of any person who is sentenced to participate in any type of community or useful public service, but nothing in this subsection (5) shall prohibit a governmental entity or private nonprofit or for-profit entity from electing to accept the provisions of the "Workers' Compensation Act of Colorado" by purchasing and keeping in force a policy of workers' compensation insurance covering such person.

The court shall assess an amount, not to exceed one hundred twenty dollars, upon every person required to perform community or useful public service pursuant to section 18-1.3-501 (2). The court may waive this fee if the court determines the defendant to be indigent. Such amount shall be used by the operating agency responsible for overseeing such person's community or useful public service program to pay the cost of administration of the program and the cost of personal services. Such amount is to be commensurate with program costs in providing services and shall be adjusted from time to time by the general assembly to insure that the operating agencies shall be financially self-supporting. The proceeds from such amounts shall be used by the operating agency only for defraying the cost of personal services and other operating expenses related to the administration of the program, a general liability policy covering such person, and, if such person will be covered by workers' compensation insurance pursuant to subsection (5) of this section or an insurance policy providing such or similar coverage, the cost of purchasing and keeping in force such insurance coverage and shall not be used by the operating agency for any other purpose.

18-1.3-508. Definite sentence not void. If, through oversight or otherwise, any person is sentenced or committed to the custody of the executive director of the department of corrections for the commission of a misdemeanor for a definite period of time, the sentence or commitment shall not for that reason be void, but the person so sentenced or committed shall be subject to the liabilities and entitled to the benefits which are applicable to those persons who are properly sentenced.

18-1.3-509. Credit for time served on misdemeanor sentences. A person who is confined for a misdemeanor offense prior to the imposition of a sentence for the misdemeanor offense shall be entitled to credit against the term of his or her sentence for the entire period of the confinement. At the time of sentencing, the court shall make a finding of the amount of presentence confinement to which the offender is entitled and shall include the finding in the mittimus. The period of confinement shall be deducted from the offender's sentence by the county jail.

PART 6 RESTITUTION

18-1.3-601. Legislative declaration. (1) The general assembly finds and declares that:
Crime victims endure undue suffering and hardship resulting from physical injury, emotional and psychological injury, or loss of property;
Persons found guilty of causing such suffering and hardship should be under a moral and legal obligation to make full restitution to those harmed by their misconduct;
The payment of restitution by criminal offenders to their victims is a mechanism for the rehabilitation of offenders;
Restitution is recognized as a deterrent to future criminality;
An effective criminal justice system requires timely restitution to victims of crime and to members of the immediate families of such victims in order to lessen the financial burdens inflicted upon them, to compensate them for their suffering and hardship, and to preserve the individual dignity of victims;
Former procedures for restitution assessment, collection, and distribution have proven to be inadequate and inconsistent from case to case;
The purposes of this part 6 are to facilitate:
The establishment of programs and procedures to provide for and collect full restitution for victims of crime in the most expeditious manner; and
The effective and timely assessment, collection, and distribution of restitution requires the cooperation and collaboration of all criminal justice agencies and departments.
(2) It is the intent of the general assembly that restitution be ordered, collected, and disbursed to the victims of crime and their immediate families. Such restitution will aid the offender in reintegration as a productive member of society. This part 6 shall be liberally construed to accomplish all such purposes.

18-1.3-602. Definitions. As used in this part 6, unless the context otherwise requires:

"Collections investigator" means a person employed by the judicial department whose primary responsibility is to administer, enforce, and collect on with respect to fines, fees, restitution, or any other accounts receivable of the court, judicial district, or judicial department.

"Conviction" means a verdict of guilty by a judge or jury or a plea of guilty or nolo contendere that is accepted by the court for a felony, misdemeanor, petty offense, or traffic misdemeanor offense, or adjudication for an offense that would constitute a criminal offense if committed byan adult. "Conviction" also includes having received a deferred judgment and sentence or deferred adjudication; except that a person shall not be deemed to have been convicted if the person has successfully completed a deferred sentence or deferred adjudication.

(2.3) "Moneyadvanced bya governmental agencyfor a service animal" means costs incurred by a peace officer, law enforcement agency, fire department, fire protection district, or governmental search and rescue agency for the veterinary treatment and disposal of a service animal that was harmed while aiding in official duties and for the training of an animal to become a service animal to replace a service animal that was harmed while aiding in official duties, as applicable.

(2.5) Repealed.

(a) "Restitution" means any pecuniary loss suffered by a victim and includes but is not limited to all out-of-pocket expenses, interest, loss of use of money, anticipated future expenses, rewards paid by victims, money advanced by law enforcement agencies, money advanced by a governmental agency for a service animal, adjustment expenses, and other losses or injuries proximately caused by an offender's conduct and that can be reasonably calculated and recompensed in money. "Restitution" does not include damages for physical or mental pain and suffering, loss of consortium, loss of enjoyment of life, loss of future earnings, or punitive damages.

(a.5) "Restitution" includes, for a person convicted of assault in the first, second, or third degree, as described in section 18-3-202, 18-3-203, or 18-3-204, all or any portion of the financial obligations of medical tests performed on and treatment prescribed for a victim, peace officer, firefighter, emergency medical care provider, or emergency medical service provider.

"Restitution" may also include extraordinary direct public and all private investigative costs.

(I) "Restitution" shall also include all costs incurred by a government agency or private entity to:

Remove, clean up, or remediate a place used to manufacture or attempt to manufacture a controlled substance or which contains a controlled substance or which contains chemicals, supplies, or equipment used or intended to be used in the manufacturing of a controlled substance;

Store, preserve, or test evidence of a controlled substance violation; or

Sell and provide for the care of and provision for an animal disposed of under the animal cruelty laws in accordance with part 2 of article 9 of this title or article 42 of title 35, C.R.S.

(II) Costs under this paragraph (c) shall include, but are not limited to, overtime wages for peace officers or other government employees, the operating expenses for any equipment utilized, and the costs of any property designed for one-time use, such as protective clothing.

"Restitution" shall also include costs incurred by a governmental agency or insurer that provides medical benefits, health benefits, or nonmedical support services directly related to a medical or health condition to a victim for losses or injuries proximately caused by an offender's conduct, including but not limited to costs incurred by medicaid and other care programs for indigent persons.

(3.5) "Service animal" means any animal, the services of which are used to aid the performance of official duties by a peace officer, law enforcement agency, fire department, fire protection district, or governmental search and rescue agency.

(a) "Victim" means any person aggrieved by the conduct of an offender and includes but is not limited to the following:

Anyperson against whom anyfelony, misdemeanor, petty, or traffic misdemeanor offense has been perpetrated or attempted;

Any person harmed by an offender's criminal conduct in the course of a scheme, conspiracy, or pattern of criminal activity;

Anyperson who has suffered losses because of a contractual relationship with, including but not limited to an insurer, or because of liability under section 14-6-110, C.R.S., for a person described in subparagraph (I) or (II) of this paragraph (a);

Any victim compensation board that has paid a victim compensation claim;

If any person described in subparagraph (I) or (II) of this paragraph (a) is deceased or incapacitated, the person's spouse, parent, legal guardian, natural or adopted child, child living with the victim, sibling, grandparent, significant other, as defined in section 24-4.1-302 (4), C.R.S., or other lawful representative;

Any person who had to expend resources for the purposes described in paragraphs (b), (c), and (d) of subsection (3) of this section.

"Victim" shall not include a person who is accountable for the crime or a crime arising from the same conduct, criminal episode, or plan as defined under the law of this state or of the United States.

Any "victim" under the age of eighteen is considered incapacitated, unless that person is legally emancipated or the court orders otherwise.

It is the intent of the general assembly that this definition of the term "victim" shall apply to this part 6 and shall not be applied to any other provision of the laws of the state of Colorado that refers to the term "victim".

Notwithstanding any other provision of this section, "victim" includes a person less than eighteen years of age who has been trafficked by an offender, as described in section 18-3-503 or 18- 3-504.

18-1.3-603. Assessment of restitution - corrective orders. (1) Every order of conviction of a felony, misdemeanor, petty, or traffic misdemeanor offense, except any order of conviction for a state traffic misdemeanor offense issued by a municipal or county court in which the prosecuting attorney is acting as a special deputy district attorney pursuant to an agreement with the district attorney's office, shall include consideration of restitution. Each such order shall include one or more of the following:

An order of a specific amount of restitution be paid by the defendant;

An order that the defendant is obligated to pay restitution, but that the specific amount of restitution shall be determined within the ninety-one days immediately following the order of conviction, unless good cause is shown for extending the time period by which the restitution amount shall be determined;

An order, in addition to or in place of a specific amount of restitution, that the defendant pay restitution covering the actual costs of specific future treatment of any victim of the crime; or

Contain a specific finding that no victim of the crime suffered a pecuniary loss and therefore no order for the payment of restitution is being entered. The court shall base its order for restitution upon information presented to the court by the prosecuting attorney, who shall compile such information through victim impact statements or other means to determine the amount of restitution and the identities of the victims. Further, the prosecuting attorney shall present this information to the court prior to the order of conviction or within ninety-one days, if it is not available prior to the order of conviction. The court may extend this date if it finds that there are extenuating circumstances affecting the prosecuting attorney's ability to determine restitution.

Any order for restitution may be:

Increased if additional victims or additional losses not known to the judge or the prosecutor at the time the order of restitution was entered are later discovered and the final amount of restitution due has not been set by the court; or

Decreased:

With the consent of the prosecuting attorney and the victim or victims to whom the restitution is owed; or

If the defendant has otherwise compensated the victim or victims for the pecuniarylosses suffered.

(a) (I) Any order for restitution entered pursuant to this section is a final civil judgment in favor of the state and any victim. Notwithstanding any other civil or criminal statute or rule, any such judgment remains in force until the restitution is paid in full. The provisions of article 18.5 of title 16, C.R.S., apply notwithstanding the termination of a deferred judgment and sentence or a deferred adjudication, the entry of an order of expungement pursuant to section 19-1-306, C.R.S., or an order to seal entered pursuant to part 7 of article 72 of title 24, C.R.S.

(II) Notwithstanding the provisions of subparagraph (I) of this paragraph (a), two years after the presentation of the defendant's original death certificate to the clerk of the court or the court collections investigator, the court may terminate the remaining balance of the judgment and order for restitution if, following notice by the clerk of the court or the court collections investigator to the district attorney, the district attorney does not object and there is no evidence of a continuing source of income of the defendant to pay restitution. The termination of a judgment and order pursuant to this subparagraph (II) does not terminate an associated judgment against a defendant who is jointly and severally liable with the deceased defendant.

Any order for restitution made pursuant to this section is also an order that:

The defendant owes simple interest from the date of the entry of the order at the rate of eight percent per annum; and

The defendant owes all reasonable and necessary attorney fees and costs incurred in collecting such order due to the defendant's nonpayment.

The entry of an order for restitution under this section creates a lien by operation of law against the defendant's personal property and any interest that the defendant may have in any personal property.

Any order of restitution imposed shall be considered a debt for "willful and malicious" injury for purposes of exceptions to discharge in bankruptcy as provided in 11 U.S.C. sec. 523.

The clerk of the court is authorized to adjust the unpaid balance in the case upon proof that any restitution or related interest amounts have been or will be satisfied outside of the court registry and receipting process regardless of when the restitution order and judgment were entered. The accounting adjustment does not modify a court's order.

If more than one defendant owes restitution to the same victim for the same pecuniary loss, the orders for restitution shall be joint and several obligations of the defendants.

Any amount paid to a victim under an order of restitution shall be set off against any amount later recovered as compensatory damages by such victim in any federal or state civil proceeding.

When a person's means of identification or financial information was used without that person's authorization in connection with a conviction for any crime in violation of part 2, 3, or 4 of article 4, part 1, 2, 3, or 7 of article 5, or article 5.5 of this title, the sentencing court may issue such orders as are necessary to correct a public record that contains false information resulting from any violation of such laws. In addition, the restitution order shall include any costs incurred by the victim related to section 16-5-103, C.R.S.

(a) Notwithstanding the provisions of subsection (1) of this section, for a non-felony conviction under title 42, C.R.S., the court shall order restitution concerning only the portion of the victim's pecuniaryloss for which the victim cannot be compensated under a policy of insurance, self- insurance, an indemnity agreement, or a risk management fund.

The court, in determining the restitution amount, shall consider whether the defendant or the vehicle driven by the defendant at the time of the offense was covered by:

A complying policy of insurance or certificate of self-insurance as required by the laws of this state;

Self-insurance including but not limited to insurance coverage pursuant to the provisions of part 15 of article 30 of title 24, C.R.S.; or

Any other insurance or indemnity agreement that would indemnify the defendant for any damages sustained by the victim.

(I) Except as otherwise provided in this paragraph (c), a court may not award restitution to a victim concerning a pecuniary loss for which the victim has received or is entitled to receive benefits or reimbursement under a policy of insurance or other indemnity agreement.

(II) (A) A court may award a victim restitution for a deductible amount under his or her policy of insurance.

(B) (Deleted by amendment, L. 2004, p. 904, § 28, effective May 21, 2004.)

(I) (Deleted by amendment, L. 2004, p. 904, § 28, effective May 21, 2004.)

(II) Nothing in this paragraph (d) shall prohibit a nonowner driver or passenger in the vehicle from being awarded restitution if the driver or passenger was not covered by his or her own medical payments coverage policy.

(I) Notwithstanding any provision of law to the contrary, an insurance company, risk management fund, or public entity shall not be obligated to defend a defendant in a hearing concerning restitution. No court shall interpret an indemnity or insurance contract so as to obligate

an insurance company, risk management fund, or public entity to defend a defendant at a restitution hearing absent a specific agreement.

(II) Notwithstanding any provision of law, indemnity contract, or insurance contract to the contrary, an insurance company, risk management fund, or public entity shall not be obligated to pay or otherwise satisfy a civil judgment entered pursuant to this part 6, or to indemnify a defendant for an amount awarded in a restitution order.

Nothing in this article shall be construed to limit or abrogate the rights and immunities set forth in the "Colorado Governmental Immunity Act", article 10 of title 24, C.R.S.

The provisions of this subsection (8) shall not preclude the court, pursuant to article 4.1 of title 24, C.R.S., from ordering restitution to reimburse an expenditure made by a victim compensation fund.

For a conviction for human trafficking for involuntary servitude, as described in section 18-3-503, or for human trafficking for sexual servitude, as described in section 18-3-504, the court shall order restitution, if appropriate, pursuant to this section even if the victim is unavailable to accept payment of restitution.

(a) If, as a result of the defendant's conduct, a crime victim compensation board has provided assistance to or on behalf of a victim pursuant to article 4.1 of title 24, C.R.S., the amount of assistance provided and requested by the crime victim compensation board is presumed to be a direct result of the defendant's criminal conduct and must be considered by the court in determining the amount of restitution ordered.

The amount of assistance provided is established by either:

A list of the amount of money paid to each provider; or

If the identity or location of a provider would pose a threat to the safety or welfare of the victim, summary data reflecting what total payments were made for:

Medical and dental expenses;

56

Funeral or burial expenses;
Mental health counseling;
Wage or support losses; or
Other expenses.
Records of a crime victim compensation board relating to a claimed amount of restitution are subject to the provisions of section 24-4.1-107.5, C.R.S.

PART 7 FINES AND COSTS

18-1.3-701. Judgment for costs and fines. (1) (a) Where any person, association, or corporation is convicted of an offense, or any juvenile is adjudicated a juvenile delinquent for the commission of an act that would have been a criminal offense if committed by an adult, the court shall give judgment in favor of the state of Colorado, the appropriate prosecuting attorney, or the appropriate law enforcement agency and against the offender or juvenile for the amount of the costs

of prosecution, the amount of the cost of care, and any fine imposed. No fine shall be imposed for conviction of a felony except as provided in section 18-1.3-401 or 18-7-203 (2) (a). Such judgments shall be enforceable in the same manner as are civil judgments, and, in addition, the provisions of section 16-11-101.6, C.R.S., and section 18-1.3-702 apply. A county clerk and recorder may not charge a fee for the recording of a transcript or satisfaction of a judgment entered pursuant to this section.
Except as otherwise provided in paragraph (c) of this subsection (1), on and after July 1, 2010, all judgments collected pursuant to this section for fees and court costs shall be transmitted to the state treasurer for deposit in the judicial stabilization cash fund created in section 13-32-101 (6), C.R.S. Judgments collected pursuant to this section for fees for interpreters or auxiliary services provided pursuant to section 13-90-204, C.R.S., and reimbursed pursuant to section 13-90-210, C.R.S., shall be remitted to the Colorado commission for the deaf and hard of hearing in the department of human services created in section 26-21-104, C.R.S.
The costs assessed pursuant to subsection (1) of this section or section 16-18-101, C.R.S., may include:
Any docket fee required by article 32 of title 13, C.R.S., or any other fee or tax required by statute to be paid to the clerk of the court;
The jury fee required by section 13-71-144, C.R.S.;
Any fees required to be paid to sheriffs pursuant to section 30-1-104, C.R.S.;
Any fees of the court reporter for all or any part of a transcript necessarily obtained for use in the case, including the fees provided for in section 16-18-101 (2), C.R.S., and including the fees for a transcript of any preliminary hearing;
(d.5) The actual costs paid to any expert witness;
(I) The witness fees and mileage paid pursuant to article 33 of title 13, C.R.S., and section 16-9-203, C.R.S.;
(II) For any person required to travel more than fifty miles from the person's place of residence to the place where specified in the subpoena, in addition to the witness fee and mileage specified in subparagraph (I) of this paragraph (e):
Actual lodging expenses incurred; and
Actual rental car, taxi, or other transportation costs incurred;
(e.5) If a person under eighteen years of age is required to appear, the amount that a parent or guardian of the person was paid for transportation and lodging expenses incurred while accompanying the person;
Any fees for exemplification and copies of papers necessarily obtained for use in the case;
Any costs of taking depositions for the perpetuation of testimony, including reporter's fees, witness fees, expert witness fees, mileage for witnesses, and sheriff fees for service of subpoenas;
Any statutory fees for service of process or statutory fees for any required publications; (h.5) Any fees for interpreters required during depositions or during trials;
Any item specifically authorized by statute to be included as part of the costs;
On proper motion of the prosecuting attorney and at the discretion of the court, any other reasonable and necessary costs incurred by the prosecuting attorney or Colorado state patrol that are

directly the result of the successful prosecution of the defendant for a violation of section 42-4-1301, C.R.S., including the costs resulting from the collection and analysis of any chemical test upon the defendant pursuant to section 42-4-1301.1, C.R.S., which costs shall be reimbursed by the defendant directly to the Colorado state patrol.
(j.5) On proper motion of the prosecuting attorney and at the discretion of the court, any other reasonable and necessary costs incurred by the prosecuting attorney or law enforcement agency other than the Colorado state patrol that are directly the result of the successful prosecution of the defendant for a violation of section 42-4-1301, C.R.S., including the costs resulting from the collection and analysis of any chemical test upon the defendant pursuant to section 42-4-1301.1, C.R.S., which costs the court shall assess against the defendant, collect from the defendant, and transfer to the law enforcement agency that performed the chemical tests.
Any costs incurred in obtaining a governor's warrant pursuant to section 16-19-108,
C.R.S.;
Any costs incurred by the law enforcement agency in photocopying reports, developing
film, and purchasing videotape as necessary for use in the case;
Any costs of participation in a diversion program if the offender or juvenile unsuccessfully participated in a diversion program prior to the conviction or adjudication.
Where any person, association, or corporation is granted probation, the court shall order the offender to make such payments toward the cost of care as are appropriate under the circumstances. In setting the amount of such payments, the court shall take into consideration and make allowances for any restitution ordered to the victim or victims of a crime, which shall take priority over any payments ordered pursuant to this article, and for the maintenance and support of the offender's spouse, dependent children, or other persons having a legal right to support and maintenance from the estate of the offender. If the court determines that the offender has a sufficient estate to pay all or part of the cost of care, the court shall determine the amount which shall be paid by the offender for the cost of care, which amount shall in no event be in excess of the per capita cost of supervising an offender on probation.
Where any person is sentenced to a term of imprisonment, whether to a county jail or the department of corrections, the court shall order such person to make such payments toward the cost of care as are appropriate under the circumstances. In setting the amount of such payments, the court shall take into consideration and make allowances for any restitution ordered to the victim or victims of a crime, which shall take priority over any payments ordered pursuant to this article, and for the maintenance and support of the inmate's spouse, dependent children, or any other persons having a legal right to support and maintenance out of the offender's estate. The court shall also consider the financial needs of the offender for the six-month period immediately following the offender's release, for the purpose of allowing said offender to seek employment. If the court determines that the person has a sufficient estate to pay all or part of the cost of care, the court shall determine the amount which shall be paid by the offender, which amount in no event shall be in excess of the per capita cost of maintaining prisoners in the institution or facility in which the offender has been residing prior to

sentencing for the purpose of reimbursing the appropriate law enforcement agency and the per capita cost of maintaining prisoners in the department of corrections for the purpose of paying the cost of care after sentencing.

As used in this section, unless the context otherwise requires:

"Cost of care" means the cost to the department or the local government charged with the custody of an offender for providing room, board, clothing, medical care, and other normal living expenses for an offender confined to a jail or correctional facility, or any costs associated with maintaining an offender in a home detention program contracted for by the department of public safety, as determined by the executive director of the department of corrections or the executive director of the department of public safety, whichever is appropriate, or the cost of supervision of probation when the offender is granted probation, or the cost of supervision of parole when the offender is placed on parole by the state board of parole, as determined by the court.

"Estate" means any tangible or intangible properties, real or personal, belonging to or due to an offender, including income or payments to such person received or earned prior to or during incarceration from salary or wages, bonuses, annuities, pensions, or retirement benefits, or any source whatsoever except federal benefits of any kind. Real property that is held in joint ownership or ownership in common with an offender's spouse, while being used and occupied by the spouse as a place of residence, shall not be considered a part of the estate of the offender for the purposes of this section.

After the set-offs for restitution and for maintenance and support as provided in subsection (4) of this section, any amounts recovered pursuant to this section that are available to reimburse the costs of providing medical care shall be used to reimburse the state for the state's financial participation for medical assistance if medical care is provided for the inmate or an infant of a female inmate under the "Colorado Medical Assistance Act", articles 4, 5, and 6 of title 25.5, C.R.S.


18-1.3-702. Monetary payments - due process required. (1) (a) When the court imposes a sentence, enters a judgment, or issues an order that obligates the defendant to pay a monetary amount, the court may direct as follows:

That the defendant pay the entire monetary amount at the time sentence is pronounced;

That the defendant pay the entire monetary amount at some later date;

That the defendant pay as directed by the court or the court's designated official:

At a future date certain in its entirety;

By periodic payments, which may include payments at intervals, referred to in this section as a "payment plan"; or

By other payment arrangement as determined by the court or the court's designated official;

When the defendant is sentenced to a period of probation as well as payment of a monetary amount, that payment of the monetary amount be made a condition of probation.

A court's designated official shall report to the court on any failure to pay.

As used in this section, "court's designated official" includes, but is not limited to, a "collections investigator" as defined in section 18-1.3-602 (1).

When the court imposes a sentence, enters a judgment, or issues an order that obligates a defendant to pay any monetary amount, the court shall instruct the defendant as follows:

If at any time the defendant is unable to pay the monetary amount due, the defendant must contact the court's designated official or appear before the court to explain why he or she is

unable to pay the monetary amount;

If the defendant lacks the present ability to pay the monetary amount due without undue hardship to the defendant or the defendant's dependents, the court shall not jail the defendant for failure to pay; and

If the defendant has the ability to pay the monetary amount as directed by the court or the court's designee but willfully fails to pay, the defendant may be imprisoned for failure to comply with the court's lawful order to pay pursuant to the terms of this section.

Incarceration for failure to pay is prohibited absent provision of the following procedural protections:

When a defendant is unable to pay a monetary amount due without undue hardship to himself or herself or his or her dependents, the court shall not imprison the defendant for his or her failure to pay;

Except in the case of a corporation, if the defendant failed to pay a monetary amount due and the record indicates that the defendant has willfully failed to pay that monetary amount, the court, when appropriate, may consider a motion to impose part or all of a suspended sentence, may consider a motion to revoke probation, or may institute proceedings for contempt of court. When instituting contempt of court proceedings, the court, including a municipal court, shall provide all procedural protections mandated in rule 107 of the Colorado rules of civil procedure or rule 407 of the Colorado rules of county court civil procedure.

The court shall not find the defendant in contempt of court, nor impose a suspended sentence, nor revoke probation, nor order the defendant to jail for failure to pay unless the court has made findings on the record, after providing notice to the defendant and a hearing, that the defendant has the ability to comply with the court's order to pay a monetary amount due without undue hardship to the defendant or the defendant's dependents and that the defendant has not made a good-faith effort to comply with the order. If the defendant fails to appear at the hearing referenced in this paragraph (c) after receiving notice, the court may issue a warrant for his or her arrest for failure to appear.

The court shall not accept a defendant's guilty plea for contempt of court for failure to pay or failure to comply with the court's order to pay a monetary amount unless the court has made findings on the record that the defendant has the ability to comply with the court's order to pay a monetary amount due without undue hardship to the defendant or the defendant's dependents and that the defendant has not made a good-faith effort to comply with the order; and

The court shall not issue a warrant for failure to pay money, failure to appear to pay money, or failure to appear at any post-sentencing court appearance wherein the defendant was required to appear if he or she failed to pay a monetary amount; however, a court may issue an arrest warrant or incarcerate a defendant related to his or her failure to pay a monetary amount only through the procedures described in paragraphs (a) to (d) of this subsection (3).

For purposes of this section, a defendant or a defendant's dependents are considered to suffer undue hardship if he, she, or they would be deprived of money needed for basic living necessities, such as food, shelter, clothing, necessary medical expenses, or child support. In determining whether a defendant is able to comply with an order to pay a monetary amount without undue hardship to the defendant or the defendant's dependents, the court shall consider:

Whether the defendant is experiencing homelessness;

The defendant's present employment, income, and expenses;

The defendant's outstanding debts and liabilities, both secured and unsecured;

Whether the defendant has qualified for and is receiving any form of public assistance, including food stamps, temporary assistance for needy families, medicaid, or supplemental security income benefits;

The availability and convertibility, without undue hardship to the defendant or the defendant's dependents, of any real or personal property owned by the defendant;

Whether the defendant resides in public housing;

Whether the defendant's family income is less than two hundred percent of the federal poverty line, adjusted for family size; and

Any other circumstances that would impair the defendant's ability to pay.

If the court finds a defendant in contempt of court for willful failure to pay, the court may direct that the defendant be imprisoned until the monetary payment ordered by the court is made, but the court shall specify a maximum period of imprisonment subject to the following limits:

When the monetary amount was imposed for a felony, the period shall not exceed one year;

When the monetary amount was imposed for a misdemeanor, the period shall not exceed one-third of the maximum term of imprisonment authorized for the misdemeanor;

When the monetary amount was imposed for a petty offense, a traffic violation, or a violation of a municipal ordinance, any of which is punishable by a possible jail sentence, the period shall not exceed fifteen days;

There shall be no imprisonment in those cases when no imprisonment is provided for in the possible sentence; and

When a sentence of imprisonment and a monetary amount was imposed, the aggregate of the period and the term of the sentence shall not exceed the maximum term of imprisonment authorized for the offense.

This section applies to all courts of record in Colorado, including but not limited to municipal courts.

Nothing in this section prevents the collection of a monetary amount in the same manner as a judgment in a civil action.

PART 8 SPECIAL PROCEEDINGS -
SENTENCING OF HABITUAL CRIMINALS

18-1.3-801. Punishment for habitual criminals. (1) (a) A person shall be adjudged an habitual criminal and shall be punished by a term in the department of corrections of life imprisonment if the person:

Is convicted of:

Any class 1 or 2 felony or level 1 drug felony; or

Any class 3 felony that is a crime of violence, as defined in section 18-1.3-406 (2); and

Has been twice convicted previously for any of the offenses described in subparagraph of this paragraph (a).

A felony described in subparagraph (I) of paragraph (a) of this subsection (1) is:

One based upon charges separately brought and tried, and arising out of separate and distinct criminal episodes, in this or any other state; or

A crime under the laws of any other state, the United States, or any territory subject to the jurisdiction of the United States, which, if committed within this state, would be such a felony described in paragraph (a) of this subsection (1).

No person sentenced pursuant to this subsection (1) shall be eligible for parole until such person has served at least forty calendar years.

Nothing in this subsection (1) prohibits the governor from issuing a pardon or a clemency order on a case-by-case basis; however, the governor shall submit a report to the general assembly on each such pardon or clemency order in accordance with section 7 of article IV of the state constitution.

Nothing in this subsection (1) is to be construed to prohibit a person convicted of a class 1 felony from being sentenced pursuant to section 18-1.3-1201, 18-1.3-1302, or 18-1.4-102.

This subsection (1) shall not apply to a person convicted of first or second degree burglary, which person shall be subject to subsections (1.5), (2), and (2.5) of this section and section 18-1.3-804.

(1.5) Except as otherwise provided in subsection (5) of this section, every person convicted in this state of any class 1, 2, 3, 4, or 5 felony or level 1, 2, or 3 drug felony who, within ten years of the date of the commission of the said offense, has been twice previously convicted upon charges separately brought and tried, and arising out of separate and distinct criminal episodes, either in this state or elsewhere, of a felony or, under the laws of any other state, the United States, or any territory subject to the jurisdiction of the United States, of a crime which, if committed within this state, would be a felony shall be adjudged an habitual criminal and shall be punished:

For the felony offense of which such person is convicted by imprisonment in the department of corrections for a term of three times the maximum of the presumptive range pursuant to section 18-1.3-401 for the class or level of felony of which such person is convicted; or

For the level 1 drug felony offense of which such person is convicted by imprisonment in the department of corrections for a term of forty-eight years.

(a) (I) Except as otherwise provided in paragraph (b) of this subsection (2) and in subsection (5) of this section, every person convicted in this state of any felony, who has been three times previously convicted, upon charges separately brought and tried, and arising out of separate and distinct criminal episodes, either in this state or elsewhere, of a felony or, under the laws of any other state, the United States, or any territory subject to the jurisdiction of the United States, of a crime which, if committed within this state, would be a felony, shall be adjudged an habitual criminal and shall be punished:

For the felony offense of which such person is convicted by imprisonment in the department of corrections for a term of four times the maximum of the presumptive range pursuant to section 18-1.3-401 for the class or level of felony of which such person is convicted; or

For the level 1 drug felony offense of which such person is convicted by imprisonment

in the department of corrections for a term of sixty-four years.

Such former conviction or convictions and judgment or judgments shall be set forth in apt words in the indictment or information. Nothing in this part 8 shall abrogate or affect the punishment by death in any and all crimes punishable by death on or after July 1, 1972.

(b) The provisions of paragraph (a) of this subsection (2) shall not apply to a conviction for a level 4 drug felony pursuant to section 18-18-403.5 (2), or a conviction for a level 4 drug felony for attempt or conspiracy to commit unlawful possession of a controlled substance, as described in section 18-18-403.5 (2), if the amount of the schedule I or schedule II controlled substance possessed is not more than four grams or not more than two grams of methamphetamine, heroin, cathinones, or ketamine or not more than four milligrams of flunitrazepam, even if the person has been previously convicted of three or more qualifying felony convictions.

(2.5) Any person who is convicted and sentenced pursuant to subsection (2) of this section, or section 16-13-101 (2), C.R.S., as it existed prior to October 1, 2002, who is thereafter convicted of a felony which is a crime of violence pursuant to section 18-1.3-406, shall be adjudged an habitual criminal and shall be punished by a term in the department of corrections of life imprisonment. No person sentenced pursuant to this subsection (2.5) shall be eligible for parole until such person has served at least forty calendar years.

No drug law conviction shall be counted as a prior felony conviction under this section unless such prior offense would be a felony if committed in this state at the time of the commission of the new offense.

A person who meets the criteria set forth in subsection (1) of this section shall be adjudged an habitual criminal and sentenced only in accordance with that subsection and not pursuant to subsections (1.5), (2), and (2.5) of this section.

A conviction for escape, as described in section 18-8-208 (1), (2), or (3), or attempt to escape, as described in section 18-8-208.1 (1), (1.5), or (2), shall not be used for the purpose of adjudicating a person an habitual criminal as described in subsection (1.5) or subsection (2) of this section unless the conviction is based on the offender's escape or attempt to escape from a correctional facility, as defined in section 17-1-102, C.R.S., or from physical custodywithin a county jail.

18-1.3-802. Evidence of former convictions - identity. On any trial under the provisions of this section and sections 18-1.3-801 and 18-1.3-803, a duly authenticated copy of the record of former convictions and judgments of any court of record for any of said crimes against the party indicted or informed against shall be prima facie evidence of such convictions and may be used in evidence against such party. Identification photographs and fingerprints that are part of the record of such former convictions and judgments, or are part of the records kept at the place of such party's incarceration or by any custodian authorized by the executive director of the department of corrections after sentencing for any of such former convictions and judgments, shall be prima facie evidence of the identity of such party and may be used in evidence against him or her.

18-1.3-803. Verdict of jury. (1) If the allegation of previous convictions of other felony

offenses is included in an indictment or information and if a verdict of guilty of the substantive offense with which the defendant is charged is returned, the court shall conduct a separate sentencing hearing to determine whether or not the defendant has suffered such previous felony convictions. As soon as practicable, the hearing shall be conducted by the judge who presided at trial or before whom the guilty plea was entered or a replacement for said judge in the event he or she dies, resigns, is incapacitated, or is otherwise disqualified as provided in section 16-6-201, C.R.S. An information or indictment seeking the increased penalties authorized by section 18- 1.3-801 shall identify by separate counts each alleged former conviction and shall allege that the defendant on a date and at a place specified was convicted of a specific felony. If any such conviction was had outside this state, the information or indictment shall allege that the offense, if committed in this state, would be a felony.
Upon arraignment of the defendant, such defendant shall be required to admit or deny that such defendant has been previously convicted of the crimes identified in the information or indictment. If the defendant refuses to admit or deny the previous convictions, such refusal shall be treated as a denial by such defendant that the defendant has been convicted as alleged. If the defendant admits to having been convicted as alleged in any count charging a previous conviction, no proof of such previous conviction is required. Such admission shall constitute conclusive proof in determining whether the defendant has been previously convicted of an alleged felony and the court shall sentence the defendant in accordance with section 18-1.3-801.
If the defendant denies that he or she has been previously convicted as alleged in any count of an information or indictment, the trial judge, or a replacement judge as provided in subsection (1) of this section, shall determine by separate hearing and verdict whether the defendant has been convicted as alleged. The procedure in any case in which the defendant does not become a witness in his or her own behalf upon the trial of the substantive offense shall be as follows:
The jury shall render a verdict upon the issue of the defendant's guilt or innocence of the substantive offense charged;
If the verdict is that the defendant is guilty of the substantive offense charged, the trial judge, or a replacement judge as provided in subsection (1) of this section, shall proceed to try the issues of whether the defendant has been previously convicted as alleged. The prosecuting attorney has the burden of proving beyond a reasonable doubt that the defendant has been previously convicted as alleged.
(a) If, upon the trial of the issues upon the substantive offense charged, the defendant testifies in his or her own defense and denies that he or she has been previously convicted as alleged, the prosecuting attorney on rebuttal, may present all evidence relevant to the issues of previous convictions for the sole purpose of impeachment of the defendant's credibility, subject to the rules governing admission of evidence at criminal trials.
(b) If, upon the trial of the issues upon the substantive offense charged, the defendant testifies in his or her own defense and, after having denied the previous conviction under subsection
(3) of this section, admits that he or she has been previously convicted as alleged, the trial judge, or a replacement judge as provided in subsection (1) of this section, shall, in any sentencing hearing, consider any admissions of prior convictions elicited from the defendant in connection with his or her testimony on the substantive offense only as they affect the defendant's credibility. In any sentencing hearing, the prosecution shall be required to meet its burden of proving beyond a

reasonable doubt the defendant's prior convictions by evidence independent of the defendant's testimony.
(6) If the prosecuting attorney does not have any information indicating that the defendant has been previously convicted of a felony prior to the time a verdict of guilty is rendered on a felony charge and if thereafter the prosecuting attorney learns of the felony conviction prior to the time that sentence is pronounced by the court, he or she may file a new information in which it shall be alleged in separate counts that the defendant has been convicted of the particular offense upon which judgment has not been entered and that prior thereto at a specified date and place the defendant has been convicted of a felony warranting application of increased penalties authorized in this section and sections 18-1.3-801 and 18-1.3-802. The defendant shall be arraigned upon the new information, and, if the defendant denies the previous conviction, the trial judge, or a replacement judge as provided in subsection (1) of this section, shall try the issue prior to imposition of sentence.

18-1.3-804. Habitual burglary offenders - punishment - legislative declaration. (1) Every person convicted in this state of first degree burglary, first degree burglary of controlled substances, or second degree burglary of a dwelling who, within ten years of the date of the commission of the said offense, has been previously convicted upon charges separately brought and tried, either in this state or elsewhere, of first degree burglary, first degree burglary of drugs or first degree burglary of controlled substances, or second degree burglary of a dwelling or, under the laws of any other state, the United States, or any territory subject to the jurisdiction of the United States, of a felony which, if committed within this state, would be first degree burglary, first degree burglary of drugs or first degree burglary of controlled substances, or second degree burglary of a dwelling shall be adjudged a habitual burglary offender and shall be sentenced to the department of corrections for a term of incarceration greater than the maximum in the presumptive range, but not more than twice the maximum term, provided for such offense in section 18-1.3-401 (1) (a).
Every person convicted in this state of first degree burglary, first degree burglary of controlled substances, or second degree burglary of a dwelling who has been previously convicted of two or more felonies shall be subject to the applicable provisions of section 18-1.3-801.
Such former conviction or convictions and judgment or judgments shall be set forth in apt words in the indictment or information.
In no case shall any person who is subject to the provisions of this section be eligible for suspension of sentence or probation.
Insofar as they may be applicable, sections 18-1.3-802 and 18-1.3-803 shall govern trials which are held as a result of the provisions of this section.
The general assembly hereby finds and declares that the frequency of incidence of the crime of burglary, together with particularly high rates of recidivism among burglary offenders and the extensive economic impact which results from the crime of burglary, requires the special classification and punishment of habitual burglary offenders as provided in this section.

PART 9 SENTENCING OF SEX OFFENDERS

18-1.3-901. Short title. This part 9 shall be known and may be cited as the "Colorado Sex Offenders Act of 1968".

18-1.3-902. Applicability of part. The provisions of this part 9 shall apply to persons sentenced for offenses committed prior to November 1, 1998.

18-1.3-903. Definitions. As used in this part 9, unless the context otherwise requires:
guilty.

"Board" means the state board of parole.
"Conviction" means conviction after trial by court or jury or acceptance of a plea of

"Department" means the department of corrections.
"Sex offender" means a person convicted of a sex offense.
"Sex offense" means sexual assault, except misdemeanor sexual assault in the third
degree, as set forth in section 18-3-404 (2), as it existed prior to July 1, 2000; sexual assault on a child, as defined in section 18-3-405; aggravated incest, as defined in section 18-6-302; and an attempt to commit any of the offenses mentioned in this subsection (5).

18-1.3-904. Indeterminate commitment. The district court having jurisdiction may, subject to the requirements of this part 9, in lieu of the sentence otherwise provided by law, commit a sex offender to the custody of the department for an indeterminate term having a minimum of one day and a maximum of his or her natural life.

18-1.3-905. Requirements before acceptance of a plea of guilty. Before the district court may accept a plea of guilty from any person charged with a sex offense, the court shall, in addition to any other requirement of law, advise the defendant that he or she may be committed to the custody of the department, including any penal institution under the jurisdiction of the department, as provided in section 18-1.3-904.

18-1.3-906. Commencement of proceedings. Within twenty-one days after the conviction of a sex offense, upon the motion of the district attorney, the defendant, or the court, the court shall commence proceedings under this part 9 by ordering the district attorney to prepare a notice of the commencement of proceedings and to serve that notice upon the defendant personally.

18-1.3-907.          Defendant to be advised of rights. (1)      Upon the commencement of
proceedings, the court shall advise the defendant, orally and in writing, that:
The defendant is to be examined in accordance with the provisions of section 18-1.3-908;
The defendant has a right to counsel, and, if the defendant is indigent, counsel will be appointed to represent him or her;
The defendant has a right to remain silent;
An evidentiary hearing will be held pursuant to section 18-1.3-911, and the defendant and his or her counsel will be furnished with copies of all reports prepared for the court pursuant to sections 18-1.3-908 and 18-1.3-909 at least fourteen days prior to the evidentiary hearing.
(2) The written advisement of rights may be incorporated into the notice of commencement of proceedings.

18-1.3-908. Psychiatric examination and report. (1) (a) After advising the defendant of his or her rights, the court shall forthwith commit the defendant to the Colorado mental health institute at Pueblo, the university of Colorado psychiatric hospital, or the county jail.
If committed to the Colorado mental health institute at Pueblo or the university of Colorado psychiatric hospital, the defendant shall be examined by two psychiatrists of the receiving institution.
If committed to the county jail, the defendant shall be examined by two psychiatrists appointed by the court.
(a) The examining psychiatrists shall make independent written reports to the court which shall contain the opinion of the psychiatrist as to whether the defendant, if at large, constitutes a threat of bodily harm to members of the public.
The written reports shall also contain opinions concerning:
Whether the defendant is mentally deficient;
Whether the defendant could benefit from psychiatric treatment; and
Whether the defendant could be adequately supervised on probation.
The examinations shall be made and the reports filed with the court and the probation department within sixty-three days after the commencement of proceedings, and this time may not be enlarged by the court.

18-1.3-909. Report of probation department. (1) Upon the commencement of proceedings under this part 9, the court shall order an investigation and report to be made by the probation officer similar to the presentence report provided for in section 16-11-102, C.R.S.
(2) The report shall be filed with the court within seventy-seven days after the commencement of proceedings, and this time may not be enlarged by the court.

18-1.3-910. Termination of proceedings. After reviewing the reports of the psychiatrists and the probation officer, the court may terminate proceedings under this part 9 and proceed with sentencing as otherwise provided by law.

18-1.3-911. Evidentiary hearing. (1) (a) The court shall set a hearing date at least fourteen days and no more than twenty-eight days after service upon the defendant and his or her counsel of the reports required by sections 18-1.3-908 and 18-1.3-909.
(b) The court may, in its discretion, upon the motion of the defendant, continue the hearing an additional twenty-one days.
(a) The court shall, upon motion of the district attorney or the defendant, subpoena all witnesses required by the moving party in accordance with the Colorado rules of criminal procedure.
(b) The district attorney shall serve upon the defendant and his or her counsel a list of all witnesses to be called by the district attorney at least fourteen days before the evidentiary hearing.
In the evidentiary hearing, the court shall receive evidence bearing on the issue of whether the defendant, if at large, constitutes a threat of bodily harm to members of the public.
In the evidentiary hearing, the following procedure shall govern:
The district attorney may call and examine witnesses, and the defendant shall be allowed to cross-examine those witnesses.
The defendant may call and examine witnesses, and the district attorney shall be allowed to cross-examine those witnesses.
The defendant may call and cross-examine as adverse witnesses the psychiatrists and probation officers who have filed reports pursuant to sections

18-1.3-908 and 18-1.3-909.
The reports of the psychiatrists and probation officers filed with the court pursuant to sections 18-1.3-908 and 18-1.3-909 may be received into evidence.
Except as otherwise provided in this section, the laws of this state concerning evidence in criminal trials shall govern in the evidentiary hearing.

18-1.3-912. Findings of fact and conclusions of law. (1) After the evidentiary hearing, the court shall, within seven days, make oral or written findings of fact and conclusions of law.
If the court finds beyond a reasonable doubt that the defendant, if at large, constitutes a threat of bodily harm to members of the public, the court shall commit the defendant pursuant to section 18-1.3-904.
If the court does not find as provided in subsection (2) of this section, it shall terminate proceedings under this part 9 and proceed with sentencing as otherwise provided by law.
If the findings and conclusions are oral, they shall be reduced to writing and filed within fourteen days, and the defendant shall not be committed to the custody of the department pursuant to section 18-1.3-904 until the findings and conclusions are filed.

18-1.3-913. Appeal. The defendant may appeal an adverse finding made pursuant to section 18-1.3-912 in the same manner as is provided by law for other criminal appeals.

18-1.3-914. Time allowed on sentence. If the proceedings under this part 9 are terminated by the court, as provided in section 18-1.3-910 or 18-1.3-912 (3), the court shall deduct the time

from the commencement of proceedings to the termination of proceedings from the minimum sentence of the defendant.

18-1.3-915. Costs. The costs of the maintenance of the prisoner during the pendency of proceedings under this part 9 and the costs of the psychiatric examinations and reports shall be paid by the state of Colorado.

18-1.3-916. Diagnostic center as receiving center. The diagnostic center, as defined in section 17-40-101 (1.5), C.R.S., shall be the receiving center for all persons committed pursuant to section 18-1.3-904.
PART 10 LIFETIME SUPERVISION OF
SEX OFFENDERS

18-1.3-1001. Legislative declaration. The general assembly hereby finds that the majority of persons who commit sex offenses, if incarcerated or supervised without treatment, will continue to present a danger to the public when released from incarceration and supervision. The general assembly also finds that keeping all sex offenders in lifetime incarceration imposes an unacceptably high cost in both state dollars and loss of human potential. The general assembly further finds that some sex offenders respond well to treatment and can function as safe, responsible, and contributing members of society, so long as they receive treatment and supervision. The general assembly therefore declares that a program under which sex offenders may receive treatment and supervision for the rest of their lives, if necessary, is necessary for the safety, health, and welfare of the state.

18-1.3-1002. Short title. This part 10 shall be known and may be cited as the "Colorado Sex Offender Lifetime Supervision Act of 1998".

18-1.3-1003. Definitions. As used in this part 10, unless the context otherwise requires:

"Department" means the department of corrections.
"Management board" means the sex offender management board created in section 16- 11.7-103, C.R.S.
"Parole board" means the state board of parole created in section 17-2-201, C.R.S.
"Sex offender" means a person who is convicted of or pleads guilty or nolo contendere to a sex offense.
(a) "Sex offense" means any of the following offenses:

(A) Sexual assault, as described in section 18-3-402; or
(B) Sexual assault in the first degree, as described in section 18-3-402 as it existed prior to July 1, 2000;
Sexual assault in the second degree, as described in section 18-3-403 as it existed prior to July 1, 2000;
(A) Felony unlawful sexual contact, as described in section 18-3-404 (2); or
(B) Felony sexual assault in the third degree, as described in section 18-3-404 (2) as it existed prior to July 1, 2000;
Sexual assault on a child, as described in section 18-3-405;
Sexual assault on a child by one in a position of trust, as described in section 18-3-405.3;
Aggravated sexual assault on a client by a psychotherapist, as described in section 18-3- 405.5 (1);
Enticement of a child, as described in section 18-3-305;
Incest, as described in section 18-6-301;
Aggravated incest, as described in section 18-6-302;
Patronizing a prostituted child, as described in section 18-7-406;
Class 4 felony internet luring of a child, in violation of section 18-3-306 (3); or
Internet sexual exploitation of a child, in violation of section 18-3-405.4.
(b) "Sex offense" also includes criminal attempt, conspiracy, or solicitation to commit any of the offenses specified in paragraph (a) of this subsection (5) if such criminal attempt, conspiracy, or solicitation would constitute a class 2, 3, or 4 felony.

18-1.3-1004. Indeterminate sentence. (1) (a) Except as otherwise provided in this subsection (1) and in subsection (2) of this section, the district court having jurisdiction shall sentence a sex offender to the custody of the department for an indeterminate term of at least the minimum of the presumptive range specified in section 18-1.3-401 for the level of offense committed and a maximum of the sex offender's natural life.

If the sex offender committed a sex offense that constitutes a crime of violence, as defined in section 18-1.3-406, the district court shall sentence the sex offender to the custody of the department for an indeterminate term of at least the midpoint in the presumptive range for the level of offense committed and a maximum of the sex offender's natural life.

If the sex offender committed a sex offense that makes him or her eligible for sentencing as an habitual sex offender against children pursuant to section 18-3-412, the district court shall sentence the sex offender to the custody of the department for an indeterminate term of at least three times the upper limit of the presumptive range for the level of offense committed and a maximum of the sex offender's natural life.

If the sex offender committed a sex offense that constitutes a sexual offense, as defined in section 18-3-415.5, and the sex offender, prior to committing the offense, had notice that he or she had tested positive for the human immunodeficiency virus (HIV) and HIV infection, and the infectious agent of the HIV infection was in fact transmitted, the district court shall sentence the sex offender to the custody of the department for an indeterminate term of at least the upper limit of the presumptive range for the level of offense committed and a maximum of the sex offender's natural life.

(I) Notwithstanding any other provision of law, the district court shall sentence a sex

offender to the custody of the department for an indeterminate term as specified in subparagraph (II) of this paragraph (e) if the sex offender:

Committed a class 2, class 3, or class 4 sex offense in violation of section 18-3-402, 18- 3-405, or 18-3-405.3 when the act includes sexual intrusion as defined in section 18-3-401 (5) or sexual penetration as defined in section 18-3-401 (6);

Committed the act against a child who was under twelve years of age at the time of the offense; and

Was at least eighteen years of age and at least ten years older than the child.

(II) The district court shall sentence a sex offender to the department of corrections for an indeterminate term of incarceration of:

At least ten to sixteen years for a class 4 felony to a maximum of the person's natural life, as provided in this subsection (1), if he or she committed a crime as described in subparagraph

of this paragraph (e);

At least eighteen to thirty-two years for a class 3 felony to a maximum of the person's natural life, as provided in this subsection (1), if he or she committed a crime as described in subparagraph (I) of this paragraph (e); and

At least twenty-four to forty-eight years for a class 2 felony, to a maximum of the person's natural life, as provided in this subsection (1), if he or she committed a crime as described in subparagraph (I) of this paragraph (e).

(III) If the defendant is placed on parole, the parole board shall order the defendant to wear electronic monitoring for the duration of his or her period of parole.

(a) The district court having jurisdiction, based on consideration of the evaluation conducted pursuant to section 16-11.7-104, C.R.S., and the factors specified in section 18-1.3-203, may sentence a sex offender to probation for an indeterminate period of at least ten years for a class 4 felony or twenty years for a class 2 or 3 felony and a maximum of the sex offender's natural life; except that, if the sex offender committed a sex offense that constitutes a crime of violence, as defined in section 18-1.3-406, or committed a sex offense that makes him or her eligible for sentencing as a habitual sex offender against children pursuant to section 18-3-412, or a sex offense requiring sentencing pursuant to paragraph (e) of subsection (1) of this section, the court shall sentence the sex offender to the department of corrections as provided in subsection (1) of this section. For any sex offender sentenced to probation pursuant to this subsection (2), the court shall order that the sex offender, as a condition of probation, participate in an intensive supervision probation program established pursuant to section 18-1.3-1007, until further order of the court.

(b) The court, as a condition of probation, may sentence a sex offender to a residential community corrections program pursuant to section 18-1.3-301 for a minimum period specified by the court. Following completion of the minimum period, the sex offender may be released to intensive supervision probation as provided in section 18-1.3-1008 (1.5).

Each sex offender sentenced pursuant to this section shall be required as a part of the sentence to undergo treatment to the extent appropriate pursuant to section 16-11.7-105, C.R.S.

Repealed.

(a) Any sex offender sentenced pursuant to subsection (1) of this section and convicted

of one or more additional crimes arising out of the same incident as the sex offense shall be sentenced for the sex offense and such other crimes so that the sentences are served consecutively rather than concurrently.

(b) (I) Except as otherwise provided in subparagraph (II) of this paragraph (b), if a sex offender sentenced pursuant to this part 10 is convicted of a subsequent crime prior to being discharged from parole pursuant to section 18-1.3-1006 or discharged from probation pursuant to section 18-1.3-1008, any sentence imposed for the second crime shall not supersede the sex offender's sentence pursuant to the provisions of this part 10. If the sex offender commits the subsequent crime while he or she is on parole or probation and the sex offender receives a sentence to the department of corrections for the subsequent crime, the sex offender's parole or probation shall be deemed revoked pursuant to section 18-1.3-1010, and the sex offender shall continue to be subject to the provisions of this part 10.

(II) The provisions of subparagraph (I) of this paragraph (b) shall not apply if the sex offender commits a subsequent crime that is a class 1 felony.


18-1.3-1005. Parole - intensive supervision program. (1) The department shall establish an intensive supervision parole program for sex offenders sentenced to incarceration and subsequently released on parole pursuant to this part 10. In addition, the parole board may require a person, as a condition of parole, to participate in the intensive supervision parole program established pursuant to this section if the person is convicted of:

Indecent exposure, as described in section 18-7-302;

Criminal attempt, conspiracy, or solicitation to commit any of the offenses specified in section 18-1.3-1003 (5) (a), which attempt, conspiracy, or solicitation would constitute a class 5 felony; or

Any of the offenses specified in section 16-22-102 (9) (j), (9) (k), (9) (l), (9) (n), (9) (o), (9) (p), (9) (q), (9) (r), or (9) (s), C.R.S.

(1.5) In addition to the persons specified in subsection (1) of this section, the parole board shall require, as a condition of parole, any person convicted of felony failure to register as a sex offender, as described in section 18-3-412.5, who is sentenced to incarceration and subsequently released on parole, to participate in the intensive supervision parole program established pursuant to this section.

The department shall require that sex offenders and any other persons in the intensive supervision parole program established pursuant to this section receive the highest level of supervision that is provided to parolees. The intensive supervision parole program may include, but is not limited to, severely restricted activities, daily contact between the sex offender or other person and the community parole officer, monitored curfew, home visitation, employment visitation and monitoring, drug and alcohol screening, treatment referrals and monitoring, including physiological monitoring, and payment of restitution. In addition, the intensive supervision parole program shall be designed to minimize the risk to the public to the greatest extent possible.

The executive director of the department shall establish and enforce standards and criteria for administration of the intensive supervision parole program created pursuant to this section.

18-1.3-1006. Release from incarceration - parole - conditions. (1) (a) On completion of the minimum period of incarceration specified in a sex offender's indeterminate sentence, less any earned time credited to the sex offender pursuant to section 17-22.5-405, C.R.S., the parole board shall schedule a hearing to determine whether the sex offender may be released on parole. In determining whether to release the sex offender on parole, the parole board shall determine whether the sex offender has successfully progressed in treatment and would not pose an undue threat to the community if released under appropriate treatment and monitoring requirements and whether there is a strong and reasonable probability that the person will not thereafter violate the law. The department shall make recommendations to the parole board concerning whether the sex offender should be released on parole and the level of treatment and monitoring that should be imposed as a condition of parole. The recommendation shall be based on the criteria established by the management board pursuant to section 18-1.3-1009.

If a sex offender is released on parole pursuant to this section, the sex offender's sentence to incarceration shall continue and shall not be deemed discharged until such time as the parole board may discharge the sex offender from parole pursuant to subsection (3) of this section. The period of parole for any sex offender convicted of a class 4 felony shall be an indeterminate term of at least ten years and a maximum of the remainder of the sex offender's natural life. The period of parole for any sex offender convicted of a class 2 or 3 felony shall be an indeterminate term of at least twenty years and a maximum of the remainder of the sex offender's natural life.

If the parole board does not release the sex offender on parole pursuant to paragraph (a) of this subsection (1), the parole board shall review such denial pursuant to the time periods set forth in section 17-2-201 (4) (a), C.R.S. At each review, the department shall make recommendations, based on the criteria established by the management board pursuant to section 18-1.3-1009, concerning whether the sex offender should be released on parole.

(a) As a condition of release on parole pursuant to this section, a sex offender shall participate in the intensive supervision parole program created by the department pursuant to section 18-1.3-1005. Participation in the intensive supervision parole program shall continue until the sex offender can demonstrate that he or she has successfully progressed in treatment and would not pose an undue threat to the community if paroled to a lower level of supervision, at which time the sex offender's community parole officer may petition the parole board for a reduction in the sex offender's level of supervision. The sex offender's community parole officer and treatment provider shall make recommendations to the parole board concerning whether the sex offender has met the requirements specified in this subsection (2) such that the level of parole supervision should be reduced. The recommendations shall be based on the criteria established by the management board pursuant to section 18-1.3-1009.

(b) Following reduction in a sex offender's level of parole supervision pursuant to paragraph

of this subsection (2), the sex offender's community parole officer may return the sex offender to the intensive supervision parole program if the community parole officer determines that an increased level of supervision is necessary to protect the public safety. The community parole officer shall notify the parole board as soon as possible after returning the sex offender to the intensive supervision parole program. To subsequently reduce the sex offender's level of supervision, the community parole officer may petition the parole board as provided in paragraph (a) of this

subsection (2).

(a) On completion of twenty years on parole for any sex offender convicted of a class 2 or 3 felony or on completion of ten years of parole for any sex offender convicted of a class 4 felony, the parole board shall schedule a hearing to determine whether the sex offender may be discharged from parole. In determining whether to discharge the sex offender from parole, the parole board shall determine whether the sex offender has successfully progressed in treatment and would not pose an undue threat to the community if allowed to live in the community without treatment or supervision. The sex offender's community parole officer and treatment provider shall make recommendations to the parole board concerning whether the sex offender has met the requirements specified in this subsection (3) such that the sex offender should be discharged from parole. The recommendations shall be based on the criteria established by the management board pursuant to section 18-1.3-1009.

If the parole board does not discharge the sex offender from parole pursuant to paragraph

of this subsection (3), the parole board shall review such denial at least once every three years until it determines that the sex offender meets the criteria for discharge specified in paragraph (a) of this subsection (3). At each review, the sex offender's community parole officer and treatment provider shall make recommendations, based on the criteria established by the management board pursuant to section 18-1.3-1009, concerning whether the sex offender should be discharged.

In determining whether to release a sex offender on parole, reduce the level of supervision, or discharge a sex offender from parole pursuant to this section, the parole board shall consider the recommendations of the department and the sex offender's community parole officer and treatment provider. If the parole board chooses not to follow the recommendations made, it shall make findings on the record in support of its decision.

18-1.3-1007. Probation - intensive supervision program. (1) (a) The judicial department shall establish an intensive supervision probation program for sex offenders sentenced to probation pursuant to this part 10. In addition, the court shall require a person, as a condition of probation, to participate in the intensive supervision probation program established pursuant to this section if the person is convicted of one of the following offenses and sentenced to probation:

Indecent exposure, as described in section 18-7-302 (4);

Criminal attempt, conspiracy, or solicitation to commit any of the offenses specified in section 18-1.3-1003 (5) (a), which attempt, conspiracy, or solicitation would constitute a class 5 felony;

Any of the offenses specified in section 16-22-102 (9) (j), (9) (k), (9) (l), (9) (n), (9) (o), (9) (p), (9) (q), (9) (r), or (9) (s), C.R.S.;

Any felony offense that involves unlawful sexual behavior or any felony offense with an underlying factual basis, as determined by the court, resulting in a conviction or plea of guilty or nolo contendere on or after July 1, 2001;

Sexual assault in the third degree, in violation of section 18-3-404 (2), as it existed prior to July 1, 2000.

The judicial department may establish the intensive supervision probation program in any judicial district or combination of judicial districts.

(1.5) In addition to the persons specified in subsection (1) of this section, the court may

require any person convicted of felony failure to register as a sex offender, as described in section 18-3-412.5, and sentenced to probation to participate, as a condition of probation and until further order of the court, in the intensive supervision probation program established pursuant to this section.

The judicial department shall require that sex offenders and any other persons participating in the intensive supervision probation program created to this section receive the highest level of supervision that is provided to probationers. The intensive supervision probation program may include but not be limited to severely restricted activities, daily contact between the sex offender or other person and the probation officer, monitored curfew, home visitation, employment visitation and monitoring, drug and alcohol screening, treatment referrals and monitoring, including physiological monitoring, and payment of restitution. In addition, the intensive supervision probation program shall be designed to minimize the risk to the public to the greatest extent possible.

The judicial department shall establish and enforce standards and criteria for administration of the intensive supervision probation program created pursuant to this section.

For the purposes of this section, "convicted" means having entered a plea of guilty, including a plea of guilty entered pursuant to a deferred sentence under section 18-1.3-102, or a plea of no contest, accepted by the court, or having received a verdict of guilty by a judge or jury.

18-1.3-1008. Probation - conditions - release. (1) If the court sentences a sex offender to probation, in addition to any conditions imposed pursuant to section 18-1.3-204, the court shall require as a condition of probation that the sex offender participate until further order of the court in the intensive supervision probation program created pursuant to section 18-1.3-1007.

(1.5) If the court as a condition of probation sentences a sex offender to a residential communitycorrections program, following completion of the minimum period of sentence specified by the court, the community corrections program shall notify the judicial department when it determines that the sex offender has successfully progressed in treatment and would not pose an undue threat to the community if allowed to live in the community while continuing on intensive supervision probation. The community corrections program shall base its determination on the criteria established by the management board pursuant to section 18-1.3-1009. The judicial department shall file the recommendations of the community corrections program with the court. Upon order of the court, the sex offender shall be released from the community corrections program, and the court shall order the sex offender, as a condition of probation, to participate in the intensive supervision program created in section 18-1.3-1007. The sex offender shall participate in such program until further order of the court.

On completion of twenty years of probation for any sex offender convicted of a class 2 or 3 felony or on completion of ten years of probation for any sex offender convicted of a class 4 felony, the court shall schedule a review hearing to determine whether the sex offender should be discharged from probation. In making its determination, the court shall determine whether the sex offender has successfully progressed in treatment and would not pose an undue threat to the community if allowed to live in the community without treatment or supervision. The sex offender's probation officer and treatment provider shall make recommendations to the court concerning

whether the sex offender has met the requirements of this section such that he or she should be discharged from probation.

(a) In determining whether to discharge a sex offender from probation pursuant to this section, the court shall consider the recommendations of the sex offender's probation officer and treatment provider. The recommendations of the probation officer and the treatment provider shall be based on the criteria established by the management board pursuant to section 18-1.3-1009. If the court chooses not to follow the recommendations made, the court shall make findings on the record in support of its decision.

(b) If the court does not discharge the sex offender from probation pursuant to paragraph (a) of this subsection (3), the court shall review such denial at least once every three years until it determines that the sex offender meets the criteria for discharge as specified in paragraph (a) of this subsection (3). At each review, the sex offender's probation officer and treatment provider shall make recommendations, based on the criteria established bythe management board pursuant to section 18- 1.3-1009, concerning whether the sex offender should be discharged.

18-1.3-1009. Criteria for release from incarceration, reduction in supervision, and discharge. (1) On or before July 1, 1999, the management board, in collaboration with the department of corrections, the judicial department, and the parole board, shall establish:

The criteria by and the manner in which a sex offender may demonstrate that he or she would not pose an undue threat to the community if released on parole or to a lower level of supervision while on parole or probation or if discharged from parole or probation. The court and the parole board may use the criteria to assist in making decisions concerning release of a sex offender, reduction of the level of supervision for a sex offender, and discharge of a sex offender.

The methods of determining whether a sex offender has successfully progressed in treatment; and

Standards for community entities that provide supervision and treatment specifically designed for sex offenders who have developmental disabilities. At a minimum, the standards shall determine whether an entity would provide adequate support and supervision to minimize any threat that the sex offender may pose to the community.

18-1.3-1010. Arrest of parolee or probationer - revocation. (1) (a) A sex offender paroled pursuant to section 18-1.3-1006 is subject to arrest and revocation of parole as provided in sections 17-2-103 and 17-2-103.5, C.R.S. At anyrevocation proceeding, the sex offender's communityparole officer and the treatment provider shall submit written recommendations concerning the level of treatment and monitoring that should be imposed as a condition of parole if parole is not revoked or whether the sex offender poses a sufficient threat to the community that parole should be revoked. The recommendations shall be based on the criteria established by the management board pursuant to section 18-1.3-1009. If the parole board revokes the sex offender's parole, the sex offender shall continue to be subject to the provisions of this part 10.

(b) At a revocation hearing held pursuant to this subsection (1), the parole board shall consider the recommendations of the community parole officer and the treatment provider, in

addition to evidence concerning any of the grounds for revocation of parole specified in sections 17- 2-103 and 17-2-103.5, C.R.S. If the parole board chooses not to follow the recommendations made, it shall make findings on the record in support of its decision.

(2) (a) A sex offender sentenced to probation pursuant to section 18-1.3-1004 (2) is subject to arrest and revocation of probation as provided in sections 16-11-205 and 16-11-206, C.R.S. At any revocation proceeding, the sex offender's probation officer and the sex offender's treatment provider shall submit recommendations concerning the level of treatment and monitoring that should be imposed as a condition of probation if probation is not revoked or whether the sex offender poses a sufficient threat to the community that probation should be revoked. The recommendations shall be based on the criteria established by the management board pursuant to section 18-1.3-1009. If the court revokes the sex offender's probation, the court shall sentence the sex offender as provided in section 18-1.3-1004, and the sex offender shall be subject to the provisions of this part 10.

(b) At a revocation hearing held pursuant to this subsection (2), the court shall consider the recommendations of the probation officer and the treatment provider, in addition to evidence concerning anyof the grounds for revocation of probation specified in sections 16-11-205 and 16-11- 206, C.R.S. If the court chooses not to follow the recommendations made, it shall make findings on the record in support of its decision.

18-1.3-1011. Annual report. (1) On or before November 1, 2000, and on or before each November 1 thereafter, the department of corrections, the department of public safety, and the judicial department shall submit a report to the judiciary committees of the house of representatives and the senate, or any successor committees, and to the joint budget committee of the general assembly specifying, at a minimum:

The impact on the prison population, the parole population, and the probation population in the state due to the extended length of incarceration and supervision provided for in sections 18- 1.3-1004, 18-1.3-1006, and 18-1.3-1008;

The number of offenders placed in the intensive supervision parole program and the intensive supervision probation program and the length of supervision of offenders in said programs;

The number of sex offenders sentenced pursuant to this part 10 who received parole release hearings and the number released on parole during the preceding twelve months, if any;

The number of sex offenders sentenced pursuant to this part 10 who received parole or probation discharge hearings and the number discharged from parole or probation during the preceding twelve months, if any;

The number of sex offenders sentenced pursuant to this part 10 who received parole or probation revocation hearings and the number whose parole or probation was revoked during the preceding twelve months, if any;

A summary of the evaluation instruments developed by the management board and use of the evaluation instruments in evaluating sex offenders pursuant to this part 10;

The availability of sex offender treatment providers throughout the state, including location of the treatment providers, the services provided, and the amount paid by offenders and by the state for the services provided, and the manner of regulation and review of the services provided by sex offender treatment providers;

The average number of sex offenders sentenced pursuant to this part 10 that participated in phase I and phase II of the department's sex offender treatment and monitoring program during each month of the preceding twelve months;

The number of sex offenders sentenced pursuant to this part 10 who were denied admission to treatment in phase I and phase II of the department's sex offender treatment and monitoring program for reasons other than length of remaining sentence during each month of the preceding twelve months;

The number of sex offenders sentenced pursuant to this part 10 who were terminated from phase I and phase II of the department's sex offender treatment and monitoring program during the preceding twelve months and the reason for termination in each case;

The average length of participation by sex offenders sentenced pursuant to this part 10 in phase I and phase II of the department's sex offender treatment and monitoring program during the preceding twelve months;

The number of sex offenders sentenced pursuant to this part 10 who were denied readmission to phase I and phase II of the department's sex offender treatment and monitoring program after having previously been terminated from the program during the preceding twelve months;

The number of sex offenders sentenced pursuant to this part 10 who were recommended by the department's sex offender treatment and monitoring program to the parole board for release on parole during the preceding twelve months and whether the recommendation was followed in each case; and

The number of sex offenders sentenced pursuant to this part 10 who were recommended by the department's sex offender treatment and monitoring program for placement in community corrections during the preceding twelve months and whether the recommendation was followed in each case.


18-1.3-1012. Applicability of part. The provisions of this part 10 shall apply to any person who commits a sex offense on or after November 1, 1998.

PART 11

SPECIAL PROCEEDINGS - PRETRIAL MOTIONS IN CLASS 1 FELONY CASES ALLEGING THAT A DEFENDANT IS A MENTALLY RETARDED DEFENDANT


18-1.3-1101. Definitions. As used in this part 11:

"Defendant" means any person charged with a class 1 felony.
"Mentallyretarded defendant" means anydefendant with significantlysubaverage general intellectual functioning existing concurrently with substantial deficits in adaptive behavior and manifested and documented during the developmental period. The requirement for documentation

may be excused by the court upon a finding that extraordinary circumstances exist.


18-1.3-1102. Pretrial motion by defendant in class 1 felony case - determination whether defendant is mentally retarded - procedure. (1) Any defendant may file a motion with the trial court in which the defendant may allege that such defendant is a mentally retarded defendant. Such motion shall be filed at least ninety-one days prior to trial.
The court shall hold a hearing upon any motion filed pursuant to subsection (1) of this section and shall make a determination regarding such motion no later than fourteen days prior to trial. At such hearing, the defendant shall be permitted to present evidence with regard to such motion and the prosecution shall be permitted to offer evidence in rebuttal. The defendant shall have the burden of proof to show by clear and convincing evidence that such defendant is mentally retarded.
The court shall enter specific findings of fact and conclusions of law regarding whether or not the defendant is a mentally retarded defendant as defined in section 18-1.3-1101.


18-1.3-1103. Mentally retarded defendant - death penalty not imposed thereon. A sentence of death shall not be imposed upon any defendant who is determined to be a mentally retarded defendant pursuant to section 18-1.3-1102. If anyperson who is determined to be a mentally retarded defendant is found guilty of a class 1 felony, such defendant shall be sentenced to life imprisonment.


18-1.3-1104. Evaluation and report. (1) When the defendant files a motion alleging that the defendant is a mentally retarded defendant, the court shall order one or more evaluations of the defendant with regard to such motion.
In ordering an evaluation of the defendant pursuant to subsection (1) of this section, the court shall specify the place where the evaluation is to be conducted and the period of time allocated for the evaluation. In determining the place where the evaluation is to be conducted, the court shall give priority to the place where the defendant is in custody, unless the nature and circumstances of the evaluation requires designation of a different location. The court shall direct one or more psychologists who are recommended by the executive director of the department of health care policy and financing pursuant to section 25.5-10-239, C.R.S., or his or her designee, to evaluate the defendant. For good cause shown, upon motion of the prosecution or the defendant or upon the court's own motion, the court may order such further or other evaluation as it deems necessary. Nothing in this section shall abridge the right of the defendant to procure an evaluation as provided in section 18-1.3-1105.
The defendant shall have a privilege against self-incrimination that may be invoked prior to or during the course of an evaluation under this section. A defendant's failure to cooperate with the evaluators or other personnel conducting the evaluation may be admissible in the defendant's mental retardation hearing.
To aid in the formation of an opinion as to mental retardation, it is permissible in the

course of an evaluation under this section to use statements of the defendant and any other evidence, including but not limited to the circumstances surrounding the commission of the offense as well as the medical and social history of the defendant, in evaluating the defendant.

A written report of the evaluation shall be prepared in triplicate and delivered to the appropriate clerk of the court. The clerk shall furnish a copy of the report to both the prosecuting attorney and the counsel for the defendant.

The report of evaluation shall include, but is not limited to:

The name of each expert who evaluated the defendant;

A description of the nature, content, extent, and results of the evaluation and any tests conducted; and

Diagnosis and an opinion as to whether the defendant is mentally retarded.

Nothing in this section shall be construed to preclude the application of section 16-8-109, C.R.S.

18-1.3-1105. Evaluation at insistence of defendant. (1) If the defendant wishes to be evaluated by an expert in mental retardation of the defendant's choice in connection with the mental retardation hearing under this part 11, the court, upon timely motion, shall order that the evaluator chosen by the defendant be given reasonable opportunity to conduct the evaluation.

(2) Whenever an expert is endorsed as a witness by the defendant, a copy of any report of an evaluation of the defendant shall be furnished to the prosecution within a reasonable time but not less than thirty-five days prior to the mental retardation hearing.

PART 12

SPECIAL PROCEEDINGS - SENTENCING IN CLASS 1 FELONIES

18-1.3-1201. Imposition of sentence in class 1 felonies - appellate review. (1) (a) Upon conviction of guilt of a defendant of a class 1 felony, the trial court shall conduct a separate sentencing hearing to determine whether the defendant should be sentenced to death or life imprisonment, unless the defendant was under the age of eighteen years at the time of the commission of the offense or unless the defendant has been determined to be a mentally retarded defendant pursuant to part 11 of this article, in either of which cases, the defendant shall be sentenced to life imprisonment. The hearing shall be conducted by the trial judge before the trial jury as soon as practicable. Alternate jurors shall not be excused from the case prior to submission of the issue of guilt to the trial jury and shall remain separately sequestered until a verdict is entered by the trial jury. If the verdict of the trial jury is that the defendant is guilty of a class 1 felony, the alternate jurors shall sit as alternate jurors on the issue of punishment. If, for any reason satisfactory to the court, any member or members of the trial jury are excused from participation in the sentencing hearing, the trial judge shall replace each juror or jurors with an alternate juror or jurors. If a trial jury was waived or if the defendant pled guilty, the hearing shall be conducted before the trial judge. The

court shall instruct the defendant when waiving his or her right to a jury trial or when pleading guilty, that he or she is also waiving his or her right to a jury determination of the sentence at the sentencing hearing.

(a.5) and (a.7) (Deleted by amendment, L. 2002, 3rd Ex. Sess., p. 7, § 2, effective July 12, 2002.)

All admissible evidence presented byeither the prosecuting attorneyor the defendant that

the court deems relevant to the nature of the crime, and the character, background, and history of the defendant, including any evidence presented in the guilt phase of the trial, any matters relating to any of the aggravating or mitigating factors enumerated in subsections (4) and (5) of this section, and any matters relating to the personal characteristics of the victim and the impact of the crimes on the victim's family may be presented. Any such evidence, including but not limited to the testimony of members of the victim's immediate family, as defined in section 24-4.1-302 (6), C.R.S., which the court deems to have probative value may be received, as long as each party is given an opportunity to rebut such evidence. The prosecuting attorney and the defendant or the defendant's counsel shall be permitted to present arguments for or against a sentence of death. The jury shall be instructed that life imprisonment means imprisonment for life without the possibility of parole.

(Deleted by amendment, L. 2002, 3rd Ex. Sess., p. 7, § 2, effective July 12, 2002.)

The burden of proof as to the aggravating factors enumerated in subsection (5) of this section shall be beyond a reasonable doubt. There shall be no burden of proof as to proving or disproving mitigating factors.

(a) After hearing all the evidence and arguments of the prosecuting attorney and the defendant, the jury shall deliberate and render a verdict based upon the following considerations:

Whether at least one aggravating factor has been proved as enumerated in subsection (5) of this section;

Whether sufficient mitigating factors exist which outweigh any aggravating factor or factors found to exist; and

Based on the considerations in subparagraphs (I) and (II) of this paragraph (a), whether the defendant should be sentenced to death or life imprisonment.

(I) In the event that no aggravating factors are found to exist as enumerated in subsection

(5) of this section, the jury shall render a verdict of life imprisonment, and the court shall sentence the defendant to life imprisonment.

(II) The jury shall not render a verdict of death unless it unanimously finds and specifies in writing that:

At least one aggravating factor has been proved; and

There are insufficient mitigating factors to outweigh the aggravating factor or factors that were proved.

In the event that the jury's verdict is to sentence to death, such verdict shall be unanimous and shall be binding upon the court unless the court determines, and sets forth in writing the basis and reasons for such determination, that the verdict of the jury is clearly erroneous as contrary to the weight of the evidence, in which case the court shall sentence the defendant to life imprisonment.

If the jury's verdict is not unanimous, the jury shall be discharged, and the court shall sentence the defendant to life imprisonment.

(2.5) In all cases where the sentencing hearing is held before the court alone, the court shall

determine whether the defendant should be sentenced to death or life imprisonment in the same manner in which a jury determines its verdict under paragraphs (a) and (b) of subsection (2) of this section. The sentence of the court shall be supported by specific written findings of fact based upon the circumstances as set forth in subsections (4) and (5) of this section and upon the records of the trial and sentencing hearing.

(3) (a) The provisions of this subsection (3) shall apply only in a class 1 felony case in which the prosecuting attorney has filed a statement of intent to seek the death penalty pursuant to rule 32.1
of the Colorado rules of criminal procedure.

The prosecuting attorney shall provide the defendant with the following information and materials not later than twenty-one days after the prosecution files its written intention to seek the death penalty or within such other time frame as the supreme court may establish by rule; except that any reports, recorded statements, and notes, including results of physical or mental examinations and scientific tests, experiments, or comparisons, of any expert whom the prosecuting attorney intends to call as a witness at the sentencing hearing shall be provided to the defense as soon as practicable but not later than sixty-three days before trial:

A list of all aggravating factors that are known to the prosecuting attorney at that time and that the prosecuting attorney intends to prove at the sentencing hearing;

A list of all witnesses whom the prosecuting attorney may call at the sentencing hearing, specifying for each the witness' name, address, and date of birth and the subject matter of the witness' testimony;

The written and recorded statements, including any notes of those statements, for each witness whom the prosecuting attorney may call at the sentencing hearing;

(Deleted by amendment, L. 2002, 3rd Ex. Sess., p. 7, § 2, effective July 12, 2002.)

A list of books, papers, documents, photographs, or tangible objects that the prosecuting attorney may introduce at the sentencing hearing; and

All material or information that tends to mitigate or negate the finding of any of the aggravating factors the prosecuting attorney intends to prove at the sentencing hearing.

(b.5) Upon receipt of the information required to be disclosed by the defendant pursuant to paragraph (c) of this subsection (3), the prosecuting attorney shall notify the defendant as soon as practicable of any additional witnesses whom the prosecuting attorney intends to call in response to the defendant's disclosures.

The defendant shall provide the prosecuting attorney with the following information and materials no later than thirty-five days before the first trial date set for the beginning of the defendant's trial or within such other time frame as the supreme court may establish by rule; however, any reports, recorded statements, and notes, including results of physical or mental examinations and scientific tests, experiments, or comparisons, of any expert whom the defense intends to call as a witness at the sentencing hearing shall be provided to the prosecuting attorney as soon as practicable but not later than thirty-five days before trial:

A list of all witnesses whom the defendant may call at the sentencing hearing, specifying for each the witness' name, address, and date of birth and the subject matter of the witness' testimony;

The written and recorded statements, including any notes of those statements, of each witness whom the defendant may call at the sentencing hearing; and

(Deleted by amendment, L. 2002, 3rd Ex. Sess., p. 7, § 2, effective July 12, 2002.)

A list of books, papers, documents, photographs, or tangible objects that the defendant may introduce at the sentencing hearing.

(c.5) (I) Any material subject to this subsection (3) that the defendant believes contains information that is privileged to the extent that the prosecution cannot be aware of it in connection with its preparation for, or conduct of, the trial to determine guilt on the substantive charges against the defendant shall be submitted by the defendant to the trial judge under seal no later than forty-nine days before trial.

(II) The trial judge shall review any such material submitted under seal pursuant to subparagraph (I) of this paragraph (c.5) to determine whether it is in fact privileged. Any material the trial judge finds not to be privileged shall be provided forthwith to the prosecuting attorney. Any material submitted under seal that the trial judge finds to be privileged shall be provided forthwith to the prosecution if the defendant is convicted of a class 1 felony.

(I) Except as otherwise provided in subparagraph (II) of this paragraph (d), if the witnesses disclosed by the defendant pursuant to paragraph (c) of this subsection (3) include witnesses who may provide evidence concerning the defendant's mental condition at the sentencing hearing conducted pursuant to this section, the trial court, at the request of the prosecuting attorney, shall order that the defendant be examined and a report of said examination be prepared pursuant to section 16-8-106, C.R.S.

(II) The court shall not order an examination pursuant to subparagraph (I) of this paragraph

if:

Such an examination was previously performed and a report was prepared in the same case; and

The report included an opinion concerning how any mental disease or defect of the defendant or condition of mind caused by mental disease or defect of the defendant affects the mitigating factors that the defendant may raise at the sentencing hearing held pursuant to this section.

If the witnesses disclosed by the defendant pursuant to paragraph (c) of this subsection

include witnesses who may provide evidence concerning the defendant's mental condition at a sentencing hearing conducted pursuant to this section, the provisions of section 16-8-109, C.R.S., concerning testimony of lay witnesses shall apply to said sentencing hearing.

There is a continuing duty on the part of the prosecuting attorney and the defendant to disclose the information and materials specified in this subsection (3). If, after complying with the duty to disclose the information and materials described in this subsection (3), either party discovers or obtains any additional information and materials that are subject to disclosure under this subsection (3), the party shall promptly notify the other party and provide the other party with complete access to the information and materials.

The trial court, upon a showing of extraordinary circumstances that could not have been foreseen and prevented, may grant an extension of time to comply with the requirements of this subsection (3).

If it is brought to the attention of the court that either the prosecuting attorney or the defendant has failed to comply with the provisions of this subsection (3) or with an order issued pursuant to this subsection (3), the court may enter any order against such party that the court deems just under the circumstances, including but not limited to an order to permit the discovery or

inspection of information and materials not previously disclosed, to grant a continuance, to prohibit the offending party from introducing the information and materials not disclosed, or to impose sanctions against the offending party.

For purposes of this section, mitigating factors shall be the following factors:

The age of the defendant at the time of the crime; or

The defendant's capacity to appreciate wrongfulness of the defendant's conduct or to conform the defendant's conduct to the requirements of law was significantly impaired, but not so impaired as to constitute a defense to prosecution; or

The defendant was under unusual and substantial duress, although not such duress as to constitute a defense to prosecution; or

The defendant was a principal in the offense which was committed by another, but the defendant's participation was relatively minor, although not so minor as to constitute a defense to prosecution; or

The defendant could not reasonably have foreseen that the defendant's conduct in the course of the commission of the offense for which the defendant was convicted would cause, or would create a grave risk of causing, death to another person; or

The emotional state of the defendant at the time the crime was committed; or

The absence of any significant prior conviction; or

The extent of the defendant's cooperation with law enforcement officers or agencies and with the office of the prosecuting district attorney; or

The influence of drugs or alcohol; or

The good faith, although mistaken, belief by the defendant that circumstances existed which constituted a moral justification for the defendant's conduct; or

The defendant is not a continuing threat to society; or

Any other evidence which in the court's opinion bears on the question of mitigation.

For purposes of this section, the following are aggravating factors:

The class 1 felony was committed by a person under sentence of imprisonment for a class 1, 2, or 3 felony as defined by Colorado law or United States law, or for a crime committed against another state or the United States which would constitute a class 1, 2, or 3 felony as defined by Colorado law; or

The defendant was previously convicted in this state of a class 1 or 2 felony involving violence as specified in section 18-1.3-406, or was previously convicted by another state or the United States of an offense which would constitute a class 1 or 2 felony involving violence as defined by Colorado law in section 18-1.3-406; or

The defendant intentionally killed any of the following persons while the person was engaged in the course of the performance of the person's official duties, and the defendant knew or reasonably should have known that the victim was a person engaged in the performance of the person's official duties, or the victim was intentionally killed in retaliation for the performance of the victim's official duties:

A peace officer or former peace officer as described in section 16-2.5-101, C.R.S.; or

A firefighter as defined in section 24-33.5-1202 (4), C.R.S.; or

(II.5) An emergency medical service provider, as defined in section 18-3-201 (1); or

A judge, referee, or former judge or referee of any court of record in the state or federal

system or in any other state court system or a judge or former judge in any municipal court in this state or in any other state. For purposes of this subparagraph (III), the term "referee" shall include a hearing officer or any other officer who exercises judicial functions.

An elected state, county, or municipal official; or

A federal law enforcement officer or agent or former federal law enforcement officer or agent; or

The defendant intentionally killed a person kidnapped or being held as a hostage by the defendant or by anyone associated with the defendant; or

The defendant has been a party to an agreement to kill another person in furtherance of which a person has been intentionally killed; or

The defendant committed the offense while lying in wait, from ambush, or by use of an explosive or incendiary device or a chemical, biological, or radiological weapon. As used in this paragraph (f), "explosive or incendiary device" means:

Dynamite and all other forms of high explosives; or

Any explosive bomb, grenade, missile, or similar device; or

Any incendiary bomb or grenade, fire bomb, or similar device, including any device which consists of or includes a breakable container including a flammable liquid or compound, and a wick composed of any material which, when ignited, is capable of igniting such flammable liquid or compound, and can be carried or thrown by one individual acting alone.

The defendant committed a class 1, 2, or 3 felony and, in the course of or in furtherance of such or immediate flight therefrom, the defendant intentionally caused the death of a person other than one of the participants; or

The class 1 felony was committed for pecuniary gain; or

In the commission of the offense, the defendant knowingly created a grave risk of death to another person in addition to the victim of the offense; or

The defendant committed the offense in an especiallyheinous, cruel, or depraved manner;

or

The class 1 felony was committed for the purpose of avoiding or preventing a lawful

arrest or prosecution or effecting an escape from custody. This factor shall include the intentional killing of a witness to a criminal offense.

The defendant unlawfully and intentionally, knowingly, or with universal malice manifesting extreme indifference to the value of human life generally, killed two or more persons during the commission of the same criminal episode; or

The defendant intentionally killed a child who has not yet attained twelve years of age;

or

The defendant committed the class 1 felony against the victim because of the victim's

race, color, ancestry, religion, or national origin; or

The defendant's possession of the weapon used to commit the class 1 felony constituted a felony offense under the laws of this state or the United States; or

The defendant intentionally killed more than one person in more than one criminal episode; or

The victim was a pregnant woman, and the defendant intentionally killed the victim, knowing she was pregnant.

(a) Whenever a sentence of death is imposed upon a person pursuant to the provisions of this section, the supreme court shall review the propriety of that sentence, having regard to the nature of the offense, the character and record of the offender, the public interest, and the manner in which the sentence was imposed, including the sufficiency and accuracy of the information on which it was based. The procedures to be employed in the review shall be as provided by supreme court rule. The supreme court shall combine its review pursuant to this subsection (6) with consideration of any appeal that may be filed pursuant to part 2 of article 12 of title 16, C.R.S.

(b) A sentence of death shall not be imposed pursuant to this section if the supreme court determines that the sentence was imposed under the influence of passion or prejudice or any other arbitrary factor or that the evidence presented does not support the finding of statutory aggravating circumstances.

(a) If any provisions of this section are determined by the United States supreme court or by the Colorado supreme court to render this section unconstitutional or invalid such that this section does not constitute a valid and operative death penalty statute for class 1 felonies, but severance of such provisions would, through operation of the remaining provisions of this section, maintain this section as a valid and operative death penalty statute for class 1 felonies, it is the intent of the general assembly that those remaining provisions are severable and are to have full force and effect.

(b) If any death sentence is imposed upon a defendant pursuant to the provisions of this section and, on appellate review including consideration pursuant to subsection (8) of this section, the imposition of such death sentence upon such defendant is held invalid for reasons other than unconstitutionality of the death penalty or insufficiency of the evidence to support the sentence, the case shall be remanded to the trial court to set a new sentencing hearing before a newly impaneled jury or, if the defendant pled guilty or waived the right to jury sentencing, before the trial judge; except that, if the prosecutor informs the trial court that, in the opinion of the prosecutor, capital punishment would no longer be in the interest of justice, said defendant shall be returned to the trial court and shall then be sentenced to life imprisonment. If a death sentence imposed pursuant to this section is held invalid based on unconstitutionality of the death penalty or insufficiency of the evidence to support the sentence, said defendant shall be returned to the trial court and shall then be sentenced to life imprisonment.

If, on appeal, the supreme court finds one or more of the aggravating factors that were found to support a sentence to death to be invalid for any reason, the supreme court may determine whether the sentence of death should be affirmed on appeal by:

Reweighing the remaining aggravating factor or factors and all mitigating factors and then determining whether death is the appropriate punishment in the case; or

Applying harmless error analysis by considering whether, if the sentencing body had not considered the invalid aggravating factor, it would have nonetheless sentenced the defendant to death; or

If the supreme court finds the sentencing body's consideration of an aggravating factor was improper because the aggravating factor was not given a constitutionally narrow construction, determining whether, beyond a reasonable doubt, the sentencing body would have returned a verdict of death had the aggravating factor been properly narrowed; or

Employing any other constitutionally permissible method of review.

18-1.3-1202. Death penalty inflicted by lethal injection. The manner of inflicting the punishment of death shall be by the administration of a lethal injection within the time prescribed in this part 12, unless for good cause the court or governor may prolong the time. For the purposes of this part 12, "lethal injection" means a continuous intravenous injection of a lethal quantity of sodium thiopental or other equally or more effective substance sufficient to cause death. The manner of inflicting the punishment of death shall, in all circumstances, be by the administration of a lethal injection regardless of the date of the commission of the offense or offenses for which the death penalty is imposed.

18-1.3-1203. Genetic testing prior to execution. Prior to the execution of the death penalty pursuant to this part 12, the judicial department shall obtain the chemical testing of a biological substance sample from the convicted offender to determine the genetic markers thereof.

18-1.3-1204. Implements - sentence executed by executive director. The executive director of the department of corrections, at the expense of the state of Colorado, shall provide a suitable and efficient room or place, enclosed from public view, within the walls of the correctional facilities at Canon City and therein at all times have in preparation all necessary implements requisite for carrying into execution the death penalty by means of the administration of a lethal injection. The execution shall be performed in the room or place by a person selected by the executive director and trained to administer intravenous injections. Death shall be pronounced by a licensed physician or a coroner according to accepted medical standards.

18-1.3-1205. Week of execution - warrant. When a person is convicted of a class 1 felony, the punishment for which is death, and the convicted person is sentenced to suffer the penalty of death, the judge passing such sentence shall appoint and designate in the warrant of conviction a week of time within which the sentence must be executed; the end of such week so appointed shall be not fewer than ninety-one days nor more than one hundred twenty-six days from the day of passing the sentence. Said warrant shall be directed to the executive director of the department of corrections or the executive director's designee commanding said executive director or designee to execute the sentence imposed upon some day within the week of time designated in the warrant and shall be delivered to the sheriff of the county in which such conviction is had, who, within three days thereafter, shall proceed to the correctional facilities at Cañon City and deliver the convicted person, together with the warrant, to said executive director or designee, who shall keep the convict in confinement until execution of the death penalty. Persons shall be permitted access to the inmate pursuant to prison rules. Such rules shall provide, at a minimum, for the inmate's attendants, counsel, and physician, a spiritual adviser selected by the inmate, and members of the inmate's family to have access to the inmate.

18-1.3-1206. Execution - witnesses. The particular day and hour of the execution of said sentence within the week specified in said warrant shall be fixed by the executive director of the department of corrections or the executive director's designee, and the executive director shall be present thereat or shall appoint some other representative among the officials or officers of the correctional facilities at Canon City to be present in his or her place and stead. There shall also be present a physician and such guards, attendants, and other persons as the executive director or the executive director's designee in his or her discretion deems necessary to conduct the execution. In addition, there may be present such witnesses as the executive director or the executive director's designee in his or her discretion deems desirable, not to exceed eighteen persons. The executive director or the executive director's designee shall notify the governor of the day and hour for the execution as soon as it has been fixed.

18-1.3-1207. Record and certificate of execution. The executive director of the department of corrections or his or her designee shall keep a book of record, to be known as record of executions, in which shall be entered the reports specified in this section. Immediately after the execution, a postmortem examination of the body of the convict shall be made by the attending physician, who shall enter in said book of record the nature and extent of the examination and sign and certify to the same. The executive director or his or her designee shall also immediately make and enter in said book a report, setting forth the time of such execution and that the convict (naming him or her) was then and there executed in conformity to the sentence specified in the warrant of the court (naming such court) to him or her directed and in accordance with the provisions of this part 12, and shall insert in said report the names of all the persons who were present and witnessed the execution, and shall procure each of such persons to sign said report with his or her full name and place of residence before leaving the place of execution. The executive director or his or her designee shall thereupon attach his or her certificate to said report, certifying to the truth and correctness thereof, and shall immediately deliver a certified transcript of the record entry to the court which sentenced the convict.

PART 13

SPECIAL PROCEEDINGS - APPLICABILITY OF PROCEDURE IN CLASS 1 FELONY CASES FOR CRIMES COMMITTED ON OR AFTER JULY 1, 1988, AND PRIOR TO SEPTEMBER 20, 1991

18-1.3-1301. Applicability of procedure for the imposition of sentences in class 1 felony cases. (1) It is the expressed intention of the general assembly that there be no hiatus in the imposition of the death penalty as a sentence for the commission of a class 1 felony in the state of Colorado as a result of the holding of the Colorado supreme court in People v. Young, 814 P.2d 834 (Colo. 1991). Toward that end, the provisions of former section 16-11-103, C.R.S., as it existed prior to the enactment of senate bill 78, enacted at the second regular session of the fifty-sixth general

assembly, and as it currently exists as section 18-1.3-1201, to the extent such provisions were not automatically revitalized by the operation of law, are reenacted as section 18-1.3-1302 and are hereby made applicable to offenses committed on or after July 1, 1988, and prior to September 20, 1991. (2) It is the intent of the general assembly that this part 13 is independent from former section 16-11-103, C.R.S., now section 18-1.3-1201, and that if any provision of this part 13 or the application thereof to any person or circumstance is held to be invalid or unconstitutional, such invalidity or unconstitutionality shall not affect the application of section 18-1.3-1201 to any offense committed on or after September 20, 1991.

18-1.3-1302. Imposition of sentences in class 1 felonies for crimes committed on or after July 1, 1988, and prior to September 20, 1991 - appellate review. (1) (a) Upon conviction of guilt of a defendant of a class 1 felony, the trial court shall conduct a separate sentencing hearing to determine whether the defendant should be sentenced to death or life imprisonment, unless the defendant was under the age of eighteen years at the time of the commission of the offense, in which case the defendant shall be sentenced to life imprisonment. The hearing shall be conducted by the trial judge before the trial jury as soon as practicable. Alternate jurors shall not be excused from the case prior to submission of the issue of guilt to the trial jury and shall remain separately sequestered until a verdict is entered by the trial jury. If the verdict of the trial jury is that the defendant is guilty of a class 1 felony, the alternate jurors shall sit as alternate jurors on the issue of punishment. If, for any reason satisfactory to the court, any member or members of the trial jury are excused from participation in the sentencing hearing, the trial judge shall replace such juror or jurors with an alternate juror or jurors. If a trial jury was waived or if the defendant pleaded guilty, the hearing shall be conducted before the trial judge.
All admissible evidence presented by either the prosecuting attorney or the defendant that the court deems relevant to the nature of the crime, and the character, background, and history of the defendant, including any evidence presented in the guilt phase of the trial, and any matters relating to any of the aggravating or mitigating factors enumerated in subsections (4) and (5) of this section may be presented. Any such evidence which the court deems to have probative value may be received, as long as each party is given an opportunity to rebut such evidence. The prosecuting attorney and the defendant or the defendant's counsel shall be permitted to present arguments for or against a sentence of death. For offenses committed before July 1, 1985, the jury shall be instructed that life imprisonment means life without the possibility of parole for twenty calendar years. For offenses committed on or after July 1, 1985, the jury shall be instructed that life imprisonment means life without the possibility of parole for forty calendar years.
Both the prosecuting attorney and the defense shall notify each other of the names and addresses of any witnesses to be called in the sentencing hearing and the subject matter of such testimony. Such discovery shall be provided within a reasonable amount of time as determined by order of the court and shall be provided not less than twenty-four hours prior to the commencement of the sentencing hearing. Unless good cause is shown, noncompliance with this paragraph (c) shall result in the exclusion of such evidence without further sanction.
The burden of proof as to the aggravating factors enumerated in subsection (5) of this

section shall be beyond a reasonable doubt. There shall be no burden of proof as to proving or disproving mitigating factors.
(a) After hearing all the evidence and arguments of the prosecuting attorney and the defendant, the jury shall deliberate and render a verdict based upon the following considerations:
Whether at least one aggravating factor has been proved as enumerated in subsection (5) of this section;
Whether sufficient mitigating factors exist which outweigh any aggravating factor or factors found to exist; and
Based on the considerations in subparagraphs (I) and (II) of this paragraph (a), whether the defendant should be sentenced to death or life imprisonment.
(I) In the event that no aggravating factors are found to exist as enumerated in subsection
of this section, the jury shall render a verdict of life imprisonment, and the court shall sentence the defendant to life imprisonment.
(II) The jury shall not render a verdict of death unless it finds and specifies in writing that:
At least one aggravating factor has been proved; and
There are insufficient mitigating factors to outweigh the aggravating factor or factors that were proved.
In the event that the jury's verdict is to sentence to death, such verdict shall be unanimous and shall be binding upon the court unless the court determines, and sets forth in writing the basis and reasons for such determination, that the verdict of the jury is clearly erroneous as contrary to the weight of the evidence, in which case the court shall sentence the defendant to life imprisonment.
If the jury's verdict is not unanimous, the jury shall be discharged, and the court shall sentence the defendant to life imprisonment.
In all cases where the sentencing hearing is held before the court alone, the court shall determine whether the defendant should be sentenced to death or life imprisonment in the same manner in which a jury determines its verdict under paragraphs (a) and (b) of subsection (2) of this section. The sentence of the court shall be supported by specific written findings of fact based upon the circumstances as set forth in subsections (4) and (5) of this section and upon the records of the trial and the sentencing hearing.
For purposes of this section, mitigating factors shall be the following factors:
The age of the defendant at the time of the crime; or
The defendant's capacity to appreciate wrongfulness of the defendant's conduct or to conform the defendant's conduct to the requirements of law was significantly impaired, but not so impaired as to constitute a defense to prosecution; or
The defendant was under unusual and substantial duress, although not such duress as to constitute a defense to prosecution; or
The defendant was a principal in the offense which was committed by another, but the defendant's participation was relatively minor, although not so minor as to constitute a defense to prosecution; or
The defendant could not reasonably have foreseen that the defendant's conduct in the course of the commission of the offense for which the defendant was convicted would cause, or would create a grave risk of causing, death to another person; or
The emotional state of the defendant at the time the crime was committed; or

The absence of any significant prior conviction; or
The extent of the defendant's cooperation with law enforcement officers or agencies and with the office of the prosecuting district attorney; or
The influence of drugs or alcohol; or
The good faith, although mistaken, belief by the defendant that circumstances existed which constituted a moral justification for the defendant's conduct; or
The defendant is not a continuing threat to society; or
Any other evidence which in the court's opinion bears on the question of mitigation.
For purposes of this section, aggravating factors shall be the following factors:

The class 1 felony was committed by a person under sentence of imprisonment for a class 1, 2, or 3 felony as defined by Colorado law or United States law, or for a crime committed against another state or the United States which would constitute a class 1, 2, or 3 felony as defined by Colorado law; or
The defendant was previously convicted in this state of a class 1 or 2 felony involving violence as specified in section 18-1.3-406, or was previously convicted by another state or the United States of an offense which would constitute a class 1 or 2 felony involving violence as defined by Colorado law in section 18-1.3-406; or
The defendant intentionally killed any of the following persons while such person was engaged in the course of the performance of such person's official duties, and the defendant knew or reasonably should have known that such victim was such a person engaged in the performance of such

person's official duties, or the victim was intentionally killed in retaliation for the performance of the victim's official duties:

A peace officer or former peace officer as described in section 16-2.5-101, C.R.S.; or

A firefighter as defined in section 24-33.5-1202 (4), C.R.S.; or

A judge, referee, or former judge or referee of any court of record in the state or federal system or in any other state court system or a judge or former judge in any municipal court in this state or in any other state. For purposes of this subparagraph (III), the term "referee" shall include a hearing officer or any other officer who exercises judicial functions.

An elected state, county, or municipal official; or

A federal law enforcement officer or agent or former federal law enforcement officer or agent; or

The defendant intentionally killed a person kidnapped or being held as a hostage by the defendant or by anyone associated with the defendant; or

The defendant has been a party to an agreement to kill another person in furtherance of which a person has been intentionally killed; or

The defendant committed the offense while lying in wait, from ambush, or by use of an explosive or incendiary device. As used in this paragraph (f), "explosive or incendiary device" means:

Dynamite and all other forms of high explosives; or

Any explosive bomb, grenade, missile, or similar device; or

Any incendiary bomb or grenade, fire bomb, or similar device, including any device which consists of or includes a breakable container including a flammable liquid or compound, and

a wick composed of any material which, when ignited, is capable of igniting such flammable liquid or compound, and can be carried or thrown by one individual acting alone.

The defendant committed or attempted to commit a class 1, 2, or 3 felony and, in the course of or in furtherance of such or immediate flight therefrom, the defendant intentionally caused the death of a person other than one of the participants; or

The class 1 felony was committed for pecuniary gain; or

In the commission of the offense, the defendant knowingly created a grave risk of death to another person in addition to the victim of the offense; or

The defendant committed the offense in an especially heinous, cruel, or depraved manner;

or

The class 1 felony was committed for the purpose of avoiding or preventing a lawful

arrest or prosecution or effecting an escape from custody. This factor shall include the intentional killing of a witness to a criminal offense.

(a) Whenever a sentence of death is imposed upon a person pursuant to the provisions of this section, the supreme court shall review the propriety of that sentence, having regard to the nature of the offense, the character and record of the offender, the public interest, and the manner in which the sentence was imposed, including the sufficiency and accuracy of the information on which it was based. The procedures to be employed in the review shall be as provided by supreme court rule. The supreme court shall combine its review pursuant to this subsection (6) with consideration of any appeal that may be filed pursuant to part 2 of article 12 of title 16, C.R.S.

(b) A sentence of death shall not be imposed pursuant to this section if the supreme court determines that the sentence was imposed under the influence of passion or prejudice or any other arbitrary factor or that the evidence presented does not support the finding of statutory aggravating circumstances.

(a) If any provision of this section or the application thereof to any person or circumstances is held invalid or unconstitutional, such invalidity or unconstitutionality shall not affect other provisions or applications of this section, which can be given effect without the invalid or unconstitutional provision or application, and to this end the provisions of this section are declared to be severable.

If any death sentence imposed upon a defendant pursuant to the provisions of this section and the imposition of such death sentence upon such defendant is held invalid or unconstitutional, said defendant shall be returned to the trial court and shall then be sentenced to life imprisonment.

PART 14

COMPETENCY OF PERSONS TO BE EXECUTED

18-1.3-1401. Definitions. As used in this part 14, unless the context otherwise requires:

"Colorado mental health institute" means the Colorado mental health institute at Pueblo.

"Mentally incompetent to be executed" means that, due to a mental disease or defect, a person who has been sentenced to death is presently unaware that he or she is to be punished for the

crime of murder or that the impending punishment for that crime is death.

18-1.3-1402. Mental competency to be executed - presumptions. (1) A person who is sentenced to death shall not be executed so long as the person is mentally incompetent to be executed.

(2) Any convicted person who is sentenced to death is presumed mentally competent to be executed. A convicted person may be found mentally incompetent to be executed only on clear and convincing evidence of such condition. The party asserting that the convicted person is mentally incompetent to be executed bears the burden of proof regarding such condition and the burden of producing evidence of such condition.

18-1.3-1403. Mental incompetency to be executed - filing of motion. (1) (a) If, after a sentence of death is imposed, the executive director of the department of corrections, the convicted person's attorney, or an attorney for the state has a good faith reason to believe that the convicted person may be mentally incompetent to be executed, the executive director, the convicted person's attorney, or the state attorney may file a motion raising the issue of whether the convicted person is mentally incompetent to be executed. The motion shall be filed in the district court in the judicial district in which the convicted person was sentenced and shall be directed to the judge who presided over the convicted person's sentencing hearing. If that judge is unavailable, the chief judge of the same judicial district shall decide the motion. The motion shall be filed in both the district court clerk's office and the office of the judge who will hear the motion. On the same day the motion and accompanying materials are filed with the court, the motion and all accompanying materials shall be served upon the office of the prosecuting attorney who tried the case and the attorney general's office.

(b) If the judge who presided at the sentencing hearing has a good faith reason to believe that the convicted person may be mentally incompetent to be executed, the judge shall so advise the convicted person's attorney or shall appoint an attorney to investigate the issue and file any motions the attorney deems appropriate under this part 14.

(2) (a) A motion filed pursuant to subsection (1) of this section shall set forth the facts relating to the convicted person's conviction and sentence and

73

the facts giving rise to the belief that the convicted person may be mentally incompetent to be executed and shall request the district court to order that the convicted person be examined for mental incompetency to be executed. The motion shall be accompanied by the names and addresses of any mental health experts who have examined the convicted person with respect to the issue of whether the convicted person is mentally incompetent to be executed and the results of those examinations, as well as any records of any other mental health examinations, treatment, or reports that are not privileged and are available to the moving party or in the moving party's possession. If the moving party has any question regarding whether any such report is privileged, the report shall be submitted to the court ex parte and the court shall make a determination as to release of the report. If the moving party is the convicted person's attorney, the convicted person shall be deemed to have waived any claim of confidentiality or privilege as to communications made by the convicted person to any physician, psychiatrist, or

psychologist in the course of examination or treatment for any mental health condition for which the convicted person has received treatment, and the moving party shall include any records of any other mental health examinations, treatment, or reports.

(b) On receipt of a motion raising the issue of whether a convicted person is mentally incompetent to be executed, the clerk of the district court shall transmit copies of the motion to the supreme court. The clerk of the district court shall transmit copies of all subsequent filings to the supreme court as they are received.


18-1.3-1404. Mental incompetency to be executed - examination. (1) (a) On receipt of a motion filed pursuant to section 18-1.3-1403, the district court shall determine whether the motion is timely, as prescribed by section 18-1.3-1405, and whether it presents reasonable grounds for ordering an examination. Prior to making any determinations, the district court shall ensure that the prosecution has an opportunity to respond to the motion and to submit any additional information for consideration. The district court shall also provide an opportunity for the executive director of the department of corrections, the convicted person's attorney, or an attorney for the state to respond to the motion and to submit additional information for consideration. All responses and additional submissions shall be filed with the court within three days following the filing of the motion. Within seven days following the filing of the motion, the district court shall determine whether there are reasonable grounds for ordering the examination, based on the motion and any supporting information, any information submitted by the prosecuting attorney or any other responding party, and the record in the case, including transcripts of previous hearings and orders.

(b) The district court shall issue a stay of execution upon a showing of reasonable grounds for granting the stay. A stay of execution may be requested only by the convicted person's attorney, the executive director of the department of corrections, or an attorney for the state.

(a) If the court finds there are no reasonable grounds for the requested examination, the court shall dismiss the motion. If the court finds the motion is timely and there are reasonable grounds for ordering an examination, the court may order the convicted person to submit to physical, neurological, psychiatric, psychological, or other examinations or evaluations that are reasonably necessary to adequately determine whether the convicted person is mentally incompetent to be executed.

The Colorado mental health institute shall create and maintain a list of licensed, qualified psychiatrists and psychologists who shall be available to perform the examinations required pursuant to this part 14.

If the court determines an examination is necessary, the court shall appoint one or more licensed psychiatrists to observe and examine the convicted person. In making such appointment, the court may select one or more licensed psychiatrists from the list prepared by the Colorado mental health institute pursuant to paragraph (b) of this subsection (2) or appoint another qualified, licensed psychiatrist. If requested in the motion for competency examination or by motion of the executive director of the department of corrections, the prosecution, or the attorney for the convicted person or by request of the appointed psychiatrist, and for good cause shown, the court may order further examinations, including the services of licensed psychologists, licensed physicians, or psychiatrists. All examinations shall be completed and reports filed with the court within thirty-five days following the court's initial appointment of experts.

(a) Any examination ordered pursuant to this section shall be conducted at a department of corrections facility.

(b) At the time of appointment of experts, the parties shall disclose to the appointed experts and to each other the names and addresses of any other previously undisclosed mental health experts who have examined the convicted person and the results of the examinations, as well as any and all records of any other previously undisclosed mental health examinations, treatment, or reports that are not privileged. If the party has any question regarding whether any such records are privileged, the records shall be submitted to the court ex parte and the court shall make a determination as to release of the record. The appointed experts shall make copies of their reports available to all of the parties at the time of filing the reports with the court. The experts' reports shall indicate whether the convicted person has a mental disease or defect which renders the convicted person mentally incompetent to be executed.

The convicted person shall submit to and cooperate in all examinations or evaluations ordered by the court, regardless of which party selects the examining mental health expert. The district court shall consider any relevant evidence concerning the issue of the convicted person's competency to be executed, including but not limited to the convicted person's refusal to be examined or evaluated.

(a) After the examinations are completed and reports are filed, the court shall conduct a hearing within seven days following the court's receipt of all reports from appointed experts. The hearing shall be limited to the sole issue of whether the convicted person is mentally incompetent to be executed. At the hearing, all parties may present evidence, cross-examine witnesses, and present argument or, by stipulation, may submit the matter for the court's determination on the basis of the experts' reports or other evidence.

(b) The Colorado rules of evidence shall apply to each hearing held pursuant to this section. The transcript of the hearing shall be forwarded to the Colorado supreme court within three days following the conclusion of the hearing.

(a) Within three days following the conclusion of the hearing held pursuant to subsection

of this section, the district court, either on the record or by written ruling, shall specifically state its findings on the motion raising the issue of whether the convicted person is mentally incompetent to be executed. If the ruling is in written form, it shall be transmitted by facsimile or electronic mail to all parties and the Colorado supreme court on the same day of its issuance.

If the court finds the convicted person is not mentally incompetent to be executed, the court shall immediately remand the convicted person to the custody of the executive director of the department of corrections who shall execute the judgment as specified in the warrant issued pursuant to section 18-1.3-1205. If the week specified in the warrant has passed, the district court shall issue a new warrant designating a week of time within which the sentence shall be executed.

If the court finds the convicted person is mentally incompetent to be executed, the court shall stay the execution and shall immediately transmit a copy of its order to the Colorado supreme court.

The time frames specified in this section shall apply only if the motion filed pursuant to section 18-1.3-1403 is filed within one hundred nineteen days prior to the convicted person's execution date. In all other cases, the court shall establish time frames for filing of responses and additional submissions and for completion of the examinations and shall hear and rule on the motion as expeditiously as possible.


18-1.3-1405. Mentally incompetent to be executed - untimely or successive motions. (1) A motion raising the issue of whether a convicted person is mentally incompetent to be executed that is filed pursuant to section 18-1.3-1404 fewer than thirty-five days before the scheduled execution is untimely and shall not be considered by the court unless it is accompanied by both of the following:

At least one affidavit from a licensed physician, licensed psychiatrist, or licensed psychologist who has examined the convicted person that states the physician's, psychiatrist's, or psychologist's opinion that the convicted person is mentally incompetent to be executed; and

A statement that establishes good cause for the failure to file the motion in a timely manner.

(2) (a) Except as provided in paragraph (b) of this subsection (2), if the court has determined, pursuant to section 18-1.3-1404 or 18-1.3-1406 (3), that a convicted person is not mentally incompetent to be executed, no further consideration of the convicted person's mental incompetence to be executed may be granted by the court.

(b) A successive motion raising the issue of whether a convicted person is mentally incompetent to be executed maybe filed onlyif the successive motion is accompanied by an affidavit from a licensed physician, licensed psychiatrist, or licensed psychologist who has examined the convicted person that shows a substantial change of circumstances since the previous motion was denied or the prior determination of restoration to competency to be executed was made and the showing is sufficient to raise a significant question regarding whether the convicted person is mentally incompetent to be executed.

18-1.3-1406. Persons mentally incompetent to be executed - restoration to competency. (1) The court may order a restoration hearing at any time on its own motion, on motion of an attorney for the state, or on motion of the convicted person's attorney. The court shall order a hearing if the executive director of the department of corrections files a report that the convicted person is no longer mentally incompetent to be executed.

At the hearing, if the question is contested, the burden of submitting evidence and the burden of proof by clear and convincing evidence shall be upon the party asserting that the convicted person is mentally competent to be executed.

At the hearing, the court shall determine whether the convicted person is mentally competent to be executed and, if so, shall order that the execution be conducted according to the original warrant issued pursuant to section 18-1.3-1205, if unexpired, or shall issue a new warrant appointing a time for execution of the judgment.

18-1.3-1407. Appeal of determination of mental incompetency to be executed. (1) Within seven days after the district court rules on a motion raising the issue of

whether a convicted person is mentally incompetent to be executed filed pursuant to this part 14, a party may file with the Colorado supreme court a petition to obtain a review of the district court's decision and requesting a stay of execution pending the review.

(2) The supreme court shall expedite its review of the district court's decision and, if the designated week of execution in an existing warrant of conviction has not passed, shall not take more than seven days to render its decision.

## ARTICLE 1.4  Class 1 Felonies Committed - July 1, 1995, through July 12, 2002

18-1.4-101. Applicability of procedure for the imposition of sentences in class 1 felony cases. (1) It is the expressed intention of the general assembly that there be no hiatus in the imposition of the death penalty as a sentence for the commission of a class 1 felony in the state of Colorado as a result of the holding of the United States supreme court in Ring v. Arizona, 536 U.S. 584 (2002). Toward that end, the provisions of section 16-11-103, C.R.S., as it existed prior to the passage of Senate Bill 95-54, enacted at the first regular session of the sixtieth general assembly, are reenacted as section 18-1.4-102, and are hereby made applicable to offenses committed on or after July 1, 1995, and prior to July 12, 2002.

It is the expressed intention of the general assembly that the adoption of section 18-1.4- 102 shall not be construed by any court as a legislative statement that the provisions of Senate Bill 95-54, enacted at the first regular session of the sixtieth general assembly, are unconstitutional in any way or that any death sentence obtained pursuant to the provisions of Senate Bill 95-54, enacted at the first regular session of the sixtieth general assembly, is invalid in any way.

It is the expressed intention of the general assembly that this article is independent from section 16-11-103, C.R.S., as it existed prior to October 1, 2002, and section 18-1.3-1201 and that, if any provision of this article or the application thereof to any person or circumstances is held invalid or unconstitutional, such invalidity or unconstitutionality shall not affect the application of section 16-11-103, C.R.S., as it existed prior to October 1, 2002, and section 18-1.3-1201 to any offense committed on or after the effective date of amendments to said sections enacted at the third extraordinary session of the sixty-third general assembly.

18-1.4-102. Imposition of sentence in class 1 felonies for crimes committed on or after July 1, 1995, and prior to July 12, 2002 - appellate review. (1) (a) Upon conviction of guilt of a defendant of a class 1 felony, the trial court shall conduct a separate sentencing hearing to determine whether the defendant should be sentenced to death or life imprisonment, unless the defendant was under the age of eighteen years at the time of the commission of the offense, or unless

the defendant has been determined to be a mentally retarded defendant pursuant to part 4 of article 9 of title 16, C.R.S., as it existed prior to October 1, 2002, in either of which cases, the defendant shall be sentenced to life imprisonment. The hearing shall be conducted by the trial judge before the trial jury as soon as practicable. Alternate jurors shall not be excused from the case prior to submission of the issue of guilt to the trial jury and shall remain separatelysequestered until a verdict is entered by the trial jury. If the verdict of the trial jury is that the defendant is guilty of a class 1 felony, the alternate jurors shall sit as alternate jurors on the issue of punishment. If, for any reason satisfactory to the court, any member or members of the trial jury are excused from participation in the sentencing hearing, the trial judge shall replace such juror or jurors with an alternate juror or jurors. If a trial jury was waived or if the defendant pled guilty, the hearing shall be conducted before the trial judge. The court shall instruct the defendant when waiving his or her right to a jury trial or when pleading guilty, that he or she is also waiving his or her right to a jury determination of the sentence at the sentencing hearing.

All admissible evidence presented byeither the prosecuting attorneyor the defendant that the court deems relevant to the nature of the crime, and the character, background, and history of the defendant, including any evidence presented in the guilt phase of the trial, any matters relating to any of the aggravating or mitigating factors enumerated in subsections (4) and (5) of this section, and any matters relating to the personal characteristics of the victim and the impact of the crimes on the victim's family may be presented. Any such evidence, including but not limited to the testimony of members of the victim's immediate family, as defined in section 24-4.1-302 (6), C.R.S., which the court deems to have probative value may be received, as long as each party is given an opportunity to rebut such evidence. The prosecuting attorney and the defendant or the defendant's counsel shall be permitted to present arguments for or against a sentence of death. The jury shall be instructed that life imprisonment means imprisonment for life without the possibility of parole.

(Deleted by amendment, L. 2002, 3rd Ex. Sess., p. 24, § 14, effective July 12, 2002.)

The burden of proof as to the aggravating factors enumerated in subsection (5) of this section shall be beyond a reasonable doubt. There shall be no burden of proof as to proving or disproving mitigating factors.

If, as of July 12, 2002, the prosecution has announced it will be seeking the death sentence as the punishment for a conviction of a class 1 felony and a defendant has been convicted at trial of a class 1 felony or has pled guilty to a class 1 felony, but a sentencing hearing to determine whether that defendant shall be sentenced to death or life imprisonment has not yet been held, a jury shall be impaneled to determine the sentence at the sentencing hearing pursuant to the procedures set forth in this section or, if the defendant pled guilty or waived the right to jury sentencing, the sentence shall be determined by the trial judge.

(a) After hearing all the evidence and arguments of the prosecuting attorney and the defendant, the jury shall deliberate and render a verdict based upon the following considerations:

Whether at least one aggravating factor has been proved as enumerated in subsection (5) of this section;

Whether sufficient mitigating factors exist which outweigh any aggravating factor or factors found to exist; and

Based on the considerations in subparagraphs (I) and (II) of this paragraph (a), whether the defendant should be sentenced to death or life imprisonment.

(I) In the event that no aggravating factors are found to exist as enumerated in subsection

of this section, the jury shall render a verdict of life imprisonment, and the court shall sentence the defendant to life imprisonment.

(II) The jury shall not render a verdict of death unless it finds and specifies in writing that:

At least one aggravating factor has been proved; and

There are insufficient mitigating factors to outweigh the aggravating factor or factors that were proved.

In the event that the jury's verdict is to sentence to death, such verdict shall be unanimous and shall be binding upon the court unless the court determines, and sets forth in writing the basis and reasons for such determination, that the verdict of the jury is clearly erroneous as contrary to the weight of the evidence, in which case the court shall sentence the defendant to life imprisonment.

If the jury's verdict is not unanimous, the jury shall be discharged, and the court shall sentence the defendant to life imprisonment.

In all cases where the sentencing hearing is held before the court alone, the court shall determine whether the defendant should be sentenced to death or life imprisonment in the same manner in which a jury determines its verdict under paragraphs (a) and (b) of subsection (2) of this section. The sentence of the court shall be supported by specific written findings of fact based upon the circumstances as set forth in subsections (4) and (5) of this section and upon the records of the trial and the sentencing hearing.

(3.5) (a) The provisions of this subsection (3.5) shall apply only in a class 1 felony case in which the prosecuting attorney has filed a statement of intent to seek the death penalty pursuant to rule 32.1 (b) of the Colorado rules of criminal procedure.

The prosecuting attorney shall provide the defendant with the following information and materials not later than twenty-one days after the prosecution files its written intention to seek the death penalty or within such other time frame as the supreme court may establish by rule; except that any reports, recorded statements, and notes, including results of physical or mental examinations and scientific tests, experiments, or comparisons, of any expert whom the prosecuting attorney intends to call as a witness at the sentencing hearing shall be provided to the defense as soon as practicable but not later than sixty-three days before trial:

A list of all aggravating factors that are known to the prosecuting attorney at that time and that the prosecuting attorney intends to prove at the sentencing hearing;

A list of all witnesses whom the prosecuting attorney may call at the sentencing hearing, specifying for each the witness' name, address, and date of birth and the subject matter of the witness' testimony;

The written and recorded statements, including any notes of those statements, for each witness whom the prosecuting attorney may call at the sentencing hearing;

A list of books, papers, documents, photographs, or tangible objects that the prosecuting attorney may introduce at the sentencing hearing; and

All material or information that tends to mitigate or negate the finding of any of the aggravating factors the prosecuting attorney intends to prove at the sentencing hearing.

Upon receipt of the information required to be disclosed by the defendant pursuant to paragraph (d) of this subsection (3.5), the prosecuting attorney shall notify the defendant as soon as practicable of any additional witnesses whom the prosecuting attorney intends to call in response to

the defendant's disclosures.

The defendant shall provide the prosecuting attorney with the following information and materials no later than thirty-five days before the first trial date set for the beginning of the defendant's trial or within such other time frame as the supreme court may establish by rule; however, any reports, recorded statements, and notes, including results of physical or mental examinations and scientific tests, experiments, or comparisons, of any expert whom the defense intends to call as a witness at the sentencing hearing shall be provided to the prosecuting attorney as soon as practicable but not later than thirty-five days before trial:

A list of all witnesses whom the defendant may call at the sentencing hearing, specifying for each the witness' name, address, and date of birth and the subject matter of the witness' testimony;

The written and recorded statements, including any notes of those statements, of each witness whom the defendant may call at the sentencing hearing; and

A list of books, papers, documents, photographs, or tangible objects that the defendant may introduce at the sentencing hearing.

(I) Any material subject to this subsection (3.5) that the defendant believes contains information that is privileged to the extent that the prosecution cannot be aware of it in connection with its preparation for, or conduct of, the trial to determine guilt on the substantive charges against the defendant shall be submitted by the defendant to the trial judge under seal no later than forty-nine days before trial.

(II) The trial judge shall review any such material submitted under seal pursuant to subparagraph (I) of this paragraph (e) to determine whether it is in fact privileged. Any material the trial judge finds not to be privileged shall be provided forthwith to the prosecuting attorney. Any material submitted under seal that the trial judge finds to be privileged shall be provided forthwith to the prosecution if the defendant is convicted of a class 1 felony.

(I) Except as otherwise provided in subparagraph (II) of this paragraph (f), if the witnesses disclosed by the defendant pursuant to paragraph (d) of this subsection (3.5) include witnesses who may provide evidence concerning the defendant's mental condition at the sentencing hearing conducted pursuant to this section, the trial court, at the request of the prosecuting attorney, shall order that the defendant be examined and a report of said examination be prepared pursuant to section 16-8-106, C.R.S.

(II) The court shall not order an examination pursuant to subparagraph (I) of this paragraph

if:

Such an examination was previously performed and a report was prepared in the same

case; and

The report included an opinion concerning how any mental disease or defect of the defendant or condition of mind caused by mental disease or defect of the defendant affects the mitigating factors that the defendant may raise at the sentencing hearing held pursuant to this section.

If the witnesses disclosed by the defendant pursuant to paragraph (d) of this subsection (3.5) include witnesses who may provide evidence concerning the defendant's mental condition at a sentencing hearing conducted pursuant to this section, the provisions of section 16-8-109, C.R.S., concerning testimony of lay witnesses shall apply to said sentencing hearing.

There is a continuing duty on the part of the prosecuting attorney and the defendant to disclose the information and materials specified in this subsection (3.5). If, after complying with the duty to disclose the information and materials described in this subsection (3.5), either party discovers or obtains any additional information and materials that are subject to disclosure under this subsection (3.5), the party shall promptly notify the other party and provide the other party with complete access to the information and materials. The trial court, upon a showing of extraordinary circumstances that could not have been foreseen and prevented, may grant an extension of time to comply with the requirements of this subsection (3.5).

If it is brought to the attention of the court that either the prosecuting attorney or the defendant has failed to comply with the provisions of this subsection (3.5) or with an order issued pursuant to this subsection (3.5), the court may enter any order against such party that the court deems just under the circumstances, including but not limited to an order to permit the discovery or inspection of information and materials not previously disclosed, to grant a continuance, to prohibit the offending party from introducing the information and materials not disclosed, or to impose sanctions against the offending party.

For purposes of this section, mitigating factors shall be the following factors:

The age of the defendant at the time of the crime; or

The defendant's capacity to appreciate wrongfulness of the defendant's conduct or to conform the defendant's conduct to the requirements of law was significantly impaired, but not so impaired as to constitute a defense to prosecution; or

The defendant was under unusual and substantial duress, although not such duress as to constitute a defense to prosecution; or

The defendant was a principal in the offense which was committed by another, but the defendant's participation was relatively minor, although not so minor as to constitute a defense to prosecution; or

The defendant could not reasonably have foreseen that the defendant's conduct in the course of the commission of the offense for which the defendant was convicted would cause, or would create a grave risk of causing, death to another person; or

The emotional state of the defendant at the time the crime was committed; or

The absence of any significant prior conviction; or

The extent of the defendant's cooperation with law enforcement officers or agencies and with the office of the prosecuting district attorney; or

The influence of drugs or alcohol; or

The good faith, although mistaken, belief by the defendant that circumstances existed which constituted a moral justification for the defendant's conduct; or

The defendant is not a continuing threat to society; or

Any other evidence which in the court's opinion bears on the question of mitigation.

For purposes of this section, aggravating factors shall be the following factors:

The class 1 felony was committed by a person under sentence of imprisonment for a class 1, 2, or 3 felony as defined by Colorado law or United States law, or for a crime committed against another state or the United States which would constitute a class 1, 2, or 3 felony as defined by Colorado law; or

The defendant was previously convicted in this state of a class 1 or 2 felony involving violence as specified in section 16-11-309, C.R.S., as it existed prior to October 1, 2002, or section 18-1.3-406, or was previously convicted by another state or the United States of an offense which would constitute a class 1 or 2 felony involving violence as defined by Colorado law in section 16- 11-309, C.R.S., as it existed prior to October 1, 2002, or section 18-1.3-406; or

The defendant intentionally killed any of the following persons while such person was engaged in the course of the performance of such person's official duties, and the defendant knew or reasonably should have known that such victim was such a person engaged in the performance of such person's official duties, or the victim was intentionally killed in retaliation for the performance of the victim's official duties:

A peace officer or former peace officer as described in section 16-2.5-101, C.R.S.; or

A firefighter as defined in section 24-33.5-1202 (4), C.R.S.; or

A judge, referee, or former judge or referee of any court of record in the state or federal system or in any other state court system or a judge or former judge in any municipal court in this state or in any other state. For purposes of this subparagraph (III), the term "referee" shall include a hearing officer or any other officer who exercises judicial functions.

An elected state, county, or municipal official; or

A federal law enforcement officer or agent or former federal law enforcement officer or agent; or

The defendant intentionally killed a person kidnapped or being held as a hostage by the defendant or by anyone associated with the defendant; or

The defendant has been a party to an agreement to kill another person in furtherance of which a person has been intentionally killed; or

The defendant committed the offense while lying in wait, from ambush, or by use of an explosive or incendiary device. As used in this paragraph (f), "explosive or incendiary device" means:

Dynamite and all other forms of high explosives; or

Any explosive bomb, grenade, missile, or similar device; or

Any incendiary bomb or grenade, fire bomb, or similar device, including any device which consists of or includes a breakable container including a flammable liquid or compound, and a wick composed of any material which, when ignited, is capable of igniting such flammable liquid or compound, and can be carried or thrown by one individual acting alone.

The defendant committed a class 1, 2, or 3 felony and, in the course of or in furtherance of such or immediate flight therefrom, the defendant intentionally caused the death of a person other than one of the participants; or

The class 1 felony was committed for pecuniary gain; or

In the commission of the offense, the defendant knowingly created a grave risk of death to another person in addition to the victim of the offense; or

The defendant committed the offense in an especiallyheinous, cruel, or depraved manner;

or

The class 1 felony was committed for the purpose of avoiding or preventing a lawful

arrest or prosecution or effecting an escape from custody. This factor shall include the intentional killing of a witness to a criminal offense.

The defendant unlawfully and intentionally, knowingly, or with universal malice manifesting extreme indifference to the value of human life generally, killed two or more persons during the commission of the same criminal episode; or

The defendant intentionally killed a child who has not yet attained twelve years of age;

or

(I) The defendant committed the class 1 felony against the victim because of the victim's

race, color, ancestry, religion, or national origin.

(II) The provisions of this paragraph (n) shall apply to offenses committed on or after July 1, 1998.

(I) The defendant's possession of the weapon used to commit the class 1 felony constituted a felony offense under the laws of this state or the United States.

(II) The provisions of this paragraph (o) shall apply to offenses committed on or after August 2, 2000.

(a) Whenever a sentence of death is imposed upon a person pursuant to the provisions of this section, the supreme court shall review the propriety of that sentence, having regard to the nature of the offense, the character and record of the offender, the public interest, and the manner in which the sentence was imposed, including the sufficiency and accuracy of the information on which it was based. The procedures to be employed in the review shall be as provided by supreme court rule. The supreme court shall combine its review pursuant to this subsection (6) with consideration of any appeal that may be filed pursuant to part 2 of article 12 of title 16, C.R.S.

(b) A sentence of death shall not be imposed pursuant to this section if the supreme court determines that the sentence was imposed under the influence of passion or prejudice or any other arbitrary factor or that the evidence presented does not support the finding of statutory aggravating circumstances.

(a) It is the expressed intent of the general assembly that there be in place a valid and operative procedure for the imposition of a sentence of death concerning class 1 felonies committed on or after July 1, 1995, and prior to July 12, 2002. Towards that end, if any provisions of this section are determined by the United States supreme court or by the Colorado supreme court to render this section unconstitutional or invalid such that this section does not constitute a valid and operative death penalty statute concerning such class 1 felonies, but severance of such provisions would, through operation of the remaining provisions of this section, maintain this section as a valid and operative death penalty statute concerning such class 1 felonies, it is the intent of the general assembly that those remaining provisions are severable and are to have full force and effect. If, instead, any provisions of this section are determined by the United States supreme court or by the Colorado supreme court to render this section unconstitutional or invalid such that this section does not constitute a valid and operative death penalty statute concerning such class 1 felonies, and severance of such provisions would not, through operation of the remaining provisions of this section, render this section a valid and operative death penalty statute concerning such offenses, it is the intent of the general assembly that this entire article be void and inoperative.

(b) If any death sentence is imposed upon a defendant pursuant to the provisions of this section and, on appellate review including consideration pursuant to subsection (9) of this section, the imposition of such death sentence upon such defendant is held invalid for reasons other than unconstitutionality of the death penalty or insufficiency of the evidence to support the sentence, the

case shall be remanded to the trial court to set a new sentencing hearing before a newly impaneled jury or, if the defendant pled guilty or waived the right to jury sentencing, before the trial judge; except that, if the prosecutor informs the trial court that, in the opinion of the prosecutor, capital punishment would no longer be in the interest of justice, said defendant shall be returned to the trial court and shall then be sentenced to life imprisonment. If a death sentence imposed pursuant to this section is held invalid based on unconstitutionality of the death penalty or insufficiency of the evidence to support the sentence, said defendant shall be returned to the trial court and shall then be sentenced to life imprisonment.

When reviewing a sentence of death imposed by a three-judge panel, if the Colorado supreme court concludes that any one or more of the determinations made by the three-judge panel were constitutionally required to have been made by a jury, the supreme court may:

Examine the record and the jury's verdicts or the defendant's guilty pleas at the guilt phase of the trial and determine whether any of the aggravating factors found to exist by the three- judge panel were also fairly determined to exist beyond a reasonable doubt by the jury's verdicts or the defendant's guilty pleas; and

(I) If the supreme court determines that one or more aggravating factors were fairly determined to exist beyond a reasonable doubt by the jury's verdicts or the defendant's guilty pleas, the supreme court shall determine whether the sentence of death should be affirmed on appeal by proceeding in accordance with the provisions of paragraphs (a) to (d) of subsection (9) of this section; or

(II) If the supreme court determines there were no aggravating factors fairly determined to exist beyond a reasonable doubt by the jury's verdicts or the defendant's guilty pleas, the supreme court shall remand the case to the trial court for a sentencing hearing before a newly impaneled jury.

If, on appeal, the supreme court finds one or more of the aggravating factors that were found to support a sentence to death to be invalid for any reason, the supreme court may determine whether the sentence of death should be affirmed on appeal by:

Reweighing the remaining aggravating factor or factors and all mitigating factors and then determining whether death is the appropriate punishment in the case; or

Applying harmless error analysis by considering whether, if the sentencing body had not considered the invalid aggravating factor, it would have nonetheless sentenced the defendant to death; or

If the supreme court finds the sentencing body's consideration of an aggravating factor was improper because the aggravating factor was not given a constitutionally narrow construction, determining whether, beyond a reasonable doubt, the sentencing body would have returned a verdict of death had the aggravating factor been properly narrowed; or

Employing any other constitutionally permissible method of review.

### ARTICLE 1.5   Criminal Justice Commission

18-1.5-101 to 18-1.5-105.  (Repealed)

### ARTICLE 1.7   Treatment of Persons with Mental Illness Involved in the Criminal Justice System

18-1.7-101 to 18-1.7-106. (Repealed)

### ARTICLE 1.8   Interagency Task Force on Trafficking in Persons

18-1.8-101.  (Repealed)

### ARTICLE 1.9   Continuing Examination of the Treatment of Persons with Mental Illness Who are Involved in the Justice System

18-1.9-101. Legislative declaration. (1)  The general assembly hereby finds that:

In November of 1998, the Colorado department of corrections reported that ten percent of its correctional population met the diagnostic criteria for serious mental illness, which number was double the number identified two years earlier, and five to six times the number documented in 1988, only ten years earlier;

The Colorado department of corrections estimates that in 2002, sixteen percent of its inmate population met the diagnostic criteria for major mental illness;

The Colorado division of youth corrections estimates that twenty-four percent of juveniles in the juvenile justice system are diagnosed with mental illness;

A study conducted in 1995 found that approximately six percent of the persons held in county jails and in community corrections throughout the state had been diagnosed as persons with serious mental illness;

It is estimated that nationally, nearly nine percent of all adults and juveniles on probation have been identified as having serious mental illness;

For the 1998-99 fiscal year, approximately forty-four percent of the inpatient population at the Colorado mental health institute at Pueblo had been committed following the return of a verdict of not guilty by reason of insanity or a determination by the court that the person was incompetent to stand trial due to mental illness;

Persons with mental illness, as a direct or indirect result of their condition, are in many instances more likely than persons who do not have mental illness to be involved in the criminal and juvenile justice systems;

The existing procedures and diagnostic tools used bypersons working in the criminal and juvenile justice systems may not be sufficient to identify appropriately and diagnose persons with mental illness who are involved in the criminal and juvenile justice systems;

The criminal and juvenile justice systems may not be structured in such a manner as to provide the level of treatment and care for persons with mental illness that is necessary to ensure the safety of these persons, of other persons in the criminal and juvenile justice systems, and of the community at large;

Studies show that, for offenders under community supervision, treatment of the mental illness of the offender decreases repeat arrests by forty-four percent; and

The ongoing supervision, care, and monitoring, especially with regard to medication, of persons with mental illness who are released from incarceration are crucial to ensuring the safety of the community.

The general assembly further finds that pursuant to the findings in a report requested by the joint budget committee in 1999 that recommended cross-system collaboration and communication as a method for reducing the number of persons with mental illness who are involved in the criminal and juvenile justice systems, the legislative oversight committee and advisory task force for the examination of the treatment of persons with mental illness who are involved in the criminal justice system were created in 1999 and extended for an additional three years in 2000. Over the course of four years, the legislative oversight committee and advisorytask force began to address, but did not finish addressing, the issues specified in subsection (1) of this section, through both legislative and non-legislative solutions including, but not limited to:

Community-based intensive treatment management programs for juveniles involved in the juvenile justice system;

An expedited application process for aid to the needy disabled benefits for persons with mental illness upon release from incarceration;

Standardized inter-agency screening to detect mental illness in adults who are involved in the criminal justice system and juveniles who are involved in the juvenile justice system;

Training of law enforcement officers to recognize and safely deal with persons who have mental illness through the use of crisis intervention teams; and

Creating local initiative committee pilot programs for the management of community-
based programs for adults with mental illness who are involved in the criminal justice system.

Experts involved in cross-system collaboration and communication to reduce the number of persons with mental illness who are involved in the criminal and juvenile justice systems recommend a five-year plan to continue the work of the task force and the legislative oversight committee in order to more fully effectuate solutions to these issues.

Therefore, the general assembly declares that it is necessary to create a task force to continue to examine the identification, diagnosis, and treatment of persons with mental illness who are involved in the state criminal and juvenile justice systems and to make additional recommendations to a legislative oversight committee for the continuing development of legislative proposals related to this issue.

18-1.9-102. Definitions. As used in this article, unless the context otherwise requires:

"Committee" means the legislative oversight committee established pursuant to section 18-1.9-103.

(1.5) "Co-occurring disorder" means a disorder that commonlycoincides with mental illness and may include, but is not limited to, substance abuse, developmental disability, fetal alcohol syndrome, and traumatic brain injury.

"Task force" means the task force concerning the treatment of persons with mental illness in the criminal and juvenile justice systems established pursuant to section 18-1.9-104.

18-1.9-103. Legislative oversight committee concerning the treatment of persons with mental illness in the criminal and juvenile justice systems - creation - duties. (1) Creation.

There is hereby created a legislative oversight committee concerning the treatment of persons with mental illness in the criminal and juvenile justice systems.

The committee shall consist of six members. The president of the senate, the minority leader of the senate, and the speaker of the house of representatives shall appoint the members of the committee, as follows:

The president of the senate shall appoint two senators to serve on the committee, and the minority leader of the senate shall appoint one senator to serve on the committee;

The speaker of the house of representatives shall appoint three representatives to serve on the committee, no more than two of whom shall be members of the same political party;

The terms of the members appointed by the speaker of the house of representatives, the president of the senate, and the minority leader of the senate and who are serving on March 22, 2007, shall be extended to and expire on or shall terminate on the convening date of the first regular session of the sixty-seventh general assembly. As soon as practicable after such convening date, the speaker, the president, and the minority leader of the senate shall each appoint or reappoint members in the same manner as provided in subparagraphs (I) and (II) of this paragraph (b). Thereafter, the terms of members appointed or reappointed by the speaker, the president, and the minority leader of the senate shall expire on the convening date of the first regular session of each general assembly, and all subsequent appointments and reappointments by the speaker, the president, and the minority

leader of the senate shall be made as soon as practicable after such convening date. The person making the original appointment or reappointment shall fill any vacancy by appointment for the remainder of an unexpired term. Members appointed or reappointed by the speaker, the president, and the minority leader of the senate shall serve at the pleasure of the appointing authority and shall continue in office until the member's successor is appointed.

The president of the senate shall select the first chair of the committee, and the speaker of the house of representatives shall select the first vice-chair. The chair and vice-chair shall alternate annually thereafter between the two houses. The chair and vice-chair of the committee may establish such organizational and procedural rules as are necessary for the operation of the committee.

(I) Members of the committee may receive payment of per diem and reimbursement for actual and necessary expenses authorized pursuant to section 2-2-307, C.R.S.

(II) The director of research of the legislative council and the director of the office of legislative legal services may supply staff assistance to the committee as they deem appropriate, within existing appropriations. If staff assistance is not available within existing appropriations, then the director of research of the legislative council and the director of the office of legislative legal services may supply staff assistance to the task force only if moneys are credited to the treatment of persons with mental illness in the criminal and juvenile justice systems cash fund created in section 18-1.9-106 in an amount sufficient to fund staff assistance.

(2) Duties. (a) Beginning in 2005 and continuing each year thereafter, the committee shall meet at least three times each year and at such other times as it deems necessary.

(I) The committee shall be responsible for the oversight of the task force and shall submit annual reports to the general assemblyregarding the findings and recommendations of the task force. In addition, the committee may recommend legislative changes that shall be treated as bills recommended by an interim legislative committee for purposes of any introduction deadlines or bill limitations imposed by the joint rules of the general assembly.

(II) The provisions of subparagraph (I) of this paragraph (b) shall not apply during the suspension of the committee during the 2010 interim.

(I) The committee shall submit a report to the general assembly by January 15, 2005, and by each January 15 thereafter. The annual reports must summarize the issues addressing the treatment of persons with mental illness who are involved in the criminal and juvenile justice systems that have been considered and recommended legislative proposals, if any.

(II) The general assembly reviewed the reporting requirements in subparagraph (I) of this paragraph (c) during the 2008 regular session and continued the requirements.

18-1.9-104. Task force concerning treatment of persons with mental illness in the criminal and juvenile justice systems - creation - membership - duties. (1) Creation. (a) There is hereby created a task force concerning treatment of persons with mental illness in the criminal and juvenile justice systems in Colorado. The task force shall consist of thirty-two members appointed as provided in paragraphs (b) and (c) of this subsection (1).

The chief justice of the Colorado supreme court shall appoint four members who represent the judicial department, two of whom shall represent the division of probation within the

department, one of whom shall have experience handling juvenile justice matters within the department, and one of whom shall have experience handling adult criminal justice matters within the department.

The chair and vice-chair of the committee shall appoint twenty-eight members as follows:

One member who represents the division of criminal justice within the department of public safety;

Two members who represent the department of corrections, one of whom represents the division of parole within the department;

Two members who represent local law enforcement agencies, one of whom shall be in active service and the other one of whom shall have experience dealing with juveniles in the juvenile justice system;

Five members who represent the department of human services, as follows:

One member who represents the unit within the department of human services that is responsible for mental health and drug and alcohol abuse services;

One member who represents the division of youth corrections;

One member who represents the unit within the department of human services that is responsible for child welfare services;

(Deleted by amendment, L. 2009, p. 140, § 3, effective August 5, 2009.)

One member who represents the Colorado mental health institute at Pueblo; and

One member who represents the mental health planning and advisory committee within the department of human services;

One member who represents the interests of county departments of social services;

One member who represents the department of education;

One member who represents the state attorney general's office;

One member who represents the district attorneys within the state;

Two members who represent the criminal defense bar within the state, one of whom shall have experience representing juveniles in the juvenile justice system;

Two members who are licensed mental health professionals practicing within the state, one of whom shall have experience treating juveniles;

One member who represents community mental health centers within the state;

One member who is a person with knowledge of public benefits and public housing within the state;

One member who is a practicing forensic professional within the state;

Three members of the public as follows:

One member who has mental illness and has been involved in the criminal justice system in this state;

One member who has an adult family member who has mental illness and has been involved in the criminal justice system in this state; and

One member who is the parent of a child who has mental illness and has been involved in the juvenile justice system in this state;

One member who represents the department of health care policy and financing;

One member who represents the department of labor and employment;

One member who represents the office of the child's representative; and

One member who represents the office of the alternate defense counsel.

A vacancy occurring in a position filled by the chief justice of the Colorado supreme court pursuant to paragraph (b) of this subsection (1) shall be filled as soon as possible by the chief justice of the Colorado supreme court in accordance with the limitations specified in paragraph (b) of this subsection (1). In addition, the chief justice of the Colorado supreme court may remove and replace any appointment to the task force made pursuant to paragraph (b) of this subsection (1).

A vacancy occurring in a position filled by the chair and vice-chair of the committee pursuant to paragraph (c) of this subsection (1) shall be filled as soon as possible by the chair and vice-chair of the committee in accordance with the limitations specified in paragraph (c) of this subsection (1). In addition, the chair and vice-chair of the committee may remove and replace any appointment to the task force made pursuant to paragraph (c) of this subsection (1).

In making appointments to the task force, the appointing authorities shall ensure that the membership of the task force reflects the ethnic, cultural, and gender diversity of the state and includes representation of all areas of the state.

Issues for study. The task force shall examine the identification, diagnosis, and treatment of persons with mental illness who are involved in the state criminal and juvenile justice systems, including an examination of liability, safety, and cost as they relate to these issues. The task force shall specifically consider, but need not be limited to, the following issues:

On or before July 1, 2005:

The diagnosis, treatment, and housing of juveniles with mental illness who are involved in the criminal justice system or the juvenile justice system; and

The adoption of a common framework for effectively addressing the mental health issues, including competency and co-occurring disorders, of juveniles who are involved in the criminal justice system or the juvenile justice system;

On or before July 1, 2006:

The prosecution of and sentencing alternatives for persons with mental illness that may involve treatment and ongoing supervision;

The civil commitment of persons with mental illness who have been criminally convicted, found not guilty by reason of insanity, or found to be incompetent to stand trial; and

The development of a plan to most effectively and collaboratively serve the population of juveniles involved in the criminal justice system or the juvenile justice system;

(b.5) Repealed.

On or before July 1, 2007:

The diagnosis, treatment, and housing of adults with mental illness who are involved in the criminal justice system;

The ongoing treatment, housing, and supervision, especially with regard to medication, of adults and juveniles who are involved in the criminal and juvenile justice systems and who are incarcerated or housed within the community and the availability of public benefits for such persons;

The ongoing assistance and supervision, especially with regard to medication, of persons with mental illness after discharge from sentence; and

The identification of alternative entities to exercise jurisdiction regarding release for persons found not guilty by reason of insanity, such as the development and use of a psychiatric

security review board, including recommendations related to the indeterminate nature of the commitment imposed;

On or before July 1, 2008, the identification, diagnosis, and treatment of minority persons with mental illness, women with mental illness, and persons with co-occurring disorders, in the criminal and juvenile justice systems;

On or before July 1, 2009:

The early identification, diagnosis, and treatment of adults and juveniles with mental illness who are involved in the criminal and juvenile justice systems;

The modification of the criminal and juvenile justice systems to most effectively serve adults and juveniles with mental illness who are involved in these systems;

The implementation of appropriate diagnostic tools to identify persons in the criminal and juvenile justice systems with mental illness; and

Any other issues concerning persons with mental illness who are involved in the state criminal and juvenile justice systems that arise during the course of the task force study;

Beginning July 1, 2011, through July 1, 2014:

The diagnosis, treatment, and housing of persons with mental illness or co-occurring disorders who are convicted of crimes, or incarcerated or who plead guilty, nolo contendere, or not guilty by reason of insanity or who are found to be incompetent to stand trial;

The diagnosis, treatment, and housing of juveniles with mental illness or co-occurring disorders who are adjudicated, detained, or committed for offenses that would constitute crimes if committed by adults or who plead guilty, nolo contendere, or not guilty by reason of insanity or who are found to be incompetent to stand trial;

The ongoing treatment, housing, and supervision, especially with regard to medication, of adults and juveniles who are involved in the criminal and juvenile justice systems and who are incarcerated or housed within the community and the availability of public benefits for these persons; and

The safety of the staff who treat or supervise persons with mental illness and the use of force against persons with mental illness;

On or after July 1, 2014:

Housing for a person with mental illness after his or her release from the criminal or juvenile justice system;

Medication consistency, delivery, and availability;

Best practices for suicide prevention, within and outside of correctional facilities;

Treatment of co-occurring disorders;

Awareness of and training for enhanced staff safety, including expanding training opportunities for providers; and

Enhanced data collection related to issues affecting persons with mental illness in the criminal and juvenile justice systems.

Additional duties of the task force. The task force shall provide guidance and make findings and recommendations to the committee for its development of reports and legislative recommendations for modification of the criminal and juvenile justice systems, with respect to persons with mental illness who are involved in these systems. In addition, the task force shall:

On or before August 1, 2004, and by each August 1 thereafter, select a chair and a vice- chair from among its members;

Meet at least six times each year, or more often as directed by the chair of the committee;

Communicate with and obtain input from groups throughout the state affected by the issues identified in subsection (2) of this section;

Create subcommittees as needed to carry out the duties of the task force. The subcommittees may consist, in part, of persons who are not members of the task force. Such persons may vote on issues before the subcommittee but shall not be entitled to a vote at meetings of the task force.

Submit a report to the committee by October 1, 2004, and by each October 1 thereafter, that, at a minimum, specifies:

Issues to be studied in upcoming task force meetings and a prioritization of those issues;

Findings and recommendations regarding issues of prior consideration by the task force;

Legislative proposals of the task force that identify the policy issues involved, the agencies responsible for the implementation of the changes, and the funding sources required for implementation.

Flexibility. No requirement set forth in subsection (2) of this section shall prohibit the task force from studying, presenting findings and recommendations on, or requesting permission to draft legislative proposals concerning any issue described in subsection (2) of this section at any time during the existence of the task force.

Compensation. Members of the task force shall serve without compensation. However, members of the task force appointed pursuant to subparagraph (XIV) of paragraph (c) of subsection

(1) of this section may receive reimbursement for actual and necessary expenses associated with their duties on the task force.

(6)     Coordination. The task force may work with other task forces, committees, or organizations that are pursuing policy initiatives similar to those addressed in subsection (2) of this section. The task force shall consider developing relationships with other task forces, committees, and organizations to leverage efficient policy-making opportunities through collaborative efforts.

18-1.9-105. Task force funding - staff support. (1) The division of criminal justice of the department of public safety, on behalf of the task force, is authorized to receive and expend contributions, grants, services, and in-kind donations from any public or private entity for any direct or indirect costs associated with the duties of the task force set forth in this article.

(2) The director of research of the legislative council, the director of the office of legislative legal services, the director of the division of criminal justice within the department of public safety, and the executive directors of the departments represented on the task force may supply staff assistance to the task force as they deem appropriate within existing appropriations. If staff assistance is not available from a governmental agency within

existing appropriations, then the executive directors of the departments represented on the task force, the director of research of the legislative council, and the director of the office of legislative legal services may supply staff assistance to the task force only if moneys are credited to the treatment of persons with mental illness in the criminal and juvenile justice systems cash fund created in section 18-1.9-106 in an amount sufficient to fund staff assistance. The task force may also accept staff support from the private sector.

18-1.9-106. Treatment of persons with mental illness in the criminal and juvenile justice systems cash fund. (1) All private and public funds received through grants, contributions, and donations pursuant to this article shall be transmitted to the state treasurer, who shall credit the same to the treatment of persons with mental illness in the criminal and juvenile justice systems cash fund, which fund is hereby created and referred to in this section as the "fund". The moneys in the fund shall be subject to annual appropriation by the general assembly for the direct and indirect costs associated with the implementation of this article. All moneys in the fund not expended for the purpose of this article may be invested by the state treasurer as provided by law. All interest and income derived from the investment and deposit of moneys in the fund shall be credited to the fund. Any unexpended and unencumbered moneys remaining in the fund at the end of a fiscal year shall remain in the fund and shall not be credited or transferred to the general fund or another fund. All unexpended and unencumbered moneys remaining in the fund as of July 1, 2020, shall be transferred to the general fund.
(1.5) Repealed.
(2) Compensation as provided in sections 18-1.9-103 (1) (d) and 18-1.9-105 (2) for members of the general assembly and for staff assistance to the committee and task force provided by the director of research of the legislative council and the director of the office of legislative legal services shall be approved by the chair of the legislative council and paid by vouchers and warrants drawn as provided by law from moneys appropriated for such purpose and allocated to the legislative council from the fund.

18-1.9-107. Repeal of article. This article is repealed, effective July 1, 2020.

### ARTICLE 2 Inchoate Offenses

## PART 1 ATTEMPTS

18-2-101. Criminal attempt. (1) A person commits criminal attempt if, acting with the kind of culpability otherwise required for commission of an offense, he engages in conduct constituting a substantial step toward the commission of the offense. A substantial step is any conduct, whether act, omission, or possession, which is strongly corroborative of the firmness of the actor's purpose

to complete the commission of the offense. Factual or legal impossibility of committing the offense is not a defense if the offense could have been committed had the attendant circumstances been as the actor believed them to be, nor is it a defense that the crime attempted was actually perpetrated by the accused.
A person who engages in conduct intending to aid another to commit an offense commits criminal attempt if the conduct would establish his complicity under section 18-1-603 were the offense committed by the other person, even if the other is not guilty of committing or attempting the offense.
It is an affirmative defense to a charge under this section that the defendant abandoned his effort to commit the crime or otherwise prevented its commission, under circumstances manifesting the complete and voluntary renunciation of his criminal intent.
(3.5) Criminal attempt to commit any crime for which a court is required to sentence a defendant for a crime of violence in accordance with section 18-1.3-406 is itself a crime of violence for the purposes of that section.
Criminal attempt to commit a class 1 felony is a class 2 felony; criminal attempt to commit a class 2 felony is a class 3 felony; criminal attempt to commit a class 3 felony is a class 4 felony; criminal attempt to commit a class 4 felony is a class 5 felony; criminal attempt to commit a class 5 or 6 felony is a class 6 felony.
Criminal attempt to commit a felony which is defined by any statute other than one contained in this title and for which no penalty is specifically provided is a class 6 felony.
Criminal attempt to commit a class 1 misdemeanor is a class 2 misdemeanor.

Criminal attempt to commit a misdemeanor other than a class 1 misdemeanor is a class 3 misdemeanor.
Criminal attempt to commit a petty offense is a crime of the same class as the offense
itself.
The provisions of subsections (4) to (8) of this section shall not apply to a person who
commits criminal attempt to escape. A person who commits criminal attempt to escape shall be punished as provided in section 18-8-208.1.
(a) Except as otherwise provided by law, criminal attempt to commit a level 1 drug felony is a level 2 drug felony; criminal attempt to commit a level 2 drug felony is a level 3 drug felony; criminal attempt to commit a level 3 drug felony is a level 4 drug felony; and criminal attempt to commit a level 4 drug felony is a level 4 drug felony.
(b) Except as otherwise provided by law, criminal attempt to commit a level 1 drug misdemeanor is a level 2 drug misdemeanor; and criminal attempt to commit a level 2 drug misdemeanor is a level 2 drug misdemeanor.

## PART 2 CRIMINAL CONSPIRACY

18-2-201. Conspiracy. (1) A person commits conspiracy to commit a crime if, with the

intent to promote or facilitate its commission, he agrees with another person or persons that they, or one or more of them, will engage in conduct which constitutes a crime or an attempt to commit a crime, or he agrees to aid the other person or persons in the planning or commission of a crime or of an attempt to commit such crime.
No person may be convicted of conspiracy to commit a crime, unless an overt act in pursuance of that conspiracy is proved to have been done by him or by a person with whom he conspired.
If a person knows that one with whom he conspires to commit a crime has conspired with another person or persons to commit the same crime, he is guilty of conspiring to commit a crime with the other person or persons, whether or not he knows their identity.
If a person conspires to commit a number of crimes, he is guilty of only one conspiracy so long as such multiple crimes are part of a single criminal episode.
(4.5) Conspiracy to commit any crime for which a court is required to sentence a defendant for a crime of violence in accordance with section 18-1.3-

406 is itself a crime of violence for the purposes of that section.

If a person conspires to commit a felony which is defined by any statute other than one contained in this title and for which conspiracy no penalty is specifically provided, he is guilty of a class 6 felony. If a person conspires to commit a misdemeanor which is defined by any statute other than one contained in this title and for which conspiracy no penalty is specifically provided, he is guilty of a class 3 misdemeanor.

18-2-202. Joinder and venue in conspiracy prosecutions. (1) Subject to the provisions of subsection (2) of this section, two or more persons charged with criminal conspiracy may be prosecuted jointly if:

They are charged with conspiring with one another; or

They are charged with being involved in conspiracies that are so related as to constitute different aspects of a scheme of organized criminal conduct. In such case it is immaterial that the persons charged are not parties to the same conspiracy.

In any joint prosecution under subsection (1) of this section:

No defendant shall be charged with a conspiracy in any judicial district other than one in which he entered into the conspiracy or in which an overt act pursuant to such conspiracy was done by him or by a person with whom he conspired; and

Neither the liability of anydefendant nor the admissibility against him of evidence of acts or declarations of another shall be enlarged by this joinder; and

The court shall order a severance or take a special verdict as to any defendant who so requests, if it deems it necessary or appropriate to promote the fair determination of his guilt or innocence.

18-2-203. Renunciation of criminal purpose. It is an affirmative defense to a charge of conspiracy that the offender, after conspiring to commit a crime, thwarted the success of the conspiracy, under circumstances manifesting a complete and voluntary renunciation of his criminal

intent.

18-2-204. Duration of conspiracy. (1) Conspiracy is a continuing course of conduct which terminates when the crime or crimes which are its object are committed or the agreement that they be committed is abandoned by the defendant and by those with whom he conspired.

Abandonment is presumed if neither the defendant nor anyone with whom he conspired does any overt act in pursuance of the conspiracy during the applicable period of limitation.

If an individual abandons the agreement, the conspiracy is terminated as to him only if and when he gives timely notice to those with whom he conspired of his abandonment and the notice is evidenced by circumstances corroborating the giving of the same, or he informs the law enforcement authorities, having jurisdiction, of the existence of the conspiracy and of his participation therein.

18-2-205. Incapacity, irresponsibility, or immunity of party to conspiracy. (1) It is immaterial to the liability of a person who conspires with another to commit a crime that:

He or the person with whom he conspires does not occupy a particular position or have a particular characteristic which is an element of the crime, if he believes that one of them does; or

The person with whom he conspires is irresponsible or has an immunity to prosecution or conviction for the commission of the crime.

18-2-206. Penalties for criminal conspiracy - when convictions barred. (1) Conspiracy to commit a class 1 felony is a class 2 felony; conspiracy to commit a class 2 felony is a class 3 felony; conspiracy to commit a class 3 felony is a class 4 felony; conspiracy to commit a class 4 felony is a class 5 felony; conspiracy to commit a class 5 or 6 felony is a class 6 felony.

A person may not be convicted of conspiracy to commit an offense if he is acquitted of the offense which is the object of the conspiracy where the sole evidence of conspiracy is the evidence establishing the commission of the offense which is the object of the conspiracy.

If the particular conduct charged to constitute a criminal conspiracy is so inherently unlikely to result or culminate in the commission of a crime that neither that conduct nor the offender presents a public danger warranting the grading of the offense under this section, the court may enter judgment and impose sentence for a crime of a lesser class or, in extreme cases, may dismiss the prosecution.

Conspiracy to commit a class 1 misdemeanor is a class 2 misdemeanor.

Conspiracy to commit a misdemeanor other than a class 1 misdemeanor is a class 3 misdemeanor.

Conspiracy to commit a petty offense is a crime of the same class as the offense itself.

(a) Except as otherwise provided by law, conspiracy to commit a level 1 drug felony is a level 2 drug felony; conspiracy to commit a level 2 drug felony is a level 3 drug felony; conspiracy to commit a level 3 drug felony is a level 4 drug felony; and conspiracy to commit a level 4 drug

felony is a level 4 drug felony.

(b) Except as otherwise provided by law, conspiracy to commit a level 1 drug misdemeanor is a level 2 drug misdemeanor; and conspiracy to commit a level 2 drug misdemeanor is a level 2 drug misdemeanor.

PART 3 CRIMINAL SOLICITATION

18-2-301. Criminal solicitation. (1) Except as to bona fide acts of persons authorized by law to investigate and detect the commission of offenses by others, a person is guilty of criminal solicitation if he or she commands, induces, entreats, or otherwise attempts to persuade another person, or offers his or her services or another's services to a third person, to commit a felony, whether as principal or accomplice, with intent to promote or facilitate the commission of that crime, and under circumstances strongly corroborative of that intent.

It is a defense to a prosecution under this section that, if the criminal object were achieved, the defendant would be the sole victim of the offense or the offense is so defined that his conduct would be inevitably incident to its commission or he otherwise would not be guilty under the statute defining the offense or under section 18-1-603 dealing with complicity.

It is no defense to a prosecution under this section that the person solicited could not be guilty of the offense because of lack of responsibility or culpability, or other incapacity.

It is an affirmative defense to a prosecution under this section that the defendant, after soliciting another person to commit a felony, persuaded him not to do so or otherwise prevented the commission of the felony, under circumstances manifesting a complete and voluntary renunciation of the defendant's criminal intent.

Criminal solicitation is subject to the penalties provided for criminal attempt in section 18-2-101.

## PART 4 RENUNCIATION AND ABANDONMENT

18-2-401. Nonavailability of defenses. (1) Renunciation and abandonment are not voluntary and complete so as to be a defense to prosecution under this article if they are motivated in whole or in part by:

A belief that a circumstance exists which increases the probability of detection or apprehension of the defendant or another or which makes more difficult the consummation of the crime; or

A decision to postpone the crime until another time or to substitute another victim or another but similar objective.

### ARTICLE 3 Offenses Against the Person

## PART 1

## HOMICIDE AND RELATED OFFENSES

18-3-101. Definition of terms. As used in this part 1, unless the context otherwise requires:

"Homicide" means the killing of a person by another.

"Person", when referring to the victim of a homicide, means a human being who had been born and was alive at the time of the homicidal act.

(2.5) One in a "position of trust" includes, but is not limited to, any person who is a parent or acting in the place of a parent and charged with any of a parent's rights, duties, or responsibilities concerning a child, including a guardian or someone otherwise responsible for the general supervision of a child's welfare, or a person who is charged with any duty or responsibility for the health, education, welfare, or supervision of a child, including foster care, child care, family care, or institutional care, either independently or through another, no matter how brief, at the time of an unlawful act.

The term "after deliberation" means not only intentionally but also that the decision to commit the act has been made after the exercise of reflection and judgment concerning the act. An act committed after deliberation is never one which has been committed in a hasty or impulsive manner.

18-3-102. Murder in the first degree. (1) A person commits the crime of murder in the first degree if:

After deliberation and with the intent to cause the death of a person other than himself, he causes the death of that person or of another person; or

Acting either alone or with one or more persons, he or she commits or attempts to commit arson, robbery, burglary, kidnapping, sexual assault as prohibited by section 18-3-402, sexual assault in the first or second degree as prohibited by section 18-3-402 or 18-3-403 as those sections existed prior to July 1, 2000, or a class 3 felony for sexual assault on a child as provided in section 18-3-405 (2), or the crime of escape as provided in section 18-8-208, and, in the course of or in furtherance of the crime that he or she is committing or attempting to commit, or of immediate flight therefrom, the death of a person, other than one of the participants, is caused by anyone; or

By perjury or subornation of perjury he procures the conviction and execution of any

innocent person; or

Under circumstances evidencing an attitude of universal malice manifesting extreme indifference to the value of human life generally, he knowingly engages in conduct which creates a grave risk of death to a person, or persons, other than himself, and thereby causes the death of another; or

He or she commits unlawful distribution, dispensation, or sale of a controlled substance to a person under the age of eighteen years on school grounds as provided in section 18-18-407 (2), and the death of such person is caused by the use of such controlled substance; or

The person knowingly causes the death of a child who has not yet attained twelve years of age and the person committing the offense is one in a position of trust with respect to the victim.

It is an affirmative defense to a charge of violating subsection (1) (b) of this section that the defendant:

Was not the only participant in the underlying crime; and

Did not commit the homicidal act or in any way solicit, request, command, importune, cause, or aid the commission thereof; and

Was not armed with a deadly weapon; and

Had no reasonable ground to believe that any other participant was armed with such a weapon, instrument, article, or substance; and

Did not engage himself in or intend to engage in and had no reasonable ground to believe that any other participant intended to engage in conduct likely to result in death or serious bodily injury; and

Endeavored to disengage himself from the commission of the underlying crime or flight therefrom immediately upon having reasonable grounds to believe that another participant is armed with a deadly weapon, instrument, article, or substance, or intended to engage in conduct likely to result in death or serious bodily injury.

Murder in the first degree is a class 1 felony.

The statutory privilege between patient and physician and between husband and wife shall not be available for excluding or refusing testimony in any prosecution for the crime of murder in the first degree as described in paragraph (f) of subsection (1) of this section.

18-3-103. Murder in the second degree. (1) A person commits the crime of murder in the second degree if the person knowingly causes the death of a person.

Diminished responsibility due to self-induced intoxication is not a defense to murder in the second degree.

(2.5) (Deleted by amendment, L. 96, p. 1844, § 12, effective July 1, 1996.)

(a) Except as otherwise provided in paragraph (b) of this subsection (3), murder in the second degree is a class 2 felony.

(b) Notwithstanding the provisions of paragraph (a) of this subsection (3), murder in the second degree is a class 3 felony where the act causing the death was performed upon a sudden heat of passion, caused by a serious and highly provoking act of the intended victim, affecting the defendant sufficiently to excite an irresistible passion in a reasonable person; but, if between the

provocation and the killing there is an interval sufficient for the voice of reason and humanity to be heard, the killing is a class 2 felony.
A defendant convicted pursuant to subsection (1) of this section shall be sentenced by the court in accordance with the provisions of section 18-1.3-406.


18-3-104. Manslaughter. (1) A person commits the crime of manslaughter if:
Such person recklessly causes the death of another person; or
Such person intentionally causes or aids another person to commit suicide.
(Deleted by amendment, L. 96, p. 1844, § 13, effective July 1, 1996.)
Manslaughter is a class 4 felony.
This section shall not apply to a person, including a proxy decision-maker as such person is described in section 15-18.5-103, C.R.S., who complies with any advance medical directive in accordance with the provisions of title 15, C.R.S., including a medical durable power of attorney, a living will, or a cardiopulmonary resuscitation (CPR) directive.
(a) This section shall not apply to a medical caregiver with prescriptive authority or authority to administer medication who prescribes or administers medication for palliative care to a terminally ill patient with the consent of the terminally ill patient or his or her agent.
For purposes of this subsection (4):
"Agent" means a person appointed to represent the interests of the terminally ill patient by a medical power of attorney, power of attorney, health care proxy, or any other similar statutory or regular procedure used for designation of such person.
"Medical caregiver" means a physician, registered nurse, nurse practitioner, physician assistant, or anesthesiologist assistant licensed by this state.
"Palliative care" means medical care and treatment provided by a licensed medical caregiver to a patient with an advanced chronic or terminal illness whose condition may not be responsive to curative treatment and who is, therefore, receiving treatment that relieves pain and suffering and supports the best possible quality of his or her life.
Paragraph (a) of this subsection (4) shall not be interpreted to permit a medical caregiver to assist in the suicide of the patient.


18-3-105. Criminally negligent homicide. Any person who causes the death of another person by conduct amounting to criminal negligence commits criminally negligent homicide which is a class 5 felony.


18-3-106. Vehicular homicide. (1) (a) If a person operates or drives a motor vehicle in a reckless manner, and such conduct is the proximate cause of the death of another, such person commits vehicular homicide.
(I) If a person operates or drives a motor vehicle while under the influence of alcohol or one or more drugs, or a combination of both alcohol and one or more drugs, and such conduct is the proximate cause of the death of another, such person commits vehicular homicide. This is a strict

liability crime.
For the purposes of this subsection (1), one or more drugs means any drug, as defined in section 27-80-203 (13), C.R.S., any controlled substance, as defined in section 18-18-102 (5), and any inhaled glue, aerosol, or other toxic vapor or vapors, as defined in section 18-18-412.
The fact that any person charged with a violation of this subsection (1) is or has been entitled to use one or more drugs under the laws of this state shall not constitute a defense against any charge of violating this subsection (1).
"Driving under the influence" means driving a vehicle when a person has consumed alcohol or one or more drugs, or a combination of alcohol and one or more drugs, which alcohol alone, or one or more drugs alone, or alcohol combined with one or more drugs affect such person to a degree that such person is substantially incapable, either mentally or physically, or both mentally and physically, of exercising clear judgment, sufficient physical control, or due care in the safe operation of a vehicle.
Vehicular homicide, in violation of paragraph (a) of this subsection (1), is a class 4 felony. Vehicular homicide, in violation of paragraph (b) of this subsection (1), is a class 3 felony.
In any prosecution for a violation of subsection (1) of this section, the amount of alcohol in the defendant's blood or breath at the time of the commission of the alleged offense, or within a reasonable time thereafter, as shown by analysis of the defendant's blood or breath, gives rise to the following:
If there was at such time 0.05 or less grams of alcohol per one hundred milliliters of blood, or if there was at such time 0.05 or less grams of alcohol per two hundred ten liters of breath, it shall be presumed that the defendant was not under the influence of alcohol.
If there was at such time in excess of 0.05 but less than 0.08 grams of alcohol per one hundred milliliters of blood, or if there was at such time in excess of 0.05 but less than 0.08 grams of alcohol per two hundred ten liters of breath, such fact may be considered with other competent evidence in determining whether or not the defendant was under the influence of alcohol.
If there was at such time 0.08 or more grams of alcohol per one hundred milliliters of blood, or if there was at such time 0.08 or more grams of alcohol per two hundred ten liters of breath, such fact gives rise to the permissible inference that the defendant was under the influence of alcohol.
If at such time the driver's blood contained five nanograms or more of delta 9- tetrahydrocannabinol per milliliter in whole blood, as shown by analysis of the defendant's blood, such fact gives rise to a permissible inference that the defendant was under the influence of one or more drugs.
The limitations of subsection (2) of this section shall not be construed as limiting the introduction, reception, or consideration of any other competent evidence bearing upon the question of whether or not the defendant was under the influence of alcohol.
(a) If a law enforcement officer has probable cause to believe that any person was driving a motor vehicle in violation of paragraph (b) of subsection (1) of this section, the person, upon the request of the law enforcement officer, shall take, and complete, and cooperate in the completing of any test or tests of the person's blood, breath, saliva, or urine for the purpose of determining the alcoholic or drug content within his or her system. The type of test or tests shall be determined by the law enforcement officer requiring the test or tests. If the person refuses to take, or to complete,

or to cooperate in the completing of any test or tests, the test or tests may be performed at the direction of a law enforcement officer having probable cause, without the person's authorization or consent. If any person refuses to take or complete, or cooperate in the taking or completing of any test or tests required by this paragraph (a), the person shall be subject to license revocation pursuant to the provisions of section 42-2-126 (3), C.R.S. When the test or tests show that the amount of alcohol in a person's blood was in violation of the limits provided for in section 42-2-126 (3) (a), (3) (b), (3) (d), or (3) (e), C.R.S., the person shall be subject to license revocation pursuant to the provisions of section 42-2-126, C.R.S.
Any person who is required to submit to testing shall cooperate with the person authorized to obtain specimens of his blood, breath, saliva, or urine, including the signing of any release or consent forms required by any person, hospital, clinic, or association authorized to obtain such specimens. If such person does not cooperate with the person, hospital, clinic, or association authorized to obtain such specimens, including the signing of any release or consent forms, such noncooperation shall be considered a refusal to submit to testing.
The tests shall be administered at the direction of a law enforcement officer having probable cause to believe that the person committed a violation of

subparagraph (I) of paragraph (b) of subsection (1) of this section and in accordance with rules and regulations prescribed by the state board of health concerning the health of the person being tested and the accuracy of such testing. Strict compliance with such rules and regulations shall not be a prerequisite to the admissibility of test results at trial unless the court finds that the extent of noncompliance with a board of health rule has so impaired the validity and reliability of the testing method and the test results as to render the evidence inadmissible. In all other circumstances, failure to strictly comply with such rules and regulations shall only be considered in the weight to be given to the test results and not to the admissibility of such test results. It shall not be a prerequisite to the admissibility of test results at trial that the prosecution present testimony concerning the composition of any kit used to obtain blood, urine, saliva, or breath specimens. A sufficient evidentiary foundation concerning the compliance of such kits with the rules and regulations of the department of public health and environment shall be established by the introduction of a copy of the manufacturer's or supplier's certificate of compliance with such rules and regulations if such certificate specifies the contents, sterility, chemical makeup, and amounts of chemicals contained in such kit.

No person except a physician, a registered nurse, a paramedic as certified in part 2 of article 3.5 of title 25, C.R.S., an emergency medical service provider as defined in part 1 of article

3.5 of title 25, C.R.S., or a person whose normal duties include withdrawing blood samples under the supervision of a physician or registered nurse is entitled to withdraw blood for the purpose of determining the alcoholic or drug content of the blood for purposes of this section. In a trial for a violation of paragraph (b) of subsection (1) of this section, testimony of a law enforcement officer that he or she witnessed the taking of a blood specimen by a person who he or she reasonably believed was authorized to withdraw blood specimens is sufficient evidence that the person was authorized, and testimony from the person who obtained the blood specimens concerning the person's authorization to obtain blood specimens is not a prerequisite to the admissibility of test results concerning the blood specimens obtained. No civil liability shall attach to any person authorized to obtain blood, breath, saliva, or urine specimens or to any hospital, clinic, or association in or for which such specimens are obtained pursuant to this subsection (4) as a result of the act of

obtaining the specimens from a person if the specimens were obtained according to the rules prescribed by the state board of health; except that such provision does not relieve the person from liability for negligence in obtaining any specimen sample.

Any person who is dead or unconscious shall be tested to determine the alcohol or drug content of his blood or any drug content of his system as provided in this subsection (4). If a test cannot be administered to a person who is unconscious, hospitalized, or undergoing medical treatment because the test would endanger the person's life or health, the law enforcement agency shall be allowed to test any blood, urine, or saliva which was obtained and not utilized by a health care provider and shall have access to that portion of the analysis and results of any tests administered by such provider which shows the alcohol or drug content of the person's blood or any drug content within his system. Such test results shall not be considered privileged communications and the provisions of section 13-90-107, C.R.S., relating to the physician-patient privilege shall not apply. Any person who is dead, in addition to the tests prescribed, shall also have his blood checked for carbon monoxide content and for the presence of drugs, as prescribed by the department of public health and environment. Such information obtained shall be made a part of the accident report.

If a person refuses to take, or to complete, or to cooperate in the completing of any test or tests as provided in this subsection (4) and such person subsequently stands trial for a violation of subsection (1) (b) of this section, the refusal to take or to complete, or to cooperate with the completing of any test or tests shall be admissible into evidence at the trial, and a person may not claim the privilege against self-incrimination with regard to the admission of his refusal to take, or to complete, or to cooperate with the completing of any test or tests.

Notwithstanding any provision in section 42-4-1301.1, C.R.S., concerning requirements which relate to the manner in which tests are administered, the test or tests taken pursuant to the provisions of this section may be used for the purposes of driver's license revocation proceedings under section 42-2-126, C.R.S., and for the purposes of prosecutions for violations of section 42-4- 1301 (1) or (2), C.R.S.

In all actions, suits, and judicial proceedings in any court of this state concerning alcohol- related or drug-related traffic offenses, the court shall take judicial notice of methods of testing a person's alcohol or drug level and of the design and operation of devices, as certified by the department of public health and environment, for testing a person's blood, breath, saliva, or urine to determine his alcohol or drug level. This subsection (5) shall not prevent the necessity of establishing during a trial that the testing devices used were working properly and that such testing devices were properly operated. Nothing in this subsection (5) shall preclude a defendant from offering evidence concerning the accuracy of testing devices.

18-3-107. First degree murder of a peace officer, firefighter, or emergency medical service provider - legislative declaration. (1) A person who commits murder in the first degree, as defined in section 18-3-102, and the victim is a peace officer, firefighter, or emergency medical service provider, engaged in the performance of his or her duties, commits the felony crime of first degree murder of a peace officer, firefighter, or emergency medical service provider.

As used in this section, "peace officer, firefighter, or emergency medical service provider engaged in the performance of his or her duties" means a peace officer as described in section 16-

2.5-101, C.R.S., a firefighter, as defined in section 18-3-201 (1.5), or an emergency medical service provider, as defined in section 18-3-201 (1), who is engaged or acting in, or who is present for the purpose of engaging or acting in, the performance of any duty, service, or function imposed, authorized, required, or permitted by law to be performed by a peace officer, firefighter, or emergency medical service provider, whether or not the peace officer, firefighter, or emergency medical service provider is within the territorial limits of his or her jurisdiction, if the peace officer, firefighter, or emergency medical service provider is in uniform or the person committing an assault upon or offense against or otherwise acting toward the peace officer, firefighter, or emergency medical service provider knows or reasonably should know that the victim is a peace officer, firefighter, or emergency medical service provider.

A person convicted of first degree murder of a peace officer, firefighter, or emergency medical service provider shall be punished by life imprisonment without the possibility of parole for the rest of his or her natural life, unless a proceeding held to determine sentence according to the procedure set forth in section 18-1.3-1201, 18-1.3-1302, or 18-1.4-102 results in a verdict that requires imposition of the death penalty, in which event the person shall be sentenced to death. Nothing in this subsection (3) is construed as limiting the power of the governor to grant reprieves, commutations, and pardons pursuant to section 7 of article IV of the Colorado constitution.

In the event the death penalty as provided for in this section is held to be unconstitutional by the Colorado supreme court or the United States supreme court, a person convicted of first degree murder of a peace officer, firefighter, or emergency medical service provider under subsection (1) of this section shall be punished by life imprisonment without the possibility of parole. In such circumstance, the court which previously sentenced a person to death shall cause the person to be brought before the court, and the court shall sentence the person to life imprisonment without the possibility of parole.

The general assembly recognizes that protection of peace officers, firefighters, and emergency medical service providers from crime is a major concern of our state because society depends on peace officers, firefighters, and emergency medical service providers for protection against crime and other dangers and because peace officers, firefighters, and emergency medical service providers are disproportionately damaged by crime because their duty to protect society often places them in dangerous circumstances. Society as a whole benefits from affording special protection to peace officers, firefighters, and emergency medical service providers because the protection deters crimes against them and allows them to better serve and protect our state. The general assembly therefore finds that the penalties for first degree murder of a peace officer, firefighter, or emergency medical service provider should be more severe than the penalty for first degree murder of other members of society.

PART 2 ASSAULTS

18-3-201. Definitions. As used in sections 18-3-201 to 18-3-204, unless the context otherwise requires:

"Emergency medical care provider" means a doctor, intern, nurse, nurse's aide, physician's assistant, ambulance attendant or operator, air ambulance pilot, paramedic, or any other member of a hospital or health care facility staff or security force who is involved in providing emergency medical care at a hospital or health care facility, or in an air ambulance or ambulance as defined in section 25-3.5-103 (1) and (1.5), C.R.S.
(1.3) "Emergency medical service provider" has the same meaning as set forth in section 25- 3.5-103 (8), C.R.S. The term refers to both paid and volunteer emergency medical service providers. (1.5) "Firefighter" means an officer or member of a fire department or fire protection or fire- fighting agency of the state, or any municipal or quasi-municipal corporation in this state, whether
that person is a volunteer or receives compensation for services rendered as such firefighter.
"Peace officer, firefighter, or emergency medical service provider engaged in the performance of his or her duties" means a peace officer, as described in section 16-2.5-101, C.R.S., a firefighter, or an emergency medical service provider, who is engaged or acting in, or who is present for the purpose of engaging or acting in, the performance of any duty, service, or function imposed, authorized, required, or permitted by law to be performed by a peace officer, firefighter, or emergency medical service provider, whether or not the peace officer, firefighter, or emergency medical service provider is within the territorial limits of his or her jurisdiction, if the peace officer, firefighter, or emergency medical service provider is in uniform or the person committing an assault upon or offense against or otherwise acting toward the peace officer, firefighter, or emergency medical service provider knows or reasonably should know that the victim is a peace officer, firefighter, or emergency medical service provider. For the purposes of this subsection (2) and this part 2, the term "peace officer" includes countyenforcement personnel designated pursuant to section 29-7-101 (3), C.R.S.

18-3-202. Assault in the first degree. (1) A person commits the crime of assault in the first degree if:
With intent to cause serious bodily injury to another person, he causes serious bodily injury to any person by means of a deadly weapon; or
With intent to disfigure another person seriously and permanently, or to destroy, amputate, or disable permanently a member or organ of his body, he causes such an injury to any person; or
Under circumstances manifesting extreme indifference to the value of human life, he knowingly engages in conduct which creates a grave risk of death to another person, and thereby causes serious bodily injury to any person; or
Repealed.
With intent to cause serious bodily injury upon the person of a peace officer, firefighter, or emergency medical service provider, he or she threatens with a deadly weapon a peace officer, firefighter, or emergency medical service provider engaged in the performance of his or her duties, and the offender knows or reasonably should know that the victim is a peace officer, firefighter, or emergency medical service provider acting in the performance of his or her duties; or
(e.5) With intent to cause serious bodily injury upon the person of a judge of a court of competent jurisdiction or an officer of said court, he threatens with a deadly  weapon a judge of a

court of competent jurisdiction or an officer of said court, and the offender knows or reasonably should know that the victim is a judge of a court of competent jurisdiction or an officer of said court; or
While lawfully confined or in custody as a result of being charged with or convicted of a crime or as a result of being charged as a delinquent child or adjudicated as a delinquent child and with intent to cause serious bodily injury to a person employed by or under contract with a detention facility, as defined in section 18-8-203 (3), or to a person employed by the division in the department of human services responsible for youth services and who is a youth services counselor or is in the youth services worker classification series, he or she threatens with a deadly weapon such a person engaged in the performance of his or her duties and the offender knows or reasonably should know that the victim is such a person engaged in the performance of his or her duties while employed by or under contract with a detention facility or while employed by the division in the department of human services responsible for youth services. A sentence imposed pursuant to this paragraph (f) shall be served in the department of corrections and shall run consecutively with any sentences being served by the offender. A person who participates in a work release program, a furlough, or any other similar authorized supervised or unsupervised absence from a detention facility, as defined in section 18-8-203 (3), and who is required to report back to the detention facility at a specified time shall be deemed to be in custody.
With the intent to cause serious bodily injury, he or she applies sufficient pressure to impede or restrict the breathing or circulation of the blood of another person by applying such pressure to the neck or by blocking the nose or mouth of the other person and thereby causes serious bodily injury.
(a) If assault in the first degree is committed under circumstances where the act causing the injury is performed upon a sudden heat of passion, caused by a serious and highly provoking act of the intended victim, affecting the person causing the injury sufficiently to excite an irresistible passion in a reasonable person, and without an interval between the provocation and the injury sufficient for the voice of reason and humanity to be heard, it is a class 5 felony.
If assault in the first degree is committed without the circumstances provided in paragraph (a) of this subsection (2), it is a class 3 felony.
If a defendant is convicted of assault in the first degree pursuant to subsection (1) of this section, the court shall sentence the defendant in accordance with the provisions of section 18-1.3- 406.
Repealed.
Repealed.

18-3-203. Assault in the second degree. (1) A person commits the crime of assault in the second degree if:
Repealed.
With intent to cause bodily injury to another person, he or she causes such injury to any person by means of a deadly weapon; or
With intent to prevent one whom he or she knows, or should know, to be a peace officer, firefighter,  emergency  medical  care  provider,  or emergency  medical  service  provider  from

performing a lawful duty, he or she intentionally causes bodily injury to any person; or
(c.5) With intent to prevent one whom he or she knows, or should know, to be a peace officer, firefighter, or emergency medical service provider from performing a lawful duty, he or she intentionally causes serious bodily injury to any person; or
He recklessly causes serious bodily injury to another person by means of a deadly weapon; or
For a purpose other than lawful medical or therapeutic treatment, he intentionally causes stupor, unconsciousness, or other physical or mental

impairment or injury to another person by administering to him, without his consent, a drug, substance, or preparation capable of producing the intended harm; or

While lawfully confined or in custody, he or she knowingly and violently applies physical force against the person of a peace officer, firefighter, or emergency medical service provider engaged in the performance of his or her duties, or a judge of a court of competent jurisdiction, or an officer of said court, or, while lawfully confined or in custody as a result of being charged with or convicted of a crime or as a result of being charged as a delinquent child or adjudicated as a delinquent child, he or she knowingly and violently applies physical force against a person engaged in the performance of his or her duties while employed by or under contract with a detention facility, as defined in section 18-8-203 (3), or while employed by the division in the department of human services responsible for youth services and who is a youth services counselor or is in the youth services worker classification series, and the person committing the offense knows or reasonably should know that the victim is a peace officer, firefighter, or emergency medical service provider engaged in the performance of his or her duties, or a judge of a court of competent jurisdiction, or an officer of said court, or a person engaged in the performance of his or her duties while employed by or under contract with a detention facility or while employed by the division in the department of human services responsible for youth services. A sentence imposed pursuant to this paragraph (f) shall be served in the department of corrections and shall run consecutively with any sentences being served by the offender; except that, if the offense is committed against a person employed by the division in the department of human services responsible for youth services, the court may grant probation or a suspended sentence in whole or in part, and the sentence may run concurrently or consecutivelywith anysentences being served. A person who participates in a work release program, a furlough, or any other similar authorized supervised or unsupervised absence from a detention facility, as defined in section 18-8-203 (3), and who is required to report back to the detention facility at a specified time is deemed to be in custody.

(f.5) (I) While lawfully confined in a detention facility within this state, a person with intent to infect, injure, harm, harass, annoy, threaten, or alarm a person in a detention facility whom the actor knows or reasonably should know to be an employee of a detention facility, causes such employee to come into contact with blood, seminal fluid, urine, feces, saliva, mucus, vomit, or any toxic, caustic, or hazardous material by any means, including but not limited to throwing, tossing, or expelling such fluid or material.

Repealed.

(A) As used in this paragraph (f.5), "detention facility" means any building, structure, enclosure, vehicle, institution, or place, whether permanent or temporary, fixed or mobile, where persons are or may be lawfully held in custody or confinement under the authority of the state of

Colorado or any political subdivision of the state of Colorado.

(B) As used in this paragraph (f.5), "employee of a detention facility" includes employees of the department of corrections, employees of any agency or person operating a detention facility, law enforcement personnel, and any other persons who are present in or in the vicinity of a detention facility and are performing services for a detention facility. "Employee of a detention facility" does not include a person lawfully confined in a detention facility.

With intent to cause bodily injury to another person, he or she causes serious bodily injury to that person or another; or

With intent to infect, injure, or harm another person whom the actor knows or reasonably should know to be engaged in the performance of his or her duties as a peace officer, a firefighter, an emergency medical care provider, or an emergency medical service provider, he or she causes such person to come into contact with blood, seminal fluid, urine, feces, saliva, mucus, vomit, or any toxic, caustic, or hazardous material by any means, including by throwing, tossing, or expelling such fluid or material; or

With the intent to cause bodily injury, he or she applies sufficient pressure to impede or restrict the breathing or circulation of the blood of another person by applying such pressure to the neck or by blocking the nose or mouth of the other person and thereby causes bodily injury.

(a) If assault in the second degree is committed under circumstances where the act causing the injury is performed upon a sudden heat of passion, caused by a serious and highly provoking act of the intended victim, affecting the person causing the injury sufficiently to excite an irresistible passion in a reasonable person, and without an interval between the provocation and the injury sufficient for the voice of reason and humanity to be heard, it is a class 6 felony.

If assault in the second degree is committed without the circumstances provided in paragraph (a) of this subsection (2), it is a class 4 felony.

(b.5) Assault in the second degree by any person under subsection (1) of this section without the circumstances provided in paragraph (a) of this subsection (2) is a class 3 felony if the person who is assaulted, other than a participant in the crime, suffered serious bodily injury during the commission or attempted commission of or flight from the commission or attempted commission of murder, robbery, arson, burglary, escape, kidnapping in the first degree, sexual assault, sexual assault in the first or second degree as such offenses existed prior to July 1, 2000, or class 3 felony sexual assault on a child.

(I) If a defendant is convicted of assault in the second degree pursuant to paragraph (c.5) of subsection (1) of this section or paragraph (b.5) of this subsection (2), except with respect to sexual assault or sexual assault in the first degree as it existed prior to July 1, 2000, the court shall sentence the defendant in accordance with the provisions of section 18-1.3-406. A defendant convicted of assault in the second degree pursuant to paragraph (b.5) of this subsection (2) with respect to sexual assault or sexual assault in the first degree as it existed prior to July 1, 2000, shall be sentenced in accordance with section 18-1.3-401 (8) (e) or (8) (e.5).

(II) If a defendant is convicted of assault in the second degree pursuant to paragraph (b), (c), (d), or (g) of subsection (1) of this section, the court shall sentence the offender in accordance with section 18-1.3-406; except that, notwithstanding the provisions of section 18-1.3-406, the court is not required to sentence the defendant to the department of corrections for a mandatory term of incarceration.

Repealed.

18-3-204. Assault in the third degree. (1) A person commits the crime of assault in the third degree if:

The person knowingly or recklessly causes bodily injury to another person or with criminal negligence the person causes bodily injury to another person by means of a deadly weapon; or

The person, with intent to harass, annoy, threaten, or alarm another person whom the actor knows or reasonably should know to be a peace officer, a firefighter, an emergency medical care provider, or an emergency medical service provider, causes the other person to come into contact with blood, seminal fluid, urine, feces, saliva, mucus, vomit, or toxic, caustic, or hazardous material by any means, including throwing, tossing, or expelling the fluid or material.

Repealed.

Assault in the third degree is a class 1 misdemeanor and is an extraordinary risk crime that is subject to the modified sentencing range specified in section 18-1.3-501 (3).

Repealed.

18-3-205. Vehicular assault. (1) (a) If a person operates or drives a motor vehicle in a reckless manner, and this conduct is the proximate cause of serious bodily injury to another, such person commits vehicular assault.

(I) If a person operates or drives a motor vehicle while under the influence of alcohol or one or more drugs, or a combination of both alcohol and one or more drugs, and this conduct is the proximate cause of a serious bodily injury to another, such person commits vehicular assault. This is a strict liability crime.

For the purposes of this subsection (1), one or more drugs means any drug, as defined in section 27-80-203 (13), C.R.S., any controlled substance, as defined in section 18-18-102 (5), and any inhaled glue, aerosol, or other toxic vapor or vapors, as defined in section 18-18-412.

The fact that any person charged with a violation of this subsection (1) is or has been entitled to use one or more drugs under the laws of this state shall not constitute a defense against any charge of violating this subsection (1).

"Driving under the influence" means driving a vehicle when a person has consumed alcohol or one or more drugs, or a combination of alcohol and one or more drugs, which alcohol alone, or one or more drugs alone, or alcohol combined with one or more drugs affect such person to a degree that such person is substantially incapable, either mentally or physically, or both mentally and physically, of exercising clear judgment, sufficient physical control, or due care in the safe operation of a vehicle.

Vehicular assault, in violation of paragraph (a) of this subsection (1), is a class 5 felony. Vehicular assault, in violation of paragraph (b) of this subsection (1), is a class 4 felony.

In any prosecution for a violation of subsection (1) of this section, the amount of alcohol in the defendant's blood or breath at the time of the commission of the alleged offense, or within a

reasonable time thereafter, as shown by analysis of the defendant's blood or breath, gives rise to the following:

If there was at such time 0.05 or less grams of alcohol per one hundred milliliters of blood, or if there was at such time 0.05 or less grams of alcohol per two hundred ten liters of breath, it shall be presumed that the defendant was not under the influence of alcohol.

If there was at such time in excess of 0.05 but less than 0.08 grams of alcohol per one hundred milliliters of blood, or if there was at such time in excess of 0.05 but less than 0.08 grams of alcohol per two hundred ten liters of breath, such fact may be considered with other competent evidence in determining whether or not the defendant was under the influence of alcohol.

If there was at such time 0.08 or more grams of alcohol per one hundred milliliters of blood, or if there was at such time 0.08 or more grams of alcohol per two hundred ten liters of breath, such fact gives rise to the permissible inference that the defendant was under the influence of alcohol.

If at such time the driver's blood contained five nanograms or more of delta 9- tetrahydrocannabinol per milliliter in whole blood, as shown by analysis of the defendant's blood, such fact gives rise to a permissible inference that the defendant was under the influence of one or more drugs.

The limitations of subsection (2) of this section shall not be construed as limiting the introduction, reception, or consideration of any other competent evidence bearing upon the question of whether or not the defendant was under the influence of alcohol.

(a) If a law enforcement officer has probable cause to believe that any person was driving a motor vehicle in violation of paragraph (b) of subsection (1) of this section, the person, upon the request of the law enforcement officer, shall take, and complete, and cooperate in the completing of any test or tests of the person's blood, breath, saliva, or urine for the purpose of determining the alcoholic or drug content within his or her system. The type of test or tests shall be determined by the law enforcement officer requiring the test or tests. If the person refuses to take, or to complete, or to cooperate in the completing of any test or tests, the test or tests may be performed at the direction of a law enforcement officer having probable cause, without the person's authorization or consent. If any person refuses to take, or to complete, or to cooperate in the taking or completing of any test or tests required by this paragraph (a), the person shall be subject to license revocation pursuant to the provisions of section 42-2-126 (3), C.R.S. When the test or tests show that the amount of alcohol in a person's blood was in violation of the limits provided for in section 42-2-126

(a), (3) (b), (3) (d), or (3) (e), C.R.S., the person shall be subject to license revocation pursuant to the provisions of section 42-2-126, C.R.S.

Any person who is required to submit to testing shall cooperate with the person authorized to obtain specimens of his blood, breath, saliva, or urine, including the signing of any release or consent forms required by any person, hospital, clinic, or association authorized to obtain such specimens. If such person does not cooperate with the person, hospital, clinic, or association authorized to obtain such specimens, including the signing of any release or consent forms, such noncooperation shall be considered a refusal to submit to testing.

The tests shall be administered at the direction of a law enforcement officer having probable cause to believe that the person committed a violation of subparagraph (I) of paragraph (b) of subsection (1) of this section and in accordance with rules and regulations prescribed by the state

board of health concerning the health of the person being tested and the accuracy of such testing. Strict compliance with such rules and regulations shall not be a prerequisite to the admissibility of test results at trial unless the court finds that the extent of noncompliance with a board of health rule has so impaired the validity and reliability of the testing method and the test results as to render the evidence inadmissible. In all other circumstances, failure to strictly comply with such rules and regulations shall only be considered in the weight to be given to the test results and not to the admissibility of such test results. It shall not be a prerequisite to the admissibility of test results at trial that the prosecution present testimony concerning the composition of any kit used to obtain blood, urine, saliva, or breath specimens. A sufficient evidentiary foundation concerning the compliance of such kits with the rules and regulations of the department of public health and environment shall be established by the introduction of a copy of the manufacturer's or supplier's certificate of compliance with such rules and regulations if such certificate specifies the contents, sterility, chemical makeup, and amounts of chemicals contained in such kit.

No person except a physician, a registered nurse, a paramedic as certified in part 2 of article 3.5 of title 25, C.R.S., an emergency medical service provider as defined in part 1 of article

3.5 of title 25, C.R.S., or a person whose normal duties include withdrawing blood samples under the supervision of a physician or registered nurse is entitled to withdraw blood to determine the alcoholic or drug content of the blood for purposes of this section. In a trial for a violation of paragraph (b) of subsection (1) of this section, testimony of a law enforcement officer that the officer witnessed the taking of a blood specimen by a person who the officer reasonably believed was authorized to withdraw blood specimens is sufficient evidence that the person was authorized, and testimony from the person who obtained the blood specimens concerning the person's authorization to obtain blood specimens is not a prerequisite to the admissibility of test results concerning the blood specimens obtained. No civil liability shall attach to a person authorized to obtain blood, breath, saliva, or urine specimens or to a hospital, clinic, or association in or for which the specimens are obtained in accordance with this subsection (4) as a result of the act of obtaining the specimens from any person if the specimens were obtained according to the rules prescribed by the state board of health; except that the provision does not relieve the person from liability for negligence in obtaining the specimen sample.

Any person who is dead or unconscious shall be tested to determine the alcohol or drug content of his blood or any drug content of his system as provided in this subsection (4). If a test cannot be administered to a person who is unconscious, hospitalized, or undergoing medical treatment because the test would endanger the person's life or health, the law enforcement agency shall be allowed to test any blood, urine, or saliva which was obtained and not utilized by a health care provider and shall have access to that portion of the analysis and results of any tests administered by such provider which shows the alcohol or drug content of the person's blood or any drug content within his system. Such test results shall not be considered privileged communications, and the provisions of section 13-90-107, C.R.S., relating to the physician-patient privilege shall not apply. Any person who is dead, in addition to the tests prescribed, shall also have his blood checked for carbon monoxide content and for the presence of drugs, as prescribed by the department of public health and environment. Such information obtained shall be made a part of the accident report.

If a person refuses to take, or to complete, or to cooperate in the completing of any test or tests as provided in this subsection (4) and such person subsequently stands trial for a violation

of subsection (1) (b) of this section, the refusal to take, or to complete, or to cooperate with the completing of any test or tests shall be admissible into evidence at the trial, and a person may not claim the privilege against self-incrimination with regard to the admission of his refusal to take, or to complete, or to cooperate with the completing of any test or tests.

Notwithstanding any provision in section 42-4-1301.1, C.R.S., concerning requirements which relate to the manner in which tests are administered, the test or tests taken pursuant to the provisions of this section may be used for the purposes of driver's license revocation proceedings under section 42-2-126, C.R.S., and for the purposes of prosecutions for violations of section 42-4- 1301 (1) or (2), C.R.S.

In all actions, suits, and judicial proceedings in any court of this state concerning alcohol- related or drug-related traffic offenses, the court shall take judicial notice of methods of testing a person's alcohol or drug level and of the design and operation of devices, as certified by the department of public health and environment, for testing a person's blood, breath, saliva, or urine to determine his alcohol or drug level. This subsection (5) shall not prevent the necessityof establishing during a trial that the testing devices used were working properly and that such testing devices were properly operated. Nothing in this subsection (5) shall preclude a defendant from offering evidence concerning the accuracy of testing devices.


18-3-206. Menacing. (1) A person commits the crime of menacing if, by any threat or physical action, he or she knowingly places or attempts to place another person in fear of imminent serious bodily injury. Menacing is a class 3 misdemeanor, but, it is a class 5 felony if committed:

By the use of a deadly weapon or any article used or fashioned in a manner to cause a person to reasonably believe that the article is a deadly weapon; or

By the person representing verbally or otherwise that he or she is armed with a deadly weapon.


18-3-207. Criminal extortion - aggravated extortion. (1) A person commits criminal extortion if:

The person, without legal authority and with the intent to induce another person against that other person's will to perform an act or to refrain from performing a lawful act, makes a substantial threat to confine or restrain, cause economic hardship or bodily injury to, or damage the property or reputation of, the threatened person or another person; and

The person threatens to cause the results described in paragraph (a) of this subsection (1)

by:

90

Performing or causing an unlawful act to be performed; or

Invoking action by a third party, including but not limited to, the state or any of its

political subdivisions, whose interests are not substantially related to the interests pursued by the person making the threat.

(1.5) A person commits criminal extortion if the person, with the intent to induce another person against that other person's will to give the person money or another item of value, threatens to report to law enforcement officials the immigration status of the threatened person or another

person.

A person commits aggravated criminal extortion if, in addition to the acts described in

subsection (1) of this section, the person threatens to cause the results described in paragraph (a) of subsection (1) of this section by means of chemical, biological, or harmful radioactive agents, weapons, or poison.

For the purposes of this section, "substantial threat" means a threat that is reasonably likely to induce a belief that the threat will be carried out and is one that threatens that significant confinement, restraint, injury, or damage will occur.

Criminal extortion, as described in subsections (1) and (1.5) of this section, is a class 4 felony. Aggravated criminal extortion, as described in subsection (2) of this section, is a class 3 felony.


18-3-208. Reckless endangerment. A person who recklessly engages in conduct which creates a substantial risk of serious bodily injury to another person commits reckless endangerment, which is a class 3 misdemeanor.


18-3-209. Assault on the elderly or persons with disabilities - legislative declaration. (Repealed)

PART 3 KIDNAPPING

18-3-301. First degree kidnapping. (1) Any person who does any of the following acts with the intent thereby to force the victim or any other person to make any concession or give up anything of value in order to secure a release of a person under the offender's actual or apparent control commits first degree kidnapping:

Forcibly seizes and carries any person from one place to another; or

Entices or persuades any person to go from one place to another; or

Imprisons or forcibly secretes any person.

Whoever commits first degree kidnapping is guilty of a class 1 felony if the person kidnapped shall have suffered bodily injury; but no person convicted of first degree kidnapping shall suffer the death penalty if the person kidnapped was liberated alive prior to the conviction of the kidnapper.

Whoever commits first degree kidnapping commits a class 2 felony if, prior to his conviction, the person kidnapped was liberated unharmed.


18-3-302. Second degree kidnapping. (1) Any person who knowingly seizes and carries any person from one place to another, without his consent and without lawful justification, commits

second degree kidnapping.

Any person who takes, entices, or decoys away any child not his own under the age of eighteen years with intent to keep or conceal the child from his parent or guardian or with intent to sell, trade, or barter such child for consideration commits second degree kidnapping.

Second degree kidnapping is a class 2 felony if any of the following circumstances exist:

The person kidnapped is a victim of a sexual offense pursuant to part 4 of this article; or

The person kidnapped is a victim of a robbery.

(a) Unless it is a class 2 felony under subsection (3) of this section, second degree kidnapping is a class 3 felony if any of the following circumstances exist:

The kidnapping is accomplished with intent to sell, trade, or barter the victim for consideration; or

The kidnapping is accomplished by the use of a deadly weapon or any article used or fashioned in a manner to cause a person to reasonably believe that the article is a deadly weapon; or

The kidnapping is accomplished by the perpetrator representing verbally or otherwise that he or she is armed with a deadly weapon.

(b) A defendant convicted of second degree kidnapping committed under any of the circumstances set forth in this subsection (4) shall be sentenced by the court in accordance with the provisions of section 18-1.3-406.

Second degree kidnapping is a class 4 felony, except as provided in subsections (3) and

of this section.


18-3-303. False imprisonment. (1) Any person who knowingly confines or detains another without the other's consent and without proper legal authority commits false imprisonment. This section shall not apply to a peace officer acting in good faith within the scope of his or her duties.

False imprisonment is a class 2 misdemeanor; except that false imprisonment is a class 5 felony if:

The person uses force or threat of force to confine or detain the other person; and

The person confines or detains the other person for twelve hours or longer.


18-3-304. Violation of custody order or order relating to parental responsibilities. (1) Except as otherwise provided in subsection (2.5) of this section, any person, including a natural or foster parent, who, knowing that he or she has no privilege to do so or heedless in that regard, takes or entices any child under the age of eighteen years from the custody or care of the child's parents, guardian, or other lawful custodian or person with parental responsibilities with respect to the child commits a class 5 felony.

Except as otherwise provided in subsection (2.5) of this section, any parent or other person who violates an order of any district or juvenile court of this state, granting the custody of a child or parental responsibilities with respect to a child under the age of eighteen years to any person, agency, or institution, with the intent to deprive the lawful custodian or person with parental responsibilities of the custody or care of a child under the age of eighteen years, commits a class 5 felony.

(2.5) Any person who, in the course of committing the offenses described in subsections (1) and (2) of this section, removes a child under the age of eighteen years from this country commits a class 4 felony.

It shall be an affirmative defense either that the offender reasonably believed that his conduct was necessary to preserve the child from danger to his welfare, or that the child, being at the time more than fourteen years old, was taken away at his own instigation without enticement and without purpose to commit a criminal offense with or against the child.

Any criminal action charged pursuant to this section may be tried in either the county where the act is committed or in which the court issuing the orders granting custody or allocating parental responsibilities is located, if such court is within this state.

Repealed.

18-3-305. Enticement of a child. (1) A person commits the crime of enticement of a child if he or she invites or persuades, or attempts to invite or persuade, a child under the age of fifteen years to enter any vehicle, building, room, or secluded place with the intent to commit sexual assault or unlawful sexual contact upon said child. It is not necessary to a prosecution for attempt under this subsection (1) that the child have perceived the defendant's act of enticement.

Enticement of a child is a class 4 felony. It is a class 3 felony if the defendant has a previous conviction for enticement of a child or sexual assault on a child or for conspiracy to commit or the attempted commission of either offense, or if the enticement of a child results in bodily injury to that child. When a person is convicted, pleads nolo contendere, or receives a deferred sentence for a violation of the provisions of this section and the court knows the person is a current or former employee of a school district in this state or holds a license or authorization pursuant to the provisions of article 60.5 of title 22, C.R.S., the court shall report such fact to the department of education.

18-3-306. Internet luring of a child. (1) An actor commits internet luring of a child if the actor knowingly communicates over a computer or computer network, telephone network, or data network or by a text message or instant message to a person who the actor knows or believes to be under fifteen years of age and, in that communication or in any subsequent communication by computer, computer network, telephone network, data network, text message, or instant message, describes explicit sexual conduct as defined in section 18-6-403 (2) (e), and, in connection with that description, makes a statement persuading or inviting the person to meet the actor for any purpose, and the actor is more than four years older than the person or than the age the actor believes the person to be.

It shall not be a defense to this section that a meeting did not occur.

and (b) (Deleted by amendment, L. 2007, p. 1688, § 8, effective July 1, 2007.)

Internet luring of a child is a class 5 felony; except that luring of a child is a class 4 felony if committed with the intent to meet for the purpose of engaging in sexual exploitation as

defined in section 18-6-403 or sexual contact as defined in section 18-3-401.

For purposes of this section, "in connection with" means communications that further, advance, promote, or have a continuity of purpose and may occur before, during, or after the invitation to meet.

PART 4

UNLAWFUL SEXUAL BEHAVIOR

18-3-401. Definitions. As used in this part 4, unless the context otherwise requires:

"Actor" means the person accused of a sexual offense pursuant to this part 4.

(1.5) "Consent" means cooperation in act or attitude pursuant to an exercise of free will and with knowledge of the nature of the act. A current or previous relationship shall not be sufficient to constitute consent under the provisions of this part 4. Submission under the influence of fear shall not constitute consent. Nothing in this definition shall be construed to affect the admissibility of evidence or the burden of proof in regard to the issue of consent under this part 4.

(1.7) "Diagnostic test" means a human immunodeficiency virus (HIV) screening test followed by a supplemental HIV test for confirmation in those instances when the HIV screening test is repeatedly reactive.

"Intimate parts" means the external genitalia or the perineum or the anus or the buttocks or the pubes or the breast of any person.

(2.4) "Medical-reporting victim" means a victim who seeks medical treatment services following a sexual assault but who elects not to participate in the criminal justice system at the time the victim receives medical services.

(2.5) "Pattern of sexual abuse" means the commission of two or more incidents of sexual contact involving a child when such offenses are committed by an actor upon the same victim.

"Physically helpless" means unconscious, asleep, or otherwise unable to indicate willingness to act.

(3.5) One in a "position of trust" includes, but is not limited to, any person who is a parent or acting in the place of a parent and charged with any of a parent's rights, duties, or responsibilities concerning a child, including a guardian or someone otherwise responsible for the general supervision of a child's welfare, or a person who is charged with any duty or responsibility for the health, education, welfare, or supervision of a child, including foster care, child care, family care, or institutional care, either independently or through another, no matter how brief, at the time of an unlawful act.

"Sexual contact" means the knowing touching of the victim's intimate parts by the actor, or of the actor's intimate parts by the victim, or the knowing touching of the clothing covering the immediate area of the victim's or actor's intimate parts if that sexual contact is for the purposes of sexual arousal, gratification, or abuse.

"Sexual intrusion" means any intrusion, however slight, by any object or any part of a person's body, except the mouth, tongue, or penis, into the genital or anal opening of another person's body if that sexual intrusion can reasonably be construed as being for the purposes of sexual arousal,

gratification, or abuse.

"Sexual penetration" means sexual intercourse, cunnilingus, fellatio, analingus, or anal intercourse. Emission need not be proved as an element of any sexual penetration. Any penetration, however slight, is sufficient to complete the crime.

"Victim" means the person alleging to have been subjected to a criminal sexual assault.

18-3-402. Sexual assault. (1) Any actor who knowingly inflicts sexual intrusion or sexual penetration on a victim commits sexual assault if:

The actor causes submission of the victim by means of sufficient consequence reasonably calculated to cause submission against the victim's will; or

The actor knows that the victim is incapable of appraising the nature of the victim's conduct; or

The actor knows that the victim submits erroneously, believing the actor to be the victim's spouse; or

At the time of the commission of the act, the victim is less than fifteen years of age and the actor is at least four years older than the victim and is not the spouse of the victim; or

At the time of the commission of the act, the victim is at least fifteen years of age but less than seventeen years of age and the actor is at least ten years older than the victim and is not the spouse of the victim; or

The victim is in custody of law or detained in a hospital or other institution and the actor has supervisory or disciplinary authority over the victim and uses this position of authority to coerce the victim to submit, unless the act is incident to a lawful search; or

The actor, while purporting to offer a medical service, engages in treatment or examination of a victim for other than a bona fide medical purpose or in a manner substantially inconsistent with reasonable medical practices; or

The victim is physically helpless and the actor knows the victim is physically helpless and the victim has not consented.

(2)  Sexual assault is a class 4 felony, except as provided in subsections (3), (3.5), (4), and of this section.

If committed under the circumstances of paragraph (e) of subsection (1) of this section, sexual assault is a class 1 misdemeanor and is an extraordinary risk crime that is subject to the modified sentencing range specified in section 18-1.3-501 (3).

(3.5) Sexual assault is a class 3 felony if committed under the circumstances described in paragraph (h) of subsection (1) of this section.

Sexual assault is a class 3 felony if it is attended by any one or more of the following circumstances:

The actor causes submission of the victim through the actual application of physical force or physical violence; or

The actor causes submission of the victim by threat of imminent death, serious bodily injury, extreme pain, or kidnapping, to be inflicted on anyone, and the victim believes that the actor has the present ability to execute these threats; or

The actor causes submission of the victim by threatening to retaliate in the future against

the victim, or any other person, and the victim reasonably believes that the actor will execute this threat. As used in this paragraph (c), "to retaliate" includes threats of kidnapping, death, serious bodily injury, or extreme pain; or

The actor has substantially impaired the victim's power to appraise or control the victim's conduct by employing, without the victim's consent, any drug, intoxicant, or other means for the purpose of causing submission.

(Deleted by amendment, L. 2002, p. 1578, § 2, effective July 1, 2002.)

(a) Sexual assault is a class 2 felony if any one or more of the following circumstances exist:

In the commission of the sexual assault, the actor is physically aided or abetted by one or more other persons; or

The victim suffers serious bodily injury; or

The actor is armed with a deadly weapon or an article used or fashioned in a manner to cause a person to reasonably believe that the article is a deadly weapon or represents verbally or otherwise that the actor is armed with a deadly weapon and uses the deadly weapon, article, or representation to cause submission of the victim.

(b) (I) If a defendant is convicted of sexual assault pursuant to this subsection (5), the court shall sentence the defendant in accordance with section 18-1.3-401 (8) (e). A person convicted solely of sexual assault pursuant to this subsection (5) shall not be sentenced under the crime of violence provisions of section 18-1.3-406 (2). Any sentence for a conviction under this subsection (5) shall be consecutive to any sentence for a conviction for a crime of violence under section 18-1.3-406.

(II) The provisions of this paragraph (b) shall apply to offenses committed prior to November 1, 1998.

Any person convicted of felony sexual assault committed on or after November 1, 1998, under any of the circumstances described in this section shall be sentenced in accordance with the provisions of part 10 of article 1.3 of this title.

A person who is convicted on or after July 1, 2013, of a sexual assault under this section, upon conviction, shall be advised by the court that the person has no right:

To notification of the termination of parental rights and no standing to object to the termination of parental rights for a child conceived as a result of the commission of that offense;

To allocation of parental responsibilities, including parenting time and decision-making responsibilities for a child conceived as a result of the commission of that offense;

Of inheritance from a child conceived as a result of the commission of that offense; and

To notification of or the right to object to the adoption of a child conceived as a result of the commission of that offense.


18-3-403.  Sexual assault in the second degree. (Repealed)


18-3-404.  Unlawful sexual contact. (1) Any actor who knowingly subjects a victim to any sexual contact commits unlawful sexual contact if:

The actor knows that the victim does not consent; or

The actor knows that the victim is incapable of appraising the nature of the victim's conduct; or

The victim is physically helpless and the actor knows that the victim is physically helpless and the victim has not consented; or

The actor has substantially impaired the victim's power to appraise or control the victim's conduct by employing, without the victim's consent, any drug, intoxicant, or other means for the purpose of causing submission; or

Repealed.

The victim is in custody of law or detained in a hospital or other institution and the actor has supervisory or disciplinary authority over the victim and uses this position of authority, unless incident to a lawful search, to coerce the victim to submit; or

The actor engages in treatment or examination of a victim for other than bona fide medical purposes or in a manner substantially inconsistent with reasonable medical practices.

(1.5) Any person who knowingly, with or without sexual contact, induces or coerces a child by any of the means set forth in section 18-3-402 to expose intimate parts or to engage in any sexual contact, intrusion, or penetration with another person, for the purpose of the actor's own sexual gratification, commits unlawful sexual contact. For the purposes of this subsection (1.5), the term "child" means any person under the age of eighteen years.

(1.7)  Repealed.

(a) Unlawful sexual contact is a class 1 misdemeanor and is an extraordinary risk crime that is subject to the modified sentencing range specified in section 18-1.3-501 (3).

(b) Notwithstanding the provisions of paragraph (a) of this subsection (2), unlawful sexual contact is a class 4 felony if the actor compels the victim to submit by use of such force, intimidation, or threat as specified in section 18-3-402 (4) (a), (4) (b), or (4) (c) or if the actor engages in the conduct described in paragraph (g) of subsection (1) of this section or subsection (1.5) of this section.

If a defendant is convicted of the class 4 felony of unlawful sexual contact pursuant to paragraph (b) of subsection (2) of this section, the court shall sentence the defendant in accordance with the provisions of section 18-1.3-406; except that this subsection (3) shall not apply if the actor engages in the conduct described in paragraph (g) of subsection (1) of this section.

A person who is convicted on or after July 1, 2013, of unlawful sexual contact under this section, upon conviction, shall be advised by the court that the person has no right:

To notification of the termination of parental rights and no standing to object to the termination of parental rights for a child conceived as a result of the commission of that offense;

To allocation of parental responsibilities, including parenting time and decision-making responsibilities for a child conceived as a result of the commission of that offense;

Of inheritance from a child conceived as a result of the commission of that offense; and

To notification of or the right to object to the adoption of a child conceived as a result of the commission of that offense.


18-3-405. Sexual assault on a child. (1) Any actor who knowingly subjects another not his or her spouse to any sexual contact commits sexual assault on a child if the victim is less than fifteen

years of age and the actor is at least four years older than the victim.

Sexual assault on a child is a class 4 felony, but it is a class 3 felony if:

The actor applies force against the victim in order to accomplish or facilitate sexual contact; or

The actor, in order to accomplish or facilitate sexual contact, threatens imminent death, serious bodily injury, extreme pain, or kidnapping against the victim or another person, and the victim believes that the actor has the present ability to execute the threat; or

The actor, in order to accomplish or facilitate sexual contact, threatens retaliation by causing in the future the death or serious bodily injury, extreme pain, or kidnapping against the victim or another person, and the victim believes that the actor will execute the threat; or

The actor commits the offense as a part of a pattern of sexual abuse as described in subsection (1) of this section. No specific date or time must be alleged for the pattern of sexual abuse; except that the acts constituting the pattern of sexual abuse, whether charged in the information or indictment or committed prior to or at any time after the offense charged in the information or indictment, shall be subject to the provisions of section 16-5-401 (1) (a), C.R.S., concerning sex offenses against children. The offense charged in the information or indictment shall constitute one of the incidents of sexual contact involving a child necessary to form a pattern of sexual abuse as defined in section 18-3-401 (2.5).

If a defendant is convicted of the class 3 felony of sexual assault on a child pursuant to paragraphs (a) to (d) of subsection (2) of this section, the court shall sentence the defendant in accordance with the provisions of section 18-1.3-406.

A person who is convicted on or after July 1, 2013, of sexual assault on a child under this section, upon conviction, shall be advised by the court that the person has no right:

To notification of the termination of parental rights and no standing to object to the termination of parental rights for a child conceived as a result of the commission of that offense;

To allocation of parental responsibilities, including parenting time and decision-making responsibilities for a child conceived as a result of the commission of that offense;

Of inheritance from a child conceived as a result of the commission of that offense; and

To notification of or the right to object to the adoption of a child conceived as a result of the commission of that offense.


18-3-405.3. Sexual assault on a child by one in a position of trust. (1) Any actor who knowingly subjects another not his or her spouse to any sexual contact commits sexual assault on a child by one in a position of trust if the victim is a child less than eighteen years of age and the actor committing the offense is one in a position of trust with respect to the victim.

Sexual assault on a child by one in a position of trust is a class 3 felony if:

The victim is less than fifteen years of age; or

The actor commits the offense as a part of a pattern of sexual abuse as described in subsection (1) of this section. No specific date or time need be alleged for the pattern of sexual abuse; except that the acts constituting the pattern of sexual abuse whether charged in the information or indictment or committed prior to or at any time after the offense charged in the information or indictment, shall be subject to the provisions of section 16-5-401 (1) (a), C.R.S.,

concerning sex offenses against children. The offense charged in the information or indictment shall constitute one of the incidents of sexual contact involving a child necessary to form a pattern of sexual abuse as defined in section 18-3-401 (2.5).

Sexual assault on a child by one in a position of trust is a class 4 felony if the victim is fifteen years of age or older but less than eighteen years of age and the offense is not committed as part of a pattern of sexual abuse, as described in paragraph (b) of subsection (2) of this section.

If a defendant is convicted of the class 3 felony of sexual assault on a child pursuant to paragraph (b) of subsection (2) of this section, the court shall sentence the defendant in accordance with the provisions of section 18-1.3-406.

A person who is convicted on or after July 1, 2013, of sexual assault on a child by one in a position of trust under this section, upon conviction, shall be advised by the court that the person has no right:

To notification of the termination of parental rights and no standing to object to the termination of parental rights for a child conceived as a result of the commission of that offense;

To allocation of parental responsibilities, including parenting time and decision-making responsibilities for a child conceived as a result of the commission of that offense;

Of inheritance from a child conceived as a result of the commission of that offense; and

To notification of or the right to object to the adoption of a child conceived as a result of the commission of that offense.


18-3-405.4. Internet sexual exploitation of a child. (1) An actor commits internet sexual exploitation of a child if the actor knowingly importunes, invites, or entices through communication via a computer network or system, telephone network, or data network or by a text message or instant message, a person whom the actor knows or believes to be under fifteen years of age and at least four years younger than the actor, to:

Expose or touch the person's own or another person's intimate parts while communicating with the actor via a computer network or system, telephone network, or data network or by a text message or instant message; or

Observe the actor's intimate parts via a computer network or system, telephone network, or data network or by a text message or instant message.

(Deleted by amendment, L. 2009, (HB 09-1163), ch. 343, p. 1797, § 1, effective July 1, 2009.)
Internet sexual exploitation of a child is a class 4 felony.

18-3-405.5. Sexual assault on a client by a psychotherapist. (1) (a) Any actor who knowingly inflicts sexual penetration or sexual intrusion on a victim commits aggravated sexual assault on a client if:
The actor is a psychotherapist and the victim is a client of the psychotherapist; or
The actor is a psychotherapist and the victim is a client and the sexual penetration or intrusion occurred by means of therapeutic deception.
(b)  Aggravated sexual assault on a client is a class 4 felony.

(a) Any actor who knowingly subjects a victim to any sexual contact commits sexual assault on a client if:
The actor is a psychotherapist and the victim is a client of the psychotherapist; or
The actor is a psychotherapist and the victim is a client and the sexual contact occurred by means of therapeutic deception.
(b)  Sexual assault on a client is a class 1 misdemeanor.
Consent by the client to the sexual penetration, intrusion, or contact shall not constitute a defense to such offense.
As used in this section, unless the context otherwise requires:
"Client" means a person who seeks or receives psychotherapy from a psychotherapist.
"Psychotherapist" means anyperson who performs or purports to perform psychotherapy, whether the person is licensed or registered by the state pursuant to title 12, C.R.S., or certified by the state pursuant to part 5 of article 1 of title 25, C.R.S.
"Psychotherapy" means the treatment, diagnosis, or counseling in a professional relationship to assist individuals or groups to alleviate mental disorders, understand unconscious or conscious motivation, resolve emotional, relationship, or attitudinal conflicts, or modify behaviors which interfere with effective emotional, social, or intellectual functioning.
"Therapeutic deception" means a representation by a psychotherapist that sexual contact, penetration, or intrusion by the psychotherapist is consistent with or part of the client's treatment.
A person who is convicted on or after July 1, 2013, of sexual assault on a client by a psychotherapist under this section, upon conviction, shall be advised by the court that the person has no right:
To notification of the termination of parental rights and no standing to object to the termination of parental rights for a child conceived as a result of the commission of that offense;
To allocation of parental responsibilities, including parenting time and decision-making responsibilities for a child conceived as a result of the commission of that offense;
Of inheritance from a child conceived as a result of the commission of that offense; and
To notification of or the right to object to the adoption of a child conceived as a result of the commission of that offense.

18-3-405.6. Invasion of privacy for sexual gratification. (1) A person who knowingly observes or takes a photograph of another person's intimate parts without that person's consent, in a situation where the person observed or photographed has a reasonable expectation of privacy, for the purpose of the observer's own sexual gratification, commits unlawful invasion of privacy for sexual gratification.
(a) Except as otherwise provided in paragraph (b) of this subsection (2), invasion of privacy for sexual gratification is a class 1 misdemeanor and is an extraordinary risk crime subject to the modified sentencing range specified in section 18-1.3-501 (3).
Invasion of privacy for sexual gratification is a class 6 felony and is an extraordinary risk crime subject to the modified sentencing range specified in section 18-1.3-401 (10) if either of the following circumstances exist:
The offense is committed subsequent to a prior conviction, as defined in section 16-22-

102 (3), C.R.S., for unlawful sexual behavior as defined in section 16-22-102 (9), C.R.S.; or
The person observes or takes a photograph of the intimate parts of a person under fifteen years of age. This subparagraph (II) shall not apply if the defendant is less than four years older than the person observed or photographed.
For purposes of this section, "photograph" includes a photograph, motion picture, videotape, live feed, print, negative, slide, or other mechanically, electronically, or chemically produced or reproduced visual material.

18-3-406.  Criminality of conduct. (Repealed)

18-3-407. Victim's and witness's prior history - evidentiary hearing - victim's identity - protective order. (1) Evidence of specific instances of the victim's or a witness's prior or subsequent sexual conduct, opinion evidence of the victim's or a witness's sexual conduct, and reputation evidence of the victim's or a witness's sexual conduct may be admissible only at trial and shall not be admitted in any other proceeding except at a proceeding pursuant to paragraph (c) of subsection (2) of this section. At trial, such evidence shall be presumed to be irrelevant except:
Evidence of the victim's or witness' prior or subsequent sexual conduct with the actor;
Evidence of specific instances of sexual activity showing the source or origin of semen, pregnancy, disease, or any similar evidence of sexual intercourse offered for the purpose of showing that the act or acts charged were or were not committed by the defendant.
In any criminal prosecution for class 4 felony internet luring of a child, as described in section 18-3-306 (3) or under sections 18-3-402 to 18-3-405.5, 18-3-504, 18-6-301, 18-6-302, 18-6- 403, 18-6-404, and any offense described in part 4 of article 7 of this title, or for attempt or conspiracy to commit any of said crimes, if evidence, that is not excepted under subsection (1) of this section, of specific instances of the victim's or a witness's prior or subsequent sexual conduct, or opinion evidence of the victim's or a witness's sexual conduct, or reputation evidence of the victim's or a witness's sexual conduct, or evidence that the victim or a witness has a history of false reporting of sexual assaults is to be offered at trial, the following procedure shall be followed:
A written motion shall be made at least thirty-five days prior to trial, unless later for good cause shown, to the court and to the opposing parties stating that the moving party has an offer of proof of the relevancy and materiality of evidence of specific instances of the victim's or witness' prior or subsequent sexual conduct, or opinion evidence of the victim's or witness' sexual conduct, or reputation evidence of the victim's or witness' sexual conduct, or evidence that the victim or witness has a history of false reporting of sexual assaults that is proposed to be presented.
The written motion shall be accompanied by an affidavit in which the offer of proof shall be stated.
If the court finds that the offer of proof is sufficient, the court shall notify the other party of such. If the prosecution stipulates to the facts contained in the offer of proof, the court shall rule on the motion based upon the offer of proof without an evidentiary hearing. Otherwise, the court shall set a

hearing to be held in camera prior to trial. In such hearing, to the extent the facts are in dispute, the court may allow the questioning of the victim or witness regarding the offer of proof

made by the moving party or otherwise allow a presentation of the offer of proof, including but not limited to the presentation of witnesses.

An in camera hearing may be held during trial if evidence first becomes available at the time of the trial or for good cause shown.

At the conclusion of the hearing, or by written order if no hearing is held, if the court finds that the evidence proposed to be offered regarding the sexual conduct of the victim or witness is relevant to a material issue to the case, the court shall order that evidence may be introduced and prescribe the nature of the evidence or questions to be permitted. The moving party may then offer evidence pursuant to the order of the court.

All motions and supporting documents filed pursuant to this section shall be filed under seal and may be unsealed only if the court rules the evidence is admissible and the case proceeds to trial. If the court determines that only part of the evidence contained in the motion is admissible, only that portion of the motion and supporting documents pertaining to the admissible portion may be unsealed.

The court shall seal all court transcripts, tape recordings, and records of proceedings, other than minute orders, of a hearing held pursuant to this section. The court may unseal the transcripts, tape recordings, and records only if the court rules the evidence is admissible and the case proceeds to trial. If the court determines that only part of the evidence is admissible, only the portion of the hearing pertaining to the admissible evidence may be unsealed.

(a) In a criminal prosecution including an offense described in subsection (2) of this section, the court may, at any time upon motion of the prosecution or on the court's own motion, issue a protective order pursuant to the Colorado rules of criminal procedure concerning disclosure of information relating to the victim or a witness. The court may punish a violation of a protective order by contempt of court.

(b) The victim who would be the subject of the protective order may object to the motion for a protective order.


18-3-407.5. Victim evidence - forensic evidence - electronic lie detector exam without victim's consent prohibited. (1) A law enforcement agency with jurisdiction over a sexual assault must pay for any direct cost associated with the collection of forensic evidence from a victim who reports the assault to the law enforcement agency.

A law enforcement agency, prosecuting officer, or other government official may not ask or require a victim of a sexual offense to submit to a polygraph examination or any form of a mechanical or electrical lie detector examination as a condition for proceeding with any criminal investigation or prosecution of an offense. A law enforcement agency shall conduct the examination only with the victim's written informed consent. Consent shall not be considered informed unless the law enforcement agency informs the victim in writing of the victim's right to refuse to submit to the examination. In addition, the law enforcement agency shall orally provide to the victim information about the potential uses of the results of the examination.

(a) A law enforcement agency, prosecuting officer, or other government official may not ask or require a victim of a sexual offense to participate in the criminal justice system process or cooperate with the law enforcement agency, prosecuting officer, or other government official as a

condition of receiving a forensic medical examination that includes the collection of evidence.

A victim of a sexual offense shall not bear the cost of a forensic medical examination that includes the collection of evidence that is used for the purpose of evidence collection even if the victim does not want to participate in the criminal justice system or otherwise cooperate with the law enforcement agency, prosecuting officer, or other government official. The division of criminal justice in the department of public safety shall pay the cost of the examination.

When personnel at a medical facility perform a medical forensic examination that includes the collection of evidence based on the request of a victim of a sexual offense and the medical facility performing the examination knows where the crime occurred, the facility shall contact the law enforcement agency in whose jurisdiction the crime occurred regarding preservation of the evidence. If the medical facility does not know where the crime occurred, the facility shall contact its local law enforcement agency regarding preservation of the evidence. Notwithstanding any other statutory requirements regarding storage of biological evidence, the law enforcement agency contacted by the medical facility shall retrieve the evidence from the facility and store it for at least two years.

A law enforcement agency shall not submit medical forensic evidence associated with an anonymous report submitted pursuant to section 12-36-135, C.R.S., to the Colorado bureau of investigation or any other laboratory for testing as described in section 24-33.5-113, C.R.S. Medical forensic evidence associated with a medical report submitted pursuant to section 12-36-135, C.R.S., when the victim has consented to evidence testing, shall be submitted to the Colorado bureau of investigation or another laboratory and tested, pursuant to section 24-33.5-113, C.R.S., regardless of whether the victim has chosen to participate in the criminal justice system.


18-3-407.7. Sexual assault victim emergency payment program - creation - eligibility. (1) There is hereby created the sexual assault victim emergency payment program, referred to in this section as the "program", in the division of criminal justice in the department of public safety. The purpose of the program is to assist medical-reporting victims of sexual assault with medical expenses associated with a sexual assault that are not otherwise covered pursuant to section 18-3-407.5 or any other victim compensation program.

(a) A medical-reporting victim must request and receive a medical forensic examination to be eligible to have medical costs and fees covered through the program. The division of criminal justice shall develop a policy for administering the program. The policy must include a requirement to establish a cap for the amount payable per victim based on actual and reasonable costs and available funds, but the minimum cap must not be less than one thousand dollars. The program must cover medical fees and costs associated with obtaining the medical forensic examination, including but not limited to emergencydepartment fees and costs, laboratoryfees, prescription medication, and physician's fees, as long as funds are available. The program may also cover medical fees and costs for injuries directly related to the sexual assault. The program may also pay for any uncovered direct costs of the medical forensic examination for a medical-reporting victim. The total amount paid for all expenses must not exceed the annual cap established by the division of criminal justice.

The program shall be the payor of last resort.

A hospital shall limit the amounts charged for emergency or associated fees and costs

eligible for payment pursuant to paragraph (a) of this subsection (2) to not more than the lowest negotiated rate from a private health plan.

The division of criminal justice may waive any requirement set forth in this section for good cause shown or in the interests of justice, if it is so required.


18-3-408. Jury instruction prohibited. In anycriminal prosecution under sections 18-3-402 to 18-3-405, or for attempt or conspiracy to commit any crime under sections 18-3-402 to 18-3-405, the jury shall not be instructed to examine with caution the testimony of the victim solely because of the nature of the charge, nor shall the jury be instructed that such a charge is easy to make but difficult to defend against, nor shall any similar instruction be given. However, the jury shall be instructed not to allow gender bias or any kind of prejudice based upon gender to influence the decision of the jury.


18-3-408.5. Jury instruction on consent - when required. (1) In any criminal prosecution for a crime listed in subsection (2) of this section or for attempt or conspiracy to commit a crime listed in subsection (2) of this section, upon request of any party to the proceedings, the jury shall be instructed on the definition of consent as set forth in section 18-3-401 (1.5). Notwithstanding the provisions of section 18-1-505 (4), an instruction on the definition of consent given pursuant to this section shall not constitute an affirmative defense, but shall only act as a defense to the elements of the offense.

The provisions of subsection (1) of this section shall apply to the following crimes:

Sexual assault as described in section 18-3-402 (1) (a);

Sexual assault as described in section 18-3-402 (1) (b), (1) (c), or (1) (e), as they existed prior to July 1, 2000, for offenses committed prior to July 1, 2000;

Sexual assault in the second degree as described in section 18-3-403 (1) (a) or (1) (b), as they existed prior to July 1, 2000, for offenses committed prior to July 1, 2000;

Unlawful sexual contact as described in section 18-3-404 (1) (a), (1) (c), or (1) (d);

Unlawful sexual contact as described in section 18-3-404 (1.7), as it existed prior to July 1, 2010, for offenses committed prior to July 1, 2010;

Invasion of privacy for sexual gratification as described in section 18-3-405.6; or

Criminal invasion of privacy in violation of section 18-7-801.


18-3-409. Marital defense. Any marital relationship, whether established statutorily, putatively, or by common law, between an actor and a victim shall not be a defense to any offense under this part 4 unless such defense is specifically set forth in the applicable statutory section by having the elements of the offense specifically exclude a spouse.


18-3-410. Medical exception. The provisions of this part 4 shall not apply to any act performed for bona fide medical purposes if such act is performed in a manner which is not

inconsistent with reasonable medical practices.


18-3-411. Sex offenses against children - "unlawful sexual offense" defined - limitation for commencing proceedings - evidence - statutory privilege. (1) As used in this section, "unlawful sexual offense" means enticement of a child, as described in section 18-3-305, sexual assault, as described in section 18-3-402, when the victim at the time of the commission of the act is a child less than fifteen years of age, sexual assault in the first degree, as described in section 18-3- 402, as it existed prior to July 1, 2000, when the victim at the time of the commission of the act is a child less than fifteen years of age; sexual assault in the second degree, as described in section 18- 3-403 (1) (a), (1) (b), (1) (c), (1) (d), (1) (g), or (1) (h), as it existed prior to July 1, 2000, when the victim at the time of the commission of the act is a child less than fifteen years of age, or as described in section 18-3-403 (1) (e), as it existed prior to July 1, 2000, when the victim is less than fifteen years of age and the actor is at least four years older than the victim; unlawful sexual contact, as described in section 18-3-404 (1) (a), (1) (b), (1) (c), (1) (d), (1) (f), or (1) (g), when the victim at the time of the commission of the act is a child less than fifteen years of age; sexual assault in the third degree, as described in section 18-3-404 (1) (a), (1) (b), (1) (c), (1) (d), (1) (f), or (1) (g), as it existed prior to July 1, 2000, when the victim at the time of the commission of the act is a child less than fifteen years of age; sexual assault on a child, as described in section 18-3-405; sexual assault on a child by one in a position of trust, as described in section 18-3-405.3; aggravated incest, as described in section 18-6-302; human trafficking of a minor for sexual servitude, as described in section 18-3-504 (2), C.R.S.; sexual exploitation of a child, as described in section 18-6-403; procurement of a child for sexual exploitation, as described in section 18-6-404; indecent exposure, as described in section 18-7-302, soliciting for child prostitution, as described in section 18-7-402; pandering of a child, as described in section 18-7-403; procurement of a child, as described in section 18-7-403.5; keeping a place of child prostitution, as described in section 18-7-404; pimping of a child, as described in section 18-7-405; inducement of child prostitution, as described in section 18- 7-405.5; patronizing a prostituted child, as described in section 18-7-406; class 4 felony internet luring of a child, as described in section 18-3-306 (3); internet sexual exploitation of a child, as described in section 18-3-405.4; or criminal attempt, conspiracy, or solicitation to commit any of the acts specified in this subsection (1).

No person shall be prosecuted, tried, or punished for a misdemeanor offense specified in section 18-3-402 or 18-3-404, unless the indictment, information, complaint, or action for the same is found or instituted within five years after the commission of the offense. The limitation for commencing criminal proceedings and juvenile delinquencyproceedings concerning unlawful sexual offenses that are felonies shall be governed by section 16-5-401 (1) (a), C.R.S.

Out-of-court statements made by a child describing any act or attempted act of sexual contact, intrusion, or penetration, as defined in section 18-3-401, performed or attempted to be performed with, by, or on the child declarant, not otherwise admissible by a statute or court rule which provides an exception to the objection of hearsay, may be admissible in any proceeding in which the child is a victim of an unlawful sexual offense pursuant to the provisions of section 13-25- 129, C.R.S.

All cases involving the commission of an unlawful sexual offense shall take precedence

before the court; the court shall hear these cases as soon as possible after they are filed.

The statutory privilege between the husband and the wife shall not be available for excluding or refusing testimony in any prosecution of an unlawful sexual offense.


18-3-412. Habitual sex offenders against children - indictment or information - verdict of the jury. (1) For the purpose of this section, "unlawful sexual offense" means sexual assault, as described in section 18-3-402, when the victim at the time of the commission of the act is a child less than fifteen years of age, sexual assault in the first degree, as described in section 18-3-402, as it existed prior to July 1, 2000, when the victim at the time of the commission of the act is a child less than fifteen years of age; sexual assault in the second degree, as described in section 18-3-403 (1) (a), (1) (b), (1) (c), (1) (d), (1) (g), or (1) (h), as it existed prior to July 1, 2000, when the victim at the time of the commission of the act is a child less than fifteen years of age, or as described in section 18-3-403 (1) (e), as it existed prior to July 1, 2000, when the victim is less than fifteen years of age and the actor is at least four years older than the victim; unlawful sexual contact, as described in section 18-3-404 (1) (a), (1) (b), (1) (c), (1) (d), (1) (f), or (1) (g), when the victim at the time of the commission of the act is a child less than fifteen years of age; sexual assault in the third degree, as described

97

in section 18-3-404 (1) (a), (1) (b), (1) (c), (1) (d), (1) (f), or (1) (g), as it existed prior to July 1, 2000, when the victim at the time of the commission of the act is a child less than fifteen years of age; sexual assault on a child, as described in section 18-3-405; sexual assault on a child by one in a position of trust, as described in section 18-3-405.3; aggravated incest, as described in section 18-6-302; human trafficking of a minor for sexual servitude, as described in section 18-3-504 (2), C.R.S.; sexual exploitation of a child, as described in section 18-6-403; procurement of a child for sexual exploitation, as described in section 18-6-404; soliciting for child prostitution, as described in section 18-7-402; pandering of a child, as described in section 18-7-403; procurement of a child, as described in section 18-7-403.5; keeping a place of child prostitution, as described in section 18-7-404; pimping of a child, as described in section 18-7-405; inducement of child prostitution, as described in section 18-7-405.5; patronizing a prostituted child, as described in section 18-7-406; or criminal attempt, conspiracy, or solicitation to commit any of the acts specified in this subsection (1).

Every person convicted in this state of an unlawful sexual offense who has been previously convicted upon charges prior to the commission of the present act, which were separately brought, either in this state or elsewhere, of an unlawful sexual offense or who has been previously convicted under the laws of any other state, the United States, or any territory subject to the jurisdiction of the United States of an unlawful act that, if committed within this state, would be an unlawful sexual offense shall be adjudged an habitual sex offender against children. If the second or subsequent unlawful sexual offense for which a defendant is convicted constitutes a felony, the court shall impose a sentence to the department of corrections of not less than three times the upper limit of the presumptive range for that class felony as set out in section 18-1.3-401. If the second or subsequent unlawful sexual offense for which a defendant is convicted constitutes a misdemeanor, the court shall impose a sentence to the county jail of not less than three times the maximum sentence for that class misdemeanor as set out in section 18-1.3-501.

Any previous conviction of an unlawful sexual offense shall be set forth in apt words in

the complaint, indictment, or information. For purposes of trial, a duly authenticated copy of the record of previous convictions and judgments of any court of record for any of said crimes of the party indicted, charged, or informed against shall be prima facie evidence of such convictions and may be used in evidence against such party. A duly authenticated copy of the records of institutions of treatment or incarceration, including, but not limited to, records pertaining to identification of the party indicted, charged, or informed against, shall be prima facie evidence of the facts contained therein and may be used in evidence against such party.

Any person who is subject to the provisions of this section shall not be eligible for suspension of sentence.

The procedures specified in section 18-1.3-803 shall govern in a trial to which the provisions of this section are alleged to apply based on a previous conviction or convictions for an unlawful sexual offense as set out in the complaint, indictment, or information.


18-3-412.5. Failure to register as a sex offender. (1) A person who is required to register pursuant to article 22 of title 16, C.R.S., and who fails to comply with any of the requirements placed on registrants by said article, including but not limited to committing any of the acts specified in this subsection (1), commits the offense of failure to register as a sex offender:

Failure to register pursuant to article 22 of title 16, C.R.S.;

Submission of a registration form containing false information or submission of an incomplete registration form;

Failure to provide information or knowingly providing false information to a probation department employee, to a community corrections administrator or his or her designee, or to a judge or magistrate when receiving notice pursuant to section 16-22-106 (1), (2), or (3), C.R.S., of the duty to register;

If the person has been sentenced to a county jail, otherwise incarcerated, or committed, due to conviction of or disposition or adjudication for an offense specified in section 16-22-103, C.R.S., failure to provide notice of the address where the person intends to reside upon release as required in sections 16-22-106 and 16-22-107, C.R.S.;

Knowingly providing false information to a sheriff or his or her designee, department of corrections personnel, or department of human services personnel concerning the address where the person intends to reside upon release from the county jail, the department of corrections, or the department of human services. Providing false information shall include, but is not limited to, providing false information as described in section 16-22-107 (4) (b), C.R.S.

Failure when registering to provide the person's current name and any former names;

Failure to register with the local law enforcement agency in each jurisdiction in which the person resides upon changing an address, establishing an additional residence, or legally changing names;

Failure to provide the person's correct date of birth, to sit for or otherwise provide a current photograph or image, to provide a current set of fingerprints, or to provide the person's correct address;

Failure to complete a cancellation of registration form and file the form with the local law enforcement agency of the jurisdiction in which the person will no longer reside;

When the person's place of residence is a trailer or motor home, failure to register an address at which the trailer or motor home is lawfully located pursuant to section 16-22-109 (1) (a.3), C.R.S.;

Failure to register an e-mail address, instant-messaging identity, or chat room identity prior to using the address or identity if the person is required to register that information pursuant to section 16-22-108 (2.5), C.R.S.

(1.5) (a) In a prosecution for a violation of this section, it is an affirmative defense that:

Uncontrollable circumstances prevented the person from complying;

The person did not contribute to the creation of the circumstances in reckless disregard of the requirement to comply; and

The person complied as soon as the circumstances ceased to exist.

(b) In order to assert the affirmative defense pursuant to this subsection (1.5), the defendant shall provide notice to the prosecuting attorney as soon as practicable, but not later than thirty-five days prior to trial, of his or her notice of intent to rely upon the affirmative defense. The notice shall include a description of the uncontrollable circumstance or circumstances and the dates the uncontrollable circumstances began and ceased to exist in addition to the names and addresses of any witnesses the defendant plans to call to support the affirmative defense. The prosecuting attorney shall advise the defendant of the names and addresses of any additional witnesses who may be called to refute such affirmative defense as soon as practicable after their names become known. Upon the request of the prosecution, the court shall first rule as a matter of law whether the claimed facts and circumstances would, if established, constitute sufficient evidence to support submission to the jury.

(a) Failure to register as a sex offender is a class 6 felony if the person was convicted of felony unlawful sexual behavior, or of another offense, the underlying factual basis of which includes felony unlawful sexual behavior, or if the person received a disposition or was adjudicated for an offense that would constitute felony unlawful sexual behavior if committed by an adult, or for another offense, the underlying factual basis of which involves felony unlawful sexual behavior; except that any second or subsequent offense of failure to register as a sex offender by such person is a class 5 felony.

Any person convicted of felony failure to register as a sex offender shall be sentenced pursuant to the provisions of section 18-1.3-401. If such person is sentenced to probation, the court may require, as a condition of probation, that the person participate until further order of the court in an intensive supervision probation program established pursuant to section 18-1.3-1007. If such person is sentenced to incarceration and subsequently released on parole, the parole board may require, as a condition of parole, that the person participate in an intensive supervision parole program established pursuant to section 18-1.3-1005.

A person who is convicted of a felony sex offense in another state or jurisdiction, including but not limited to a military or federal jurisdiction, and who commits failure to register as a sex offender in this state commits felony failure to register as a sex offender as specified in paragraph (a) of this subsection (2) and shall be sentenced as provided in paragraph (b) of this subsection (2).

(a) Failure to register as a sex offender is a class 1 misdemeanor if the person was convicted of misdemeanor unlawful sexual behavior, or of another offense, the underlying factual basis of which involves misdemeanor unlawful sexual behavior, or if the person received a

disposition or was adjudicated for an offense that would constitute misdemeanor unlawful sexual behavior if committed by an adult, or for another offense, the underlying factual basis of which involves misdemeanor unlawful sexual behavior. A class 1 misdemeanor conviction pursuant to this subsection (3) is an extraordinary risk crime that is subject to the modified sentencing range specified in section 18-1.3-501 (3).

(b) A person who is convicted of a misdemeanor sex offense in another state or jurisdiction, including but not limited to a military or federal jurisdiction, and who commits failure to register as a sex offender in this state commits misdemeanor failure to register as a sex offender as specified in paragraph (a) of this subsection (3).

(a) Any juvenile who receives a disposition or is adjudicated for a delinquent act of failure to register as a sex offender that would constitute a felony if committed by an adult shall be sentenced to a forty-five-day mandatory minimum detention sentence; except that any juvenile who receives a disposition or is adjudicated for a second or subsequent delinquent act of failure to register as a sex offender that would constitute a felony if committed by an adult shall be placed or committed out of the home for not less than one year.

(b) Any juvenile who receives a disposition or is adjudicated for a delinquent act of failure to register as a sex offender that would constitute a misdemeanor if committed by an adult shall be sentenced to a thirty-day mandatory minimum detention sentence; except that any juvenile who receives a disposition or is adjudicated for a second or subsequent delinquent act of failure to register as a sex offender that would constitute a misdemeanor if committed by an adult shall be sentenced to a forty-five-day mandatory minimum detention sentence.

For purposes of this section, unless the context otherwise requires, "unlawful sexual behavior" has the same meaning as set forth in section 16-22-102 (9), C.R.S.

(a) When a peace officer determines that there is probable cause to believe that a crime of failure to register as a sex offender has been committed by a person required to register as a sexually violent predator in this state pursuant to article 22 of title 16, C.R.S., or in any other state, the officer shall arrest the person suspected of the crime. It shall be a condition of any bond posted by such person that the person shall register pursuant to the provisions of section 16-22-108, C.R.S., within seven days after release from incarceration.

(b) When a peace officer makes a warrantless arrest pursuant to this subsection (6), the peace officer shall immediately notify the Colorado bureau of investigation of the arrest. Upon receiving the notification, the Colorado bureau of investigation shall notify the jurisdiction where the sexually violent predator last registered. The jurisdiction where the sexually violent predator last registered, if it is not the jurisdiction where the probable cause arrest is made, shall coordinate with the arresting jurisdiction immediately to determine the appropriate jurisdiction that will file the charge. If the sexually violent predator is being held in custody after the arrest, the appropriate jurisdiction shall have no less than seven days after the date of the arrest to charge the sexually violent predator.


18-3-412.6. Failure to verify location as a sex offender. (1) A person who is required to register pursuant to article 22 of title 16, C.R.S., and who lacks a fixed residence, as defined in that article, and who fails to comply with the provisions of section 16-22-109 (3.5) (c) (I) or 16-22-109 (3.5) (c) (II), C.R.S., commits the offense of failure to verify location as a sex offender.

(a) In a prosecution for a violation of this section, it is an affirmative defense that:
Uncontrollable circumstances prevented the person from complying; and
The person did not contribute to the creation of the circumstances in reckless disregard of the requirement to comply; and
The person complied as soon as the circumstances ceased to exist.
(b) In order to assert the affirmative defense pursuant to this subsection (2), the defendant shall provide notice to the prosecuting attorney as soon as practicable, but not later than thirty days prior to trial, of his or her notice of intent to rely upon the affirmative defense. The notice shall include a description of the uncontrollable circumstance or circumstances and the dates that the uncontrollable circumstances began and ceased to exist in addition to the names and addresses of any witnesses the defendant plans to call to support the affirmative defense. The prosecuting attorney shall advise the defendant of the names and addresses of any additional witnesses who may be called to refute the affirmative defense as soon as practicable after their names become known. Upon the request of the prosecution, the court shall first rule as a matter of law whether the claimed facts and circumstances would, if established, constitute sufficient evidence to support submission to the jury.
Failure to verify location as a sex offender is an unclassified misdemeanor punishable by a sentence of up to thirty days in the county jail; except that a third or subsequent violation of this section is an unclassified misdemeanor punishable by up to one year in the county jail.
Failure to verify location as a sex offender is not a sexual offense subject to the provisions of sections 16-11.7-104 and 16-11.7-105, C.R.S., and, notwithstanding any other provision of law to the contrary, offenders convicted of a violation of this section are not eligible for probation pursuant to part 2 of article 1.3 of this title.


18-3-413. Video tape depositions - children - victims of sexual offenses. (1) When a defendant has been charged with an unlawful sexual offense, as defined in section 18-3-411 (1), or incest, as defined in section 18-6-301, and when the victim at the time of the commission of the act is a child less than fifteen years of age, the prosecution may apply to the court for an order that a deposition be taken of the victim's testimony and that the deposition be recorded and preserved on video tape.

The prosecution shall apply for the order in writing at least three days prior to the taking of the deposition. The defendant shall receive reasonable notice of the taking of the deposition.

Upon timely receipt of the application, the court shall make a preliminary finding regarding whether, at the time of trial, the victim is likely to be medically unavailable or otherwise unavailable within the meaning of rule 804 (a) of the Colorado rules of evidence. Such finding shall be based on, but not be limited to, recommendations from the child's therapist or any other person having direct contact with the child, whose recommendations are based on specific behavioral indicators exhibited by the child. If the court so finds, it shall order that the deposition be taken, pursuant to rule 15 (d) of the Colorado rules of criminal procedure, and preserved on video tape. The prosecution shall transmit the video tape to the clerk of the court in which the action is pending.

If at the time of trial the court finds that further testimony would cause the victim emotional trauma so that the victim is medically unavailable or otherwise unavailable within the meaning of rule 804 (a) of the Colorado rules of evidence, the court may admit the video tape of the victim's deposition as former testimony under rule 804 (b) (1) of the Colorado rules of evidence.

Nothing in this section shall prevent the admission into evidence of any videotaped statements of children which would qualify for admission pursuant to section 13-25-129, C.R.S., or any other statute or rule of evidence.

18-3-413.5. Use of closed circuit television - child victims of sexual offenses. (Repealed)

18-3-414. Payment of treatment costs for the victim or victims of a sexual offense against a child. (1) In addition to any other penalty provided by law, the court may order any person who is convicted of an unlawful sexual offense, as defined in section 18-3-411 (1), or of incest, as defined in section 18-6-301, when the victim was under the age of fifteen at the time of the commission of the offense, to meet all or any portion of the financial obligations of treatment prescribed for the victim or victims of his or her offense.
(2) At the time of sentencing, the court may order that an offender described in subsection
of this section be put on a period of probation for the purpose of paying the treatment costs of the victim or victims.

18-3-414.5. Sexually violent predators - assessment - annual report. (1) As used in this section, unless the context otherwise requires:
"Sexually violent predator" means an offender:
Who is eighteen years of age or older as of the date the offense is committed or who is less than eighteen years of age as of the date the offense is committed but is tried as an adult pursuant to section 19-2-517 or 19-2-518, C.R.S.;
Who has been convicted on or after July 1, 1999, of one of the following offenses, or of an attempt, solicitation, or conspiracy to commit one of the following offenses, committed on or after July 1, 1997:
Sexual assault, in violation of section 18-3-402 or sexual assault in the first degree, in violation of section 18-3-402, as it existed prior to July 1, 2000;
Sexual assault in the second degree, in violation of section 18-3-403, as it existed prior to July 1, 2000;
Unlawful sexual contact, in violation of section 18-3-404 (1.5) or (2) or sexual assault in the third degree, in violation of section 18-3-404 (1.5) or (2), as it existed prior to July 1, 2000;
Sexual assault on a child, in violation of section 18-3-405; or
Sexual assault on a child by one in a position of trust, in violation of section 18-3-405.3;
Whose victim was a stranger to the offender or a person with whom the offender established or promoted a relationship primarily for the purpose of sexual victimization; and
Who, based upon the results of a risk assessment screening instrument developed by the division of criminal justice in consultation with and approved by the sex offender management

board established pursuant to section 16-11.7-103 (1), C.R.S., is likely to subsequently commit one or more of the offenses specified in subparagraph (II) of this paragraph (a) under the circumstances described in subparagraph (III) of this paragraph (a).
"Convicted" includes having received a verdict of guilty by a judge or jury, having pleaded guilty or nolo contendere, or having received a deferred judgment and sentence.
When a defendant is convicted of one of the offenses specified in subparagraph (II) of paragraph (a) of subsection (1) of this section, the probation department shall, in coordination with the evaluator completing the mental health sex offense specific evaluation, complete the sexually violent predator risk assessment, unless the evaluation and assessment have been completed within the six months prior to the conviction or the defendant has been previously designated a sexually violent predator. Based on the results of the assessment, the court shall make specific findings of fact and enter an order concerning whether the defendant is a sexually violent predator. If the defendant is found to be a sexually violent predator, the defendant shall be required to register pursuant to the provisions of section 16-22-108, C.R.S., and shall be subject to community notification pursuant to part 9 of article 13 of title 16, C.R.S. If the department of corrections receives a mittimus that indicates that the court did not make a specific finding of fact or enter an order regarding whether the defendant is a sexually violent predator, the department shall immediately notify the court and, if necessary, return the defendant to the custody of the sheriff for delivery to the court, and the court shall make a finding or enter an order regarding whether the defendant is a sexually violent predator; except that this provision shall not apply if the court was not required to enter the order when imposing the original sentence in the case.
When considering release on parole or discharge for an offender who was convicted of one of the offenses specified in subparagraph (II) of paragraph (a) of subsection (1) of this section, if there has been no previous court order, the parole board shall make specific findings concerning whether the offender is a sexually violent predator, based on the results of a sexually violent predator assessment. If no previous assessment has been completed, the parole board shall order the department of corrections to complete a sexually violent predator assessment. If the parole board finds that the offender is a sexually violent predator, the offender shall be required to register pursuant to the provisions of section 16-22-108, C.R.S., and shall be subject to community notification pursuant to part 9 of article 13 of title 16, C.R.S.
On or before January 15, 2008, and on or before January 15 each year thereafter, the judicial department and the department of corrections shall jointly submit to the judiciary committees of the senate and the house of representatives, or any successor committees, to the division of criminal justice in the department of public safety, and to the governor a report specifying the following information:
The number of offenders evaluated pursuant to this section in the preceding twelve months;
The number of sexually violent predators identified pursuant to this section in the preceding twelve months;
The total number of sexually violent predators in the custody of the department of corrections at the time of the report, specifying those incarcerated, those housed in community corrections, and those on parole, including the level of supervision for each sexually violent predator on parole;

The length of the sentence imposed on each sexually violent predator in the custody of the department of corrections at the time of the report;
The number of sexually violent predators discharged from parole during the preceding twelve months;
The total number of sexually violent predators on probation at the time of the report and the level of supervision of each sexually violent predator on probation; and
The number of sexually violent predators discharged from probation during the preceding twelve months.

18-3-415. Testing for persons charged with sexual offense. The court shall order any adult or juvenile who is bound over for trial for any sexual offense involving sexual penetration as defined in section 18-3-401 (6), subsequent to a preliminary hearing or after having waived the right to a preliminary hearing, or any person who is indicted for or is convicted of any such offense, to submit to a diagnostic test for a sexually transmitted infection pursuant to section 18-3-415.5. The results of the diagnostic test must be reported to the court or the court's designee, who shall then disclose the results to any victim of the sexual offense who requests such disclosure. Review and disclosure of diagnostic test results by the courts are closed and confidential, and any transaction records relating thereto are also closed and confidential. Disclosure of diagnostic test results must comply with the requirements of section 25-4-410 (2), C.R.S. If the person who is bound over for trial or who is indicted for or convicted of any such offense voluntarily submits to a diagnostic test for sexually transmitted infections, the fact of such person's voluntary submission is admissible in mitigation of sentence if the person is convicted of the charged offense.

18-3-415.5. Testing persons charged with certain sexual offenses for serious sexually transmitted infections - mandatory sentencing. (1) For purposes of this section, "sexual offense" is limited to a sexual offense that consists of sexual penetration, as defined in section 18-3-401 (6), involving sexual intercourse or anal intercourse, and "HIV" has the same meaning set forth in section 25-4-402 (4).

The court shall order any adult or juvenile who is bound over for trial subsequent to a preliminary hearing or after having waived the right to a preliminary hearing on a charge of committing a sexual offense to submit to a diagnostic test for the human immunodeficiency virus (HIV) and HIV infection, said diagnostic test to be ordered in conjunction with the diagnostic test ordered pursuant to section 18-3-415. The results of the diagnostic test must be reported to the district attorney. The district attorney shall keep the results of such diagnostic test strictly confidential, except for purposes of pleading and proving the mandatory sentencing provisions specified in subsection (5) of this section.

(a) If the person tested pursuant to subsection (2) of this section tests positive for the human immunodeficiency virus (HIV) and HIV infection, the district attorney may contact the state department of public health and environment or any county, district, or municipal public health agency to determine whether the person had been notified prior to the date of the offense for which the person has been bound over for trial that he or she tested positive for the human

immunodeficiency virus (HIV) and HIV infection.

If the district attorney determines that the person tested pursuant to subsection (2) of this section had notice of his or her HIV infection prior to the date the offense was committed, the district attorney may file an indictment or information alleging such knowledge and seeking the mandatory sentencing provisions authorized in subsection (5) of this section. Any such allegation must be kept confidential from the jury and under seal of court. The state department of public health and environment or any county, district, or municipal public health agency shall provide documentary evidence limited to whether the person tested pursuant to subsection (2) of this section had notice of or had discussion concerning his or her HIV infection and the date of such notice or discussion. The parties may stipulate that the person identified in the documents as having notice or discussion of his or her HIV infection is the person tested pursuant to subsection (2) of this section. Such stipulation shall constitute conclusive proof that said person had notice of his or her HIV infection prior to committing the substantive offense, and the court shall sentence said person in accordance with subsection (5) of this section.

If the parties do not stipulate as provided in paragraph (c) of this subsection (3), an officer or employee of the state department of public health and environment or of the county, district, or municipal public health agency who has had contact with the person tested pursuant to subsection (2) of this section regarding his or her HIV infection and can identify the person shall provide, for purposes of pretrial preparation and in court proceedings, oral and documentary evidence limited to whether the person had notice of or had discussion concerning his or her HIV infection and the date of such notice or discussion. If the state department or the county, district, or municipal public health agency no longer employs an officer or employee who has had contact with the person tested pursuant to subsection (2) of this section regarding the person's HIV infection, the state department or the county, district, or municipal public health agency shall provide:

The names of and current addresses, if available, for each former officer or employee who had contact with the person tested pursuant to subsection (2) of this section regarding the person's HIV infection;

Documentary evidence concerning whether the person tested pursuant to subsection (2) of this section was provided notice of or had discussion concerning his or her HIV infection and the date of such notice or discussion; and

If none of said former officers or employees are available, any officer or employee who has knowledge regarding whether the person tested pursuant to subsection (2) of this section was provided notice of or had discussion concerning his or her HIV infection and the date of such notice or discussion. The officer or employee shall provide such evidence for the purposes of pretrial preparation and in court proceedings.

Nothing in this section shall be interpreted as abridging the confidentiality requirements imposed on the state department of public health and environment and the county, district, and municipal public health agencies pursuant to part 4 of article 4 of title 25, C.R.S., with regard to any person or entity other than as specified in this section.

(a) If a verdict of guilty is returned on the substantive offense with which the person tested pursuant to subsection (2) of this section is charged, the court shall conduct a separate sentencing hearing as soon as practicable to determine whether said person had notice of his or her HIV infection prior to the date the offense was committed, as alleged. The judge who presided at trial

or before whom the guilty plea was entered or a replacement for said judge in the event he or she dies, resigns, is incapacitated, or is otherwise disqualified as provided in section 16-6-201, C.R.S, shall conduct the hearing. At the sentencing hearing, the district attorney has the burden of proving beyond a reasonable doubt that:

The person had notice of his or her HIV infection prior to the date the offense was committed, as alleged; and

The infectious agent of the HIV infection was in fact transmitted.

(b) If the court determines that the person tested pursuant to subsection (2) of this section had notice of the HIV infection prior to the date the offense was committed and the infectious agent of the HIV infection was in fact transmitted, the judge shall sentence the person to a mandatory term of incarceration of at least the upper limit of the presumptive range for the level of offense committed, up to the remainder of the person's natural life, as provided in section 18-1.3-1004.

18-3-416. Reports of convictions to department of education. When a person is convicted, pleads nolo contendere, or receives a deferred sentence for a violation of the provisions of this part 4 when the victim is a child and the court knows the person is a current or former employee of a school district in this state or holds a license or authorization pursuant to the provisions of article of title 22, C.R.S., the court shall report such fact to the department of education.

18-3-417. Reports of sexual assault by applicants, registrants, or licensed professionals. When the director of the division of professions and occupations or a board or commission within the division of professions and occupations in the department of regulatory agencies refers a case to the office of expedited settlement or the office of the attorney general for disciplinary action related to an alleged offense described in this part 4, the office of expedited settlement or the office of the attorney general shall forward the victim's contact information to a victim's advocate in the office of the attorney general. The victim's advocate shall make reasonable efforts to advise the victim of the right to pursue criminal action, the right to pursue civil action, the applicable statutes of limitations, and contact information for the police, sheriff, and community- based resources in the jurisdiction where the alleged offense occurred. This provision shall not prohibit additional reporting of criminal offenses by the attorney general.

PART 5

HUMAN TRAFFICKING AND SLAVERY

18-3-501. Legislative declaration. (1) The general assemblyherebyfinds and declares that:
Human trafficking constitutes a serious problem in Colorado and across the nation;
Human trafficking is abhorrent to a civilized society and deserving of the most diligent response from the state;
Human trafficking often involves minors who have been forced into involuntary

servitude and commercial sexual activity;
Human trafficking can take many forms but generally includes the use of physical abuse, threats of harm, or fear of other consequences to prevent victims from reporting the activity; and
Human trafficking creates a cycle of violence, impacting victims, families, and communities.
The general assembly further finds and declares that:
Legislation is required to combat this despicable practice, to make it easier to prosecute and punish persons who engage in human trafficking, and to protect the victims; and
The general assembly supports a comprehensive approach to combating human trafficking, which approach includes prevention, protection, prosecution, and partnerships.
Now, therefore, the general assembly joins the federal government and other states around the nation in passing legislation in order to combat human trafficking and protect the victims.

18-3-502. Definitions. As used in this part 5, unless the context otherwise requires:
"Adult" means a person eighteen years of age or older.
"Coercing" means inducing a person to act or to refrain from acting, if the inducement is accomplished by any one or more of the following means:
The use or threat of the use of force against, abduction of, causing of serious harm to, or physical restraint of a person;
The use of a plan, pattern, or statement for the purpose of causing the person to believe that failure to perform the act or failure to refrain from performing the act will result in the use of force against, abduction of, causing of serious harm to, or physical restraint of that person or another person;
Using or threatening to use the law or the legal process, whether administrative, civil, or criminal, in any manner or for any purpose for which the law was not designed;
Threatening to notify law enforcement officials that a person is present in the United States in violation of federal immigration laws;
The destruction or taking, or a threat to destroy or take, a person's identification document or other property;
Controlling or threatening to control a person's access to a controlled substance, as defined in section 18-18-102 (5);
The use of debt bondage; or
The exploitation of a person's physical or mental impairment, where such impairment has a substantial adverse effect on the person's cognitive or volitional functions.
"Commercial sexual activity" means sexual activity for which anything of value is given to, promised to, or received by a person.
"Debt bondage" means:
Demanding commercial sexual activity as payment toward or satisfaction of a real or purported debt; or
Demanding labor or services as payment toward or satisfaction of a real or purported debt and failing to apply the reasonable value of the labor or services toward the liquidation of the debt; or

Demanding labor or services where the length of the labor or services is not limited and the nature of the labor or services is not defined.
"Identification document" means a real or purported passport, driver's license, immigration document, travel document, or other government-issued identification document, including a document issued by a foreign government.
"Maintain" means to provide sustenance or care for a minor and includes but is not limited to providing shelter, food, clothing, drugs, medical care, or communication services.

"Makes available" means to facilitate contact between a minor and another person.
"Minor" means a person less than eighteen years of age.
"Person" has the same meaning as set forth in section 2-4-401 (8), C.R.S.
"Serious harm" means bodilyinjuryor anyother harm, whether physical or nonphysical, including psychological, financial, or reputational harm, which is sufficiently serious, under all the surrounding circumstances, to compel a reasonable person to perform or continue to perform labor or services or sexual activity to avoid incurring the harm.
"Sexual activity" means:
Sexual contact, as defined in section 18-3-401 (4);
Sexual intrusion, as defined in section 18-3-401 (5);
Sexual penetration, as defined in section 18-3-401 (6);
Sexual exploitation of a child, pursuant to section 18-6-403 (3) (a) and (3) (d); or
An obscene performance, as defined in section 18-7-101.
"Victim" means a person who is alleged to have been, or who has been, subjected to human trafficking, as described in section 18-3-503 or section 18-3-504.

18-3-503. Human trafficking for involuntary servitude - human trafficking of a minor for involuntary servitude. (1) A person who knowingly sells, recruits, harbors, transports, transfers, isolates, entices, provides, receives, or obtains byanymeans another person for the purpose of coercing the other person to perform labor or services commits human trafficking for involuntary servitude.
(2) Human trafficking for involuntary servitude is a class 3 felony; except that human trafficking of a minor for involuntary servitude is a class 2

felony.

18-3-504. Human trafficking for sexual servitude - human trafficking of a minor for sexual servitude. (1) (a) A person who knowingly sells, recruits, harbors, transports, transfers, isolates, entices, provides, receives, or obtains by any means another person for the purpose of coercing the person to engage in commercial sexual activity commits human trafficking for sexual servitude.

(b) Human trafficking for sexual servitude is a class 3 felony.

(a) A person who knowingly sells, recruits, harbors, transports, transfers, isolates, entices, provides, receives, obtains by any means, maintains, or makes available a minor for the purpose of commercial sexual activity commits human trafficking of a minor for sexual servitude.

Human trafficking of a minor for sexual servitude is a class 2 felony.

In any prosecution under this subsection (2), it is not a defense that:

The minor consented to being sold, recruited, harbored, transported, transferred, isolated, enticed, provided, received, obtained, or maintained by the defendant for the purpose of engaging in commercial sexual activity;

The minor consented to participating in commercial sexual activity;

The defendant did not know the minor's age or reasonably believed the minor to be eighteen years of age or older; or

The minor or another person represented the minor to be eighteen years of age or older.

A person does not need to receive any of the proceeds of any commercial sexual activity to commit an offense described in this section.

Conviction for an offense described in this section does not preclude conviction for an offense described in article 6 or 7 of this title based in whole or in part on the same or related conduct, and the court shall not require the prosecution to elect at trial between such offenses.

18-3-505. Human trafficking council - created - duties - repeal. (1) (a) There is created in the department of public safety the Colorado human trafficking council, referred to within this section as the "council". The purpose of the council is to bring together leadership from community- based and statewide anti-trafficking efforts, to build and enhance collaboration among communities and counties within the state, to establish and improve comprehensive services for victims and survivors of human trafficking, to assist in the successful prosecution of human traffickers, and to help prevent human trafficking in Colorado.

(b) The membership of the council shall reflect, to the extent possible, representation of urban and rural areas of the state and a balance of expertise, both governmental and non- governmental, in issues relating to human trafficking. The council shall include members with expertise in child welfare and human services to address the unique needs of child victims, including those child victims who are involved in the child welfare system. The membership of the council shall consist of the following persons, who shall be appointed as follows:

Two representatives from the department of human services, each to be appointed by the executive director of the department of human services;

A representative of the department of law, to be appointed by the attorney general;

A representative of the state department of labor and employment, to be appointed by the executive director of the department of labor and employment;

A representative of the division of the Colorado state patrol that addresses human smuggling and human trafficking pursuant to section 24-33.5-211, C.R.S., to be appointed by the executive director of the department of public safety;

A representative of a statewide association of police chiefs, to be appointed by the governor or his or her designee;

A representative of a statewide association of county sheriffs, to be appointed by the governor or his or her designee;

A representative of a statewide coalition for victims of sexual assault, to be appointed by the governor or his or her designee;

A representative of a statewide organization that provides services to crime victims, to be appointed by the governor or his or her designee;

A representative of a statewide immigrant rights organization, to be appointed by the governor or his or her designee;

A representative of a statewide organization of district attorneys, to be appointed by the governor or his or her designee;

A representative of a statewide organization of criminal defense attorneys, to be appointed by the governor or his or her designee;

At least three but not more than five persons, each representing a regional or city-wide human trafficking task force or coalition, each to be appointed by the governor or his or her designee;

A representative of a nonprofit organization that facilitates the treatment or housing of human trafficking victims, to be appointed by the governor or his or her designee;

A representative of a college or university department that conducts research on human trafficking, to be appointed by the governor or his or her designee;

A representative of a statewide organization that provides legal advocacy to abused, neglected, and at-risk children, to be appointed by the governor or his or her designee;

Two representatives of organizations that provide direct services to victims of human trafficking, to be appointed by the governor or his or her designee;

One representative of a faith-based organization that assists victims of human trafficking, to be appointed by the governor or his or her designee;

Two persons, each of whom is a director of a county department of social services, one from an urban county and the other from a rural county, each to be appointed by the governor or his or her designee;

One person who provides child welfare services for a county department of social services, to be appointed by the governor or his or her designee;

Two persons who are former victims of human trafficking, one who is a former victim of human trafficking for involuntary servitude and one who is a former victim of human trafficking for sexual servitude, each to be appointed by the governor or his or her designee;

A representative of a child advocacy center;

One person to be appointed by the commissioner of agriculture; and

One person representing the judicial branch, to be appointed by the chief justice of the supreme court.

Each appointing authority described in subsection (1) of this section shall make his or her appointments to the council on or before August 1, 2014. The members of the council shall elect presiding officers for the council, including a chair and vice-chair, from among the council members appointed pursuant to subsection (1) of this section, which presiding officers shall serve terms of two years. Council members may reelect a presiding officer. Each member of the council shall serve at the pleasure of his or her appointing authority for a term of four years. The appointing authority may reappoint the member for an additional term or terms. Members of the council shall serve without compensation but may be reimbursed for actual travel expenses incurred in the performance of their duties.

The council shall hold its first meeting on or before November 1, 2014, at a time and place to be designated by the executive director of the department of public safety, or by his or her

designee. The council shall meet at least four times each year and shall carry out the following duties:

On or before January 1, 2016, make recommendations to the judiciary committees of the house of representatives and senate, or any successor committees, concerning:

Whether the general assembly should establish standards and a process for the certification of organizations that provide services to victims of human trafficking;

Whether the general assembly should establish a grant program for organizations that provide services to victims of human trafficking, including consideration of how such a grant program may be funded; and

Whether the general assembly should enact legislation concerning:

The prosecution of or granting of immunity to a child victim of commercial sexual exploitation for offenses related to that exploitation;

The creation of other legal protections, including statutory defenses for child victims of commercial sexual exploitation for offenses related to that exploitation and the creation of any necessary changes to title 19, C.R.S., to implement those legal protections or defenses; or

Standards, guidelines, or mandates regarding the appropriate assessment, placement, and treatment of child victims of commercial sexual exploitation through title 19, C.R.S., including but not limited to the use of locked placement.

(a.5) The recommendations submitted pursuant to paragraph (a) of this subsection (4) must include a full explanation of each recommendation with a discussion of the benefits of each recommendation, any problems that might be encountered, and how those problems, if any, might be mitigated.

On or before January 1, 2017, and on or before January 17 of each year thereafter, submit a report to the judiciary committees of the house of representatives and senate, or any successor committees, summarizing the activities of the council during the preceding year;

Consider and make, as it deems necessary, recommendations to the judiciary committees of the house of representatives and senate, or to any successor committees, concerning any statutory changes that the council deems necessary to facilitate the prosecution and punishment of persons who engage in, and to protect the victims of, human trafficking;

Develop an implementation plan for a public awareness campaign to educate the public about human trafficking and place victims services contact information in places where victims of human trafficking are likely to see it;

Develop training standards and curricula for organizations that provide assistance to victims of human trafficking, for persons who work in or who frequent places where human trafficking victims are likely to appear, and for law enforcement agencies;

Identify best practices for the prevention of human trafficking, particularly for the prevention of child sex trafficking;

Collect data relating to the prevalence of, and the efforts of law enforcement to combat, human trafficking in Colorado. The council shall annuallyreport the data to the judiciary committees of the house of representatives and senate, or to any successor committees.

Research and pursue funding opportunities for the council;

On or after January 1, 2019, perform a post-enactment review of section 18-7-201.3 and

report its findings to the judiciary committees of the senate and house of representatives, or any successor committees.

The department of public safety is authorized to accept and expend gifts, grants, and donations for the purpose of assisting the council in fulfilling its duties pursuant to this section.

This section is repealed, effective September 1, 2019. Before repeal, the department of regulatory agencies shall review the council pursuant to section 2-3-1203, C.R.S.

PART 6 STALKING

18-3-601. Legislative declaration. (1) The general assemblyherebyfinds and declares that:

Stalking is a serious problem in this state and nationwide;

Although stalking often involves persons who have had an intimate relationship with one another, it can also involve persons who have little or no past relationship;

A stalker will often maintain strong, unshakable, and irrational emotional feelings for his or her victim and may likewise believe that the victim either returns these feelings of affection or will do so if the stalker is persistent enough. Further, the stalker often maintains this belief, despite a trivial or nonexistent basis for it and despite rejection, lack of reciprocation, efforts to restrict or avoid the stalker, and other facts that conflict with this belief.

A stalker may also develop jealousy and animosity for persons who are in relationships with the victim, including family members, employers and co-workers, and friends, perceiving them as obstacles or as threats to the stalker's own "relationship" with the victim;

Because stalking involves highlyinappropriate intensity, persistence, and possessiveness, it entails great unpredictability and creates great stress and fear for the victim;

Stalking involves severe intrusions on the victim's personal privacy and autonomy, with an immediate and long-lasting impact on quality of life as well as risks to security and safety of the victim and persons close to the victim, even in the absence of express threats of physical harm.

The general assembly hereby recognizes the seriousness posed by stalking and adopts the provisions of this part 6 with the goal of encouraging and authorizing effective intervention before stalking can escalate into behavior that has even more serious consequences.

18-3-602. Stalking - penalty - definitions - Vonnie's law. (1) A person commits stalking if directly, or indirectly through another person, the person knowingly:

Makes a credible threat to another person and, in connection with the threat, repeatedly follows, approaches, contacts, or places under surveillance that person, a member of that person's immediate family, or someone with whom that person has or has had a continuing relationship; or

Makes a credible threat to another person and, in connection with the threat, repeatedly makes any form of communication with that person, a member of that person's immediate family, or someone with whom that person has or has had a continuing relationship, regardless of whether a conversation ensues; or

Repeatedly follows, approaches, contacts, places under surveillance, or makes any form of communication with another person, a member of that person's immediate family, or someone with whom that person has or has had a continuing relationship in a manner that would cause a reasonable person to suffer serious emotional distress and does cause that person, a member of that person's immediate family, or someone with whom that person has or has had a continuing relationship to suffer serious emotional distress. For purposes of this paragraph (c), a victim need not show that he or she received professional treatment or counseling to show that he or she suffered serious emotional distress.

For the purposes of this part 6:

Conduct "in connection with" a credible threat means acts that further, advance, promote, or have a continuity of purpose, and may occur before, during, or after the credible threat.

"Credible threat" means a threat, physical action, or repeated conduct that would cause a reasonable person to be in fear for the person's safety or the safety of his or her immediate family or of someone with whom the person has or has had a continuing relationship. The threat need not be directly expressed if the totality of the conduct would cause a reasonable person such fear.

"Immediate family" includes the person's spouse and the person's parent, grandparent, sibling, or child.

"Repeated" or "repeatedly" means on more than one occasion.

A person who commits stalking:

Commits a class 5 felony for a first offense except as otherwise provided in subsection

of this section; or

Commits a class 4 felony for a second or subsequent offense, if the offense occurs within seven years after the date of a prior offense for which the person was convicted.

Stalking is an extraordinary risk crime that is subject to the modified presumptive sentencing range specified in section 18-1.3-401 (10).

If, at the time of the offense, there was a temporary or permanent protection order, injunction, or condition of bond, probation, or parole or any other court order in effect against the person, prohibiting the behavior described in this section, the person commits a class 4 felony.

Nothing in this section shall be construed to alter or diminish the inherent authority of the court to enforce its orders through civil or criminal contempt proceedings; however, before a criminal contempt proceeding is heard before the court, notice of the proceedings shall be provided to the district attorney for the judicial district of the court where the proceedings are to be heard and the district attorney for the judicial district in which the alleged act of criminal contempt occurred. The district attorney for either district shall be allowed to appear and argue for the imposition of contempt sanctions.

A peace officer shall have a duty to respond as soon as reasonably possible to a report of stalking and to cooperate with the alleged victim in investigating the report.

(a) When a person is arrested for an alleged violation of this section, the fixing of bail for the crime of stalking shall be done in accordance with section 16-4-105 (4), C.R.S., and a protection order shall issue in accordance with section 18-1-1001 (5).

(b) This subsection (8) shall be known and may be cited as "Vonnie's law".

When a violation under this section is committed in connection with a violation of a

court order, including but not limited to any protection order or any order that sets forth the conditions of a bond, any sentences imposed pursuant to this section and pursuant to section 18-6-

or any sentence imposed in a contempt proceeding for violation of the court order shall be served consecutively and not concurrently.

ARTICLE 3.5

Offenses Against Pregnant Women

18-3.5-101. Definitions. As used in this article, unless the context otherwise requires:

"Consent" has the same meaning as provided in section 18-1-505.

"Intentionally" or "with intent" has the same meaning as provided in section 18-1-501.

"Knowingly" has the same meaning as provided in section 18-1-501.

"Pregnancy", for purposes of this article only and notwithstanding any other definition or use to the contrary, means the presence of an implanted human embryo or fetus within the uterus of a woman.

"Recklessly" shall have the same meaning as provided in section 18-1-501.

"Unlawful termination of pregnancy" means the termination of a pregnancy by any means other than birth or a medical procedure, instrument, agent, or drug, for which the consent of the pregnant woman, or a person authorized by law to act on her behalf, has been obtained, or for which the pregnant woman's consent is implied by law.

18-3.5-102. Exclusions. (1) Nothing in this article shall permit the prosecution of a person for any act of providing medical, osteopathic, surgical, mental health, dental, nursing, optometric, healing, wellness, or pharmaceutical care; furnishing inpatient or outpatient hospital or clinic services; furnishing telemedicine services; or furnishing any service related to assisted reproduction or genetic testing.

(2) Nothing in this article shall permit the prosecution of a woman for any act or any failure to act with regard to her own pregnancy.

18-3.5-103. Unlawful termination of pregnancy in the first degree. (1) A person commits the offense of unlawful termination of pregnancy in the first degree if, with the intent to terminate unlawfully the pregnancy of a woman, the person unlawfully terminates the woman's pregnancy.

Unlawful termination of pregnancy in the first degree is a class 3 felony but is a class 2 felony if the woman dies as a result of the unlawful termination of a pregnancy.

A defendant convicted pursuant to subsection (1) of this section shall be sentenced by

the court in accordance with the provisions of section 18-1.3-406.

18-3.5-104. Unlawful termination of pregnancy in the second degree. (1) A person commits the offense of unlawful termination of pregnancy in the second degree if the person knowingly causes the unlawful termination of the pregnancy of a woman.

(a) Except as otherwise provided in paragraph (b) of this subsection (2), unlawful termination of pregnancy in the second degree is a class 4 felony.

(b) If unlawful termination of pregnancy in the second degree is committed under circumstances where the act causing the unlawful termination of pregnancy is performed upon a sudden heat of passion, caused by a serious and highly provoking act of the intended victim, affecting the person causing the unlawful termination of pregnancy sufficiently to excite an irresistible passion in a reasonable person, and without an interval between the provocation and the unlawful termination of pregnancy sufficient for the voice of reason and humanity to be heard, it is a class 5 felony.

A defendant convicted pursuant to subsection (1) of this section shall be sentenced by the court in accordance with the provisions of section 18-1.3-406.

18-3.5-105. Unlawful termination of pregnancy in the third degree. (1) A person commits the offense of unlawful termination of pregnancy in the third degree if, under circumstances manifesting extreme indifference to the value of human life, the person knowingly engages in conduct that creates a grave risk of death to another person, and thereby causes the unlawful termination of the pregnancy of a woman.
(2) Unlawful termination of pregnancy in the third degree is a class 5 felony.


18-3.5-106. Unlawful termination of pregnancy in the fourth degree. (1) A person commits the offense of unlawful termination of pregnancy in the fourth degree if the person recklessly causes the unlawful termination of the pregnancy of a woman at such time as the person knew or reasonably should have known that the woman was pregnant.
(2) (a) Unlawful termination of pregnancy in the fourth degree is a class 6 felony.
(b) Unlawful termination of pregnancy in the fourth degree by any person is a class 5 felony if the pregnancy of the woman, other than a participant in the crime, is unlawfully terminated during the commission or attempted commission of or flight from the commission or attempted commission of murder, assault in the first or second degree, robbery, arson, burglary, escape, kidnapping in the first degree, sexual assault, sexual assault in the first or second degree as such offenses existed prior to July 1, 2000, or class 3 felony sexual assault on a child, but only to the extent that the person is a principal in the criminal act or attempted criminal act, as described in section 18-1-603.


18-3.5-107. Vehicular unlawful termination of pregnancy. (1) If a person operates or drives a motor vehicle in a reckless manner, and this conduct is the proximate cause of the unlawful

termination of the pregnancy of a woman, such person commits vehicular unlawful termination of pregnancy.
(2) Vehicular unlawful termination of pregnancy in violation of subsection (1) of this section is a class 5 felony.


18-3.5-108. Aggravated vehicular unlawful termination of pregnancy - definitions. (1) (a) If a person operates or drives a motor vehicle while under the influence of alcohol or one or more drugs, or a combination of both alcohol and one or more drugs, and this conduct is the proximate cause of the unlawful termination of the pregnancy of a woman, such person commits aggravated vehicular unlawful termination of pregnancy. This is a strict liability crime.
As used in this subsection (1):
"Driving under the influence" means driving a vehicle when a person has consumed alcohol or one or more drugs, or a combination of alcohol and one or more drugs, which alcohol alone, or one or more drugs alone, or alcohol combined with one or more drugs affect such person to a degree that such person is substantially incapable, either mentally or physically, or both mentally and physically, of exercising clear judgment, sufficient physical control, or due care in the safe operation of a vehicle.
"One or more drugs" means all substances defined as a drug in section 12-42.5-102 (13), C.R.S., and all controlled substances defined in section 18-18-102 (5), and glue-sniffing, aerosol inhalation, or the inhalation of any other toxic vapor or vapors as defined in section 18-18-412.
The fact that a person charged with a violation of this subsection (1) is or has been entitled to use one or more drugs under the laws of this state shall not constitute a defense against any charge of violating this subsection (1).
Aggravated vehicular unlawful termination of pregnancy, in violation of paragraph (a) of subsection (1) of this section, is a class 4 felony.
In any prosecution for a violation of subsection (1) of this section, the amount of alcohol in the defendant's blood or breath at the time of the commission of the alleged offense or within a reasonable time thereafter, as shown by analysis of the defendant's blood or breath, shall give rise to the following presumptions:
If there was at such time 0.05 or less grams of alcohol per one hundred milliliters of blood, or if there was at such time 0.05 or less grams of alcohol per two hundred ten liters of breath, it shall be presumed that the defendant was not under the influence of alcohol.
If there was at such time in excess of 0.05 grams but less than 0.08 grams of alcohol per one hundred milliliters of blood, or if there was at such time in excess of 0.05 grams but less than
0.08 grams of alcohol per two hundred ten liters of breath, such fact may be considered with other competent evidence in determining whether or not the defendant was under the influence of alcohol.
If there was at such time 0.08 or more grams of alcohol per one hundred milliliters of blood, or if there was at such time 0.08 or more grams of alcohol per two hundred ten liters of breath, it shall be presumed that the defendant was under the influence of alcohol.
The limitations of subsection (3) of this section shall not be construed as limiting the introduction, reception, or consideration of any other competent evidence bearing upon the question

of whether or not the defendant was under the influence of alcohol.
(a) If a law enforcement officer has probable cause to believe that a person was driving a motor vehicle in violation of paragraph (a) of subsection (1) of this section, the person, upon the request of the law enforcement officer, shall take and complete, and cooperate in completing, any test or tests of the person's blood, breath, saliva, or urine for the purpose of determining the alcohol or drug content within his or her system. The type of test or tests shall be determined by the law enforcement officer requiring the test or tests. If the person refuses to take, complete, or cooperate in completing any test or tests, the test or tests may be performed at the direction of a law enforcement officer having probable cause, without the person's authorization or consent. If a person refuses to take, complete, or cooperate in taking or completing any test or tests required by this paragraph (a), the person shall be subject to license revocation pursuant to the provisions of section 42-2-126 (3), C.R.S. When the test or tests show that the amount of alcohol in a person's blood was in violation of the limits provided for in section 42-2-126 (3) (a), (3) (b), (3) (d), or (3) (e), C.R.S., the person shall be subject to license revocation pursuant to the provisions of section 42-2-126, C.R.S.
Any person who is required to submit to testing shall cooperate with the person authorized to obtain specimens of his or her blood, breath, saliva, or urine, including the signing of any release or consent forms required by any person, hospital, clinic, or association authorized to obtain such specimens. If such person does not cooperate with the person, hospital, clinic, or association authorized to obtain such specimens, including the signing of any release or consent forms, such noncooperation shall be considered a refusal to submit to testing.
The tests shall be administered at the direction of a law enforcement officer having probable cause to believe that the person committed a violation of paragraph (a) of subsection (1) of this section and in accordance with rules and regulations prescribed by the state board of health concerning the health of the person being tested and the accuracy of the testing. Strict compliance with the rules and regulations shall not be a prerequisite to the admissibility of test results at trial unless the court finds that the extent of noncompliance with a board of health rule has so impaired the validity and reliability of the testing method and the test results as to render the evidence inadmissible. In all other circumstances, failure to strictly comply with such rules and regulations shall only be considered in the weight to be given to the test results and not to the admissibility of the test results. It shall not be a prerequisite to the admissibility of test results at trial that the prosecution present testimony concerning the composition of any kit used to obtain blood, urine, saliva, or breath specimens. A sufficient evidentiary foundation concerning the compliance of such kits with the rules and

regulations of the department of public health and environment shall be established by the introduction of a copy of the manufacturer's or supplier's certificate of compliance with the rules and regulations if the certificate specifies the contents, sterility, chemical makeup, and amounts of chemicals contained in such kit.

No person except a physician, a registered nurse, an emergency medical service provider as certified in part 2 of article 3.5 of title 25, C.R.S., an emergency medical technician as defined in part 1 of article 3.5 of title 25, C.R.S., or a person whose normal duties include withdrawing blood samples under the supervision of a physician or registered nurse shall be entitled to withdraw blood for the purpose of determining the alcohol or drug content therein. In any trial for a violation of paragraph (b) of subsection (1) of this section, testimony of a law enforcement officer that he or she

witnessed the taking of a blood specimen by a person who he or she reasonably believed was authorized to withdraw blood specimens shall be sufficient evidence that the person was so authorized, and testimony from the person who obtained the blood specimens concerning the person's authorization to obtain blood specimens shall not be a prerequisite to the admissibility of test results concerning the blood specimens obtained. No civil liability shall attach to any person authorized to obtain blood, breath, saliva, or urine specimens or to any hospital, clinic, or association in or for which such specimens are obtained pursuant to this subsection (5) as a result of the act of obtaining such specimens from any person if such specimens were obtained according to the rules and regulations prescribed by the state board of health; except that this subsection (5) shall not relieve any such person from liability for negligence in the obtaining of any specimen sample.

Any person who is dead or unconscious shall be tested to determine the alcohol or drug content of his or her blood or any drug content of his or her system as provided in this subsection (5). If a test cannot be administered to a person who is unconscious, hospitalized, or undergoing medical treatment because the test would endanger the person's life or health, the law enforcement agency shall be allowed to test any blood, urine, or saliva that was obtained and not utilized by a health care provider and shall have access to that portion of the analysis and results of any tests administered by the provider that show the alcohol or drug content of the person's blood or any drug content within his or her system. Such test results shall not be considered privileged communications, and the provisions of section 13-90-107, C.R.S., relating to the physician-patient privilege shall not apply.

Any person who is dead, in addition to the tests prescribed, shall also have his or her blood checked for carbon monoxide content and for the presence of drugs, as prescribed by the department of public health and environment. Any information obtained shall be made a part of the law enforcement officer's accident report.

If a person refuses to take, complete, or cooperate in completing any test or tests as provided in this subsection (5) and the person subsequently stands trial for a violation of paragraph

of subsection (1) of this section, the refusal to take, complete, or cooperate with completing any test or tests shall be admissible into evidence at the trial, and the person may not claim the privilege against self-incrimination with regard to the admission of his or her refusal to take, complete, or cooperate with completing any test or tests.

(g) Notwithstanding any provision of section 42-4-1301.1, C.R.S., concerning requirements that relate to the manner in which tests are administered, the test or tests taken pursuant to the provisions of this section may be used for the purposes of driver's license revocation proceedings under section 42-2-126, C.R.S., and for the purposes of prosecutions for violations of section 42-4-1301 (1) or (2), C.R.S.

In all actions, suits, and judicial proceedings in any court of this state concerning alcohol-related or drug-related traffic offenses, the court shall take judicial notice of methods of testing a person's alcohol or drug level and of the design and operation of devices, as certified by the department of public health and environment, for testing a person's blood, breath, saliva, or urine to determine his or her alcohol or drug level. This subsection (6) shall not prevent the necessity of establishing during a trial that the testing devices used were working properly and that such testing devices were properly operated. Nothing in this subsection (6) shall preclude a defendant from offering evidence concerning the accuracy of testing devices.

18-3.5-109. Careless driving resulting in unlawful termination of pregnancy - penalty. (1) A person who drives a motor vehicle, bicycle, electrical assisted bicycle, or low-power scooter in a careless and imprudent manner, without due regard for the width, grade, curves, corners, traffic, and use of the streets and highways and all other attendant circumstances and causes the unlawful termination of a pregnancy of a woman is guilty of careless driving, resulting in unlawful termination of pregnancy. A person convicted of careless driving of a bicycle or electrical assisted bicycle resulting in the unlawful termination of pregnancy shall not be subject to the provisions of section 42-2-127, C.R.S.

(2) Any person who violates any provision of this section commits a class 1 misdemeanor traffic offense.

18-3.5-110. Construction. Nothing in this article shall be construed to confer the status of "person" upon a human embryo, fetus, or unborn child at any stage of development prior to live birth.

### ARTICLE 4  Offenses Against Property

PART 1 ARSON

18-4-101. Definitions. As used in this article, unless the context otherwise requires:

"Building" means a structure which has the capacity to contain, and is designed for the shelter of, man, animals, or property, and includes a ship, trailer, sleeping car, airplane, or other vehicle or place adapted for overnight accommodations of persons or animals, or for carrying on of business therein, whether or not a person or animal is actually present.

"Occupied structure" means any area, place, facility, or enclosure which, for particular purposes, may be used by persons or animals upon occasion, whether or not included within the definition of "building" in subsection (1) of this section, and which is in fact occupied by a person or animal, and known by the defendant to be thus occupied at the time he acts in violation of one or more of sections 18-4-102 to 18-4-105.

Property is that of "another" if anyone other than the defendant has a possessory or proprietary interest therein.

If a building is divided into units for separate occupancy, any unit not occupied by the defendant is a "building of another".

18-4-102. First degree arson. (1) A person who knowingly sets fire to, burns, causes to be burned, or by the use of any explosive damages or destroys, or causes to be damaged or destroyed, any building or occupied structure of another without his consent commits first degree arson.

First degree arson is a class 3 felony.

A defendant convicted of committing first degree arson by the use of any explosive shall be sentenced by the court in accordance with the provisions of section 18-1.3-406.

18-4-103. Second degree arson. (1) A person who knowingly sets fire to, burns, causes to be burned, or by the use of any explosive damages or destroys, or causes to be damaged or destroyed, any property of another without his consent, other than a building or occupied structure, commits second degree arson.

Second degree arson is a class 4 felony, if the damage is one hundred dollars or more.

Second degree arson is a class 2 misdemeanor, if the damage is less than one hundred dollars.

18-4-104. Third degree arson. (1) A person who, by means of fire or explosives, intentionally damages any property with intent to defraud commits third degree arson.

(2) Third degree arson is a class 4 felony.

18-4-105. Fourth degree arson. (1) A person who knowingly or recklessly starts or maintains a fire or causes an explosion, on his own property or that of another, and by so doing places another in danger of death or serious bodily injury or places anybuilding or occupied structure of another in danger of damage commits fourth degree arson.

Fourth degree arson is a class 4 felony if a person is thus endangered.

Fourth degree arson is a class 2 misdemeanor if only property is thus endangered and the value of the property is one hundred dollars or more.

Fourth degree arson is a class 3 misdemeanor if only property is thus endangered and the value of the property is less than one hundred dollars.

It shall not be an arson offense pursuant to this section if:

A person starts and maintains a fire as a controlled agricultural burn in a reasonably cautious manner; and

No person suffers any of the following as a result of the fire:

Bodily injury;

Serious bodily injury; or

Death.

For purposes of this section, "controlled agricultural burn" means a technique used in farming to clear the land of any existing crop residue, kill weeds and weed seeds, or reduce fuel buildup and decrease the likelihood of a future fire.

PART 2

BURGLARY AND RELATED OFFENSES

18-4-201. Definitions. As used in this article, unless the context otherwise requires:

"Premises" means any real estate and all improvements erected thereon.

"Separate building" means each unit of a building consisting of two or more units separately secured or occupied.

A person "enters unlawfully" or "remains unlawfully" in or upon premises when the person is not licensed, invited, or otherwise privileged to do so. A person who, regardless of his or her intent, enters or remains in or upon premises that are at the time open to the public does so with license and privilege unless the person defies a lawful order not to enter or remain, personally communicated to him or her by the owner of the premises or some other authorized person. A license or privilege to enter or remain in a building that is only partly open to the public is not a license or privilege to enter or remain in that part of the building that is not open to the public. Except as is otherwise provided in section 33-6-116 (1), C.R.S., a person who enters or remains upon unimproved and apparently unused land that is neither fenced nor otherwise enclosed in a manner designed to exclude intruders does so with license and privilege unless notice against trespass is personally communicated to the person by the owner of the land or some other authorized person or unless notice forbidding entry is given by posting with signs at intervals of not more than four hundred forty yards or, if there is a readily identifiable entrance to the land, by posting with signs at such entrance to the private land or the forbidden part of the land. In the case of a designated access road not otherwise posted, said notice shall be posted at the entrance to private land and shall be substantially as follows: "ENTERING PRIVATE PROPERTY REMAIN ON ROADS".

18-4-202. First degree burglary. (1) A person commits first degree burglary if the person knowingly enters unlawfully, or remains unlawfully after a lawful or unlawful entry, in a building or occupied structure with intent to commit therein a crime, other than trespass as defined in this article, against another person or property, and if in effecting entry or while in the building or occupied structure or in immediate flight therefrom, the person or another participant in the crime assaults or menaces any person, the person or another participant is armed with explosives, or the person or another participant uses a deadly weapon or possesses and threatens the use of a deadly weapon.

First degree burglary is a class 3 felony.

If under the circumstances stated in subsection (1) of this section the property involved is a controlled substance, as defined in section 18-18-102 (5), within a pharmacy or other place having lawful possession thereof, such person commits first degree burglary of controlled substances, which is a class 2 felony.

18-4-202.1. Habitual burglary offenders - punishment - legislative declaration. (Repealed)

18-4-203. Second degree burglary. (1) A person commits second degree burglary, if the person knowingly breaks an entrance into, enters unlawfully in, or remains unlawfully after a lawful or unlawful entry in a building or occupied structure with intent to commit therein a crime against another person or property.

Second degree burglary is a class 4 felony, but it is a class 3 felony if:

It is a burglary of a dwelling; or

It is a burglary, the objective of which is the theft of a controlled substance, as defined in section 18-18-102 (5), lawfully kept within any building or occupied structure.

18-4-204. Third degree burglary. (1) A person commits third degree burglary if with intent to commit a crime he enters or breaks into any vault, safe, cash register, coin vending machine, product dispenser, moneydepository, safetydeposit box, coin telephone, coin box, or other apparatus or equipment whether or not coin operated.

(2) Third degree burglary is a class 5 felony, but it is a class 4 felony if it is a burglary, the objective of which is the theft of a controlled substance, as defined in section 18-18-102 (5), lawfully kept in or upon the property burglarized.

18-4-205. Possession of burglary tools. (1) A person commits possession of burglary tools if he possesses any explosive, tool, instrument, or other article adapted, designed, or commonly used for committing or facilitating the commission of an offense involving forcible entry into premises or theft by a physical taking, and intends to use the thing possessed, or knows that some person intends to use the thing possessed, in the commission of such an offense.

(2) Possession of burglary tools is a class 5 felony.

## PART 3 ROBBERY

18-4-301. Robbery. (1) A person who knowingly takes anything of value from the person or presence of another by the use of force, threats, or intimidation commits robbery.

Robbery is a class 4 felony.

18-4-302. Aggravated robbery. (1) A person who commits robbery is guilty of aggravated

robbery if during the act of robbery or immediate flight therefrom:

He is armed with a deadly weapon with intent, if resisted, to kill, maim, or wound the person robbed or any other person; or

He knowingly wounds or strikes the person robbed or any other person with a deadly weapon or by the use of force, threats, or intimidation with a deadly weapon knowingly puts the person robbed or any other person in reasonable fear of death or bodily injury; or

He has present a confederate, aiding or abetting the perpetration of the robbery, armed with a deadly weapon, with the intent, either on the part of the defendant or confederate, if resistance is offered, to kill, maim, or wound the person robbed or any other person, or by the use of force, threats, or intimidation puts the person robbed or any other person in reasonable fear of death or bodily injury; or

He possesses any article used or fashioned in a manner to lead any person who is present reasonably to believe it to be a deadly weapon or represents verbally or otherwise that he is then and there so armed.

Repealed.

Aggravated robbery is a class 3 felony and is an extraordinary risk crime that is subject to the modified presumptive sentencing range specified in section 18-1.3-401 (10).

If a defendant is convicted of aggravated robbery pursuant to paragraph (b) of subsection

of this section, the court shall sentence the defendant in accordance with the provisions of section 18-1.3-406.

18-4-303. Aggravated robbery of controlled substances. (1) A person who takes any controlled substance, as defined in section 18-18-102 (5), from any pharmacy or other place having lawful possession thereof or from any pharmacist or other person having lawful possession thereof under the aggravating circumstances defined in section 18-4-302 is guilty of aggravated robbery of controlled substances.

Aggravated robbery of controlled substances is a class 2 felony.

18-4-304. Robbery of the elderly or disabled - legislative declaration. (Repealed)

18-4-305. Use of photographs, video tapes, or films of property. Pursuant to section 13- 25-130, C.R.S., photographs, video tapes, or films of property over which a person is alleged to have exerted unauthorized control or otherwise to have obtained unlawfully are competent evidence if the photographs, video tapes, or films are admissible into evidence under the rules of law governing the admissibility of photographs, video tapes, or films into evidence.

## PART 4 THEFT

18-4-401. Theft. (1) A person commits theft when he or she knowingly obtains, retains, or exercises control over anything of value of another without authorization or by threat or deception; or receives, loans money by pawn or pledge on, or disposes of anything of value or belonging to another that he or she knows or believes to have been stolen, and:

Intends to deprive the other person permanently of the use or benefit of the thing of

value;

Knowingly uses, conceals, or abandons the thing of value in such manner as to deprive

the other person permanently of its use or benefit;

Uses, conceals, or abandons the thing of value intending that such use, concealment, or abandonment will deprive the other person permanently of its use or benefit;

Demands any consideration to which he or she is not legally entitled as a condition of restoring the thing of value to the other person; or

Knowingly retains the thing of value more than seventy-two hours after the agreed-upon time of return in any lease or hire agreement.

(1.5) For the purposes of this section, a thing of value is that of "another" if anyone other than the defendant has a possessory or proprietary interest therein.

Theft is:

(Deleted by amendment, L. 2007, p. 1690, § 3, effective July 1, 2007.)

A class 1 petty offense if the value of the thing involved is less than fifty dollars; (b.5) Repealed.

A class 3 misdemeanor if the value of the thing involved is fifty dollars or more but less than three hundred dollars;

A class 2 misdemeanor if the value of the thing involved is three hundred dollars or more but less than seven hundred fifty dollars;

A class 1 misdemeanor if the value of the thing involved is seven hundred fifty dollars or more but less than two thousand dollars;

A class 6 felony if the value of the thing involved is two thousand dollars or more but less than five thousand dollars;

A class 5 felony if the value of the thing involved is five thousand dollars or more but less than twenty thousand dollars;

A class 4 felony if the value of the thing involved is twenty thousand dollars or more but less than one hundred thousand dollars;

A class 3 felony if the value of the thing involved is one hundred thousand dollars or more but less than one million dollars; and

A class 2 felony if the value of the thing involved is one million dollars or more.

and (3.1) Repealed.

(a) When a person commits theft twice or more within a period of six months, two or more of the thefts may be aggregated and charged in a single count, in which event the thefts so aggregated and charged shall constitute a single offense, the penalty for which shall be based on the aggregate value of the things involved, pursuant to subsection (2) of this section.

(b) When a person commits theft twice or more against the same person pursuant to one scheme or course of conduct, the thefts may be aggregated and charged in a single count, in which

event they shall constitute a single offense, the penalty for which shall be based on the aggregate value of the things involved, pursuant to subsection (2) of this section.

Theft from the person of another by means other than the use of force, threat, or intimidation is a class 5 felony without regard to the value of the thing taken.

In every indictment or information charging a violation of this section, it shall be sufficient to allege that, on or about a day certain, the defendant committed the crime of theft by unlawfully taking a thing or things of value of a person or persons named in the indictment or information. The prosecuting attorney shall at the request of the defendant provide a bill of particulars.

Repealed.

A municipality shall have concurrent power to prohibit theft, by ordinance, where the value of the thing involved is less than one thousand dollars.

(a) If a person is convicted of or pleads guilty or nolo contendere to theft by deception and the underlying factual basis of the case involves the mortgage lending process, a minimum fine of the amount of pecuniary harm resulting from the theft shall be mandatory, in addition to any other penalty the court may impose.

A court shall not accept a plea of guilty or nolo contendere to another offense from a person charged with a violation of this section that involves the mortgage lending process unless the plea agreement contains an order of restitution in accordance with part 6 of article 1.3 of this title that compensates the victim for any costs to the victim caused by the offense.

The district attorneys and the attorney general have concurrent jurisdiction to investigate and prosecute a violation of this section that involves making false statements or filing or facilitating the use of a document known to contain a false statement or material omission relied upon by another person in the mortgage lending process.

Documents involved in the mortgage lending process include, but are not limited to, uniform residential loan applications or other loan applications; appraisal reports; HUD-1 settlement statements; supporting personal documentation for loan applications such as W-2 forms, verifications of income and employment, bank statements, tax returns, and payroll stubs; and any required disclosures.

For the purposes of this subsection (9):

"Mortgage lending process" means the process through which a person seeks or obtains a residential mortgage loan, including, without limitation, solicitation, application, or origination; negotiation of terms; third-party provider services; underwriting; signing and closing; funding of the loan; and perfecting and releasing the mortgage.

"Residential mortgage loan" means a loan or agreement to extend credit, made to a person and secured by a mortgage or lien on residential real property, including, but not limited to, the refinancing or renewal of a loan secured by residential real property.

"Residential real property" means real property used as a residence and containing no more than four families housed separately.


18-4-402. Theft of rental property. (Repealed)


18-4-403. Statutory intent. If any law of this state refers to or mentions larceny, stealing, embezzlement (except embezzlement of public moneys), false pretenses, confidence games, or shoplifting, that law shall be interpreted as if the word "theft" were substituted therefor; and in the enactment of sections 18-4-401 to 18-4-403 it is the intent of the general assembly to define one crime of theft and to incorporate therein such crimes, thereby removing distinctions and technicalities which previously existed in the pleading and proof of such crimes.


18-4-404. Obtaining control over any stolen thing of value - conviction. Every person who obtains control over any stolen thing of value, knowing the thing of value to have been stolen by another, may be tried, convicted, and punished whether or not the principal is charged, tried, or convicted.


18-4-405. Rights in stolen property. All property obtained by theft, robbery, or burglary shall be restored to the owner, and no sale, whether in good faith on the part of the purchaser or not, shall divest the owner of his right to such property. The owner may maintain an action not only against the taker thereof but also against any person in whose possession he finds the property. In any such action, the owner may recover two hundred dollars or three times the amount of the actual damages sustained by him, whichever is greater, and may also recover costs of the action and reasonable attorney fees; but monetary damages and attorney fees shall not be recoverable from a good-faith purchaser or good-faith holder of the property.


18-4-406. Concealment of goods. If any person willfully conceals unpurchased goods, wares, or merchandise owned or held by and offered or displayed for sale by any store or other mercantile establishment, whether the concealment be on his own person or otherwise and whether on or off the premises of said store or mercantile establishment, such concealment constitutes prima facie evidence that the person intended to commit the crime of theft.


18-4-407. Questioning of person suspected of theft without liability. If any person triggers an alarm or a theft detection device as defined in section 18-4-417 (2) or conceals upon his person or otherwise carries away any unpurchased goods, wares, or merchandise held or owned by any store or mercantile establishment, the merchant or any employee thereof or any peace officer, acting in good faith and upon probable cause based upon reasonable grounds therefor, may detain and question such person, in a reasonable manner for the purpose of ascertaining whether the person is guilty of theft. Such questioning of a person by a merchant, merchant's employee, or peace or police officer does not render the merchant, merchant's employee, or peace officer civilly or criminally liable for slander, false arrest, false imprisonment, malicious prosecution, or unlawful detention.

**18-4-408. Theft of trade secrets - penalty.** (1) Any person who, with intent to deprive or withhold from the owner thereof the control of a trade secret, or with an intent to appropriate a trade secret to his own use or to the use of another, steals or discloses to an unauthorized person a trade secret, or, without authority, makes or causes to be made a copy of an article representing a trade secret, commits theft of a trade secret.

As used in this section:

"Article" means any object, material, device, or substance, or copy thereof, including any writing, record, recording, drawing, sample, specimen, prototype, model, photograph, microorganism, blueprint, or map.

"Copy" means any facsimile, replica, photograph, or other reproduction of an article, and any note, drawing, or sketch made of or from an article.

"Representing" means describing, depicting, containing, constituting, reflecting, or recording.

"Trade secret" means the whole or any portion or phase of any scientific or technical information, design, process, procedure, formula, improvement, confidential business or financial information, listing of names, addresses, or telephone numbers, or other information relating to any business or profession which is secret and of value. To be a trade secret the owner thereof must have taken measures to prevent the secret from becoming available to persons other than those selected by the owner to have access thereto for limited purposes.

(a) Theft of a trade secret is a class 1 misdemeanor. A second or subsequent offense under this section committed within five years after the date of a prior conviction is a class 5 felony.

(b) Notwithstanding section 16-5-401 (1) (a), C.R.S., any prosecution for violation of this section shall be commenced within three years after discovery of the offense.

**18-4-409. Aggravated motor vehicle theft.** (1) As used in this section, unless the context otherwise requires:

"Motor vehicle" means all vehicles of whatever description propelled by any power other than muscular, except vehicles running on rails.

"Vehicle identification number" means the serial number placed upon the motor vehicle by the manufacturer thereof or assigned to the motor vehicle by the department of revenue.

A person commits aggravated motor vehicle theft in the first degree if he or she knowingly obtains or exercises control over the motor vehicle of another without authorization or by threat or deception and:

Retains possession or control of the motor vehicle for more than twenty-four hours; or

Attempts to alter or disguise or alters or disguises the appearance of the motor vehicle; or

Attempts to alter or remove or alters or removes the vehicle identification number; or

Uses the motor vehicle in the commission of a crime other than a traffic offense; or

Causes five hundred dollars or more property damage, including but not limited to property damage to the motor vehicle involved, in the course of obtaining control over or in the exercise of control of the motor vehicle; or

Causes bodily injury to another person while he or she is in the exercise of control of the motor vehicle; or

Removes the motor vehicle from this state for a period of time in excess of twelve hours; or

Unlawfully attaches or otherwise displays in or upon the motor vehicle license plates other than those officially issued for the motor vehicle.

Aggravated motor vehicle theft in the first degree is a:

Class 5 felony if the value of the motor vehicle or motor vehicles involved is less than twenty thousand dollars;

(a.5) Class 4 felony if the value of the motor vehicle or motor vehicles involved is twenty thousand dollars or more but less than one hundred thousand dollars;

Class 3 felony if the value of the motor vehicle or motor vehicles involved is more than one hundred thousand dollars or if the defendant has twice previously been convicted or adjudicated of charges separately brought and tried either in this state or elsewhere of an offense involving theft of a motor vehicle under the laws of this state, any other state, the United States, or any territory subject to the jurisdiction of the United States.

A person commits aggravated motor vehicle theft in the second degree if he or she knowingly obtains or exercises control over the motor vehicle of another without authorization or by threat or deception and if none of the aggravating factors in subsection (2) of this section are present. Aggravated motor vehicle theft in the second degree is a:

Class 5 felony if the value of the motor vehicle or motor vehicles involved is twenty thousand dollars or more;

Class 6 felony if the value of the motor vehicle or motor vehicles involved is one thousand dollars or more but less than twenty thousand dollars;

Class 1 misdemeanor if the value of the motor vehicle or motor vehicles involved is less than one thousand dollars.

(4.5) Whenever a person is convicted of, pleads guilty or nolo contendere to, receives a deferred judgment or sentence for, or is adjudicated a juvenile delinquent for, a violation of this section, the offender's driver's license shall be revoked as provided in section 42-2-125, C.R.S.

Consistent with section 18-1-202, if the theft of a motor vehicle occurs in one jurisdiction and the motor vehicle is recovered in another jurisdiction, the offender may be tried in the jurisdiction where the theft occurred, in any jurisdiction through which the motor vehicle was operated or transported, or in the jurisdiction in which the motor vehicle was recovered.

**18-4-410. Theft by receiving. (Repealed)**

**18-4-411. Transactions for profit in stolen goods.** If any person obtains control over stolen property knowing or believing the property to have been stolen, and such offense involves two or more separate stolen things of value each of which is the property of a separate owner, such commission of theft constitutes prima facie evidence that the person is engaged in the business of buying, selling, or otherwise disposing of stolen goods for a profit.

**18-4-411.5. Interagency task force on organized retail theft - legislative declaration - repeal. (Repealed)**

**18-4-412. Theft of medical records or medical information - penalty.** (1) Any person who, without proper authorization, knowingly obtains a medical record or medical information with the intent to appropriate the medical record or medical information to his own use or to the use of another, who steals or discloses to an unauthorized person a medical record or medical information, or who, without authority, makes or causes to be made a copy of a medical record or medical information commits theft of a medical record or medical information.

As used in this section:

"Medical record" means the written or graphic documentation, sound recording, or computer record pertaining to medical, mental health, and health care services, including medical marijuana services, performed at the direction of a physician or other licensed health care provider on behalf of a patient by physicians, dentists, nurses, service providers, emergency medical service providers, mental health professionals, prehospital providers, or other health care personnel. "Medical record" includes such diagnostic documentation as X rays, electrocardiograms, electroencephalograms, and other test results. "Medical record" includes data entered into the prescription drug monitoring program under section 12-42.5-403, C.R.S.

"Medical information" means any information contained in the medical record or any information pertaining to the medical, mental health, and health care services performed at the direction of a physician or other licensed health care provider which is protected by the physician- patient privilege established by section 13-90-107 (1) (d), C.R.S.

"Proper authorization" means:

A written authorization signed by the patient or his or her duly designated representative;

or

An appropriate order of court; or

Authorized possession pursuant to law or regulation for claims processing, possession

for medical audit or quality assurance purposes, possession by a consulting physician to the patient, or possession by hospital personnel for record-keeping and billing purposes; or

Authorized possession pursuant to section 18-3-415, 18-3-415.5, 25-1-122, or 30-10- 606 (6), C.R.S.; or

Authorized possession bya law enforcement officer or agency, acting in official capacity and pursuant to an official investigation.

"Copy" means any facsimile, replica, photograph, sound recording, magnetic or electronic recording, or other reproduction of a medical record and any note, drawing, or sketch made of or from a medical record.

Theft of a medical record or medical information is a class 6 felony.

The obtaining, accessing, use, or disclosure of relevant medical records or medical information pursuant to 18 U.S.C. sec. 922 (t) and sections 24-33.5-424, 13-5-142, and 13-9-123, C.R.S., by the Colorado bureau of investigation, the clerk of the court of any judicial district in the

state, the clerk of the probate court of the city and county of Denver, or by any of their employees and accessing such records and information through the NICS system shall not constitute theft of a medical record or medical information under this section.

This section shall not apply to covered entities, their business associates, or health oversight agencies as each is defined in the federal "Health Insurance Portability and Accountability Act of 1996" as amended by the federal "Health Information Technology for Economic and Clinical Health Act" and the respective implementing regulations.


18-4-413. Mandatory sentencing for repeated felony theft from a store - store defined. (1) For purposes of this section and section 18-4-414, "store" means any establishment primarily engaged in the sale of goods at retail.

Any person convicted of felony theft, which felony theft was from a store, who within the immediately preceding four years was twice convicted of felony theft, which felony theft was each time from a store, shall be sentenced to at least the minimum term provided for such offense. A person convicted under this section shall not be eligible for probation or suspension of sentence.

The mandatory sentencing requirements specified in subsection (2) of this section shall not apply when the person is being sentenced pursuant to section 18-4-401 (4).


18-4-414. Evidence of value. (1) For purposes of this part 4, when theft occurs from a store, evidence of the retail value of the thing involved shall be prima facie evidence of the value of the thing involved. Evidence offered to prove retail value may include, but shall not be limited to, affixed labels and tags, signs, shelf tags, and notices.

(2) For the purposes of this part 4, in all cases where theft occurs, evidence of the value of the thing involved may be established through the sale price of other similar property and may include, but shall not be limited to, testimony regarding affixed labels and tags, signs, shelf tags, and notices tending to indicate the price of the thing involved. Hearsay evidence shall not be excluded in determining the value of the thing involved.


18-4-415. Use of photographs, video tapes, or films of property. Pursuant to section 13- 25-130, C.R.S., photographs, video tapes, or films of property over which a person is alleged to have exerted unauthorized control or otherwise to have obtained unlawfully are competent evidence if the photographs, video tapes, or films are admissible into evidence under the rules of law governing the admissibility of photographs, video tapes, or films into evidence.


18-4-416. Theft by resale of a lift ticket or coupon. Any unauthorized person who, with the intent to profit therefrom, resells or offers to resell any ticket, pass, badge, pin, coupon, or other device which then entitles the bearer to the use, benefit, or enjoyment of any skiing service or skiing facility commits a class 2 petty offense. The penalty of a violation of this section shall be a fine in an amount not to exceed three hundred dollars. Under no circumstances shall a person being charged

with this class 2 petty offense be arrested by any peace officer, and a summons to the appropriate court of jurisdiction shall be issued to the accused person.


18-4-417. Unlawful acts - theft detection devices. (1) (a) It is unlawful for any person to knowingly manufacture, distribute, or sell a theft detection shielding device or a theft detection deactivating device with the knowledge that some person intends to use the device in the commission of an offense involving theft.

It is unlawful for any person to possess a theft detection shielding device or a theft detection deactivating device with the intent to use the device possessed, or with the knowledge that some person intends to use the device possessed, in the commission of an offense involving theft.

It is unlawful for any person to knowingly deactivate or remove a theft detection device or any component thereof in any store or mercantile establishment without authorization prior to purchase.

As used in this section:

"Theft detection deactivating device" means any tool, instrument, mechanism, or other article adapted, designed, engineered, used, or operated to inactivate, incapacitate, or remove a theft detection device without authorization. "Theft detection deactivating device" includes, but is not limited to, jumper wires, wire cutters, and electronic article surveillance removal devices.

"Theft detection device" means an electronic or magnetic mechanism, machine, apparatus, tag, or article designed and operated for the purpose of detecting the unauthorized removal of merchandise from a store or mercantile establishment.

"Theft detection shielding device" means any tool, instrument, mechanism, or article adapted, designed, engineered, used, or operated to avoid detection by a theft detection device during the commission of an offense involving theft. "Theft detection shielding device" includes, but is not limited to, foil-lined or otherwise modified clothing, bags, purses, or containers capable of and for the sole purpose of avoiding detection devices. Any person who violates any of the provisions of subsection (1) of this section commits a class 1 misdemeanor.


18-4-418.  Fuel piracy. (Repealed)


18-4-419.  Newspaper theft. (Repealed)


18-4-420. Chop shop activity - ownership or operation of a chop shop - altered or removed identification number - penalties - definitions. (1) A person commits ownership or operation of a chop shop if he or she knowingly:
Owns or operates a chop shop, knowing that it is a chop shop, or conspires with another person to own or operate a chop shop, knowing that it is a chop shop;

Transports an unlawfully obtained motor vehicle or major component motor vehicle part to or from a chop shop, knowing that it is a chop shop; or
Sells or transfers to, or purchases or receives from, a chop shop, knowing that it is a chop shop, an unlawfully obtained motor vehicle or major component motor vehicle part.
A violation of paragraph (a) of subsection (1) of this section is a class 4 felony. A violation of paragraph (b) or (c) of subsection (1) of this section is a class 5 felony.
(a) A person commits altering or removing a vehicle identification number if he or she knowingly:
Removes, changes, alters, counterfeits, defaces, destroys, disguises, falsifies, forges, or obliterates the vehicle identification number, manufacturer's number, or engine number of a motor vehicle or major component motor vehicle part with an intent to misrepresent the identity or prevent the identification of a motor vehicle or major component motor vehicle part; or
Possesses, purchases, disposes of, sells, or transfers a motor vehicle or a major component motor vehicle part with knowledge that it contains a removed, changed, altered, counterfeited, defaced, destroyed, disguised, falsified, forged, or obliterated vehicle identification number, manufacturer's number, or engine number unless such motor vehicle or major component motor vehicle part is otherwise in compliance with the provisions of section 42-5-110, C.R.S.
(b) This subsection (3) does not apply to a private party or to an agent of a private party that is acting with the authorization of a law enforcement agency to lawfully seize, retain, recycle, transport, or otherwise dispose of a motor vehicle or major component motor vehicle part with a vehicle identification number, manufacturer number, or engine number that is removed, changed, altered, counterfeited, defaced, destroyed, disguised, falsified, forged, or obliterated.
Altering or removing a vehicle identification number is a class 5 felony.
As used in this section, unless the context otherwise requires:
"Chop shop" means any building, lot, facility, or other structure or premise where:
Any person or persons possess, receive, store, disassemble, or alter, including the alteration or concealment of any identifying feature or number, an unlawfully obtained motor vehicle or major component motor vehicle part for the purpose of using, selling, or disposing of the motor vehicle or major component motor vehicle part; or
Two or more unlawfully obtained motor vehicles are present for the purpose of alteration, sale, or disposal; or
Six or more unlawfully obtained major component motor vehicle parts from two or more motor vehicles are present for the purpose of alteration, sale, or disposal.
"Major component motor vehicle part" means any of the following parts of a motor vehicle:
The engine;
The transmission;
A front fender;
The hood;
Any door allowing entrance to or egress from the passenger compartment of the vehicle;
The front or rear bumper;
A rear quarter panel;
The deck lid, tailgate, or hatchback;

The trunk floor pan;
The cargo box of a pickup truck;
The frame, or if the vehicle has a unitized body, the supporting structure or structures that serve as the frame;
The cab of a truck;
The body of a passenger vehicle;
An airbag or airbag assembly;
A wheel or tire; or
Any other part of a motor vehicle that is comparable in design or function to any of the parts that have been listed, or that have been labeled with a unique traceable identification number, by the manufacturer of the motor vehicle or part.
"Motor vehicle" means all vehicles of whatever description that are propelled by any power other than muscular power; except that "motor vehicle" does not include vehicles that run on rails.
"Unlawfully obtained" means obtained by theft, fraud, or deceit or obtained without the permission of the owner.
PART 5 TRESPASS, TAMPERING, AND
CRIMINAL MISCHIEF


18-4-501. Criminal mischief. (1) A person commits criminal mischief when he or she knowingly damages the real or personal property of one or more other persons, including property owned by the person jointly with another person or property owned by the person in which another person has a possessory or proprietary interest, in the course of a single criminal episode.

(2) and (3) Repealed.

Criminal mischief is:

A class 3 misdemeanor when the aggregate damage to the real or personal property is less than three hundred dollars;

A class 2 misdemeanor when the aggregate damage to the real or personal property is three hundred dollars or more but less than seven hundred fifty dollars;

A class 1 misdemeanor when the aggregate damage to the real or personal property is seven hundred fifty dollars or more but less than one thousand dollars;

A class 6 felony when the aggregate damage to the real or personal property is one thousand dollars or more but less than five thousand dollars;

A class 5 felony when the aggregate damage to the real or personal property is five thousand dollars or more but less than twenty thousand dollars;

A class 4 felony when the aggregate damage to the real or personal property is twenty thousand dollars or more but less than one hundred thousand dollars;

A class 3 felony when the aggregate damage to the real or personal property is one hundred thousand dollars or more but less than one million dollars; and

A class 2 felony when the aggregate damage to the real or personal property is one million dollars or more.

18-4-502. First degree criminal trespass. A person commits the crime of first degree criminal trespass if such person knowingly and unlawfully enters or remains in a dwelling of another or if such person enters any motor vehicle with intent to commit a crime therein. First degree criminal trespass is a class 5 felony.

18-4-503. Second degree criminal trespass. (1) A person commits the crime of second degree criminal trespass if such person:

Unlawfully enters or remains in or upon the premises of another which are enclosed in a manner designed to exclude intruders or are fenced; or

Knowingly and unlawfully enters or remains in or upon the common areas of a hotel, motel, condominium, or apartment building; or

Knowingly and unlawfully enters or remains in a motor vehicle of another.

Second degree criminal trespass is a class 3 misdemeanor, but:

It is a class 2 misdemeanor if the premises have been classified by the county assessor for the county in which the land is situated as agricultural land pursuant to section 39-1-102 (1.6),

C.R.S.; and

It is a class 4 felony if the person trespasses on premises so classified as agricultural land with the intent to commit a felony thereon.

Whenever a person is convicted of, pleads guilty or nolo contendere to, receives a deferred judgment or sentence for, or is adjudicated a juvenile delinquent for, a violation of paragraph (c) of subsection (1) of this section, the offender's driver's license shall be revoked as provided in section 42-2-125, C.R.S.

18-4-504. Third degree criminal trespass. (1) A person commits the crime of third degree criminal trespass if such person unlawfully enters or remains in or upon premises of another.

Third degree criminal trespass is a class 1 petty offense, but:

It is a class 3 misdemeanor if the premises have been classified by the county assessor for the county in which the land is situated as agricultural land pursuant to section 39-1-102 (1.6),

C.R.S.; and

It is a class 5 felony if the person trespasses on premises so classified as agricultural land with the intent to commit a felony thereon.

18-4-504.5. Definition of premises. As used in sections 18-4-503 and 18-4-504, "premises" means real property, buildings, and other improvements thereon, and the stream banks and beds of any nonnavigable fresh water streams flowing through such real property.

18-4-505. First degree criminal tampering. Except as provided in sections 18-4-506.3 and 18-4-506.5, a person commits the crime of first degree criminal tampering if, with intent to cause interruption or impairment of a service rendered to the public by a utility or by an institution providing health or safety protection, he tampers with property of a utility or institution. First degree criminal tampering is a class 1 misdemeanor.

18-4-506. Second degree criminal tampering. Except as provided in sections 18-4-506.3 and 18-4-506.5, a person commits the crime of second degree criminal tampering if he tampers with property of another with intent to cause injury, inconvenience, or annoyance to that person or to another or if he knowingly makes an unauthorized connection with property of a utility. Second degree criminal tampering is a class 2 misdemeanor.

18-4-506.3. Tampering with equipment associated with oil or gas gathering operations - penalty. (1) Any person who in any manner knowingly destroys, breaks, removes, or otherwise tampers with or attempts to destroy, break, remove, or otherwise tamper with any equipment associated with oil or gas gathering operations commits a class 2 misdemeanor.

(2) Any person who in any manner, without the consent of the owner or operator, knowingly alters, obstructs, interrupts, or interferes with or attempts to alter, obstruct, interrupt, or interfere with the action of any equipment used or associated with oil or gas gathering operations commits a class 2 misdemeanor.

18-4-506.5. Tampering with a utility meter - penalty. (1) Any person who connects any pipe, tube, stopcock, wire, cord, socket, motor, or other instrument or contrivance with any main, service pipe, or other medium conducting or supplying gas, water, or electricity to any building without the knowledge and consent of the person supplying such gas, water, or electricity commits a class 2 misdemeanor.

Any person who in any manner alters, obstructs, or interferes with the action of any meter provided for measuring or registering the quantity of gas, water, or electricity passing through said meter without the knowledge and consent of the person owning said meter commits a class 2 misdemeanor.

Nothing in this section shall be construed to apply to any licensed electrical or plumbing contractor while performing usual and ordinary services in accordance with recognized customs and standards.

18-4-507. Defacing or destruction of written instruments. Every person who defaces or destroys any written instrument evidencing a property right, whether vested or contingent, with the intent to defraud commits a class 1 misdemeanor.

18-4-508. Defacing, destroying, or removing landmarks, monuments, or accessories. (1) Any person who knowingly cuts, fells, alters, or removes any certain boundary tree knowing such is a boundary tree, monument, or other allowed landmark, to the damage of any person, or any person who intentionally defaces, removes, pulls down, injures, or destroys any location stake, side post, corner post, landmark, or monument, or any other legal land boundary monument in this state, designating or intending to designate the location, boundary, or name of any mining claim, lode, or vein of mineral, or the name of the discoverer or date of discovery thereof, commits a class 2 misdemeanor.
(2) Any person who knowingly removes or knowingly causes to be removed any public land survey monument, as defined by section 38-53-103 (18), C.R.S., or control corner, as defined in section 38-53-103 (6), C.R.S., or a restoration of any such monument or who knowingly removes or knowingly causes to be removed any bearing tree knowing such is a bearing tree or other accessory, as defined by section 38-53-103 (1), C.R.S., even if said person has title to the land on which said monument or accessory is located, commits a class 2 misdemeanor unless, prior to such removal, said person has caused a Colorado professional land surveyor to establish at least two witness corners or reference marks for each such monument or accessory removed and has filed or caused to be filed a monument record pursuant to article 53 of title 38, C.R.S.

18-4-509. Defacing property - definitions. (1) (a) Any person who destroys, defaces, removes, or damages any historical monument commits the crime of defacing property.
Any person who defaces or causes, aids in, or permits the defacing of public or private property without the consent of the owner by any method of defacement, including but not limited to painting, drawing, writing, or otherwise marring the surface of the property by use of paint, spray paint, ink, or any other substance or object, commits the crime of defacing property.
(I) Any person who, with regard to a cave that is public property or the property of another, knowingly performs any of the following acts without the consent of the owner commits the crime of defacing property:
Breaking or damaging any lock, fastening, door, or structure designed to enclose or protect any such cave;
Defacing, damaging, or breaking from any part of such cave any cave resource; or
Removing from such cave any cave resource.
(II) For purposes of this section:
"Cave" means any naturally occurring void, cavity, recess, lava tube, or system of interconnected passages that occurs beneath the surface of the earth or within a cliff or ledge, including any cave resource therein, but not including any mine, tunnel, aqueduct, or other artificial excavation, and that is large enough to permit an individual to enter, regardless of whether the entrance is naturally formed or has been artificially created or enlarged. "Cave" includes any natural pit, sinkhole, or other feature that is an extension of the entrance.
"Cave resource" includes any material or substance occurring naturally in caves, such as animal life, plant life, paleontological deposits, sediments, minerals, speleogens, and speleothems. (B.5) "Juvenile" shall have the same meaning as set forth in section 19-1-103 (68), C.R.S.

"Speleogen" means relief features on the walls, ceiling, or floor of any cave that are part of the surrounding rock, including, but not limited to, anastomoses, scallops, meander niches, petromorphs, and rock pendants in solution caves and similar features unique to volcanic caves.
"Speleothem" means any natural mineral formation or deposit occurring in a cave, including, but not limited to, any stalactite, stalagmite, helictite, cave flower, flowstone, concretion, drapery, rimstone, or formation of clay or mud.
(2) (a) (I) Defacing property is a class 2 misdemeanor; except that:
A second or subsequent conviction for the offense of defacing property is a class 1 misdemeanor and the court shall impose a mandatory minimum fine of seven hundred fifty dollars upon conviction; and
If a person violates paragraph (b) of subsection (1) of this section twice or more within a period of six months, the damages caused by two or more of the violations may be aggregated and charged in a single count, in which event the violations so aggregated and charged shall constitute a single offense, and, if the aggregate damages are five hundred dollars or more, it is a class 1 misdemeanor and the court shall impose a mandatory minimum fine of seven hundred fifty dollars upon conviction.
In sentencing a person who violates this section, the court has discretion to impose alternatives in sentencing as described in part 1 of article 1.3 of this title, including but not limited to restorative justice practices, as defined in section 18-1-901 (3) (o.5), or in the case of a juvenile offender, to impose restorative justice, as defined in section 19-1-103 (94.1), C.R.S.
The court may suspend all or part of the mandatory minimum fine associated with a conviction under this section upon the offender's successful completion of any sentence alternative imposed by the court pursuant to subparagraph (II) of this paragraph (a).
Fifty percent of the fines collected pursuant to this paragraph (a) shall be credited to the highwayusers tax fund, created in section 43-4-201, C.R.S., and allocated and expended as specified in section 43-4-205 (5.5) (a), C.R.S., and fifty percent of the fines collected pursuant to this paragraph (a) shall be credited to the juvenile diversion cash fund created in section 19-2-303.5, C.R.S.; except that the fines collected pursuant to paragraph (c) of subsection (1) of this section shall be credited to the Colorado travel and tourism promotion fund created in section 24-49.7-106, C.R.S.
Any person convicted of defacing property pursuant to paragraph (b) or (c) of subsection
of this section shall be ordered by the court to personally make repairs to any property damaged, or properties similarly damaged, if possible. If the property cannot be repaired, the court shall order a person convicted of defacing property to replace or compensate the owner for the damaged property but may, in the case of a violation of paragraph (b) of subsection (1) of this section, limit such compensation to two thousand five hundred dollars.
Repealed.

18-4-510. Defacing posted notice. Any person who knowingly mars, destroys, or removes any posted notice authorized by law commits a class 1 petty offense.

18-4-511. Littering of public or private property. (1) Any person who deposits, throws,

or leaves any litter on any public or private property or in any waters commits littering.

It shall be an affirmative defense that:

Such property is an area designated by law for the disposal of such material and the person is authorized by the proper public authority to so use the property; or

The litter is placed in a receptacle or container installed on such property for that purpose; or

Such person is the owner or tenant in lawful possession of such property, or he has first obtained written consent of the owner or tenant in lawful possession, or the act is done under the personal direction of said owner or tenant.

(a) The term "litter" as used in this section means all rubbish, waste material, refuse, garbage, trash, debris, or other foreign substances, solid or liquid, of every form, size, kind, and description.

(b) The phrase "public or private property" as used in this section includes, but is not limited to, the right-of-wayof any road or highway, anybody of water or watercourse, including frozen areas or the shores or beaches thereof, any park, playground, or building, any refuge, conservation, or recreation area, and any residential, farm, or ranch properties or timberlands.

Except as otherwise provided in sections 33-15-108 (2) and 42-4-1406, C.R.S., littering is a class 2 petty offense punishable, upon conviction, by a mandatory fine of not less than twenty dollars nor more than five hundred dollars upon a first conviction, by a mandatory fine of not less than fifty dollars nor more than one thousand dollars upon a second conviction, and by a mandatory fine of not less than one hundred dollars nor more than one thousand dollars upon a third or subsequent conviction.

It is in the discretion of the court, upon the conviction of any person and the imposition of a fine under this section, to suspend any or all of the fine in excess of the mandatory minimum fine upon the condition that the convicted person gather and remove from specified public property or specified private property, with prior permission of the owner or tenant in lawful possession thereof, any litter found thereon, or upon the condition that the convicted person pick up litter at a time prescribed by and a place within the jurisdiction of the court for not less than eight hours upon a first conviction or for not less than sixteen hours upon a second or subsequent conviction.

Whenever litter is thrown, deposited, dropped, or dumped from any motor vehicle in violation of this section, the operator of said motor vehicle is presumed to have caused or permitted the litter to be so thrown, deposited, dropped, or dumped therefrom.

In addition to those law enforcement officers and agencies of this state and the political subdivisions thereof authorized to enforce this section, the officers of the Colorado state patrol and the district wildlife managers and other commissioned officers of the division of parks and wildlife are expressly authorized, empowered, and directed to enforce the provisions of this section.


18-4-512. Abandonment of a motor vehicle. (1) Any person who abandons any motor vehicle upon a street, highway, right-of-way, or any other public property, or upon any private property without the express consent of the owner or person in lawful charge of that private property commits abandonment of a motor vehicle.

To "abandon" means to leave a thing with the intention not to retain possession of or

assert ownership over it. The intent need not coincide with the act of leaving.

It is prima facie evidence of the necessary intent that:

The motor vehicle has been left for more than seven days unattended and unmoved; or

License plates or other identifying marks have been removed from the motor vehicle; or

The motor vehicle has been damaged or is deteriorated so extensively that it has value only for junk or salvage; or

The owner has been notified by a law enforcement agency to remove the motor vehicle, and it has not been removed within three days after notification.

Abandonment of a motor vehicle is a class 3 misdemeanor.


18-4-513. Criminal use of a noxious substance. (1) Any person who deposits on the land or in the building or vehicle of another, without his consent, any stink bomb or device, irritant, or offensive-smelling substance with the intent to interfere with another's use or enjoyment of the land, building, or vehicle commits a class 3 misdemeanor.

(2) It shall be an affirmative defense that a peace officer in the performance of his duties reasonably used a noxious substance.


18-4-514. Use of photographs, video tapes, or films of property. Pursuant to section 13- 25-130, C.R.S., photographs, video tapes, or films of property over which a person is alleged to have exerted unauthorized control or otherwise to have obtained unlawfully are competent evidence if the photographs, video tapes, or films are admissible into evidence under the rules of law governing the admissibility of photographs, video tapes, or films into evidence.


18-4-515. Entry to survey property - exception to criminal trespass. (1) Effective July 1, 1992, no person shall be in violation of the trespass laws of this part 5 if the requirements of this section are met. The provisions of this section provide an exception to the trespass laws only and do not affect or supersede the provisions and requirements of articles 1 to 7 of title 38, C.R.S., concerning condemnation proceedings, notwithstanding any laws to the contrary.

(2) Any person who is licensed as a professional land surveyor pursuant to section 12-25- 214, C.R.S., or who is under the direct supervision of such a person as an employee, agent, or representative, may enter public or private land to investigate and utilize boundary evidence and to perform boundary surveys if the notice requirement in this subsection (2) is met. The notice of the pending survey shall contain the identity of the party for whom the survey is being performed and the purpose for which the survey will be performed, the employer of the surveyor, the identity of the surveyor, the dates the land will be entered, the time, location, and timetable for such entry, the estimated completion date, the estimated number of entries that will be required, and a statement requesting the landowner to provide the surveyor with the name of each person who occupies the land as a tenant or lessee, whether on a permanent or a temporary basis. Nothing in this subsection

(2) shall be deemed to confer liability upon a landowner who fails or refuses to provide such requested statement. At least fourteen days before the desired date of entry the professional land

surveyor shall cause such notice to be given to the landowner by certified mail, return receipt requested, and by regular mail. Any landowner may waive the requirement that notice be given by certified mail, return receipt requested, and by regular mail. The waivers described in this subsection may be given orally or in writing.

If a landowner does not acknowledge receipt of the notice within fourteen days of such receipt, the professional land surveyor or other persons described in subsection (2) of this section shall have the right to enter the land pursuant to the specifications given in the notice. If a landowner acknowledges receipt of the notice within fourteen days of receipt, such landowner has the right to modify the time and other provisions of the

116

surveyor's access, as long as such modifications do not unreasonably restrict completion of the survey.

All persons described in subsection (2) of this section who enter land pursuant to and for a purpose described in this section shall carry upon their person at all times during entry and stay upon the land sufficient identification to identify themselves and their employer or principal, and shall present such identification upon request.

Persons described in subsection (2) of this section shall be liable for actual damages caused during entry and stay upon a landowner's land. No professional land surveyor or person under such surveyor's direct supervision shall have a civil cause of action against a landowner or lessee for personal injury or propertydamage incurred while on the land for purposes consistent with those described in subsection (2) of this section, except when such damages and injurywere willfully or deliberately caused by the landowner.

18-4-516. Criminal operation of a device in motion picture theater. (1) A person who, while within a motion picture theater, knowingly operates an audiovisual recording function of a device for the purpose of recording a motion picture, while a motion picture is being exhibited, without the consent of the owner or lessee of the motion picture theater, commits the offense of criminal operation of a device in a motion picture theater. Criminal operation of a device in a motion picture theater is a class 1 misdemeanor.

If a person operates or appears to operate an audiovisual recording function for the purpose of recording a motion picture in a motion picture theater, the owner or lessee of a facility in which a motion picture is being exhibited, or the authorized agent or employee of the owner of lessee, or any peace or police officer, acting in good faith and upon probable cause based upon reasonable grounds therefor, may detain and question such person, in a reasonable manner for the purpose of ascertaining whether the person is guilty of criminal operation of a device in motion picture theater. Such questioning of a person by the owner or lessee of a motion picture theater, or the authorized agent or employee of the owner or lessee, or peace or police officer does not render the owner or lessee of a motion picture theater, or the authorized agent or employee of the owner or lessee, or peace or police officer civilly or criminally liable for slander, false arrest, false imprisonment, malicious prosecution, or unlawful detention.

This section does not prevent a lawfully authorized investigative, law enforcement, or intelligence-gathering employee or agent of the state or federal government, while operating within the scope of lawfullyauthorized investigative, protective, law enforcement, or intelligence-gathering activities, from operating an audiovisual recording function of a device in a motion picture theater.

Nothing in this section prevents prosecution under any other provision of law providing for greater penalty.

As used in this section:

"Audiovisual recording function" means the capability of a device to record or transmit a motion picture or any part thereof by means of any technology now known or hereafter developed.

"Motion picture theater" means a movie theater, screening room, or other venue when used primarily for the exhibition of motion pictures.

PART 6

THEFT OF SOUND RECORDINGS

18-4-601. Definitions. As used in this part 6, unless the context otherwise requires:

"Aggregate wholesale value" means the average wholesale value of lawfully manufactured and authorized sound or audio-visual recordings corresponding to the number of nonconforming recorded articles involved in the offense. Proof of the specific wholesale value of each nonconforming device shall not be required.

(1.3) "Article" means a tangible medium on which sounds, images, or both are recorded or otherwise stored, including an original phonograph record, disc, tape, audio or video cassette, wire, film, memory card, flash drive, hard drive, data storage device, or other medium now existing or developed later on which sounds, images, or both are or can be recorded or otherwise stored, or a copy or reproduction that duplicates, in whole or in part, the original.

(1.5) "Copyright" means the ownership rights that accrue to an owner and relate solely to the common law copyright accruing to such owner. The term "copyright" does not include a federal copyright, which inures to the benefit of owners pursuant to Public Law 92-140, as amended by Public Law 93-573, which became effective February 15, 1972. For the purposes of this part 6, no common law copyright shall exist for a period longer than fifty-six years after an original copyright accrues to an owner.

(1.7) "Manufacturer" means the person who actuallymakes a recording or causes a recording to be made. "Manufacturer" does not include a person who manufactures a medium upon which sounds or images can be recorded or stored, or who manufactures the cartridge or casing itself, unless such person actually makes the recording or causes the recording to be made.

"Owner" means the person who owns the copyright on the original fixation of sounds embodied in the master phonograph record, master disc, master tape, master film, or other device used for reproducing sounds on phonograph records, discs, tapes, films, or other articles upon which sound is recorded and from which the transferred recorded sounds are directly derived.

"Person" means any individual, firm, partnership, corporation, or association.

18-4-602. Unlawful transfer for sale. (1) A person who knowinglyand without the consent of the owner transfers any copyrighted sounds recorded on a phonograph record, video disc, wire, tape, film, or other article on which sounds are recorded with the intent to sell such article on which

such sounds are so transferred or to cause the same to be sold for profit or to be used to promote the sale of any product commits unlawful transfer for sale.

(2) Unlawful transfer for sale is a class 6 felony.

18-4-603. Unlawful trafficking in unlawfully transferred articles. (1) A person who knowingly, or who reasonablyshould have such knowledge, advertises, offers for sale or resale, sells or resells, distributes, or possesses for any of the purposes provided in this subsection (1) any article that has been transferred without consent of the owner as provided in section 18-4-602 commits unlawful trafficking in unlawfully transferred articles.

(2) Each act of unlawful trafficking in unlawfully transferred articles is a class 3 misdemeanor.

18-4-604. Dealing in unlawfully packaged recorded articles. (1) A person who knowingly and for commercial advantage or private financial gain advertises, offers for sale or resale, sells or resells, transports, or possesses for any of the purposes provided in this subsection (1) any article on which sounds are recorded, the cover, box, jacket, or label of which does not clearly and conspicuously disclose the actual name and address of the manufacturer, commits dealing in unlawfully packaged recorded articles.

(2) Dealing in unlawfully packaged recorded articles is a class 1 misdemeanor. If the offense involves more than one hundred unlawfully packaged recorded articles or the offense is a second or subsequent offense, the court shall assess a fine of at least one thousand dollars.

18-4-604.3. Unlawful recording of a live performance. (1) A person who, without the consent of the owner of the right to record a live performance, records or causes to be recorded the live performance on a phonograph record, compact disc, video disc, wire, tape, film, or other article on which a live performance is recorded with the intent to sell the article on which the live performance is recorded or to cause the same to be sold for profit or to be used to promote the sale of any product commits unlawful recording of a live performance.

In the absence of a written agreement or law to the contrary, the performer or performers of a live performance are presumed to own the rights to record the live performance.

For purposes of this section, a person who is authorized to maintain custody and control of business records that reflect whether the owner of the live performance consented to having the live performance recorded is a competent witness in a proceeding regarding the issue of consent.

Unlawful recording of a live performance is a class 1 misdemeanor.

As used in this section, "live performance" means a recitation, rendering, or playing of a series of images, musical, spoken, or other sounds, or a combination of images and sounds, in an audible sequence.

18-4-604.7. Trafficking in unlawfully recorded live performance. (1) A person who knows or reasonablyshould know that an article has been recorded in violation of section 18-4-604.3 and advertises, offers for sale or resale, sells or resells, or distributes the article, or possesses the article for any of the said purposes, commits trafficking in an unlawfully recorded live performance.

Each act of trafficking in an unlawfully recorded live performance is a class 1 misdemeanor.

18-4-605. Applicability. (1) This part 6 shall not apply to:

Any broadcaster who, in connection with or as part of a radio, television, or cable broadcast transmission or for the purpose of archival preservation, transfers any copyrighted sounds recorded on a sound recording;

Any person who transfers copyrighted sounds in the home for personal use and without compensation for such transfer.

(2) This part 6 shall neither enlarge nor diminish the rights of the respective parties in a civil litigation concerning the subject matter of this part 6.

18-4-606. Confiscation and disposition of items. (1) A law enforcement officer shall, upon discovery, confiscate all unlawfully labeled, transferred, or recorded articles possessed for the purposes of selling or distributing in violation of this part 6 and all equipment and components used or intended to be used to knowingly and unlawfully transfer, manufacture, or record articles for the purposes of selling or distributing in violation of this part 6.

(2) Notwithstanding any other provision of law, recorded articles and equipment and components that are confiscated pursuant to subsection (1) of this section are contraband and shall be delivered to the district attorney in the county in which the confiscation was made. Upon conviction of the person, the district attorney may request a court order for destruction of the recorded articles and a court order for distribution of the equipment and components. Upon conviction of the person and motion of the district attorney, the court shall order the recorded articles to be destroyed or otherwise disposed of if the court finds that the person claiming title to the recorded articles possessed the recorded articles for the purposes of selling or distributing in violation of this part 6. The court shall order the equipment and components distributed to a charitable or educational organization if the court finds that the person claiming title to the equipment possessed the equipment to record nonconforming articles for the purposes of selling or distributing in violation of this part 6.

18-4-607. Restitution. Notwithstanding any other provision of law, upon conviction of a violation of this part 6, the convicted person shall be ordered to make restitution to the owner or lawful producer of the master sound or audio-visual recording, or to the trade association representing the owner or lawful producer who suffered injury resulting from the crime. The order of restitution shall be based on the aggregate wholesale value of lawfully manufactured and authorized recordings corresponding to the number of nonconforming recorded articles involved in

the offense unless a greater value can be proven. The order of restitution shall also include investigative costs relating to the offense.

PART 7

THEFT OF CABLE TELEVISION SERVICE

18-4-701. Theft of cable service - definitions. (1) As used in this part 7, unless the context otherwise requires:

"Cable operator" means any person who:

Provides cable service over a cable system in which such person directly or through one or more affiliates owns a significant interest; or

Controls or is responsible for the management and operation of such cable system through any arrangement.

"Cable service" means:

The one-way transmission to subscribers of a video programming service;

Two-way interactive services delivered over a cable system;

Subscriber interaction, if any, that is required for the selection or use of such video programming or interactive service.

"Cable system" means a facility consisting of a set of closed transmission paths and associated signal operation, reception, and control equipment that is designed to provide cable service.

A person commits theft of cable service if such person knowingly:

Obtains cable service from a cable operator by trick, artifice, deception, use of an unauthorized device or decoder, or other means without authorization or with the intent to deprive such cable operator of lawful compensation for the services rendered;

(I) Makes or maintains, without authority from or payment to a cable operator, a connection or connections, whether physical, electrical, mechanical, acoustical, or otherwise with any cable, wire, component, or other device used for the distribution of cable services.

(II) Notwithstanding subparagraph (I) of this paragraph (b), this paragraph (b) shall not include circumstances where a person has attached a wire or cable to extend service that the person has paid for or that has been authorized to an additional outlet, or where the cable operator has failed to disconnect a previously authorized cable service.

Modifies, alters, or maintains a modification or alteration to a device installed or capable of being installed with the authorization of a cable operator, which modification or alteration is for the purpose of intercepting or receiving cable service carried by such cable operator without authority from or payment to such cable operator;

Possesses without authority, with the intent to receive cable operator services without authorization from or payment to a cable operator, a device or printed circuit board designed in whole or in part to facilitate the following acts:

To receive cable services offered for sale over a cable system; or

To perform or facilitate the performance of any act set forth in paragraphs (a) to (c) of

this subsection (2).

Manufactures, imports into this state, distributes, sells, leases, or offers or advertises for sale or lease, with the intent to receive cable services or with the intent to promote the reception of cable services without payment or authorization from a cable operator, any device, printed circuit board, or plan or kit for a device or printed circuit board designed in whole or in part to facilitate the following acts:

To receive any cable services offered for sale over a cable system; or

To perform or facilitate the performance of any act set forth in paragraphs (a) to (c) of this subsection (2).

Fails to return or surrender equipment used to receive cable service and provided by a cable operator, after such service has been terminated for any reason.

This section does not apply to satellite dishes.

Any person who violates this section commits a class 2 misdemeanor.


18-4-702. Civil action - damages. (1) (a) A licensed or duly permitted cable operator may bring a civil action for damages against any person who commits civil theft of cable service.

Civil theft of cable service is the willful or intentional commission of any act described in section 18-4-701 (2).

No plaintiff that files an action pursuant to this section for theft of cable services shall be required to plead damages with particularity as a condition precedent for maintaining such an action.

There is a rebuttable presumption that a violation of section 18-4-701 (2) (a) has occurred if there exists in the actual possession of the person a device that permits the reception of unauthorized cable services for which no payment has been made to a cable operator and no legitimate purpose exists.

There is a rebuttable presumption that a violation of section 18-4-701 (2) (b) has occurred if cable service to the person's business or residential property was disconnected by a cable operator, notification of such action by certified mail was provided to such person, and a connection of such service exists at such person's business or residential property after the date of the disconnection.

There is a rebuttable presumption that a violation of section 18-4-701 (2) (c) has occurred if the cable operator, as a matter of standard procedure:

Places written warning labels on its converters or decoders explaining that tampering with such devices is a violation of law and a converter or decoder is found to have been tampered with, altered, or modified so as to allow the reception or interception of cable services without authority from or payment to a cable operator; or

Seals its converters or decoders with a label or mechanical device and the label or device has been removed or broken.

There is a rebuttable presumption that a violation of section 18-4-701 (2) (d) has occurred if a person possesses ten or more devices or printed circuit boards. If such rebuttable presumption is not overcome, the court shall find that such person committed civil theft of cable service willfully and for purposes of commercial advantage and shall increase the damages award in accordance with paragraph (a) of subsection (3) of this section.

There is a rebuttable presumption that a violation of section 18-4-701 (2) (e) has occurred if the person, while engaging in any of the prohibited acts, made apparent to the buyer that the product would enable the buyer to obtain cable service without payment to a cable operator. If such rebuttable presumption is not overcome, the court shall find that such person committed civil theft of cable service willfully and for purposes of commercial advantage and shall increase the damages award in accordance with paragraph (a) of subsection (3) of this section.

There is a rebuttable presumption that a violation of section 18-4-701 (2) (f) has occurred if a cable operator mailed by certified mail to the person, at the provided address, a written demand requesting the return of an operator-owned converter, decoder, or other device and the person failed to return said device or to make reasonable arrangements to do so within fifteen days after the date of such notice. Such reasonable arrangements may include requesting that the cable operator collect the equipment, subject to the cable operator's policies.

In any civil action brought pursuant to this section, a cable operator shall be entitled, upon proof of civil theft of cable service, to recover the greater of the following amounts as damages:

Four thousand dollars; or

Three times the amount of any actual damages sustained.

(a) Notwithstanding any provision of subsection (2) of this section to the contrary, a court may increase the award of damages in any civil action brought pursuant to this section by an amount of not more than fifty thousand dollars if such court finds that civil theft of cable service was committed willfully and for the purpose of commercial advantage.

In any civil action described in paragraph (a) of this subsection (3), a cable operator need not prove that the final purchaser actually used the device, plan, kit, or printed circuit board without authorization from or payment to a cable operator.

No attempt by a person to limit or shift legal liability in an action described in this subsection (3) by requiring purchasers to sign a disclaimer acknowledging their responsibility to report use of a device, plan, kit, or printed circuit board to a cable operator shall be effective, and any such disclaimer shall be void.

(Deleted by amendment, L. 98, p. 830, § 57, effective August 5, 1998.)

In any action for civil theft of cable service, the prevailing party shall be awarded reasonable attorney fees and direct costs incurred as a result of such theft, including, but not limited to, the costs of any investigation, disconnection or reconnection, service calls, employees, equipment, and expert witnesses and costs of the civil action.

A cable operator may seek an injunction to enjoin or restrain a violation of this section and damages arising from such violation in the same action.


18-4-703. Severability. If any provision of this part 7 or the application thereof to any person or circumstances is held invalid, such invalidity shall not affect the other provisions or applications of this part 7 which can be given effect without the invalid provision or application, and to this end the provisions of this part 7 are declared to be severable.

PART 8

THEFT OF PUBLIC TRANSPORTATION SERVICES

18-4-801 and 18-4-802. (Repealed)

## ARTICLE 5  Offenses Involving Fraud

PART 1

FORGERY, SIMULATION, IMPERSONATION, AND RELATED OFFENSES

18-5-101. Definitions. As used in sections 18-5-101 to 18-5-110, unless the context otherwise requires:
"Complete written instrument" means one which purports to be a genuine written instrument fully drawn with respect to every essential feature thereof.
(1.5) "Document-making implement" means any implement or impression, including, but not limited to, a template or a computerized template or form, specially designed or primarily used for making identification documents, false identification documents, or another document-making implement.
To "falsely alter" a written instrument means to change a written instrument without the authority of anyone entitled to grant such authority, whether it be in complete or incomplete form, by means of erasure, obliteration, deletion, insertion of new matter, transposition of matter, or any other means, so that such instrument in its thus altered form falsely appears or purports to be in all respects an authentic creation of or fully authorized by its ostensible maker.

To "falsely complete" a written instrument means:
To transform an incomplete written instrument into a complete one by adding, inserting, or changing matter without the authority of anyone entitled to grant that authority, so that the complete written instrument falsely appears or purports to be in all respects an authentic creation of or fully authorized by its ostensible maker; or
To transform an incomplete written instrument into a complete one by adding or inserting materially false information or adding or inserting a materially false statement. A materially false statement is a false assertion that affects the action, conduct, or decision of the person who receives or is intended to receive the asserted information in a manner that directly or indirectly benefits the person making the assertion.
To "falsely make" a written instrument means to make or draw a written instrument,

whether complete or incomplete, which purports to be an authentic creation of its ostensible maker, but which is not, either because the ostensible maker is fictitious or because, if real, he did not authorize the making or the drawing thereof.
"Forged instrument" means a written instrument which has been falsely made, completed, or altered.
"Government" means the United States, any state, county, municipality, or other political unit, any department, agency, or subdivision of any of the foregoing, or any corporation or other entity established by law to carry out governmental functions.
(6.5) "Identification document" means a document made or issued by or under the authority of the United States government, a state, political subdivision of a state, a foreign government, political subdivision of a foreign government, an international governmental, or an international quasi-governmental organization which, when completed with information concerning a particular individual, is of a type intended or commonly accepted for the purpose of identification of individuals.
"Incomplete written instrument" means one which contains some matter by way of content or authentication but which requires additional matter in order to render it a complete written instrument.
(7.5) "Produce" includes alter, authenticate, or assemble.
"Utter" means to transfer, pass, or deliver, or attempt or cause to be transferred, passed, or delivered, to another person any written instrument, article, or thing.
"Written instrument" means any paper, document, or other instrument containing written or printed matter or the equivalent thereof, used for purposes of reciting, embodying, conveying, or recording information, and any money, credit card, token, stamp, seal, badge, or trademark or any evidence or symbol of value, right, privilege, or identification, which is capable of being used to the advantage or disadvantage of some person.

18-5-102. Forgery. (1) A person commits forgery, if, with intent to defraud, such person falsely makes, completes, alters, or utters a written instrument which is or purports to be, or which is calculated to become or to represent if completed:
Part of an issue of money, stamps, securities, or other valuable instruments issued by a government or government agency; or
Part of an issue of stock, bonds, or other instruments representing interests in or claims against a corporate or other organization or its property; or
A deed, will, codicil, contract, assignment, commercial instrument, promissory note, check, or other instrument which does or may evidence, create, transfer, terminate, or otherwise affect a legal right, interest, obligation, or status; or
A public record or an instrument filed or required by law to be filed or legally fileable in or with a public office or public servant; or
A written instrument officially issued or created by a public office, public servant, or government agency; or
Part of an issue of tokens, transfers, certificates, or other articles manufactured and designed for use in transportation fees upon public conveyances, or as symbols of value usable in

place of money for the purchase of property or services available to the public for compensation; or
Part of an issue of lottery tickets or shares designed for use in the lottery held pursuant to part 2 of article 35 of title 24, C.R.S.; or
A document-making implement that may be used or is used in the production of a false identification document or in the production of another document-making implement to produce false identification documents.
Forgery is a class 5 felony.
Uttering a forged document to a peace officer shall create a presumption that the person intended to defraud such peace officer.

18-5-103. Second degree forgery. (Repealed)

18-5-104. Second degree forgery. (1) A person commits second degree forgery if, with intent to defraud, such person falsely makes, completes, alters, or utters a written instrument of a kind not described in section 18-5-102 or 18-5-104.5.
(2) Second degree forgery is a class 1 misdemeanor.

18-5-104.5. Use of forged academic record. (1) A person commits use of a forged academic record if, with intent to seek employment or with intent to seek admission to a public or private institution of higher education in this state or for the purpose of securing a scholarship or other form of financial assistance from the institution itself or from other public or private sources of financial assistance, such person falsely makes, completes, alters, or utters a written instrument which is or purports to be, or is calculated to become or to represent if completed, a bona fide academic record of an institution of secondary or higher education.

For purposes of this section:

"Academic record" means a transcript, diploma, grade report, or similar document of an institution of secondary or higher education.

"Financial assistance" means financial assistance for educational purposes, including, but not limited to, loans, scholarships, grants, fellowships, assistantships, work-study programs, or other forms of financial aid.

Use of a forged academic record is a class 1 misdemeanor.


18-5-105. Criminal possession of a forged instrument. A person commits a class 6 felony when, with knowledge that it is forged and with intent to use to defraud, such person possesses any forged instrument of a kind described in section 18-5-102.


18-5-106. Criminal possession of second degree forged instrument. (Repealed)


18-5-107. Criminal possession of second degree forged instrument. A person commits a class 2 misdemeanor, when, with knowledge that it is forged, and with intent to defraud, such person possesses any forged instrument of a kind covered by section 18-5-104.


18-5-108. Merger of offenses. A person may not be convicted of both forgery and criminal possession of a forged instrument with respect to the same written instrument.


18-5-109. Criminal possession of forgery devices. (1) A person commits criminal possession of forgery devices when:

Such person makes or possesses with knowledge of its character any plate, die, or other device, apparatus, equipment, or article specifically designed for use in counterfeiting, unlawfully simulating, or otherwise forging written instruments or counterfeit marks; or

Such person makes or possesses any device, apparatus, equipment, or article capable of or adaptable to a use specified in paragraph (a) of this subsection (1), with intent to use it, or to aid or permit another to use it, for purposes of forgery or the production of counterfeit marks; or

Such person illegally possesses a genuine plate, die, or other device used in the production of written instruments or counterfeit marks, with intent to fraudulently use the same; or

Such person unlawfully makes, produces, possesses, or utters a document-making implement knowing that such document-making implement may be used or is used in the production of a false identification document or counterfeit mark or another implement for the production of false identification documents or counterfeit marks.

Criminal possession of forgery devices is a class 6 felony.

As used in this section, "counterfeit mark" has the meaning set forth in section 18-5- 110.5 (3) (a).


18-5-110. Criminal simulation. (1) A person commits a criminal simulation, when:

With intent to defraud, he makes, alters, or represents any object in such fashion that it appears to have an antiquity, rarity, source or authorship, ingredient, or composition which it does not in fact have; or

With knowledge of its true character and with intent to use to defraud, he utters, misrepresents, or possesses any object made or altered as specified in paragraph (a) of this subsection (1).

(2) Criminal simulation is a class 1 misdemeanor.


18-5-110.5. Trademark counterfeiting. (1) A person commits trademark counterfeiting if such person intentionally manufactures, displays, advertises, distributes, offers for sale, sells, or possesses with intent to sell or distribute marks, goods, or services that the person knows are, bear, or are identified by one or more counterfeit marks and has possession, custody, or control of more

than twenty-five items bearing a counterfeit mark.

(a) Trademark counterfeiting is:

A class 2 misdemeanor if a person has not previously been convicted under this section and the violation involves fewer than one hundred items that are, bear, or are identified by a counterfeit mark or the total retail value of all goods or services that are, bear, or are identified by a counterfeit mark is less than one thousand dollars;

A class 1 misdemeanor if:

A person has one or more previous convictions under this section; or

The violation involves one hundred or more items that are, bear, or are identified by a counterfeit mark or the total retail value of all goods or services that are, bear, or are identified by a counterfeit mark is one thousand dollars or more.

In addition to the penalties specified in paragraph (a) of this subsection (2), any person convicted under this section shall be liable for a fine in an amount equal to three times the total retail value of all goods or services that bear or are identified by a counterfeit mark unless extenuating circumstances are shown by such person.

The remedies provided in this section are in addition to, and not in lieu of, any other civil or criminal penalties or remedies provided by law.

For purposes of this section:

"Counterfeit mark" means a mark identical to or substantially indistinguishable from a trademark that, without the permission of the owner of the trademark, is:

Affixed or designed to be affixed to, or displayed or otherwise associated with, goods;

or

Displayed in advertising for, or otherwise associated with, services.

(I) "Retail value" means the counterfeiter's regular selling price for the goods or services that bear or are identified by a counterfeit mark.

In the case of items bearing a counterfeit mark that are components of a finished product, "retail value" means the counterfeiter's regular selling price for the finished product.

For purposes of subsection (2) of this section, the quantity or retail value of goods or services shall include the aggregate quantity or retail value of all marks, goods, and services that are, bear, or are identified by counterfeit marks.

"Trademark" means any trademark registered under the laws of this state or of the United States.

In a trial under this section, any state or federal certificate of registration of a trademark shall be prima facie evidence of the facts stated therein.


18-5-111. Unlawfully using slugs. (1) A person commits unlawfully using slugs, if:

With intent to defraud the vendor of property or a service sold by means of a coin machine, he knowingly inserts, deposits, or uses a slug in such machine or causes the machine to be operated by any other unauthorized means; or

He makes, possesses, or disposes of a slug or slugs with intent to enable a person to use it or them fraudulently in a coin machine.

"Coin machine" means a coin box, turnstile, vending machine, or other mechanical or

electronic device or receptacle designed to receive a coin or bill of a certain denomination or token made for the purpose and, in return for the insertion or deposit thereof, to offer, to provide, to assist in providing, or to permit the acquisition of some property or some public or private service.

"Slug" means any object or article which, by virtue of its size, shape, or any other quality, is capable of being inserted, deposited, or otherwise used in a coin machine as an improper but effective substitute for a genuine coin, bill, or token, and of thereby enabling a person to obtain without valid consideration the property or service sold through the machine.

Unlawfully using slugs is a class 3 misdemeanor.


18-5-112. Obtaining signature by deception. (1) A person commits obtaining signature by deception if, by deception and with intent to defraud or to acquire a benefit for himself or another, he causes another to sign or execute a written instrument.

As used in this section, "by deception" means by knowingly:

Creating or confirming another's impression which is false and which the deceiver does not believe to be true; or

Failing to correct a false impression held by another which the deceiver previously has created or confirmed; or

Preventing another from acquiring information pertinent to any matter material to a proper understanding of any transaction in which the signature of such person is procured.

Obtaining signatures by deception is a class 2 misdemeanor.


18-5-113. Criminal impersonation. (1) A person commits criminal impersonation if he or she knowingly:

Assumes a false or fictitious identity or legal capacity, and in such identity or capacity he or she:

Marries, or pretends to marry, or to sustain the marriage relation toward another without the connivance of the latter;

Becomes bail or surety for a party in an action or proceeding, civil or criminal, before a court or officer authorized to take the bail or surety; or

Confesses a judgment, or subscribes, verifies, publishes, acknowledges, or proves a written instrument which by law may be recorded, with the intent that the same may be delivered as true; or

Assumes a false or fictitious identity or capacity, legal or other, and in such identity or capacity he or she:

Performs an act that, if done by the person falsely impersonated, might subject such person to an action or special proceeding, civil or criminal, or to liability, charge, forfeiture, or penalty; or

Performs any other act with intent to unlawfully gain a benefit for himself, herself, or another or to injure or defraud another.

Criminal impersonation is a class 6 felony.

For the purposes of subsection (1) of this section, using false or fictitious personal identifying information, as defined in section 18-5-901 (13), shall constitute the assumption of a false or fictitious identity or capacity.


18-5-114. Offering a false instrument for recording. (1) A person commits offering a false instrument for recording in the first degree if, knowing that a written instrument relating to or affecting real or personal property or directly affecting contractual relationships contains a material false statement or material false information, and with intent to defraud, he presents or offers it to a public office or a public employee, with the knowledge or belief that it will be registered, filed, or recorded or become a part of the records of that public office or public employee.

Offering a false instrument for recording in the first degree is a class 5 felony.

A person commits offering a false instrument for recording in the second degree if, knowing that a written instrument relating to or affecting real or personal property or directly affecting contractual relationships contains a material false statement or material false information, he presents or offers it to a public office or a public employee, with the knowledge or belief that it will be registered, filed, or recorded or become a part of the records of that public office or public employee.

Offering a false instrument for recording in the second degree is a class 1 misdemeanor.


18-5-115. Charitable fraud. (Repealed)


18-5-116. Controlled substances - inducing consumption by fraudulent means. (1) It is unlawful for any person, surreptitiously or by means of fraud, misrepresentation, suppression of truth, deception, or subterfuge, to cause any other person to unknowingly consume or receive the direct administration of any controlled substance, as defined in section 18-18-102 (5); except that nothing in this section shall diminish the scope of health care authorized by law.

Any person who violates the provisions of this section commits a class 4 felony.

122

18-5-117.  Unlawful possession of personal identifying information. (Repealed)

18-5-118.  Offenses involving forgery of a penalty assessment notice issued to a minor under the age of eighteen years - suspension of driving privilege.  (Repealed)

18-5-119.  Theft of personal identifying information. (Repealed)

18-5-120.  Gathering personal information by deception. (Repealed)

PART 2

FRAUD IN OBTAINING PROPERTY OR SERVICES

18-5-201.  Definitions. (Repealed)

18-5-201.1.  Definitions relating to guaranteed check cards. (Repealed)

18-5-202.  Fraudulent use of a credit device. (Repealed)

18-5-202.1.  Fraudulent use of guaranteed check card. (Repealed)

18-5-203.  Theft of credit device or guaranteed check card. (Repealed)

18-5-204.  Criminal possession of credit device or guaranteed check card. (Repealed)

18-5-205.  Fraud by check - definitions - penalties. (1) As used in this section, unless the context otherwise requires:
"Check" means a written, unconditional order to pay a sum certain in money, drawn on a bank, payable on demand, and signed by the drawer.
"Check", for the purposes of this section only, also includes a negotiable order of withdrawal and a share draft.
"Drawee" means the bank upon which a check is drawn or a bank, savings and loan association, or credit union on which a negotiable order of withdrawal or a share draft is drawn.
"Drawer" means a person, either real or fictitious, whose name appears on a check as the primary obligor, whether the actual signature be that of himself or of a person authorized to draw the check on himself.
"Insufficient funds" means a drawer has insufficient funds with the drawee to pay a check when the drawer has no checking account, negotiable order of withdrawal account, or share draft account with the drawee or has funds in such an account with the drawee in an amount less than the amount of the check plus the amount of all other checks outstanding at the time of issuance; and a check dishonored for "no account" shall also be deemed to be dishonored for "insufficient funds".
"Issue". A person issues a check when he makes, draws, delivers, or passes it or causes it to be made, drawn, delivered, or passed.

"Negotiable order of withdrawal" and "share draft" mean negotiable or transferable instruments drawn on a negotiable order of withdrawal account or a share draft account, as the case may be, for the purpose of making payments to third persons or otherwise.
"Negotiable order of withdrawal account" means an account in a bank or savings and loan association and "share draft account" means an account in a credit union, on which payment of interest or dividends may be made on a deposit with respect to which the bank or savings and loan association or the credit union, as the case may be, may require the depositor to give notice of an intended withdrawal not less than thirty days before the withdrawal is made, even though in practice such notice is not required and the depositor is allowed to make withdrawal by negotiable order of withdrawal or share draft.
Any person, knowing he has insufficient funds with the drawee, who, with intent to defraud, issues a check for the payment of services, wages, salary, commissions, labor, rent, money, property, or other thing of value, commits fraud by check.
Fraud by check is:
(Deleted by amendment, L. 2007, p. 1693,  8, effective July 1, 2007.)
(a.5) A class 1 petty offense if the fraudulent check was for the sum of less than fifty dollars or if the offender is convicted of fraud by check involving the issuance of two or more checks within a sixty-day period in the state of Colorado totaling less than fifty dollars in the aggregate;

(a.7) A class 3 misdemeanor if the fraudulent check was for the sum of fifty dollars or more but less than three hundred dollars or if the offender is convicted of fraud by check involving the issuance of two or more checks within a sixty-day period in the state of Colorado totaling fifty dollars or more but less than three hundred dollars in the aggregate;
A class 2 misdemeanor if the fraudulent check was for the sum of three hundred dollars or more but less than seven hundred fifty dollars or if the offender is convicted of fraud by check involving the issuance of two or more checks within a sixty-day period in the state of Colorado totaling three hundred dollars or more but less than seven hundred fifty dollars in the aggregate;

(b.5) (Deleted by amendment, L. 2014.)
A class 1 misdemeanor if the fraudulent check was for the sum of seven hundred fifty dollars or more but less than two thousand dollars or if the

offender is convicted of fraud by check involving the issuance of two or more checks within a sixty-day period in the state of Colorado totaling seven hundred fifty dollars or more but less than two thousand dollars in the aggregate;

A class 6 felony if the fraudulent check was for the sum of two thousand dollars or more or if the offender is convicted of fraud by check involving the issuance of two or more checks within a sixty-day period in the state of Colorado totaling two thousand dollars or more in the aggregate;

A class 6 felony if the fraudulent check was drawn on an account which did not exist or which has been closed for a period of thirty days or more prior to the issuance of said check.

Any person having acquired rights with respect to a check which is not paid because the drawer has insufficient funds shall have standing to file a complaint under this section, whether or not he is the payee, holder, or bearer of the check.

Any person who opens a checking account, negotiable order of withdrawal account, or

share draft account using false identification or an assumed name for the purpose of issuing fraudulent checks commits a class 2 misdemeanor.

If deferred prosecution is ordered, the court as a condition of supervision shall require the defendant to make restitution on all checks issued by the defendant that are unpaid as of the date of commencement of the supervision in addition to other terms and conditions appropriate for the treatment or rehabilitation of the defendant.

A bank, savings and loan association, or credit union is not civilly or criminally liable for releasing information relating to the drawer's account to a sheriff, deputy sheriff, undersheriff, police officer, agent of the Colorado bureau of investigation, division of gaming investigator, division of lottery investigator, parks and outdoor recreation officer, Colorado wildlife officer, district attorney, assistant district attorney, deputy district attorney, or authorized investigator for a district attorney or the attorney general investigating or prosecuting a charge under this section.

This section does not relieve the prosecution from the necessity of establishing the required culpable mental state. However, for purposes of this section, the issuer's knowledge of insufficient funds is presumed, except in the case of a postdated check or order, if:

He has no account upon which the check or order is drawn with the bank or other drawee at the time he issues the check or order; or

He has insufficient funds upon deposit with the bank or other drawee to pay the check or order, on presentation within thirty days after issue.

Restitution for offenses described in this section may be collected as a condition of pretrial diversion by a district attorney, an employee of a district attorney's office, or a person under contract with a district attorney's office. Such collection is governed by the provisions of article 18.5 of title 16, C.R.S., and is not the collection of a debt.

18-5-206. Defrauding a secured creditor or debtor. (1) If a person, with intent to defraud a creditor by defeating, impairing, or rendering worthless or unenforceable any security interest, sells, assigns, transfers, conveys, pledges, encumbers, conceals, destroys, or disposes of any collateral subject to a security interest, the person commits:

(Deleted by amendment, L. 2007, p. 1694, 9, effective July 1, 2007.)

A class 1 petty offense if the value of the collateral is less than fifty dollars; (b.5)  (Deleted by amendment, L. 2014.)

A class 3 misdemeanor if the value of the collateral is fifty dollars or more but less than three hundred dollars;

A class 2 misdemeanor if the value of the collateral is three hundred dollars or more but less than seven hundred fifty dollars;

A class 1 misdemeanor if the value of the collateral is seven hundred fifty dollars or more but less than two thousand dollars;

A class 6 felony if the value of the collateral is two thousand dollars or more but less than five thousand dollars;

A class 5 felony if the value of the collateral is five thousand dollars or more but less than twenty thousand dollars;

A class 4 felony if the value of the collateral is twenty thousand dollars or more but less

than one hundred thousand dollars;

A class 3 felony if the value of the collateral is one hundred thousand dollars or more but less than one million dollars; and

A class 2 felony if the value of the collateral is one million dollars or more.

If a creditor, with intent to defraud a debtor, sells, assigns, transfers, conveys, pledges, buys, or encumbers a promissory note or contract signed by the debtor, the creditor commits:

(Deleted by amendment, L. 2007, p. 1694, 9, effective July 1, 2007.)

A class 1 petty offense if the amount owing on the note or contract is less than fifty dollars;

(b.5)  (Deleted by amendment, L. 2014.)

A class 3 misdemeanor if the amount owing on the note or contract is fifty dollars or more but less than three hundred dollars;

A class 2 misdemeanor if the amount owing on the note or contract is three hundred dollars or more but less than seven hundred fifty dollars;

A class 1 misdemeanor if the amount owing on the note or contract is seven hundred fifty dollars or more but less than two thousand dollars;

A class 6 felony if the amount owing on the note or contract is two thousand dollars or more but less than five thousand dollars;

A class 5 felony if the amount owing on the note or contract is five thousand dollars or more but less than twenty thousand dollars;

A class 4 felony if the amount owing on the note or contract is twenty thousand dollars or more but less than one hundred thousand dollars;

A class 3 felony if the amount owing on the note or contract is one hundred thousand dollars or more but less than one million dollars; and

A class 2 felony if the amount owing on the note or contract is one million dollars or more.

18-5-207. Purchase on credit to defraud. A person who purchases any personal property on credit and thereafter, before paying for it, sells, hypothecates, pledges, or disposes of it with intent to defraud the seller or vendor commits a class 2 misdemeanor.

18-5-208. Dual contracts to induce loan. It is a class 3 misdemeanor for any person to knowingly make, issue, deliver, or receive dual contracts for the purchase or sale of real property. The term "dual contracts", either written or oral, means two separate contracts concerning the same parcel of real property, one of which states the true and actual purchase price and one of which states a purchase price in excess of the true and actual purchase price, and is used, or intended to be used, to induce persons to make a loan or a loan commitment on such real property in reliance upon the stated inflated value.

18-5-209. Issuing a false financial statement - obtaining a financial transaction device

by false statements. (1) A person commits issuing a false financial statement if, with intent to defraud, he:

Knowingly makes or utters a written instrument which purports to describe the financial condition or ability to pay of himself or another person and which is false in some material respect and reasonably relied upon; or

Represents in writing that a written instrument purporting to describe another person's financial condition or ability to pay as of a prior date is accurate with respect to that person's current financial condition or ability to pay, knowing the instrument to be materially false in that respect and reasonably relied upon.

Issuing a false financial statement is a class 2 misdemeanor.

A person commits issuing a false financial statement for purposes of obtaining a financial transaction device, as defined in section 18-5-701 (3), if, with intent to defraud, upon filing an application for a financial transaction device with an issuer, he knowingly makes or causes to be made a false statement or report, which is false in some material respect and reasonably relied upon, relative to his name, occupation, financial condition, assets, or liabilities or willfully and substantially overvalues any assets or willfully omits or substantially undervalues any indebtedness for the purpose of influencing the issuer to issue a financial transaction device.

Issuing a false financial statement for purposes of obtaining a financial transaction device when such device is used to obtain property or services or money is a class 1 misdemeanor.

Issuing two or more false financial statements for purposes of obtaining two or more financial transaction devices when such devices are used to obtain property or services or money is a class 6 felony.

18-5-210. Receiving deposits in a failing financial institution. A person commits a class 6 felony if, as an officer, manager, or other person participating in the direction of a financial institution, he knowingly receives or permits the receipt of a deposit or investment, knowing that the institution is insolvent. A financial institution is insolvent within the meaning of this section when from any cause it is unable to pay its obligations in the ordinary or usual course of business or its liabilities exceed its assets.

18-5-211. Insurance fraud - definitions. (1) A person commits insurance fraud if the person does any of the following:

With an intent to defraud presents or causes to be presented an application for the issuance or renewal of an insurance policy, which application, or documentation in support of such application or renewal, contains false material information or withholds material information that is requested by the insurer and results in the issuance of an insurance policy or insurance coverage for the applicant or another;

With an intent to defraud presents or causes to be presented any claim for a loss or injury, which claim contains false material information or withholds material information;

With an intent to defraud causes or participates, or purports to be involved, in a vehicular collision, or any other vehicular accident, for the purpose of presenting any false or fraudulent

insurance claim;

With an intent to defraud presents or causes to be presented a claim for the payment of a loss where the loss or damage claimed preexisted the execution of the applicable contract of insurance unless otherwise permitted under the contract of insurance or policy; or

With an intent to defraud presents or causes to be presented any written, oral, or electronic material or statement as part of, in support of or in opposition to, a claim for payment or other benefit pursuant to an insurance policy, knowing that the statement contains false material information or withholds material information.

An insurance producer or agent of an insurance producer commits insurance fraud if he or she knowingly moves, diverts, or misappropriates premium funds belonging to an insurer or unearned premium funds belonging to an insured or applicant for insurance from a producer's trust or other account without the authorization of the owner of the funds or other lawful justification.

An insurance producer or agent of an insurance producer commits insurance fraud if he or she with an intent to defraud creates, utters, or presents a certificate or any other evidence of insurance containing false information to any person or entity.

Insurance fraud committed in violation of paragraph (a) of subsection (1) of this section is a class 1 misdemeanor. Insurance fraud committed in violation of paragraphs (b) to (e) of subsection (1) of this section or subsection (2) or (3) of this section is a class 5 felony.

The commissioner of insurance shall revoke the license to conduct business in this state of any licensed insurance producer under article 2 of title 10, C.R.S., who is convicted of any provision under this section.

Nothing in this section precludes a prosecutor from prosecuting any other offense.

As used in this section, unless the context otherwise requires:

"Claim" means a demand for money, property, or services pursuant to a contract of insurance as well as any documentation in support of such claim whether submitted contemporaneously with the claim or at a different time. A claim and any supporting information may be in written, oral, electronic, or digital form.

"Insurance" has the same meaning as defined in section 10-1-102 (12), C.R.S.

"Insurance producer" has the same meaning as defined in section 10-2-103 (6), C.R.S.

"Insurer" has the same meaning as defined in section 10-1-102 (13), C.R.S.

"Material information" is a statement or assertion directly pertaining to an application for insurance or an insurance claim that a reasonable person making such an assertion knows or should know will affect the action, conduct, or decision of the person who receives or is intended to receive the asserted information in a manner that would directly or indirectly benefit the person making the assertion.

PART 3 FRAUDULENT AND DECEPTIVE
SALES AND BUSINESS PRACTICES

18-5-301. Fraud in effecting sales. (1) A person commits a class 2 misdemeanor if, in the course of business, he knowingly:

Uses or possesses for use a false weight or measure, or any other device for falsely determining or recording any quality or quantity; or

Sells, offers, or exposes for sale or delivers less than the represented quantity of any commodity or service; or

Takes or attempts to take more than the represented quantity of any commodity or service when as buyer he furnishes the weight or measure; or

Sells, offers, or exposes for sale an adulterated or mislabeled commodity. "Adulterated" means varying from the standard of composition or quality prescribed by or pursuant to any statute of the state of Colorado or the United States providing criminal penalties for such variance, or set by established commercial usage. "Mislabeled" means varying from the standard of truth or disclosure in labeling prescribed or pursuant to any statute of the state of Colorado or the United States providing criminal penalties for such variance, or set by established commercial usage; or

Makes a false or misleading statement in any advertisement addressed to the public or to a substantial segment thereof for the purpose of promoting the purchase or sale of property or services.

Repealed.

18-5-302. Unlawful activity concerning the selling of land. (1) Any person who, after once selling, bartering, or disposing of any land, or executing any bond or agreement for sale of any land, again sells, barters, or disposes of the same tract of land or any part thereof, or executes any bond or agreement to sell or barter or dispose of the same land or any part thereof, to any other person, with intent to defraud, commits selling land twice. Selling land twice is a class 5 felony.

Any person who knowingly makes a false representation as to the existence of an ownership interest in land which he has as a seller or which his principal has, and which is relied upon, commits a class 6 felony.

A person who signs a lien waiver for a construction loan under section 38-22-119, C.R.S., and knowingly fails to timely pay any debts resulting from a construction agreement covered by the waiver commits a class 1 misdemeanor, unless there is a bona fide dispute as to the existence or amount of the debt.

18-5-303. Bait advertising. (1) A person commits bait advertising if, in any manner, including advertising or any other means of communication, he offers property or services as part of a scheme or plan, with the intent, plan, or purpose not to sell or provide the advertised property or services at all, or not at the price at which he offered them, or not in a quantity sufficient to meet the reasonable expected public demand, unless the quantity is specifically stated in the advertisement.

It shall be an affirmative defense that a television or radio broadcasting station or a publisher or printer of a newspaper, magazine, or other form of printed advertising which

broadcasted, published, or printed a false advertisement prohibited by section 18-5-301 (1) (e) or a bait advertisement prohibited by subsection (1) of this section or a telephone company which furnished service to a subscriber did so without knowledge of the advertiser's or subscriber's intent, plan, or purpose.

Bait advertising is a class 2 misdemeanor.

18-5-304. False statements as to circulation. It is a class 1 petty offense for any person engaged in the publication of any newspaper, magazine, periodical, or other advertising medium published in the state of Colorado or for any employee of any such publisher knowingly to make any statement concerning the circulation of the newspaper, magazine, periodical, or other advertising medium which is untrue or misleading where such publisher fixes his charges for advertising space in the publication on the amount of its circulation.

18-5-305. Identification number - altering - possession. (1) A person commits the crime of altering identification number if, with intent that identification of an article be hindered or prevented, he obscures an identification number or in the course of business he sells, offers for sale, leases, or otherwise disposes of an article knowing that an identification number thereon is obscured.

"Identification number" means a serial or motor number placed by the manufacturer upon an article as a permanent individual identifying mark.

"Obscure" means to destroy, remove, alter, conceal, or deface so as to render illegible by ordinary means of inspection.

Possession of an article on which an identification number is obscured is prima facie evidence that the person possessing it obscured the number with intent to hinder or prevent identification of the article, and that he knows that the identification number is obscured, unless, prior to his arrest or the issuance of a warrant for a search of the premises where the article is kept, whichever is earlier, he reports possession of the article to the police or other appropriate law enforcement agency.

Altering identification number is a class 3 misdemeanor.

18-5-306. Counterfeit or imitation controlled substances. (Repealed)

18-5-307. Fee paid to private employment agencies. (1) As used in this section:

"Applicant" means any person applying to a private employment agency in order to secure employment with any person, firm, association, or corporation other than the private employment agency.

"Employment" means every character of service rendered or to be rendered for wages, salary, commission, or other form of remuneration.

(b.5) "Fee-paid position" means a position of employment which is available to an applicant where no fee or cost accrues to the applicant as a condition of obtaining such position.

(I) "Private employment agency" means any nongovernmental person, firm, association, or corporation which secures or attempts to secure employment, arranges an interview between an applicant and a specific employer other than itself, or, by any form of advertising or representation, holds itself out to a prospective applicant as able to secure employment for the applicant with any person, firm, association, or corporation other than itself, or engages in employment counseling and in connection therewith supplies or represents that it is able to supply employers or available jobs, where an applicant may become liable for the payment of a fee, either directly or indirectly.

(II) "Private employment agency" also means any nongovernmental person, firm, association, or corporation which provides a list of potential employers or available jobs in a publication, if the primary purpose of the publication, as represented by the provider, is to enable applicants to find employment or to list available jobs and if the applicant is charged more than twenty dollars within any period of time of thirty days or less for access to the publication or revisions or updates thereof, unless the listings of all jobs in the publication are initiated by employers rather than the provider.

Any fee paid by an applicant to a private employment agency shall be by written contractual agreement which includes specific provisions for refunds and extended payment options. The exclusion of said options from the contractual agreement shall be explicitly stated in said agreement.

No fee shall be charged by a private employment agency until an applicant is placed in employment.

In the event employment terminates for any reason within one hundred calendar days, an applicant shall not be required to pay a fee to a private employment agency in excess of one percent of the total fee for each calendar day elapsed between the beginning and termination of employment. For purposes of this subsection (4), the amount of the total fee shall be based on the actual gross income earned, annualized in accordance with the contractual fee schedule.

In the event employment terminates for any reason within one hundred calendar days, a private employment agency shall refund any portion of a fee paid by an applicant in excess of the limits specified in subsection (4) of this section. Such a refund shall be made in full within seven calendar days of said agency's receipt of written notification of the termination of employment; except that, if it has not been determined within that period of time that the instrument used to pay the fee is backed by sufficient funds, the refund is due upon such determination. If a refund is not made when due, the private employment agency is liable to the applicant for the refund due plus an additional sum equal to the amount of the refund.

(5.5) It shall be unlawful for any private employment agency knowingly to do or cause to be done any of the following:

Send an applicant to any fictitious job or position or make any false representation concerning the availability of employment;

Send an applicant to any place where a strike or lockout exists or is impending without notifying the applicant of the circumstances;

Conspire or arrange with any employer to secure the discharge of an employee or give or receive any gratuity or divide or share with an employer any fee, charge, or remuneration received from any applicant for employment;

Circulate or publish, by advertisement or otherwise, any false statements or representations to persons seeking employment or to employers seeking employees;

Fail to refund fees to an applicant where such refund is due pursuant to subsection (5) of this section;

Advertise or represent the availability of fee-paid positions where no cost accrues to the applicant if hired in such a manner as to confuse such position with other available positions which are not available on a fee-paid basis;

Advertise or represent that an available position is available on a free or no fee basis or otherwise indicate that no charge or cost accrues to anyone when in fact the employer is obligated to pay a fee contingent upon the acceptance of employment of the applicant;

Advertise for any position, including personnel for its own staff, without identifying in the advertisement that it is a private employment agency.

A private employment agency or any employee of such agency commits a misdemeanor if said agency or employee knowingly violates any provision of this section. An agency found guilty of such a crime shall be subject to a fine of not more than one thousand dollars per conviction, and any employee of such agency found directly responsible for committing acts in violation of this section shall be subject to a fine of not more than one thousand dollars, or by imprisonment for not more than one year in the county jail, or by both such fine and imprisonment.

A private employment agency which has been convicted of a misdemeanor pursuant to this article, or any person connected therewith pursuant to paragraph (c) of subsection (1) of this section prior to conducting business in this state after such conviction, regardless of how classified as person, firm, association, or corporation, shall file with the department of labor and employment a cash or corporate surety bond in the sum of twenty thousand dollars. Such bond shall be executed by the private employment agency as principal and by a surety company authorized to do business in this state. Said private employment agency shall maintain such bond in effect as long as it conducts business in this state. Any person who suffers loss or damage as the result of a violation of this article, including any person who is owed a refund or any part thereof pursuant to subsections and (5) of this section, may recover against the bond to the extent of the loss or damage suffered. A surety on any bond filed under the provisions of this section shall be released therefrom after such surety serves written notice thereof to the department of labor and employment at least sixty days prior to such release. Said release shall not discharge or otherwise affect any claim for loss or damage which occurred while said bond was in effect or which occurred under any contract executed during any period of time when said bond was in effect, except when another bond is filed in a like amount and provides indemnification for any such loss. The sole responsibilities of the department of labor and employment under this subsection (7) shall be to serve as a repository of bonds filed pursuant to this subsection (7) and to notify the district attorney in the county in which a private employment agencyis located when the department of labor and employment receives written notice from a surety seeking release from a bond that has been filed with the department of labor and employment by said private employment agency pursuant to this subsection (7). A private employment agency that violates the provisions of this section with regard to any three or more different applicants in any one-year period shall be deemed a class 1 public nuisance and shall be subject to the provisions of part 3 of article 13 of title 16, C.R.S. Any surety bond filed by such agency shall be forfeited and the proceeds distributed as provided in section 16-13-311, C.R.S.

18-5-308. Electronic mail fraud. (1) A person commits electronic mail fraud if he or she violates any provision of 18 U.S.C. sec. 1037 (a).

This section shall not apply to a provider of internet access service, as defined in 47 U.S.C. sec. 231, who does not initiate the commercial electronic mail message.

Electronic mail fraud is a class 2 misdemeanor; except that a second or subsequent offense within two years is a class 1 misdemeanor.

18-5-309. Money laundering - illegal investments - penalty - definitions. (1) A person commits money laundering if he or she:

Conducts or attempts to conduct a financial transaction that involves money or any other thing of value that he or she knows or believes to be the proceeds, in any form, of a criminal offense:

With the intent to promote the commission of a criminal offense; or

With knowledge or a belief that the transaction is designed in whole or in part to:

Conceal or disguise the nature, location, source, ownership, or control of the proceeds of a criminal offense; or

Avoid a transaction reporting requirement under federal law;

Transports, transmits, or transfers a monetary instrument or moneys:

With the intent to promote the commission of a criminal offense; or

With knowledge or a belief that the monetary instrument or moneys represent the proceeds of a criminal offense and that the transportation, transmission, or transfer is designed, in whole or in part, to:

Conceal or disguise the nature, location, source, ownership, or control of the proceeds of a criminal offense; or

Avoid a transaction reporting requirement under federal law; or

Intentionally conducts a financial transaction involving property that is represented to be the proceeds of a criminal offense, or involving property that the person knows or believes to have been used to conduct or facilitate a criminal offense, to:

Promote the commission of a criminal offense;

Conceal or disguise the nature, location, source, ownership, or control of property that the person believes to be the proceeds of a criminal offense; or

Avoid a transaction reporting requirement under federal law.

Money laundering is a class 3 felony.

As used in this section, unless the context otherwise requires:

"Conducts or attempts to conduct a financial transaction" includes, but is not limited to, initiating, concluding, or participating in the initiation or conclusion of a transaction.

"Financial transaction" means a transaction involving:

The movement of moneys by wire or other means;

One or more monetary instruments;

The transfer of title to any real property, vehicle, vessel, or aircraft; or

The use of a financial institution.

"Monetary instrument" means:

Coin or currency of the United States or any other country; a traveler's check; a personal check; a bank check; a cashier's check; a money order; a bank draft of any country; or gold, silver, or platinum bullion or coins;

An investment security or negotiable instrument in bearer form or in other form such that title passes upon delivery; or

A gift card or other device that is the equivalent of money and can be used to obtain cash, property, or services.

"Represent" includes, but is not limited to, the making of a representation by a peace officer, a federal officer, or another person acting at the direction of, or with the approval of, a peace officer or federal officer.

"Transaction" includes a purchase, sale, loan, pledge, gift, transfer, delivery, or other disposition and, with respect to a financial institution, includes a deposit; a withdrawal; a transfer between accounts; an exchange of currency; a loan; an extension of credit; a purchase or sale of any stock, bond, certificate of deposit, or other monetary instrument; the use of a safe deposit box; or any other payment, transfer, or delivery by, through, or to a financial institution by whatever means.

PART 4

BRIBERY AND RIGGING OF CONTESTS

18-5-401. Commercial bribery and breach of duty to act disinterestedly. (1) A person commits a class 6 felony if he solicits, accepts, or agrees to accept any benefit as consideration for knowingly violating or agreeing to violate a duty of fidelity to which he is subject as:

Agent or employee; or

Trustee, guardian, or other fiduciary; or

Lawyer, physician, accountant, appraiser, or other professional adviser; or

Officer, director, partner, manager, or other participant in the direction of the affairs of an incorporated or unincorporated association; or

Duly elected or appointed representative or trustee of a labor organization or employee welfare trust fund; or

Arbitrator or other purportedly disinterested adjudicator or referee.

A person who holds himself out to the public as being engaged in the business of making disinterested selection, appraisal, or criticism of commodities, property, or services commits a class 6 felony if he knowingly solicits, accepts, or agrees to accept any benefit to alter, modify, or change his selection, appraisal, or criticism.

A person commits a class 6 felony if he confers or offers or agrees to confer any benefit the acceptance of which would be a felony under subsections (1) and (2) of this section.

18-5-402. Rigging publicly exhibited contests. (1)  A person commits a class 3

misdemeanor if, with the intent to prevent a publicly exhibited or advertised contest from being conducted in accordance with the rules and usages purporting to govern it, he:

Confers or offers or agrees to confer any benefit upon, or threatens any detriment to a participant, official, or other person associated with the contest or exhibition; or

Tampers with any person, animal, or thing; or

Knowingly solicits, accepts, or agrees to accept any benefit the conferring of which is prohibited by paragraph (a) of this subsection (1).

A person commits a class 3 misdemeanor if he knowingly engages in, sponsors, produces, judges, or otherwise participates in a publicly exhibited or advertised contest knowing that the contest is not being conducted in compliance with the rules and usages purporting to govern it, by reason of conduct prohibited by this section.

18-5-403. Bribery in sports. (1) As used in this section:

"Sports contest" means any professional or amateur sport or athletic game, race, or contest viewed by the public.

"Sports participant" means any person who participates or expects to participate in a sports contest as a player, contestant, or member of a team, or as a coach, manager, trainer, owner, or other person directly associated with a player, contestant, team, or entry.

"Sports official" means any person who acts or expects to act in a sports contest as an umpire, referee, judge, or otherwise to officiate at a sports contest.

A person commits bribery in sports if:

He confers, or offers or agrees to confer, any benefit upon or threatens any detriment to a sports participant with intent to influence him not to give his best efforts in a sports contest; or

He confers, or offers or agrees to confer, any benefit upon or threatens any detriment to a sports official with intent to influence him to perform his duties improperly; or

Being a sports participant, he knowingly accepts, agrees to accept, or solicits any benefit from another person upon an understanding that he will thereby be influenced not to give his best efforts in a sports contest; or

Being a sports official, he knowingly accepts, agrees to accept, or solicits any benefit from another person upon an understanding that he will perform his duties improperly; or

With intent to influence the outcome of a sports contest, he tampers with any sports participant, sports official, or any animal or equipment or other thing involved in the conduct or operation of a sports contest in a manner contrary to the rules and usages purporting to govern such a contest.

Bribery in sports is a class 6 felony.

PART 5 OFFENSES RELATING TO
THE UNIFORM COMMERCIAL CODE

18-5-501. Definitions. The definitions set forth in the "Uniform Commercial Code", title 4, C.R.S., shall apply to sections 18-5-502 to 18-5-511.

18-5-502. Failure to pay over assigned accounts. Where, under the terms of an assignment of an account, as defined in section 4-9-102 (a) (2), C.R.S., the assignor, being permitted to collect the proceeds from the debtor, is to pay over to the assignee any of the proceeds and, after collection thereof, the assignor willfully and wrongfully fails to pay over to the assignee the proceeds amounting to one thousand dollars or more, the person commits a class 5 felony. Where the amount of the proceeds withheld by the assignor is less than one thousand dollars, the person commits a class 1 misdemeanor.

18-5-503. Criminal liability of transferor of a bulk transfer. (Repealed)

18-5-504. Concealment or removal of secured property. If a person who has given a security interest in personal property, as security interest is defined in section 4-1-201 (b) (35), C.R.S., or other person with actual knowledge of the security interest, during the existence of the securityinterest, knowinglyconceals or removes the encumbered propertyfrom the state of Colorado without written consent of the secured creditor, the person commits a class 5 felony where the value of the property concealed or removed is one thousand dollars or more. Where the value of the property concealed or removed is less than one thousand dollars, the person commits a class 1 misdemeanor.

18-5-505. Failure to pay over proceeds unlawful. Where, under the terms of an instrument creating a security interest in personal property, as security interest is defined in section 4-1-201 (b) (35), C.R.S., the person giving the security interest and retaining possession of the encumbered property and having liberty of sale or other disposition, is required to account to the secured creditor for the proceeds of the sale or other disposition, and willfully and wrongfully fails to pay to the secured creditor the amounts due on account thereof, the person giving the security interest commits a class 5 felony where the amount of the proceeds withheld is one thousand dollars or more. If the amount of the proceeds withheld is less than one thousand dollars, the person commits a class 1 misdemeanor.

18-5-506. Fraudulent receipt - penalty. A warehouse, as defined in section 4-7-102 (a) (13), C.R.S., or any officer, agent, or servant of a warehouse, that issues or aids in issuing a receipt knowing that the goods for which the receipt is issued have not been actually received by the warehouse, or are not under the warehouse's actual control at the time of issuing the receipt, commits

a class 6 felony.

18-5-507. False statement in receipt - penalty. A warehouse, as defined in section 4-7-102
(a) (13), C.R.S., or any officer, agent, or servant of a warehouse, that fraudulently issues or aids in fraudulently issuing a receipt for goods knowing that it contains any false statement, commits a class 2 misdemeanor.

18-5-508. Duplicate receipt not marked - penalty. A warehouse, as defined in section 4-7- 102 (a) (13), C.R.S., or any officer, agent, or servant of a warehouse, that issues or aids in issuing a duplicate or additional negotiable receipt for goods knowing that a former negotiable receipt for the same goods or any part of them is outstanding and uncancelled, without placing upon the face thereof the word "duplicate", except in case of a lost or destroyed receipt after proceedings as provided for in section 4-7-601, C.R.S., commits a class 6 felony.

18-5-509. Warehouse's goods mingled - receipts - penalty. Where there are deposited with or held by a warehouse, as defined in section 4-7-102 (a) (13), C.R.S., goods of which the warehouse is owner, either solely or jointly or in common with others, the warehouse or any of the warehouse's officers, agents, or servants that, knowing this ownership, issue or aid in issuing a negotiable receipt for the goods that does not state such ownership commits a class 2 misdemeanor.

18-5-510. Delivery of goods without receipt - penalty. A warehouse, as defined in section 4-7-102 (a) (13), C.R.S., or any officer, agent, or servant of a warehouse, that delivers goods out of the possession of such warehouse, knowing that a negotiable receipt the negotiation of which would transfer the right of the possession of those goods is outstanding and uncancelled, without obtaining the possession of that receipt at or before the time of the delivery, except the cases provided for in section 4-7-601, C.R.S., commits a class 2 misdemeanor.

18-5-511. Mortgaged goods receipt - penalty. Any person who deposits goods to which the person does not have title, or upon which there is a security interest in personal property, as security interest is defined in section 4-1-201 (b) (35), C.R.S., and who takes for such goods a negotiable receipt that the person afterwards negotiates for value with intent to deceive and without disclosing the person's want of title or the existence of such security interest, commits a class 2 misdemeanor.

18-5-512. Issuance of bad check. (1) In adopting this section, the general assembly declares as a matter of policy that the issuance and delivery of a known bad check by any person is, in itself, not only harmful to the person to whom it is given but is also injurious to the community

at large and is, therefore, a proper subject for criminal sanction without regard to the purpose for which the check was given.
"Insufficient funds" means not having a sufficient balance in account with a bank or other drawee for the payment of a check or order when the check or order is presented for payment and it remains unpaid thirty days after such presentment.
Except as provided in section 18-5-205, a person commits a class 3 misdemeanor if he issues or passes a check or similar sight order for the payment of money, knowing that the issuer does not have sufficient funds in or on deposit with the bank or other drawee for the payment in full of the check or order as well as all other checks or orders outstanding at the time of issuance.
This section does not relieve the prosecution from the necessity of establishing the required knowledge by evidence. However, for purposes of this section, the issuer's knowledge of insufficient funds is presumed, except in the case of a postdated check or order, if:
He has no account with the bank or other drawee at the time he issues the check or order;
or
He has insufficient funds upon deposit with the bank or other drawee to pay the check

or order, on presentation within thirty days after issue.

A bank shall not be civilly or criminally liable for releasing information relating to the issuer's account to a sheriff, deputy sheriff, undersheriff, police officer, agent of the Colorado bureau of investigation, division of gaming investigator, division of lottery investigator, parks and outdoor recreation officer, Colorado wildlife officer, district attorney, assistant district attorney, deputy district attorney, or authorized investigator for a district attorney investigating or prosecuting a charge under this section.

Restitution for offenses described in this section may be collected as a condition of pretrial diversion by a district attorney, an employee of a district attorney's office, or a person under contract with a district attorney's office. Such collection is governed by the provisions of article 18.5 of title 16, C.R.S., and is not the collection of a debt.

PART 6

IMITATION CONTROLLED SUBSTANCES ACT

18-5-601 to 18-5-606. (Repealed)

PART 7

FINANCIAL TRANSACTION DEVICE CRIME ACT

18-5-701. Definitions. As used in this part 7, unless the context otherwise requires:

"Account holder" means the person or business entity named on the face of a financial transaction device to whom or for whose benefit the financial transaction device is issued by an issuer.

"Automated banking device" means any machine which, when properly activated by a financial transaction device or a personal identification code, may be used for any of the purposes for which a financial transaction device may be used.

"Financial transaction device" means any instrument or device whether known as a credit card, banking card, debit card, electronic fund transfer card, or guaranteed check card, or account number representing a financial account or affecting the financial interest, standing, or obligation of or to the account holder, that can be used to obtain cash, goods, property, or services or to make financial payments, but shall not include a "check", a "negotiable order of withdrawal", and a "share draft" as defined in section 18-5-205.

"Issuer" means any person or banking, financial, or business institution, corporation, or other business entity that assigns financial rights byacquiring, distributing, controlling, or cancelling a financial transaction device.

"Personal identification code" means any grouping of letters, numbers, or symbols assigned to the account holder of a financial transaction device by the issuer to permit authorized electronic use of that financial transaction device.

"Sales form" means any written record of a financial transaction involving use of a financial transaction device.

18-5-702. Unauthorized use of a financial transaction device. (1) A person commits unauthorized use of a financial transaction device if he uses such device for the purpose of obtaining cash, credit, property, or services or for making financial payment, with intent to defraud, and with notice that either:

The financial transaction device has expired, has been revoked, or has been cancelled;

or

For any reason his use of the financial transaction device is unauthorized either by the

issuer thereof or by the account holder.

For purposes of paragraphs (a) and (b) of subsection (1) of this section, "notice" includes either notice given in person or notice given in writing to the account holder. The sending of a notice in writing by registered or certified mail, return receipt requested, duly stamped and addressed to such account holder at his last address known to the issuer, evidenced by a signed returned receipt signed by the account holder, is prima facie evidence that the notice was received.

Unauthorized use of a financial transaction device is:

(Deleted by amendment, L. 2007, p. 1695, 13, effective July 1, 2007.)

A class 1 petty offense if the value of the cash, credit, property, or services obtained or of the financial payments made is less than fifty dollars;

A class 3 misdemeanor if the value of the cash, credit, property, or services obtained or of the financial payments made is fifty dollars or more but less than three hundred dollars;

A class 2 misdemeanor if the value of the cash, credit, property, or services obtained or of the financial payments made is three hundred dollars or more but less than seven hundred fifty dollars;

A class 1 misdemeanor if the value of the cash, credit, property, or services obtained or of the financial payments made is seven hundred fifty dollars or more but less than two thousand

dollars;

A class 6 felony if the value of the cash, credit, property, or services obtained or of the financial payments made is two thousand dollars or more but less than five thousand dollars;

A class 5 felony if the value of the cash, credit, property, or services obtained or of the financial payments made is five thousand dollars or more but less than twenty thousand dollars;

A class 4 felony if the value of the cash, credit, property, or services obtained or of the financial payments made is twenty thousand dollars or more but less than one hundred thousand dollars;

A class 3 felony if the value of the cash, credit, property, or services obtained or of the financial payments made is one hundred thousand dollars or more but less than one million dollars; and

A class 2 felony if the value of the cash, credit, property, or services obtained or of the financial payments made is one million dollars or more.

The value of the cash, credit, property, or services obtained and the financial payments made shall be the total value of the cash, credit, property, or services obtained or financial payments made by unauthorized use of a single financial transaction device within a six-month period from the date of the first unauthorized use.

18-5-703. Criminal possession of a financial transaction device. (Repealed)


18-5-704. Sale or possession for sale of a financial transaction device. (Repealed)


18-5-705. Criminal possession or sale of a blank financial transaction device. (1) A person commits criminal possession or sale of a blank financial transaction device if, without the authorization of the issuer or manufacturer, he has in his possession or under his control or receives from another person, with intent to use, deliver, circulate, or sell it or with intent to cause the use, delivery, circulation, or sale of it, or sells any financial transaction device which has not been embossed or magneticallyencoded with the name of the account holder, personal identification code, expiration date, or other proprietary institutional information.
Criminal possession of a blank financial transaction device is a class 6 felony.


felony.

Criminal possession of two or more blank financial transaction devices is a class 5

Delivery, circulation, or sale of one blank financial transaction device is a class 5 felony.
Delivery, circulation, or sale of two or more blank financial transaction devices is a class 3 felony.
For purposes of this section, a blank financial transaction device is one that has at least one or more characteristics of a financial transaction device but does not contain all of the characteristics of a completed financial transaction device.

18-5-706. Criminal possession of forgery devices. (1) A person commits possession of forgery devices if he possesses any tools, photographic equipment, printing equipment, or any other device adapted, designed, or commonly used for committing or facilitating the commission of an offense involving the unauthorized manufacture, printing, embossing, or magnetic encoding of a financial transaction device or the altering or addition of any uniform product codes, optical characters, or holographic images to a financial transaction device, and intends to use the thing possessed, or knows that some person intends to use the thing possessed, in the commission of such an offense.
Possession of a forgery device is a class 6 felony.

18-5-707. Unlawful manufacture of a financial transaction device. (1) A person commits unlawful manufacture of a financial transaction device if, with intent to defraud, he:
Falsely makes or manufactures, by printing, embossing, or magnetically encoding, a financial transaction device; or
Falsely alters or adds uniform product codes, optical characters, or holographic images to a device which is or purports to be, or which is calculated to become or to represent if completed, a financial transaction device; or
Falsely completes a financial transaction device by adding to an incomplete device to make it a complete one.
As used in this section, unless the context otherwise requires:
To "falsely alter" a financial transaction device means to change such device without the authority of anyone entitled to grant such authority, whether it be in complete or incomplete form, by means of erasure, obliteration, deletion, insertion of new matter, transposition of matter, or any other means, so that such device in its thus altered form falsely appears or purports to be in all respects an authentic creation of or fully authorized by its ostensible issuer.
To "falsely complete" a financial transaction device means to transform an incomplete device into a complete one by adding, inserting, or changing matter without the authority of anyone entitled to grant that authority, so that the complete device falsely appears or purports to be in all respects an authentic creation of or fully authorized by its ostensible issuer.
To "falsely make" a financial transaction device means to make or manufacture a device, whether complete or incomplete, which purports to be an authentic creation of its ostensible issuer, but which is not, either because the ostensible issuer is fictitious or because, if real, he did not authorize the making or the manufacturing thereof.
Unlawful manufacture of a financial transaction device is a class 5 felony.
PART 8 EQUITY SKIMMING
AND RELATED OFFENSES

18-5-801. Definitions. As used in this part 8, unless the context otherwise requires:
"Lease" means any grant of use and possession for consideration, with or without an option to buy.
"Real property" means land and any interest or estate in land and includes a manufactured home as defined in section 42-1-102 (106) (b), C.R.S.
"Rent" means any moneys or any other thing of value received as a payment or as a deposit for the privilege of living in or using real property.
"Security interest" means an interest in personal property which secures payment or performance of an obligation.
"Vehicle" means any device of conveyance capable of moving itself or of being moved from place to place upon wheels or a track or by water or air, whether or not intended for the transport of persons or property, and includes any space within such "vehicle" adapted for overnight accommodation of persons or animals or for the carrying on of business. "Vehicle" does not include a manufactured home as defined in section 42-1-102 (106) (b), C.R.S.

18-5-802. Equity skimming of real property. (1) A person commits the crime of equity skimming of real property if the person knowingly:
Acquires an interest in real property that is encumbered by a loan secured by a mortgage or deed of trust and the loan is in arrears at the time the person acquires the interest or is placed in default within eighteen months after the person acquires the interest; and
Either:
Fails to apply all rent derived from the person's interest in the real property first toward the satisfaction of all outstanding payments due on the loan and second toward any fees due to any association of real property owners that charges such fees for the upkeep of the housing facility, or common area including buildings and grounds thereof, of which the real property is a part before appropriating the remainder of such rent or any part thereof for any other purpose except for the purpose of repairs necessary to prevent waste of the real property; or
After a foreclosure in which title has vested pursuant to section 38-38-501, C.R.S., collects rent on behalf of any person other than the owner of the real property.
Repealed.
Equity skimming of real property is a class 5 felony.
It shall be an affirmative defense to this section:
That all deficiencies in all underlying encumbrances at the time of acquisition have been fully satisfied and brought current and that, in addition, any regular payments on the underlying encumbrances during the succeeding nine months after the date of acquisition have been timely paid in full; except that this shall not be an affirmative defense to a crime that includes the element set forth in subparagraph (II) of paragraph (b) of subsection (1) of this section;
That any fees due to an association of real property owners for the upkeep of the housing facility, or common area including buildings and grounds thereof, of which the real property is a part have been paid in full.
The provisions of this section shall not apply to any bona fide lender who accepts a deed in lieu of foreclosure or who forecloses upon the real property.

The provisions of this section shall not apply to any bona fide purchaser who acquires fee title in any real property without agreeing to pay all underlying encumbrances and takes fee title subject to all underlying encumbrances, if the following written, verbatim warning was provided to the seller in capital letters of no less than ten-point, bold-faced type and acknowledged by the seller's signature:

WARNING: PURCHASER,      , WILL NOT ASSUME OR PAY ANY PRESENT MORTGAGE, DEEDS OF TRUST, OR OTHER LIENS OR ENCUMBRANCES AGAINST THE PROPERTY. THE SELLER,           , UNDERSTANDS HE/SHE WILL REMAIN RESPONSIBLE FOR ALL PAYMENTS DUE ON SUCH MORTGAGES, DEEDS OF TRUST, OR OTHER LIENS OR ENCUMBRANCES AND FOR ANY DEFICIENCY JUDGMENT UPON FORECLOSURE.

I HAVE HAD THE FOREGOING READ TO ME AND UNDERSTAND THE PURCHASER, , WILL NOT ASSUME ANY PRESENT MORTGAGES, DEEDS OF TRUST, OR OTHER LIENS OR ENCUMBRANCES AGAINST THE PROPERTY DESCRIBED AS       .

DATE     SELLER  .

18-5-803. Equity skimming of a vehicle. (1) A person commits equity skimming of a vehicle if, knowing the vehicle is subject to a security interest, lien, or lease, he accepts possession of or exercises any control over the vehicle in exchange for consideration given which may be verbal assurance or otherwise, and:
Obtains or exercises control over the vehicle of another and then sells or leases the vehicle to a third partywithout first obtaining written authorization from the secured creditor, lessor, or lienholder for the transaction of the sale or lease to the third party, unless the entire balance of the security interest, lien, or lease is paid or satisfied within thirty days of said transaction; or
Arranges the sale or lease of the vehicle of another to a third party without first obtaining written authorization from the secured creditor, lessor, or lienholder for the transaction of the sale or lease to the third party and exercises control over any part of the funds received, unless the entire balance of the security interest, lien, or lease is paid or satisfied within thirty days of said transaction; or
Knowingly fails to ascertain on a monthly basis whether payments are due to the secured creditor, lienholder, or lessor and to apply all funds he receives for any lease or sale of the vehicle toward the satisfaction of any outstanding payment due to the secured creditor, lienholder, or lessor in a timely manner.
(2) Equity skimming of a vehicle is a class 6 felony.

18-5-804. Civil action. A condominium association, a property owners' association, or any

like association of real property owners which charges fees for the upkeep of a housing facility, a housing project, or a common area thereof may proceed pursuant to rule 102 of the Colorado rules of civil procedure if such fees have not been received by the condominium association, property owners' association, or any like association for a period of ninety days or more.

PART 9

IDENTITY THEFT AND RELATED OFFENSES

18-5-901. Definitions. As used in this part 9, unless the context otherwise requires:
"Account holder" means any person or business entity named on or associated with the account or named on the face of a financial device to whom or for whose benefit the financial device is issued by an issuer.
"Extension of credit" means any loan or agreement, express or implied, whereby the repayment or satisfaction of any debt or claim, whether acknowledged or disputed, valid or invalid, and however arising, may or will be deferred.
To "falsely alter" a written instrument or financial device means to change a written instrument or financial device without the authority of anyone entitled to grant such authority, whether it be in complete or incomplete form, by means of erasure, obliteration, deletion, insertion of new matter, transposition of matter, or any other means, so that the written instrument or financial device in its thus altered form falsely appears or purports to be in all respects an authentic creation of or fully authorized by its ostensible maker.
To "falsely complete" a written instrument or financial device means:
To transform an incomplete written instrument or financial device into a complete one by adding, inserting, or changing matter without the authority of anyone entitled to grant that authority, so that the complete written instrument or financial device falsely appears or purports to be in all respects an authentic creation of or fully authorized by its ostensible maker; or
To transform an incomplete written instrument or financial device into a complete one byadding or inserting materiallyfalse information or adding or inserting a materiallyfalse statement. A materially false statement is a false assertion that affects the action, conduct, or decision of the person who receives or is intended to receive the asserted information in a manner that directly or indirectly benefits the person making the assertion.
To "falsely make" a written instrument or financial device means to make or draw a written instrument or financial device, whether it be in complete or incomplete form, that purports to be an authentic creation of its ostensible maker, but that is not, either because the ostensible maker is fictitious or because, if real, the ostensible maker did not authorize the making or the drawing of the written instrument or financial device.
"Financial device" means anyinstrument or device that can be used to obtain cash, credit, property, services, or any other thing of value or to make financial payments, including but not limited to:
A credit card, banking card, debit card, electronic fund transfer card, or guaranteed check card;

A check;
A negotiable order of withdrawal;
A share draft; or
A money order.
"Financial identifying information" means any of the following that can be used, alone or in conjunction with any other information, to obtain cash, credit, property, services, or any other thing of value or to make a financial payment:
A personal identification number, credit card number, banking card number, checking account number, debit card number, electronic fund transfer card number, guaranteed check card number, or routing number; or
A number representing a financial account or a number affecting the financial interest, standing, or obligation of or to the account holder.
"Government" means:
The United States and its departments, agencies, or subdivisions;
A state, county, municipality, or other political unit and its departments, agencies, or subdivisions; and

133

A corporation or other entity established by law to carry out governmental functions.

"Issuer" means a person, a banking, financial, or business institution, or a corporation or other business entity that assigns financial rights by acquiring, distributing, controlling, or cancelling an account or a financial device.

"Number" includes, without limitation, any grouping or combination of letters, numbers, or symbols.

"Of another" means that of a natural person, living or dead, or a business entity as defined in section 16-3-301.1 (11) (b), C.R.S.

"Personal identification number" means a number assigned to an account holder by an issuer to permit authorized use of an account or financial device.

"Personal identifying information" means information that may be used, alone or in conjunction with any other information, to identify a specific individual, including but not limited to a name; a date of birth; a social securitynumber; a password; a pass code; an official, government- issued driver's license or identification card number; a government passport number; biometric data; or an employer, student, or military identification number.

"Utter" means to transfer, pass, or deliver, or to attempt or cause to be transferred, passed, or delivered, to another person a written instrument or financial device, article, or thing.


"Written instrument" means a paper, document, or other instrument containing written or printed matter or the equivalent thereof, used for purposes of reciting, embodying, conveying, or recording information, and any money, token, stamp, seal, badge, or trademark or any evidence or symbol of value, right, privilege, or identification, that is capable of being used to the advantage or disadvantage of another.


18-5-902. Identity theft. (1) A person commits identity theft if he or she:

Knowingly uses the personal identifying information, financial identifying information,


or financial device of another without permission or lawful authority with the intent to obtain cash, credit, property, services, or any other thing of value or to make a financial payment;

Knowingly possesses the personal identifying information, financial identifying information, or financial device of another without permission or lawful authority, with the intent to use or to aid or permit some other person to use such information or device to obtain cash, credit, property, services, or any other thing of value or to make a financial payment;

With the intent to defraud, falsely makes, completes, alters, or utters a written instrument or financial device containing any personal identifying information or financial identifying information of another;

Knowingly possesses the personal identifying information or financial identifying information of another without permission or lawful authority to use in applying for or completing an application for a financial device or other extension of credit;

Knowingly uses or possesses the personal identifying information of another without permission or lawful authority with the intent to obtain a government-issued document; or

(Deleted by amendment, L. 2009, (SB 09-093), ch. 326, p. 1737, § 1, effective July 1, 2009.)

Identity theft is a class 4 felony.

The court shall be required to sentence the defendant to the department of corrections for a term of at least the minimum of the presumptive range and may sentence the defendant to a maximum of twice the presumptive range if:

The defendant is convicted of identity theft or of attempt, conspiracy, or solicitation to commit identity theft; and

The defendant has a prior conviction for a violation of this part 9 or a prior conviction for an offense committed in any other state, the United States, or any other territory subject to the jurisdiction of the United States that would constitute a violation of this part 9 if committed in this state, or for attempt, conspiracy, or solicitation to commit a violation of this part 9 or for attempt, conspiracy, or solicitation to commit an offense in another jurisdiction that would constitute a violation of this part 9 if committed in this state.

18-5-903. Criminal possession of a financial device. (1) A person commits criminal possession of a financial device if the person has in his or her possession or under his or her control any financial device that the person knows, or reasonably should know, to be lost, stolen, or delivered under mistake as to the identity or address of the account holder.

(2) (a) Criminal possession of one financial device is a class 1 misdemeanor.

Criminal possession of two or more financial devices is a class 6 felony.

Criminal possession of four or more financial devices, of which at least two are issued to different account holders, is a class 5 felony.

18-5-903.5. Criminal possession of an identification document. (1) A person commits criminal possession of an identification document if the person knowingly has in his or her possession or under his or her control another person's actual driver's license, actual government-

issued identification card, actual social security card, or actual passport, knowing that he or she does so without permission or lawful authority.

(2) (a) Criminal possession of one or more identification documents issued to the same person is a class 1 misdemeanor.

(b) Criminal possession of two or more identification documents, of which at least two are issued to different persons, is a class 6 felony.

18-5-904. Gathering identity information by deception. (1) A person commits gathering identity information by deception if he or she knowingly makes or conveys a materially false statement, without permission or lawful authority, with the intent to obtain, record, or access the personal identifying information or financial identifying information of another.

(2) Gathering identity information by deception is a class 5 felony.

18-5-905. Possession of identity theft tools. (1) A person commits possession of identity theft tools if he or she possesses anytools, equipment, computer, computer network, scanner, printer, or other article adapted, designed, or commonly used for committing or facilitating the commission of the offense of identity theft as described in section 18-5-902, and intends to use the thing possessed, or knows that a person intends to use the thing possessed, in the commission of the offense of identity theft.

(2) Possession of identity theft tools is a class 5 felony.

## ARTICLE 5.5 Computer Crime

18-5.5-101. Definitions. As used in this article, unless the context otherwise requires:

"Authorization" means the express consent of a person which may include an employee's job description to use said person's computer, computer network, computer program, computer software, computer system, property, or services as those terms are defined in this section.

"Computer" means an electronic, magnetic, optical, electromagnetic, or other data processing device which performs logical, arithmetic, memory, or storage functions by the manipulations of electronic, magnetic, radio wave, or light wave impulses, and includes all input, output, processing, storage, software, or communication facilities which are connected or related to or operating in conjunction with such a device.

"Computer network" means the interconnection of communication lines (including microwave or other means of electronic communication) with a computer through remote terminals,

or a complex consisting of two or more interconnected computers.

"Computer program" means a series of instructions or statements, in a form acceptable to a computer, which permits the functioning of a computer system in a manner designed to provide appropriate products from such computer system.

"Computer software" means computer programs, procedures, and associated documentation concerned with the operation of a computer system.

"Computer system" means a set of related, connected or unconnected, computer equipment, devices, and software.

(6.3) "Damage" includes, but is not limited to, any impairment to the integrity of availability of information, data, computer program, computer software, or services on or via a computer, computer network, or computer system or part thereof.

(6.7) "Exceed authorized access" means to access a computer with authorization and to use such access to obtain or alter information, data, computer program, or computer software that the person is not entitled to so obtain or alter.

"Financial instrument" means any check, draft, money order, certificate of deposit, letter of credit, bill of exchange, credit card, debit card, or marketable security.

"Property" includes, but is not limited to, financial instruments, information, including electronically produced data, and computer software and programs in either machine or human readable form, and any other tangible or intangible item of value.

"Services" includes, but is not limited to, computer time, data processing, and storage functions.

To "use" means to instruct, communicate with, store data in, retrieve data from, or otherwise make use of any resources of a computer, computer system, or computer network.

18-5.5-102. Computer crime. (1) A person commits computer crime if the person knowingly:

Accesses a computer, computer network, or computer system or any part thereof without authorization; exceeds authorized access to a computer,

135

computer network, or computer system or any part thereof; or uses a computer, computer network, or computer system or any part thereof without authorization or in excess of authorized access; or

Accesses any computer, computer network, or computer system, or any part thereof for the purpose of devising or executing any scheme or artifice to defraud; or

Accesses any computer, computer network, or computer system, or any part thereof to obtain, by means of false or fraudulent pretenses, representations, or promises, money; property; services; passwords or similar information through which a computer, computer network, or computer system or any part thereof may be accessed; or other thing of value; or

Accesses any computer, computer network, or computer system, or any part thereof to commit theft; or

Without authorization or in excess of authorized access alters, damages, interrupts, or causes the interruption or impairment of the proper functioning of, or causes any damage to, any computer, computer network, computer system, computer software, program, application, documentation, or data contained in such computer, computer network, or computer system or any

part thereof; or

Causes the transmission of a computer program, software, information, code, data, or command by means of a computer, computer network, or computer system or any part thereof with the intent to cause damage to or to cause the interruption or impairment of the proper functioning of or that actually causes damage to or the interruption or impairment of the proper functioning of any computer, computer network, computer system, or part thereof; or

Uses or causes to be used a software application that runs automated tasks over the internet to access a computer, computer network, or computer system, or any part thereof, that circumvents or disables any electronic queues, waiting periods, or other technological measure intended by the seller to limit the number of event tickets that may be purchased by any single person in an online event ticket sale as defined in section 6-1-720, C.R.S. (Deleted by amendment, L. 2000, p. 695, § 8, effective July 1, 2000.)

(a) Except as provided in paragraphs (b) and (c) of this subsection (3), if the loss, damage, value of services, or thing of value taken, or cost of restoration or repair caused by a violation of this section is:

Less than fifty dollars, computer crime is a class 1 petty offense;

Fifty dollars or more but less than three hundred dollars, computer crime is a class 3 misdemeanor;

Three hundred dollars or more but less than seven hundred fifty dollars, computer crime is a class 2 misdemeanor;

Seven hundred fifty dollars or more but less than two thousand dollars, computer crime is a class 1 misdemeanor;

Two thousand dollars or more but less than five thousand dollars, computer crime is a class 6 felony;

Five thousand dollars or more but less than twenty thousand dollars, computer crime is a class 5 felony;

Twenty thousand dollars or more but less than one hundred thousand dollars, computer crime is a class 4 felony;

One hundred thousand dollars or more but less than one million dollars, computer crime is a class 3 felony; and

One million dollars or more, computer crime is a class 2 felony.

Computer crime committed in violation of paragraph (a) of subsection (1) of this section is a class 2 misdemeanor; except that, if the person has previously been convicted under this section, a previous version of this section, or a statute of another state of similar content and purport, computer crime committed in violation of paragraph (a) of subsection (1) of this section is a class 6 felony.

(I) Computer crime committed in violation of paragraph (g) of subsection (1) of this section is a class 1 misdemeanor.

If computer crime is committed to obtain event tickets, each ticket purchased shall constitute a separate offense.

Paragraph (g) of subsection (1) of this section shall not prohibit the resale of tickets in a secondary market by a person other than the event sponsor or promoter.

Consistent with section 18-1-202, a prosecution for a violation of paragraph (g) of

subsection (1) of this section may be tried in the county where the event has been, or will be, held.

### ARTICLE 6  Offenses Involving the Family Relations

PART 1 ABORTION

18-6-101 to 18-6-105.  (Repealed)

PART 2 BIGAMY

18-6-201. Bigamy. (1)  Any married person who, while still married, marries, enters into a civil union, or cohabits in this state with another person commits bigamy, unless as an affirmative defense it appears that at the time of the cohabitation, subsequent marriage, or subsequent civil union:

The accused reasonably believed the prior spouse to be dead; or

The prior spouse had been continually absent for a period of five years during which time the accused did not know the prior spouse to be alive; or

The accused reasonably believed that he or she was legally eligible to remarry or legally eligible to enter into a civil union.

(1.5) Any person who is a partner in a civil union, while still legally in a civil union, who marries, enters into another civil union, or cohabits in the state with another person other than a current partner in a civil union, commits bigamy, unless as an affirmative defense it appears that at the time of the cohabitation or subsequent marriage or subsequent civil union:

The accused reasonably believed the prior partner to be dead; or

The prior partner had been continually absent for a period of five years during which time the accused did not know the prior partner to be alive; or

The accused reasonably believed that he or she was legally eligible to marry or legally eligible to enter into a civil union.

(2)  Bigamy is a class 6 felony.

18-6-202. Marrying a bigamist. Any unmarried person who knowingly marries or cohabits with another in this state under circumstances known to him which would render the other person guilty of bigamy under the laws of this state commits marrying a bigamist, which is a class 2 misdemeanor.

18-6-203. Definitions. As used in sections 18-6-201 and 18-6-202, "cohabitation" means to live together under the representation of being married.

PART 3 INCEST

18-6-301. Incest. (1) Any person who knowingly marries, inflicts sexual penetration or sexual intrusion on, or subjects to sexual contact, as defined in section 18-3-401, an ancestor or descendant, including a natural child, child by adoption, or stepchild twenty-one years of age or older, a brother or sister of the whole or half blood, or an uncle, aunt, nephew, or niece of the whole blood commits incest, which is a class 4 felony. For the purpose of this section only, "descendant" includes a child by adoption and a stepchild, but only if the person is not legally married to the child by adoption or the stepchild.

When a person is convicted of, pleads nolo contendere to, or receives a deferred sentence for a violation of the provisions of this section and the victim is a child who is under eighteen years of age and the court knows the person is a current or former employee of a school district or a charter school in this state or holds a license or authorization pursuant to the provisions of article 60.5 of title 22, C.R.S., the court shall report such fact to the department of education.

18-6-302. Aggravated incest. (1) A person commits aggravated incest when he or she knowingly:

Marries his or her natural child or inflicts sexual penetration or sexual intrusion on or subjects to sexual contact, as defined in section 18-3-401, his or her natural child, stepchild, or child by adoption, but this paragraph (a) shall not apply when the person is legally married to the stepchild or child by adoption. For the purpose of this paragraph (a) only, "child" means a person under twenty-one years of age.

Marries, inflicts sexual penetration or sexual intrusion on, or subjects to sexual contact, as defined in section 18-3-401, a descendant, a brother or sister of the whole or half blood, or an uncle, aunt, nephew, or niece of the whole blood who is under ten years of age.

Aggravated incest is a class 3 felony.

When a person is convicted, pleads nolo contendere, or receives a deferred sentence for a violation of the provisions of this section and the court knows the person is a current or former employee of a school district in this state or holds a license or authorization pursuant to the provisions of article 60.5 of title 22, C.R.S., the court shall report such fact to the department of

education.

18-6-303. Sentencing. (1) The court may suspend a portion of the sentence of any person who is convicted of a violation committed prior to November 1, 1998, of any offense listed in this part 3 who is not a habitual sex offender against children, as described in section 18-3-412, if the offender receives a presentence evaluation that recommends a treatment program and the offender satisfactorily completes the recommended treatment program.

In addition to any other penalty provided by law, the court may sentence a defendant who is convicted of a first offense pursuant to this part 3, committed prior to November 1, 1998, to a period of probation for purposes of treatment that, when added to any time served, does not exceed the maximum sentence imposable for the offense.

The court shall sentence a defendant who is convicted of any offense specified in this part 3 committed on or after November 1, 1998, pursuant to the provisions of part 10 of article 1.3 of this title.

PART 4 WRONGS TO CHILDREN

18-6-401. Child abuse. (1) (a) A person commits child abuse if such person causes an injury to a child's life or health, or permits a child to be unreasonably placed in a situation that poses a threat of injury to the child's life or health, or engages in a continued pattern of conduct that results in malnourishment, lack of proper medical care, cruel punishment, mistreatment, or an accumulation of injuries that ultimately results in the death of a child or serious bodily injury to a child.

(I) Except as otherwise provided in subparagraph (III) of this paragraph (b), a person commits child abuse if such person excises or infibulates, in whole or in part, the labia majora, labia minora, vulva, or clitoris of a female child. A parent, guardian, or other person legally responsible for a female child or charged with the care or custody of a female child commits child abuse if he or she allows the excision or infibulation, in whole or in part, of such child's labia majora, labia minora, vulva, or clitoris.

Belief that the conduct described in subparagraph (I) of this paragraph (b) is required as a matter of custom, ritual, or standard practice or consent to the conduct by the child on whom it is performed or by the child's parent or legal guardian shall not be an affirmative defense to a charge of child abuse under this paragraph (b).

A surgical procedure as described in subparagraph (I) of this paragraph (b) is not a crime if the procedure:

Is necessary to preserve the health of the child on whom it is performed and is performed by a person licensed to practice medicine under article 36 of title 12, C.R.S.; or

Is performed on a child who is in labor or who has just given birth and is performed for medical purposes connected with that labor or birth by a person licensed to practice medicine under article 36 of title 12, C.R.S.

If the district attorney having jurisdiction over a case arising under this paragraph (b) has a reasonable belief that any person arrested or charged pursuant to this paragraph (b) is not a citizen or national of the United States, the district attorney shall report such information to the immigration and naturalization service, or any successor agency, in an expeditious manner.

(I) A person commits child abuse if, in the presence of a child, or on the premises where a child is found, or where a child resides, or in a vehicle containing a child, the person knowingly engages in the manufacture or attempted manufacture of a controlled substance, as defined by section 18-18-102 (5), or knowingly possesses ephedrine, pseudoephedrine, or phenylpropanolamine, or their salts, isomers, or salts of isomers, with the intent to use the product as an immediate precursor in the manufacture of a controlled substance. It shall be no defense to the crime of child abuse, as described in this subparagraph (I), that the defendant did not know a child was present, a child could be found, a child resided on the premises, or that a vehicle contained a child.

A parent or lawful guardian of a child or a person having the care or custody of a child who knowingly allows the child to be present at or reside at a premises or to be in a vehicle where the parent, guardian, or person having care or custody of the child knows or reasonably should know another person is engaged in the manufacture or attempted manufacture of methamphetamine commits child abuse.

A parent or lawful guardian of a child or a person having the care or custody of a child who knowingly allows the child to be present at or reside at a premises or to be in a vehicle where the parent, guardian, or person having care or custody of the child knows or reasonably should know another person possesses ephedrine, pseudoephedrine, or phenylpropanolamine, or their salts, isomers, or salts of isomers, with the intent to use the product as an immediate precursor in the manufacture of methamphetamine commits child abuse.

In this section, "child" means a person under the age of sixteen years.

The statutory privilege between patient and physician and between husband and wife shall not be available for excluding or refusing testimony in any prosecution for a violation of this section.

No person, other than the perpetrator, complicitor, coconspirator, or accessory, who reports an instance of child abuse to law enforcement officials shall be subjected to criminal or civil liability for any consequence of making such report unless he knows at the time of making it that it is untrue.

Deferred prosecution is authorized for a first offense under this section unless the provisions of subsection (7.5) of this section or section 18-6-401.2

apply.

Repealed.

(a) Where death or injury results, the following shall apply:

When a person acts knowingly or recklessly and the child abuse results in death to the child, it is a class 2 felony except as provided in paragraph (c) of this subsection (7).

When a person acts with criminal negligence and the child abuse results in death to the child, it is a class 3 felony.

When a person acts knowingly or recklessly and the child abuse results in serious bodily injury to the child, it is a class 3 felony.

When a person acts with criminal negligence and the child abuse results in serious bodily injury to the child, it is a class 4 felony.

When a person acts knowingly or recklessly and the child abuse results in any injury other than serious bodily injury, it is a class 1 misdemeanor; except that, if it is committed under the circumstances described in paragraph (e) of this subsection (7), then it is a class 5 felony.

When a person acts with criminal negligence and the child abuse results in any injury other than serious bodily injury to the child, it is a class 2 misdemeanor; except that, if it is committed under the circumstances described in paragraph (e) of this subsection (7), then it is a class 5 felony.

Where no death or injury results, the following shall apply:

An act of child abuse when a person acts knowingly or recklessly is a class 2 misdemeanor; except that, if it is committed under the circumstances described in paragraph (e) of this subsection (7), then it is a class 5 felony.

An act of child abuse when a person acts with criminal negligence is a class 3 misdemeanor; except that, if it is committed under the circumstances described in paragraph (e) of this subsection (7), then it is a class 5 felony.

When a person knowingly causes the death of a child who has not yet attained twelve years of age and the person committing the offense is one in a position of trust with respect to the child, such person commits the crime of murder in the first degree as described in section 18-3-102 (1) (f).

When a person commits child abuse as described in paragraph (c) of subsection (1) of this section, it is a class 3 felony.

A person who has previously been convicted of a violation of this section or of an offense in any other state, the United States, or any territory subject to the jurisdiction of the United States that would constitute child abuse if committed in this state and who commits child abuse as provided in subparagraph (V) or (VI) of paragraph (a) of this subsection (7) or as provided in subparagraph

or (II) of paragraph (b) of this subsection (7) commits a class 5 felony if the trier of fact finds that the new offense involved any of the following acts:

The defendant, who was in a position of trust, as described in section 18-3-401 (3.5), in relation to the child, participated in a continued pattern of conduct that resulted in the child's malnourishment or failed to ensure the child's access to proper medical care;

The defendant participated in a continued pattern of cruel punishment or unreasonable isolation or confinement of the child;

The defendant made repeated threats of harm or death to the child or to a significant person in the child's life, which threats were made in the presence of the child;

The defendant committed a continued pattern of acts of domestic violence, as that term is defined in section 18-6-800.3, in the presence of the child; or

The defendant participated in a continued pattern of extreme deprivation of hygienic or sanitary conditions in the child's daily living environment.

(7.3) Felony child abuse is an extraordinary risk crime that is subject to the modified presumptive sentencing range specified in section 18-1.3-401 (10). Misdemeanor child abuse is an extraordinary risk crime that is subject to the modified sentencing range specified in section 18-1.3- 501 (3).

(7.5) If a defendant is convicted of the class 2 or class 3 felony of child abuse under subparagraph (I) or (III) of paragraph (a) of subsection (7) of this section, the court shall sentence

the defendant in accordance with section 18-1.3-401 (8) (d).

Repealed.

If a parent is charged with permitting a child to be unreasonably placed in a situation that poses a threat of injury to the child's life or health, pursuant to paragraph (a) of subsection (1) of this section, and the child was seventy-two hours old or younger at the time of the alleged offense, it is an affirmative defense to the charge that the parent safely, reasonably, and knowingly handed the child over to a firefighter, as defined in section 18-3-201 (1.5), or to a hospital staff member who engages in the admission, care, or treatment of patients, when the firefighter is at a fire station or the hospital staff member is at a hospital.

18-6-401.1. Child abuse - limitation for commencing proceedings - evidence - statutory privilege. (1) For the purposes of this section, "child abuse" means child abuse as defined in section 18-6-401 (1).

No person shall be prosecuted, tried, or punished for an act of child abuse other than the misdemeanor offenses specified in section 18-6-401 (7) (a) (V), (7) (a) (VI), and (7) (b), unless the indictment, information, complaint, or action for the same is found or instituted within ten years after commission of the offense. No person shall be prosecuted, tried, or punished for the misdemeanor offenses specified in section 18-6-401 (7) (a) (V), (7) (a) (VI), and (7) (b), unless the indictment, information, complaint, or action for the same is found or instituted within five years after the commission of the offense.

Out-of-court statements made by a child describing any act of child abuse performed on the child declarant, not otherwise admissible by a statute or court rule which provides an exception to the objection of hearsay, may be admissible in any proceeding in which the child is a victim of an act of child abuse pursuant to the provisions of section 13-25-129, C.R.S.

All cases involving the commission of an act of child abuse shall take precedence before the court; the court shall hear these cases as soon as possible after they are filed.

The statutory privilege between the victim-patient and his physician and between the husband and the wife shall not be available for excluding or refusing testimony in any prosecution of an act of child abuse.

18-6-401.2. Habitual child abusers - indictment or information - verdict of the jury. (1) For the purposes of this section, "child abuse" means child abuse as defined in section 18- 6-401 (1).

Every person convicted in this state of an act of child abuse who has been previously convicted upon charges prior to the commission of the present act, which were separately brought, either in this state or elsewhere, of an act of child abuse or who has been previously convicted under the laws of any other state, the United States, or any territory subject to the jurisdiction of the United States of an unlawful act which, if committed within this state, would be an act of child abuse shall be adjudged an habitual child abuser. If the second or subsequent act of child abuse for which a defendant is convicted constitutes a class 3 felony under section 18-6-401 (7) (a) (II) or a class 4 felony under section 18-6-401 (7) (a) (IV), the sentence imposed shall be served in the department

of corrections and shall not be less than the upper limit of the presumptive range for that class felony as set out in section 18-1.3-401. If the second or subsequent act of child abuse for which a defendant is convicted constitutes a misdemeanor, the sentence imposed shall be served in the county jail

138

and shall not be less than the maximum sentence for that class misdemeanor as set out in section 18-1.3- 501.

Any previous conviction of an act of child abuse shall be set forth in apt words in the complaint, indictment, or information. For purposes of trial, a duly authenticated copy of the record of previous convictions and judgments of any court of record for any of said crimes of the party indicted, charged, or informed against shall be prima facie evidence of such convictions and may be used in evidence against such party. A duly authenticated copy of the records of institutions of treatment or incarceration, including, but not limited to, records pertaining to identification of the party indicted, charged, or informed against, shall be prima facie evidence of the facts contained therein and may be used in evidence against such party.

Any person who is subject to the provisions of this section shall not be eligible for probation or suspension of sentence or deferred prosecution. The procedures specified in section 18-1.3-803 shall govern in a trial to which the provisions of this section are alleged to apply based on a previous conviction or convictions for an act of child abuse as set out in the complaint, indictment, or information.

18-6-401.3. Video tape depositions - children - victims of child abuse. (1) When a defendant has been charged with an act of child abuse, as defined in section 18-6-401 (1), and when the victim at the time of the commission of the act is a child less than fifteen years of age, the prosecution may apply to the court for an order that a deposition be taken of the victim's testimony and that the deposition be recorded and preserved on video tape. The prosecution shall apply for the order in writing at least three days prior to the taking of the deposition. The defendant shall receive reasonable notice of the taking of the deposition.

Upon timely receipt of the application, the court shall make a preliminary finding regarding whether, at the time of trial, the victim is likely to be medically unavailable or otherwise unavailable within the meaning of rule 804 (a) of the Colorado rules of evidence. Such finding shall be based on, but not be limited to, recommendations from the child's therapist or any other person having direct contact with the child, whose recommendations are based on specific behavioral indicators exhibited by the child. If the court so finds, it shall order that the deposition be taken, pursuant to rule 15 (d) of the Colorado rules of criminal procedure, and preserved on video tape. The prosecution shall transmit the video tape to the clerk of the court in which the action is pending.

If at the time of trial the court finds that further testimony would cause the victim emotional trauma so that the victim is medically unavailable or otherwise unavailable within the meaning of rule 804 (a) of the Colorado rules of evidence, the court may admit the video tape of the victim's deposition as former testimony under rule 804 (b) (1) of the Colorado rules of evidence.

Nothing in this section shall prevent the admission into evidence of any videotaped statements of children that would qualify for admission pursuant to section 13-25-129, C.R.S., or

any other statute or rule of evidence.

18-6-401.4. Payment of treatment costs for the victim or victims of an act of child abuse. (1) In addition to any other penalty provided by law, the court may order any person who is convicted of an act of child abuse, as defined in section 18-6-401 (1), to meet all or any portion of the financial obligations of treatment prescribed for the victim or victims of his offense.

(2) At the time of sentencing, the court may order that an offender described in subsection of this section be put on a period of probation for the purpose of paying the treatment costs of the victim or victims.

18-6-402. Trafficking in children. (Repealed)

18-6-403. Sexual exploitation of a child. (1) The general assembly hereby finds and declares: That the sexual exploitation of children constitutes a wrongful invasion of the child's right of privacy and results in social, developmental, and emotional injury to the child; that a child below the age of eighteen years is incapable of giving informed consent to the use of his or her body for a sexual purpose; and that to protect children from sexual exploitation it is necessary to prohibit the production of material which involves or is derived from such exploitation and to exclude all such material from the channels of trade and commerce.

(1.5) The general assembly further finds and declares that the mere possession or control of any sexually exploitative material results in continuing victimization of our children by the fact that such material is a permanent record of an act or acts of sexual abuse of a child; that each time such material is shown or viewed, the child is harmed; that such material is used to break down the will and resistance of other children to encourage them to participate in similar acts of sexual abuse; that laws banning the production and distribution of such material are insufficient to halt this abuse; that in order to stop the sexual exploitation and abuse of our children, it is necessary for the state to ban the possession of any sexually exploitative materials; and that the state has a compelling interest in outlawing the possession of any sexually exploitative materials in order to protect societyas a whole, and particularly the privacy, health, and emotional welfare of its children.

As used in this section, unless the context otherwise requires:

"Child" means a person who is less than eighteen years of age.

(Deleted by amendment, L. 2003, p. 1882, 1, effective July 1, 2003.)

"Erotic fondling" means touching a person's clothed or unclothed genitals or pubic area, developing or undeveloped genitals or pubic area (if the person is a child), buttocks, breasts, or developing or undeveloped breast area (if the person is a child), for the purpose of real or simulated overt sexual gratification or stimulation of one or more of the persons involved. "Erotic fondling" shall not be construed to include physical contact, even if affectionate, which is not for the purpose of real or simulated overt sexual gratification or stimulation of one or more of the persons involved.

"Erotic nudity" means the display of the human male or female genitals or pubic area, the undeveloped or developing genitals or pubic area of the human male or female child, the human

breasts, or the undeveloped or developing breast area of the human child, for the purpose of real or simulated overt sexual gratification or stimulation of one or more of the persons involved.

"Explicit sexual conduct" means sexual intercourse, erotic fondling, erotic nudity, masturbation, sadomasochism, or sexual excitement.

"Masturbation" means the real or simulated touching, rubbing, or otherwise stimulating of a person's own clothed or unclothed genitals or pubic area, developing or undeveloped genitals or pubic area (if the person is a child), buttocks, breasts, or developing or undeveloped breast area (if the person is a child), by manual manipulation or self-induced or with an artificial instrument, for the purpose of real or simulated overt sexual gratification or arousal of the person.

"Sadomasochism" means:

Real or simulated flagellation or torture for the purpose of real or simulated sexual stimulation or gratification; or

The real or simulated condition of being fettered, bound, or otherwise physically restrained for sexual stimulation or gratification of a person.

"Sexual excitement" means the real or simulated condition of human male or female genitals when in a state of real or simulated overt sexual stimulation or arousal.

"Sexual intercourse" means real or simulated intercourse, whether genital-genital, oral- genital, anal-genital, or oral-anal, between persons of the same or opposite sex, or between a human and an animal, or with an artificial genital.

"Sexually exploitative material" means any photograph, motion picture, video, recording or broadcast of moving visual images, print, negative, slide, or other mechanically, electronically, chemically, or digitally reproduced visual material that depicts a child engaged in, participating in, observing, or being used for explicit sexual conduct.

"Video", "recording or broadcast", or "motion picture" means any material that depicts a moving image of a child engaged in, participating in, observing, or being used for explicit sexual conduct.

A person commits sexual exploitation of a child if, for any purpose, he or she knowingly:

Causes, induces, entices, or permits a child to engage in, or be used for, any explicit sexual conduct for the making of any sexually exploitative material; or

Prepares, arranges for, publishes, including but not limited to publishing through digital or electronic means, produces, promotes, makes, sells, finances, offers, exhibits, advertises, deals in, or distributes, including but not limited to distributing through digital or electronic means, any sexually exploitative material; or

(b.5) Possesses or controls any sexually exploitative material for any purpose; except that this paragraph (b.5) does not apply to peace officers or court personnel in the performance of their official duties, nor does it apply to physicians, psychologists, therapists, or social workers, so long as such persons are licensed in the state of Colorado and the persons possess such materials in the course of a bona fide treatment or evaluation program at the treatment or evaluation site; or

Possesses with the intent to deal in, sell, or distribute, including but not limited to distributing through digital or electronic means, any sexually exploitative material; or

Causes, induces, entices, or permits a child to engage in, or be used for, any explicit sexual conduct for the purpose of producing a performance. (Deleted by amendment, L. 2003, p. 1882, 1, effective July 1, 2003.)

(a) Except as provided in paragraph (b) of this subsection (5), sexual exploitation of a child is a class 3 felony.

Sexual exploitation of a child by possession of sexually exploitative material pursuant to paragraph (b.5) of subsection (3) of this section is a class 5 felony; except that said offense is a class 4 felony if:

It is a second or subsequent offense; or

The possession is of a video, recording or broadcast of moving visual images, or motion picture or more than twenty different items qualifying as sexually exploitative material.

If any provision of this section or the application thereof to any person or circumstances is held invalid, such invalidity shall not affect other provisions or applications of this section which can be given effect without the invalid provision or application, and to this end the provisions of this section are declared to be severable.

18-6-404. Procurement of a child for sexual exploitation. Any person who intentionally gives, transports, provides, or makes available, or who offers to give, transport, provide, or make available, to another person a child for the purpose of sexual exploitation of a child commits procurement of a child for sexual exploitation, which is a class 3 felony.

18-6-405. Reports of convictions to department of education. (1) When a person is convicted, pleads nolo contendere, or receives a deferred sentence for a violation of the provisions of this part 4 and the court knows the person is a current or former employee of a school district in this state or holds a license or authorization pursuant to the provisions of article 60.5 of title 22, C.R.S., the court shall report such fact to the department of education. Repealed.

PART 5 ADULTERY

18-6-501. Adultery. (Repealed)

PART 6 HARBORING A MINOR

18-6-601. Harboring a minor. (1) (a) A person commits the crime of harboring a minor if the person knowingly provides shelter to a minor without the consent of a parent, guardian, custodian of the minor, or the person with whom the child resides the majority of the time pursuant to a court order allocating parental responsibilities and if the person intentionally:

Fails to release the minor to a law enforcement officer after being requested to do so by the officer; or

Fails to disclose the location of the minor to a law enforcement officer when requested to do so, if the person knows the location of the minor and had either taken the minor to that location or had assisted the minor in reaching that location; or

Obstructs a law enforcement officer from taking the minor into custody; or

Assists the minor in avoiding or attempting to avoid the custody of a law enforcement officer; or

Fails to notify the parent, guardian, custodian of the minor, or the person with whom the child resides the majority of the time pursuant to a court order allocating parental responsibilities or a law enforcement officer that the minor is being sheltered within twenty-four hours after shelter has been provided.

If the shelter provided to the minor is by a licensed child care facility, including a licensed homeless youth shelter, the minor, despite the minor's status, may reside at such facility or shelter for a period not to exceed two weeks after the time of intake, pursuant to the procedures set forth in article 5.7 of title 26, C.R.S.

It is a defense to a prosecution under this section that the defendant had custody of the minor or lawful parenting time with the minor pursuant to a court order.

(2) Harboring a minor is a class 2 misdemeanor.

PART 7 CONTRIBUTING TO DELINQUENCY

18-6-701. Contributing to the delinquency of a minor. (1) Any person who induces, aids, or encourages a child to violate any federal or state law, municipal or county ordinance, or court order commits contributing to the delinquency of a minor. For the purposes of this section, the term "child" means any person under the age of eighteen years.

Contributing to the delinquency of a minor is a class 4 felony.

When a person is convicted, pleads nolo contendere, or receives a deferred sentence for a violation of the provisions of this section and the court knows the person is a current or former employee of a school district in this state or holds a license or authorization pursuant to the provisions of article 60.5 of title 22, C.R.S., the court shall report such fact to the department of education.

## PART 8 DOMESTIC VIOLENCE

18-6-800.3. Definitions. As used in this part 8, unless the context otherwise requires:

"Domestic violence" means an act or threatened act of violence upon a person with whom the actor is or has been involved in an intimate relationship. "Domestic violence" also includes any other crime against a person, or against property, including an animal, or any municipal ordinance violation against a person, or against property, including an animal, when used as a method of coercion, control, punishment, intimidation, or revenge directed against a person with whom the actor is or has been involved in an intimate relationship.

"Intimate relationship" means a relationship between spouses, former spouses, past or present unmarried couples, or persons who are both the parents of the same child regardless of whether the persons have been married or have lived together at any time.

18-6-801. Domestic violence - sentencing. (1) (a) In addition to any sentence that is imposed upon a person for violation of any criminal law under this title, any person who is convicted of any crime, the underlying factual basis of which has been found by the court on the record to include an act of domestic violence, as defined in section 18-6-800.3 (1), or any crime against property, whether or not such crime is a felony, when such crime is used as a method of coercion, control, punishment, intimidation, or revenge directed against a person with whom the actor is or has been involved in an intimate relationship shall be ordered to complete a treatment program and a treatment evaluation that conform with the standards adopted by the domestic violence offender management board as required by section 16-11.8-103 (4), C.R.S. If an intake evaluation conducted by an approved treatment program provider discloses that sentencing to a treatment program would be inappropriate, the person shall be referred back to the court for alternative disposition.

The court may order a treatment evaluation to be conducted prior to sentencing if a treatment evaluation would assist the court in determining an appropriate sentence. The person ordered to undergo such evaluation shall be required to pay the cost of the treatment evaluation. If such treatment evaluation recommends treatment, and if the court so finds, the person shall be ordered to complete a treatment program that conforms with the standards adopted by the domestic violence offender management board as required by section 16-11.8-103 (4), C.R.S.

Nothing in this subsection (1) shall preclude the court from ordering domestic violence treatment in any appropriate case.

Subsection (1) of this section shall not apply to persons sentenced to the department of corrections.

A person charged with the commission of a crime, the underlying factual basis of which includes an act of domestic violence as defined in section 18-6-800.3 (1), shall not be entitled to plead guilty or plead nolo contendere to an offense which does not include the domestic violence designation required in section 16-21-103, C.R.S., unless the prosecuting attorney makes a good faith representation on the record that such attorney would not be able to establish a prima facie case that the person and the alleged victim were currently or formerly involved in an intimate relationship if the defendant were brought to trial on the original domestic violence offense and upon such a finding by the court. The prosecuting attorney's record and the court's findings shall specify the relationship in the alleged domestic violence case which the prosecuting attorney is not able to prove beyond a reasonable doubt and the reasons therefor. No court shall accept a plea of guilty or nolo contendere to an offense which does not include the domestic violence designation required in section 16-21-

103, C.R.S., when the facts of the case indicate that the underlying factual basis includes an act of domestic violence as defined in section 18-6-800.3 (1) unless there is a good faith representation by the prosecuting attorney that he or she would be unable to establish a prima facie case if the defendant were brought to trial on the original offense.

No person accused or convicted of a crime, the underlying factual basis of which has been found by the court on the record to include an act of domestic violence, as defined in section 18-6-800.3 (1), shall be eligible for home detention in the home of the victim pursuant to section 18-1.3-105 or 18-1.3-106. Nothing in this subsection (4) is intended to prohibit a court from ordering a deferred sentence for a person accused or convicted of a crime, the underlying factual basis of which has been found by the court on the record to include an act of domestic violence, as defined in section 18-6-800.3 (1).

Before granting probation, the court shall consider the safety of the victim and the victim's children if probation is granted.

Nothing in this section shall preclude the ability of a municipality to enact concurrent ordinances.

(a) Any misdemeanor offense that includes an act of domestic violence is a class 5 felony if the defendant at the time of sentencing has been previously convicted of three or more prior offenses that included an act of domestic violence and that were separately brought and tried and arising out of separate criminal episodes.

The prior convictions must be set forth in apt words in the indictment or information. For the purposes of this section, "conviction" includes any federal, state, or municipal conviction for a felony, misdemeanor, or municipal ordinance violation.

Trials in cases alleging that the defendant is an habitual domestic violence offender pursuant to this subsection (7) must be conducted in accordance with the rules of criminal procedure for felonies. The trier of fact shall determine whether an offense charged includes an act of domestic violence. Following a conviction for an offense which underlying factual basis includes an act of domestic violence:

If any prior conviction included a determination by a jury or was admitted by the defendant that the offense included an act of domestic violence, the court shall proceed to sentencing without further findings as to that prior conviction by the jury or by the court, if no jury trial is had;

For any prior conviction in which the factual basis was found by the court to include an act of domestic violence, but did not include a finding of domestic violence by a jury or that was not admitted by the defendant, the trial court shall proceed to a sentencing stage of the proceedings. The prosecution shall present evidence to the trier of fact that the prior conviction included an act of domestic violence. The prosecution has the burden of proof beyond a reasonable doubt.

At the sentencing stage, the following applies:

A finding of domestic violence made by a court at the time of the prior conviction constitutes prima facie evidence that the crime involved domestic violence;

Evidence of the prior conviction is admissible through the use of certified documents under seal, or the court may take judicial notice of a prior conviction;

Evidence admitted in the guilt stage of the trial, including testimony of the defendant and other acts admitted pursuant to section 18-6-801.5, may be considered by the finder of fact.

(a) In addition to any sentence that is imposed upon a defendant for violation of any criminal law under this title, if a defendant is convicted of any crime, the underlying factual basis of which is found by the court on the record to be a misdemeanor crime of domestic violence, as defined in 18 U.S.C. sec. 921 (a) (33), or that is punishable by a term of imprisonment exceeding one year and includes an act of domestic violence, as defined in section 18-6-800.3 (1), the court:

Shall order the defendant to:

Refrain from possessing or purchasing any firearm or ammunition for the duration of the order; and

Relinquish any firearm or ammunition in the defendant's immediate possession or control or subject to the defendant's immediate possession or control; and

May require that before the defendant is released from custody on bond, the defendant shall relinquish, for the duration of the order, any firearm or ammunition in the defendant's immediate possession or control or subject to the defendant's immediate possession or control.

Upon issuance of an order to relinquish one or more firearms or ammunition pursuant to paragraph (a) of this subsection (8), the defendant shall relinquish any firearm or ammunition not more than twenty-four hours after being served with the order; except that a court may allow a defendant up to seventy-two hours to relinquish a firearm or up to five days to relinquish ammunition pursuant to this paragraph (b) if the defendant demonstrates to the satisfaction of the court that he or she is unable to comply within twenty-four hours. To satisfy this requirement, the defendant may:

Sell or transfer possession of the firearm or ammunition to a federally licensed firearms dealer described in 18 U.S.C. sec. 923, as amended; except that this provision shall not be interpreted to require any federally licensed firearms dealer to purchase or accept possession of any firearm or ammunition;

Arrange for the storage of the firearm or ammunition by a law enforcement agency; except that this provision shall not be interpreted to require any law enforcement agency to provide storage of firearms or ammunition for any person; or

Sell or otherwise transfer the firearm or ammunition to a private party who may legally possess the firearm or ammunition; except that a defendant who sells or transfers a firearm pursuant to this subparagraph (III) shall satisfy all of the provisions of section 18-12-112, concerning private firearms transfers, including but not limited to the performance of a criminal background check of the transferee.

If a defendant is unable to satisfy the provisions of paragraph (b) of this subsection (8) because he or she is incarcerated or otherwise held in the custody of a law enforcement agency, the court shall require the defendant to satisfy such provisions not more than twenty-four hours after his or her release from incarceration or custody or be held in contempt of court. Notwithstanding any provision of this paragraph (c), the court may, in its discretion, require the defendant to relinquish any firearm or ammunition in the defendant's immediate possession or control or subject to the defendant's immediate possession or control before the end of the defendant's incarceration. In such a case, a defendant's failure to relinquish a firearm or ammunition as required shall constitute contempt of court.

A federally licensed firearms dealer who takes possession of a firearm or ammunition pursuant to this subsection (8) shall issue a receipt to the defendant at the time of relinquishment. The federally licensed firearms dealer shall not return the firearm or ammunition to the defendant

unless the dealer:

Contacts the bureau to request that a background check of the defendant be performed; and check.

Obtains approval of the transfer from the bureau after the performance of the background

A local law enforcement agency may elect to store firearms or ammunition for persons
pursuant to this subsection (8). If an agency so elects:
The agency may charge a fee for such storage, the amount of which shall not exceed the direct and indirect costs incurred by the agency in providing such storage;
The agency may establish policies for disposal of abandoned or stolen firearms or ammunition; and
The agency shall issue a receipt to each defendant at the time the defendant relinquishes possession of a firearm or ammunition.
If a local law enforcement agency elects to store firearms or ammunition for a defendant pursuant to this subsection (8), the law enforcement agency shall not return the firearm or ammunition to the defendant unless the agency:
Contacts the bureau to request that a background check of the defendant be performed;
and check.

Obtains approval of the transfer from the bureau after the performance of the background

(I) A law enforcement agency that elects to store a firearm or ammunition for a defendant pursuant to this subsection (8) may elect to cease storing the firearm or ammunition. A law enforcement agency that elects to cease storing a firearm or ammunition for a defendant shall notify the defendant of such decision and request that the defendant immediately make arrangements for the transfer of the possession of the firearm or ammunition to the defendant or, if the defendant is prohibited from possessing a firearm, to another person who is legally permitted to possess a firearm.

(II) If a law enforcement agency elects to cease storing a firearm or ammunition for a defendant and notifies the defendant as described in subparagraph (I) of this paragraph (g), the law enforcement agency may dispose of the firearm or ammunition if the defendant fails to make arrangements for the transfer of the firearm or ammunition and complete said transfer within ninety days of receiving such notification.

If a defendant sells or otherwise transfers a firearm or ammunition to a private party who may legally possess the firearm or ammunition, as described in subparagraph (III) of paragraph (b) of this subsection (8), the defendant shall acquire:

From the transferee, a written receipt acknowledging the transfer, which receipt shall be dated and signed by the defendant and the transferee; and

From the licensed gun dealer who requests from the bureau a background check of the transferee, as described in section 18-12-112, a written statement of the results of the background check.

(I) Not more than three business days after the relinquishment, the defendant shall file a copy of the receipt issued pursuant to paragraph (d), (e), or (h) of this subsection (8), and, if applicable, the written statement of the results of a background check performed on the transferee, as described in subparagraph (II) of paragraph (h) of this subsection (8), with the court as proof of

the relinquishment. If a defendant fails to timely file a receipt or written statement as described in this paragraph (i):

The failure constitutes a class 2 misdemeanor, and the defendant shall be punished as provided in section 18-1.3-501; and

The court shall issue a warrant for the defendant's arrest.

(II) In any subsequent prosecution for a violation of this paragraph (i), the court shall take judicial notice of the defendant's failure to file a receipt or written statement, which will constitute prima facie evidence that the defendant has violated this paragraph (i), and testimony of the clerk of the court or his or her deputy is not required.

(I) A law enforcement agency that elects in good faith to not store a firearm or ammunition for a defendant pursuant to sub-subparagraph (B) of subparagraph (III) of paragraph (b) of this subsection (8) shall not be held criminally or civilly liable for such election not to act.

(II) A law enforcement agency that returns possession of a firearm or ammunition to a defendant in good faith as permitted by paragraph (f) of this subsection (8) shall not be held criminally or civilly liable for such action.


18-6-801.5. Domestic violence - evidence of similar transactions. (1) The general assembly hereby finds that domestic violence is frequently cyclical in nature, involves patterns of abuse, and can consist of harm with escalating levels of seriousness. The general assembly therefore declares that evidence of similar transactions can be helpful and is necessary in some situations in prosecuting crimes involving domestic violence.

In criminal prosecutions involving domestic violence in which the defendant and the victim named in the information have engaged in an intimate relationship as of the time alleged in the information, evidence of any other acts of domestic violence between the defendant and the victim named in the information, and between the defendant and other persons, constitute other acts or transactions for the purposes of this section, and the court may authorize the admission of evidence as provided in subsection (3) of this section.

The proponent of evidence of other acts or transactions under this section shall advise the trial court by offer of proof of such evidence and shall specify whether the evidence is offered to show a common plan, scheme, design, identity, modus operandi, motive, or guilty knowledge or for some other purpose.

Upon the offer of proof under subsection (3) of this section, the trial court shall determine whether the probative value of the evidence of similar acts or transactions is substantially outweighed by the danger of unfair prejudice to the defendant, confusion of the issues, or misleading of the jury if the evidence is allowed or by considerations of undue delay, waste of time, or needless presentation of cumulative evidence.

Upon admitting evidence of other acts or transactions into evidence pursuant to this section and again in the general charge to the jury, the trial court shall direct the jury as to the limited purpose for which the evidence is admitted and for which the jury may consider it.


18-6-801.6. Domestic violence - summons and complaint. Any person completing or preparing a summons, complaint, summons and complaint, indictment, information, or application for an arrest warrant shall indicate on the face of such document whether the facts forming the basis of the alleged criminal act, if proven, could constitute domestic violence as defined in section 18-6- 800.3 (1).


18-6-802. Domestic violence - local board - treatment programs - liability immunity - repeal. (Repealed)


18-6-802.5. Domestic violence - treatment programs. Any defendant who is sentenced to a treatment program pursuant to section 18-6-801 or who is ordered to complete an evaluation pursuant to section 18-6-801 (1) shall pay for the evaluation and treatment programs on a sliding fee basis, as provided in the standardized procedures for the treatment evaluation of domestic violence offenders and the guidelines and standards for a system of programs for the treatment of domestic violence offenders adopted by the domestic violence offender management board pursuant to section 16-11.8-103, C.R.S.


18-6-803. Commission - manual of standards for treatment of domestic violence perpetrators - repeal. (Repealed)


18-6-803.5. Crime of violation of a protection order - penalty - peace officers' duties - definitions. (1) A person commits the crime of violation of a protection order if, after the person has been personally served with a protection order that identifies the person as a restrained person or otherwise has acquired from the court or law enforcement personnel actual knowledge of the contents of a protection order that identifies the person as a restrained person, the person:

Contacts, harasses, injures, intimidates, molests, threatens, or touches the protected person or protected property, including an animal, identified in the protection order or enters or remains on premises or comes within a specified distance of the protected person, protected property, including an animal, or premises or violates any other provision of the protection order to protect the protected person from imminent danger to life or health, and

144

such conduct is prohibited by the protection order;

Except as permitted pursuant to section 18-13-126 (1) (b), hires, employs, or otherwise contracts with another person to locate or assist in the location of the protected person; or

Violates a civil protection order issued pursuant to section 13-14-105.5, C.R.S., or pursuant to section 18-1-1001 (9) by:

Possessing or attempting to purchase or receive a firearm or ammunition while the protection order is in effect; or

Failing to timely file a receipt or written statement with the court as described in section 13-14-105.5 (9), C.R.S., or in section 18-1-1001 (9) (i) or 18-6-801 (8) (i).

(1.5) As used in this section:

"Protected person" means the person or persons identified in the protection order as the person or persons for whose benefit the protection order was issued.

(a.5) (I) "Protection order" means any order that prohibits the restrained person from contacting, harassing, injuring, intimidating, molesting, threatening, or touching anyprotected person or protected animal, or from entering or remaining on premises, or from coming within a specified distance of a protected person or protected animal or premises or any other provision to protect the protected person or protected animal from imminent danger to life or health, that is issued by a court of this state or a municipal court, and that is issued pursuant to:

Article 14 of title 13, C.R.S., section 18-1-1001, section 19-2-707, C.R.S., section 19-4- 111, C.R.S., or rule 365 of the Colorado rules of county court civil procedure;

(B) Sections 14-4-101 to 14-4-105, C.R.S., section 14-10-107, C.R.S., section 14-10-108,

C.R.S., or section 19-3-316, C.R.S., as those sections existed prior to July 1, 2004;

An order issued as part of the proceedings concerning a criminal municipal ordinance violation; or

Any other order of a court that prohibits a person from contacting, harassing, injuring, intimidating, molesting, threatening, or touching any person, or from entering or remaining on premises, or from coming within a specified distance of a protected person or premises.

(II) For purposes of this section only, "protection order" includes any order that amends, modifies, supplements, or supersedes the initial protection order. "Protection order" also includes any restraining order entered prior to July 1, 2003, and any foreign protection order as defined in section 13-14-110, C.R.S.

"Registry" means the computerized information system created in section 18-6-803.7 or the national crime information center created pursuant to 28 U.S.C. sec. 534.

"Restrained person" means the person identified in the order as the person prohibited from doing the specified act or acts.

(Deleted by amendment, L. 2003, p. 1003, § 6, effective July 1, 2003.)

(a) Violation of a protection order is a class 2 misdemeanor; except that, if the restrained person has previously been convicted of violating this section or a former version of this section or an analogous municipal ordinance, or if the protection order is issued pursuant to section 18-1-1001, the violation is a class 1 misdemeanor.

(a.5) A second or subsequent violation of a protection order is an extraordinary risk crime that is subject to the modified sentencing range specified in section 18-1.3-501 (3).

(Deleted by amendment, L. 95, p. 567, 3, effective July 1, 1995.)

Nothing in this section shall preclude the ability of a municipality to enact concurrent ordinances. Any sentence imposed for a violation of this section shall run consecutively and not concurrently with any sentence imposed for any crime which gave rise to the issuing of the protection order.

(a) Whenever a protection order is issued, the protected person shall be provided with a copy of such order. A peace officer shall use every reasonable means to enforce a protection order.

A peace officer shall arrest, or, if an arrest would be impractical under the circumstances, seek a warrant for the arrest of a restrained person when the peace officer has information amounting to probable cause that:

The restrained person has violated or attempted to violate any provision of a protection order; and

The restrained person has been properly served with a copy of the protection order or the restrained person has received actual notice of the existence and substance of such order.

In making the probable cause determination described in paragraph (b) of this subsection (3), a peace officer shall assume that the information received from the registry is accurate. A peace officer shall enforce a valid protection order whether or not there is a record of the protection order in the registry.

The arrest and detention of a restrained person is governed by applicable constitutional and applicable state rules of criminal procedure. The arrested person shall be removed from the scene of the arrest and shall be taken to the peace officer's station for booking, whereupon the arrested person may be held or released in accordance with the adopted bonding schedules for the jurisdiction in which the arrest is made, or the arrested person may be taken to the jail in the county where the protection order was issued. The law enforcement agency or any other locally designated agency shall make all reasonable efforts to contact the protected party upon the arrest of the restrained person. The prosecuting attorney shall present any available arrest affidavits and the criminal history of the restrained person to the court at the time of the first appearance of the restrained person before the court. The arresting agency arresting the restrained person shall forward to the issuing court a copy of such agency's report, a list of witnesses to the violation, and, if applicable, a list of any charges filed or requested against the restrained person. The agency shall give a copy of the agency's report, witness list, and charging list to the protected party. The agency shall delete the address and telephone number of a witness from the list sent to the court upon request of such witness, and such address and telephone number shall not thereafter be made available to any person, except law enforcement officials and the prosecuting agency, without order of the court.

If a restrained person is on bond in connection with a violation or attempted violation of a protection order in this or any other state and is subsequently arrested for violating or attempting to violate a protection order, the arresting agency shall notify the prosecuting attorney who shall file a motion with the court which issued the prior bond for the revocation of the bond and for the issuance of a warrant for the arrest of the restrained person if such court is satisfied that probable cause exists to believe that a violation of the protection order issued by the court has occurred.

A peace officer arresting a person for violating a protection order or otherwise enforcing a protection order shall not be held criminally or civilly liable for such arrest or enforcement unless the peace officer acts in bad faith and with malice or does not act in compliance with rules adopted by the Colorado supreme court.

(a) A peace officer is authorized to use every reasonable means to protect the alleged victim or the alleged victim's children to prevent further violence. Such peace officer may transport, or obtain transportation for, the alleged victim to shelter. Upon the request of the protected person, the peace officer may also transport the minor child of the protected person, who is not an emancipated minor, to the same shelter if such shelter is willing to accept the child, whether or not there is a custody order or an order allocating parental responsibilities with respect to such child or an order for the care and control of the child and whether or not the other parent objects. A peace officer who transports a minor child over the objection of the other parent shall not be held liable for

any damages that may result from interference with the custody, parental responsibilities, care, and control of or access to a minor child in complying with this subsection (6).

(b) For purposes of this subsection (6), "shelter" means a battered women's shelter, a friend's or family member's home, or such other safe haven as may be designated by the protected person and which is within a reasonable distance from the location at which the peace officer found the victim. The protection order shall contain in capital letters and bold print a notice informing the protected person that such protected person may either initiate contempt proceedings against the restrained person if the order is issued in a civil action or request the prosecuting attorney to initiate contempt proceedings if the order is issued in a criminal action.

A protection order issued in the state of Colorado shall contain a statement that:

The order or injunction shall be accorded full faith and credit and be enforced in every civil or criminal court of the United States, another state, an Indian tribe, or a United States territory pursuant to 18 U.S.C. sec. 2265;

The issuing court had jurisdiction over the parties and subject matter; and

The defendant was given reasonable notice and opportunity to be heard.

A criminal action charged pursuant to this section may be tried either in the county where the offense is committed or in the county in which the court that issued the protection order is located, if such court is within this state.


18-6-803.6. Duties of peace officers and prosecuting agencies - preservation of evidence. (1) When a peace officer determines that there is probable cause to believe that a crime or offense involving domestic violence, as defined in section 18-6-800.3 (1), has been committed, the officer shall, without undue delay, arrest the person suspected of its commission pursuant to the provisions in subsection (2) of this section, if applicable, and charge the person with the appropriate crime or offense. Nothing in this subsection (1) shall be construed to require a peace officer to arrest both parties involved in an alleged act of domestic violence when both claim to have been victims of such domestic violence. Additionally, nothing in this subsection (1) shall be construed to require a peace officer to arrest either party involved in an alleged act of domestic violence when a peace officer determines there is no probable cause to believe that a crime or offense of domestic violence has been committed. The arrested person shall be removed from the scene of the arrest and shall be taken to the peace officer's station for booking, whereupon the arrested person may be held or released in accordance with the adopted bonding schedules for the jurisdiction in which the arrest is made.

If a peace officer receives complaints of domestic violence from two or more opposing persons, the officer shall evaluate each complaint separately to determine if a crime has been committed by one or more persons. In determining whether a crime has been committed by one or more persons, the officer shall consider the following:

Any prior complaints of domestic violence;

The relative severity of the injuries inflicted on each person;

The likelihood of future injury to each person; and

The possibility that one of the persons acted in self-defense.

(a) A peace officer is authorized to use every reasonable means to protect the alleged

victim or the alleged victim's children to prevent further violence. Such peace officer may transport, or obtain transportation for, the alleged victim to shelter. Upon the request of the protected person, the peace officer may also transport the minor child of the protected person, who is not an emancipated minor, to the same shelter if such shelter is willing to accept the child, whether or not there is a custody order or an order for the care and control of the child or an order allocating parental responsibilities with respect to the child and whether or not the other parent objects. A peace officer who transports a minor child over the objection of the other parent shall not be held liable for any damages that may result from interference with the custody, parental responsibilities, care, and control of or access to a minor child in complying with this subsection (3).

(b) For purposes of this subsection (3), "shelter" means a battered women's shelter, a friend's or family member's home, or such other safe haven as may be designated by the protected person and which is within a reasonable distance from the location at which the peace officer found the victim.

(a) The arresting agency shall make reasonable efforts to collect and preserve any pertinent evidence until the time of final disposition of the matter, including, but not limited to, the following:

Any dispatch tape recording relating to the event;

Any on-scene video or audio tape recordings;

Any medical records of treatment of the alleged victim or the defendant; and

Any other relevant physical evidence or witness statements.

(b) However, in the absence of bad faith, any failure to collect or preserve any evidence listed in paragraph (a) of this subsection (4) shall not be grounds to dismiss the matter.

(4.5) When a peace officer responds to a call or is otherwise responding to a report about an alleged offense involving domestic violence, as defined in section 18-6-800.3 (1), or other domestic dispute, the officer shall include in his or her written or oral report concerning such incident whether children may have seen or heard the alleged offense; except that, in the absence of bad faith, the failure of a peace officer to note that a child may have seen or heard the alleged offense shall not be grounds to dismiss the matter.

A peace officer shall not be held civilly or criminally liable for acting pursuant to this section if the peace officer acts in good faith and without malice.


18-6-803.7. Central registry of protection orders - creation. (1) As used in this section:

"Bureau" means the Colorado bureau of investigation.

"Protected person" means the person or persons identified in the protection order as the person or persons for whose benefit the protection order was issued.

(b.5) (I) "Protection order" means any order that prohibits the restrained person from contacting, harassing, injuring, intimidating, molesting, threatening, or touching any protected person, or from entering or remaining on premises, or from coming within a specified distance of a protected person or premises, that is issued by a court of this state or an authorized municipal court, and that is issued pursuant to:

Article 14 of title 13, C.R.S., section 18-1-1001, section 19-2-707, C.R.S., section 19-4-

111, C.R.S., or rule 365 of the Colorado rules of county court civil procedure;

(B) Sections 14-4-101 to 14-4-105, C.R.S., section 14-10-107, C.R.S., section 14-10-108, C.R.S., or section 19-3-316, C.R.S., as those sections existed prior to July 1, 2004; or

(C) An order issued as part of the proceedings concerning a criminal municipal ordinance violation.

(II) "Protection order" also includes any restraining order entered prior to July 1, 2003, and any foreign protection order as described in section 13-14-110, C.R.S.

"Registry" means a computerized information system.

"Restrained person" means the person identified in the order as the person prohibited from doing the specified act or acts.

(Deleted by amendment, L. 2003, p. 1007, § 7, effective July 1, 2003.)

"Subsequent order" means an order which amends, modifies, supplements, or supersedes a protection order.

(a) There is hereby created in the bureau a computerized central registry of protection orders which shall be accessible to any state law enforcement agencyor to any local law enforcement agencyhaving a terminal which communicates with the bureau. The central registry computers shall communicate with computers operated by the state judicial department.

Protection orders and subsequent orders shall be entered into the registry by the clerk of the court issuing the protection order; except that orders issued pursuant to sections 18-1-1001 and 19-2-707, C.R.S., shall be entered into the registry only at the discretion of the court or upon motion of the district attorney. The clerk of the court issuing the protection order shall be responsible for updating the registry electronically in a timely manner to ensure the notice is as complete and accurate as is reasonably possible with regard to the information specified in subsection (3) of this section.

The restrained person's attorney, if present at the time the protection order or subsequent order is issued, shall notify the restrained person of the contents of such order if the restrained person was absent when such order was issued.

Protection orders and subsequent orders shall be placed in the registry not later than twenty-four hours after they have been issued; except that, if the court issuing the protection order or subsequent order specifies that it be placed in the registry immediately, such order shall be placed in the registry immediately.

Upon reaching the expiration date of a protection order or subsequent order, if any, the bureau shall note the termination in the registry.

In the event the protection order or subsequent order does not have a termination date, the clerk of the issuing court shall be responsible for noting the termination of the protection order or subsequent order in the registry.

(a) In addition to any information, notice, or warning required by law, a protection order or subsequent order entered into the registry shall contain the following information, if such information is available:

The name, date of birth, sex, and physical description of the restrained person to the extent known;

The date the order was issued and the effective date of the order if such date is different from the date the order was issued;

The names of the protected persons and their dates of birth;

If the protection order is one prohibiting the restrained person from entering in, remaining upon, or coming within a specified distance of certain premises, the address of the premises and the distance limitation;

The expiration date of the protection order, if any;

Whether the restrained person has been served with the protection order and, if so, the date and time of service;

The amount of bail and any conditions of bond which the court has set in the event the restrained person has violated a protection order; and

An indication whether the conditions of the protection order are also conditions of a bail bond for a felony charge.

(b) If available, the protection order or subsequent order shall contain the fingerprint-based state identification number issued by the bureau to the restrained person.


18-6-803.8. Foreign protection orders. (Repealed)


18-6-803.9. Assaults and deaths related to domestic violence - report. The Colorado bureau of investigation shall prepare a report by November 1, 1995, and by November 1 of each year thereafter, to the governor, the president of the senate, and the speaker of the house of representatives on the number of assaults related to and the number of deaths caused directly by domestic violence, including, but not limited to, homicides of victims, self-defense killings of alleged perpetrators, and incidental killings of children, peace officers, persons at work, neighbors, and bystanders in the course of episodes of domestic violence.


18-6-804. Repeal of part. (Repealed)


18-6-805. Repeal of sections. (Repealed)

ARTICLE 6.5


Wrongs to At-risk Adults


18-6.5-101. Legislative declaration. The general assembly recognizes that fear of mistreatment is one of the major personal concerns of at-risk persons and that at-risk persons are more vulnerable to and disproportionately damaged by crime in general but, more specifically, by

abuse, exploitation, and neglect because they are less able to protect themselves against offenders, a number of whom are in positions of trust, and because they are more likely to receive serious injury from crimes committed against them and not to fully recover from such injury. At-risk persons are more impacted by crime than the general population because they tend to suffer great relative deprivation, financially, physically, and psychologically, as a result of the abuses against them. A significant number of at-risk persons are not as physically, intellectually, or emotionally equipped to protect themselves or aid in their own security as non-at-risk persons in society. They are far more susceptible than the general population to the adverse long-term effects of crimes committed against them, including abuse, exploitation, and neglect. The general assembly therefore finds that penalties for specified crimes committed against at-risk persons should be more severe than the penalties for the commission of the same crimes against other members of society.


18-6.5-102. Definitions. As used in this article, unless the context otherwise requires:

person:

"Abuse" means any of the following acts or omissions committed against an at-risk

The nonaccidental infliction of bodily injury, serious bodily injury, or death;
Confinement or restraint that is unreasonable under generally accepted caretaking
standards; or
Subjection to sexual conduct or contact classified as a crime under this title.
"At-risk adult" means any person who is seventy years of age or older or any person who is eighteen years of age or older and is a person with a disability as said term is defined in subsection
of this section.
(2.5) "At-risk adult with IDD" means a person who is eighteen years of age or older and is a person with an intellectual and developmental disability, as defined in section 25.5-10-202 (26) (a), C.R.S.
"At-risk elder" means any person who is seventy years of age or older.
"At-risk juvenile" means any person who is under the age of eighteen years and is a person with a disability as said term is defined in subsection (11) of this section.
(4.5) "At-risk person" means an at-risk adult, an at-risk adult with IDD, an at-risk elder, or an at-risk juvenile.
"Caretaker" means a person who:
Is responsible for the care of an at-risk person as a result of a family or legal relationship;
Has assumed responsibility for the care of an at-risk person; or
Is paid to provide care or services to an at-risk person.
(a) "Caretaker neglect" means neglect that occurs when adequate food, clothing, shelter, psychological care, physical care, medical care, habilitation, supervision, or any other treatment necessary for the health or safety of an at-risk person is not secured for an at-risk person or is not provided by a caretaker in a timely manner and with the degree of care that a reasonable person in the same situation would exercise, or a caretaker knowingly uses harassment, undue influence, or intimidation to create a hostile or fearful environment for an at-risk person.
Notwithstanding the provisions of paragraph (a) of this subsection (6), the withholding,

withdrawing, or refusing of any medication, any medical procedure or device, or any treatment, including but not limited to resuscitation, cardiac pacing, mechanical ventilation, dialysis, and artificial nutrition and hydration, in accordance with any valid medical directive or order or as described in a palliative plan of care, is not deemed caretaker neglect.
As used in this subsection (6), "medical directive or order" includes a medical durable power of attorney, a declaration as to medical treatment executed pursuant to section 15-18-104, C.R.S., a medical order for scope of treatment form executed pursuant to article 18.7 of title 15, C.R.S., and a CPR directive executed pursuant to article 18.6 of title 15, C.R.S.
"Clergy member" means a priest; rabbi; duly ordained, commissioned, or licensed minister of a church; member of a religious order; or recognized leader of any religious body.
"Convicted" and "conviction" mean a plea of guilty accepted by the court, including a plea of guilty entered pursuant to a deferred sentence under section 18-1.3-102, a verdict of guilty by a judge or jury, or a plea of no contest accepted by the court.
"Crime against an at-risk person" means any offense listed in section 18-6.5-103 or criminal attempt, conspiracy, or solicitation to commit any of those offenses.
"Exploitation" means an act or omission committed by a person who:
Uses deception, harassment, intimidation, or undue influence to permanently or temporarily deprive an at-risk person of the use, benefit, or possession of any thing of value;
Employs the services of a third party for the profit or advantage of the person or another person to the detriment of the at-risk person;
Forces, compels, coerces, or entices an at-risk person to perform services for the profit or advantage of the person or another person against the will of the at-risk person; or
Misuses the property of an at-risk person in a manner that adversely affects the at-risk person's ability to receive health care or health care benefits or to pay bills for basic needs or obligations.
(10.5) "Mistreated" or "mistreatment" means:
Abuse;
Caretaker neglect; or
Exploitation.
"Person with a disability" means any person who:
Is impaired because of the loss of or permanent loss of use of a hand or foot or because of blindness or the permanent impairment of vision of both eyes to such a degree as to constitute virtual blindness;
Is unable to walk, see, hear, or speak;
Is unable to breathe without mechanical assistance;
Is a person with an intellectual and developmental disability as defined in section 25.5- 10-202, C.R.S.;
Is a person with a mental illness as the term is defined in section 27-65-102 (14), C.R.S.;
Is mentally impaired as the term is defined in section 24-34-501 (1.3) (b) (II), C.R.S.;
Is blind as that term is defined in section 26-2-103 (3), C.R.S.; or
Is receiving care and treatment for a developmental disability under article 10.5 of title 27, C.R.S.
"Position of trust" means assuming a responsibility, duty, or fiduciary relationship

toward an at-risk adult or at-risk juvenile.
"Undue influence" means the use of influence to take advantage of an at-risk person's vulnerable state of mind, neediness, pain, or emotional distress.


18-6.5-103. Crimes against at-risk persons - classifications. (1) Crimes against at-risk persons are as prescribed in this section.
Any person whose conduct amounts to criminal negligence, as defined in section 18-1- 501 (3), commits:
A class 4 felony if such negligence results in the death of an at-risk person;
A class 5 felony if such negligence results in serious bodily injury to an at-risk person; and
A class 6 felony if such negligence results in bodily injury to an at-risk person.

(a) Any person who commits a crime of assault in the first degree, as such crime is described in section 18-3-202, and the victim is an at-risk person, commits a class 4 felony if the circumstances described in section 18-3-202 (2) (a) are present and a class 2 felony if such circumstances are not present.

Any person who commits a crime of assault in the second degree, as such crime is described in section 18-3-203, and the victim is an at-risk person, commits a class 5 felony if the circumstances described in section 18-3-203 (2) (a) are present and a class 3 felony if such circumstances are not present.

Any person who commits a crime of assault in the third degree, as such crime is described in section 18-3-204, and the victim is an at-risk person, commits a class 6 felony.

Any person who commits robbery, as such crime is described in section 18-4-301 (1), and the victim is an at-risk person, commits a class 3 felony. If the offender is convicted of robbery of an at-risk person, the court shall sentence the defendant to the department of corrections for at least the presumptive sentence under section 18-1.3-401 (1).

Any person who commits theft, and commits any element or portion of the offense in the presence of the victim, as such crime is described in section 18-4-401 (1), and the victim is an at-risk person, or who commits theft against an at-risk person while acting in a position of trust, whether or not in the presence of the victim, or who commits theft against an at-risk person knowing the victim is an at-risk person, whether in the presence of the victim or not, commits a class 5 felony if the value of the thing involved is less than five hundred dollars or a class 3 felony if the value of the thing involved is five hundred dollars or more. Theft from the person of an at-risk person by means other than the use of force, threat, or intimidation is a class 4 felony without regard to the value of the thing taken.

(5.5) (Deleted by amendment, L. 2016.)

Any person who knowingly commits caretaker neglect against an at-risk person or knowingly acts in a manner likely to be injurious to the physical or mental welfare of an at-risk person commits a class 1 misdemeanor.

(a) Any person who commits a crime of sexual assault, as such crime is described in section 18-3-402, sexual assault in the first degree, as such crime was described in section 18-3-402,

as it existed prior to July 1, 2000, and the victim is an at-risk person, commits a class 2 felony.

Any person who commits a crime of sexual assault in the second degree, as such crime was described in section 18-3-403, as it existed prior to July 1, 2000, and the victim is an at-risk person, commits a class 3 felony.

Any person who commits unlawful sexual contact, as such crime is described in section 18-3-404, or sexual assault in the third degree, as such crime was described in section 18-3-404, as it existed prior to July 1, 2000, and the victim is an at-risk person, commits a class 6 felony; except that the person commits a class 3 felony if the person compels the victim to submit by use of such force, intimidation, or threat as specified in section 18-3-402 (4) (a), (4) (b), or (4) (c), or if the actor engages in the conduct described in section 18-3-404 (1) (g) or (1.5).

Any person who commits sexual assault on a child, as such crime is described in section 18-3-405, and the victim is an at-risk juvenile, commits a class 3 felony; except that, if the circumstances described in section 18-3-405 (2) (a), (2) (b), (2) (c), or (2) (d) are present, the person commits a class 2 felony.

Any person who commits sexual assault on a child by one in a position of trust, as such crime is described in section 18-3-405.3, and the victim is an at-risk juvenile, commits a class 2 felony if the victim is less than fifteen years of age or a class 3 felony if the victim is fifteen years of age or older but less than eighteen years of age.

Any person who commits sexual assault on a client by a psychotherapist, as such crime is described in section 18-3-405.5, and the victim is an at-risk person, commits a class 3 felony if the circumstances described in section 18-3-405.5 (1) exist or a class 6 felony if such circumstances are not present.

(7.5) (a) A person commits criminal exploitation of an at-risk person when he or she knowingly uses deception, harassment, intimidation, or undue influence to permanently or temporarily deprive an at-risk person of the use, benefit, or possession of any thing of value.

(b) Criminal exploitation of an at-risk person is a class 3 felony if the thing of value is five hundred dollars or greater. Criminal exploitation of an at-risk person is a class 5 felony if the thing of value is less than five hundred dollars.

(Deleted by amendment, L. 2016.)


18-6.5-103.5. Video tape depositions - at-risk adult victims and witnesses. (1) In any case in which a defendant is charged with a crime against an at-risk adult or at-risk elder, or in any case involving a victim or witness who is an at-risk adult or at-risk elder, the prosecution may file a motion with the court at any time prior to commencement of the trial for an order that a deposition be taken of the testimony of the victim or witness and that the deposition be recorded and preserved on a video imaging format.

The prosecution shall file a motion requesting a recorded deposition at least fourteen days prior to the taking of the deposition. The defendant shall receive reasonable notice of the taking of the deposition. The defendant shall have the right to be present and to be represented by counsel at the deposition; except that for good cause shown, the court may permit the filing of a motion requesting a recorded deposition less than fourteen days prior to taking the deposition.

(a) (I) Upon receipt of the motion, the court shall schedule the deposition to take place within fourteen days without further findings, except for good cause shown by the prosecution if the motion asks for the deposition to be taken in less than fourteen days, if the victim is an at-risk elder.

Except for depositions of at-risk elder victims as described in subparagraph (I) of this paragraph (a), upon the filing of the motion by the prosecution stating reasons the victim or witness may be unavailable at trial, the court may order a deposition for an at-risk adult victim or witness or at-risk elder witness. Filing the motion creates a rebuttable presumption that a deposition should be taken to prevent injustice. The court may deny the motion for deposition upon a finding that granting the motion will not prevent injustice. The prosecution may file a new request for a deposition if circumstances change prior to trial.

Both the prosecution and the defendant shall provide all available discovery no later than five days before the scheduled deposition. If the discovery has not been provided as set forth in this subparagraph (III), either party may file a motion with the court to reschedule the deposition in order to obtain the necessary discovery to adequately prepare for the deposition.

(b) The deposition must be taken, preserved on a video imaging format, and conducted pursuant to rule 15 (d) of the Colorado rules of criminal procedure; except that after consultation with the chief judge of the judicial district, the trial court may appoint an active or senior district or county court judge to serve in its place and preside over all aspects of the taking of the deposition. After the deposition is taken, the prosecution shall transmit the recording to the clerk of the court in which the action is pending.

If at the time of trial the court finds that the victim or witness is medically unavailable or otherwise unavailable within the meaning of rule 804 (a) of the Colorado rules of evidence, the court may admit the recording of the victim's or witness' deposition as former testimony under rule 804 (b) (1) of the Colorado rules of evidence.


18-6.5-104. Statutory privilege not allowed. The statutory privileges provided in section 13-90-107 (1), C.R.S., are not available for excluding or refusing testimony in any prosecution for a crime committed against an at-risk person pursuant to this article.

18-6.5-105. Preferential trial dates of cases involving crimes against at-risk persons. Consistent with the constitutional right to a speedytrial, all cases involving the commission of a crime against an at-risk person must take precedence before the court, and the court shall hear these cases as soon as possible after they are filed.

18-6.5-106. Payment of treatment costs for victims of crimes against at-risk persons - restitution. (1) In addition to any other penalty provided by law, the court may order any person who is convicted of a crime against an at-risk person, as set forth in this article, to meet all or any portion of the financial obligations of treatment prescribed for the victim or victims of such person's offense.
(2) At the time of sentencing, the court may order that an offender described in subsection

(1) of this section be put on a period of probation for the purpose of paying the treatment costs of the victim or victims, which, when added to any time served, does not exceed the maximum sentence imposable for the offense.
(3) If an at-risk person has sustained monetary damages as a result of the commission of a crime described in this article against such person, the court shall order the offender to provide restitution pursuant to article 18.5 of title 16 and article 28 of title 17, C.R.S. If, after a reasonable period not to exceed one hundred eighty-two days, the offender has not, in the opinion of the court, completed adequate restitution, the offender's probation may be revoked. However, any remaining amount of restitution continues to have the full force and effect of a final judgment and remain enforceable pursuant to article 18.5 of title 16, C.R.S.

18-6.5-107. Surcharge - collection and distribution of funds - crimes against at-risk persons surcharge fund - creation - report. (1) Each person who is convicted of a crime against an at-risk person or who is convicted of identity theft pursuant to section 18-5-902, when the victim is an at-risk person, shall be required to pay a surcharge to the clerk of the court for the judicial district in which the conviction occurs.
Surcharges pursuant to subsection (1) of this section shall be in the following amounts:
For each class 2 felony of which a person is convicted, one thousand five hundred dollars;
For each class 3 felony of which a person is convicted, one thousand dollars;
For each class 4 felony of which a person is convicted, five hundred dollars;
For each class 5 felony of which a person is convicted, three hundred seventy-five dollars;
For each class 6 felony of which a person is convicted, two hundred fifty dollars;
For each class 1 misdemeanor of which a person is convicted, two hundred dollars;
For each class 2 misdemeanor of which a person is convicted, one hundred fifty dollars; and

For each class 3 misdemeanor of which a person is convicted, seventy-five dollars.

The clerk of the court shall allocate the surcharge required pursuant to this section as follows:

Five percent shall be retained by the clerk of the court for administrative costs incurred pursuant to this subsection (3). Such amount retained shall be transmitted to the state treasurer for deposit in the judicial stabilization cash fund created in section 13-32-101 (6), C.R.S.

Ninety-five percent shall be transferred to the state treasurer, who shall credit the same to the crimes against at-risk persons surcharge fund created pursuant to subsection (4) of this section.

(a) There is created in the state treasurythe crimes against at-risk persons surcharge fund, referred to in this section as the "fund", that consists of money received by the state treasurer pursuant to this section. The money in the fund is subject to annual appropriation by the general assembly to the state office on aging in the department of human services, created pursuant to section 26-11-202, C.R.S., for distribution to a fiscal agent that is an affiliate of a national organization that serves individuals affected by a disability and chronic condition across the life span and is working with the state of Colorado to implement the lifespan respite care program, referred to in this section

as the "fiscal agent". Provided that programs selected to receive money from the fund meet the guidelines for distribution pursuant to paragraph (b) of this subsection (4), the fiscal agent shall award money to programs selected by a statewide coalition of nonprofit or not-for-profit organizations that focus on the needs of caregivers of at-risk persons.

The state office on aging in the department of human services shall establish guidelines for the distribution of the moneys from the fund, including but not limited to:

Procedures for programs to use in applying for an award of moneys from the fund;

Procedures for the fiscal agent to use in reporting to the state office on aging pursuant to paragraph (e) of this subsection (4); and

Accountability and performance standards for programs that receive moneys from the fund.

Notwithstanding any provisions of paragraph (a) of this subsection (4) to the contrary, the fiscal agent may use a portion of the money that it receives pursuant to paragraph (a) of this subsection (4) for training and to facilitate the coordination of programs that provide respite services for caregivers of at-risk persons. The fiscal agent shall distribute the remainder of the money directly to the programs.

Each program that receives moneys from the fund shall:

Provide respite services that allow a caregiver to have a break from caregiving;

Have a signed agreement and protocol with the fiscal agent;

Conduct a fingerprint-based criminal history record check of staff and providers; and

Satisfy the accountability and performance standards established by the state office on aging pursuant to subparagraph (III) of paragraph (b) of this subsection (4).

The fiscal agent shall report to the state office on aging in the department of human services on a regular basis to be specified by the state office on aging. The report shall include, but need not be limited to:

A list of all programs that received moneys from the fund in the preceding fiscal year;

A description of how each program that received moneys from the fund in the preceding fiscal year used those moneys; and

Documentation demonstrating that each program that received moneys from the fund in the preceding fiscal year satisfied all of the criteria specified in paragraph (d) of this subsection (4).

The state office on aging shall not expend any moneys until the fund has enough money to pay the expenses necessary to administer the fund.

All interest derived from the deposit and investment of moneys in the fund shall be credited to the fund. Any moneys not appropriated by the general assembly shall remain in the fund and shall not be transferred or revert to the general fund of the state at the end of any fiscal year.

The court may waive all or any portion of the surcharge required by subsection (1) of this section if the court finds that a person convicted of a crime against an at-risk person is indigent or financially unable to pay all or any portion of the surcharge. The court may waive only that portion of the surcharge that the court finds that the person convicted of a crime against an at-risk person is financially unable to pay.

18-6.5-108. Mandatory reports of mistreatment of at-risk elders and at-risk adults with IDD - list of reporters - penalties. (1) (a) On and after July 1, 2016, a person specified in paragraph of this subsection (1) who observes the mistreatment of an at-risk elder or an at-risk adult with IDD, or who has reasonable cause to believe that an at-risk elder or an at-risk adult with IDD has been mistreated or is at imminent risk of mistreatment, shall report such fact to a law enforcement agency not more than twenty-four hours after making the observation or discovery.

The following persons, whether paid or unpaid, shall report as required by paragraph (a) of this subsection (1):

Any person providing health care or health-care-related services, including general medical, surgical, or nursing services; medical, surgical, or nursing speciality services; dental services; vision services; pharmacy services; chiropractic services; or physical, occupational, musical, or other therapies;

Hospital and long-term care facility personnel engaged in the admission, care, or treatment of patients;

First responders including emergency medical service providers, fire protection personnel, law enforcement officers, and persons employed by, contracting with, or volunteering with any law enforcement agency, including victim advocates;

Medical examiners and coroners;

Code enforcement officers;

Veterinarians;

Psychologists, addiction counselors, professional counselors, marriage and family therapists, and registered psychotherapists, as those persons are defined in article 43 of title 12, C.R.S.;

Social workers, as defined in part 4 of article 43 of title 12, C.R.S.;

Staff of community-centered boards;

Staff, consultants, or independent contractors of service agencies as defined in section 25.5-10-202 (34), C.R.S.;

Staff or consultants for a licensed or unlicensed, certified or uncertified, care facility, agency, home, or governing board, including but not limited to long-term care facilities, home care agencies, or home health providers;

Staff of, or consultants for, a home care placement agency, as defined in section 25-27.5-102 (5), C.R.S.;

Persons performing case management or assistant services for at-risk elders or at-risk adults with IDD;

Staff of county departments of human or social services;

Staff of the state departments of human services, public health and environment, or health care policy and financing;

Staff of senior congregate centers or senior research or outreach organizations;

Staff, and staff of contracted providers, of area agencies on aging, except the long- term care ombudsmen;

Employees, contractors, and volunteers operating specialized transportation services for at-risk elders and at-risk adults with IDD;

Court-appointed guardians and conservators;

Personnel at schools serving persons in preschool through twelfth grade;

Clergy members; except that the reporting requirement described in paragraph (a) of this subsection (1) does not apply to a person who acquires reasonable cause to believe that an at-risk elder or an at-risk adult with IDD has been mistreated or has been exploited or is at imminent risk of mistreatment or exploitation during a communication about which the person may not be examined as a witness pursuant to section 13-90-107 (1) (c), C.R.S., unless the person also acquires such reasonable cause from a source other than such a communication; and

(A) Personnel of banks, savings and loan associations, credit unions, and other lending or financial institutions who directly observe in person the mistreatment of an at-risk elder or who have reasonable cause to believe that an at-risk elder has been mistreated or is at imminent risk of mistreatment; and

(B) Personnel of banks, savings and loan associations, credit unions, and other lending or financial institutions who directly observe in person the mistreatment of an at-risk adult with IDD or who have reasonable cause to believe that an at-risk adult with IDD has been mistreated or is at imminent risk of mistreatment by reason of actual knowledge of facts or circumstances indicating the mistreatment.

A person who willfully violates paragraph (a) of this subsection (1) commits a class 3 misdemeanor and shall be punished in accordance with section 18-1.3-501.

Notwithstanding the provisions of paragraph (a) of this subsection (1), a person described in paragraph (b) of this subsection (1) is not required to report the mistreatment of an at-risk elder or an at-risk adult with IDD if the person knows that another person has already reported to a law enforcement agency the same mistreatment that would have been the basis of the person's own report.

(a) A law enforcement agency that receives a report of mistreatment of an at-risk elder or an at-risk adult with IDD shall acquire, to the extent possible, the following information from the person making the report:

The name, age, address, and contact information of the at-risk elder or at-risk adult with IDD;

The name, age, address, and contact information of the person making the report;

The name, age, address, and contact information of the caretaker of the at-risk elder or at-risk adult with IDD, if any;

The name of the alleged perpetrator;

The nature and extent of any injury, whether physical or financial, to the at-risk elder or at-risk adult with IDD;

The nature and extent of the condition that required the report to be made; and

Any other pertinent information.

Not more than twenty-four hours after receiving a report of mistreatment of an at-risk elder or an at-risk adult with IDD, a law enforcement agency shall provide the report to the county department for the county in which the at-risk elder or at-risk adult with IDD resides and the district attorney's office of the location where the mistreatment occurred.

The law enforcement agency shall complete a criminal investigation when appropriate. The law enforcement agency shall provide a summary report of the investigation to the county

department for the county in which the at-risk elder or at-risk adult with IDD resides and to the district attorney's office of the location where the mistreatment occurred.

A person, including but not limited to a person specified in paragraph (b) of subsection

(1) of this section, who reports mistreatment of an at-risk elder or an at-risk adult with IDD to a law enforcement agency pursuant to subsection (1) of this section is immune from suit and liability for damages in any civil action or criminal prosecution if the report was made in good faith; except that such a person is not immune if he or she is the alleged perpetrator of the mistreatment.

(4) A person, including but not limited to a person specified in paragraph (b) of subsection

(1) of this section, who knowingly makes a false report of mistreatment of an at-risk elder or an at- risk adult with IDD to a law enforcement agency commits a class 3 misdemeanor and must be punished as provided in section 18-1.3-501 and is liable for damages proximately caused thereby.

(5) The reporting duty described in subsection (1) of this section does not create a civil duty of care or establishing a civil standard of care that is owed to an at-risk elder or an at-risk adult with IDD by a person specified in paragraph (b) of subsection (1) of this section.

18-6.5-109. At-risk adults with intellectual and developmental disabilities mandatory reporting implementation task force - report - repeal.  (Repealed)

### ARTICLE 7   Offenses Relating to Morals

PART 1 OBSCENITY - OFFENSES

18-7-101. Definitions. As used in this part 1, unless the context otherwise requires:

"Material" means anything tangible that is capable of being used or adapted to arouse interest, whether through the medium of reading, observation, sound, or in any other manner, but does not include an actual three-dimensional obscene device.

(1.5)  "Minor" means a person under eighteen years of age.

"Obscene" means material or a performance that:

The average person, applying contemporarycommunity standards, would find that taken as a whole appeals to the prurient interest in sex;

Depicts or describes:

Patently offensive representations or descriptions of ultimate sex acts, normal or perverted, actual or simulated, including sexual intercourse, sodomy, and sexual bestiality; or

Patently offensive representations or descriptions of masturbation, excretory functions,

sadism, masochism, lewd exhibition of the genitals, the male or female genitals in a state of sexual stimulation or arousal, or covered male genitals in a discernibly turgid state; and

Taken as a whole, lacks serious literary, artistic, political, or scientific value.

"Obscene device" means a device including a dildo or artificial vagina, designed or marketed as useful primarily for the stimulation of human genital organs.

"Patently offensive" means so offensive on its face as to affront current community standards of tolerance.

"Performance" means a play, motion picture, dance, or other exhibition performed before an audience.

"Promote" means to manufacture, issue, sell, give, provide, lend, mail, deliver, transfer, transmit, publish, distribute, circulate, disseminate, present, exhibit, or advertise, or to offer or agree to do the same.

(6.5)  "Prurient interest" means a shameful or morbid interest.

"Simulated" means the explicit depiction or description of any of the types of conduct set forth in paragraph (b) of subsection (2) of this section, which creates the appearance of such conduct.

"Wholesale promote" means to manufacture, issue, sell, provide, mail, deliver, transfer, transmit, publish, distribute, circulate, disseminate, or to offer or agree to do the same for purpose of resale.

If any of the depictions or descriptions of sexual conduct described in this section are declared by a court of competent jurisdiction to be unlawfully included herein, this declaration shall not invalidate this section as to other patently offensive sexual conduct included herein.

18-7-102. Obscenity. (1) (a) Except as otherwise provided in subsection (1.5) of this section, a person commits wholesale promotion of obscenity if, knowing its content and character, such person wholesale promotes or possesses with intent to wholesale promote anyobscene material.

(b)  Wholesale promotion of obscenity is a class 1 misdemeanor.

(1.5) (a) A person commits wholesale promotion of obscenity to a minor if, knowing its content and character, such person wholesale promotes to a minor or possesses with intent to wholesale promote to a minor any obscene material.

(b)  Wholesale promotion of obscenity to a minor is a class 6 felony.

(a) Except as otherwise provided in subsection (2.5) of this section, a person commits promotion of obscenity if, knowing its content and character, such person:

Promotes or possesses with intent to promote any obscene material; or

Produces, presents, or directs an obscene performance or participates in a portion thereof that is obscene or that contributes to its obscenity.

(b)  Promotion of obscenity is a class 2 misdemeanor.

(2.5) (a) A person commits promotion of obscenity to a minor if, knowing its content and character, such person:

154

Promotes to a minor or possesses with intent to promote to a minor any obscene material; or

Produces, presents, or directs an obscene performance involving a minor or participates

in a portion thereof that is obscene or that contributes to its obscenity.

(b) Promotion of obscenity to a minor is a class 6 felony.

Repealed.

A person who possesses six or more identical obscene materials is presumed to possess them with intent to promote the same.

This section does not apply to a person who possesses or distributes obscene material or participates in conduct otherwise proscribed by this section when the possession, participation, or conduct occurs in the course of law enforcement activities.

This section does not apply to a person's conduct otherwise proscribed by this section which occurs in that person's residence as long as that person does not engage in the wholesale promotion or promotion of obscene material in his residence.


18-7-103. Injunctions to restrain the promotion of obscene materials. (1) The district courts of this state and the judges thereof shall have full power, authority, and jurisdiction to enjoin the wholesale promotion, promotion, or display of obscene materials as specified in this section and to issue all necessary and proper restraining orders, injunctions, and writs and processes in connection therewith not inconsistent with this article.

The district attorney of the county in which a person, firm, or corporation wholesale promotes, promotes, or displays, or is about to wholesale promote, promote, or display, or has in his, her, or its possession with intent to wholesale promote, promote, or display, or is about to acquire possession with intent to wholesale promote, promote, or displayanyobscene material maymaintain an action for injunction against such person, firm, or corporation to prevent the wholesale promotion, promotion, or display or further wholesale promotion, promotion, or display of said material described or identified in said suit for injunction.

This article shall not authorize the issuance of temporary restraining orders except where exigent circumstances require the same. In matters of exigent circumstances, the restraining order shall provide that the action must be commenced on the earliest possible date. No temporary restraining order may be issued to restrain the continued exhibitions of a motion picture being shown commercially before the public, notwithstanding the existence of exigent circumstances.

No temporaryrestraining order or temporaryinjunction may be issued except after notice to the person, firm, or corporation sought to be enjoined and only after all parties have been offered or afforded an opportunity to be heard. A person, firm, or corporation shall be deemed to have been offered or afforded an opportunity to be heard if notice has been given and he, she, or it fails to appear. At such hearing, evidence shall be presented and witnesses examined.

Before or after the commencement of the hearing on an application for a temporary injunction, the court may, and on motion of the party sought to be restrained shall, order the trial on the action on the merits to be advanced and consolidated with the hearing on the application. Where such hearings are not so consolidated, and a temporary injunction or restraining order is issued, the court shall hold a final hearing and a trial of the issues within one day after joinder of issue, and a decision shall be rendered within two days of the conclusion of the trial. If a final hearing is not held within one day after joinder of issue or a decision not rendered within two days of the conclusion of the trial, the injunction shall be dissolved. No temporary injunction or restraining order shall issue

until after a showing of probable cause to believe that the material or display is obscene and a showing of probable success on the merits. Any such temporary injunction or restraining order shall provide that the defendant may not be punished for contempt if the material is found not to be obscene after joinder of issue, final hearing, and trial.

Nothing contained in this article shall prevent the court from issuing a temporary restraining order forbidding the removing, destroying, deleting, splicing, or otherwise altering of any motion picture alleged to be obscene.

Any person, firm, or corporation sought to be permanently enjoined shall be entitled to a full adversary trial of the issues within one day after the joinder of issue, and a decision shall be rendered by the court within two days of the conclusion of the trial. If the defendant in any suit for a permanent injunction filed under the terms of this article shall fail to answer or otherwise join issue within the time required to file his, her, or its answer, the court, on motion of the party applying for the injunction, shall enter a general denial for the defendant and set a date for hearing on the question raised in the suit for injunction within fourteen days following the entry of the general denial entered by the court. The court shall render its decision within two days after the conclusion of the hearing.

In the event that a final order or judgment of injunction is entered against the person, firm, or corporation sought to be enjoined, such final order or judgment shall contain a provision directing the person, firm, or corporation to surrender to the sheriff of the county in which the action was brought any of the material described in subsection (2) of this section, and such sheriff shall be directed to seize and destroy the same six months after the entry of the said final order unless criminal proceedings or an indictment is brought before that time, in which event, said material may be used as evidence in such criminal proceeding.

In any action brought as herein provided, the district attorney shall not be required to file any undertaking, bond, or security before the issuance of any injunction order provided for above, shall not be liable for costs, and shall not be liable for damages sustained by reason of the injunction order in cases where judgment is rendered in favor of the person, firm, or corporation sought to be enjoined.

Every person, firm, or corporation who wholesale promotes, promotes, displays, or acquires possession with intent to wholesale promote, promote, or display any of the material described in subsection (2) of this section, after the service upon him of a summons and complaint in an action brought pursuant to this article, is chargeable with knowledge of the contents.


18-7-104. Applicability of this part 1. (Repealed)


18-7-104.5. Remedies under the "Colorado Organized Crime Control Act". When a person or persons, through an enterprise, engage in a pattern of racketeering activity for which the predicate offenses are the promotion or wholesale promotion of obscenity, pursuant to article 17 of this title, the difference in the fair market value of real property in the vicinity of the location of such enterprise from what the value would be if such enterprise or any part thereof were not located in the vicinity, as established by the opinion testimony of experts or otherwise, shall be deemed a compensable injury for which the owners of victimized real property can exercise all civil remedies

set forth in article 17 of this title, in addition to any other measure of damages provable pursuant to article 17 of this title.


18-7-105. Severability. If any provision of this part 1 is found by a court of competent jurisdiction to be unconstitutional, the remaining provisions of

155

this part 1 are valid, unless it appears to the court that the valid provisions of this part 1 are so essentially and inseparably connected with, and so dependent upon, the void provision that it cannot be presumed that the general assembly would have enacted the valid provisions without the void provision or unless the court determines that the valid provisions, standing alone, are incomplete and are incapable of being executed in accordance with the legislative intent.

18-7-106. Constitutional questions expedited. (Repealed)

18-7-107. Posting a private image for harassment - definitions. (1) (a) An actor who is eighteen years of age or older commits the offense of posting a private image for harassment if he or she posts or distributes through the use of social media or any website any photograph, video, or other image displaying the private intimate parts of an identified or identifiable person eighteen years of age or older:
With the intent to harass the depicted person and inflict serious emotional distress upon the depicted person;
(A) Without the depicted person's consent; or
(B) When the actor knew or should have known that the depicted person had a reasonable expectation that the image would remain private; and
The conduct results in serious emotional distress of the depicted person.
Posting a private image for harassment is a class 1 misdemeanor.
Notwithstanding the provisions of section 18-1.3-501 (1) (a), in addition to any other sentence the court may impose, the court shall fine the defendant up to ten thousand dollars. The fines collected pursuant to this paragraph (c) shall be credited to the crime victim compensation fund created in section 24-4.1-117, C.R.S.
It shall not be an offense under this section if the photograph, video, or image is related to a newsworthy event.
Nothing in this section precludes punishment under any section of law providing for greater punishment.
(a) An individual whose private intimate parts have been posted in accordance with this section may bring a civil action against the person who caused the posting of the private images and is entitled to injunctive relief, the greater of ten thousand dollars or actual damages incurred as a result of the posting of the private images, exemplary damages, and reasonable attorney fees and costs.
(b) An individual whose private intimate parts have been posted in accordance with this section shall retain a protectable right of authorship regarding the commercial use of the private

image.
Nothing in this section shall be construed to impose liability on the provider of an
interactive computer service, as defined in 47 U.S.C. sec. 230 (f) (2), an information service, as defined in 47 U.S.C. sec. 153, or a
telecommunications service, as defined in 47 U.S.C. sec. 153, for content provided by another person.
For purposes of this section, unless the context otherwise requires:
"Newsworthy event" means a matter of public interest, of public concern, or related to a public figure who is intimately involved in the resolution of important public questions or, by reason of his or her fame, shapes events in areas of concern to society.
"Private intimate parts" means external genitalia or the perineum or the anus or the pubes of any person or the breast of a female.
"Social media" means any electronic medium, including an interactive computer service, telephone network, or data network, that allows users to create, share, and view user-generated content, including but not limited to videos, still photographs, blogs, video blogs, podcasts, instant messages, electronic mail, or internet website profiles.

18-7-108. Posting a private image for pecuniary gain - definitions. (1) (a) An actor who is eighteen years of age or older commits the offense of posting a private image for pecuniary gain if he or she posts or distributes through social media or any website any photograph, video, or other image displaying the private intimate parts of an identified or identifiable person eighteen years of age or older:
With the intent to obtain a pecuniary benefit from any person as a result of the posting, viewing, or removal of the private image; and
(A) When the actor has not obtained the depicted person's consent; or
(B) When the actor knew or should have known that the depicted person had a reasonable expectation that the image would remain private.
Posting a private image for pecuniary gain is a class 1 misdemeanor.
Notwithstanding the provisions of section 18-1.3-501 (1) (a), in addition to any other sentence the court may impose, the court shall fine the defendant up to ten thousand dollars. The fines collected pursuant to this paragraph (c) shall be credited to the crime victim compensation fund created in section 24-4.1-117, C.R.S.
It shall not be an offense under this section if the photograph, video, or image is related to a newsworthy event.
Nothing in this section precludes punishment under any section of law providing for greater punishment.
(a) An individual whose private intimate parts have been posted in accordance with this section may bring a civil action against the person who caused the posting of the private images and is entitled to injunctive relief, the greater of ten thousand dollars or actual damages incurred as a result of the posting of the private images, exemplary damages, and reasonable attorney fees and costs.
(b) An individual whose private intimate parts have been posted in accordance with this section shall retain a protectable right of authorship regarding the commercial use of the private

image.
Nothing in this section shall be construed to impose liability on the provider of an
interactive computer service, as defined in 47 U.S.C. sec. 230 (f) (2), an information service, as defined in 47 U.S.C. sec. 153, or a
telecommunications service, as defined in 47 U.S.C. sec. 153, for content provided by another person.
For purposes of this section, unless the context otherwise requires:
"Newsworthy event" means a matter of public interest, of public concern, or related to a public figure who is intimately involved in the resolution of important public questions or, by reason of his or her fame, shapes events in areas of concern to society.
"Private intimate parts" means external genitalia or the perineum or the anus or the pubes of any person or the breast of a female.
"Social media" means any electronic medium, including an interactive computer service, telephone network, or data network, that allows users to create, share, and view user-generated content, including but not limited to videos, still photographs, blogs, video blogs, podcasts, instant messages, electronic mail, or internet website profiles.

PART 2 PROSTITUTION

18-7-201. Prostitution prohibited. (1) Any person who performs or offers or agrees to perform any act of sexual intercourse, fellatio, cunnilingus, masturbation, or anal intercourse with any person not his spouse in exchange for money or other thing of value commits prostitution.

(a) "Fellatio", as used in this section, means any act of oral stimulation of the penis.

"Cunnilingus", as used in this section, means any act of oral stimulation of the vulva or clitoris.

"Masturbation", as used in this section, means stimulation of the genital organs by manual or other bodily contact exclusive of sexual intercourse.

"Anal intercourse", as used in this section, means contact between human beings of the genital organs of one and the anus of another.

Prostitution is a class 3 misdemeanor.

18-7-201.3. Affirmative defense - human trafficking - expungement of record protective order - definitions. (1) A person charged with prostitution, as described in section 18-7-201 or any corresponding municipal code or ordinance, for an offense committed on or after July 1, 2015, which offense was committed as a direct result of being a victim of human trafficking, may assert as an affirmative defense that he or she is a victim of human trafficking as defined in subsection (4) of this section. To assert the affirmative defense pursuant to this subsection (1), the person charged with the offense must demonstrate by a preponderance of the evidence that he or she was a victim of human trafficking at the time of the offense. An official determination or documentation is not required to assert an affirmative defense pursuant to this subsection (1), but official documentation from a

federal, state, local, or tribal government agency indicating that the defendant was a victim at the time of the offense creates a presumption that his or her participation in the offense was a direct result of being a victim.

(a) On or after January 1, 2016, a person charged with or convicted of prostitution, as described in section 18-7-201 or any corresponding municipal code or ordinance, for an offense committed before July 1, 2015, which offense was committed as a direct result of being a victim of human trafficking, as defined in subsection (4) of this section, may apply to the court for a sealing of his or her records pursuant to section 24-72-702 or 24-72-706, C.R.S., as applicable.

A juvenile charged with or adjudicated of prostitution, as described in section 18-7-201 or any corresponding municipal code or ordinance, for an offense committed before July 1, 2015, which offense was committed as a direct result of being a victim of human trafficking, as defined in subsection (4) of this section, may apply to the court for expungement of his or her record pursuant to section 19-1-306, C.R.S.

An official determination or documentation is not required to grant a motion pursuant to this subsection (2), but official documentation from a federal, state, local, or tribal government agency indicating that the defendant was a victim at the time of the offense creates a presumption that his or her participation in the offense was a direct result of being a victim.

At the request of a person who asserted the affirmative defense pursuant to subsection

of this section, the court may at any time issue a protective order concerning protecting the confidentiality of the person asserting the affirmative defense.

As used in this section, unless the context otherwise requires:

"Human trafficking" means an offense described in part 5 of article 3 of this title or any conduct that, if it occurred prior to the enactment of such part 5, would constitute an offense of human trafficking pursuant to part 5 of article 3 of this title.

"Victim of human trafficking" means a "victim" as defined in section 18-3-502 (12).

18-7-201.5. Acquired immune deficiency syndrome testing for persons convicted of prostitution. (Repealed)

18-7-201.7. Prostitution with knowledge of being infected with acquired immune deficiency syndrome. (Repealed)

he:

18-7-202. Soliciting for prostitution. (1) A person commits soliciting for prostitution if

Solicits another for the purpose of prostitution; or

Arranges or offers to arrange a meeting of persons for the purpose of prostitution; or

Directs another to a place knowing such direction is for the purpose of prostitution.

Soliciting for prostitution is a class 3 misdemeanor. A person who is convicted of

soliciting for prostitution may be required to pay a fine of not more than five thousand dollars in

addition to any penalty imposed by the court pursuant to section 18-1.3-501, which additional fine shall be transferred to the state treasurer, who shall transfer the same to the prostitution enforcement cash fund created in section 24-33.5-513, C.R.S.

18-7-203. Pandering. (1) Any person who does any of the following for money or other thing of value commits pandering:

Inducing a person by menacing or criminal intimidation to commit prostitution; or

Knowingly arranging or offering to arrange a situation in which a person may practice prostitution.

(2) (a) Pandering under paragraph (a) of subsection (1) of this section is a class 5 felony. A person who is convicted of pandering under paragraph (a) of subsection (1) of this section shall be required to pay a fine of not less than five thousand dollars and not more than ten thousand dollars in addition to any penalty imposed by the court pursuant to section 18-1.3-401, which additional fine shall be transferred to the state treasurer, who shall transfer the same to the prostitution enforcement cash fund created in section 24-33.5-513, C.R.S.

(b) Pandering under paragraph (b) of subsection (1) of this section is a class 3 misdemeanor. A person who is convicted of pandering under paragraph (b) of subsection (1) of this section shall be required to pay a fine of not less than five thousand dollars and not more than ten thousand dollars in addition to any penalty imposed by the court pursuant to section 18-1.3-501, which additional fine shall be transferred to the state treasurer, who shall transfer the same to the prostitution enforcement cash fund created in section 24-33.5-513, C.R.S.

18-7-204. Keeping a place of prostitution. (1) Any person who has or exercises control over the use of any place which offers seclusion or shelter for the practice of prostitution and who performs any one or more of the following commits keeping a place of prostitution if he:

Knowingly grants or permits the use of such place for the purpose of prostitution; or

Permits the continued use of such place for the purpose of prostitution after becoming aware of facts or circumstances from which he should reasonably know that the place is being used for purposes of prostitution.

Keeping a place of prostitution is a class 2 misdemeanor.

18-7-205. Patronizing a prostitute. (1) Anyperson who performs anyof the following with a person not his spouse commits patronizing a prostitute:

Engages in an act of sexual intercourse or of deviate sexual conduct with a prostitute; or

Enters or remains in a place of prostitution with intent to engage in an act of sexual intercourse or deviate sexual conduct.

(2) Patronizing a prostitute is a class 1 misdemeanor. A person who is convicted of patronizing a prostitute may be required to pay a fine of not more than five thousand dollars in addition to any penalty imposed by the court pursuant to section 18-1.3-401 or 18-1.3-503, which additional fine shall be transferred to the state treasurer, who shall transfer the same to the

prostitution enforcement cash fund created in section 24-33.5-513, C.R.S.

18-7-205.5. Acquired immune deficiency syndrome testing for persons convicted of patronizing a prostitute. (Repealed)

18-7-205.7. Patronizing a prostitute with knowledge of being infected with acquired immune deficiency syndrome. (Repealed)

18-7-206. Pimping. Any person who knowingly lives on or is supported or maintained in whole or in part by money or other thing of value earned, received, procured, or realized by any other person through prostitution commits pimping, which is a class 3 felony.

18-7-207. Prostitute making display. Any person who by word, gesture, or action endeavors to further the practice of prostitution in any public place or within public view commits a class 1 petty offense.

18-7-208. Promoting sexual immorality. (Repealed)

PART 3 PUBLIC INDECENCY

18-7-301. Public indecency. (1) Any person who performs any of the following in a public place or where the conduct may reasonably be expected to be viewed by members of the public commits public indecency:

An act of sexual intercourse; or

(Deleted by amendment, L. 2010, (HB 10-1334), ch. 359, p. 1707, § 1, effective August 11, 2010.)

A lewd exposure of an intimate part as defined by section 18-3-401 (2) of the body, not including the genitals, done with intent to arouse or to satisfy the sexual desire of any person; or

A lewd fondling or caress of the body of another person; or

A knowing exposure of the person's genitals to the view of a person under circumstances in which such conduct is likely to cause affront or alarm to the other person.

(a) Except as otherwise provided in paragraph (b) of this subsection (2), public indecency is a class 1 petty offense.

(b) Public indecency as described in paragraph (e) of subsection (1) of this section is a class 1 misdemeanor if the violation is committed subsequent to a conviction for a violation of paragraph

158

(e) of subsection (1) of this section or for a violation of a comparable offense in any other state or in the United States, or for a violation of a comparable municipal ordinance.
(Deleted by amendment, L. 2010, (HB 10-1334), ch. 359, p. 1707, § 1, effective August 11, 2010.)

18-7-302. Indecent exposure. (1) A person commits indecent exposure:
If he or she knowingly exposes his or her genitals to the view of any person under circumstances in which such conduct is likely to cause affront or alarm to the other person with the intent to arouse or to satisfy the sexual desire of any person;
If he or she knowingly performs an act of masturbation in a manner which exposes the act to the view of any person under circumstances in which such conduct is likely to cause affront or alarm to the other person.
(a) (Deleted by amendment, L. 2003, p. 1435, § 31, effective July 1, 2003.)
(b) Indecent exposure is a class 1 misdemeanor.
(Deleted by amendment, L. 2002, p. 1587, § 21, effective July 1, 2002.)
Indecent exposure is a class 6 felony if the violation is committed subsequent to two prior convictions of a violation of this section or of a violation of a comparable offense in any other state or in the United States, or of a violation of a comparable municipal ordinance.
For purposes of this section, "masturbation" means the real or simulated touching, rubbing, or otherwise stimulating of a person's own genitals or pubic area for the purpose of sexual gratification or arousal of the person, regardless of whether the genitals or pubic area is exposed or covered.

PART 4

CHILD PROSTITUTION

18-7-401. Definitions. As used in this part 4, unless the context otherwise requires:
"Anal intercourse" means contact between human beings of the genital organs of one and the anus of another.
"Child" means a person under the age of eighteen years.
"Cunnilingus" means any act of oral stimulation of the vulva or clitoris.
"Fellatio" means any act of oral stimulation of the penis.
"Masturbation" means stimulation of the genital organs by manual or other bodily contact, or by any object, exclusive of sexual intercourse.
"Prostitution by a child" means either a child performing or offering or agreeing to perform any act of sexual intercourse, fellatio, cunnilingus, masturbation, or anal intercourse with any person not the child's spouse in exchange for money or other thing of value or any person performing or offering or agreeing to perform any act of sexual intercourse, fellatio, cunnilingus, masturbation, or anal intercourse with any child not the person's spouse in exchange for money or other thing of value.

"Prostitution of a child" means either inducing a child to perform or offer or agree to perform any act of sexual intercourse, fellatio, cunnilingus, masturbation, or anal intercourse with any person not the child's spouse by coercion or by any threat or intimidation or inducing a child, by coercion or by any threat or intimidation or in exchange for money or other thing of value, to allow any person not the child's spouse to perform or offer or agree to perform any act of sexual intercourse, fellatio, cunnilingus, masturbation, or anal intercourse with or upon such child. Such coercion, threat, or intimidation need not constitute an independent criminal offense and shall be determined solely through its intended or its actual effect upon the child.

18-7-402. Soliciting for child prostitution. (1) A person commits soliciting for child prostitution if he:
Solicits another for the purpose of prostitution of a child or by a child;
Arranges or offers to arrange a meeting of persons for the purpose of prostitution of a child or by a child; or
Directs another to a place knowing such direction is for the purpose of prostitution of a child or by a child.
Soliciting for child prostitution is a class 3 felony.

18-7-403. Pandering of a child. (1) Any person who does any of the following for money or other thing of value commits pandering of a child:
Inducing a child by menacing or criminal intimidation to commit prostitution; or
Knowingly arranging or offering to arrange a situation in which a child may practice prostitution.
Pandering under paragraph (a) of subsection (1) of this section is a class 2 felony. Pandering under paragraph (b) of subsection (1) of this section is a class 3 felony.

18-7-403.5. Procurement of a child. Any person who intentionally gives, transports, provides, or makes available, or who offers to give, transport, provide, or make available, to another person a child for the purpose of prostitution of the child commits procurement of a child, which is a class 3 felony.

18-7-404. Keeping a place of child prostitution. (1) Any person who has or exercises control over the use of any place which offers seclusion or shelter for the practice of prostitution and who performs any one or more of the following commits keeping a place of child prostitution if he:
Knowingly grants or permits the use of such place for the purpose of prostitution of a child or by a child; or
Permits the continued use of such place for the purpose of prostitution of a child or by a child after becoming aware of facts or circumstances from which he should reasonably know that the place is being used for purposes of such prostitution.

(2) Keeping a place of child prostitution is a class 3 felony.

18-7-405. Pimping of a child. Any person who knowingly lives on or is supported or maintained in whole or in part by money or other thing of value earned, received, procured, or realized by a child through prostitution commits pimping of a child, which is a class 3 felony.

18-7-405.5. Inducement of child prostitution. (1) Any person who by word or action, other than conduct specified in section 18-7-403 (1)(a), induces a child to engage in an act which is prostitution by a child, as defined in section 18-7-401 (6), commits inducement of child prostitution. Inducement of child prostitution is a class 3 felony.

18-7-406. Patronizing a prostituted child. (1) Any person who performs any of the following with a child not his spouse commits patronizing a prostituted child:
Engages in an act which is prostitution of a child or by a child, as defined in section 18-7- 401 (6) or (7); or
Enters or remains in a place of prostitution with intent to engage in an act which is prostitution of a child or by a child, as defined in section 18-7-401 (6) or (7).
(2) Patronizing a prostituted child is a class 3 felony.

18-7-407. Criminality of conduct. In any criminal prosecution under sections 18-7-402 to 18-7-407, it shall be no defense that the defendant did not know the child's age or that he reasonably believed the child to be eighteen years of age or older.

18-7-408. Severability. If any provision of this part 4 or the application thereof to any person or circumstances is held invalid, such invalidity shall not affect other provisions of this part 4 which may be given effect without the invalid provision or application, and, to this end, the provisions of this part 4 are declared to be severable.

18-7-409. Reports of convictions to department of education. When a person is convicted, pleads nolo contendere, or receives a deferred sentence for a violation of the provisions of this part 4 and the court knows the person is a current or former employee of a school district in this state or holds a license or authorization pursuant to the provisions of article 60.5 of title 22, C.R.S., the court shall report such fact to the department of education.

PART 5

SEXUALLY EXPLICIT MATERIALS

HARMFUL TO CHILDREN

18-7-501. Definitions. As used in this part 5, unless the context otherwise requires:
"Child" means a person under the age of eighteen years.
"Harmful to children" means that quality of any description or representation, in whatever form, of sexually explicit nudity, sexual conduct, sexual excitement, or sadomasochistic abuse, when it:
Taken as a whole, predominantly appeals to the prurient interest in sex of children;
Is patently offensive to prevailing standards in the adult community as a whole with respect to what is suitable material for children; and
Is, when taken as a whole, lacking in serious literary, artistic, political, and scientific value for children.
"Knowingly" means having general knowledge of, or reason to know, or a belief or ground for belief which warrants further inspection or inquiry, or both, of:
The character and content of any material described herein which is reasonably susceptible of examination; and
The age of the child; however, an honest mistake shall constitute an excuse from liability hereunder if a reasonable bona fide attempt is made to ascertain the true age of such child.
"Sadomasochistic abuse" means actual or explicitly simulated flagellation or torture by or upon a person who is nude or clad in undergarments, a mask or bizarre costume, or the condition of being fettered, bound, or otherwise physically restrained on the part of one so clothed.
"Sexual conduct" means actual or explicitly simulated acts of masturbation, homosexuality, sexual intercourse, sodomy, or physical contact in an act of apparent sexual stimulation or gratification with a person's clothed or unclothed genitals, pubic area, buttocks, or, if such be female, breast.
"Sexual excitement" means the condition of human male or female genitals when in a state of sexual stimulation or arousal.
"Sexually explicit nudity" means a state of undress so as to expose the human male or female genitals, pubic area, or buttocks with less than a full opaque covering, or the showing of the female breast with less than a fully opaque covering of any portion thereof below the top of the areola, or the depiction of covered or uncovered male genitals in a discernibly turgid state.

18-7-502. Unlawful acts. (1) It shall be unlawful for any person knowingly to sell or loan for monetary consideration to a child:
Any picture, photograph, drawing, sculpture, motion picture film, or similar visual representation or image of a person or portion of the human body which depicts sexually explicit nudity, sexual conduct, or sadomasochistic abuse and which, taken as a whole, is harmful to children; or
Any book, pamphlet, magazine, printed matter however reproduced, or sound recording which contains anymatter enumerated in paragraph (a) of this subsection (1), or explicit and detailed verbal descriptions or narrative accounts of sexual excitement, sexual conduct, or sadomasochistic

abuse and which, taken as a whole, is harmful to children.
It shall be unlawful for any person knowingly to sell to a child an admission ticket or pass, or knowingly to admit a child to premises whereon there is exhibited a motion picture, show, or other presentation which, in whole or in part, depicts sexually explicit nudity, sexual conduct, or sadomasochistic abuse and which is harmful to children or to exhibit any such motion picture at any such premises which are not designed to prevent viewing from any public way of such motion picture by children not admitted to any such premises.
It shall be unlawful for any child falsely to represent to any person mentioned in subsection (1) or (2) of this section, or to his agent, that he is eighteen years of age or older, with the intent to procure any material set forth in subsection (1) of this section, or with the intent to procure his admission to any motion picture, show, or other presentation, as set forth in subsection (2) of this section.
It shall be unlawful for any person knowingly to make a false representation to any person mentioned in subsection (1) or (2) of this section, or to his agent, that he is the parent or guardian of any juvenile, or that any child is eighteen years of age or older, with the intent to procure any material set forth in subsection (1) of this section, or with the intent to procure any child's admission to any motion picture, show, or other presentation, as set forth in subsection (2) of this section.
It shall be unlawful for any person knowingly to exhibit, expose, or display in public at newsstands or any other business or commercial establishment

frequented by children or where children are or may be invited as part of the general public:

Any picture, photograph, drawing, sculpture, motion picture film, or similar visual representation or image of a person or portion of the human body which depicts sexually explicit nudity, sexual conduct, or sadomasochistic abuse and which is harmful to children; or

Any book, pamphlet, magazine, printed matter however reproduced, or sound recording which contains any matter enumerated in paragraph (a) of this subsection (5), or explicit verbal descriptions or narrative accounts of sexual excitement, sexual conduct, or sadomasochistic abuse and which, taken as a whole, is harmful to children.

A violation of any provision of this section is a class 2 misdemeanor.

**18-7-503. Applicability.** (1) Nothing contained in this part 5 shall be construed to apply to:

The purchase, distribution, exhibition, or loan of any work of art, book, magazine, or other printed or manuscript material by any accredited museum, library, school, or institution of higher education;

The exhibition or performance of any play, drama, tableau, or motion picture by any theatre, museum, school, or institution of higher education, either supported by public appropriation or which is an accredited institution supported by private funds.

**18-7-504. Severability.** If any provision of this part 5 or the application thereof to any person or circumstances is held invalid, such invalidity shall not affect other provisions of this part 5 which may be given effect without the invalid provision or application, and, to this end, the

provisions of this part 5 are declared to be severable.

## PART 6

## VISUAL REPRESENTATIONS CONTAINING ACTUAL VIOLENCE

**18-7-601. Dispensing violent films to minors - misdemeanors.** (1) No person shall sell, rent, or otherwise furnish to a minor any video tape, video disc, film representation, or other form of motion picture if:

The average person, applying contemporary community standards, would find that the work, taken as a whole, predominantly appeals to the interest in violence; and

The work depicts or describes, in a patently offensive way, repeated acts of actual, not simulated, violence resulting in serious bodily injury or death; and

The work, taken as a whole, lacks serious literary, artistic, political, or scientific value.

For the purposes of this section, "minor" means any person under eighteen years of age, and "serious bodily injury" shall be defined as provided in section 18-1-901 (3) (p).

Any person who violates subsection (1) of this section is guilty of a misdemeanor and, upon conviction thereof, shall be punished by a fine of one thousand dollars; except that, for a second or subsequent offense, the fine shall be five thousand dollars.

## PART 7

## SEXUAL CONDUCT IN A CORRECTIONAL INSTITUTION

**18-7-701. Sexual conduct in a correctional institution.** (1) An employee, contract employee, or volunteer of a correctional institution or an individual who performs work or volunteer functions in a correctional institution who engages in sexual conduct with a person who is in lawful custody in a correctional institution commits the offense of sexual conduct in a correctional institution.

For purposes of this section:

"Correctional institution" means a correctional facility, as defined in section 17-1-102 (1.7), C.R.S., a local jail, as defined in section 17-1-102 (7), C.R.S., operated by or under contract with the department of corrections, a jail, a facility operated by or under contract with the department of human services in which juveniles are or may be lawfully held for detention or commitment for the commission of a crime, or a facility of a community corrections program as defined in section 17-27-102 (3), C.R.S.

"Sexual conduct" means sexual contact as defined in section 18-3-401 (4), sexual intrusion as defined in section 18-3-401 (5), or sexual penetration as defined in section 18-3-401 (6). "Sexual conduct" does not include acts of an employee of a correctional institution or a person who has custody of another person that are performed to carry out the necessary duties of the employee

or the person with custody.

Sexual conduct in a correctional institution is a class 5 felony if the sexual conduct includes sexual intrusion or sexual penetration and is committed by an employee or contract employee of a correctional institution or by an employee, contract employee, or individual who performs work functions in a correctional institution or for the department of corrections, the department of human services, or a community corrections program.

Sexual conduct in a correctional institution is a class 6 felony if:

The sexual conduct consists solely of sexual contact and is committed by an employee or contract employee of a correctional institution or by an employee, contract employee, or individual who performs work functions in a correctional institution or for the department of corrections, the department of human services, or a community corrections program;

The sexual conduct includes sexual intrusion or sexual penetration and is committed by a volunteer.

Sexual conduct in a correctional institution is a class 1 misdemeanor if the sexual conduct consists solely of sexual contact and is committed by a volunteer.

## PART 8

## CRIMINAL INVASION OF PRIVACY

**18-7-801. Criminal invasion of privacy.** (1) A person who knowingly observes or takes a photograph of another person's intimate parts, as defined in section 18-3-401 (2), without that person's consent, in a situation where the person observed or photographed has a reasonable expectation of privacy,

161

commits criminal invasion of privacy.

Criminal invasion of privacy is a class 2 misdemeanor.

For the purposes of this section, "photograph" includes a photograph, motion picture, videotape, live feed, print, negative, slide, or other mechanically, electronically, digitally, or chemically reproduced visual material.

### ARTICLE 8   Offenses - Governmental Operations

PART 1 OBSTRUCTION OF PUBLIC JUSTICE

18-8-101.  Definitions. As used in this article, unless the context otherwise requires:

"Government" has the same meaning as described in section 18-1-901 (3) (i).

"Governmental function" has the same meaning as described in section 18-1-901 (3) (j). (2.5)  "Peace officer" has the same meaning as described in section 16-2.5-101, C.R.S.

"Public servant" has the same meaning as described in section 18-1-901 (3) (o).

18-8-102. Obstructing government operations. (1) A person commits obstructing government operations if he intentionally obstructs, impairs, or hinders the performance of a governmental function by a public servant, by using or threatening to use violence, force, or physical interference or obstacle.

It shall be an affirmative defense that:

The obstruction, impairment, or hindrance was of unlawful action by a public servant;
or
The obstruction, impairment, or hindrance was of the making of an arrest; or
The obstruction, impairment, or hindrance of a governmental function was by lawful activities in connection with a labor dispute with the government.

Obstructing government operations is a class 3 misdemeanor.

18-8-103. Resisting arrest. (1) A person commits resisting arrest if he knowingly prevents or attempts to prevent a peace officer, acting under color of his official authority, from effecting an arrest of the actor or another, by:

Using or threatening to use physical force or violence against the peace officer or another;
or
Using any other means which creates a substantial risk of causing bodily injury to the peace officer or another.

It is no defense to a prosecution under this section that the peace officer was attempting to make an arrest which in fact was unlawful, if he was acting under color of his official authority, and in attempting to make the arrest he was not resorting to unreasonable or excessive force giving rise to the right of self-defense. A peace officer acts "under color of his official authority" when, in the regular course of assigned duties, he is called upon to make, and does make, a judgment in good faith based upon surrounding facts and circumstances that an arrest should be made by him.

The term "peace officer" as used in this section and section 18-8-104 means a peace officer in uniform or, if out of uniform, one who has identified himself by exhibiting his credentials as such peace officer to the person whose arrest is attempted.

Resisting arrest is a class 2 misdemeanor.

18-8-104. Obstructing a peace officer, firefighter, emergency medical services provider, rescue specialist, or volunteer. (1) (a) A person commits obstructing a peace officer, firefighter, emergency medical services provider, rescue specialist, or volunteer when, by using or threatening to use violence, force, physical interference, or an obstacle, such person knowingly obstructs,

impairs, or hinders the enforcement of the penal law or the preservation of the peace by a peace officer, acting under color of his or her official authority; knowingly obstructs, impairs, or hinders the prevention, control, or abatement of fire by a firefighter, acting under color of his or her official authority; knowingly obstructs, impairs, or hinders the administration of medical treatment or emergency assistance by an emergency medical service provider or rescue specialist, acting under color of his or her official authority; or knowingly obstructs, impairs, or hinders the administration of emergency care or emergency assistance by a volunteer, acting in good faith to render such care or assistance without compensation at the place of an emergency or accident.

(b) To assure that animals used in law enforcement or fire prevention activities are protected from harm, a person commits obstructing a peace officer or firefighter when, by using or threatening to use violence, force, physical interference, or an obstacle, he or she knowingly obstructs, impairs, or hinders any such animal.

It is not a defense to a prosecution under this section that the peace officer was acting in an illegal manner, if he or she was acting under color of his or her official authority. A peace officer acts "under color of his or her official authority" if, in the regular course of assigned duties, he or she makes a judgment in good faith based on surrounding facts and circumstances that he or she must act to enforce the law or preserve the peace.

Repealed.

Obstructing a peace officer, firefighter, emergency medical service provider, rescue specialist, or volunteer is a class 2 misdemeanor.

For purposes of this section, unless the context otherwise requires:

"Emergency medical service provider" means a member of a public or private emergency medical service agency, whether that person is a volunteer or receives compensation for services rendered as such emergency medical service provider.

"Rescue specialist" means a member of a public or private rescue agency, whether that person is a volunteer or receives compensation for services rendered as such rescue specialist.

18-8-105. Accessory to crime. (1) A person is an accessory to crime if, with intent to hinder, delay, or prevent the discovery, detection, apprehension, prosecution, conviction, or punishment of another for the commission of a crime, he renders assistance to such person.

"Render assistance" means to:

Harbor or conceal the other; or

(a.5) Harbor or conceal the victim or a witness to the crime; or

Warn such person of impending discovery or apprehension; except that this does not apply to a warning given in an effort to bring such person into compliance with the law; or

Provide such person with money, transportation, weapon, disguise, or other thing to be used in avoiding discovery or apprehension; or

By force, intimidation, or deception, obstruct anyone in the performance of any act which might aid in the discovery, detection, apprehension, prosecution, conviction, or punishment of such person; or

Conceal, destroy, or alter any physical or testimonial evidence that might aid in the discovery, detection, apprehension, prosecution, conviction, or punishment of such person.

Being an accessory to crime is a class 4 felony if the offender knows that the person being assisted has committed, or has been convicted of, or is charged by pending information, indictment, or complaint with a crime, and if that crime is designated by this code as a class 1 or class 2 felony.

Being an accessory to crime is a class 5 felony if the offender knows that the person being assisted is suspected of or wanted for a crime, and if that crime is designated by this code as a class 1 or class 2 felony.

Being an accessory to crime is a class 5 felony if the offender knows that the person being assisted has committed, or has been convicted of, or is charged by pending information, indictment, or complaint with a crime, or is suspected of or wanted for a crime, and if that crime is designated by this code as a felony other than a class 1 or class 2 felony; except that being an accessory to a class 6 felony is a class 6 felony.

Being an accessory to crime is a class 1 petty offense if the offender knows that the person being assisted has committed, or has been convicted of, or is charged by pending information, indictment, or complaint with a crime, or is suspected of or wanted for a crime, and if that crime is designated by this code as a misdemeanor of any class.

18-8-106. Refusal to permit inspections. (1) A person commits a class 1 petty offense if, knowing that a public servant is legally authorized to inspect property:

He refuses to produce or make available the property for inspection at a reasonable hour; or

If the property is available for inspection he refuses to permit the inspection at a reasonable hour.

For purposes of this section, "property" means any real or personal property, including books, records, and documents which are owned, possessed, or otherwise subject to the control of the defendant. A "legally authorized inspection" means any lawful search, sampling, testing, or other examination of property, in connection with the regulation of a business or occupation, that is authorized by statute or lawful regulatory provision.

18-8-107. Refusing to aid a peace officer. A person, eighteen years of age or older, commits a class 1 petty offense when, upon command by a person known to him to be a peace officer, he unreasonably refuses or fails to aid the peace officer in effecting or securing an arrest or preventing the commission by another of any offense.

18-8-108. Compounding. (1) A person commits compounding if he accepts or agrees to accept any pecuniary benefit as consideration for:

Refraining from seeking prosecution of an offender; or

Refraining from reporting to law enforcement authorities the commission or suspected commission of any crime or information relating to a crime.

It is an affirmative defense to prosecution under this section that the benefit received by

the defendant did not exceed an amount which the defendant reasonably believed to be due as restitution or indemnification for harm caused by the crime.

Compounding is a class 3 misdemeanor.

18-8-109. Concealing death. Any person who conceals the death of another person and thereby prevents a determination of the cause or circumstances of death commits a class 1 misdemeanor. For the purpose of this section only, "another person" includes a fetus born dead.

18-8-110. False report of explosives, weapons, or harmful substances. Any person who reports to any other person that a bomb or other explosive, any chemical or biological agent, any poison or weapon, or any harmful radioactive substance has been placed in any public or private place or vehicle designed for the transportation of persons or property, knowing that the report is false, commits a class 6 felony.

18-8-111. False reporting to authorities. (1) A person commits false reporting to authorities, if:

He or she knowingly:

Causes by any means, including but not limited to activation, a false alarm of fire or other emergency or a false emergency exit alarm to sound or to be transmitted to or within an official or volunteer fire department, ambulance service, law enforcement agency, or any other government agency which deals with emergencies involving danger to life or property; or

Prevents by any means, including but not limited to deactivation, a legitimate fire alarm, emergency exit alarm, or other emergency alarm from sounding or from being transmitted to or within an official or volunteer fire department, ambulance service, law enforcement agency, or any other government agency that deals with emergencies involving danger to life or property; or

He makes a report or knowingly causes the transmission of a report to law enforcement authorities of a crime or other incident within their official concern when he knows that it did not occur; or

He or she makes a report or knowingly causes the transmission of a report to law enforcement authorities pretending to furnish information relating to an offense or other incident within their official concern when he or she knows that he or she has no such information or knows that the information is false; or

He or she knowingly provides false identifying information to law enforcement authorities.

False reporting to authorities is a class 3 misdemeanor; except that if it is committed in violation of paragraph (a) of subsection (1) of this section and committed during the commission of another criminal offense, it is a class 2 misdemeanor.

For purposes of this section, "identifying information" means a person's name, address, birth date, social security number, or driver's license or Colorado identification number.

18-8-112. Impersonating a peace officer. (1) A person who falsely pretends to be a peace officer and performs an act in that pretended capacity commits impersonating a peace officer.
(2) Impersonating a peace officer is a class 6 felony.


18-8-113. Impersonating a public servant. (1) A person commits impersonating a public servant if he falsely pretends to be a public servant other than a peace officer and performs any act in that pretended capacity.
It is no defense to a prosecution under this section that the office the actor pretended to hold did not in fact exist.
Impersonating a public servant is a class 3 misdemeanor.


18-8-114. Abuse of public records. (1) A person commits a class 1 misdemeanor if:
The person knowingly makes a false entry in or falsely alters any public record; or
Knowing the person lacks the authority to do so, the person knowingly destroys, mutilates, conceals, removes, or impairs the availability of any public record; or
Knowing the person lacks the authority to retain the record, the person refuses to deliver up a public record in the person's possession upon proper request of any person lawfully entitled to receive such record; or
Knowing the person has not been authorized by the custodian of the public record to do so, the person knowingly alters any public record.
(2) As used in this section, the term "public record" includes all official books, papers, or records created, received, or used by or in any governmental office or agency.


18-8-115. Duty to report a crime - liability for disclosure. It is the duty of every corporation or person who has reasonable grounds to believe that a crime has been committed to report promptly the suspected crime to law enforcement authorities. Notwithstanding any other provision of the law to the contrary, a corporation or person may disclose information concerning a suspected crime to other persons or corporations for the purpose of giving notice of the possibility that other such criminal conduct may be attempted which may affect the persons or corporations notified. When acting in good faith, such corporation or person shall be immune from any civil liability for such reporting or disclosure. This duty shall exist notwithstanding any other provision of the law to the contrary; except that this section shall not require disclosure of any communication privileged by law.


18-8-116. Disarming a peace officer. (1) A person commits disarming a peace officer if he or she knowingly, without justification and without consent, removes the firearm or self-defense electronic control device, direct-contact stun device, or other similar device of a peace officer who is acting under color of his or her official authority.

Disarming a peace officer is a class 5 felony.
The term "peace officer" as used in this section means a peace officer in uniform or, if out of uniform, one who has identified himself by exhibiting his credentials as such peace officer to the person.


18-8-117. Unlawful sale of publicly provided services or appointments - definitions. (1) A person commits an unlawful sale of public services if the person does any of the following with respect to a government service or an appointment to receive a government service and if a government entity makes the service or appointment publicly available without charge:
The person reserves or obtains the service or appointment, and the person sells the service or appointment;
The person reserves or obtains, with the intent to sell, the service or appointment;
The person reserves or obtains the service or appointment, and the person appends the service or appointment to another good or service the person offers for sale; or
The person falsely represents to the potential customer that the person has obtained or secured the service or appointment, and the person attempts to sell the service or appointment.

This section does not apply when the person:
Has consent from the government entity to sell the specific service or appointment obtained or reserved; or
Is obtaining and selling or offering to sell only information.
Unlawful sale of public services is a class 1 misdemeanor, as defined in section 18-1.3-501.
As used in this section, "government entity" means the state of Colorado, a political subdivision of Colorado, or an agency of either the state of Colorado or a political subdivision of Colorado.

PART 2

ESCAPE AND OFFENSES RELATING TO CUSTODY


18-8-201. Aiding escape. (1) Any person who knowingly aids, abets, or assists another person to escape or attempt to escape from custody or confinement commits the offense of aiding escape.
"Escape" is deemed to be a continuing activity commencing with the conception of the design to escape and continuing until the escapee is returned to custody or the attempt to escape is thwarted or abandoned.
"Assist" includes anyactivity characterized as "rendering assistance" in section 18-8-105.
Aiding escape is a class 2 felony if the person aided was in custody or confinement as a result of conviction of a class 1 or class 2 felony.

Aiding escape is a class 3 felony if the person aided was in custody or confinement and charged with or held for any felony or convicted of any felony other than a class 1 or class 2 felony.
Aiding escape is a class 1 misdemeanor if the person aided was in custody or confinement and charged with, held for, or convicted of a misdemeanor

164

or a petty offense.

18-8-201.1. Aiding escape from an institution for the care and treatment of persons with mental illness. Any person who knowingly aids the escape of a person who is an inmate of an institution for the care and treatment of persons with mental illness and who knows the person aided is confined in such institution pursuant to a commitment under article 8 of title 16, C.R.S., commits the offense of aiding escape from an institution for the care and treatment of persons with mental illness, which is a class 5 felony.

18-8-202. Inducing prisoners to absent selves. Any person who invites, entices, solicits, or induces any prisoner in custody or confinement to absent himself from his work or who substantially delays or hinders a prisoner in his work commits a class 1 petty offense.

18-8-203. Introducing contraband in the first degree. (1) A person commits introducing contraband in the first degree if he or she knowingly and unlawfully:
Introduces or attempts to introduce a dangerous instrument, malt, vinous, or spirituous liquor, as defined in section 12-47-103, C.R.S., fermented malt beverage, as defined in section 12- 46-103, C.R.S., controlled substance, as defined in section 18-18-102 (5), or marijuana or marijuana concentrate, as defined in section 27-80-203 (15) and (16), C.R.S., into a detention facility or at any location where an inmate is or is likely to be located, while the inmate is in the custody and under the jurisdiction of a political subdivision of the state of Colorado or the department of corrections, but not on parole; or
Being a person confined in a detention facility, makes any dangerous instrument, controlled substance, marijuana or marijuana concentrate, or alcohol.
Introducing contraband in the first degree is a class 4 felony.
"Detention facility" means any building, structure, enclosure, vehicle, institution, work site, or place, whether permanent or temporary, fixed or mobile, where persons are or may be lawfully held in custody or confinement under the jurisdiction of the department of corrections or under the authority of the United States, the state of Colorado, or any political subdivision of the state of Colorado.
"Dangerous instrument" as used in this section and in section 18-8-204.1, means a firearm, explosive device or substance (including ammunition), knife or sharpened instrument, poison, acid, bludgeon, or projective device, or any other device, instrument, material, or substance which is readily capable of causing or inducing fear of death or bodily injury, the use of which is not specifically authorized.

18-8-204. Introducing contraband in the second degree. (1)     A person commits introducing contraband in the second degree if he or she knowingly and unlawfully:
Introduces or attempts to introduce contraband into a detention facility; or
Being a person confined in a detention facility, makes any contraband, as defined in subsection (2) of this section.
(1.5) A person confined in a detention facility commits introducing contraband in the second degree if he or she knowingly and unlawfully introduces or attempts to introduce contraband into a detention facility or at any location where an inmate is likely to be located, while such inmate is in the custody and under the jurisdiction of a political subdivision of the state of Colorado or the department of corrections, but not on parole.
"Contraband" as used in this section means any of the following, but does not include any article or thing referred to in section 18-8-203:
Any key, key pattern, key replica, or lock pick;
Any tool or instrument that could be used to cut fence or wire, dig, pry, or file;

value;

Any money or coin of United States or foreign currency or any written instrument of

Any uncancelled postage stamp or implement of the United States postal service;

Any counterfeit or forged identification card;

Any combustible material other than safety matches;

Any drug, other than a controlled substance as defined in section 18-18-102 (5), in quantities other than those authorized by a physician;

Any mask, wig, disguise, or other means of altering normal physical appearance which could hinder ready identification;

Any drug paraphernalia as defined in section 18-18-426;

Any material which is "obscene" as defined in section 18-7-101;

Any chain, rope, or ladder;

Any article or thing that poses or may pose a threat to the security of the detention facility as determined by the administrative head of the detention facility if reasonable notice is given that such article or thing is contraband;

For purposes of a facility of the department of corrections or any private contract prison, any cigarettes or tobacco products, as defined in section 39-28.5-101 (5), C.R.S.; or

Any portable electronic communication device, including but not limited to cellular telephones; cloned cellular telephones as defined in section 18-9-309; public, private, or family-style radios; pagers; personal digital assistants; any other device capable of transmitting or intercepting cellular or radio signals between providers and users of telecommunication and data services; and portable computers; except those devices authorized by the executive director of the department of corrections or his or her designee.

Introducing contraband in the second degree is a class 6 felony.


18-8-204.1. Possession of contraband in the first degree. (1) A person being confined in a detention facility commits the crime of possession of contraband in the first degree if he knowingly

obtains or has in his possession contraband as listed in section 18-8-203 (1) (a) or alcohol; except that this subsection (1) shall not apply to contraband specified in section 18-18-405.

Possession of contraband in the first degree, other than a dangerous instrument, is a class 6 felony.

Possession of contraband in the first degree involving a dangerous instrument is a class 4 felony.


18-8-204.2. Possession of contraband in the second degree. (1) A person being confined in a detention facility commits the crime of possession of contraband in the second degree if he knowingly obtains or has in his possession contraband as defined in section 18-8-204 (2) unless possession is authorized by rule or regulation promulgated by the administrative head of the detention facility.

Possession of contraband in the second degree is a class 1 misdemeanor.


18-8-205. Aiding escape from civil process. Any person who aids, abets, or assists the escape of a person in legal custody under civil process commits a class 1 petty offense.


18-8-206. Assault during escape. (1) Any person confined in any lawful place of confinement within the state who, while escaping or attempting to escape, commits an assault with intent to commit bodily injury upon the person of another with a deadly weapon, or by any means of force likely to produce serious bodily injury, commits:

A class 1 felony, if the person has been convicted of a class 1 felony; or

A class 2 felony, if the person has been convicted of a felony other than a class 1 felony; or

A class 3 felony, if the person was in custody or confinement and held for or charged with but not convicted of a felony; or

A class 3 felony, if the person was in custody or confinement and charged with, held for, or convicted of a misdemeanor or a petty offense.


18-8-207. Holding hostages. Any person in lawful custody or confinement within the state who, while escaping or attempting to escape, holds as hostage any person or by force or threat of force holds any person against his will commits a class 2 felony.


18-8-208. Escapes. (1) A person commits a class 2 felony if, while being in custody or confinement following conviction of a class 1 or class 2 felony, he knowingly escapes from said custody or confinement.

A person commits a class 3 felony if, while being in custody or confinement following conviction of a felony other than a class 1 or class 2 felony, he knowingly escapes from said custody

or confinement.

A person commits a class 4 felony if, while being in custody or confinement and held for or charged with but not convicted of a felony, he knowingly escapes from said custody or confinement.

A person commits a class 3 misdemeanor if, while being in custody or confinement following conviction of a misdemeanor or petty offense or a violation of a municipal ordinance, he or she knowingly escapes from said place of custody or confinement.

(4.5) A person commits a class 3 misdemeanor if he or she has been committed to the division of youth corrections in the department of human services for a delinquent act, is over eighteen years of age, and escapes from a staff secure facility as defined in section 19-1-103 (101.5), C.R.S., other than a state-operated locked facility.

A person commits a class 1 petty offense if, while being in custody or confinement and held for or charged with but not convicted of a misdemeanor or petty offense or violation of a municipal ordinance, he or she knowingly escapes from said custody or confinement.

A person who knowingly escapes confinement while being confined pursuant to a commitment under article 8 of title 16, C.R.S.:

Commits a class 1 misdemeanor if the person had been charged with a misdemeanor at the proceeding in which the person was committed;

Commits a class 1 misdemeanor if the person had been charged with a felony at the proceeding in which the person was committed, if in the escape the person does not travel from the state of Colorado;

Commits a class 5 felony if the person had been charged with a felony at the proceeding in which the person was committed, if in the escape the person travels outside of the state of Colorado.

In a prosecution for an offense under subsection (6) of this section, it shall be a defense for any person who, while being confined pursuant to a commitment under article 8 of title 16, C.R.S., escapes and who voluntarily returns to the place of confinement.

A person commits a class 5 felony if he knowingly escapes while in custody or confinement pursuant to the provisions of article 19 of title 16, C.R.S. The minimum sentences provided by sections 18-1.3-401, 18-1.3-501, and 18-1.3-503, respectively, for violation of the provisions of this section shall be mandatory, and the court shall not grant probation or a suspended sentence, in whole or in part; except that the court may grant a suspended sentence if the court is sentencing a person to the youthful offender system pursuant to section 18-1.3-407. The provisions of this subsection (9) do not apply to subsection (4.5) of this section.

Repealed.

A person who is placed in a community corrections program for purposes of obtaining residential treatment as a condition of probation pursuant to section 18-1.3-204 (2.2) or 18-1.3-301

(b) is not in custody or confinement for purposes of this section.


18-8-208.1. Attempt to escape. (1) Except as otherwise provided in subsection (1.5) of this section, if a person, while in custody or confinement following conviction of a felony, knowingly

attempts to escape from said custody or confinement, he or she commits a class 4 felony. The sentence imposed pursuant to this subsection (1) shall run consecutively with any sentences being served by the offender.

(1.5) If a person, while in custody or confinement following conviction of a felony and either serving a direct sentence to a community corrections program pursuant to section 18-1.3-301, or having been placed in an intensive supervision parole program pursuant to section 17-27.5-101, C.R.S., knowingly attempts to escape from his or her custody or confinement, he or she commits a class 5 felony. The sentence imposed pursuant to this subsection (1.5) may run concurrently or consecutively with any sentence being served by the offender.

If a person, while in custody or confinement and held for or charged with but not convicted of a felony, knowingly attempts to escape from said custody or confinement, he commits a class 5 felony. If the person is convicted of the felony or other crime for which he was originally in custody or confinement, the sentence imposed pursuant to this subsection (2) shall run consecutively with any sentences being served by the offender.

If a person, while in custody or confinement following conviction of a misdemeanor or petty offense, knowingly attempts to escape from said custody or confinement, he is guilty of a misdemeanor and, upon conviction thereof, shall be punished by imprisonment in the county jail for not less than two months nor more than four months. The sentence imposed pursuant to this subsection (3) shall run consecutively with any sentences being served by the offender.

If a person, while in custody or confinement and held for or charged with but not convicted of a misdemeanor or petty offense, knowingly attempts to escape from said custody or confinement, he is guilty of a petty offense and, upon conviction thereof, shall be punished by imprisonment in the county jail for not less than two months nor more than four months. If the person is convicted of the misdemeanor or petty offense for which he was originally in custody or confinement, the sentence imposed pursuant to this subsection (4) shall run consecutively with any sentences being served by the offender.

The sentences imposed by subsections (1), (1.5), and (2) of this section and the minimum sentences imposed by subsections (3) and (4) of this section shall be mandatory, and the court shall not grant probation or a suspended sentence, in whole or in part; except that the court may grant a suspended sentence if the court is sentencing a person to the youthful offender system pursuant to section 18-1.3-407.

A person who participates in a work release program, a home detention program, as defined in section 18-1.3-106 (1.1), a furlough, an intensive supervision program, or any other similar authorized supervised or unsupervised absence from a detention facility, as defined in section 18-8-203 (3), and who is required to report back to the detention facility at a specified time shall be deemed to be in custody.

Any person held in a staff secure facility, as defined in section 19-1-103 (101.5), C.R.S., shall be deemed to be in custody or confinement for purposes of this section.


18-8-209. Concurrent and consecutive sentences. (1) Except as otherwise provided in subsection (2) of this section, any sentence imposed following conviction of an offense under sections 18-8-201 to 18-8-208 or section 18-8-211 shall run consecutively and not concurrentlywith

any sentence which the offender was serving at the time of the conduct prohibited by those sections.

(2) If an offender was serving a direct sentence to a communitycorrections program pursuant to section 18-1.3-301 or was in an intensive supervision parole program pursuant to section 17-27.5- 101, C.R.S., at the time he or she committed an offense specified in section 18-8-201 or 18-8-208, the sentence imposed following a conviction of said offense may run concurrently with any sentence the offender was serving at the time he or she committed said offense.


18-8-210. Persons in custody or confinement for unclassified offenses. For the purpose of determining the grade and classification of an offense under sections 18-8-201, 18-8-206, and 18- 8-208, a person in custody or confinement for an offense which is unclassified or was not classified under this code at the time the custody or confinement began is deemed to have been in custody or confinement for a class 2 misdemeanor if such custody or confinement was for a misdemeanor offense or a class 5 felony if such custody or confinement was for a felony offense.


18-8-210.1. Persons in custody or confinement - juvenile offenders. For the purposes of this part 2, any reference to custody, confinement, charged with, held for, convicted of, a felony, misdemeanor, or petty offense shall be deemed to include a juvenile who is detained or committed for the commission of an act which would constitute such a felony, misdemeanor, or petty offense if committed by an adult or who is the subject of a petition filed pursuant to article 2 of title 19, C.R.S., alleging the commission of such a delinquent act or a juvenile who has been adjudicated a juvenile delinquent as provided for in article 2 of title 19, C.R.S., for an act which would constitute a felony, misdemeanor, or petty offense if committed by an adult.


18-8-210.2. Persons in custody or confinement. For the purposes of this part 2, any reference to custody, confinement, charged with, held for, or convicted of, a felony, misdemeanor, or petty offense shall be deemed to include any felony, misdemeanor, or petty offense under the laws of this state and any felony, misdemeanor, or petty offense having similar elements under the laws of another state, the United States, or any territory subject to the jurisdiction of the United States.

18-8-211. Riots in detention facilities. (1) A person confined in any detention facility within the state commits active participation in a riot when he, with two or more other persons, actively participates in violent conduct that creates grave danger of, or does cause, damage to property or injury to persons and substantially obstructs the performance of institutional functions, or commands, induces, entreats, or otherwise attempts to persuade others to engage in such conduct.

Active participation in a riot by any person while confined in anydetention facilitywithin the state:

Is a class 3 felony if the participant employs in the course of such participation a deadly weapon, as defined in section 18-1-901 (3) (e), destructive device, as defined in section 18-9-101 (1), or any article used or fashioned in a manner to cause a person to reasonably believe that the

article is a deadly weapon, or if the participant, in the course of such participation, represents verbally or otherwise that he or she is armed with a deadly weapon; or

Is a felony if the participant does not employ any such weapon or device in the course of such participation, and, upon conviction thereof, the punishment shall be imprisonment in a detention facility for not less than two years nor more than ten years.

A person confined in any detention facility in this state commits a class 5 felony if, during a riot or when a riot is impending, he intentionally disobeys an order of a detention officer to move, disperse, or refrain from specified activities in the immediate vicinity of the riot or impending riot.

"Detention facility", as used in this section, means any building, structure, enclosure, vehicle, institution, or place, whether permanent or temporary, fixed or mobile, where persons are or may be lawfully held in custody or confinement under the authority of the state of Colorado or any political subdivision of the state of Colorado.

18-8-212. Violation of bail bond conditions. (1) A person who is released on bail bond of whatever kind, and either before, during, or after release is accused by complaint, information, indictment, or the filing of a delinquency petition of any felony arising from the conduct for which he was arrested, commits a class 6 felony if he knowingly fails to appear for trial or other proceedings in the case in which the bail bond was filed or if he knowingly violates the conditions of the bail bond.

A person who is released on bail bond of whatever kind, and either before, during, or after release is accused by complaint, information, indictment, or the filing of a delinquency petition of any misdemeanor arising from the conduct for which he was arrested, commits a class 3 misdemeanor if he knowingly fails to appear for trial or other proceedings in the case in which the bail bond was filed or if he knowingly violates the conditions of the bail bond.

The court shall sentence any person who is convicted of a misdemeanor offense in violation of section 18-6-803.5, or a felony offense in violation of section 18-8-704, 18-8-705, 18-8- 706, or 18-8-707, involving a victim or witness in the underlying offense while on bond in the underlying case to imprisonment of not less than one year for violation of subsection (1) of this section and not less than six months for violation of subsection (2) of this section. The court shall order the sentence to be served consecutively with any sentence for the offense on which the person is on bail if the underlying sentence is a sentence to incarceration.

(3.5) A person who is on bond for a sex offense as defined in section 18-1.3-1003 who is convicted under this section for a bond violation shall not be eligible for probation or a suspended sentence and shall be sentenced to imprisonment of not less than one year. Any such sentence shall be served consecutively with any sentence for the offense on which the person is on bail.

A criminal action charged pursuant to this section may be tried either in the county where the offense is committed or in the county in which the court that issued the bond is located, if such court is within this state.

18-8-213. Unauthorized residency by an adult offender from another state. (1) A

person commits the crime of unauthorized residency by an adult offender if the person, in order to stay in the state, is required to have the permission of the compact administrator or a designated deputy of the compact administrator of the interstate compact for adult offender supervision established pursuant to part 28 of article 60 of title 24, C.R.S., and the person:

Is not a resident of this state, has not been accepted by the compact administrator of the interstate compact for adult offender supervision established pursuant to part 28 of article 60 of title 24, C.R.S., and is found residing in this state; or

Is a resident of this state, has not been accepted by the compact administrator of the interstate compact for adult offender supervision established pursuant to part 28 of article 60 of title 24, C.R.S., and is found residing in this state more than ninety days after his or her transfer from the receiving state.

(2) Unauthorized residency by a parolee or probationer is a class 5 felony.

PART 3

BRIBERY AND CORRUPT INFLUENCES

18-8-301. Definitions. The definitions contained in section 18-8-101 are applicable to this part 3, unless the context otherwise requires, and, in addition to those definitions:

"Benefit" means any gain or advantage to the beneficiary, including any gain or advantage to a third person pursuant to the desire or consent of the beneficiary.

"Party officer" means a person who holds any position or office in a political party, whether by election, appointment, or otherwise.

"Pecuniary benefit" is benefit in the form of money, property, commercial interests, or anything else the primary significance of which is economic gain.

"Public servant", as used in sections 18-8-302 to 18-8-308, includes persons who presently occupy the position of a public servant as defined in section 18-8-101 (3) or have been elected, appointed, or designated to become a public servant although not yet occupying that position.

18-8-302. Bribery. (1) A person commits the crime of bribery, if:

He offers, confers, or agrees to confer any pecuniary benefit upon a public servant with the intent to influence the public servant's vote, opinion, judgment, exercise of discretion, or other action in his official capacity; or

While a public servant, he solicits, accepts, or agrees to accept any pecuniary benefit upon an agreement or understanding that his vote, opinion, judgment, exercise of discretion, or other action as a public servant will thereby be influenced.

It is no defense to a prosecution under this section that the person sought to be influenced was not qualified to act in the desired way, whether because he had not yet assumed office, lacked jurisdiction, or for any other reason.

Bribery is a class 3 felony.


if he:

18-8-303. Compensation for past official behavior. (1) A person commits a class 6 felony,

Solicits, accepts, or agrees to accept any pecuniary benefit as compensation for having,
as a public servant, given a decision, opinion, recommendation, or vote favorable to another or for having otherwise exercised a discretion in his favor, whether or not he has in so doing violated his duty; or
Offers, confers, or agrees to confer compensation, acceptance of which is prohibited by this section.

18-8-304. Soliciting unlawful compensation. A public servant commits a class 2 misdemeanor if he requests a pecuniary benefit for the performance of an official action knowing that he was required to perform that action without compensation or at a level of compensation lower than that requested.

18-8-305. Trading in public office. (1) A person commits trading in public office if:
He offers, confers, or agrees to confer any pecuniary benefit upon a public servant or party officer upon an agreement or understanding that he or a particular person will or may be appointed to a public office or designated or nominated as a candidate for public office; or
While a public servant or party officer, he solicits, accepts, or agrees to accept any pecuniary benefit from another upon an agreement or understanding that a particular person will or may be appointed to a public office or designated or nominated as a candidate for public office.

It shall be an affirmative defense that the pecuniary benefit was a customary contribution to political campaign funds solicited and received by lawfully constituted political parties.
Trading in public office is a class 1 misdemeanor.

18-8-306. Attempt to influence a public servant. Any person who attempts to influence any public servant by means of deceit or by threat of violence or economic reprisal against any person or property, with the intent thereby to alter or affect the public servant's decision, vote, opinion, or action concerning any matter which is to be considered or performed by him or the agency or body of which he is a member, commits a class 4 felony.

18-8-307. Designation of supplier prohibited. (1) No public servant shall require or direct a bidder or contractor to deal with a particular person in procuring any goods or service required in submitting a bid to or fulfilling a contract with any government.
Any provision in invitations to bid or any contract documents prohibited by this section are against public policy and void.

It shall be an affirmative defense that the defendant was a public servant acting within the scope of his authority exercising the right to reject any material, subcontractor, service, bond, or contract tendered by a bidder or contractor because it does not meet bona fide specifications or requirements relating to quality, availability, form, experience, or financial responsibility.
Any public servant who violates the provisions of subsection (1) of this section commits a class 6 felony.

18-8-308. Failing to disclose a conflict of interest. (1) A public servant commits failing to disclose a conflict of interest if he exercises any substantial discretionary function in connection with a government contract, purchase, payment, or other pecuniary transaction without having given seventy-two hours' actual advance written notice to the secretary of state and to the governing body of the government which employs the public servant of the existence of a known potential conflicting interest of the public servant in the transaction with reference to which he is about to act in his official capacity.
A "potential conflicting interest" exists when the public servant is a director, president, general manager, or similar executive officer or owns or controls directly or indirectly a substantial interest in any nongovernmental entity participating in the transaction.
Failing to disclose a conflict of interest is a class 2 misdemeanor.

PART 4

ABUSE OF PUBLIC OFFICE

18-8-401. Definitions. The definitions contained in sections 18-8-101 and 18-8-301 are applicable to this part 4, unless a different meaning is plainly required.

18-8-402. Misuse of official information. (1) Any public servant, in contemplation of official action by himself or by a governmental unit with which he is associated or in reliance on information to which he has access in his official capacity and which has not been made public, commits misuse of official information if he:
Acquires a pecuniary interest in any property, transaction, or enterprise which may be affected by such information or official action; or
Speculates or wagers on the basis of such information or official action; or
Aids, advises, or encourages another to do any of the foregoing with intent to confer on any person a special pecuniary benefit.
Misuse of official information is a class 6 felony.

18-8-403. Official oppression. (1) A public servant, while acting or purporting to act in an official capacity or taking advantage of such actual or purported capacity, commits official

oppression if, with actual knowledge that his conduct is illegal, he:
Subjects another to arrest, detention, search, seizure, mistreatment, dispossession, assessment, or lien; or
Has legal authority and jurisdiction of any person legally restrained of his liberty and denies the person restrained the reasonable opportunity to consult in private with a licensed attorney- at-law, if there is no danger of imminent escape and the person in custody expresses a desire to consult with such attorney.

Official oppression is a class 2 misdemeanor.

18-8-404. First degree official misconduct. (1) A public servant commits first degree official misconduct if, with intent to obtain a benefit for the public servant or another or maliciously to cause harm to another, he or she knowingly:
Commits an act relating to his office but constituting an unauthorized exercise of his official function; or
Refrains from performing a duty imposed upon him by law; or
Violates any statute or lawfully adopted rule or regulation relating to his office.
First degree official misconduct is a class 2 misdemeanor.

18-8-405. Second degree official misconduct. (1) A public servant commits second degree official misconduct if he knowingly, arbitrarily, and capriciously:
Refrains from performing a duty imposed upon him by law; or
Violates any statute or lawfully adopted rule or regulation relating to his office.
(2) Second degree official misconduct is a class 1 petty offense.

18-8-406. Issuing a false certificate. A person commits a class 6 felony, if, being a public servant authorized by law to make and issue official certificates or other official written instruments, he makes and issues such an instrument containing a statement which he knows to be false.

18-8-407. Embezzlement of public property. (1) Every public servant who lawfully or unlawfully comes into possession of any public moneys or public property of whatever description, being the property of the state or of any political subdivision of the state, and who knowingly converts any of such public moneys or property to his own use or to any use other than the public use authorized by law is guilty of embezzlement of public property. Every person convicted under the provisions of this section shall be forever thereafter ineligible and disqualified from being a member of the general assembly of this state or from holding any office of trust or profit in this state.
(2) Embezzlement of public property is a class 5 felony.

18-8-408. Designation of insurer prohibited. (1) No public servant shall, directly or

indirectly, require or direct a bidder on any public building or construction contract which is about to be or has been competitively bid to obtain from a particular insurer, agent, or broker any surety bond or contract of insurance required in such bid or contract or required by any law, ordinance, or regulation.
Any such public servant who violates any of the provisions of subsection (1) of this section commits a class 1 petty offense.
Any provisions in invitations to bid or in any contract documents prohibited by this section are declared void as against the public policy of this state. Nothing in this section shall be construed to prevent any such public servant acting on behalf of the government from exercising the right to approve or reject a surety bond or contract of insurance as to its form or sufficiency or the lack of financial capability of an insurer selected by a bidder.
This section shall apply only to contracts entered into on or after July 1, 1977.

18-8-409. Violation of rules and regulations of judicial nominating commissions not subject to criminal prosecution. A person who violates a rule or regulation promulgated by any judicial nominating commission shall not be subject to criminal prosecution.

PART 5

PERJURY AND RELATED OFFENSES

18-8-501. Definitions. The definitions in sections 18-8-101 and 18-8-301 are applicable to this part 5, and, in addition to those definitions:
"Materially false statement" means any false statement, regardless of its admissibility under the rules of evidence, which could have affected the course or outcome of an official proceeding, or the action or decision of a public servant, or the performance of a governmental function.
(a) "Oath" includes an affirmation and every other mode authorized by law of attesting to the truth of that which is stated. For the purposes of this section, written statements shall also be treated as if made under oath if:
The statement was made on or pursuant to a form bearing notice, authorized by law, to the effect that false statements made therein are punishable; or
The statement recites that it was made under oath, the declarant was aware of such recitation at the time he made the statement and intended that the statement should be represented as a sworn statement, and the statement was in fact so represented by its delivery or utterance with the signed jurat of an officer authorized to administer oaths appended thereto; or
The statement is made, used, or offered with the intent that it be accepted as compliance with a statute, rule, or regulation which requires a statement under oath or other like form of attestation to the truth of the matter contained in the statement; or
The statement meets the requirements for an unsworn declaration under the "Uniform

Unsworn Foreign Declarations Act", part 3 of article 55 of title 12, C.R.S.
(b) An oath is "required or authorized by law" when the use of the oath is specifically provided for by statute, court rule, or appropriate regulatory provision.
"Official proceeding" means a proceeding heard before any legislative, judicial, administrative, or other government agency, or official authorized to hear evidence under oath, including any magistrate, hearing examiner, commissioner, notary, or other person taking testimony or depositions in any such proceedings.

18-8-502. Perjury in the first degree. (1) A person commits perjury in the first degree if in any official proceeding he knowingly makes a materially false statement, which he does not believe to be true, under an oath required or authorized by law.
Knowledge of the materiality of the statement is not an element of this crime, and the defendant's mistaken belief that his statement was not material

171

is not a defense, although it may be considered by the court in imposing sentence.
Perjury in the first degree is a class 4 felony.

18-8-503. Perjury in the second degree. (1) A person commits perjury in the second degree if, other than in an official proceeding, with an intent to mislead a public servant in the performance of his duty, he makes a materially false statement, which he does not believe to be true, under an oath required or authorized by law.
(2) Perjury in the second degree is a class 1 misdemeanor.

18-8-503.5. Perjury on a motor vehicle registration application. (Repealed)

18-8-504. False swearing. (1) A person commits false swearing if he knowingly makes a materially false statement, other than those prohibited by sections 18-8-502 and 18-8-503, which he does not believe to be true, under an oath required or authorized by law.
(2) False swearing is a class 1 petty offense.

18-8-505. Perjury or false swearing - inconsistent statements. (1) Where a person charged with perjury or false swearing has made inconsistent material statements under oath, both having been made within the period of the statute of limitations, the prosecution may proceed by setting forth the inconsistent statements in a single count alleging in the alternative that one or the other was false and not believed by the defendant. In such case it shall not be necessary for the prosecution to prove which statement was false but only that one or the other statement was false and not believed by the defendant to be true.
The highest offense of which a person may be convicted in such an instance shall be determined by hypothetically assuming each statement to be false. If the assumption establishes

perjury of different degrees, the person may be convicted of the lesser degree at most. If perjury or false swearing is established by the making of the two statements, the person may be convicted of false swearing at the most.

18-8-506. Perjury and false swearing - proof. In any prosecution for perjury or false swearing, except a prosecution based upon inconsistent statements pursuant to section 18-8-505, falsity of a statement may not be established solely through contradiction by the uncorroborated testimony of a single witness.

18-8-507. Perjury and false swearing - previous criminal action. No prosecution may be brought under section 18-8-502, 18-8-503, or 18-8-504 if the substance of the defendant's false statement is the entry of a plea of not guilty in a previous criminal action in which he or she was accused of an offense.

18-8-508. Perjury - retraction. No person shall be convicted of perjury in the first degree if he retracted his false statement in the course of the same proceeding in which it was made. Statements made in separate hearings at separate stages of the same trial or administrative proceeding shall be deemed to have been made in the course of the same proceeding. Retraction is an affirmative defense.

18-8-509. Perjury and false swearing - irregularities no defense. (1) It is no defense to a prosecution under sections 18-8-502 to 18-8-504 that:
The defendant was not competent, for reasons other than mental disability or immaturity, to make the false statement alleged;
The statement was inadmissible under the law of evidence;
The oath was administered or taken in an irregular manner; or
The person administering the oath lacked authority to do so, if the taking of the oath was required by law.

PART 6

OFFENSES RELATING TO JUDICIAL AND OTHER PROCEEDINGS

18-8-601. Definitions. The definitions contained in sections 18-8-101, 18-8-301, and 18-8-501 are applicable to the provisions of this part 6, and, in addition to those definitions:
"Juror" means any person who is a member of any jury or grand jury impaneled by any court of this state or by any public servant authorized by law to impanel a jury. The term "juror" also

includes any person who has been drawn or summoned to attend as a prospective juror.
"Testimony" includes oral or written statements, documents, or any other evidence that may be offered by or through a witness in an official proceeding.

18-8-602. Bribing a witness. (Repealed)

18-8-603. Bribe-receiving by a witness. (1) A witness or a person believing he is to be called as a witness in any official proceeding commits a class 4 felony if he intentionally solicits, accepts, or agrees to accept any benefit upon an agreement or understanding that:
He will testify falsely or unlawfully withhold testimony; or
He will attempt to avoid legal process summoning him to testify; or
He will attempt to absent himself from an official proceeding to which he has been legally summoned.

18-8-604. Intimidating a witness. (Repealed)


18-8-605. Tampering with a witness. (Repealed)


18-8-606. Bribing a juror. (1) A person commits bribing a juror if he offers, confers, or agrees to confer any benefit upon a juror with intent to influence the juror's vote, opinion, decision, or other action as a juror.

(2) Bribing a juror is a class 4 felony.


18-8-607. Bribe-receiving by a juror. (1) A person commits bribe-receiving by a juror if he intentionally solicits, accepts, or agrees to accept any benefit upon an agreement or understanding that his vote, opinion, decision, or other action as a juror will thereby be influenced.
(2) Bribe-receiving by a juror is a class 4 felony.


18-8-608. Intimidating a juror. (1) A person commits intimidating a juror if he intentionally attempts by use of a threat of harm or injury to any person or property to influence a juror's vote, opinion, decision, or other action as a juror.
(2) Intimidating a juror is a class 4 felony.


18-8-609. Jury-tampering. (1) A person commits jury-tampering if, with intent to influence

a juror's vote, opinion, decision, or other action in a case, he attempts directly or indirectly to communicate with a juror other than as a part of the proceedings in the trial of the case.
(1.5) A person commits jury-tampering if he knowingly participates in the fraudulent processing or selection of jurors or prospective jurors.
Jury-tampering is a class 5 felony; except that jury-tampering in any class 1 felony trial is a class 4 felony.


18-8-610. Tampering with physical evidence. (1) A person commits tampering with physical evidence if, believing that an official proceeding is pending or about to be instituted and acting without legal right or authority, he:
Destroys, mutilates, conceals, removes, or alters physical evidence with intent to impair its verity or availability in the pending or prospective official proceeding; or
Knowingly makes, presents, or offers any false or altered physical evidence with intent that it be introduced in the pending or prospective official proceeding.
"Physical evidence", as used in this section, includes any article, object, document, record, or other thing of physical substance; except that "physical evidence" does not include a human body, part of a human body, or human remains subject to a violation of section 18-8-610.5.
Tampering with physical evidence is a class 6 felony.


18-8-610.5. Tampering with a deceased human body. (1) A person commits tampering with a deceased human body if, believing that an official proceeding is pending, in progress, or about to be instituted and acting without legal right or authority, the person willfully destroys, mutilates, conceals, removes, or alters a human body, part of a human body, or human remains with intent to impair its or their appearance or availability in the official proceedings.
(2) Tampering with a deceased human body is a class 3 felony.


18-8-611. Simulating legal process. (1) A person commits simulating legal process if he knowingly delivers or causes to be delivered to another a request for the payment of money on behalf of any creditor including himself which in form and substance simulates any legal process issued by any court of this state.
(2) Simulating legal process is a class 3 misdemeanor.


18-8-612. Failure to obey a juror summons. (1) A juror commits failure to obey a juror summons if he receives a summons to serve as a trial or grand juror as provided in section 13-71- 110, C.R.S., and knowingly fails to obey the summons without justifiable excuse.
(2) Failure to obey a juror summons is a class 3 misdemeanor.


18-8-613. Willful misrepresentation of material fact on juror questionnaire. (1) A juror

commits willful misrepresentation of a material fact if he willfully makes a misrepresentation of a material fact when he provides information on the juror questionnaire as provided in section 13-71- 115, C.R.S.
(2) Willful misrepresentation of a material fact on a juror questionnaire is a class 3 misdemeanor.


18-8-614. Willful harassment of juror by employer. (1) An employer commits willful harassment of a juror if he willfully deprives an employed juror of employment or any incidents or benefits thereof or willfully harasses, threatens, or coerces an employee because the employee receives a juror summons, responds thereto, performs any obligation or election of juror service as a trial or grand juror, or exercises any right under the "Colorado Uniform Jury Selection and Service Act", article 71 of title 13, C.R.S.
Willful harassment of a juror is a class 2 misdemeanor.

18-8-615. Retaliation against a judge. (1) (a) An individual commits retaliation against a judge if the individual makes a credible threat, as defined in section 18-3-602 (2) (b), or commits an act of harassment, as defined in section 18-9-111 (1), or an act of harm or injury upon a person or propertyas retaliation or retribution against a judge, which action is directed against or committed upon:

A judge who has served or is serving in a legal matter assigned to the judge involving the individual or a person on whose behalf the individual is acting;
A member of the judge's family;
A person in close relationship to the judge; or
A person residing in the same household with the judge.
(b) An individual commits retaliation against a judge by means of a credible threat as described in paragraph (a) of this subsection (1) if the individual knowingly makes the credible threat:
Directly to the judge; or
To another person:
If the individual intended that the communication would be relayed to the judge; or
If the other person is required by statute or ethical rule to report the communication to the judge.
Retaliation against a judge is a class 4 felony.
As used in this section, unless the context otherwise requires, "judge" means any justice of the supreme court, judge of the court of appeals, district court judge, juvenile court judge, probate court judge, water court judge, county court judge, district court magistrate, county court magistrate, municipal judge, administrative law judge, or unemployment insurance hearing officer.

18-8-616. Retaliation against a prosecutor. (1) (a) An individual commits retaliation

against a prosecutor if the individual makes a credible threat, as defined in section 18-3-602 (2) (b), or commits an act of harm or injury upon a person or property as retaliation or retribution against a prosecutor, which action is directed against or committed upon:
An elected district attorney;
A prosecutor who has served or is serving in a legal matter assigned to the prosecutor involving the individual or a person on whose behalf the individual is acting;
A member of the prosecutor's family;
A person in close relationship to the prosecutor; or
A person residing in the same household with the prosecutor.
An individual commits retaliation against a prosecutor by means of a credible threat as described in paragraph (a) of this subsection (1) if the individual knowingly makes the credible threat:
Directly to the prosecutor; or
To another person:
If the individual intended that the communication would be relayed to the prosecutor;
or
If the other person is required by statute or ethical rule to report the communication to
the prosecutor or to the court.
Retaliation against a prosecutor is a class 4 felony.
As used in this section, unless the context otherwise requires, "prosecutor" means the attorney general, deputy attorney general, assistant attorney general, district attorney, deputy district attorney, assistant district attorney, appointed special prosecutor, city attorney, United States attorney, deputy United States attorney, assistant United States attorney, or special assistant United States attorney.

PART 7

VICTIMS AND WITNESSES PROTECTION

18-8-701. Short title. This part 7 shall be known and may be cited as the "Colorado Victim and Witness Protection Act of 1984".

18-8-702. Definitions. The definitions contained in sections 18-8-301, 18-8-501, and 18-8- 601 are applicable to the provisions of this part 7, and in addition to those definitions:
"Victim" means any natural person against whom any crime has been perpetrated or attempted, as crime is defined under the laws of this state or of the United States.
"Witness" means any natural person:
Having knowledge of the existence or nonexistence of facts relating to any crime;
Whose declaration under oath is received or has been received as evidence for any purpose;
Who has reported any crime to any peace officer, correctional officer, or judicial officer;

Who has been served with a subpoena issued under the authority of any court in this state, of any other state, or of the United States; or
Who would be believed by any reasonable person to be an individual described in paragraph (a), (b), (c), or (d) of this subsection (2).

18-8-703. Bribing a witness or victim. (1) A person commits bribing a witness or victim if he or she offers, confers, or agrees to confer any benefit upon a witness, or a victim, or a person he or she believes is to be called to testify as a witness or victim in any official proceeding, or upon a member of the witness' family, a member of the victim's family, a person in close relationship to the witness or victim, or a person residing in the same household as the witness or victim with intent to:
Influence the witness or victim to testify falsely or unlawfully withhold any testimony;
or
Induce the witness or victim to avoid legal process summoning him to testify; or
Induce the witness or victim to absent himself or herself from an official proceeding.

Bribing a witness or victim is a class 4 felony.


18-8-704. Intimidating a witness or victim. (1) A person commits intimidating a witness or victim if, by use of a threat, act of harassment as defined in section 18-9-111, or act of harm or injury to any person or property directed to or committed upon a witness or a victim to any crime, a person he or she believes has been or is to be called or who would have been called to testify as a witness or a victim, a member of the witness' family, a member of the victim's family, a person in close relationship to the witness or victim, a person residing in the same household with the witness or victim, or any person who has reported a crime or who may be called to testify as a witness to or victim of any crime, he or she intentionally attempts to or does:
Influence the witness or victim to testify falsely or unlawfully withhold any testimony;
or
Induce the witness or victim to avoid legal process summoning him to testify; or
Induce the witness or victim to absent himself or herself from an official proceeding; or
Inflict such harm or injury prior to such testimony or expected testimony.
Intimidating a witness or victim is a class 4 felony.


18-8-705. Aggravated intimidation of a witness or victim. (1) A person who commits intimidating a witness or victim commits aggravated intimidation of a witness or victim if, during the act of intimidating, he:
Is armed with a deadly weapon with the intent, if resisted, to kill, maim, or wound the person being intimidated or any other person; or
Knowingly wounds the person being intimidated or any other person with a deadly weapon, or by the use of force, threats, or intimidation with a deadly weapon knowingly puts the person being intimidated or any other person in reasonable fear of death or bodily injury.

For purposes of subsection (1) of this section, possession of any article used or fashioned in a manner to lead any person reasonably to believe it to be a deadly weapon, or any verbal or other representation by the person that he is so armed, is prima facie evidence that the person is armed with a deadly weapon.
Aggravated intimidation of a witness or victim is a class 3 felony.


18-8-706. Retaliation against a witness or victim. (1) An individual commits retaliation against a witness or victim if such person uses a threat, act of harassment as defined in section 18-9- 111, or act of harm or injury upon any person or property, which action is directed to or committed upon a witness or a victim to any crime, an individual whom the person believes has been or would have been called to testify as a witness or victim, a member of the witness' family, a member of the victim's family, an individual in close relationship to the witness or victim, an individual residing in the same household with the witness or victim, as retaliation or retribution against such witness or victim.
(2) Retaliation against a witness or victim is a class 3 felony.


18-8-706.5. Retaliation against a juror. (1) An individual commits retaliation against a juror if such individual uses a threat, act of harassment as defined in section 18-9-111, or act of harm or injury upon any person or property, which action is directed to or committed upon a juror who has served for a criminal or civil trial involving the individual or a person or persons on whose behalf the individual is acting, a member of the juror's family, an individual in close relationship to the juror, or an individual residing in the same household with the juror, as retaliation or retribution against such juror.
Retaliation against a juror is a class 3 felony.


18-8-707. Tampering with a witness or victim. (1) A person commits tampering with a witness or victim if he intentionally attempts without bribery or threats to induce a witness or victim or a person he believes is to be called to testify as a witness or victim in any official proceeding or who may be called to testify as a witness to or victim of any crime to:
Testify falsely or unlawfully withhold any testimony; or
Absent himself from any official proceeding to which he has been legally summoned;
or
Avoid legal process summoning him to testify.
Tampering with a witness or victim is a class 4 felony.


18-8-708. Suit for damages by victim of intimidation or retaliation. (1) The following persons are eligible for relief pursuant to this section:
Any person who testifies as a witness or victim in any official proceeding;
Any person who may be called to testify as a witness to or victim of any crime;

Any person who is a member of the witness' or victim's family;
Any person who is in a close relationship to the witness or victim;
Any person who is residing in the same household with the witness or victim.

Any person who is eligible pursuant to subsection (1) of this section who suffers any physical injury or property damage as the result of the commission of intimidating a witness or victim pursuant to section 18-8-704, aggravated intimidation of a witness or victim pursuant to section 18-8-705, or retaliation against a witness or victim pursuant to section 18-8-706 shall, in a civil proceeding to recover for such injury or property damage, be eligible for the award of treble damages and attorney fees.
Nothing in this section shall limit the amount of recovery which a person specified in subsection (1) of this section may receive in a civil proceeding or in any other proceeding.

PART 8

OFFENSES RELATING TO USE OF FORCE BY PEACE OFFICERS

18-8-801. Definitions. As used in this part 8, unless the context otherwise requires:
"Materially false statement" has the meaning set out in section 18-8-501 (1).
"Peace officer" has the meaning set out in section 16-2.5-101, C.R.S.

18-8-802. Duty to report use of force by peace officers. (1) (a) A peace officer who, in pursuance of such officer's law enforcement duties, witnesses another peace officer, in pursuance of such other peace officer's law enforcement duties in carrying out an arrest of any person, placing any person under detention, taking any person into custody, booking any person, or in the process of crowd control or riot control, use physical force which exceeds the degree of physical force permitted pursuant to section 18-1-707 must report such use of force to such officer's immediate supervisor. At a minimum, the report required by this section shall include the date, time, and place of the occurrence, the identity, if known, and description of the participants, and a description of the events and the force used. A copy of an arrest report or other similar report required as a part of a peace officer's duties can be substituted for the report required by this section, so long as it includes such information. The report shall be made in writing within ten days of the occurrence of the use of such force.
Any peace officer who fails to report such use of force in the manner prescribed in this subsection (1) commits a class 1 misdemeanor.
Any peace officer who knowingly makes a materially false statement, which the officer does not believe to be true, in any report made pursuant to subsection (1) of this section commits false reporting to authorities pursuant to section 18-8-111 (1) (c).
No report filed pursuant to subsection (1) of this section shall be used as evidence against

a peace officer in a criminal proceeding unless there is other credible evidence which corroborates such report or in a civil action over a claim of executive or statutory privilege without a valid court order.

18-8-803. Use of excessive force. (1) Subject to the provisions of section 18-1-707, a peace officer who uses excessive force in pursuance of such officer's law enforcement duties shall be subject to the criminal laws of this state to the same degree as any other citizen, including the provisions of part 1 of article 3 of this title concerning homicide and related offenses and the provisions of part 2 of said article 3 concerning assaults.
(2) As used in this section, "excessive force" means physical force which exceeds the degree of physical force permitted pursuant to section 18-1-707. The use of excessive force shall be presumed when a peace officer continues to apply physical force in excess of the force permitted by section 18-1-707 to a person who has been rendered incapable of resisting arrest.

18-8-804. Approved policy or guidelines. Each public entity which employs any peace officer shall adopt policies or guidelines concerning the use of force by peace officers which shall be complied with by peace officers in carrying out the duties of such officers within the jurisdiction of the public entity.

### ARTICLE 9 Offenses Against Public Peace, Order, and Decency

PART 1

PUBLIC PEACE AND ORDER

18-9-101. Definitions. As used in this part 1, unless the context otherwise requires:
"Destructive device" means any material, substance, or mechanism capable of being used, either by itself or in combination with any other substance, material, or mechanism, to cause sudden and violent injury, damage, destruction, or death.
(1.4) "Funeral" means the ceremonies, rituals, and memorial services held in connection with the burial, cremation, or memorial of a deceased person, including the assembly and dispersal of the mourners.
(1.5) "Funeral site" means a church, synagogue, mosque, funeral home, mortuary, cemetery, gravesite, mausoleum, or other place where a funeral is conducted.

"Riot" means a public disturbance involving an assemblage of three or more persons which by tumultuous and violent conduct creates grave danger of damage or injury to property or persons or substantially obstructs the performance of any governmental function.

18-9-102. Inciting riot. (1) A person commits inciting riot if he:
Incites or urges a group of five or more persons to engage in a current or impending riot;
or
Gives commands, instructions, or signals to a group of five or more persons in furtherance of a riot.
A person may be convicted under section 18-2-101, 18-2-201, or 18-2-301 of attempt, conspiracy, or solicitation to incite a riot only if he engages in the prohibited conduct with respect to a current or impending riot.
Inciting riot is a class 1 misdemeanor, but, if injury to a person or damage to property results therefrom, it is a class 5 felony.

18-9-103. Arming rioters. (1) A person commits arming rioters if he:
Knowingly supplies a deadly weapon or destructive device for use in a riot; or

Teaches another to prepare or use a deadly weapon or destructive device with intent that any such thing be used in a riot.
(2) Arming rioters is a class 4 felony.

18-9-104. Engaging in a riot. (1) A person commits an offense if he or she engages in a riot. The offense is a class 4 felony if in the course of rioting the actor employs a deadly weapon, a destructive device, or any article used or fashioned in a manner to cause a person to reasonably believe that the article is a deadly weapon, or if in the course of rioting the actor represents verbally or otherwise that he or she is armed with a deadly weapon; otherwise, it is a class 2 misdemeanor.

(2) The provisions of section 18-9-102 (2) are applicable to attempt, solicitation, and conspiracy to commit an offense under this section.

18-9-105. Disobedience of public safety orders under riot conditions. A person commits a class 3 misdemeanor if, during a riot or when one is impending, he knowingly disobeys a reasonable public safety order to move, disperse, or refrain from specified activities in the immediate vicinity of the riot. A public safety order is an order designed to prevent or control disorder or promote the safety of persons or property issued by an authorized member of the police, fire, military, or other forces concerned with the riot. No such order shall apply to a news reporter or other person observing or recording the events on behalf of the public press or other news media, unless he is physically obstructing efforts by such forces to cope with the riot or impending riot. Inapplicability of the order is an affirmative defense.

18-9-106. Disorderly conduct. (1) A person commits disorderly conduct if he or she intentionally, knowingly, or recklessly:
Makes a coarse and obviously offensive utterance, gesture, or display in a public place and the utterance, gesture, or display tends to incite an immediate breach of the peace; or
(Deleted by amendment, L. 2000, p. 708, § 39, effective July 1, 2000.)
Makes unreasonable noise in a public place or near a private residence that he has no right to occupy; or
Fights with another in a public place except in an amateur or professional contest of athletic skill; or
Not being a peace officer, discharges a firearm in a public place except when engaged in lawful target practice or hunting or the ritual discharge of blank ammunition cartridges as an attendee at a funeral for a deceased person who was a veteran of the armed forces of the United States; or
Not being a peace officer, displays a deadly weapon, displays any article used or fashioned in a manner to cause a person to reasonably believe that the article is a deadly weapon, or represents verbally or otherwise that he or she is armed with a deadly weapon in a public place in a manner calculated to alarm.
Repealed.
(a) An offense under paragraph (a) or (c) of subsection (1) of this section is a class 1 petty offense; except that, if the offense is committed with intent to disrupt, impair, or interfere with a funeral, or with intent to cause severe emotional distress to a person attending a funeral, it is a class 2 misdemeanor.
An offense under paragraph (d) of subsection (1) of this section is a class 3 misdemeanor.
An offense under paragraph (e) or (f) of subsection (1) of this section is a class 2 misdemeanor.

18-9-107. Obstructing highway or other passageway. (1) An individual or corporation commits an offense if without legal privilege such individual or corporation intentionally, knowingly, or recklessly:
Obstructs a highway, street, sidewalk, railway, waterway, building entrance, elevator, aisle, stairway, or hallway to which the public or a substantial group of the public has access or any other place used for the passage of persons, vehicles, or conveyances, whether the obstruction arises from his acts alone or from his acts and the acts of others; or
Disobeys a reasonable request or order to move issued by a person the individual or corporation knows to be a peace officer, a firefighter, or a person with authority to control the use of the premises, to prevent obstruction of a highway or passageway or to maintain public safety by dispersing those gathered in dangerous proximity to a fire, riot, or other hazard.
For purposes of this section, "obstruct" means to render impassable or to render passage unreasonably inconvenient or hazardous.
An offense under this section is a class 3 misdemeanor; except that knowingly

obstructing the entrance into, or exit from, a funeral or funeral site, or knowingly obstructing a highway or other passageway where a funeral procession is taking place is a class 2 misdemeanor.

18-9-108. Disrupting lawful assembly. (1) A person commits disrupting lawful assembly if, intending to prevent or disrupt any lawful meeting, procession, or gathering, he significantly obstructs or interferes with the meeting, procession, or gathering by physical action, verbal utterance, or any other means.
Disrupting lawful assembly is a class 3 misdemeanor; except that, if the actor knows the meeting, procession, or gathering is a funeral, it is a class 2 misdemeanor.

18-9-108.5. Residential picketing - legislative declaration. (1) (a) The general assembly hereby finds that:
The protection and preservation of the home is a compelling state interest;
Residents of Colorado are entitled to enjoy a feeling of well-being, tranquility, and privacy in their homes and dwellings;
The practice of targeted residential picketing causes emotional disturbances and distress to the occupants and has the potential to incite breaches of the peace; and
The practice of targeted residential picketing does not seek to disseminate a message to the general public but, instead, seeks to harass and intrude on the privacy of the targeted resident.
(b) The general assembly further finds that ample alternative means of communication are available to those who would choose to engage in picketing outside a person's residence.
As used in this section, unless the context otherwise requires:
"Residence" means any single-family or multi-family dwelling unit that is not being used as a targeted occupant's sole place of business or as a place of public meeting.
"Targeted picketing" means picketing, with or without signs, that is specifically directed toward a residence, or one or more occupants of the residence, and that takes place on that portion of a sidewalk or street in front of the residence, in front of an adjoining residence, or on either side of the residence.
(a) It shall be unlawful for a person to engage in targeted picketing except when the person is engaging in picketing while marching, without stopping in front or on either side of a residence, over a route that proceeds a distance that extends beyond three adjacent structures to one side of the targeted residence along the one-way length and three adjacent structures to the other side of the targeted residence along the one-way length or three hundred feet to one side of the targeted residence along the one-way length and three hundred feet to the other side of the targeted residence along the one-way length, whichever distance is shorter.
(b) (I) It shall be unlawful for a person while engaged in targeted picketing to hold, carry, or otherwise display on his or her person a sign or placard

177

while he or she is on a street or sidewalk in a residential area if the person does not comply with the following restrictions:

All signs or placards shall be no greater in size than six square feet;

Each person may carry, hold, or otherwise display no more than one sign or placard.

(II) The restrictions specified pursuant to subparagraph (I) of this paragraph (b) shall not

apply to a person while engaged in targeted picketing carrying a sign or placard temporarily while transporting the sign or placard from the person's residence or business to a vehicle.

Vehicles or trailers used in targeted picketing shall not park within three residences or three hundred feet of a residence that is the subject of targeted picketing. There is a presumption that a vehicle or trailer is used in targeted picketing when signage is affixed to the vehicle containing content related to the targeted picketing.

It shall not be a violation of subsection (3) of this section unless a person has previously been ordered by a peace officer or other law enforcement official to move, disperse, or take other appropriate action to comply with this section and the person has failed to promptly comply with the warning. The warning issued by the peace officer or other law enforcement official shall indicate the required distances the person engaging in picketing must march or other conditions necessary to comply with this section. In order to ensure that an appropriate warning has been given, the local law enforcement agency shall maintain a written record indicating the name of each warned individual, the address or addresses of the targeted residence or residences, and the date and time of the warning.

A person who violates subsection (3) of this section commits an unclassified misdemeanor. The court may impose a fine of no more than five thousand dollars.

The provisions of this section shall not prohibit a local government from adopting more restrictive provisions concerning targeted picketing or carrying in a residential area more than one sign of a certain size.

18-9-109. Interference with staff, faculty, or students of educational institutions. (1) No person shall, on or near the premises or facilities of any educational institution, willfully deny to students, school officials, employees, and invitees:

Lawful freedom of movement on the premises;

Lawful use of the property or facilities of the institution;

The right of lawful ingress and egress to the institution's physical facilities.

No person shall, on the premises of any educational institution or at or in any building or other facility being used by any educational institution, willfully impede the staff or faculty of such institution in the lawful performance of their duties or willfully impede a student of the institution in the lawful pursuit of his educational activities through the use of restraint, abduction, coercion, or intimidation or when force and violence are present or threatened.

No person shall willfully refuse or fail to leave the property of or any building or other facility used by any educational institution upon being requested to do so by the chief administrative officer, his designee charged with maintaining order on the school premises and in its facilities, or a dean of such educational institution, if such person is committing, threatens to commit, or incites others to commit any act which would disrupt, impair, interfere with, or obstruct the lawful missions, processes, procedures, or functions of the institution.

It shall be an affirmative defense that the defendant was exercising his right to lawful assembly and peaceful and orderly petition for the redress of grievances, including any labor dispute between an educational institution and its employees, any contractor or subcontractor, or any employee thereof.

Any person who violates any of the provisions of this section, except subsection (6) of

this section, commits a class 3 misdemeanor.

(a) A person shall not knowingly make or convey to another person a credible threat to cause death or to cause bodily injury with a deadly weapon against:

A person the actor knows or believes to be a student, school official, or employee of an educational institution; or

An invitee who is on the premises of an educational institution.

For purposes of this subsection (6), "credible threat" means a threat or physical action that would cause a reasonable person to be in fear of bodily injury with a deadly weapon or death.

A person who violates this subsection (6) commits a class 1 misdemeanor.

18-9-110. Public buildings - trespass, interference - penalty. (1) No person shall so conduct himself at or in any public building owned, operated, or controlled by the state, or any of the political subdivisions of the state or at any building owned, operated, or controlled by the federal government as to willfully deny to any public official, public employee, or invitee on such premises the lawful rights of such official, employee, or invitee to enter, to use the facilities of, or to leave any such public building.

No person shall, at or in any such public building, willfully impede any public official or employee in the lawful performance of duties or activities through the use of restraint, abduction, coercion, or intimidation or by force and violence or threat thereof.

No person shall willfully refuse or fail to leave any such public building upon being requested to do so by the chief administrative officer or his designee charged with maintaining order in such public building, if the person has committed, is committing, threatens to commit, or incites others to commit any act which did, or would if completed, disrupt, impair, interfere with, or obstruct the lawful missions, processes, procedures, or functions being carried on in the public building.

No person shall, at any meeting or session conducted by any judicial, legislative, or administrative body or official at or in any public building, willfully impede, disrupt, or hinder the normal proceedings of such meeting or session by any act of intrusion into the chamber or other areas designated for the use of the body or official conducting the meeting or session or by any act designed to intimidate, coerce, or hinder any member of such body or official engaged in the performance of duties at such meeting or session.

No person shall, by any act of intrusion into the chamber or other areas designated for the use of any executive body or official at or in any public building, willfully impede, disrupt, or hinder the normal proceedings of such body or official.

No person, alone or in concert with another, shall picket inside any building in which the chambers, galleries, or offices of the general assembly, or either house thereof, are located, or in which the legislative office of any member of the general assembly is located, or in which a legislative hearing or meeting is being or is to be conducted.

The term "public building", as used in this section, includes any premises being temporarily used by a public officer or employee in the discharge of his official duties.

Any person who violates any of the provisions of this section commits a class 2 misdemeanor.

**18-9-111. Harassment - Kiana Arellano's law.** (1) A person commits harassment if, with intent to harass, annoy, or alarm another person, he or she:

Strikes, shoves, kicks, or otherwise touches a person or subjects him to physical contact;

or

In a public place directs obscene language or makes an obscene gesture to or at another

person; or

Follows a person in or about a public place; or

Repealed.

Directly or indirectly initiates communication with a person or directs language toward another person, anonymously or otherwise, by telephone, telephone network, data network, text message, instant message, computer, computer network, computer system, or other interactive electronic medium in a manner intended to harass or threaten bodily injury or property damage, or makes any comment, request, suggestion, or proposal by telephone, computer, computer network, computer system, or other interactive electronic medium that is obscene; or

Makes a telephone call or causes a telephone to ring repeatedly, whether or not a conversation ensues, with no purpose of legitimate conversation; or

Makes repeated communications at inconvenient hours that invade the privacy of another and interfere in the use and enjoyment of another's home or private residence or other private property; or

Repeatedly insults, taunts, challenges, or makes communications in offensively coarse language to, another in a manner likely to provoke a violent or disorderly response.

(1.5) As used in this section, unless the context otherwise requires, "obscene" means a patently offensive description of ultimate sexual acts or solicitation to commit ultimate sexual acts, whether or not said ultimate sexual acts are normal or perverted, actual or simulated, including masturbation, cunnilingus, fellatio, anilingus, or excretory functions.

(2) Harassment pursuant to subsection (1) of this section is a class 3 misdemeanor; except that harassment is a class 1 misdemeanor if the offender commits harassment pursuant to subsection

of this section with the intent to intimidate or harass another person because of that person's actual or perceived race, color, religion, ancestry, or national origin.

Any act prohibited by paragraph (e) of subsection (1) of this section may be deemed to have occurred or to have been committed at the place at which the telephone call, electronic mail, or other electronic communication was either made or received.

to (6) Repealed.

Paragraph (e) of subsection (1) of this section shall be known and may be cited as "Kiana Arellano's Law".

This section is not intended to infringe upon any right guaranteed to any person by the first amendment to the United States constitution or to prevent the expression of any religious, political, or philosophical views.

**18-9-112. Loitering - definition - legislative declaration.** (1) The word "loiter" means to be dilatory, to stand idly around, to linger, delay, or wander about, or to remain, abide, or tarry in a

public place.

A person commits a class 1 petty offense if he or she, with intent to interfere with or disrupt the school program or with intent to interfere with or endanger schoolchildren, loiters in a school building or on school grounds or within one hundred feet of school grounds when persons under the age of eighteen are present in the building or on the grounds, not having any reason or relationship involving custody of, or responsibility for, a pupil or any other specific, legitimate reason for being there, and having been asked to leave by a school administrator or his representative or by a peace officer.

It shall be an affirmative defense that the defendant's acts were lawful and he was exercising his rights of lawful assembly as a part of peaceful and orderly petition for the redress of grievances, either in the course of labor disputes or otherwise.

The general assembly hereby finds and declares that the state has a special interest in the protection of children and, particularly, in protecting children who attend schools because required to do so by the "School Attendance Law of 1963", article 33 of title 22, C.R.S., and the prohibition of loitering in subsection (2) of this section is enacted in furtherance of these interests.

**18-9-113. Desecration of venerated objects.** (1) (a) A person commits a class 3 misdemeanor if he knowingly desecrates any public monument or structure or desecrates in a public place any other object of veneration by the public.

Except as otherwise provided in section 24-80-1305, C.R.S., with respect to the disturbance of an unmarked human burial, a person commits a class 1 misdemeanor if he knowingly desecrates any place of worship or burial of human remains.

The court shall order that any person convicted pursuant to this section make restitution to cover the costs of repairing any damages to any monument, headstone, memorial marker, structure, or place that are the result of such person's conduct. Such restitution shall be paid to any person or entity that repairs such damages, as required in article 18.5 of title 16, C.R.S.

The term "desecrate" means defacing, damaging, polluting, or otherwise physically mistreating in a way that the defendant knows will outrage the sensibilities of persons likely to observe or discover his action or its result.

**18-9-114. Hindering transportation.** A person commits a class 2 misdemeanor if he knowingly and without lawful authority forcibly stops and hinders the operation of any vehicle used in providing transportation services of any kind to the public or to any person, association, or corporation.

**18-9-115. Endangering public transportation and utility transmission.** (1) A person commits endangering public transportation if such person:

Tampers with a facility of public transportation with intent to cause any damage, malfunction, nonfunction, theft, or unauthorized removal of material which would result in the creation of a substantial risk of death or serious bodily injury to anyone; or

Stops or boards a public conveyance with the intent of committing a crime thereon; or

On a public conveyance, knowingly threatens any operator, crew member, attendant, or passenger:

With death or imminent serious bodily injury; or

With a deadly weapon or with words or actions intended to induce belief that such person is armed with a deadly weapon; or

On a public conveyance:

Knowingly or recklessly causes bodily injury to another person; or

With criminal negligence causes bodily injury to another person by means of a deadly weapon.

(1.5) A person commits endangering utility transmission if such person tampers with a facility of utility transmission with intent to cause any damage, malfunction, nonfunction, theft, or unauthorized removal of material which would:

Interrupt performance of utility transmission; or

Result in a creation of a substantial risk of death or serious bodily injury to anyone.

"Public" means offered or available to the public generally, either free or upon payment of a fare, fee, rate, or tariff, or offered or made available by a school or school district to pupils regularly enrolled in public or nonpublic schools in preschool through grade twelve.

"Public conveyance" includes a passenger or freight train, airplane, bus, truck, car, boat, tramway, gondola, lift, elevator, escalator, or other device intended, designed, adapted, and used for the public carriage of persons or property.

"Facility of public transportation" includes a public conveyance and any area, structure, or device which is designed, adapted, and used to support, guide, control, permit, or facilitate the movement, starting, stopping, takeoff, landing, or servicing of a public conveyance or the loading or unloading of passengers, freight, or goods.

(4.5) "Facility of utility transmission" includes any area, structure, or device that is designed, adopted, or used to support, guide, control, permit, or facilitate transmission of:

Electrical energy in excess of thirty thousand volts; or

Water, liquid fuel, or gaseous fuel by pipeline.

Endangering public transportation or endangering utility transmission is a class 3 felony.


18-9-115.5. Violation of a restraining order related to public conveyances. Any violation of an order of court obtained pursuant to rule 65 of the Colorado rules of civil procedure, which order has specifically restrained a person from traveling in or on a particular public conveyance, shall be a class 3 misdemeanor.


18-9-116. Throwing missiles at vehicles - harassment of bicyclists. (1) Any person who knowingly projects any missile at or against any vehicle or equipment designed for the transportation of persons or property, other than a bicycle, commits a class 1 petty offense.

Any person who knowingly projects any missile at or against a bicyclist commits a class 2 misdemeanor.

As used in this section, "missile" means any object or substance.


18-9-116.5. Vehicular eluding. (1) Any person who, while operating a motor vehicle, knowingly eludes or attempts to elude a peace officer also operating a motor vehicle, and who knows or reasonably should know that he or she is being pursued by said peace officer, and who operates his or her vehicle in a reckless manner, commits vehicular eluding.

(2) (a) Vehicular eluding is a class 5 felony; except that vehicular eluding that results in bodily injury to another person is a class 4 felony and vehicular eluding that results in death to another person is a class 3 felony.

(b) Notwithstanding section 18-1.3-401, the minimum sentence within the presumptive range for a violation of this section shall be increased as follows:

For a class 5 felony, the minimum fine shall be two thousand dollars;

For a class 4 felony, the minimum fine shall be four thousand dollars; and

For a class 3 felony, the minimum fine shall be six thousand dollars.


18-9-117. Unlawful conduct on public property. (1) It is unlawful for any person to enter or remain in any public building or on any public property or to conduct himself or herself in or on the same in violation of any order, rule, or regulation concerning any matter prescribed in this subsection (1), limiting or prohibiting the use or activities or conduct in such public building or on such public property, issued by any officer or agency having the power of control, management, or supervision of the building or property. In addition to any authority granted by any other law, each such officer or agency may adopt such orders, rules, or regulations as are reasonably necessary for the administration, protection, and maintenance of such public buildings and property, specifically, orders, rules, and regulations upon the following matters:

Preservation of property, vegetation, wildlife, signs, markers, statues, buildings and grounds, and other structures, and any object of scientific, historical, or scenic interest;

Restriction or limitation of the use of such public buildings or property as to time, manner, or permitted activities;

Prohibition of activities or conduct within public buildings or on public property which may be reasonably expected to substantially interfere with the use and enjoyment of such places by others or which may constitute a general nuisance or which may interfere with, impair, or disrupt a funeral or funeral procession;

Necessary sanitation, health, and safety measures, consistent with section 25-13-113, C.R.S.;

Camping and picnicking, public meetings and assemblages, and other individual or group usages, including the place, time, and manner in which such activities may be permitted;

Use of all vehicles as to place, time, and manner of use;

Control and limitation of fires, including but not limited to the prohibition, restriction, or ban on fires or other regulation of fires to avert the start of or lessen the likelihood of wildfire, and the designation of places where fires are permitted, restricted, prohibited, or banned.

No conviction may be obtained under this section unless notice of such limitations or

prohibitions is prominently posted at all public entrances to such building or property or unless such notice is actually first given the person by the officer or agency, including any agent thereof, or by any law enforcement officer having jurisdiction or authority to enforce this section.

(a) Except as otherwise provided in paragraphs (b) and (c) of this subsection (3), any person who violates subsection (1) of this section is guilty of a class 3 misdemeanor.

Any person who violates any order, rule, or regulation adopted pursuant to paragraph (g) of subsection (1) of this section is guilty of a class 2 misdemeanor and shall be assessed a fine of not less than two hundred fifty dollars and not greater than one thousand dollars. The fine imposed by this paragraph (b) shall be mandatory and not subject to suspension. Nothing in this paragraph (b) shall be construed to limit the court's discretion in exercising other available sentencing alternatives in addition to the mandatory fine.

Any person who violates any order, rule, or regulation adopted pursuant to paragraph (c) of subsection (1) of this section concerning funerals or funeral processions is guilty of a class 2 misdemeanor.

18-9-118. Firearms, explosives, or incendiary devices in facilities of public transportation. A person commits a class 6 felony if, without legal authority, he has any loaded firearm or explosive or incendiary device, as defined in section 9-7-103, C.R.S., in his possession in, or carries, brings, or causes to be carried or brought any of such items into, any facility of public transportation, as defined in section 18-9-115 (4).

18-9-119. Failure or refusal to leave premises or property upon request of a peace officer - penalties - payment of costs. (1) The general assembly hereby finds and declares that any individual who violates any provision of this section presents a significant threat to life and property in this state; that such violations require the use of highly trained personnel and sophisticated equipment; and that any such individual, if guilty, shall be convicted of committing a crime and be required to pay for any extraordinary expenses which are a result of said violation.

Any person who barricades or refuses police entry to any premises or property through use of or threatened use of force and who knowingly refuses or fails to leave any premises or property upon being requested to do so by a peace officer who has probable cause to believe a crime is occurring and that such person constitutes a danger to himself or others commits a class 3 misdemeanor.

Any person who violates subsection (2) of this section and who, in the same criminal episode, knowingly holds another person hostage or who confines or detains such other person without his consent, without proper legal authority, and without the use of a deadly weapon commits a class 2 misdemeanor.

Any person who violates subsection (2) or (3) of this section and who, in the same criminal episode, recklesslyor knowingly causes a peace officer to believe that he possesses a deadly weapon commits a class 1 misdemeanor.

Any person who violates subsection (2) of this section and who, in the same criminal episode, knowingly holds another person hostage or who confines or detains such other person

through the possession, use, or threatened use of a deadly weapon, without the other person's consent, and without proper legal authority commits a class 4 felony.

(a) Any person convicted of a violation of this section or any person who enters a plea of guilty or nolo contendere to a violation of this section or is placed on deferred judgment and sentence for a violation of this section shall be responsible for the payment of up to a maximum of two thousand dollars for any extraordinary expenses incurred by a law enforcement agency as a result of such violation.

(b) As used in paragraph (a) of this subsection (6), "extraordinary expenses" means any cost relating to a violation of the provisions of this section, including, but not limited to, overtime wages for officers and operating expenses of any equipment utilized as a result of such violation or any damage to property occurring as a result of any violation of this section.

Any person who violates subsection (2) of this section and who, in the same criminal episode, knowingly holds another person hostage or confines or detains such other person by knowingly causing such other person to reasonably believe that he possesses a deadly weapon commits a class 5 felony. As used in this section, to "hold hostage" means to seize, imprison, entice, detain, confine, or persuade another person to remain in any premises or on any property during a violation of any provision of this section in order to seek concessions from law enforcement personnel or their representatives, or to prevent their entry to property or premises. The term includes imprisoning, enticing, detaining, confining, or persuading any child to remain in said premises or on said property in an attempt to secure said concessions.

18-9-120. Terrorist training activities - penalties - exemptions. (1) As used in this section, unless the context otherwise requires:
"Civil disorder" means any planned public disturbance involving acts of violence by an assemblage of two or more persons that causes an immediate danger of, or results in, damage or injury to property or to another person.
"Explosive or incendiary device" means:
Dynamite and all other forms of high explosives;
Any explosive bomb, grenade, missile, or similar device;
Any incendiary bomb or grenade, fire bomb, or similar device, including any device
which:
Consists of or includes a breakable receptacle containing a flammable liquid or
compound and a wick composed of any material which, when ignited, is capable of igniting such flammable liquid or compound; and
Can be carried or thrown by one person acting alone.
"Firearm" means any weapon which is designed to expel or may readily be converted to expel any projectile by the action of an explosive or the frame or receiver of any such weapon.
"Law enforcement officer" means any peace officer of this state, as described in section 16-2.5-101, C.R.S., including a member of the Colorado National Guard or any peace officer of the United States, any state, any political subdivision of a state, or the District of Columbia. "Law enforcement officer" includes, but is not limited to, any member of the National Guard, as defined

in 10 U.S.C. sec. 101 (9), any member of the organized militia of any state or territory of the United States, the Commonwealth of Puerto Rico, or the District of Columbia who is not included within the definition of National Guard, and any member of the armed forces of the United States.

Any person who teaches or demonstrates to any person the use, application, or making of any firearm, explosive or incendiary device, or technique capable of causing injury or death to any person and who knows that the same will be unlawfully used in furtherance of a civil disorder and any person who assembles with one or more other persons for the purpose of training or practicing with, or being instructed in the use of, any firearm, explosive or incendiary device, or technique capable of causing injury or death to any person with the intent to unlawfully use the same in furtherance of a civil disorder commits a class 5 felony.

(a) Nothing in this section makes unlawful any activity pursuant to section 13 of article II of the state constitution or activity of the parks and wildlife commission, any law enforcement agency, any hunting club, or any rifle club, any activity engaged in on a rifle range, pistol range, or shooting range, or any activity undertaken pursuant to any shooting school or other program or instruction, any of which activities is intended to teach the safe handling or use of firearms, archery equipment, or other weapons or techniques and is employed in connection with lawful sports or teach the use of arms for the defense of home, person, or property, or the lawful use of force as defined in part 7 of article 1 of this title, or other lawful activities.

(b) Nothing in this section shall make unlawful any act of a law enforcement officer which is performed as a part of his official duties.

18-9-121. Bias-motivated crimes. (1) The general assembly hereby finds and declares that it is the right of every person, regardless of race, color, ancestry, religion, national origin, physical or mental disability, or sexual orientation to be secure and protected from fear, intimidation, harassment, and physical harm caused by the activities of individuals and groups. The general assembly further finds that the advocacy of unlawful acts against persons or groups because of a person's or group's race, color, ancestry, religion, national origin, physical or mental disability, or sexual orientation for the purpose of inciting and provoking bodily injury or damage to property poses a threat to public order and safety and should be subject to criminal sanctions.

A person commits a bias-motivated crime if, with the intent to intimidate or harass another person because of that person's actual or perceived race, color, religion, ancestry, national origin, physical or mental disability, or sexual orientation, he or she:

Knowingly causes bodily injury to another person; or

Bywords or conduct, knowinglyplaces another person in fear of imminent lawless action directed at that person or that person's property and such words or conduct are likely to produce bodily injury to that person or damage to that person's property; or

Knowingly causes damage to or destruction of the property of another person.

Commission of a bias-motivated crime as described in paragraph (b) or (c) of subsection

of this section is a class 1 misdemeanor. Commission of a bias-motivated crime as described in paragraph (a) of subsection (2) of this section is a class 5 felony; except that commission of a bias- motivated crime as described in said paragraph (a) is a class 4 felony if the offender is  physically

aided or abetted by one or more other persons during the commission of the offense.

(3.5) (a) In determining the sentence for a first-time offender convicted of a bias-motivated crime, the court shall consider the following alternatives, which shall be in addition to and not in lieu of any other sentence received by the offender:

Sentencing the offender to pay for and complete a period of useful community service intended to benefit the public and enhance the offender's understanding of the impact of the offense upon the victim;

At the request of the victim, referring the case to a restorative justice or other suitable alternative dispute resolution program established in the judicial district pursuant to section 13-22- 313, C.R.S.

(b) In considering whether to impose the alternatives described in paragraph (a) of this subsection (3.5), the court shall consider the criminal history of the offender, the impact of the offense on the victim, the availability of the alternatives, and the nature of the offense. Nothing in this section shall be construed to require the court to impose the alternatives specified in paragraph

of this subsection (3.5).

The criminal penalty provided in this section for commission of a bias-motivated crime does not preclude the victim of such action from seeking any other remedies otherwise available under law.

For purposes of this section:

"Physical or mental disability" refers to a disability as used in the definition of the term "person with a disability" in section 18-6.5-102 (11).

"Sexual orientation" means a person's actual or perceived orientation toward heterosexuality, homosexuality, bisexuality, or transgender status.


18-9-122. Preventing passage to and from a health care facility - engaging in prohibited activities near facility. (1) The general assembly recognizes that access to health care facilities for the purpose of obtaining medical counseling and treatment is imperative for the citizens of this state; that the exercise of a person's right to protest or counsel against certain medical procedures must be balanced against another person's right to obtain medical counseling and treatment in an unobstructed manner; and that preventing the willful obstruction of a person's access to medical counseling and treatment at a health care facility is a matter of statewide concern. The general assembly therefore declares that it is appropriate to enact legislation that prohibits a person from knowingly obstructing another person's entry to or exit from a health care facility.

A person commits a class 3 misdemeanor if such person knowingly obstructs, detains, hinders, impedes, or blocks another person's entry to or exit from a health care facility.

No person shall knowingly approach another person within eight feet of such person, unless such other person consents, for the purpose of passing a leaflet or handbill to, displaying a sign to, or engaging in oral protest, education, or counseling with such other person in the public way or sidewalk area within a radius of one hundred feet from any entrance door to a health care facility. Any person who violates this subsection (3) commits a class 3 misdemeanor.

For the purposes of this section, "health care facility" means any entity that is licensed,

certified, or otherwise authorized or permitted by law to administer medical treatment in this state.

Nothing in this section shall be construed to prohibit a statutory or home rule city or county or city and county from adopting a law for the control of access to health care facilities that is no less restrictive than the provisions of this section.

In addition to, and not in lieu of, the penalties set forth in this section, a person who violates the provisions of this section shall be subject to civil liability, as provided in section 13-21- 106.7, C.R.S.


18-9-123. Bringing alcohol beverages, bottles, or cans into the major league baseball stadium. (1) (a) It shall be unlawful for any person to carry or bring into the Denver metropolitan major league baseball stadium district stadium, as defined in section 32-14-103 (5) and (10), C.R.S., and referred to in this section as the "stadium", the following:

Any alcohol beverage as defined in section 12-47-103 (2), C.R.S.; or

Any bottle or can except as provided in subsection (2) of this section.

As used in this section:

"Bottle" means a container that is made of nonporous material including but not limited to glass or ceramic, typically with a comparatively narrow neck or mouth, but excluding:

Containers made of cardboard, paper, or plastic; or

Thermos bottles.

"Can" means a container of cylindrical shape that is made of metal or metallic alloys.

Nothing in this section shall be construed to prohibit a person from bringing or carrying into the stadium a beverage, bottle, or can required in connection with the person's practice of religion, the person's medical or physical condition, or food or formula for the person's infant.

Any person who violates subsection (1) of this section commits a class 1 petty offense.

Nothing in this section shall be construed to prohibit a home rule municipality from enacting an ordinance that is at least as restrictive as or more restrictive than this section that prohibits a person from bringing any alcoholic beverage or alcoholic liquor, any bottle, or any can into the stadium.


18-9-124. Hazing - penalties - legislative declaration. (1) (a) The general assembly finds that, while some forms of initiation constitute acceptable behavior, hazing sometimes degenerates into a dangerous form of intimidation and degradation. The general assembly also recognizes that although certain criminal statutes cover the more egregious hazing activities, other activities that may not be covered by existing criminal statutes may threaten the health of students or, if not stopped early enough, may escalate into serious injury.

(b) In enacting this section, it is not the intent of the general assembly to change the penalty for any activity that is covered by any other criminal statute. It is rather the intent of the general assembly to define hazing activities not covered by any other criminal statute.

As used in this section, unless the context otherwise requires:

"Hazing" means any activity by which a person recklessly endangers the health or safety of or causes a risk of bodily injury to an individual for purposes of initiation or admission into or affiliation with any student organization; except that "hazing" does not include customary athletic events or other similar contests or competitions, or authorized training activities conducted by members of the armed forces of the state of Colorado or the United States.

"Hazing" includes but is not limited to:

Forced and prolonged physical activity;

Forced consumption of any food, beverage, medication or controlled substance, whether or not prescribed, in excess of the usual amounts for human consumption or forced consumption of any substance not generally intended for human consumption;

Prolonged deprivation of sleep, food, or drink.

It shall be unlawful for any person to engage in hazing.

Any person who violates subsection (3) of this section commits a class 3 misdemeanor.


18-9-125. Interference with a funeral. (1) A person commits interference with a funeral if he or she, knowing a funeral is being conducted:

Refuses to leave any private property within one hundred feet of the funeral site upon the request of the owner of the private property or the owner's agent; or

Refuses to leave any public property within one hundred feet of the funeral site upon the request of a public official with authority over the property or upon the request of a peace officer, and the public official or peace officer making the request has reasonable grounds to believe the person has violated a rule or regulation applicable to that property or a statute or local ordinance.

Interference with a funeral is a class 2 misdemeanor. The minimum fine prescribed by section 18-1.3-501 (1) for the offense shall be mandatory and may not be suspended in whole or in part.

Each violation of subsection (1) of this section shall constitute a separate offense for which an offender may be separately convicted and sentenced.

Any person who violates any provision of this section may also be proceeded against for violation of any other provision of law.

PART 2 CRUELTY TO ANIMALS

18-9-201. Definitions. As used in this part 2, unless the context otherwise requires:

"Abandon" means the leaving of an animal without adequate provisions for the animal's proper care by its owner, the person responsible for the animal's care or custody, or any other person having possession of such animal.

"Animal" means any living dumb creature, including a certified police working dog and a service animal as those terms are defined, respectively, in subsections (2.3) and (4.7) of this section.

(2.3) "Certified police working dog" means a dog that has current certification from a state or national agency or an association that certifies police working dogs, and that is part of a working law enforcement team.

(2.5) "Disposal" or "disposition" means adoption of an animal; return of an animal to the owner; sale of an animal under section 18-9-202.5 (4); release of an animal to a rescue group licensed pursuant to article 80 of title 35, C.R.S.; release of an animal to another pet animal facility licensed pursuant to article 80 of title 35, C.R.S.; or release of an animal to a rehabilitator licensed by the parks and wildlife division or the United States fish and wildlife service; or euthanasia.

(2.7) "Euthanasia" means to produce a humane death by techniques accepted by the American veterinary medical association.

(2.9) "Livestock" means bovine, camelids, caprine, equine, ovine, porcine, and poultry.

"Mistreatment" means every act or omission that causes or unreasonably permits the continuation of unnecessary or unjustifiable pain or suffering.

"Neglect" means failure to provide food, water, protection from the elements, or other care generally considered to be normal, usual, and accepted for an animal's health and well-being consistent with the species, breed, and type of animal.

(4.5) "Serious physical harm", as used in section 18-9-202, means any of the following:

Any physical harm that carries a substantial risk of death;

Any physical harm that causes permanent maiming or that involves some temporary, substantial maiming; or

Any physical harm that causes acute pain of a duration that results in substantial suffering.

(4.7) "Service animal" means any animal, the services of which are used to aid the performance of official duties by a fire department, fire protection district, or governmental search and rescue agency. Unless otherwise specified, "service animal" does not include a "certified police working dog" as defined in subsection (2.3) of this section.

"Sexual act with an animal" means an act between a person and an animal involving direct physical contact between the genitals of one and the mouth, anus, or genitals of the other. A sexual act with an animal may be proven without allegation or proof of penetration. Nothing in this subsection (5) shall be construed to prohibit accepted animal husbandry practices.


18-9-201.5. Scope of part 2. (1) Nothing in this part 2 shall affect accepted animal husbandry practices utilized by any person in the care of companion or livestock animals or in the extermination of undesirable pests as defined in articles 7, 10, and 43 of title 35, C.R.S.

In case of any conflict between this part 2 or section 35-43-126, C.R.S., and the wildlife statutes of the state, said wildlife statutes shall control.

Nothing in this part 2 shall affect animal care otherwise authorized by law.

Nothing in this part 2 shall affect facilities licensed under the provisions of the federal "Animal Welfare Act of 1970", 7 U.S.C. sec. 2131 et seq., as amended.


18-9-201.7. Animal cruelty prevention fund - control of fund - repeal. (Repealed)


18-9-202. Cruelty to animals - aggravated cruelty to animals - service animals. (1) (a) A person commits cruelty to animals if he or she knowingly, recklessly, or with criminal negligence overdrives, overloads, overworks, torments, deprives of necessary sustenance, unnecessarily or cruelly beats, allows to be housed in a manner that results in chronic or repeated serious physical harm, carries or confines in or upon any vehicles in a cruel or reckless manner, engages in a sexual act with an animal, or otherwise mistreats or neglects any animal, or causes or procures it to be done, or, having the charge or custody of any animal, fails to provide it with proper food, drink, or protection from the weather consistent with the species, breed, and type of animal involved, or abandons an animal.

(b) Any person who intentionally abandons a dog or cat commits the offense of cruelty to animals.

(1.5) (a) A person commits cruelty to animals if he or she recklessly or with criminal negligence tortures, needlessly mutilates, or needlessly kills an animal.

A person commits aggravated cruelty to animals if he or she knowingly tortures, needlessly mutilates, or needlessly kills an animal.

A person commits cruelty to a service animal or a certified police working dog if he or she violates the provisions of subsection (1) of this section with respect to a service animal or certified police working dog, as those terms are defined in sections 18-9-201 (2.3) and 18-9-201 (4.7), whether the service animal or certified police working dog is on duty or not on duty.

(1.6) Repealed.

(1.8) A peace officer having authority to act under this section may take possession of and impound an animal that the peace officer has probable cause to believe is a victim of a violation of subsection (1) or (1.5) of this section or is a victim of a violation of section 18-9-204 and as a result of the violation is endangered if it remains with the owner or custodian. If, in the opinion of a licensed veterinarian, an animal impounded pursuant to this subsection (1.8) is experiencing extreme pain or suffering, or is severely injured past recovery, severely disabled past recovery, or severely diseased past recovery, the animal may be euthanized without a court order.

(2) (a) Except as otherwise provided in paragraph (b) of this subsection (2), cruelty to animals, or cruelty to a service animal or certified police working dog pursuant to paragraph (c) of subsection (1.5) of this section, is a class 1 misdemeanor.

(a.5) (I) Repealed.

In addition to any other sentence imposed for a violation of this section, the court may order an offender to complete an anger management treatment program or any other appropriate treatment program.

The court shall order an evaluation to be conducted prior to sentencing to assist the court in determining an appropriate sentence. The person ordered to undergo an evaluation shall be required to pay the cost of the evaluation, unless the person qualifies for a public defender, then the cost will be paid by the judicial district. If the evaluation results in a recommendation of treatment and if the court so finds, the person shall be ordered to complete an anger management treatment program or any other treatment program that the court may deem appropriate.

Upon successful completion of an anger management treatment program or any other

treatment program deemed appropriate by the court, the court may suspend any fine imposed, except for a five hundred dollar mandatory minimum fine which shall be imposed at the time of sentencing.

In addition to any other sentence imposed upon a person for a violation of any criminal law under this title, any person convicted of a second or subsequent conviction for any crime, the underlying factual basis of which has been found by the court to include an act of cruelty to animals or cruelty to a service animal or a certified police working dog pursuant to paragraph (c) of subsection (1.5) of this section is required to pay a mandatory minimum fine of one thousand dollars and is required to complete an anger management treatment program or any other appropriate treatment program.

Nothing in this paragraph (a.5) shall preclude the court from ordering treatment in any appropriate case.

This paragraph (a.5) does not apply to the treatment of pack or draft animals by negligently overdriving, overloading, or overworking them, or the treatment of livestock and other animals used in the farm or ranch production of food, fiber, or other agricultural products when such treatment is in accordance with accepted agricultural animal husbandry practices, the treatment of animals involved in activities regulated pursuant to article 60 of title 12, C.R.S., the treatment of animals involved in research if such research facility is operating under rules set forth by the state or federal government, the treatment of animals involved in rodeos, the treatment of dogs used for legal hunting activities, wildlife nuisances, or to statutes regulating activities concerning wildlife and predator control in the state, including trapping.

(I) A second or subsequent conviction under the provisions of paragraph (a) of subsection of this section is a class 6 felony. A plea of nolo contendere accepted by the court shall be considered a conviction for the purposes of this section.

In any case where the court sentences a person convicted of a class 6 felony under the provisions of this paragraph (b) to probation, the court shall, in addition to any other condition of probation imposed, order that:

The offender, pursuant to section 18-1.3-202 (1), be committed to the county jail for ninety days; or

The offender, pursuant to section 18-1.3-105 (3), be subject to home detention for no fewer than ninety days.

In any case where an offender is committed to the county jail or placed in home detention pursuant to subparagraph (II) of this paragraph (b), the court shall enter judgment against the offender for all costs assessed pursuant to section 18-1.3-701, including, but not limited to, the cost of care.

Aggravated cruelty to animals is a class 6 felony; except that a second or subsequent conviction for the offense of aggravated cruelty to animals is a class 5 felony. A plea of nolo contendere accepted by the court shall be considered a conviction for purposes of this section.

(I) If a person is convicted of cruelty to a service animal pursuant to paragraph (c) of subsection (1.5) of this section, the court shall order him or her to make restitution to the agency or individual owning the service animal for any veterinary bills and replacement costs of the service animal if it is disabled or killed as a result of the cruelty to animals incident.

(II) If a person is convicted of cruelty to a certified police working dog pursuant to paragraph of subsection (1.5) of this section, the court shall order him or her to make restitution to the

agency or individual owning the certified police working dog for all expenses, including any immediate and ongoing veterinary expenses related to the incident, and replacement costs for the certified police working dog if it is permanently disabled or killed as a result of the cruelty to animals incident. If the court finds that the person who is convicted of cruelty to a certified police working dog pursuant to paragraph (c) of subsection (1.5) of this section did so with malicious intent, the person shall additionally make restitution to the agency or individual owning the certified working dog for all training and certification costs related to the certified police working dog.

(2.5) It shall be an affirmative defense to a charge brought under this section involving injury or death to a dog that the dog was found running, worrying, or injuring sheep, cattle, or other livestock.

(3) Nothing in this part 2 modifies in any manner the authority of the parks and wildlife commission, as established in title 33, C.R.S., or prohibits any conduct authorized or permitted under title 33, C.R.S.

18-9-202.5. Impounded animals - costs of impoundment, provision, and care - disposition - procedures - application - definition. (1) (a) (I) The owner or custodian of an animal that has been impounded by an impound agency because of alleged neglect or abuse or because of investigation of charges of cruelty to animals pursuant to section 18-9-202; animal fighting pursuant to section 18-9-204; mistreatment, neglect, or abandonment under article 42 of title 35, C.R.S.; or unlawful ownership of a dangerous dog as described in section 18-9-204.5, may prevent disposition of the animal by an impound agency by filing a payment for impoundment, care, and provision costs with the court in an amount determined by the impound agency to be sufficient to provide for the animal's care and provision at the impound agency for at least thirty days, including the day on which the animal was taken into custody.

(II) To the extent practicable, within seventy-two hours after an impoundment described under subparagraph (I) of this paragraph (a), upon request from the owner or custodian of the impounded animal, the impound agency shall allow a licensed veterinarian of the owner's or custodian's choosing and at his or her expense to examine the animal at a time and place selected by the impound agency, which examination may include taking photographs of the animal and taking biological samples for the purpose of diagnostic testing.

The owner or custodian must file the payment:

Within ten days after the animal is impounded; or

If the owner or custodian requests a hearing pursuant to subparagraph (I) of paragraph

of this subsection (1), in accordance with subparagraph (IV) of paragraph (c) of this subsection (1).

(I) Within ten days after the date of impoundment, the owner or custodian may request a hearing in a criminal court of competent jurisdiction. The owner or custodian must provide notice to the district attorney of his or her request for a hearing. If the owner or custodian requests a hearing, the court shall hold the hearing within ten days after the request is made.

At the hearing, the court shall determine, as appropriate:

Whether costs associated with the impoundment, care, and provision, as determined by the impound agency, are fair and reasonable and necessary, which costs shall be specificallyitemized

by the impound agency prior to the date of the hearing and shall include, at a minimum, an accounting of the costs of upkeep and veterinary services;

Whether there was sufficient probable cause for the impoundment; and

If the court finds probable cause for impoundment existed and the owner or custodian elects not to pay the reasonable impoundment, care, or provision costs to prevent disposition, release of the animal to the impound agency for disposition.

A warrant issued in accordance with C.R.C.P. 41 (b) authorizing seizure of the impounded animal constitutes prima facie evidence of sufficient cause for impoundment.

If probable cause is found at a hearing conducted under this paragraph (c), the owner or custodian shall file payment for costs at the hearing.

At the end of the time for which expenses are covered by an initial or any subsequent impoundment, care, and provision payment:

If the owner or custodian desires to prevent disposition of the animal, the owner or custodian must file a new payment with the court within ten days prior to the previous payment's expiration.

If the owner or custodian has not timely filed an additional payment for impoundment, care, and provision costs, the impound agency may determine disposition of the animal unless there is a court order prohibiting disposition. Unless subsection (4) of this section applies, the owner or custodian is liable for any additional costs for the care of, provision for, or disposal of the animal.

(a) Failure to pay the impoundment, care, and provision costs pursuant to subsection (1) of this section results in the forfeiture of the right to contest those costs and any ownership rights to the animal in question.

A dog that is not claimed by its owner within five days after being eligible for release from impoundment for investigation of a charge of unlawful ownership of a dangerous dog as described in section 18-9-204.5 is deemed abandoned and maybe disposed of as the impound agency deems proper.

If, in the opinion of a licensed veterinarian, an impounded animal is experiencing extreme pain or suffering or is severely injured past recovery, severely disabled past recovery, or severely diseased past recovery, the animal may be euthanized without a court order.

The court shall order an impound agency to refund to the owner or custodian all impoundment, care, and provision payments made for the animal if, after trial, a judge or jury enters or returns in favor of the owner or custodian a verdict of not guilty for all charges related to the original impoundment of the animal.

(a) With respect to the sale of an animal, the proceeds are first applied to the costs of the sale and then to the expenses for the care of and provision for the animal during impoundment and the pendencyof the sale, including expenses incurred by the impound agency that have not been paid by the owner or custodian. If the owner of the animal is convicted of cruelty to animals under section 18-9-202, animal fighting under section 18-9-204, or unlawful ownership of a dangerous dog under section 18-9-204.5 or is found by court order to have mistreated, neglected, or abandoned the animal under article 42 of title 35, C.R.S., the remaining proceeds, if any, are paid to the impound agency. If the owner of the animal is not convicted of such charges or is not found by court order to have mistreated, neglected, or abandoned the animal, the impound agency shall pay over the remaining proceeds, if any, to the owner of the animal.

If the impound agency is the department of agriculture, the department shall transmit the moneys credited for expenses to the state treasurer, who shall credit them to the animal protection fund created in section 35-42-113, C.R.S.

If the owner of the animal cannot be found, the court shall pay any remaining proceeds after all other expenses have been paid to the impound agency into the animal protection fund or, if the impound agency is not the department of agriculture, to such other impound agency as the court orders. An owner claiming the remaining proceeds must make the claim within one year after the payment of the proceeds to the impound agency. A claim not so presented to the court is forever barred unless the court, by proper order made in any case, otherwise decrees. An impound agency shall pay to the claimant any refund ordered by court decree.

At least six days prior to sale of the animal, the impound agency shall provide written notice to the owner, at the owner's last-known address, of the time and place of the sale of the animal.

If the owner of the animal is unknown, the impound agency shall publish for one week, in a newspaper of general circulation in the jurisdiction in which the animal was found, notice of sale of the animal and shall further post notice of the sale of the animal at a place provided for public notices in the jurisdiction in which the sale will take place, at least five days prior to the sale.

This subsection (4) does not apply to the disposition of an animal for a fee by:

Adoption of an animal;

Release of an animal to a rescue group licensed pursuant to article 80 of title 35, C.R.S.;

Release of an animal to another pet animal facility licensed pursuant to article 80 of title 35, C.R.S.; or

Release of an animal to a rehabilitator licensed by the parks and wildlife division or the United States fish and wildlife service.

For purposes of this section, "impound agency" means an animal shelter as defined in section 35-80-102 (1), C.R.S., the department of agriculture, created in section 24-1-123, C.R.S., or any other agency that impounds an animal pursuant to paragraph (a) of subsection (1) of this section or section 18-9-202 (1.8).

This section does not apply to animals impounded solely under article 42 of title 35, C.R.S.


18-9-203. Sheepherder abandoning sheep without notice. (Repealed)

18-9-204. Animal fighting - penalty. (1) (a) No person shall cause, sponsor, arrange, hold, or encourage a fight between animals for the purpose of monetary gain or entertainment.

For the purposes of this section, a person encourages a fight between animals for the purpose of monetary gain or entertainment if he or she:

Is knowingly present at or wagers on such a fight;

Owns, trains, transports, possesses, breeds, sells, transfers, or equips an animal with the intent that such animal will be engaged in such a fight;

Knowingly allows any such fight to occur on any property owned or controlled by him;

Knowingly allows any animal used for such a fight to be kept, boarded, housed, or trained on, or transported in, any property owned or controlled by him;

Knowingly uses any means of communication for the purpose of promoting such a fight;

or

Knowingly possesses any animal used for such a fight or any device intended to enhance the animal's fighting ability.

(a) Except as described in paragraph (b) of this subsection (2), a person who violates the provisions of this section commits a class 5 felony and, in addition to the punishment provided in section 18-1.3-401, the court shall impose upon the person a mandatory fine of at least one thousand dollars.

(b) A person who commits a second or subsequent violation of this section commits a class 4 felony and, in addition to the punishment provided in section 18-1.3-401, the court shall impose upon the person a mandatory fine of at least five thousand dollars.

Nothing in this section shall prohibit normal hunting practices as approved by the division of parks and wildlife.

Nothing in this section shall be construed to prohibit the training of animals or the use of equipment in the training of animals for any purpose not prohibited by law.

18-9-204.5. Unlawful ownership of dangerous dog - legislative declaration - definitions. (1) The general assembly hereby finds, determines, and declares that:

Dangerous dogs are a serious and widespread threat to the safety and welfare of citizens throughout the state because of the number and serious nature of attacks by such dogs; and

The regulation and control of dangerous dogs is a matter of statewide concern.

As used in this section, unless the context otherwise requires:

"Bodily injury" means any physical injury that results in severe bruising, muscle tears, or skin lacerations requiring professional medical treatment or any physical injury that requires corrective or cosmetic surgery.

(a.5) "Bureau" means the bureau of animal protection in the department of agriculture, division of animal industry, created pursuant to section 35-42-105, C.R.S.

"Dangerous dog" means any dog that:

Inflicts bodily or serious bodily injury upon or causes the death of a person or domestic animal; or

Demonstrates tendencies that would cause a reasonable person to believe that the dog may inflict bodily or serious bodily injury upon or cause the death of any person or domestic animal; or

Engages in or is trained for animal fighting as described and prohibited in section 18-9-204.

"Dog" means any domesticated animal related to the fox, wolf, coyote, or jackal.

"Domestic animal" means any dog, cat, any animal kept as a household pet, or livestock.

"Owner" or "owns" means any person, firm, corporation, or organization owning,

possessing, harboring, keeping, having financial or property interest in, or having control or custody of a domestic animal, as the term is defined in paragraph (d) of this subsection (2), including a dangerous dog as the term is defined in paragraph (b) of this subsection (2).

"Serious bodily injury" has the same meaning as such term is defined in section 18-1-901

(3) (p).

(a) A person commits ownership of a dangerous dog if such person owns, possesses, harbors, keeps, has a financial or property interest in, or has custody or control over a dangerous dog.

Any owner who violates paragraph (a) of this subsection (3) whose dog inflicts bodily injury upon any person commits a class 3 misdemeanor. Any owner involved in a second or subsequent violation under this paragraph (b) commits a class 2 misdemeanor.

Any owner who violates paragraph (a) of this subsection (3) whose dog inflicts serious bodily injury to a person commits a class 1 misdemeanor. Any owner involved in a second or subsequent violation under this paragraph (c) commits a class 6 felony.

Any owner who violates paragraph (a) of this subsection (3) whose dog causes the death of a person commits a class 5 felony.

(I) Any owner who violates paragraph (a) of this subsection (3) whose dog injures or causes the death of any domestic animal commits a class 3 misdemeanor.

Any owner of a dog that is involved in a second or subsequent violation under this paragraph (e) commits a class 2 misdemeanor. The minimum fine specified in section 18-1.3-501 for a class 2 misdemeanor shall be mandatory.

(A) The court shall order the convicted owner and any owner who enters into a deferred judgment or deferred prosecution to make restitution to the injured or dead domestic animal's owner pursuant to applicable provisions of title 16, C.R.S., governing restitution.

Restitution shall be equal to the greater of the fair market value or the replacement cost of the domestic animal on the date, but before the time, the animal was injured or destroyed plus any reasonable and necessary medical expenses incurred in treating the animal and any actual costs incurred in replacing the injured or destroyed animal.

(B.5) An owner who violates paragraph (a) of this subsection (3) and whose dog damages or destroys the property of another person commits a class 1 petty offense.

Any owner whose dog damages or destroys property shall make restitution to the owner of such property in an amount equal to the greater of the fair market value or the replacement cost of such property before its destruction plus any actual costs incurred in replacing such property.

(e.5) The court shall order any owner of a dangerous dog who has been convicted of a violation of this section to:

Confine the dangerous dog in a building or enclosure designed to be escape-proof and, whenever the dog is outside of the building or enclosure, keep the dog under the owner's control by use of a leash. The owner shall post a conspicuous warning sign on the building or enclosure notifying others that a dangerous dog is housed in the building or enclosure. In addition, if the conviction is for a second or subsequent offense, the dangerous dog shall also be muzzled whenever it is outside of the building or enclosure.

Immediately report to the bureau in writing any material change in the dangerous dog's situation, including but not limited to a change, transfer, or termination of ownership, change of address, escape, or death;

At the owner's expense, permanently identify the dangerous dog through the implantation of a microchip by a licensed veterinarian or a licensed shelter. A veterinarian or licensed shelter that implants a microchip in a dangerous dog shall report the microchipping information to the bureau within ten days after implantation of the microchip, pursuant to section 35-42-115 (2), C.R.S.

Prior to the implantation of the microchip, pay a nonrefundable dangerous dog microchip license fee of fifty dollars to the bureau;

Prior to the dangerous dog receiving any service or treatment, disclose in writing to any provider of the service or treatment, including but not limited to a veterinary health care worker, dog groomer, humane agencystaff person, pet animal care facility staff person, professional dog handler, or dog trainer, each acting in the performance of his or her respective duties, that the dangerous dog has been the subject of a conviction of a violation of this section;

Prior to a change, transfer, or termination of ownership of a dangerous dog, disclose in writing to the prospective owner that the dangerous dog has been the subject of a conviction of a violation of this section.

In addition to any other penalty set forth in this subsection (3), upon an owner's entry of a guilty plea or the return of a verdict of guilty by a judge or jury or a deferred judgment or deferred prosecution for a violation that results in bodily injury, serious bodily injury, or death to a person, the court, pursuant to applicable provisions of title 16, C.R.S., governing restitution, shall order the defendant to make restitution in accordance with said provisions.

(I) In addition to the penalties set forth in paragraphs (b) to (e) of this subsection (3), upon an owner's entry of a guilty plea or the return of a verdict of guilty by a judge or jury or a deferred judgment or deferred prosecution for a violation that results in serious bodily injury to a person or death to a person or domestic animal or for a second or subsequent violation of paragraph (b) or (e) of this subsection (3) resulting in a conviction or a deferred judgment or a deferred prosecution involving the same dog of the same owner, the court shall order that the dangerous dog be immediately confiscated and placed in a public animal shelter and shall order that, upon exhaustion of any right an owner has to appeal a conviction based on a violation of this subsection (3), the owner's dangerous dog be destroyed by euthanasia administered by a licensed veterinarian.

(II) In addition to any penalty set forth in paragraphs (b) to (e) of this subsection (3), for a second or subsequent violation of paragraph (b) or (e) of this subsection (3) resulting in a conviction or a deferred judgment or a deferred prosecution involving the same dog of a different owner, the court may order that the dangerous dog be immediately confiscated and placed in a public animal shelter and that, upon exhaustion of any right an owner has to appeal a conviction based on a violation of this subsection (3), the owner's dangerous dog be destroyed by euthanasia administered by a licensed veterinarian.

(h) (I) An affirmative defense to the violation of this subsection (3) shall be:

That, at the time of the attack by the dangerous dog which causes injury to or the death of a domestic animal, the domestic animal was at large, was an estray, and entered upon the property of the owner and the attack began, but did not necessarily end, upon such property;

That, at the time of the attack by the dangerous dog which causes injury to or the death of a domestic animal, said animal was biting or otherwise attacking the dangerous dog or its owner;

That, at the time of the attack by the dangerous dog which causes injury to or the death of a person, the victim of the attack was committing or attempting to commit a criminal offense, other than a petty offense, against the dog's owner, and the attack did not occur on the owner's property;

That, at the time of the attack by the dangerous dog which causes injury to or the death of a person, the victim of the attack was committing or attempting to commit a criminal offense, other than a petty offense, against a person on the owner's property or the property itself and the attack began, but did not necessarily end, upon such property; or

That the person who was the victim of the attack by the dangerous dog tormented, provoked, abused, or inflicted injury upon the dog in such an extreme manner which resulted in the attack.

(II) The affirmative defenses set forth in subparagraph (I) of this paragraph (h) shall not apply to any dog that has engaged in or been trained for animal fighting as said term is described in section 18-9-204.

Upon taking an owner into custody for an alleged violation of this section or the issuing of a summons and complaint to the owner, pursuant to the Colorado rules of criminal procedure and part 1 of article 4 of title 16, C.R.S., the owner's dangerous dog may be taken into custody and placed in a public animal shelter, at the owner's expense, pending final disposition of the charge against the owner. In addition, in the event the court, pursuant to the Colorado rules of criminal procedure and part 1 of article 4 of title 16, C.R.S., sets bail for an owner's release from custody pending final disposition, the court may require, as a condition of bond, that the owner's dangerous dog be placed by an impound agency, as defined in section 18-9-202.5 (5), at the owner's expense in a location selected by the impound agency including a public animal shelter, licensed boarding facility, or veterinarian's clinic, pending final disposition of the alleged violation of this section. The owner is liable for the total cost of board and care for a dog placed pursuant to this subsection (4).

(a) Nothing in this section shall be construed to prohibit a municipality from adopting any rule or law for the control of dangerous dogs; except that any such rule or law shall not regulate dangerous dogs in a manner that is specific to breed.

Nothing in this section shall be construed to abrogate a county's authority under part 1 of article 15 of title 30, C.R.S., to adopt dog control and licensing resolutions and to impose the penalties set forth in section 30-15-102, C.R.S.; except that any such resolution shall not regulate dangerous dogs in a manner that is specific to breed.

No municipality or county may destroy or dispose of a dog that is awaiting destruction or disposition as of April 21, 2004, in connection with a violation or charged violation of a municipal or county ban on one or more specific dog breeds.

The provisions of this section shall not apply to the following:

To any dog that is used by a peace officer while the officer is engaged in the performance of peace officer duties;

To any dog that inflicts bodily or serious bodily injury to any veterinary health care worker, dog groomer, humane agency personnel, professional dog handler, or trainer each acting in the performance of his or her respective duties, unless the owner is subject to a court order issued pursuant to paragraph (e.5) of subsection (3) of this section and the owner has failed to comply with the provisions of subparagraph (V) of paragraph (e.5) of subsection (3) of this section; or

To any dog that inflicts injury upon or causes the death of a domestic animal while the dog was working as a hunting dog, herding dog, or predator control dog on the property of or under the control of the dog's owner and the injury or death was to a domestic animal naturally associated with the work of such dog.

18-9-205. Disposition of fines. Any fines collected pursuant to section 18-9-204 shall be transmitted to the state treasurer, who shall then transmit the same to the county where the offense occurred for deposit in the general fund to be used for the care of the animals involved in the offense, if required, or, if not required, for any other lawful purpose.

18-9-206. Unauthorized release of an animal - penalty - restitution. (1) Any person who intentionally releases any animal which is lawfully confined for scientific, research, commercial, legal sporting, or educational purposes or for public safety purposes because the animal has been determined to be dangerous to people, has an infectious disease, or is quarantined to determine whether or not it has an infectious disease without the consent of the owner or custodian of such animal commits the offense of unauthorized release of an animal.

Unauthorized release of an animal is a class 2 misdemeanor.

Any person who is convicted of unauthorized release of an animal shall be ordered to pay restitution for any damages resulting from such release, including the cost of restoring any animal to confinement, the cost of restoring the health of any animal which is released, the cost of any damage to real or personal property which is caused by a released animal, or any cost which results if the release causes the failure of an experiment, including the costs of repeating the experiment, replacement of any animal released, and the cost of labor and materials associated with such experiment.


18-9-207. Tampering or drugging of livestock. (1) As used in this section, unless the context otherwise requires:

"Exhibition" means a show or sale of livestock at a fair or elsewhere in this state that is sponsored by or under the authority of the state or any unit of local government or any agricultural, horticultural, or livestock society, association, or corporation.

"Livestock" means any domestic animal generally used for food or in the production of food, including, but not limited to, cattle, sheep, goats, poultry, swine, or llamas.

"Sabotage" means intentionally tampering with an animal belonging to or owned by another person that has been registered, entered, or exhibited in any exhibition or raised for the apparent purpose of being entered in an exhibition.

(I) "Tamper" means any of the following:

Treatment of livestock in such a manner that food derived from the livestock would be considered adulterated under the "Colorado Food and Drug Act", part 4 of article 5 of title 25, C.R.S.;

The injection, use, or administration of any drug that is prohibited by any federal, state,

or local law or any drug that is used in a manner prohibited by federal law or the law of this state or any locality thereof;

The injection or other internal or external administration of any product or material, whether gas, solid, or liquid, to an animal for the purposes of deception, including concealing, enhancing, or transforming the true conformation, configuration, color, breed, condition, or age of the animal or making the animal appear more sound than the animal would appear otherwise;

The use or administration for cosmetic purposes of steroids, growth stimulants, or internal artificial filling, including paraffin, silicone injection, or any other substance;

The use or application of any drug or feed additive affecting the central nervous system of the animal;

The use or administration of diuretics for cosmetic purposes;

The manipulation or removal of tissue, by surgery or otherwise, so as to change, transform, or enhance the true conformation or configuration of the animal;

Subjecting the animal to inhumane conditions or procedures for the purpose of concealing, enhancing, or transforming the true conformation, configuration, condition, or age of the animal or making the animal appear more sound than the animal would appear otherwise;

Attaching to the animal's hide foreign objects, including hair or hair substitutes, cloth, and fibers, for the purpose of deception, including concealing, enhancing, or transforming the true conformation, configuration, color, breed, condition, or age of the animal or making the animal appear more sound than the animal would appear otherwise;

Substituting a different animal for the animal registered or entered in the exhibition without the permission of a responsible official of the exhibition.

(II) "Tamper" does not include any action taken or activity performed or administered by a licensed veterinarian or in accordance with instructions of a licensed veterinarian if the action or activity was undertaken for accepted medical purposes during the course of a valid veterinarian- client-patient relationship or any action taken as part of accepted grooming, ranching, commercial, or medical practices. "Tampering" shall not be construed to include normal ranching practices.

(a) No person shall commit any act in this state that would constitute tampering with or sabotaging any livestock that has been registered, entered, or exhibited in any exhibition in this state.

No person shall administer, dispense, distribute, manufacture, possess, sell, or use any drug to or for livestock unless such drug is approved by the United States food and drug administration or the United States department of agriculture; except that, if either agency has approved an application submitted for investigational use in accordance with the "Federal Food, Drug, and Cosmetic Act", the drug may be used only for the approved investigational use.

No person shall administer, distribute, possess, sell, or use any dangerous drug to or for livestock unless the drug is accompanied by a prescription issued by a licensed veterinarian entitled to practice in this state.

Any person who violates the provisions of this section commits a class 1 misdemeanor. However, in lieu of the fine provided in section 18-1.3-501, the court may impose a fine of not less than one thousand dollars or more than one hundred thousand dollars.

The name and photograph of any person convicted of violating the provisions of this section shall be made available for publication in newspapers of general circulation and trade journals.


18-9-208. Forfeiture of animals. (1) Upon the motion of the prosecuting attorney or upon the court's own motion, after the conviction of a defendant for cruelty to animals as described in section 18-9-202, or for animal fighting as described in section 18-9-204, the court may order the forfeiture of any animal owned by or in the custody of the defendant that:

Was abused, neglected, mistreated, injured, or used by the defendant during the course of the criminal episode that gave rise to such conviction;

Participated in or was affected by any act set forth in section 18-9-204 (1).

(a) If an animal is the subject of a motion made under subsection (1) of this section and is not owned by the defendant, the court may nevertheless enter an order of forfeiture of the animal if the court finds that:

The animal was abandoned prior to the criminal episode described in subsection (1) of this section;

The owner of the animal is unknown; or

The owner of the animal is known but cannot be located.

Any person who contests a motion brought under this section shall establish such person's standing as a true owner of the animal. The factors to be considered by the court in determining whether such person is a true owner shall include, but shall not be limited to, the following:

Whether the person was the primary user, custodian, or possessor of the animal;

Whether there is evidence that ownership of the animal is vested in the person;

Whether consideration was paid for the purchase of the animal, and, if so, how much of the consideration was furnished by the person.

If the court determines that a person other than the defendant is the true owner of the animal, the court may not enter an order forfeiting the animal under this section unless the court finds:

The true owner was involved in the criminal episode described in subsection (1) of this section;

The true owner knew or reasonably should have known of the criminal episode described in subsection (1) of this section and failed to take all reasonable steps available to him or her to prevent it; or

Ownership of the animal was conveyed to the true owner in order to avoid a forfeiture.

An order of forfeiture entered pursuant to this section shall provide for the immediate disposition of the forfeited animal by any means described in section 18-9-201 (2.5) other than return to the owner. If, in the opinion of a licensed veterinarian, the animal is experiencing extreme pain or suffering, or is severely injured past recovery, severely disabled past recovery, or severely diseased past recovery, the animal may be euthanized without a court order.

The owner or custodian of an animal that is the subject of a motion brought under this section shall be liable for the cost of the care, keeping, transport, or disposal of the animal. In no event shall the prosecuting attorney or the office of the prosecuting attorney be liable for such cost.

The court in its discretion may order a forfeiture authorized by this section as an element of sentencing, as a condition of probation, or as a condition of a deferred sentence.


18-9-209. Immunity for reporting cruelty to animals - false report - penalty. (1) Except as otherwise provided in subsection (2) of this section, a person who, in good faith, reports a suspected incident of cruelty to animals, service animals, or certified police working dogs, as described in section 18-9-202, to a local law enforcement agency or to the state bureau of animal protection is immune from civil liability for reporting the incident.

The provisions of subsection (1) of this section shall not apply to a person who knowingly makes a false report of animal cruelty.

A person who knowingly makes a false report of animal cruelty to a local law enforcement agency or to the state bureau of animal protection commits a class 3 misdemeanor and shall be punished as provided in section 18-1.3-501.

PART 3

OFFENSES INVOLVING COMMUNICATIONS


18-9-301. Definitions. As used in sections 18-9-301 to 18-9-305, unless the context otherwise requires:

"Aggrieved person" means a person who was a party to any intercepted wire, oral, or electronic communication or a person against whom the interception was directed.

(1.5) "Aural transfer" means a transfer containing the human voice at any point between and including the point of origin and the point of reception.

"Common carrier" means any person engaged as a common carrier for hire in intrastate, interstate, or foreign communication by wire or radio or in intrastate, interstate, or foreign radio transmission of energy.

"Contents", when used with respect to any wire, oral, or electronic communication, includes any information concerning the substance, purport, or meaning of that communication.

(3.3) "Electronic communication" means any transfer of signs, signals, writing, images, sounds, data, or intelligence of any nature transmitted in whole or in part by a wire, radio, electromagnetic, photoelectronic, or photooptical system that affects interstate or foreign commerce but does not include:

(Deleted by amendment, L. 97, p. 602, § 2, effective August 6, 1997.)

Any wire or oral communication;

Any communication made through a tone-only paging device; or

Any communication from a tracking device.

(3.5) "Electronic communication service" means any service which provides to users thereof the ability to send or receive wire or electronic communications.

(3.7) "Electronic communications system" means any wire, radio, electromagnetic, photooptical, or photoelectronic facilities for the transmission of electronic communications and any computer facilities or related electronic equipment for the electronic storage of such

communications.

"Electronic, mechanical, or other device" means any device or apparatus which can be used to intercept a wire, oral, or electronic communication, other than:

Any telephone or telegraph instrument, equipment, or facility, or any component thereof, furnished to the subscriber or user by a provider of wire or electronic communication service in the ordinary course of its business and being used by the subscriber or user in the ordinary course of its business, or furnished by such subscriber or user for connection to the facilities of such service and being used in the ordinary course of its business, or being used by a provider of wire or electronic communication service in the ordinary course of its business or by an investigative or law enforcement officer in the ordinary course of his duties;

A hearing aid or similar device being used to correct subnormal hearing to not better than normal hearing.

(4.5) "Electronic storage" means:

Any temporary, intermediate storage of a wire or electronic communication incidental to the electronic transmission thereof; and

Any storage of such communication by an electronic communication service for purposes of backup protection of such communication.

"Intercept" means the aural or other acquisition of the contents of any wire, electronic, or oral communication through the use of any electronic, mechanical, or other device.

"Investigative or law enforcement officer" means any officer of the United States or of the state of Colorado or a political subdivision thereof who is empowered by law to conduct investigations of, or to make arrests for, offenses enumerated in this part 3, and any attorney authorized by law to prosecute or participate in the prosecution of such offenses.

"Judge of competent jurisdiction" means any justice of the supreme court or a judge of any district court of the state of Colorado.

"Oral communication" means any oral communication uttered by any person believing that such communication is not subject to interception, under circumstances justifying such belief, but does not include any electronic communication.

(8.3) "Pen register" means a device which records or decodes electronic or other impulses which identify the numbers dialed or otherwise transmitted on the telephone line to which such device is attached but shall not include any device used by a provider or customer of a wire or electronic communication service for billing, or recording as an incident to billing, for communications services provided by such provider or any device used by a provider or customer of a wire communication service for cost accounting or other like purposes in the ordinary course of its business.

(8.5) "Readily accessible to the general public" means, with respect to a radio communication, that such communication is not:

Scrambled or encrypted;

Transmitted using modulation techniques having essential parameters withheld from the public with the intention of preserving the privacy of such communication;

Carried on a subcarrier or other signal subsidiary to a radio transmission;

Transmitted over a communication system provided by a common carrier, unless the

communication is a tone-only paging system communication; or

Transmitted on frequencies allocated under part 25, subpart D, E, or F of part 74, or part 94 of the rules of the federal communications commission, unless, in the case of a communication transmitted on a frequency allocated under part 74 that is not exclusively allocated to broadcast auxiliary services, the communication is a two-way voice communication by radio.

(8.7) "Trap and trace device" means a device which captures the incoming electronic or other impulses which identify the originating number of an instrument or device from which a wire or electronic communication was transmitted.

(8.9) "User" means anyperson or entitywhich uses an electronic communication service and is duly authorized by the provider of such service to engage in such use.

"Wire communication" means any aural transfer made in whole or in part through the use of facilities for the transmission of communications by the aid of wire, cable, or other like connection, including the use of such connection in a switching station, between the point of origin and the point of reception, furnished or operated by any person engaged in providing or operating such facilities for the transmission of communications and includes any electronic storage of such communication.

**18-9-302. Wiretapping and eavesdropping devices prohibited - penalty.** Anyperson who manufactures, buys, sells, or knowingly has in his possession any instrument, device, contrivance, machine, or apparatus designed or commonly used for wiretapping or eavesdropping, as prohibited in sections 18-9-303 and 18-9-304, with the intent to unlawfully use or employ or allow the same to be so used or employed, or who knowingly aids, authorizes, agrees with, employs, permits, or conspires with any person to unlawfully manufacture, buy, sell, or have the same in his possession is guilty of a class 2 misdemeanor. Upon commission of a second or subsequent offense, any person committing the same commits a class 5 felony.

**18-9-303. Wiretapping prohibited - penalty.** (1) Any person not a sender or intended receiver of a telephone or telegraph communication commits wiretapping if he:

Knowinglyoverhears, reads, takes, copies, or records a telephone, telegraph, or electronic communication without the consent of either a sender or a receiver thereof or attempts to do so; or

Intentionally overhears, reads, takes, copies, or records a telephone, telegraph, or electronic communication for the purpose of committing or aiding or abetting the commission of an unlawful act; or

Knowingly uses for any purpose or discloses to any person the contents of any such communication, or attempts to do so, while knowing or having reason to know the information was obtained in violation of this section; or

Knowingly taps or makes any connection with any telephone or telegraph line, wire, cable, or instrument belonging to another or with any electronic, mechanical, or other device belonging to another or installs any device whether connected or not which permits the interception of messages; or

Repealed.

Knowingly uses any apparatus to unlawfully do, or cause to be done, any act prohibited by this section or aids, authorizes, agrees with, employs, permits, or intentionally conspires with any person to violate the provisions of this section.

(2) Wiretapping is a class 6 felony; except that, if the wiretapping involves a cordless telephone, it is a class 1 misdemeanor.

**18-9-304. Eavesdropping prohibited - penalty.** (1) Any person not visibly present during a conversation or discussion commits eavesdropping if he:

Knowingly overhears or records such conversation or discussion without the consent of at least one of the principal parties thereto, or attempts to do so; or

Intentionally overhears or records such conversation or discussion for the purpose of committing, aiding, or abetting the commission of an unlawful act; or

Knowingly uses for any purpose, discloses, or attempts to use or disclose to any other person the contents of any such conversation or discussion while knowing or having reason to know the information was obtained in violation of this section; or

Knowingly aids, authorizes, agrees with, employs, permits, or intentionally conspires with any person to violate the provisions of this section.

(2) Eavesdropping is a class 1 misdemeanor.

**18-9-305. Exceptions.** (1) Nothing in sections 18-9-302 to 18-9-304 shall be interpreted to prevent a news agency, or an employee thereof, from using the accepted tools and equipment of that news medium in the course of reporting or investigating a public and newsworthy event; nor shall said sections prevent any person from using wiretapping or eavesdropping devices on his own premises for security or business purposes if reasonable notice of the use of such devices is given to the public.

No part of sections 18-9-302 to 18-9-304 shall apply to the normal use of services, facilities, and equipment provided by a provider of wire or electronic communication service pursuant to its tariffs on file with the public utilities commission of the state of Colorado and with the federal communications commission; and said sections shall not apply to the normal functions of any operator of a switchboard nor to any officer, agent, or employee of a provider of wire or electronic communication service or other person engaged in the business of providing service, equipment, and facilities for communication who performs an otherwise prohibited act if such act is necessary to provide the communication services, equipment, or facilities or is necessary in the construction, maintenance, repair, operations, or use of the same, including the obtaining of billing and accounting information, the protecting of the communication services, equipment, and facilities from illegal use in violation of the tariffs referred to in this subsection (2), the protecting of the provider of wire or electronic communication service from the commission of fraud against it, and the providing of requested information in response to a subpoena or court order issued by a court of competent jurisdiction or on demand of other lawful authority. It shall not be unlawful under sections 18-9-302 to 18-9-304 for an officer, employee, or agent of any provider of wire or electronic communication service or other person to provide information, facilities, or technical assistance to an investigative or law enforcement officer who, pursuant to section 16-15-102, C.R.S., is authorized to intercept a wire, oral, or electronic communication for that purpose.

A good faith reliance on a court order or the provisions of article 15 of title 16, C.R.S., shall constitute a complete defense to any criminal action brought under provision of sections 18-9- 302 to 18-9-304 or any civil action brought under any other law of the state of Colorado. This section shall not be construed in any manner which would allow an investigative or law enforcement officer of the state of Colorado to engage in any wiretapping or eavesdropping without prior authorization by a court of competent jurisdiction under the provisions of article 15 of title 16, C.R.S., except as provided in section 16-15-102 (18), C.R.S.

(4.3)  It shall not be unlawful under sections 18-9-302 to 18-9-304 for any person:

To intercept or access an electronic communication made through an electronic communications system that is configured so that such electronic communication is readily accessible to the general public;

To intercept any radio communication which is transmitted by:

Any station for the use of the general public or that relates to ships, aircraft, vehicles, or persons in distress;

Any governmental, law enforcement, civil defense, private land mobile, or public safety communications system, including police and fire, readily accessible to the general public;

A station operating on an authorized frequency within the bands allocated to the amateur, citizens band, or general mobile radio services; or

Any marine or aeronautical communications system;

To engage in any conduct which is:

Prohibited by section 633 of the federal "Communications Act of 1934", as amended; or

Excepted from the application of section 705 (a) of the federal "Communications Act of 1934", as amended, by section 705 (b) of said act;

To intercept any wire or electronic communication, the transmission of which is causing harmful interference to any lawfully operating station or consumer electronic equipment, to the extent necessary to identify the source of such interference; or

For other users of the same frequency to intercept any radio communication made through a system that utilizes frequencies monitored by individuals engaged in the provision or the use of such system, if such communication is not scrambled or encrypted.

(4.5)  It shall not be unlawful under sections 18-9-302 to 18-9-304:

To use a pen register or a trap and trace device; or

For a provider of electronic communication service to record the fact that a wire or electronic communication was initiated or completed in order to protect such provider, another provider furnishing service toward the completion of the wire or electronic communication, or a user of that service from fraudulent, unlawful, or abusive use of such service.

(4.7) A person or entity providing an electronic communication service to the public shall not intentionally divulge the contents of any communication other than a communication to such

person or entity, or an agent thereof, while in transmission on that service to any person or entity other than an addressee or intended recipient of such communication or an agent of such addressee or intended recipient; except that a person or entity providing electronic communication service to the public may divulge the contents of any such communication:

As otherwise authorized in section 16-15-102 (12), (13), (14), and (16), C.R.S., and subsections (2) and (3) of this section;

With the lawful consent of the originator or any addressee or intended recipient of such communication;

To a person employed or authorized, or whose facilities are used, to forward such communication to its destination; or

Which were inadvertently obtained by the service provider and which appear to pertain to the commission of a crime, if such divulgence is made to a law enforcement agency.

(4.9) It shall not be unlawful for a district attorney or law enforcement officer to listen to a recording of or to read a transcription of the contents of an electronic communication involving a cordless telephone when the district attorney or law enforcement officer has come into possession of such materials from a third party. In order to use such materials as evidence in a prosecution for a crime other than wiretapping or eavesdropping, the district attorney or law enforcement officer shall have a reasonable basis for believing that the recording or transcription is reliable and shall also have separate probable cause based on corroborating evidence to support a reasonable belief that the crime was committed. Nothing in this subsection (4.9) shall preclude a district attorney from prosecuting a person for a violation of section 18-9-303 or 18-9-304.

The exceptions in this section shall be affirmative defenses.


18-9-306. Abuse of telephone and telegraph service. (1) A person commits a class 3 misdemeanor, if:

As an employee of a telegraph or telephone company he knowingly divulges the contents or the purport of any message or part thereof sent or intended to be sent to any person other than one to whom said message is sent or person authorized to receive the same; or

He knowingly sends or delivers a false message or furnishes or conspires to furnish such message to an operator to be sent or delivered with intent to injure, deceive, or defraud any person, corporation, or the public; or

He knowingly and without authorization opens any sealed envelope enclosing a message with the purpose of learning the contents; or

He impersonates another, and thereby procures the delivery to himself of the message directed to such person, with the intent to use, destroy, or detain the same; or

He knowingly and without authorization reads or learns the contents or meaning of a message on its transit and uses or communicates to another any information so obtained; or

He knowingly bribes a telegraph or telephone operator or employee of a telegraph or telephone company to disclose any private message or the purport of the same received by him by reason of his trust as agent of the company or uses such information when thus obtained.


18-9-306.5. Obstruction of telephone or telegraph service. (1) A person commits obstruction of telephone or telegraph service if the person knowingly prevents, obstructs, or delays, by any means whatsoever, the sending, transmission, conveyance, or delivery in this state of any message, communication, or report by or through any telegraph or telephone line, wire, cable, or other facility or any cordless, wireless, electronic, mechanical, or other device.

Obstruction of telephone or telegraph service is a class 1 misdemeanor.


18-9-307. Refusal to yield party line. (1) The following definitions are applicable to this section:

"Party line" means a subscribers' line telephone circuit, consisting of two or more main telephone stations connected therewith, each station with a distinctive ring or telephone number.

"Emergency" means a situation in which property or human safety is in jeopardy and the prompt summoning of aid is essential.

Any person who willfully refuses to immediately yield or surrender the use of a party line when informed that the line is needed for an emergency call to a fire department, or police department, or sheriff's office or for medical aid or ambulance service commits a class 1 petty offense. This section shall not apply to persons using a party line for such an emergency call.

Any person who requests the use of a party line on the pretext that an emergency exists, knowing that no emergency in fact exists, commits a class 1 petty offense, punishable by a fine of one hundred dollars.

18-9-308. Telephone directories to contain notice. Every telephone directory published for distribution to the members of the general public shall contain a notice which explains the provisions of section 18-9-307. Such notice shall be printed in type which is no smaller than ten- point type and shall be preceded by the word "WARNING". The provisions of this section shall not apply to those directories distributed solely for business advertising purposes, commonly known as classified directories. Anyperson, firm, or corporation providing telephone service which distributes or causes to be distributed in this state telephone directories which are subject to the provisions of this section and which do not contain the notice provided for in this section commits a class 1 petty offense.

18-9-309. Telecommunications crime. (1) As used in this section and section 18-9-309.5:

"Access device" means any card, plate, code, account number, or other means of access that can be used, alone or in conjunction with another access device, to obtain telecommunications service.

(a.5) "Cellular phone" means a radio telecommunications device that may be used to obtain telecommunications services and that is programmed with an electronic serial number by or with the consent of the cellular phone manufacturer.

(a.7) "Cloned cellular phone" means a cellular phone, the electronic serial number of which

has been altered without the consent of the cellular phone's manufacturer.

(a.8) "Cloning equipment" means anyinstrument, apparatus, equipment, computer hardware, computer software, operating procedure or code, or device, whether used separately or in combination, that is designed or adapted and is used, is intended to be used, or is capable of being used:

To intercept signals, including signals transmitted to or from cellular phones, between a telecommunications provider and persons using telecommunications services or between persons using telecommunications services; or

To create cloned cellular phones.

"Credit card number" means the card number appearing on a credit card which is an identification card or plate issued to a person by any supplier of telecommunications service which permits the person to whom the card has been issued to obtain telecommunications service on credit. The term includes the number or description of the card or plate even if the card or plate itself is not produced at the time of obtaining telecommunications service.

(b.7) "Electronic serial number" means an electronic number that is programmed into a cellular phone by or with the consent of the manufacturer, transmitted by the cellular phone, and used by cellular phone telecommunications providers to validate radio transmissions as having been made by cellular phones authorized or approved by telecommunications providers.

"Illegal telecommunications equipment" means any instrument, apparatus, equipment, computer hardware, computer software, mechanism, operating procedure or code, or device, whether used separately or in combination, that is designed or adapted and is used or is intended to be used to evade the lawful charges for any telecommunications service or for concealing from any telecommunications provider or lawful authority the existence, place of origin, or destination of any telecommunication. Illegal telecommunications equipment includes cloned cellular phones.

(c.5) To "intercept signals" means to electronically capture, record, reveal, or otherwise access signals, including data, electronic serial numbers, and mobile identification numbers, that are emitted, transmitted, or received by a telecommunications provider without consent of the telecommunications provider or the person receiving or initiating the signal.

(c.7) "Mobile identification number" means the cellular phone number assigned to a cellular phone by the cellular phone telecommunications provider.

"Telecommunications device" means any instrument, apparatus, method, system, or equipment which controls, measures, directs, or facilitates telecommunications service. The term includes, but is not limited to, computer hardware, software, programs, electronic mail systems, voice mail systems, identification validation systems, and private branch exchanges.

"Telecommunications provider" means anyperson, firm, association, or any corporation, private or municipal, owning, operating, or managing any facilities used to provide telecommunications service.

"Telecommunications service" means a service which, in exchange for a pecuniary consideration, provides or offers to provide transmission of messages, signals, facsimiles, or other communication between persons who are physically separated from each other by means of telephone, telegraph, cable, wire, or the projection of energy without physical connection.

"Telephone company" means any telecommunications provider which provides local exchange telecommunications service.

A person commits a class 3 misdemeanor if he or she knowingly:

Accesses, uses, manipulates, or damages any telecommunications device without the authority of the owner or person who has the lawful possession or use thereof;

Makes, possesses, or uses illegal telecommunications equipment; except that a person who knowingly uses cloning equipment to create a cloned cellular phone commits a class 4 felony as provided in subsection (4) of this section;

Sells, gives, or furnishes to another or advertises or offer for sale illegal telecommunications equipment;

Sells, gives, or furnishes to another or advertises or offers for sale any plans or instructions for making, assembling, or using illegal telecommunications equipment; or

Sells, rents, lends, gives, publishes, or otherwise transfers or discloses to another or offers or advertises for sale or rental the number or code of a counterfeited, cancelled, expired, revoked, or nonexistent telephone number or credit card number or method of numbering or coding which is employed in the issuance of telephone numbers access devices or credit card numbers or an existing number or code or method of numbering or coding without the authority of the owner or person who has the lawful possession or use thereof.

(2.5) A person commits a class 6 felony if, within five years after a previous violation of subsection (2) of this section, the person commits a second or subsequent violation of subsection (2) of this section; except that a second or subsequent violation of subsection (2) of this section involving knowingly using cloning equipment to create a cloned cellular phone, as described in paragraph (b) of subsection (2) of this section, is a class 4 felony.

A person commits theft as defined in section 18-4-401 and shall be subject to the penalties as set forth in that section if he knowingly:

Obtains any telecommunications service by charging such service to or causing such service to be charged to an existing telephone number, access device, or credit card number without the authority of the person to whom issued or of the subscriber thereto or of the lawful holder thereof or to a nonexistent, counterfeit, expired, revoked, or cancelled credit card number, or by any method of code calling, or by installing, rearranging, or tampering with any equipment, physically or electronically, or by the use of any other fraudulent means, method, trick, or device or scheme;

Obtains telecommunications service with fraudulent intent through the use of a false or fictitious name, telephone number, address, or credit information or through the unauthorized use of the name, telephone number, address, or credit information of another.

(a) A person commits a class 4 felony if he or she knowingly uses cloning equipment to:

Intercept signals, including signals transmitted to or from cellular phones, between a telecommunications provider and persons using telecommunications services or between persons using telecommunications services; or

Create a cloned cellular phone.

A person commits a class 4 felony if he or she aids, abets, advises, or encourages one or more persons who engage in the activities described in paragraph (a) of this subsection (4).

Each violation of this subsection (4), including each instance of intercepting signals or of creating a cloned cellular phone, shall be a separate offense. The provisions of this section do not apply to:

Officers, employees, or agents of telecommunications providers who engage in conduct

prohibited by this section for the purpose of constructing, maintaining, or conducting telecommunications services or for law enforcement purposes;

Law enforcement officers and public officials in charge of jails, police premises, sheriffs' offices, department of corrections' institutions, or other penal or correctional institutions or anyother person under the color of law who engages in conduct prohibited by this section for the purpose of law enforcement or in the normal course of the officer's or official's employment activities or duties; or

Officers, employees, or agents of federal or state agencies who are authorized to monitor or intercept cellular telephone service in the normal course of the officer's, employee's, or agent's employment.

Prosecution under this section does not preclude civil liability under any applicable provision of law.

18-9-309.5. Civil remedies - injunctions - forfeiture. (1) Whenever it appears that any person is engaged in or about to engage in any act which constitutes or will constitute a violation of section 18-9-309 (2) or (3), the attorney general, the district attorney, a representative of a telecommunications provider, or any person or company harmed by such alleged violation may initiate a civil proceeding in a district court to enjoin such violation and may petition the court to issue an order for the discontinuance of telecommunications service, used in violation of section 18-9-309 (2) or (3).

An action under this section shall be brought in the county in which the subject matter of the action, or some part thereof, is located or found and shall be commenced by the filing of a complaint, which shall be verified by affidavit.

If it is shown to the satisfaction of the court, either by verified complaint or affidavit, that a person is engaged in or about to engage in any act which constitutes a violation of section 18-9-309

or (3), the court shall issue a temporary restraining order to abate and prevent the continuance or recurrence of such act. The court shall direct the sheriff to seize and retain until further order of the court any device which is being used in violation of section 18-9-309 (2) or (3). While the temporary restraining order remains in effect, all property seized pursuant to the order of the court shall remain in the custody of the court. Within fourteen days following the filing of a motion of any person adversely affected by a temporary restraining order, the court shall conduct a hearing and determine whether such temporary restraining order shall be continued pending final determination of the action. Until such hearing takes place, the temporary restraining order shall remain in full force and effect.

The court may issue a permanent injunction to restrain, abate, or prevent the continuance or recurrence of the violation of section 18-9-309 (2) or (3). The court may grant declaratory relief, mandatoryorders, or any other relief deemed necessaryto accomplish the purposes of the injunction. The court may retain jurisdiction of the case for the purpose of enforcing its orders.

If it is shown to the satisfaction of the court, either by verified complaint or affidavit, that a person is engaged in or is about to engage in any act which constitutes a violation of section 18-9-309 (2) or (3), the court may issue an order which shall be promptly served upon the person in whose name the illegal telecommunications equipment is listed, requiring the party, within a reasonable

time to be fixed by the court but not exceeding forty-eight hours from the time of service of the petition on said party, to show cause before the judge why telecommunications service should not promptly be discontinued. At the hearing the burden of proof shall be on the complainant.

Upon a finding by the court that the illegal telecommunications equipment is being used or has been used in violation of section 18-9-309 (2) or (3), the court shall issue an order requiring the telephone company which is rendering service over the device to disconnect such service. Upon receipt of such order, which shall be served upon an officer of the telephone company by the sheriff of the county in which the illegal telecommunications equipment is installed or by a duly authorized deputy, the telephone company shall proceed promptly to disconnect and remove such device and discontinue all telecommunications service until further order of the court.

The telecommunications provider who petitions the court for the removal of any illegal telecommunications equipment under this section shall be a necessary party to any proceeding or action arising out of or under section 18-9-309 (2) or (3).

No telephone company shall be liable for any damages, penalty, or forfeiture, whether civil or criminal, for any act performed in good faith and in compliance with any order issued by the court.

Property seized pursuant to the direction of the court which the court has determined to have been used in violation of section 18-9-309 (2) or (3) shall be forfeited to the state. Prior to the disposition of the seized property, a petition for the remission or mitigation of forfeiture may be filed. The court may remit or mitigate the forfeiture upon terms and conditions as the court deems reasonable if it finds that such forfeiture was incurred without willful negligence or without any intention on the petitioner to violate the law or finds the existence of such mitigating circumstances as to justify the remission or the mitigation of the forfeiture. In determining whether to remit or mitigate forfeiture, the court shall consider losses which may have been suffered by victims as the result of the use of the forfeited property.

18-9-310. Unlawful use of information - penalty. Any person who, having obtained information pursuant to a court order for wiretapping or eavesdropping, knowingly uses, publishes, or divulges the information to any person or in any manner not authorized by this part 3 commits a class 6 felony.

18-9-311. Automated dialing systems prohibited. (1) No person shall utilize an automated dialing system with a prerecorded message for the purpose of soliciting another person to purchase goods or services, whether such solicitation occurs or is intended to occur during the prerecorded message or during some further communication initiated by or resulting from the prerecorded message, unless there is an existing business relationship between

such persons and the person being called then consents to hear the prerecorded message.
Any person who violates this section commits a class 1 petty offense.

18-9-312. Hostage, endangered person, or armed person in geographical area -

telephone, electronic, cellular, or digital communications. (1) (a) Notwithstanding the provisions of sections 18-9-302 to 18-9-311, any supervising representative of a law enforcement agency shall have the authority to order a previously designated security employee of a communications or internet access provider to arrange, to the extent the necessary technology is reasonably available to the provider, to cut, reroute, or divert telephone lines or cellular or digital communications signals if the supervising representative has probable cause to believe that:
A person has taken one or more other persons hostage and is holding the hostages in the geographical area in which the supervising representative has jurisdiction; or
A person has barricaded himself or herself in a structure or a motor vehicle within the geographical area in which the supervising representative has jurisdiction and the supervising representative has a reasonable belief that the person is armed with a deadly weapon or explosive device and poses a danger to himself or herself or others.
(b) The supervising representative of a law enforcement agency may order the cutting, rerouting, or diverting of telephone lines or cellular or digital communications signals pursuant to paragraph (a) of this subsection (1) only for the purpose of preventing telephone or other electronic, cellular, or digital communication by the hostage holder or the armed person with any person other than a peace officer or a person authorized by the peace officer. The communications or internet access provider shall restore the normal operations of the telephone lines or cellular or digital communications signals as soon as practicable following resolution of the exigent circumstances. (1.5) (a) Notwithstanding the provisions of sections 18-9-302 to 18-9-311, any supervising representative of a law enforcement agency may order a previously designated security employee of a wireless telecommunications provider to provide to the law enforcement agency, without requiring the agency to obtain a court order, location information concerning the telecommunications device
of a named person if the supervising representative has probable cause to believe that:
An emergency situation exists that involves the risk of death or serious bodily injury to the named person or to another person who is in the named person's company; and
The time required to obtain a search warrant or other court order authorizing the acquisition of the information would increase such risk.
A wireless telecommunications provider may establish protocols by which the provider discloses location information, provided that such protocols shall include keeping a record of:
The name of the supervising representative of a law enforcement agency that requested the location information; and
The time and date when the request was made.
With regard to compliance with the requirements of this subsection (1.5), no cause of action may be brought against any wireless telecommunications provider, its officers, employees, agents, or other specified persons for providing location information in response to a request from a law enforcement agent with actual or apparent authority to act as a supervising representative under this subsection (1.5).
A law enforcement agency that acquires information pursuant to this subsection (1.5) shall not divulge the acquired information to any person other than to another law enforcement agency, or an employee thereof, unless the law enforcement agency has obtained a court order stating that the information was lawfully obtained and authorizing the law enforcement agency to retain the information, as described in subparagraph (I) of paragraph (d) of this subsection (1.5).

(I) Not more than forty-eight hours after ordering a previously designated security employee of a wireless telecommunications provider to provide information as described in paragraph (a) of this subsection (1.5), a law enforcement agency shall request a court order stating whether:
At the time that the supervising representative of a law enforcement agency ordered the previously designated security employee of a wireless telecommunications provider to provide the information, the supervising representative had probable cause to believe that the conditions described in paragraph (a) of this subsection (1.5) existed; and
The law enforcement agency may retain the information for a bona fide investigative purpose.
Unless a court orders that the law enforcement agency may retain the information for a bona fide investigative purpose, as described in sub-subparagraph (B) of subparagraph (I) of this paragraph (e), the law enforcement agency shall destroy the information and not retain any copy of the information for any purpose.
If the court issues an order stating that the supervising representative of the law enforcement agency did not have probable cause to believe that the conditions described in paragraph
(a) of this subsection (1.5) existed and that the information was not lawfully obtained, then neither the information nor any other evidence that is obtained as a result of the law enforcement agency's acquisition of the information may be admitted in any subsequent criminal proceeding unless the information or other evidence was also acquired independently in a lawful manner.
Any ruling by a court that the information obtained may be retained for a bona fide investigative purpose shall not be considered a ruling on the admissibility of the evidence in any criminal proceeding under the constitutional and statutory provisions of the United States or Colorado.
The serving communications or internet access provider within the geographical area of a law enforcement agency shall designate a security official employed by the provider and an alternate to provide all required assistance to law enforcement officials to carry out the purposes of this section.
Good faith reliance on an order by any supervising representative of a law enforcement agency shall constitute a complete defense to any action brought against a communications or internet access provider or any of its employees or agents in connection with actions taken under this section. A communications or internet access provider and its employees or agents shall not be liable in any civil action to any person or entity for injuries, death, or loss to any person or property incurred as a result of any act or omission resulting from, connected with, or incidental to compliance with this section.

18-9-313. Personal information on the internet - law enforcement official - victims of domestic violence, sexual assault, and stalking - definitions. (1) As used in this section:
"Immediate family" means a law enforcement official's spouse, child, or parent or any other blood relative who lives in the same residence as the law enforcement official.
(a.5) "Law enforcement official" means a peace officer as described in section 16-2.5-101, C.R.S., a judge as defined by section 18-8-615 (3), or a prosecutor, as defined in section 18-8-616

(3).
(a.9) "Participant in the address confidentiality program" means an individual accepted into the address confidentiality program in accordance with part 21 of article 30 of title 24, C.R.S.

"Personal information" means the home address, home telephone number, personal mobile telephone number, pager number, personal e-mail address, or a personal photograph of a law enforcement official or participant in the address confidentiality program; or directions to the home of a law enforcement official or participant in the address confidentiality program; or photographs of the home or vehicle of a law enforcement official or participant in the address confidentiality program.

It is unlawful for a person to knowingly make available on the internet personal information about a law enforcement official or the official's immediate family member, if the dissemination of the personal information poses an imminent and serious threat to the law enforcement official's safety or the safety of the law enforcement official's immediate family and the person making the information available on the internet knows or reasonably should know of the imminent and serious threat.

(2.5) An address confidentiality program participant may submit a written request to a state or local government official and follow the process in section 24-30-2108, C.R.S., including the presentation of a valid address confidentiality program authorization card. If a state or local government official has received the above information, then the state or local government official shall not knowingly make available on the internet personal information about such participant in the address confidentiality program or the actual address, as defined in section 24-30-2103 (1), C.R.S., of such participant in the address confidentiality program.

A violation of subsection (2) of this section is a class 1 misdemeanor.


18-9-314. Interference with lawful distribution of newspapers - definitions. (1) A person commits the offense of interference with lawful distribution of newspapers when that person obtains or exerts unauthorized control over more than five copies of an edition of a newspaper from a newspaper distribution container owned or leased by the newspaper publisher with the intent to prevent other individuals from reading that edition of the newspaper. Control is unauthorized if there is a notice on the newspaper or on the newspaper distribution container that possession of more than five copies with intent to prevent other individuals from reading that edition of the newspaper is illegal.

Interference with lawful distribution of newspapers is an unclassified misdemeanor and shall be punished by a fine of:

Up to one thousand dollars if the number of newspapers involved was one hundred or fewer or the number of newspapers involved was not determined;

Up to two thousand five hundred dollars if the number of newspapers involved was more than one hundred and fewer than five hundred;

Up to five thousand dollars if the number of newspapers involved was five hundred or more.

As used in this section:

"Edition of a newspaper" means a single press run of a newspaper.

"Newspaper" means a periodical that includes news, editorials, opinion, features, or other matters of public interest distributed on a complimentary basis. "Newspaper" includes any student periodical distributed at any institution of higher education.

"Periodical" means a publication produced on a regular interval.

Notwithstanding anyother remedies provided under this section, the newspaper publisher who is the victim of interference with lawful distribution of newspapers, an advertiser who placed an advertisement in the newspaper, or a newspaper reader who regularly reads the newspaper shall have a private civil right of action as provided in section 13-21-123, C.R.S., against the person or persons who acted in violation of subsection (1) of this section.

This section shall not apply to a person who, with the authority or permission of the person who possesses real or personal property, removes or disposes of newspapers that have been deposited in or left on that property without the authority or permission of the person who possesses the real or personal property.

ARTICLE 10

Gambling

18-10-101. Legislative declaration - construction. (1) It is declared to be the policy of the general assembly, recognizing the close relationship between professional gambling and other organized crime, to restrain all persons from seeking profit from gambling activities in this state; to restrain all persons from patronizing such activities when conducted for the profit of any person; to safeguard the public against the evils induced by common gamblers and common gambling houses; and at the same time to preserve the freedom of the press and to avoid restricting participation by individuals in sport and social pastimes which are not for profit, do not affect the public, and do not breach the peace.

(2) All the provisions of this article shall be liberally construed to achieve these ends and administered and enforced with a view to carrying out the declaration of policy stated in subsection
of this section.

18-10-102. Definitions. As used in this article, unless the context otherwise requires:

"Gain" means the direct realization of winnings; "profit" means any other realized or unrealized benefit, direct or indirect, including without limitation benefits from proprietorship, management, or unequal advantage in a series of transactions.

"Gambling" means risking any money, credit, deposit, or other thing of value for gain contingent in whole or in part upon lot, chance, the operation of a gambling device, or the happening or outcome of an event, including a sporting event, over which the person taking a risk has no control, but does not include:

Bona fide contests of skill, speed, strength, or endurance in which awards are made only to entrants or the owners of entries;

Bona fide business transactions which are valid under the law of contracts;

Other acts or transactions now or hereafter expressly authorized by law;

Any game, wager, or transaction which is incidental to a bona fide social relationship, is participated in by natural persons only, and in which no person is participating, directly or indirectly, in professional gambling; or

Repealed.

Any use of or transaction involving a crane game, as defined in section 12-47.1-103 (5.5),
C.R.S.

"Gambling device" means any device, machine, paraphernalia, or equipment that is used
or usable in the playing phases of any professional gambling activity, whether that activity consists of gambling between persons or gambling by a person involving the playing of a machine; except that the term does not include a crane game, as defined in section 12-47.1-103 (5.5), C.R.S.

"Gambling information" means a communication with respect to any wager made in the course of, and any information intended to be used for, professional gambling. In the application of this definition the following shall be presumed to be intended for use in professional gambling: Information as to wagers, betting odds, or changes in betting odds. Legitimate news reporting of an event for public dissemination is not gambling information within the meaning of this article.

"Gambling premises" means any building, room, enclosure, vehicle, vessel, or other place, whether open or enclosed, used or intended to be used for professional gambling. In the application of this definition, any place where a gambling device is found is presumed to be intended to be used for professional gambling.

"Gambling proceeds" means all money or other things of value at stake or displayed in or in connection with professional gambling.

"Gambling record" means any record, receipt, ticket, certificate, token, slip, or notation given, made, used, or intended to be used in connection with professional gambling.

"Professional gambling" means:

Aiding or inducing another to engage in gambling, with the intent to derive a profit therefrom; or

Participating in gambling and having, other than by virtue of skill or luck, a lesser chance of losing or a greater chance of winning than one or more of the other participants.

"Repeating gambling offender" means any person who is convicted of an offense under section 18-10-103 (2) or sections 18-10-105 to 18-10-107 or sections 12-47.1-809 to 12-47.1-811 or 12-47.1-818 to 12-47.1-832 or 12-47.1-839, C.R.S., or sections 18-20-103 to 18-20-114 within five years after a previous misdemeanor conviction under these sections or a former statute prohibiting gambling activities, or at any time after a previous felony conviction under any of the mentioned sections. A conviction in any jurisdiction of the United States of an offense which, if committed in this state, would be professional gambling shall warrant a prosecution in this state as a repeating gambling offender.

"Vintage slot machine" means any model slot machine, as defined in section 12-47.1- 103 (26), C.R.S., that was introduced on the market prior to January 1, 1984.

18-10-103. Gambling - professional gambling - offenses. (1) A person who engages in gambling commits a class 1 petty offense.
(2) A person who engages in professional gambling commits a class 1 misdemeanor. If he is a repeating gambling offender, it is a class 5 felony.


18-10-104. Gambling devices - gambling records - gambling proceeds. (1) Except as provided in subsection (2) of this section, all gambling devices, gambling records, and gambling proceeds are subject to seizure by any peace officer and may be confiscated and destroyed by order of a court acquiring jurisdiction. Gambling proceeds shall be forfeited to the state and shall be transmitted by court order to the general fund of the state.
(2) If a gambling device is a vintage slot machine and is not operated for gambling purposes for profit or for business purposes, it shall not be confiscated or destroyed pursuant to subsection (1) of this section. If a gambling device is confiscated and the owner shows that such gambling device is a vintage slot machine and is not used for gambling purposes, the court acquiring jurisdiction shall order such vintage slot machine returned to the person from whom it was confiscated.


18-10-105. Possession of a gambling device or record. (1) Except as provided in subsection (1.5) of this section, a person who owns, manufactures, sells, transports, possesses, or engages in any transaction designed to affect the ownership, custody, or use of a gambling device or gambling record, knowing that it is to be used in professional gambling, commits possession of a gambling device or record.
(1.5) The sale, transportation, manufacture, and remanufacture of gambling devices, including the acquisition of essential parts therefor and the assembly of such parts, is permitted if such devices are sold, transported, manufactured, and remanufactured only for transportation in interstate or foreign commerce when such transportation is not prohibited by any applicable foreign, state, or federal law. Storage of gambling devices is also permitted but only for purposes of manufacturing, remanufacturing, and transporting such devices in interstate or foreign commerce when their transportation is not prohibited. Such activities may be conducted only by persons who have registered with the United States government pursuant to the provisions of chapter 24 of Title XV of the United States Code, as amended. Such gambling devices shall not be openly displayed, except to legal buyers, or sold for use in Colorado regardless of where purchased, nor manufactured, remanufactured, or stored for purposes of manufacture, remanufacture, and transportation in violation of any applicable state or federal law. For purposes of this subsection (1.5), "legal buyer" means a buyer who resides in another state or country which does not restrict the possession of the specific gambling device in question.
(2) Possession of a gambling device or record or violation of subsection (1.5) of this section is a class 2 misdemeanor. If the offender is a repeating gambling offender, it is a class 6 felony.


18-10-106. Gambling information. (1) Whoever knowinglytransmits or receives gambling

information by telephone, telegraph, radio, semaphore, or other means or knowingly installs or maintains equipment for the transmission or receipt of gambling information commits a class 3 misdemeanor. If the offender is a repeating gambling offender, it is a class 6 felony.
(2) Facilities and equipment furnished by a public utility in the regular course of business, and which remain the property of the utility while so furnished, shall not be seized except in connection with an alleged violation of this article by the public utility and shall be forfeited only upon conviction of the public utility therefor.


18-10-107. Gambling premises. (1) Whoever as owner, lessee, agent, employee, operator, or occupant knowingly maintains, aids, or permits the maintaining of gambling premises commits maintaining gambling premises.
All gambling premises are common nuisances which shall be subject to abatement as provided by law.
Maintaining gambling premises is a class 3 misdemeanor. If the offender is a repeating gambling offender, it is a class 6 felony.


18-10-108. Exceptions. Nothing contained in this article shall be construed to modify, amend, or otherwise affect the validity of any provisions contained in articles 9, 47.1, and 60 of title 12, C.R.S.

### ARTICLE 10.5  Simulated Gambling Devices

18-10.5-101. Legislative declaration. (1) The general assembly finds, determines, and declares that:
Recently, certain individuals and companies have developed electronic machines, systems, and devices to enable gambling through pretextual sweepstakes relationships predicated on the sale of internet services, telephone cards, and other products at business locations that are or may be commonly known as internet sweepstakes cafes. These machines, systems, and devices, as more fully described in this article, appear designed to evade the existing constitutional and statutory regulations on gambling activity in Colorado and therefore are declared to be contrary to the public policy of this state.
The gambling occurring at internet sweepstakes cafes has none of the protections that are afforded to players at legal gaming sites in Colorado. This absence of uniform regulation and ongoing, governmental oversight presents a danger to consumers throughout the state of Colorado. These sites comply with none of the regulatory requirements, such as surveillance and tracking of

wagers and payouts, to assure consumers that gambling is being conducted fairly and honestly. The general assembly finds that these dangers are profound, putting at risk the financial resources of vulnerable persons and customers who are used to wagering based on clear regulatory standards and who have official lines of authority to which they may appeal when there are questionable or illegal practices used by a licensed gaming operator. The proliferation of internet sweepstakes cafes presents an increasing risk to consumers, particularly as these sweepstakes cafes have spread to sites throughout the state and are capable of operating without facing adverse consequences for their illegal, unfair, or unregulated acts;
The diversion of consumer dollars to these untaxed gambling activities not only presents the opportunity for theft but also undermines state and local programs that are funded by revenue derived from legalized gambling, including parks and recreation, historic preservation, and the state's general fund;
There is no adequate local or federal regulation of internet sweepstakes cafes, and the ability of the owners of those facilities to operate in any community in the state or to move their operations from one part of the state to another without notifying any regulatory body makes this an issue of statewide concern, appropriate for action by the general assembly;
The voters of Colorado have carefully chosen the forms of gambling to which to give their approval and the conditions under which those forms of gambling may be conducted. At no time has the question of legalization of internet sweepstakes cafes been presented to the voters of this state. Without a vote of the people, the state of Colorado cannot permit the operation of unauthorized, unregulated, and unsupervised gambling or lotteries in violation of section 2 or 9 of article XVIII of the Colorado constitution.

18-10.5-102. Definitions. As used in this article, unless the context otherwise requires:

"Electronic gaming machine" means an electrically or electronically operated machine or device that is used by a sweepstakes entrant and that displays the results of a game entry or game outcome to a participant on a screen or other mechanism at a business location, including a private club, that is owned, leased, or otherwise possessed, in whole or in part, by a person conducting the sweepstakes or by that person's partners, affiliates, subsidiaries, agents, or contractors. The term includes a machine or device that:
Uses a simulated game terminal as a representation of the prizes associated with the results of the sweepstakes entries;
Uses software that simulates a game that influences or determines the winning or value of the prize, or appears to influence or determine the winning or value of the prize;
Selects prizes from a predetermined, finite pool of entries;
Uses a mechanism that reveals the content of a predetermined sweepstakes entry;
Predetermines the prize results and stores those results for deliverywhen the sweepstakes entry is revealed;
Uses software to create a game result;
Requires a deposit of any currency or token or the use of any credit card, debit card, prepaid card, or other method of payment to activate the machine or device;

Requires direct payment into the machine or device or remote activation of the machine or device upon payment to the person offering the sweepstakes game;
Requires the purchase of a related product at additional cost in order to participate in the sweepstakes game or makes a related product available for no cost but under restrictive conditions;
Reveals a sweepstakes prize incrementally even though the progress of the images on the screen does not influence whether a prize is awarded or the value of any prize awarded; or

Determines and associates the prize with an entry or entries at the time the sweepstakes is entered.
"Enter" or "entry" means the act or process by which a person becomes eligible to receive a prize offered in a sweepstakes.
"Entrant" means a person who is or seeks to become eligible to receive a prize offered in a sweepstakes.
"Local jurisdiction" means a town, city, city and county, or the unincorporated area of a county.
"Prize" means a gift, award, gratuity, good, service, credit, or anything else of value that may be transferred to a person, whether or not possession of the prize is actually transferred or placed on an account or other record as evidence of the intent to transfer the prize. "Prize" does not include free or additional play or any intangible or virtual award that cannot be converted into money, goods, or services.
"Simulated gambling device" means a mechanically or electronically operated machine, network, system, program, or device that is used by an entrant and that displays simulated gambling displays on a screen or other mechanism at a business location, including a private club, that is owned, leased, or otherwise possessed, in whole or in part, by a person conducting the game or by that person's partners, affiliates, subsidiaries, agents, or contractors. The term includes:
A video poker game or any other kind of video card game;
A video bingo game;
A video craps game;
A video keno game;
A video lotto game;
A video roulette game;
A pot-of-gold;
An eight-liner;
A video game based on or involving the random or chance matching of different pictures, words, numbers, or symbols;
An electronic gaming machine, including a personal computer of any size or configuration that performs any of the functions of an electronic gaming machine;
A slot machine; and
A device that functions as, or simulates the play of, a slot machine.
"Sweepstakes" means any game, advertising scheme or plan, or other promotion that, with or without payment of any consideration, allows a person to enter to win or become eligible to receive a prize.

18-10.5-103. Prohibition - penalties - exemptions. (1) A person commits unlawful offering of a simulated gambling device if the person offers, facilitates, contracts for, or otherwise makes available to or for members of the public or members of an organization or club any simulated gambling device where:
The payment of consideration is required or permitted for use of the device, for admission to premises on which the device is located, or for the purchase of any product or service associated with access to or use of the device; and
As a consequence of, in connection with, or after the play of the simulated gambling device, an award of a prize is expressly or implicitly made to a person using the device.
Unlawful offering of a simulated gambling device is a class 3 misdemeanor.
Without regard to any penalty imposed under subsection (2) of this section, the attorney general and each district attorney may apply to the district court of a district in which a person who violates subsection (1) of this section is located, advertises for entrants, or does business for appropriate additional relief, including:
Injunctive relief, including a temporary restraining order or preliminary or permanent injunction, to restrain and enjoin violations of this section;
Damages, up to and including three times the total dollar amount of business transacted or facilitated by any person who violates subsection (1) of this section, payable to the local jurisdiction in which the person is located, advertises for entrants, or does business; and
Other relief the district court deems appropriate.
A person who suffers any ascertainable loss of money or of any tangible or intangible personal property as a result of a violation of this section and who also holds a license to offer gambling services under Colorado law may apply to the district court of any district where the person who violates subsection (1) of this section is or was located, advertises for entrants, or does business for appropriate additional relief, including:
Injunctive relief, including a temporary restraining order or preliminary or permanent injunction, to restrain and enjoin violations of this section;
Damages up to and including three times the actual damages sustained as a result of violations of this section;
Reasonable attorney fees and costs; and

Other relief the district court deems appropriate.

The court may award reasonable attorney fees and costs to a defendant for any action filed pursuant to subsection (4) of this section that was substantially groundless, frivolous, or vexatious.

A criminal conviction against a named defendant under subsection (2) of this section is prima facie evidence of the liability of that named defendant in an action brought under subsection

or (4) of this section.

A civil action under this section must be filed within one year after the act or transaction giving rise to the cause of action.

Conducting or assisting in the conduct of gaming wagering activities and live or simulcast racing and parimutuel wagering activities otherwise authorized by Colorado law is not a violation of this section.

Nothing in this section:

Prohibits, limits, or otherwise affects any purchase, sale, exchange, or other transaction related to stocks, bonds, futures, options, commodities, or other similar instruments or transactions occurring on a stock or commodities exchange, brokerage house, or similar entity; or

Limits or alters the application of the requirements for sweepstakes, contests, and similar activities that are otherwise established under the laws of this state.

The provision of internet or other online access, transmission, routing, storage, or other communication-related services or website design, development, storage, maintenance, billing, advertising, hypertext linking, transaction processing, or other site-related services by a telephone company, internet service provider, software developer or licensor, or other party providing similar services to customers in the normal course of its business does not violate this section even if those customers use the services to conduct a prohibited game, contest, lottery, or other activity in violation of this article; except that this subsection (10) does not exempt from criminal prosecution or civil liability a software developer, licensor, or other party whose primary purpose in providing such service is to support the offering of simulated gambling devices.

### ARTICLE 11 Offenses Involving Disloyalty

PART 1

TREASON AND RELATED OFFENSES

18-11-101. Treason. (1) A person commits treason if he levies war against the state of Colorado or adheres to its enemies, giving them aid and comfort. No person shall be convicted of treason unless upon the testimony of two witnesses to the same overt act or upon confession in open court.
(2) Treason is a class 1 felony.

18-11-102. Insurrection. (1) Any person who, with the intent by force of arms to obstruct, retard, or resist the execution of any law of this state, engages, cooperates, or participates with any armed force or with an armed force invades any portion of this state commits insurrection.
(2) Insurrection is a class 5 felony.

PART 2 ANARCHY - SEDITION

18-11-201. Advocating overthrow of government. (1) Every person who, in this state, either orally or by writing, printing, exhibiting, or circulating written or printed words or pictures, or otherwise, shall advocate, teach, incite, propose, aid, abet, encourage, or advise resistance by physical force to, or the destruction or overthrow by physical force of, constituted government in general, or of the government or laws of the United States, or of this state, under circumstances constituting a clear and present danger that violent action will result therefrom, commits sedition.
(2) Sedition is a class 5 felony.

18-11-202. Inciting destruction of life or property. Every person who, in this state, either orally or by writing, printing, exhibiting, or circulating written or printed words or pictures, shall advocate, teach, incite, propose, aid, abet, encourage, or advise the unlawful injury or destruction of private or public property by the use of physical force, violence, or bodily injury, or the unlawful injury by the use of physical force or violence of any person, or the unlawful taking of human life, as a policy or course of conduct, under circumstances constituting a clear and present danger that violent action will result therefrom, commits a class 6 felony.

18-11-203. Membership in anarchistic and seditious associations. (1) Any association, organization, society, or corporation, one of whose purposes or professed purposes is to bring about any governmental, social, industrial, or economic change in this state or in the United States by the use of sabotage, terrorism, physical force, violence, or bodily injury, or which teaches, advocates, advises, or defends the use of sabotage, terrorism, physical force, violence, or bodily injury to person or property, or threats of such injury, to accomplish such change, and which shall, by any such means, prosecute or pursue such purpose or professed purpose is declared to be anarchistic and seditious in character and to be an unlawful association.

Any person who, in this state, shall act or profess to act as an officer of any such unlawful association, or shall speak, write, or publish as a representative or professed representative of any such unlawful association, or, knowing the purpose, teachings, and doctrine of such association, shall become or continue to be a member thereof or contribute dues, money, or other things of value to it or to anyone for it commits a class 5 felony.

18-11-204. Mutilation - contempt of flag - penalty. (1) It is unlawful for any person to mutilate, deface, defile, trample upon, burn, cut, or tear any flag in public:

With intent to cast contempt or ridicule upon the flag; or

With intent to outrage the sensibilities of persons liable to observe or discover the action or its results; or

With intent to cause a breach of the peace or incitement to riot; or

Under such circumstances that it may cause a breach of the peace or incitement to riot.

"Flag", as used in this section, means any flag, ensign, banner, standard, colors, or replica or representation thereof which is an official or commonly recognized symbol of the United States of America or the state of Colorado.

Any person violating the provisions of this section commits a class 3 misdemeanor.

18-11-205. Unlawful to display flag - exceptions. (1) Any person who displays any flag other than the flag of the United States of America or the state of Colorado or any of its subdivisions, agencies, or institutions on a permanent flagstaff located on a state, county, municipal, or other public building or on its grounds within this state commits a class 1 petty offense.

(Deleted by amendment, L. 2007, p. 423, § 1, effective August 3, 2007.)

"Flag", as used in this section, means any flag, ensign, banner, standard, colors, or replica or representation thereof which is an official or commonly recognized symbol of a particular nation, state, movement, cause, or organization.

(a) This section does not apply to:

The display of the flag of the United Nations or the flag of a foreign nation displayed to identify persons officially representing such foreign nation or the property or premises of the person or nation;

The display of an appropriate flag upon ceremonial or commemorative occasions proclaimed by the president of the United States, the governor of the state of Colorado, the board of county commissioners of any county, or the mayor or other chief executive officer of a city or town within this state;

The display of the flag of any adjacent state with the flag of the state of Colorado at the ports of entry weigh stations, in recognition of the joint state port operation; or

(Deleted by amendment, L. 2007, p. 423, § 1, effective August 3, 2007.)

The display of a prisoners of war and missing in action flag or other appropriate veteran commemorative, United States or state armed forces, or military commemorative flag when displayed in accordance with 4 U.S.C. sec. 7;

The display of flags of foreign nations for special, occasional, ceremonial purposes when displayed in accordance with 4 U.S.C. sec. 7; or

The display of a flag for educational, cultural, or historical purposes with the prior permission of the chief administrative officer of the state, county, municipal, or other public building or grounds.

(b) This subsection (4) shall be an affirmative defense.

## ARTICLE 12  Offenses Relating to Firearms and Weapons

PART 1
FIREARMS AND WEAPONS - GENERAL

18-12-101. Definitions - peace officer affirmative defense. (1) As used in this article, unless the context otherwise requires:

"Adult" means any person eighteen years of age or older.

(a.3) "Ballistic knife" means any knife that has a blade which is forcefully projected from the handle by means of a spring-loaded device or explosive charge.

(a.5) "Blackjack" includes any billy, sand club, sandbag, or other hand-operated striking weapon consisting, at the striking end, of an encased piece of lead or other heavy substance and, at the handle end, a strap or springy shaft which increases the force of impact.

"Bomb" means any explosive or incendiary device or molotov cocktail as defined in section 9-7-103, C.R.S., or any chemical device which causes or can cause an explosion, which is not specifically designed for lawful and legitimate use in the hands of its possessor.

(b.5) "Bureau" means the Colorado bureau of investigation created in section 24-33.5-401, C.R.S.

"Firearm silencer" means any instrument, attachment, weapon, or appliance for causing
the firing of any gun, revolver, pistol, or other firearm to be silent or intended to lessen or muffle the noise of the firing of any such weapon.

"Gas gun" means a device designed for projecting gas-filled projectiles which release their contents after having been projected from the device and includes projectiles designed for use in such a device.

"Gravity knife" means any knife that has a blade released from the handle or sheath thereof by the force of gravity or the application of centrifugal force.

(e.5) "Handgun" means a pistol, revolver, or other firearm of any description, loaded or unloaded, from which any shot, bullet, or other missile can be discharged, the length of the barrel of which, not including any revolving, detachable, or magazine breech, does not exceed twelve inches.

(e.7) "Juvenile" means any person under the age of eighteen years.

"Knife" means any dagger, dirk, knife, or stiletto with a blade over three and one-half inches in length, or any other dangerous instrument capable of inflicting cutting, stabbing, or tearing wounds, but does not include a hunting or fishing knife carried for sports use. The issue that a knife is a hunting or fishing knife must be raised as an affirmative defense.

"Machine gun" means any firearm, whatever its size and usual designation, that shoots automatically more than one shot, without manual reloading, by a single function of the trigger.

"Short rifle" means a rifle having a barrel less than sixteen inches long or an overall length of less than twenty-six inches.

"Short shotgun" means a shotgun having a barrel or barrels less than eighteen inches long or an overall length of less than twenty-six inches.

(i.5) "Stun gun" means a device capable of temporarily immobilizing a person by the infliction of an electrical charge.

"Switchblade knife" means any knife, the blade of which opens automatically by hand

pressure applied to a button, spring, or other device in its handle.

(2) It shall be an affirmative defense to any provision of this article that the act was committed by a peace officer in the lawful discharge of his duties.

18-12-102. Possessing a dangerous or illegal weapon - affirmative defense. (1) As used in this section, the term "dangerous weapon" means a firearm silencer, machine gun, short shotgun, short rifle, or ballistic knife.

As used in this section, the term "illegal weapon" means a blackjack, gas gun, metallic knuckles, gravity knife, or switchblade knife.

A person who knowingly possesses a dangerous weapon commits a class 5 felony. Each subsequent violation of this subsection (3) by the same person shall be a class 4 felony.

A person who knowingly possesses an illegal weapon commits a class 1 misdemeanor.

It shall be an affirmative defense to the charge of possessing a dangerous weapon, or to the charge of possessing an illegal weapon, that the person so accused was a peace officer or member of the armed forces of the United States or Colorado National Guard acting in the lawful discharge of his duties, or that said person has a valid permit and license for possession of such weapon.

18-12-103. Possession of a defaced firearm. A person commits a class 1 misdemeanor if he knowingly and unlawfully possesses a firearm, the manufacturer's serial number of which, or other distinguishing number or identification mark, has been removed, defaced, altered, or destroyed, except by normal wear and tear.

18-12-103.5. Defaced firearms - contraband - destruction. (1) After a judgment of conviction under section 18-12-103 or 18-12-104 has become final, any defaced firearm upon which the judgment was based shall be deemed to be contraband, the possession of which is contrary to the public peace, health, and safety.
Defaced firearms that are deemed to be contraband shall be placed in the possession of the bureau or of a local law enforcement agency designated by the bureau and shall be destroyed or rendered permanently inoperable.

18-12-104. Defacing a firearm. A person commits a class 1 misdemeanor if such person knowingly removes, defaces, covers, alters, or destroys the manufacturer's serial number or any other distinguishing number or identification mark of a firearm.

18-12-105. Unlawfully carrying a concealed weapon - unlawful possession of weapons. (1) A person commits a class 2 misdemeanor if such person knowingly and unlawfully:
Carries a knife concealed on or about his or her person; or
Carries a firearm concealed on or about his or her person; or

Without legal authority, carries, brings, or has in such person's possession a firearm or any explosive, incendiary, or other dangerous device on the property of or within any building in which the chambers, galleries, or offices of the general assembly, or either house thereof, are located, or in which a legislative hearing or meeting is being or is to be conducted, or in which the official office of any member, officer, or employee of the general assembly is located.
(Deleted by amendment, L. 93, p. 964, § 1, effective July 1, 1993.)
It shall not be an offense if the defendant was:
A person in his or her own dwelling or place of business or on property owned or under his or her control at the time of the act of carrying; or
A person in a private automobile or other private means of conveyance who carries a weapon for lawful protection of such person's or another's person or property while traveling; or
A person who, at the time of carrying a concealed weapon, held a valid written permit to carry a concealed weapon issued pursuant to section 18-12-105.1, as it existed prior to its repeal, or, if the weapon involved was a handgun, held a valid permit to carry a concealed handgun or a temporary emergency permit issued pursuant to part 2 of this article; except that it shall be an offense under this section if the person was carrying a concealed handgun in violation of the provisions of section 18-12-214; or
A peace officer, as described in section 16-2.5-101, C.R.S., when carrying a weapon in conformance with the policy of the employing agency as provided in section 16-2.5-101 (2), C.R.S.; or
(Deleted by amendment, L. 2003, p. 1624, § 46, effective August 6, 2003.)
A United States probation officer or a United States pretrial services officer while on duty and serving in the state of Colorado under the authority of rules and regulations promulgated by the judicial conference of the United States.

18-12-105.1. Permits for concealed weapons - liability. (Repealed)

18-12-105.5. Unlawfully carrying a weapon - unlawful possession of weapons - school, college, or university grounds. (1) A person commits a class 6 felony if such person knowingly and unlawfully and without legal authority carries, brings, or has in such person's possession a deadly weapon as defined in section 18-1-901 (3) (e) in or on the real estate and all improvements erected thereon of any public or private elementary, middle, junior high, high, or vocational school or any public or private college, university, or seminary, except for the purpose of presenting an authorized public demonstration or exhibition pursuant to instruction in conjunction with an organized school or class, for the purpose of carrying out the necessary duties and functions of an employee of an educational institution that require the use of a deadly weapon, or for the purpose of participation in an authorized extracurricular activity or on an athletic team.
(Deleted by amendment, L. 2000, p. 709, § 45, effective July 1, 2000.)
It shall not be an offense under this section if:
The weapon is unloaded and remains inside a motor vehicle while upon the real estate of any public or private college, university, or seminary; or

The person is in that person's own dwelling or place of business or on property owned or under that person's control at the time of the act of carrying; or
The person is in a private automobile or other private means of conveyance and is carrying a weapon for lawful protection of that person's or another's person or property while traveling; or
The person, at the time of carrying a concealed weapon, held a valid written permit to carry a concealed weapon issued pursuant to section 18-12-105.1, as said section existed prior to its repeal; except that it shall be an offense under this section if the person was carrying a concealed handgun in violation of the provisions of section 18-12-214 (3); or
(d.5) The weapon involved was a handgun and the person held a valid permit to carry a concealed handgun or a temporary emergency permit issued pursuant to part 2 of this article; except that it shall be an offense under this section if the person was carrying a concealed handgun in violation of the provisions of section 18-12-214 (3); or
The person is a school resource officer, as defined in section 22-32-109.1 (1) (g.5), C.R.S., or a peace officer, as described in section 16-2.5-101, C.R.S., when carrying a weapon in conformance with the policy of the employing agency as provided in section 16-2.5-101 (2), C.R.S.; or
and (g) (Deleted by amendment, L. 2003, p. 1626, § 51, effective August 6, 2003.)
(h) The person has possession of the weapon for use in an educational program approved by a school which program includes, but shall not be limited to, any course designed for the repair or maintenance of weapons.

18-12-105.6. Limitation on local ordinances regarding firearms in private vehicles. (1) The general assembly hereby finds that:

A person carrying a weapon in a private automobile or other private means of conveyance for hunting or for lawful protection of such person's or another's person or property, as permitted in sections 18-12-105 (2) (b) and 18-12-105.5 (3) (c), may tend to travel within a county, city and county, or municipal jurisdiction or in or through different county, city and county, and municipal jurisdictions, en route to the person's destination;

Inconsistent laws exist in local jurisdictions with regard to the circumstances under which weapons may be carried in automobiles and other private means of conveyance;

This inconsistency creates a confusing patchwork of laws that unfairly subjects a person who lawfully travels with a weapon to criminal penalties because he or she travels within a jurisdiction or into or through another jurisdiction;

This inconsistency places citizens in the position of not knowing when they may be violating local laws while traveling within a jurisdiction or in, through, or between different jurisdictions, and therefore being unable to avoid committing a crime.

(2) (a) Based on the findings specified in subsection (1) of this section, the general assembly concludes that the carrying of weapons in private automobiles or other private means of conveyance for hunting or for lawful protection of a person's or another's person or property while traveling into, through, or within, a municipal, county, or city and county jurisdiction, regardless of the number of times the person stops in a jurisdiction, is a matter of statewide concern and is not an offense.

(b) Notwithstanding any other provision of law, no municipality, county, or city and county shall have the authority to enact or enforce any ordinance or resolution that would restrict a person's ability to travel with a weapon in a private automobile or other private means of conveyance for hunting or for lawful protection of a person's or another's person or property while traveling into, through, or within, a municipal, county, or city and county jurisdiction, regardless of the number of times the person stops in a jurisdiction.

18-12-106. Prohibited use of weapons. (1) A person commits a class 2 misdemeanor if:

He knowingly and unlawfully aims a firearm at another person; or

Recklessly or with criminal negligence he discharges a firearm or shoots a bow and arrow; or

He knowingly sets a loaded gun, trap, or device designed to cause an explosion upon being tripped or approached, and leaves it unattended by a competent person immediately present; or

The person has in his or her possession a firearm while the person is under the influence of intoxicating liquor or of a controlled substance, as defined in section 18-18-102 (5). Possession of a permit issued under section 18-12-105.1, as it existed prior to its repeal, or possession of a permit or a temporary emergency permit issued pursuant to part 2 of this article is no defense to a violation of this subsection (1).

He knowingly aims, swings, or throws a throwing star or nunchaku as defined in this paragraph (e) at another person, or he knowingly possesses a throwing star or nunchaku in a public place except for the purpose of presenting an authorized public demonstration or exhibition or pursuant to instruction in conjunction with an organized school or class. When transporting throwing stars or nunchaku for a public demonstration or exhibition or for a school or class, they shall be transported in a closed, nonaccessible container. For purposes of this paragraph (e), "nunchaku" means an instrument consisting of two sticks, clubs, bars, or rods to be used as handles, connected by a rope, cord, wire, or chain, which is in the design of a weapon used in connection with the practice of a system of self-defense, and "throwing star" means a disk having sharp radiating points or any disk-shaped bladed object which is hand-held and thrown and which is in the design of a weapon used in connection with the practice of a system of self-defense.

18-12-106.5. Use of stun guns. A person commits a class 5 felony if he knowingly and unlawfully uses a stun gun in the commission of a criminal offense.

18-12-107. Penalty for second offense. Any person who has within five years previously been convicted of a violation under section 18-12-103, 18-12-105, or 18-12-106 shall, upon conviction for a second or subsequent offense under the same section, be guilty of a class 5 felony.

18-12-107.5. Illegal discharge of a firearm - penalty. (1) Any person who knowingly or

recklessly discharges a firearm into any dwelling or any other building or occupied structure, or into any motor vehicle occupied by any person, commits the offense of illegal discharge of a firearm.

It shall not be an offense under this section if the person who discharges a firearm in violation of subsection (1) of this section is a peace officer as described in section 16-2.5-101, C.R.S., acting within the scope of such officer's authority and in the performance of such officer's duties.

Illegal discharge of a firearm is a class 5 felony.

18-12-108. Possession of weapons by previous offenders. (1) A person commits the crime of possession of a weapon by a previous offender if the person knowingly possesses, uses, or carries upon his or her person a firearm as described in section 18-1-901 (3) (h) or any other weapon that is subject to the provisions of this article subsequent to the person's conviction for a felony, or subsequent to the person's conviction for attempt or conspiracy to commit a felony, under Colorado or any other state's law or under federal law.

(a) Except as otherwise provided by paragraphs (b) and (c) of this subsection (2), a person commits a class 6 felony if the person violates subsection (1) of this section.

A person commits a class 5 felony, as provided by section 18-12-102, if the person violates subsection (1) of this section and the weapon is a dangerous weapon, as defined in section 18-12-102 (1).

A person commits a class 5 felony if the person violates subsection (1) of this section and the person's previous conviction was for burglary, arson, or any felony involving the use of force or the use of a deadly weapon and the violation of subsection (1) of this section occurs as follows:

From the date of conviction to ten years after the date of conviction, if the person was not incarcerated; or

From the date of conviction to ten years after the date of release from confinement, if such person was incarcerated or, if subject to supervision imposed as a result of conviction, ten years after the date of release from supervision.

Any sentence imposed pursuant to this subsection (2) shall run consecutively with any prior sentences being served by the offender.

A person commits the crime of possession of a weapon by a previous offender if the person knowingly possesses, uses, or carries upon his or her person a firearm as described in section 18-1-901 (3) (h) or any other weapon that is subject to the provisions of this article subsequent to the person's adjudication for an act which, if committed by an adult, would constitute a felony, or subsequent to the person's adjudication for attempt or conspiracy to commit a felony, under Colorado or any other state's law or under federal law.

(a) Except as otherwise provided by paragraphs (b) and (c) of this subsection (4), a person commits a class 6 felony if the person violates subsection

(3) of this section.

A person commits a class 5 felony, as provided by section 18-12-102, if the person violates subsection (3) of this section and the weapon is a dangerous weapon, as defined in section 18-12-102 (1).

A person commits a class 5 felony if the person commits the conduct described in subsection (3) of this section and the person's previous adjudication was based on an act that, if

committed by an adult, would constitute burglary, arson, or any felony involving the use of force or the use of a deadly weapon and the violation of subsection (3) of this section occurs as follows:

From the date of adjudication to ten years after the date of adjudication, if the person was not committed to the department of institutions, or on or after July 1, 1994, to the department of human services; or

From the date of adjudication to ten years after the date of release from commitment, if such person was committed to the department of institutions, or on or after July 1, 1994, to the department of human services or, if subject to supervision imposed as a result of an adjudication, ten years after the date of release from supervision.

Any sentence imposed pursuant to this subsection (4) shall run consecutively with any prior sentences being served by the offender.

A second or subsequent offense under paragraphs (b) and (c) of subsection (2) and paragraphs (b) and (c) of subsection (4) of this section is a class 4 felony.

(a) Upon the discharge of any inmate from the custody of the department of corrections, the department shall provide a written advisement to such inmate of the prohibited acts and penalties specified in this section. The written advisement, at a minimum, shall include the written statement specified in paragraph (c) of this subsection (6).

Any written stipulation for deferred judgment and sentence entered into by a defendant pursuant to section 18-1.3-102 shall contain a written advisement of the prohibited acts and penalties specified in this section. The written advisement, at a minimum, shall include the written statement specified in paragraph (c) of this subsection (6).

The written statement shall provide that:

(A) A person commits the crime of possession of a weapon by a previous offender in violation of this section if the person knowingly possesses, uses, or carries upon his or her person a firearm as described in section 18-1-901 (3) (h), or any other weapon that is subject to the provisions of this title subsequent to the person's conviction for a felony, or subsequent to the person's conviction for attempt or conspiracy to commit a felony, or subsequent to the person's conviction for a misdemeanor crime of domestic violence as defined in 18 U.S.C. sec. 921 (a) (33) (A), or subsequent to the person's conviction for attempt or conspiracyto commit such misdemeanor crime of domestic violence; and

(B) For the purposes of this paragraph (c), "felony" means any felony under Colorado law, federal law, or the laws of any other state; and

A violation of this section may result in a sentence of imprisonment or fine, or both.

The act of providing the written advisement described in this subsection (6) or the failure to provide such advisement may not be used as a defense to any crime charged and may not provide any basis for collateral attack on, or for appellate relief concerning, any conviction.


18-12-108.5. Possession of handguns by juveniles - prohibited - exceptions - penalty. (1) (a) Except as provided in this section, it is unlawful for any person who has not attained the age of eighteen years knowingly to have any handgun in such person's possession.

Any person possessing any handgun in violation of paragraph (a) of this subsection (1)

commits the offense of illegal possession of a handgun by a juvenile.

(I) Illegal possession of a handgun by a juvenile is a class 2 misdemeanor.

(II) For any second or subsequent offense, illegal possession of a handgun by a juvenile is a class 5 felony.

Any person under the age of eighteen years who is taken into custody by a law enforcement officer for an offense pursuant to this section shall be taken into temporary custody in the manner described in section 19-2-508, C.R.S.

This section shall not apply to:

Any person under the age of eighteen years who is:

In attendance at a hunter's safety course or a firearms safety course; or

Engaging in practice in the use of a firearm or target shooting at an established range authorized by the governing body of the jurisdiction in which such range is located or any other area where the discharge of a firearm is not prohibited; or

Engaging in an organized competition involving the use of a firearm or participating in or practicing for a performance by an organized group under 501 (c) (3) as determined by the federal internal revenue service which uses firearms as a part of such performance; or

Hunting or trapping pursuant to a valid license issued to such person pursuant to article 4 of title 33, C.R.S.; or

Traveling with any handgun in such person's possession being unloaded to or from any activity described in subparagraph (I), (II), (III), or (IV) of this paragraph (a);

Any person under the age of eighteen years who is on real property under the control of such person's parent, legal guardian, or grandparent and who has the permission of such person's parent or legal guardian to possess a handgun;

Any person under the age of eighteen years who is at such person's residence and who, with the permission of such person's parent or legal guardian, possesses a handgun for the purpose of exercising the rights contained in section 18-1-704 or section 18-1-704.5.

For the purposes of subsection (2) of this section, a handgun is "loaded" if:

There is a cartridge in the chamber of the handgun; or

There is a cartridge in the cylinder of the handgun, if the handgun is a revolver; or

The handgun, and the ammunition for such handgun, is carried on the person of a person under the age of eighteen years or is in such close proximity to such person that such person could readily gain access to the handgun and the ammunition and load the handgun.

Repealed.


18-12-108.7. Unlawfully providing or permitting a juvenile to possess a handgun - penalty - unlawfully providing a firearm other than a handgun to a juvenile - penalty. (1) (a) Any person who intentionally, knowingly, or recklessly provides a handgun with or without remuneration to any person under the age of eighteen years in violation of section 18-12-

108.5 or any person who knows of such juvenile's conduct which violates section 18-12-108.5 and fails to make reasonable efforts to prevent such violation commits the crime of unlawfully providing a handgun to a juvenile or permitting a juvenile to possess a handgun.

(b) Unlawfully providing a handgun to a juvenile or permitting a juvenile to possess a

handgun in violation of this subsection (1) is a class 4 felony.

(a) Any person who intentionally, knowingly, or recklessly provides a handgun to a juvenile or permits a juvenile to possess a handgun, even though such person is aware of a substantial risk that such juvenile will use a handgun to commit a felony offense, or who, being aware of such substantial risk, fails to make reasonable efforts to prevent the commission of the offense, commits the crime of unlawfully providing or permitting a juvenile to possess a handgun. A person shall be deemed to have violated this paragraph (a) if such person provides a handgun to or permits the possession of a handgun by any juvenile who has been convicted of a crime of violence, as defined in section 18-1.3-406, or any juvenile who has been adjudicated a juvenile delinquent for an offense which would constitute a crime of violence, as defined in section 18-1.3- 406, if such juvenile were an adult.

(b) Unlawfully providing a handgun to a juvenile or permitting a juvenile to possess a handgun in violation of this subsection (2) is a class 4 felony. With regard to firearms other than handguns, no person shall sell, rent, or transfer ownership or allow unsupervised possession of a firearm with or without remuneration to any juvenile without the consent of the juvenile's parent or legal guardian. Unlawfully providing a firearm other than a handgun to a juvenile in violation of this subsection (3) is a class 1 misdemeanor.

It shall not be an offense under this section if a person believes that a juvenile will physically harm the person if the person attempts to disarm the juvenile or prevent the juvenile from committing a violation of section 18-12-108.5.


18-12-109. Possession, use, or removal of explosives or incendiary devices - possession of components thereof - chemical, biological, and nuclear weapons - persons exempt - hoaxes. (1) As used in this section:

(I) "Explosive or incendiary device" means:

Dynamite and all other forms of high explosives, including, but not limited to, water gel, slurry, military C-4 (plastic explosives), blasting agents to include nitro-carbon-nitrate, and ammonium nitrate and fuel oil mixtures, cast primers and boosters, R.D.X., P.E.T.N., electric and nonelectric blasting caps, exploding cords commonly called detonating cord or det-cord or primacord, picric acid explosives, T.N.T. and T.N.T. mixtures, and nitroglycerin and nitroglycerin mixtures;

Any explosive bomb, grenade, missile, or similar device; and

Any incendiary bomb or grenade, fire bomb, or similar device, including any device, except kerosene lamps, which consists of or includes a breakable container including a flammable liquid or compound and a wick composed of any material which, when ignited, is capable of igniting such flammable liquid or compound and can be carried or thrown by one individual acting alone.

(II) "Explosive or incendiary device" shall not include rifle, pistol, or shotgun ammunition, or the components for handloading rifle, pistol, or shotgun ammunition.

(I) "Explosive or incendiary parts" means any substances or materials or combinations thereof which have been prepared or altered for use in the creation of an explosive or incendiary device. Such substances or materials may include, but shall not be limited to, any:

Timing device, clock, or watch which has been altered in such a manner as to be used as the arming device in an explosive;

Pipe, end caps, or metal tubing which has been prepared for a pipe bomb;

Mechanical timers, mechanical triggers, chemical time delays, electronic time delays, or commercially made or improvised items which, when used singly or in combination, may be used in the construction of a timing delay mechanism, booby trap, or activating mechanism for any explosive or incendiary device.

(II) "Explosive or incendiary parts" shall not include rifle, pistol, or shotgun ammunition, or the components for handloading rifle, pistol, or shotgun ammunition, or any signaling device customarily used in operation of railroad equipment.

Any person who knowingly possesses, controls, manufactures, gives, mails, sends, or causes to be sent an explosive or incendiary device commits a class 4 felony.

(2.5) Any person who knowingly possesses, controls, manufacturers, gives, mails, sends, or causes to be sent a chemical, biological, or radiological weapon commits a class 3 felony.

Subsection (2) of this section shall not apply to the following persons:

A peace officer while acting in his official capacity transporting or otherwise handling explosives or incendiary devices;

A member of the armed forces of the United States or Colorado National Guard while acting in his official capacity;

An authorized employee of the office of active and inactive mines in the division of reclamation, mining, and safety while acting within the scope of his or her employment;

A person possessing a valid permit issued under the provisions of article 7 of title 9, C.R.S., or an employee of such permittee acting within the scope of his employment;

A person who is exempt from the necessity of possessing a permit under the provisions of section 9-7-106 (5), C.R.S., or an employee of such exempt person acting within the scope of his employment;

A person or entityauthorized to use chemical, biological, or radiological materials in their lawful business operations while using the chemical, biological, or radiological materials in the course of legitimate business activities. Authorized users shall include clinical, environmental, veterinary, agricultural, public health, or radiological laboratories and entities otherwise licensed to possess radiological materials.

Any person who knowingly uses or causes to be used or gives, mails, sends, or causes to be sent an explosive or incendiary device or a chemical, biological, or radiological weapon or materials in the commission of or in an attempt to commit a felony commits a class 2 felony.

Any person who removes or causes to be removed or carries away any explosive or incendiary device from the premises where said explosive or incendiary device is kept by the lawful user, vendor, transporter, or manufacturer thereof, without the consent or direction of the lawful possessor, commits a class 4 felony. A person convicted of this offense shall be subjected to a mandatory minimum sentence of two years in the department of corrections.

(5.5) Any person who removes or causes to be removed or carries away any chemical, biological, or radiological weapon from the premises where said chemical, biological, or radiological weapon is kept by the lawful user, vendor, transporter, or manufacturer thereof, without the consent

or direction of the lawful possessor, commits a class 3 felony. A person convicted of this offense shall be subject to a mandatory minimum sentence of four years in the department of corrections.

Any person who possesses any explosive or incendiary parts commits a class 4 felony. (6.5) Any person who possesses any chemical weapon, biological weapon, or radiological

weapon parts commits a class 3 felony.

Any person who manufactures or possesses or who gives, mails, sends, or causes to be sent any false, facsimile, or hoax explosive or incendiary device or chemical, biological, or radiological weapon to another person or places any such purported explosive or incendiary device or chemical, biological, or radiological weapon in or upon any real or personal property commits a class 5 felony.

Any person possessing a valid permit issued under the provisions of article 7 of title 9, C.R.S., or an employee of such permittee acting within the scope of his employment, who knowingly dispenses, distributes, or sells explosive or incendiary devices to a person who is not authorized to possess or control such explosive or incendiary device commits a class 4 felony.

18-12-110. Forfeiture of firearms. Upon the motion of the prosecuting attorney after the conviction of a defendant, the court may order the forfeiture of any firearms which were used by the defendant during the course of the criminal episode which gave rise to said conviction as an element of sentencing or as a condition of probation or of a deferred sentence. Firearms forfeited under this section shall be disposed of pursuant to section 16-13-311, C.R.S.

18-12-111. Unlawful purchase of firearms. (1) Any person who knowingly purchases or otherwise obtains a firearm on behalf of or for transfer to a person who the transferor knows or reasonably should know is ineligible to possess a firearm pursuant to federal or state law commits a class 4 felony. (2) (a) Any person who is a licensed dealer, as defined in 18 U.S.C. sec. 921 (a) (11), shall post a sign displaying the provisions of subsection (1) of this section in a manner that is easily readable. The person shall post such sign in an area that is visible to the public at each location from which the person sells firearms to the general public.

Any person who violates any provision of this subsection (2) commits a class 2 petty offense and, upon conviction thereof, shall be punished by a fine of two hundred fifty dollars.

18-12-112. Private firearms transfers - background check required - penalty - definitions. (1) (a) On and after July 1, 2013, except as described in subsection (6) of this section, before any person who is not a licensed gun dealer, as defined in section 12-26.1-106 (6), C.R.S., transfers or attempts to transfer possession of a firearm to a transferee, he or she shall:

Require that a background check, in accordance with section 24-33.5-424, C.R.S., be conducted of the prospective transferee; and

Obtain approval of a transfer from the bureau after a background check has been requested by a licensed gun dealer, in accordance with section 24-33.5-424, C.R.S.

(b) As used in this section, unless the context requires otherwise, "transferee" means a person who desires to receive or acquire a firearm from a transferor. If a transferee is not a natural person, then each natural person who is authorized by the transferee to possess the firearm after the transfer shall undergo a background check, as described in paragraph (a) of this subsection (1), before taking possession of the firearm.

(a) A prospective firearm transferor who is not a licensed gun dealer shall arrange for a licensed gun dealer to obtain the background check required by this section.

A licensed gun dealer who obtains a background check on a prospective transferee shall record the transfer, as provided in section 12-26-102, C.R.S., and retain the records, as provided in section 12-26-103, C.R.S., in the same manner as when conducting a sale, rental, or exchange at retail. The licensed gun dealer shall comply with all state and federal laws, including 18 U.S.C. sec. 922, as if he or she were transferring the firearm from his or her inventory to the prospective transferee.

A licensed gun dealer who obtains a background check for a prospective firearm transferor pursuant to this section shall provide the firearm transferor and transferee a copy of the results of the background check, including the bureau's approval or disapproval of the transfer.

A licensed gun dealer may charge a fee for services rendered pursuant to this section, which fee shall not exceed ten dollars.

(a) A prospective firearm transferee under this section shall not accept possession of the firearm unless the prospective firearm transferor has obtained approval of the transfer from the bureau after a background check has been requested by a licensed gun dealer, as described in paragraph (b) of subsection (1) of this section.

(b) A prospective firearm transferee shall not knowingly provide false information to a prospective firearm transferor or to a licensed gun dealer for the purpose of acquiring a firearm.

If the bureau approves a transfer of a firearm pursuant to this section, the approval shall be valid for thirty calendar days, during which time the transferor and transferee may complete the transfer.

A person who transfers a firearm in violation of the provisions of this section may be jointly and severally liable for any civil damages proximately caused by the transferee's subsequent use of the firearm.

The provisions of this section do not apply to:

A transfer of an antique firearm, as defined in 18 U.S.C. sec. 921(a) (16), as amended, or a curio or relic, as defined in 27 CFR 478.11, as amended;

A transfer that is a bona fide gift or loan between immediate family members, which are limited to spouses, parents, children, siblings, grandparents, grandchildren, nieces, nephews, first cousins, aunts, and uncles;

A transfer that occurs by operation of law or because of the death of a person for whom the prospective transferor is an executor or administrator of an estate or a trustee of a trust created in a will;

A transfer that is temporary and occurs while in the home of the unlicensed transferee if:

The unlicensed transferee is not prohibited from possessing firearms; and
The unlicensed transferee reasonably believes that possession of the firearm is necessary

to prevent imminent death or serious bodily injury to the unlicensed transferee;
A temporary transfer of possession without transfer of ownership or a title to ownership, which transfer takes place:
At a shooting range located in or on premises owned or occupied by a duly incorporated organization organized for conservation purposes or to foster proficiency in firearms;
At a target firearm shooting competition under the auspices of, or approved by, a state agency or a nonprofit organization; or
While hunting, fishing, target shooting, or trapping if:
The hunting, fishing, target shooting, or trapping is legal in all places where the unlicensed transferee possesses the firearm; and
The unlicensed transferee holds any license or permit that is required for such hunting, fishing, target shooting, or trapping;
A transfer of a firearm that is made to facilitate the repair or maintenance of the firearm; except that this paragraph (f) does not apply unless all parties who possess the firearm as a result of the transfer may legally possess a firearm;
Any temporary transfer that occurs while in the continuous presence of the owner of the firearm;
A temporary transfer for not more than seventy-two hours. A person who transfers a firearm pursuant to this paragraph (h) may be jointly and severally liable for damages proximately caused by the transferee's subsequent unlawful use of the firearm; or
A transfer of a firearm from a person serving in the armed forces of the United States who will be deployed outside of the United States within the next thirty days to any immediate family member, which is limited to a spouse, parent, child, sibling, grandparent, grandchild, niece, nephew, first cousin, aunt, and uncle of the person.
For purposes of paragraph (f) of subsection (6) of this section:
An owner, manager, or employee of a business that repairs or maintains firearms may rely upon a transferor's statement that he or she may legally possess a firearm unless the owner, manager, or employee has actual knowledge to the contrary and may return possession of the firearm to the transferor upon completion of the repairs or maintenance without a background check;
Unless a transferor of a firearm has actual knowledge to the contrary, the transferor may rely upon the statement of an owner, manager, or employee of a business that repairs or maintains firearms that no owner, manager, or employee of the business is prohibited from possessing a firearm.
Nothing in subsection (6) of this section shall be interpreted to limit or otherwise alter the applicability of section 18-12-111 concerning the unlawful purchase or transfer of firearms.
(a) A person who violates a provision of this section commits a class 1 misdemeanor and shall be punished in accordance with section 18-1.3-501. The person shall also be prohibited from possessing a firearm for two years, beginning on the date of his or her conviction.
(b) When a person is convicted of violating a provision of this section, the state court administrator shall report the conviction to the bureau and to the national instant criminal background check system created by the federal "Brady Handgun Violence Prevention Act", Pub.L. 103-159, the relevant portion of which is codified at 18 U.S.C. sec. 922 (t). The report shall include information indicating that the person is prohibited from possessing a firearm for two years,

beginning on the date of his or her conviction.

PART 2

PERMITS TO CARRY CONCEALED HANDGUNS

18-12-201. Legislative declaration. (1) The general assembly finds that:
There exists a widespread inconsistency among jurisdictions within the state with regard to the issuance of permits to carry concealed handguns and identification of areas of the state where it is lawful to carry concealed handguns;
This inconsistency among jurisdictions creates public uncertainty regarding the areas of the state in which it is lawful to carry concealed handguns;
Inconsistency results in the arbitrary and capricious denial of permits to carry concealed handguns based on the jurisdiction of residence rather than the qualifications for obtaining a permit;
The criteria and procedures for the lawful carrying of concealed handguns historically has been regulated by state statute and should be consistent throughout the state to ensure the consistent implementation of state law; and
It is necessary that the state occupy the field of regulation of the bearing of concealed handguns since the issuance of a concealed handgun permit is based on a person's constitutional right of self-protection and there is a prevailing state interest in ensuring that no citizen is arbitrarily denied a concealed handgun permit and in ensuring that the laws controlling the use of the permit are consistent throughout the state.
Based on the findings specified in subsection (1) of this section, the general assembly hereby concludes that:
The permitting and carrying of concealed handguns is a matter of statewide concern; and
It is necessary to provide statewide uniform standards for issuing permits to carry concealed handguns for self-defense.
In accordance with the findings and conclusions specified in subsections (1) and (2) of this section, the general assembly hereby instructs each sheriff to implement and administer the provisions of this part 2. The general assembly does not delegate to the sheriffs the authority to regulate or restrict the issuance of permits provided for in this part 2 beyond the provisions of this part 2. An action or rule that encumbers the permit process by placing burdens on the applicant beyond those sworn statements and specified documents detailed in this part 2 or that creates restrictions beyond those specified in this part 2 is in conflict with the intent of this part 2 and is prohibited.

18-12-202. Definitions. As used in this part 2, unless the context otherwise requires:
Repealed.
"Certified instructor" means an instructor for a firearms safety course who is certified as a firearms instructor by:
A county, municipal, state, or federal law enforcement agency;

The peace officers standards and training board created in section 24-31-302, C.R.S.;
A federal military agency; or
A national nonprofit organization that certifies firearms instructors, operates national firearms competitions, and provides training, including courses in personal protection, in small arms safety, use, and marksmanship.
"Chronically and habitually uses alcoholic beverages to the extent that the applicant's normal faculties are impaired" means:
The applicant has at any time been committed as an alcoholic pursuant to section 27-81-111 or 27-81-112, C.R.S.; or

Within the ten-year period immediately preceding the date on which the permit application is submitted, the applicant:

Has been committed as an alcoholic pursuant to section 27-81-109 or 27-81-110, C.R.S.;

or

Has had two or more alcohol-related convictions under section 42-4-1301 (1) or (2), C.R.S., or a law of another state that has similar elements, or revocations related to misdemeanor, alcohol-related convictions under section 42-2-126, C.R.S., or a law of another state that has similar elements.

"Handgun" means a handgun as defined in section 18-12-101 (1) (e.5); except that the term does not include a machine gun as defined in section 18-12-101 (1) (g).

(a) "Handgun training class" means:

A law enforcement training firearms safety course;

A firearms safety course offered by a law enforcement agency, an institution of higher education, or a public or private institution or organization or firearms training school, that is open to the general public and is taught by a certified instructor; or

A firearms safety course or class that is offered and taught by a certified instructor.

Notwithstanding paragraph (a) of this subsection (5), "handgun training class" does not include any firearms safety course that allows a person to complete the entire course:

Via the internet or an electronic device; or

In any location other than the physical location where the certified instructor offers the course.

"Permit" means a permit to carry a concealed handgun issued pursuant to the provisions of this part 2; except that "permit" does not include a temporary emergency permit issued pursuant to section 18-12-209.

"Sheriff" means the sheriff of a county, or his or her designee, or the official who has the duties of a sheriff in a city and county, or his or her designee.

"Training certificate" means a certificate, affidavit, or other document issued by the instructor, school, club, or organization that conducts a handgun training class that evidences an applicant's successful completion of the class requirements.


18-12-203. Criteria for obtaining a permit. (1) Beginning May 17, 2003, except as otherwise provided in this section, a sheriff shall issue a permit to carry a concealed handgun to an applicant who:

Is a legal resident of the state of Colorado. For purposes of this part 2, a person who is a member of the armed forces and is stationed pursuant to permanent duty station orders at a military installation in this state, and a member of the person's immediate family living in Colorado, shall be deemed to be a legal resident of the state of Colorado.

Is twenty-one years of age or older;

Is not ineligible to possess a firearm pursuant to section 18-12-108 or federal law;

Has not been convicted of perjury under section 18-8-503, in relation to information provided or deliberately omitted on a permit application submitted pursuant to this part 2;

(I) Does not chronically and habitually use alcoholic beverages to the extent that the applicant's normal faculties are impaired.

(II) The prohibition specified in this paragraph (e) shall not apply to an applicant who provides an affidavit, signed by a professional counselor or addiction counselor who is licensed pursuant to article 43 of title 12, C.R.S., and specializes in alcohol addiction, stating that the applicant has been evaluated by the counselor and has been determined to be a recovering alcoholic who has refrained from using alcohol for at least three years.

Is not an unlawful user of or addicted to a controlled substance as defined in section 18- 18-102 (5). Whether an applicant is an unlawful user of or addicted to a controlled substance shall be determined as provided in federal law and regulations.

Is not subject to:

A protection order issued pursuant to section 18-1-1001 or section 19-2-707, C.R.S., that is in effect at the time the application is submitted; or

A permanent protection order issued pursuant to article 14 of title 13, C.R.S.; or

A temporary protection order issued pursuant to article 14 of title 13, C.R.S., that is in effect at the time the application is submitted;

Demonstrates competence with a handgun by submitting:

Evidence of experience with a firearm through participation in organized shooting competitions or current military service;

Evidence that, at the time the application is submitted, the applicant is a certified instructor;

Proof of honorable discharge from a branch of the United States armed forces within the three years preceding submittal of the application;

Proof of honorable discharge from a branch of the United States armed forces that reflects pistol qualifications obtained within the ten years preceding submittal of the application;

A certificate showing retirement from a Colorado law enforcement agency that reflects pistol qualifications obtained within the ten years preceding submittal of the application; or

A training certificate from a handgun training class obtained within the ten years preceding submittal of the application. The applicant shall submit the original training certificate or a photocopy thereof that includes the original signature of the class instructor. To the extent permitted by section 18-12-202 (5), in obtaining a training certificate from a handgun training class, the applicant shall have discretion in selecting which handgun training class to complete.

Regardless of whether an applicant meets the criteria specified in subsection (1) of this section, if the sheriff has a reasonable belief that documented previous behavior by the applicant makes it likely the applicant will present a danger to self or others if the applicant receives a permit

to carry a concealed handgun, the sheriff may deny the permit.

(a) The sheriff shall deny, revoke, or refuse to renew a permit if an applicant or a permittee fails to meet one of the criteria listed in subsection (1) of this section and may deny, revoke, or refuse to renew a permit on the grounds specified in subsection (2) of this section.

Following issuance of a permit, if the issuing sheriff has a reasonable belief that a permittee no longer meets the criteria specified in subsection (1) of this section or that the permittee presents a danger as described in subsection (2) of this section, the sheriff shall suspend the permit until such time as the matter is resolved and the issuing sheriff determines that the permittee is eligible to possess a permit as provided in this section.

If the sheriff suspends or revokes a permit, the sheriff shall notify the permittee in writing, stating the grounds for suspension or revocation and informing the permittee of the right to seek a second review by the sheriff, to submit additional information for the record, and to seek judicial review pursuant to section 18-12-207.


18-12-204. Permit contents - validity - carrying requirements. (1) (a) Each permit shall bear a color photograph of the permittee and shall display the signature of the sheriff who issues the permit. In addition, the sheriffs of this state shall ensure that all permits issued pursuant to this part 2 contain the same items of information and are the same size and the same color.

(b) A permit is valid for a period of five years after the date of issuance and may be renewed as provided in section 18-12-211. A permit issued pursuant to this part 2, including a temporary emergency permit issued pursuant to section 18-12-209, is effective in all areas of the state, except as otherwise provided in section 18-12-214.

(a) A permittee, in compliance with the terms of a permit, may carry a concealed handgun as allowed by state law. The permittee shall carry the permit, together with valid photo identification, at all times during which the permittee is in actual possession of a concealed handgun and shall produce both documents upon demand by a law enforcement officer. Failure to produce a permit upon demand by a law enforcement officer raises a rebuttable presumption that the person does not have a permit. Failure to carry and produce a permit and valid photo identification upon demand as required in this subsection (2) is a class 1 petty offense. A charge of failure to carry and produce a permit and valid photo identification upon demand pursuant to this subsection (2) shall be dismissed by the court if, at or before the permittee's scheduled court appearance, the permittee exhibits to the court a valid permit and valid photo identification, both of which were issued to the permittee prior to the date on which the permittee was charged with failure to carry and produce a permit and valid photo identification upon demand.

(b) The provisions of paragraph (a) of this subsection (2) apply to temporary emergency permits issued pursuant to section 18-12-209.

(a) A person who may lawfully possess a handgun may carry a handgun under the following circumstances without obtaining a permit and the handgun shall not be considered concealed:

The handgun is in the possession of a person who is in a private automobile or in some other private means of conveyance and who carries the handgun for a legal use, including self- defense; or

The handgun is in the possession of a person who is legally engaged in hunting activities within the state.

The provisions of this subsection (3) shall not be construed to authorize the carrying of a handgun in violation of the provisions of section 18-12-105 or 18-12-105.5.


18-12-205. Sheriff - application - procedure - background check. (1) (a) To obtain a permit, a person shall submit a permit application on a statewide standardized form developed by the sheriffs and available from each sheriff. The permit application form shall solicit only the following information from the applicant:

The applicant's full name, date of birth, and address;

The applicant's birth name, if different from the name provided pursuant to subparagraph

of this paragraph (a), and any other names the applicant may have used or by which the applicant may have been known;

The applicant's home address or addresses for the ten-year period immediately preceding submittal of the application;

Whether the applicant is a resident of this state as of the date of application and whether the applicant has a valid driver's license or other state-issued photo identification or military order proving residence; and

Whether the applicant meets the criteria for obtaining a permit specified in section 18- 12-203 (1).

(b) The permit application form shall not require the applicant to waive or release a right or privilege, including but not limited to waiver or release of privileged or confidential information contained in medical records.

(a) An applicant shall complete the permit application form and return it, in person, to the sheriff of the county or city and county in which the applicant resides or to the sheriff of the county or city and county in which the applicant maintains a secondary residence or owns or leases real property used by the applicant in a business. The applicant shall sign the completed permit application form in person before the sheriff. The applicant shall provide his or her signature voluntarily upon a sworn oath that the applicant knows the contents of the permit application and that the information contained in the permit application is true and correct. An applicant who knowingly and intentionally makes a false or misleading statement on a permit application or deliberately omits any material information requested on the application commits perjury as described in section 18-8-503. Upon conviction, the applicant shall be punished as provided in section 18-1.3-501. In addition, the applicant shall be denied the right to obtain or possess a permit, and the sheriff shall revoke the applicant's permit if issued prior to conviction.

(b) An applicant shall also submit to the sheriff a permit fee not to exceed one hundred dollars for processing the permit application. The sheriff shall set the amount of the permit fee as provided in subsection (5) of this section. In addition, the applicant shall submit an amount specified by the director of the bureau, pursuant to section 24-72-306, C.R.S., for processing the applicant's fingerprints through the bureau and through the federal bureau of investigation. Neither the permit fee nor the fingerprint processing fee shall be refundable in the event the sheriff denies the applicant's permit application or suspends or revokes the permit subsequent to issuance.

In addition to the items specified in subsection (2) of this section, an applicant, when submitting the completed permit application, shall submit the following items to the sheriff:

Documentary evidence demonstrating competence with a handgun as specified in section 18-12-203 (1) (h); and

A full frontal view color photograph of the applicant's head taken within the thirty days immediately preceding submittal of the permit application; except that the applicant need not submit a photograph if the sheriff photographs the applicant for purposes of issuing a permit. Any photograph submitted shall show the applicant's full head, including hair and facial features, and the depiction of the applicant's head shall measure one and one-eighth inches wide and one and one- fourth inches high.

(a) The sheriff shall witness an applicant's signature on the permit application as provided in subsection (2) of this section and verify that the person making application for a permit is the same person who appears in any photograph submitted and the same person who signed the permit application form. To verify the applicant's identity, the applicant shall present to the sheriff the applicant's valid Colorado driver's license or valid Colorado or military photo identification.

After verifying the applicant's identity, the sheriff shall take two complete sets of the applicant's fingerprints. The sheriff shall submit both sets of fingerprints to the bureau, and the sheriff shall not retain a set of the applicant's fingerprints.

After receipt of a permit application and the items specified in this section, the sheriff shall verify that the applicant meets the criteria specified in section 18-12-203 (1) and is not a danger as described in section 18-12-203 (2). The verification at a minimum shall include requesting the bureau to conduct a search of the national instant criminal background check system and a search of the state integrated criminal justice information system to determine whether the applicant meets the criteria specified in section 18-12-203 (1). In addition, if the applicant resides in a municipality or town, the sheriff shall consult with the police department of the municipality or town in which the applicant resides, and the sheriff may consult with other local law enforcement agencies.

The sheriff in each county or city and county in the state shall establish the amount of the new and renewal permit fees within his or her jurisdiction. The amount of the new and renewal permit fees shall comply with the limits specified in paragraph (b) of subsection (2) of this section and section 18-12-211 (1), respectively. The fee amounts shall reflect the actual direct and indirect costs to the sheriff of processing permit applications and renewal applications pursuant to this part 2.

18-12-206. Sheriff - issuance or denial of permits - report. (1) Within ninety days after the date of receipt of the items specified in section 18-12-205, a sheriff shall:

Approve the permit application and issue the permit; or

Deny the permit application based solely on the ground that the applicant fails to qualify under the criteria listed in section 18-12-203 (1) or that the applicant would be a danger as described in section 18-12-203 (2). If the sheriff denies the permit application, he or she shall notify the applicant in writing, stating the grounds for denial and informing the applicant of the right to seek a second review of the application by the sheriff, to submit additional information for the record, and to seek judicial review pursuant to section 18-12-207.

(2) If the sheriff does not receive the results of the fingerprint checks conducted by the bureau and by the federal bureau of investigation within ninety days after receiving a permit application, the sheriff shall determine whether to grant or deny the permit application without considering the fingerprint check information. If, upon receipt of the information, the sheriff finds that the permit was issued or denied erroneously, based on the criteria specified in section 18-12-203

and (2), the sheriff shall either revoke or issue the permit, whichever is appropriate.

(a) Each sheriff shall maintain a list of the persons to whom he or she issues permits pursuant to this part 2. Upon request by another criminal justice agency for law enforcement purposes, the sheriff may, at his or her discretion, share information from the list of permittees with a law enforcement agency for the purpose of determining the validity of a permit. A database maintained pursuant to this subsection (3) and any database operated by a state agency that includes permittees shall be searchable only by name.

(I) Notwithstanding the provisions of paragraph (a) of this subsection (3), on and after July 1, 2011, a sheriff shall not share information from the list of permittees with a law enforcement agency for the purpose of creating a statewide database of permittees, and any law enforcement agency that receives information concerning permittees from a sheriff shall not use the information to create or maintain a statewide database of permittees. Any information concerning a permittee that is included in a statewide database pursuant to paragraph (a) of this subsection (3) shall be removed from the database no later than July 1, 2011.

(II) Prior to the repeal in subparagraph (I) of this paragraph (b), the state auditor's office shall conduct a performance audit of the statewide database of permittees as provided in section 2-3-118, C.R.S.

Except for suspected violations of sections 18-12-105 and 18-12-105.5, a peace officer may not use or search a database of permittees maintained by a law enforcement agency to establish reasonable suspicion for a traffic stop, or when contacting an individual, to justify probable cause for a search or seizure of a person or a person's vehicle or property.

Each sheriff shall annually prepare a report specifying, at a minimum, the number of permit applications received during the year for which the report was prepared, the number of permits issued during the year, the number of permits denied during the year, the reasons for denial, the number of revocations during the year, and the reasons for the revocations. The report shall not include the name of a person who applies for a permit, regardless of whether the person receives or is denied a permit. Each sheriff shall submit the report on or before March 1, 2004, and on or before March 1 each year thereafter, to the members of the general assembly. In addition, each sheriff shall provide a copy of the annual report prepared pursuant to this subsection (4) to a member of the public upon request.

18-12-207. Judicial review - permit denial - permit suspension - permit revocation. (1) If a sheriff denies a permit application, refuses to renew a permit, or suspends or revokes a permit, the applicant or permittee may seek judicial review of the sheriff's decision. The applicant or permittee may seek judicial review either in lieu of or subsequent to the sheriff's second review.

(2) The procedure and time lines for filing a complaint, an answer, and briefs for judicial

review pursuant to this section shall be in accordance with the procedures specified in rule 106 (a)

(4) and (b) of the Colorado rules of civil procedure.

(3) Notwithstanding any other provision of law to the contrary, at a judicial review sought pursuant to this section, the sheriff shall have the burden of proving by a preponderance of the evidence that the applicant or permittee is ineligible to possess a permit under the criteria listed in section 18-12-203 (1) or, if the denial, suspension, or revocation was based on the sheriff's determination that the person would be a danger as provided in section 18-12-203 (2), the sheriff shall have the burden of proving the determination by clear and convincing evidence. Following completion of the review, the court may award attorney fees to the prevailing party.

18-12-208. Colorado bureau of investigation - duties. (1) Upon receipt of a permit applicant's fingerprints from a sheriff pursuant to section 18-12-205 (4) or upon a sheriff's request pursuant to section 18-12-211 (1), the bureau shall process the full set of fingerprints to obtain any available state criminal justice information or federal information pursuant to section 16-21-103 (5), C.R.S., and shall report any information received to the sheriff. In addition, within ten days after receiving the fingerprints, the bureau shall forward one set of the fingerprints to the federal bureau of investigation for processing to obtain any available state criminal justice information or federal information.

The bureau shall use the fingerprints received pursuant to this part 2 solely for the purposes of:

Obtaining information for the issuance or renewal of permits; and

Notifying an issuing sheriff that a permittee has been arrested for or charged with an offense that would require revocation or suspension of the permit or that a permittee has been convicted of such an offense.

On or before January 15, 2004, and on or before January 15 each year thereafter until January 15, 2007, the bureau shall provide to the general assembly a list of the jurisdictions in which the sheriff provides to the bureau the names of persons to whom the sheriff issues permits.

18-12-209. Issuance by sheriffs of temporary emergency permits. (1) Notwithstanding any provisions of this part 2 to the contrary, a sheriff, as provided in this section, may issue a temporary emergency permit to carry a concealed handgun to a person whom the sheriff has reason to believe may be in immediate danger.

(2) (a) To receive a temporary emergency permit, a person shall submit to the sheriff of the county or city and county in which the person resides or in which the circumstances giving rise to the emergency exist the items specified in section 18-12-205; except that an applicant for a temporaryemergencypermit need not submit documentaryevidence demonstrating competence with a handgun as required under section 18-12-205 (3) (a), and the applicant shall submit a temporary permit fee not to exceed twenty-five dollars, as set by the sheriff. Upon receipt of the documents and fee, the sheriff shall request that the bureau conduct a criminal history record check of the bureau files and a search of the national instant criminal background check system. The sheriff may issue a temporary emergency permit to the applicant if the sheriff determines the person may be in

immediate danger and the criminal history record check shows that the applicant meets the criteria specified in section 18-12-203; except that the applicant need not demonstrate competence with a handgun and the applicant may be eighteen years of age or older.

(b) (I) A temporary emergency permit issued pursuant to this section is valid for a period of ninety days after the date of issuance. Prior to or within ten days after expiration of a temporary emergency permit, the permittee may apply to the sheriff of the county or city and county in which the person resides or in which the circumstances giving rise to the emergency exist for renewal of the permit. The sheriff may renew a temporary emergency permit once for an additional ninety-day period; except that, if the permittee is younger than twenty-one years of age, the sheriff may renew the temporary emergency permit for subsequent ninety-day periods until the permittee reaches twenty-one years of age.

(II) If the sheriff is not the same sheriff who issued the temporary emergency permit to the permittee:

The permittee shall submit to the renewing sheriff, in addition to the materials described in section 18-12-205, a legible photocopy of the temporary emergency permit; and

The renewing sheriff shall contact the office of the sheriff who issued the temporary emergency permit and confirm that the issuing sheriff has not revoked or suspended the temporary emergency permit.

18-12-210. Maintenance of permit - address change - invalidity of permit. (1) Within thirty days after a permittee changes the address specified on his or her permit or within three business days after his or her permit is lost, stolen, or destroyed, the permittee shall notify the issuing sheriff of the change of address or permit loss, theft, or destruction. Failure to notify the sheriff pursuant to this subsection (1) is a class 1 petty offense.

If a permit is lost, stolen, or destroyed, the permit is automatically invalid. The person to whom the permit was issued may obtain a duplicate or substitute therefor upon payment of fifteen dollars to the issuing sheriff and upon submission of a notarized statement to the issuing sheriff that the permit has been lost, stolen, or destroyed.

The provisions of this section apply to temporary emergency permits issued pursuant to section 18-12-209.

18-12-211. Renewal of permits. (1) (a) Within one hundred twenty days prior to expiration of a permit, the permittee may obtain a renewal form from the sheriff of the county or city and county in which the permittee resides or from the sheriff of the county or city and county in which the permittee maintains a secondary residence or owns or leases real property used by the permittee in a business and renew the permit by submitting to the sheriff a completed renewal form, a notarized affidavit stating that the permittee remains qualified pursuant to the criteria specified in section 18- 12-203 (1) (a) to (1) (g), and the required renewal fee not to exceed fifty dollars, as set by the sheriff pursuant to section 18-12-205 (5). The renewal form must meet the requirements specified in section 18-12-205 (1) for an application.

If the sheriff is not the same sheriff who issued the permit to the permittee:

The permittee shall submit to the renewing sheriff, in addition to the materials described in paragraph (a) of this subsection (1), a legible photocopy of the permit; and

The renewing sheriff shall contact the office of the sheriff who issued the permit and confirm that the issuing sheriff has not revoked or suspended the permit.

The sheriff shall verify pursuant to section 18-12-205 (4) that the permittee meets the criteria specified in section 18-12-203 (1) (a) to (1) (g) and is not a danger as described in section 18-12-203 (2) and shall either renew or deny the renewal of the permit in accordance with the provisions of section 18-12-206 (1). If the sheriff denies renewal of a permit, the permittee may seek a second review of the renewal application by the sheriff and may submit additional information for the record. The permittee may also seek judicial review as provided in section 18-12-207.

(2) A permittee who fails to file a renewal form on or before the permit expiration date may renew the permit by paying a late fee of fifteen dollars in addition to the renewal fee established pursuant to subsection (1) of this section. No permit shall be renewed six months or more after its expiration date, and the permit shall be deemed to have permanently expired. A person whose permit has permanently expired may reapply for a permit, but the person shall submit an application for a permit and the fee required pursuant to section 18-12-205. A person who knowingly and intentionally files false or misleading information or deliberately omits material information required under this section is subject to criminal prosecution for perjury under section 18-8-503.

18-12-212. Exemption. (1) This part 2 shall not apply to law enforcement officers employed by jurisdictions outside this state, so long as the foreign employing jurisdiction exempts peace officers employed by jurisdictions within Colorado from any concealed handgun or concealed weapons laws in effect in the foreign employing jurisdiction.

Notwithstanding any provision of this part 2 to the contrary, a retired peace officer, level I or Ia, as defined in section 18-1-901 (3) (l) (I) and (3) (l) (II), as said section existed prior to its repeal in 2003, within the first five years after retirement may obtain a permit by submitting to the sheriff of the jurisdiction in which the retired peace officer resides a letter signed by the sheriff or chief of police of the jurisdiction by which the peace officer was employed immediately prior to retirement attesting that the retired officer meets the criteria specified in section 18-12-203 (1). A retired peace officer who submits a letter pursuant to this subsection (2) is not subject to the fingerprint or criminal history check requirements specified in this part 2 and is not required to pay the permit application fee. Upon receipt of a letter submitted pursuant to this subsection (2), the sheriff shall issue the permit. A permit issued pursuant to this subsection (2) may not be renewed. Upon expiration of the permit, the permittee may apply for a new permit as provided in this part 2.

18-12-213. Reciprocity. (1) A permit to carry a concealed handgun or a concealed weapon that is issued by a state that recognizes the validity of permits issued pursuant to this part 2 shall be valid in this state in all respects as a permit issued pursuant to this part 2 if the permit is issued to a person who is:

Twenty-one years of age or older; and

(I) A resident of the state that issued the permit, as demonstrated by the address stated

on a valid picture identification that is issued by the state that issued the permit and is carried by the permit holder; or

(II) A resident of Colorado for no more than ninety days, as determined by the date of issuance on a valid picture identification issued by Colorado and carried by the permit holder.

(2) For purposes of this section, a "valid picture identification" means a driver's license or a state identification issued in lieu of a driver's license.

18-12-214. Authority granted by permit - carrying restrictions. (1) (a) A permit to carry a concealed handgun authorizes the permittee to carry a concealed handgun in all areas of the state, except as specifically limited in this section. A permit does not authorize the permittee to use a handgun in a manner that would violate a provision of state law. A local government does not have authority to adopt or enforce an ordinance or resolution that would conflict with any provision of this part 2.

(b) A peace officer may temporarily disarm a permittee, incident to a lawful stop of the permittee. The peace officer shall return the handgun to the permittee prior to discharging the permittee from the scene.

A permit issued pursuant to this part 2 does not authorize a person to carry a concealed handgun into a place where the carrying of firearms is prohibited by federal law.

A permit issued pursuant to this part 2 does not authorize a person to carry a concealed handgun onto the real property, or into any improvements erected thereon, of a public elementary, middle, junior high, or high school; except that:

A permittee may have a handgun on the real property of the public school so long as the handgun remains in his or her vehicle and, if the permittee is not in the vehicle, the handgun is in a compartment within the vehicle and the vehicle is locked;

A permittee who is employed or retained by contract by a school district or charter school as a school security officer may carry a concealed handgun onto the real property, or into any improvement erected thereon, of a public elementary, middle, junior high, or high school while the permittee is on duty;

A permittee may carry a concealed handgun on undeveloped real property owned by a school district that is used for hunting or other shooting sports.

A permit issued pursuant to this part 2 does not authorize a person to carry a concealed handgun into a public building at which:

Security personnel and electronic weapons screening devices are permanently in place at each entrance to the building;

Securitypersonnel electronicallyscreen each person who enters the building to determine whether the person is carrying a weapon of any kind; and

Security personnel require each person who is carrying a weapon of any kind to leave the weapon in possession of security personnel while the person is in the building.

Nothing in this part 2 shall be construed to limit, restrict, or prohibit in any manner the existing rights of a private property owner, private tenant, private employer, or private business entity.

The provisions of this section apply to temporary emergency permits issued pursuant to section 18-12-209.

18-12-215. Immunity. (1) The bureau and a local law enforcement agency and an individual employed by the bureau or a local law enforcement agency shall not be liable for any damages that may result from good faith compliance with the provisions of this part 2.

(2) A law enforcement officer or agency, medical personnel, and an organization that offers handgun training classes and its personnel who in good faith provide information regarding an applicant shall not be liable for any damages that may result from issuance or denial of a permit.

18-12-216. Permits issued prior to May 17, 2003. (1) A permit issued pursuant to section 18-12-105.1, as it existed prior to its repeal, shall permanently expire on June 30, 2007, or on the expiration date specified on the permit, whichever occurs first. A person who submitted a full set of fingerprints to obtain a permit prior to May 17, 2003, upon expiration of the permit, may apply for renewal of the permit as provided in this part 2. A person who did not submit a full set of fingerprints to obtain a permit prior to May 17, 2003, upon expiration of the permit, may apply for a new permit as provided in this part 2.

(2) Within one hundred twenty days prior to the expiration of a permit issued pursuant to section 18-12-105.1, as it existed prior to its repeal, the issuing authority shall send a notice of expiration to the permittee to notify the permittee of the permit expiration as provided in subsection of this section and of his or her ability to renew the permit or obtain a new permit as provided in subsection (1) of this section.

PART 3

LARGE-CAPACITY AMMUNITION MAGAZINES

18-12-301. Definitions. As used in this part 3, unless the context otherwise requires:

"Bureau" means the Colorado bureau of investigation created and existing pursuant to section 24-33.5-401, C.R.S.

(a) "Large-capacity magazine" means:

A fixed or detachable magazine, box, drum, feed strip, or similar device capable of accepting, or that is designed to be readily converted to accept, more than fifteen rounds of ammunition;

A fixed, tubular shotgun magazine that holds more than twenty-eight inches of shotgun shells, including any extension device that is attached to the magazine and holds additional shotgun shells; or

A nontubular, detachable magazine, box, drum, feed strip, or similar device that is capable of accepting more than eight shotgun shells when combined with a fixed magazine.

"Large-capacity magazine" does not mean:

A feeding device that has been permanently altered so that it cannot accommodate more than fifteen rounds of ammunition;

An attached tubular device designed to accept, and capable of operating only with, .22 caliber rimfire ammunition; or

A tubular magazine that is contained in a lever-action firearm.

18-12-302. Large-capacity magazines prohibited - penalties - exceptions. (1) (a) Except as otherwise provided in this section, on and after July 1, 2013, a person who sells, transfers, or possesses a large-capacity magazine commits a class 2 misdemeanor.

Any person who violates this subsection (1) after having been convicted of a prior violation of said subsection (1) commits a class 1 misdemeanor.

Any person who violates this subsection (1) commits a class 6 felony if the person possessed a large-capacity magazine during the commission of a felony or any crime of violence, as defined in section 18-1.3-406.

(a) A person may possess a large-capacity magazine if he or she:

Owns the large-capacity magazine on July 1, 2013; and

Maintains continuous possession of the large-capacity magazine.

(b) If a person who is alleged to have violated subsection (1) of this section asserts that he or she is permitted to legally possess a large-capacity magazine pursuant to paragraph (a) of this subsection (2), the prosecution has the burden of proof to refute the assertion.

The offense described in subsection (1) of this section shall not apply to:

An entity, or any employee thereof engaged in his or her employment duties, that manufactures large-capacity magazines within Colorado exclusively for transfer to, or any licensed gun dealer, as defined in section 12-26.1-106 (6), C.R.S., or any employee thereof engaged in his or her official employment duties, that sells large-capacity magazines exclusively to:

A branch of the armed forces of the United States;

A department, agency, or political subdivision of the state of Colorado, or of any other state, or of the United States government;

A firearms retailer for the purpose of firearms sales conducted outside the state;

A foreign national government that has been approved for such transfers by the United States government; or

An out-of-state transferee who may legally possess a large-capacity magazine; or

An employee of any of the following agencies who bears a firearm in the course of his or her official duties:

A branch of the armed forces of the United States; or

A department, agency, or political subdivision of the state of Colorado, or of any other state, or of the United States government; or

A person who possesses the magazine for the sole purpose of transporting the magazine to an out-of-state entity on behalf of a manufacturer of large-capacity magazines within Colorado.

18-12-303. Identification markings for large-capacity magazines - rules. (1) A large-capacity magazine that is manufactured in Colorado on or after July 1, 2013, must include a permanent stamp or marking indicating that the large-capacity magazine was manufactured or assembled after July 1, 2013. The stamp or marking must be legibly and conspicuously engraved or cast upon the outer surface of the large-capacity magazine.

The bureau may promulgate such rules as may be necessary for the implementation of this section, including but not limited to rules requiring a large-capacity magazine that is manufactured on or after July 1, 2013, to bear identifying information in addition to the identifying information described in subsection (1) of this section.

A person who manufactures a large-capacity magazine in Colorado in violation of subsection (1) of this section commits a class 2 misdemeanor and shall be punished in accordance with section 18-1.3-501.

### ARTICLE 13  Miscellaneous Offenses

18-13-101. Abuse of a corpse. (1) A person commits abuse of a corpse if, without statutory or court-ordered authority, he or she:

Removes the body or remains of any person from a grave or other place of sepulcher without the consent of the person who has the right to dispose of the remains pursuant to section 15- 19-106, C.R.S; or

Treats the body or remains of any person in a way that would outrage normal family sensibilities.

(2)  Abuse of a corpse is a class 2 misdemeanor.


18-13-102.  Endurance contests. (Repealed)


18-13-103.  Endangering the welfare of an incompetent person. (Repealed)


18-13-104. Fighting by agreement - dueling. (1) If two or more persons shall fight by agreement in a public place, except in a sporting event authorized by law, the persons so fighting commit a class 1 petty offense.

(2) Persons who by agreement engage in a fight with deadly weapons, whether in a public or private place, commit dueling, which is a class 4 felony.


18-13-105.  Criminal libel. (Repealed)


18-13-106. Unlawful to discard or abandon iceboxes or motor vehicles and similar items. Any person abandoning or discarding, in any public or private place accessible to children, any chest, closet, piece of furniture, refrigerator, icebox, motor vehicle, or other article, having a compartment of a capacity of one and one-half cubic feet or more and having a door or lid which when closed cannot be opened easily from the inside, or who, being the owner, lessee, or manager of such place, knowingly permits such abandoned or discarded article to remain in such condition commits a class 1 petty offense.


18-13-107. Interference with persons with disabilities. (1) A person shall not falsely impersonate an individual with a disability, as that term is defined in section 24-34-301 (5.6), C.R.S.

Repealed.

A person shall not knowingly deny an individual with a disability, as defined in section 24-34-301 (5.6), C.R.S., any right or privilege protected in section 24-34-502, 24-34-502.2, 24-34- 601, 24-34-802 (1), or 24-34-803, C.R.S.

Violation of the provisions of subsection (1) of this section is a class 1 petty offense. Violation of the provisions of subsection (3) of this section is a class 3 misdemeanor.


18-13-107.3. Intentional misrepresentation of entitlement to an assistance animal - penalty - definitions. [Editor's note: This section is effective January 1, 2017.] (1) A person commits intentional misrepresentation of entitlement to an assistance animal if:

The person intentionally misrepresents entitlement to an animal in his or her possession as an assistance animal for the purpose of obtaining any of the rights or privileges set forth in state or federal law for an individual with a disability as a reasonable accommodation in housing;

The person was previously given a written or verbal warning regarding the fact that it is illegal to intentionally misrepresent entitlement to an assistance animal;

The person knows that:

The animal is not an assistance animal with regard to that person; or

The person does not have a disability.

A person who violates subsection (1) of this section commits a class 2 petty offense and, upon conviction, shall be punished as follows:

For a first offense, a fine of twenty-five dollars;

For a second offense, a fine of not less than fifty dollars but not more than two hundred dollars; and

For a third or subsequent offense, a fine of not less than one hundred dollars but not more than five hundred dollars.

(a) A defendant may petition the district court of the district in which any conviction records pertaining to the defendant's first conviction for intentional misrepresentation of entitlement

to an assistance animal, as described in subsection (1) of this section, are located for the sealing of the conviction records, except for basic identifying information.

If a petition is filed pursuant to paragraph (a) of this subsection (3) for the sealing of a record of conviction for intentional misrepresentation of entitlement to an assistance animal, the court shall order the record sealed if the following criteria are met:

The petition is filed;

The filing fee is paid or the defendant has filed a motion to file without payment with a supporting financial affidavit and the court has granted the motion;

The defendant's first conviction for intentional misrepresentation of entitlement to an assistance animal was at least three years prior to the date of the filing of the petition; and

The defendant has not had a subsequent conviction for intentional misrepresentation of entitlement to an assistance animal.

An order entered pursuant to this subsection (3) must be directed to each custodian who may have custody of any part of the conviction records that are the subject of the order. Whenever a court enters an order sealing conviction records pursuant to this subsection (3), the defendant shall provide the Colorado bureau of investigation and each custodian of the conviction records with a copy of the order and shall pay to the bureau any costs related to the sealing of his or her criminal conviction records that are in the custody of the bureau unless the court has granted the motion specified in subparagraph (II) of paragraph (b) of this subsection (3). Thereafter, the defendant may request and the court may grant an order sealing the civil case in which the conviction records were sealed.

A written finding made pursuant to section 12-36-142 (1) (a), 12-38-132.5 (1) (a), or 12- 43-226.5 (1) (a), C.R.S., is an affirmative defense to the offense established by this section. The lack of such a finding is not proof of the offense established by this section, and nothing in this section or in sections 12-36-142, 12-38-132.5, or 12-43-226.5, C.R.S., limits the means by which a person with a disability may demonstrate, pursuant to state or federal law, that the person has a disability or that the person has a disability-related need for an assistance animal.

As used in this section, unless the context otherwise requires:

"Assistance animal" means an animal that qualifies as a reasonable accommodation under the federal "Fair Housing Act", 42 U.S.C. sec. 3601 et seq., as amended or section 504 of the federal "Rehabilitation Act of 1973", 29 U.S.C. sec. 794, as amended.

"Disability" has the same meaning as set forth in the federal "Americans with Disabilities Act of 1990", 42 U.S.C. sec. 12101 et seq., and its related amendments and implementing regulations and includes a handicap as that term is defined in the federal "Fair Housing Act", 42 U.S.C. sec. 3601 et seq., as amended, and 24 CFR 100.201.

"Service animal" has the same meaning as set forth in the implementing regulations of Title II and Title III of the federal "Americans with Disabilities Act of 1990", 42 U.S.C. sec. 12101 et seq.

"State and federal law" includes section 24-34-803, C.R.S., the federal laws specified in paragraph (a) of this subsection (5), and rules and regulations implementing those laws.


18-13-107.7. Intentional misrepresentation of a service animal for a person with a

disability - penalty - sealing of conviction records - definitions. [Editor's note: This section is effective January 1, 2017.] (1) A person commits intentional misrepresentation of a service animal if:

The person intentionally misrepresents an animal in his or her possession as his or her service animal or service-animal-in-training for the purpose of obtaining any of the rights or privileges set forth in section 24-34-803, C.R.S.;

The person was previously given a written or verbal warning regarding the fact that it is illegal to intentionally misrepresent a service animal;

The person knows that the animal in question is not a service animal or service-animal- in-training.

A person who violates subsection (1) of this section commits a class 2 petty offense and, upon conviction, shall be punished as follows:

For a first offense, a fine of twenty-five dollars;

For a second offense, a fine of not less than fifty dollars but not more than two hundred dollars; and

For a third or subsequent offense, a fine of not less than one hundred dollars but not more than five hundred dollars.

(a) A defendant may petition the district court of the district in which any conviction records pertaining to the defendant's first conviction for intentional misrepresentation of a service animal, as described in subsection (1) of this section, are located for the sealing of the conviction records, except for basic identifying information.

If a petition is filed pursuant to paragraph (a) of this subsection (3) for the sealing of a record of conviction for intentional misrepresentation of a service animal, the court shall order the record sealed if the following criteria are met:

The petition is filed;

The filing fee is paid or the defendant has filed a motion to file without payment with a supporting financial affidavit and the court has granted the motion;

The defendant's first conviction for intentional misrepresentation of a service animal was at least three years prior to the date of the filing of the petition; and

The defendant has not had a subsequent conviction for intentional misrepresentation of a service animal.

An order entered pursuant to this subsection (3) must be directed to each custodian who may have custody of any part of the conviction records that are the subject of the order. Whenever a court enters an order sealing conviction records pursuant to this subsection (3), the defendant shall provide the Colorado bureau of investigation and each custodian of the conviction records with a copy of the order and shall pay to the bureau any costs related to the sealing of his or her criminal conviction records that are in the custody of the bureau unless the court has granted the motion specified in subparagraph (II) of paragraph (b) of this subsection (3). Thereafter, the defendant may request and the court may grant an order sealing the civil case in which the conviction records were sealed.

As used in this section, unless the context otherwise requires:

"Disability" has the same meaning as set forth in the federal "Americans with Disabilities Act of 1990", 42 U.S.C. sec. 12101 et seq., and its related amendments and implementing

regulations.

"Qualified individual with a disability" has the same meaning as set forth in the federal "Americans with Disabilities Act of 1990", 42 U.S.C. sec. 12101 et seq., and its related amendments and implementing regulations.

"Service animal" has the same meaning as set forth in the implementing regulations of Title II and Title III of the federal "Americans with Disabilities

Act of 1990", 42 U.S.C. sec. 12101 et seq.

"Service-animal-in-training" means a dog or miniature horse that is being individually trained to do work or perform tasks for the benefit of a qualified individual with a disability.

"Trainer of a service animal" means a person who is individually training a service animal to do work or perform tasks for the benefit of a qualified individual with a disability.

18-13-108. Removal of timber from state lands. Any person who cuts or removes any timber from any state land without lawful authority commits a class 3 misdemeanor.

18-13-109. Firing woods or prairie. (1) (a) Except as otherwise provided in subsection (2) of this section, any person who, without lawful authority and knowingly, recklessly, or with criminal negligence, sets on fire, or causes to be set on fire, any woods, prairie, or grounds of any description, other than his or her own, or who, knowingly, recklessly, or with criminal negligence, permits a fire, set or caused to be set by such person, to pass from his or her own grounds to the injury of any other person commits a class 2 misdemeanor.

(b) Any person convicted under paragraph (a) of this subsection (1) shall be assessed a fine of not less than two hundred fifty dollars and not greater than one thousand dollars. The fine imposed by this paragraph (b) shall be mandatory and not subject to suspension. Nothing in this paragraph (b) shall be construed to limit the court's discretion in exercising other available sentencing alternatives in addition to the mandatory fine.

(2) (a) Any person who knowingly violates paragraph (a) of subsection (1) of this section and who knows or reasonably should know that he or she violates any applicable order, rule, or regulation lawfully issued by a governmental authority that prohibits, bans, restricts, or otherwise regulates fires during periods of extreme fire hazard and that is designed to promote the safety of persons and property, commits a class 6 felony.

The following activities do not constitute offenses under this subsection (2):

Open burning lawfully conducted in the course of agricultural operations;

State, municipality, or county fire management operations;

Lawfully conducted prescribed or controlled burns;

Lawful activities conducted pursuant to rules, regulations, or policies adopted by the relevant state, tribal, or federal regulatory agency or agencies.

18-13-109.5. Intentionally setting wildfire. (1) A person commits the crime of intentionally setting a wildfire if he or she:

(I) Intentionally and without lawful authority sets on fire, or causes to be set on fire, any woods, prairie, or grounds of any description, other than his or her own; or

(II) Intentionally permits a fire, set or caused to be set by such person, to pass from his or her own grounds to the grounds of another; and

By so doing, places another in danger of death or serious bodily injury or places any building or occupied structure of another in danger of damage. Intentionally setting a wildfire is a class 3 felony.

For purposes of this section, "building" shall have the same meaning as set forth in section 18-4-101 (1) and "occupied structure" shall have the same meaning as set forth in section 18- 4-101 (2).

18-13-110. Air pollution violations. (Repealed)

18-13-111. Purchases of commodity metals - violations - commodity metals theft task force - creation - composition - reports - legislative declaration - definitions - repeal. (1) (a) Except as otherwise provided in subsection (3) of this section, every owner, keeper, or proprietor of a junk shop, junk store, salvage yard, or junk cart or other vehicle and every collector of or dealer in junk, salvage, or other secondhand property shall keep a book or register detailing all transactions involving commodity metals.

The owner, keeper, proprietor, collector, or dealer shall record the identification of a seller of commodity metals in the book or register and the method by which the seller verified his or her identity. The seller shall verify his or her identity by one of the following:

A valid Colorado driver's license;

An identification card issued in accordance with section 42-2-302, C.R.S.;

A valid driver's license from another state that contains a picture identification;

A military identification card;

A valid United States passport; or

An alien registration card.

(Deleted by amendment, L. 2011, (HB 11-1130), ch. 106, p. 330, § 1, effective April 13, 2011.)

The owner, keeper, proprietor, collector, or dealer shall require the seller of a commodity metal to provide for the book or register:

A signed affidavit, sworn and affirmed under penalty of law, that the seller is the owner of the commodity metal or is otherwise entitled to sell the commodity metal. The owner, keeper, proprietor, collector, or dealer shall provide the affidavit form to the seller.

The license plate number and description of the vehicle or conveyance if any, in which the commodity metal was delivered.

The owner, keeper, proprietor, collector, or dealer shall include the following in the book or register:

The date and place of each purchase of the commodity metal; and

The description and quantity of the commodity metal purchased.

The book or register shall be made available to any peace officer for inspection at any reasonable time.

(1.3) (a) A purchaser of commodity metals shall:

Sign up with the scrap theft alert system maintained by the institute of scrap recycling industries, incorporated, or its successor organization, to receive alerts regarding thefts of commodity metals in the purchaser's geographic area;

Download and maintain the scrap metal theft alerts generated by the scrap theft alert system;

Use the alerts to identify potentially stolen commodity metals, including training the purchaser's employees to use the alerts during the purchaser's daily operations.

(b) A purchaser of commodity metals shall maintain for ninety days copies of any theft alerts received and downloaded pursuant to paragraph (a) of this subsection (1.3). A purchaser shall also maintain documentation that the purchaser educates employees about, and provides to employees, scrap theft alerts.

(1.5) (a) An owner, keeper, proprietor, collector, or dealer is permitted to pay a seller in cash for any commodity metals transaction of three hundred dollars or less.

(b) If the transaction costs more than three hundred dollars, the owner, keeper, proprietor, collector, or dealer shall pay the seller of a commodity metal by check unless the seller is paid by means of any process in which a picture of the seller is taken when the money is paid.

Except as otherwise provided in subsection (3) of this section, the owner, keeper, proprietor, collector, or dealer of any commodity metal shall make a digital photographic record, video record, or other record that identifies the seller and the commodity metal that the seller is selling. The digital photographic record, video record, or other record format shall be retained for one hundred eighty days, and the owner shall permit a law enforcement officer to make inspections of the record.

The following transactions and materials are exempt from the requirements specified in subsections (1) and (2) of this section:

Any materials purchased from a regulated public utility or an original manufacturer of scrap or industrially generated scrap;

The purchase of recyclable food and beverage containers from any source; except that, for purposes of this exemption, a metal beer keg suitable for reuse shall not be considered a recyclable beverage container;

Any scrap that is involved in a transaction between dealers or governmental entities;

(Deleted by amendment, L. 2007, p. 759, §1, effective July 1, 2007.)

(Deleted by amendment, L. 2011, (HB 11-1130), ch. 106, p. 330, § 1, effective April 13, 2011.)

The information entered in the book or register, as provided in subsection (1) of this section, need not be kept for a period longer than three years after the date of purchase of the commodity metal.

A person who violates subsection (1) of this section by failing to keep a book or register, any person who knowingly gives false information with respect to the information required to be maintained in the book or register provided for in subsection (1) of this section, and any person who

violates subsection (1.3), (1.5), or (2) of this section commits:

A class 2 misdemeanor if the value of the commodity metal involved is less than five hundred dollars; or

A class 1 misdemeanor if the value of the commodity metal involved is five hundred dollars or more.

There is a rebuttable presumption that metal purchased by a dealer for the purpose of recycling is a commodity metal if the commodity metal has a value of fifty cents per pound or greater for purposes of recycling the commodity metal.

This section shall not apply to a person or entity that does not provide remuneration for commodity metals collected in drop-off curbside containers or at materials recovery sites.

For the purposes of this section, unless the context otherwise requires:

(Deleted by amendment, L. 2007, p. 759, § 1, effective July 1, 2007.)

"Book or register" means any written or electronic record of transactions kept by any owner, keeper, proprietor, collector, or dealer, including sequentially numbered receipts containing the information required by subsection (1) of this section.

(b.5) "Commodity metal" means copper; a copper alloy, including bronze or brass; or aluminum. "Commodity metal" does not include precious metals such as gold, silver, or platinum.

(Deleted by amendment, L. 2007, p. 759, § 1, effective July 1, 2007.)

"Dealer" means any person, business, or entity that buys, sells, or distributes, for the purpose of recycling, any commodity metal on a wholesale basis.

(Deleted by amendment, L. 2011, (HB 11-1130), ch. 106, p. 330, § 1, effective April 13, 2011.)

(a) There is hereby created the commodity metals theft task force, also referred to in this subsection (9) as the "task force".

The task force consists of the following ten persons or their designees:

The chief of the Colorado state patrol;

A sheriff appointed by a Colorado sheriffs' association;

A municipal police chief appointed by the Colorado association of chiefs of police;

A contractor that uses commodity metals in construction;

A representative of a national trade association or other organization that represents commodity metals recyclers, such as the institute of scrap recycling industries, incorporated, or its successor organization or another entity representing comparable interests;

A scrap metal dealer located in Colorado who is a member of the institute of scrap recycling industries, incorporated, or its successor organization;

A representative of the Colorado municipal league, or its successor entity;

A representative of Colorado counties, incorporated, or its successor entity;

A representative of a public utility that uses commodity metals; and

A representative of a railroad company that operates in Colorado.

The task force shall hold its first meeting no later than July 1, 2011. At the first meeting, the task force shall discuss the best way to distribute and use information related to theft of scrap metals, including whether and how to promote use by law enforcement agencies of the scrap theft alert system maintained by the institute of scrap recycling industries, incorporated, or its successor

organization. Thereafter, the task force shall meet on a regular basis, convening at least every October, to discuss issues related to theft of commodity metals, including sharing relevant information on theft of scrap metal, identifying ways in which Colorado's laws regulating commodity metals purchases can be improved to reduce theft, and reviewing any performance problems or communication issues. The task force is specifically directed to consider: Possible policies or practices to aid in tracking or apprehending stolen commodity metals prior to the point of sale in order to assist law enforcement personnel in theft prevention and recovery of stolen materials; recommendations regarding when and how a commodity metals purchaser should be required to apprise local law enforcement authorities if a purchased commodity metal is a potential match of a commodity metal reported stolen in the scrap theft alert system; and the creation and attributes of a civil penalty process for egregious and repeat violators of the record-keeping requirements of this section.

A member of the task force, as designated by the task force, shall report annually to the judiciary committees of the house of representatives and the senate, or any successor committees, regarding the task force's meetings, findings, and recommendations.

Members of the task force shall not be compensated for, or reimbursed for expenses incurred in, attending meetings of the task force.

This subsection (9) is repealed, effective September 1, 2025. Before the repeal, the commodity metals theft task force, created pursuant to this subsection (9), shall be reviewed as provided in section 2-3-1203, C.R.S.

(a) The general assembly hereby finds, determines, and declares that:

Thefts of commodity metals jeopardize the safety and welfare of the public, financially burden taxpayers and industry, and exhaust law enforcement resources;

Such thefts impact every community in Colorado; and

The regulation of commodity metal purchases is a matter of statewide concern.

(b) In order to continue the ability of the state to identify causes of commodity metal theft and provide realistic solutions to the theft problem, the general assembly encourages law enforcement authorities in the state to join the scrap theft alert system maintained by the institute of scrap recycling industries, incorporated, or its successor organization, and to report thefts of commodity metals occurring within their jurisdictions to this system. The general assembly also encourages commercial stakeholders affected by commodity metals theft to sign up for and participate in the scrap theft alert system.

18-13-112. Hazardous waste violations. (1) No person shall abandon any vehicle containing any hazardous waste or intentionally spill hazardous waste upon a street, highway, right- of-way, or any other public property or upon any private property without the express consent of the owner or person in lawful charge of that private property.

As used in this section:

(I) "Abandon" means to leave a thing with the intention not to retain possession of or assert ownership or control over it. The intent need not coincide with the act of leaving.

(II) It is prima facie evidence of the necessary intent that:

The vehicle has been left for more than three days unattended and unmoved; or

License plates or other identifying marks have been removed from the vehicle; or

The vehicle has been damaged or is deteriorated so extensively that it has value only for junk or salvage; or

The owner has been notified by a law enforcement agency to remove the vehicle and it has not been removed within twenty-four hours after notification.

(I) "Hazardous waste" means any waste or other material, alone, mixed with, or in combination with other wastes or materials, which because of its quantity, concentration, or physical or chemical characteristics:

Causes, or significantly contributes to, an increase in mortality or an increase in serious irreversible, or incapacitating reversible, illness; or

Poses a substantial present or potential hazard to human health or the environment when improperly treated, stored, transported, or disposed of, or otherwise improperly managed.

(II) "Hazardous waste" also means any waste or other material defined as a hazardous waste in the rules and regulations promulgated pursuant to the federal "Solid Waste Disposal Act" (42

U.S.C. 3251 et seq.), as amended by the federal "Resource Conservation and Recovery Act of 1976", as amended (42 U.S.C. 6905, 6912 (a), 6921-6927, 6930, 6974), as such rules and regulations are set forth in 40 C.F.R. Parts 122-124 and 260-265 on July 1, 1981.

"Hazardous waste" does not include:

Discharges which are point sources subject to permits under section 402 of the "Federal Water Pollution Control Act", as amended;

Source, special nuclear, or byproduct material as defined by the federal "Atomic Energy Act of 1954", as amended;

Agricultural waste;

Domestic sewage which includes final use for beneficial purposes, including fertilizer, soil conditioner, fuel, and livestock feed, of sludge from wastewater treatment plants if such sludge meets all applicable standards of the department;

Irrigation return flows;

Inert materials deposited for construction fill or topsoil placement in connection with actual or contemplated construction at such location or for changes in land contour for agricultural purposes; or

Anywaste or other materials exempted or otherwise not regulated as a hazardous waste in the rules and regulations promulgated pursuant to the federal "Solid Waste Disposal Act" (42

U.S.C. 3251 et seq.), as amended by the federal "Resource Conservation and Recovery Act of 1976", as amended (42 U.S.C. 6905, 6912 (a), 6921-6927, 6930, 6974), as such rules and regulations are set forth in 40 C.F.R. Parts 122-124 and 260-265 on July 1, 1981.

"Inert material" means non-water-soluble and nondecomposable inert solids together with such minor amounts and types of other materials as will not significantly affect the inert nature of such solids. The term includes but is not limited to earth, sand, gravel, rock, concrete which has been in a hardened state for at least sixty days, masonry, asphalt paving fragments, and such other non- water-soluble and nondecomposable inert solids.

"Vehicle" means any device which is capable of moving itself, or of being moved, from place to place upon wheels or endless tracks. The term includes but is not limited to any motor

vehicle, trailer, or semitrailer.

Any person who violates any provision of this section commits a class 4 felony.

18-13-113. Unlawful to sell metal beverage containers with detachable opening devices. (1) As used in this section:

"Beverage" means each of the following forms of liquid refreshment intended for human consumption:

Fermented malt beverages, malt liquors, beers, or any beverages obtained by the fermentation of any infusion or decoction of barley, malt, hops, or any similar product, or any combination thereof, in water;

Alcoholic beverages obtained by distillation, and mixed with water or other substances in solution;

Alcoholic beverages obtained by the fermentation of the natural sugar contents of fruits or other agricultural products containing sugar;

Mineral or soda waters;

Carbonated or noncarbonated soft drinks; or

Fruit juices or vegetable juices or fruitades.

"Beverage container" means an individual, sealed metal can which contains a beverage.

"Within Colorado" means within the exterior limits of Colorado and includes all territory within these limits owned or ceded to the United States of America.

No person shall sell or offer for sale at retail within Colorado any metal beverage container with a detachable opening device designed to detach from the beverage container when a user opens the beverage container in a manner reasonably calculated to gain access to its contents.

Subsection (2) of this section shall not apply to metal beverage containers with opening devices consisting of sensitized adhesive tape.

Any person who violates subsection (2) of this section commits a class 2 petty offense and, upon conviction thereof, shall be fined not less than fifty dollars nor more than one hundred dollars.

18-13-114. Sale of secondhand property - record - inspection - crime - definitions. (1) Every secondhand dealer, as defined in subsection (5) of this section, shall make a record, as provided in subsection (2) of this section, of each sale or trade of secondhand property made by him, his agent, or any person acting on his behalf, which sale or trade equals or exceeds thirty dollars in value for each item. Such record shall be made available to any peace officer for inspection at any reasonable time. The secondhand dealer shall mail or deliver the record of the sale or trade to the local law enforcement agency within three days of the date of such sale or trade. The secondhand dealer shall keep a copy of the record of the sale or trade for at least one year after the date of the sale or trade.

(2) The record required by this section shall be made in writing on forms designed by the Colorado bureau of investigation or a reasonable facsimile thereof as provided in subsection (3) or

of this section and shall consist of the following:

The name, address, and date of birth of the seller or trader;

The date, time, and place of the sale or trade;

An accurate and detailed account and description of the item sold or traded, including, but not limited to, any trademark, identification number, serial number, model number, brand name, or other identifying mark on such item;

The identification number from any of the following forms of identification of the seller or trader:

A valid Colorado driver's license;

An identification card issued in accordance with section 42-2-302, C.R.S.;

A valid driver's license, containing a picture, issued by another state;

A military identification card;

A valid passport;

An alien registration card; or

A nonpicture identification document issued by a state or federal government entity;

The signature of the seller or trader;

A declaration by the secondhand dealer that he is the rightful owner of the secondhand property and a description of how he obtained the property, including the serial number of such property if available or a copy of the bill of sale of such property; and

A declaration by the secondhand dealer that he has knowledge of the requirement that he mail or deliver a record of the sale or trade to the local law enforcement agency, as required by subsection (1) of this section.

Any city, municipality, city and county, or county which regulates secondhand dealers and assesses a fee as provided in section 18-13-118 shall print and provide the forms for reporting required pursuant to subsection (2) of this section.

In cities, municipalities, city and counties, and counties which do not license secondhand dealers and assess a fee as provided in section 18-13-118, the secondhand dealer shall report all the information required pursuant to subsection (2) of this section in a form acceptable to the local law enforcement agency.

As used in this section and sections 18-13-115 to 18-13-118, unless the context otherwise requires:

"Local law enforcement agency" means any marshal's office, police department, or sheriff's office with jurisdiction in the locality in which the sale or trade occurs.

"Peace officer" means any undersheriff, deputy sheriff other than one appointed with authority only to receive and serve summons and civil process, police officer, Colorado state patrol officer, town marshal, or investigator for a district attorney or the attorney general who is engaged in full-time employment by the state, a city, city and county, town, judicial district, or county within this state.

"Secondhand dealer" means any person whose principal business is that of engaging in selling or trading secondhand property. The term also includes the following: Any person whose principal business is not that of engaging in selling or trading secondhand property but who sells or trades secondhand propertythrough means commonly known as flea markets or anysimilar facilities in which secondhand property is offered for sale or trade; any person who sells or trades secondhand property from a nonpermanent location; and any person who purchases for resale any secondhand

property which carries a manufacturer or serial number. The term does not include:

A person selling or trading secondhand property so long as such property was not originally purchased for resale and so long as such person does not sell or trade secondhand property more than five weekend periods in any one calendar year, as verified by a declaration to be prepared by the seller. For the purposes of this subparagraph (I), "weekend period" means Friday through the immediately following Monday.

A person who is a retailer as defined in section 39-26-102 (8), C.R.S., or a wholesaler as defined in section 39-26-102 (18), C.R.S., and who is selling or trading secondhand property in a location which is a permanent storefront location, unless such property carries a manufacturer or serial number;

A person or organization selling or trading secondhand property at an exhibition or show which is intended to display and advertise a particular commodity or class of products, including, but not limited to, antique exhibitions, firearm exhibitions, home and garden shows, and recreational vehicle shows;

A person or organization which is charitable, nonprofit, recreational, fraternal, or political in nature or which is exempt from taxation pursuant to section 501 (c) (3) of the federal "Internal Revenue Code of 1986", as amended;

A person selling or trading firewood, Christmas trees, plants, food products, agricultural products, fungible goods, pets, livestock, or arts and crafts, excluding jewelry and items crafted of gold or silver, if sold or traded by the artist or craftsman, his immediate family, or regular employees;

A person who sells new goods exclusively, is in the business of selling such goods, is in all respects a retailer of such goods, and holds a retail license and a sales tax license in the city, county, or city and county in which the sale occurs;

An antique dealer who sells antiques, has a retail license and sales tax license in the city, county, or city and county in which the sale occurs, and sells such antiques from a permanent storefront location.

"Secondhand property" means the following items of tangible personal property sold or traded by a secondhand dealer:

Cameras, camera lenses, slide or movie projectors, projector screens, flashguns, enlargers, tripods, binoculars, telescopes, and microscopes;

Televisions, phonographs, tape recorders, video recorders, radios, tuners, speakers, turntables, amplifiers, record changers, citizens' band broadcasting units and receivers, and video games;

Skis, ski poles, ski boots, ski bindings, golf clubs, guns, jewelry, coins, luggage, boots, and furs;

Typewriters, adding machines, calculators, computers, portable air conditioners, cash registers, copying machines, dictating machines, automatic telephone answering machines, and sewing machines;

Bicycles, bicycle frames, bicycle derailleur assemblies, bicycle hand brake assemblies, and other bicycle components; and

Any item of tangible personal property which is marked with a serial or identification number and the selling price of which is thirty dollars or more, except motor vehicles, off-highway vehicles as defined in section 42-1-102 (63), C.R.S., snowmobiles, ranges, stoves, dishwashers,

refrigerators, garbage disposals, boats, airplanes, clothes washers, clothes driers, freezers, mobile homes, and nonprecious scrap metal.

(a) Any secondhand dealer who violates any of the provisions of subsection (1) or (2) of this section commits a class 1 misdemeanor. Upon a second or subsequent conviction for a violation of subsection (1) or (2) of this section within three years of the date of a prior conviction, a secondhand dealer commits a class 5 felony.

(b) Any buyer or person who trades with a secondhand dealer or any secondhand dealer who knowingly gives false information with respect to the information required by subsection (2) of this section commits a class 1 misdemeanor.

(a) Local law enforcement agencies who print and provide forms as designed by the Colorado bureau of investigation for recording the information required by subsection (2) of this section may charge a reasonable fee for each form to defray the cost of providing such form.

(b) Each local law enforcement agency may establish rules or policies requiring that secondhand dealers provide it with copies of such records. The local law enforcement agency may set forth how often such copies shall be provided to it. Each local law enforcement agency shall forward copies of records received by it to the law enforcement agencyhaving jurisdiction in the area in which the buyer or trader resides.

In the case of flea markets and similar facilities in which secondhand property is offered for sale or trade, the operator thereof shall inform each secondhand dealer of the requirements of this section and shall provide the forms for recording the information required by subsection (2) of this section. Any person who violates the provisions of this subsection (8) commits a class 3 misdemeanor.

In the case of flea markets and similar facilities in which secondhand property is offered for sale or trade, the operator thereof shall record the name and address of each secondhand dealer operating at the flea market or similar facility and the identification number of such dealer as obtained from any of the forms of identification enumerated in paragraph (d) of subsection (2) of this section. Such record shall be mailed or delivered by the operator to the local law enforcement agency within three days of the date the secondhand dealer offered secondhand property for sale or trade at the flea market or similar facility. A copy of such record shall be retained by the operator for at least one year after the date the secondhand dealer offered secondhand property for sale or trade at the flea market or similar facility.


18-13-114.5. Proof of ownership required - penalty - definitions. (1) A person who is a secondhand dealer or a dealer and retailer of new goods and who sells goods at a flea market or similar facility shall not sell or offer for sale any of the following property items without proof of ownership:
Baby food of a type usually consumed by children under three years of age;
Cosmetics;
Devices;
Drugs;
Infant formula;

Batteries; or
Razor blades.
A person required to have proof of ownership under subsection (1) of this section shall make such proof of ownership available to any peace officer for inspection at any reasonable time.
For purposes of this section:
"Cosmetic" means an article, or its components, intended to be rubbed, poured, sprinkled, or sprayed on, introduced into, or otherwise applied to, the human body, or any part of the human body, for cleansing, beautifying, promoting attractiveness, or altering appearance. "Cosmetic" does not include soap.
"Device" means an instrument, apparatus, implement, machine, contrivance, implant, in vitro reagent, or other similar or related article, including a component, part, or accessory, that is:
Recognized in the official national formulary or the United States pharmacopoeia, or any supplement to them;
Intended for use in the diagnosis of disease or other condition, or in the cure, mitigation, treatment, or prevention of disease in humans or animals; or
Intended to affect the structure or any function of the body of humans or animals and that does not achieve any of its principal intended purposes through chemical action within or on the body of humans or animals and that is not dependent upon being metabolized for the achievement of any of its principal intended purposes.
"Drug" means:
Any article recognized in an official compendium of drugs;
An article used or intended for use in the diagnosis, cure, mitigation, treatment, or prevention of disease in humans or animals;
An article, other than food, that is used or intended to affect the structure or any function of the body of humans or animals; or
An article intended for use as a component of an article specified in subparagraph (I), (II), or (III) of this paragraph (c).
"Infant formula" means a food that purports to be or is represented for special dietary use solely as a food for infants by reason of its simulation of human milk or its suitability as a complete or partial substitute for human milk.
"Proof of ownership" shall include:
The name, address, telephone number, and signature of the seller or the seller's authorized representative;
The name and address of the buyer or consignee if not sold; and
A description and quantity of the product.
A violation of this section is a class 3 misdemeanor.


18-13-115. Notice - penalties. (1) Except in the case of flea markets and similar facilities as provided in this subsection (1), every secondhand dealer shall conspicuously post a notice in a place clearly visible to all buyers and traders which sets forth the provisions of this section and of sections 18-13-114 and 18-13-116 and which sets forth the penalties for violating such sections and for violating section 18-4-401, concerning theft. Such notification shall include information to the

effect that stolen property may be confiscated by any peace officer and returned to the rightful owner without compensation to the buyer. In the case of flea markets and similar facilities, the operator thereof shall post the notice required in this subsection (1) in such a manner as to be obvious to all persons who enter the flea market or similar facility.
Each city, municipality, city and county, and county which regulates secondhand dealers as provided in section 18-13-118 shall print and provide the notices required by subsection (1) of this section to the secondhand dealers within their jurisdiction who are licensed pursuant to section 18-13-116.
In any city, municipality, city and county, and county, which does not regulate secondhand dealers as provided in section 18-13-118, the secondhand dealers shall construct a notification containing the information required by subsection (1) of this section.
Any secondhand dealer or operator of a flea market or similar facility who violates any of the provisions of subsection (1) of this section commits a class 3 misdemeanor.


18-13-116. Sales tax license. (1) Every secondhand dealer shall obtain a sales tax license as provided in section 39-26-103, C.R.S.; except that secondhand dealers and other persons operating at a flea market or similar facility shall not be required to obtain a sales tax license, but they shall be required to collect the sales tax and to remit the proceeds to the operator of the flea market or similar facility, as provided in this section. The operator shall obtain a sales tax license which is applicable to all sales occurring at the flea market or similar facility, shall collect the sales tax from each secondhand dealer operating therein who does not have his own sales tax license, and shall remit such proceeds as provided by law for the remittance of sales taxes.

(2) Any person who violates any of the provisions of subsection (1) of this section commits a class 3 misdemeanor.

**18-13-117. Record of sales.** (1) Every secondhand dealer or any person who is a dealer of new goods who is a retailer and sells such goods at a flea market or similar facility or any nonpermanent location shall keep and preserve suitable records of sales made by him and such other books or accounts as may be necessary to determine the amount of tax for the collection of which he is liable under part 1 of article 26 of title 39, C.R.S. It is the duty of every such person to keep and preserve for a period of three years all invoices of goods and merchandise purchased for resale, and all such books, invoices, and other records shall be open for examination at any time by the executive director of the department of revenue, his duly authorized agent, or any peace officer.

Any person who violates any of the provisions of subsection (1) of this section commits a class 3 misdemeanor.

**18-13-118. Regulation of secondhand dealers.** Any city, municipality, city and county, or county may enact ordinances or resolutions regulating secondhand dealers, including license requirements and assessment of fees to cover costs of administration and enforcement of such regulation; however, such ordinances may not be less stringent than the provisions of sections 18-13- 114 to 18-13-117.

**18-13-119. Health care providers - abuse of health insurance.** (1) The general assembly hereby finds, determines, and declares that:

Business practices that have the effect of eliminating the need for actual payment by the recipient of health care of required copayments and deductibles in health benefit plans interfere with contractual obligations entered into between the insured and the insurer relating to such payments; Such interference is not in the public interest when it is conducted as a regular business practice because it has the effect of increasing health care costs by removing the incentive that copayments and deductibles create in making the consumer a cost-conscious purchaser of health care; and Advertising of such practices mayaggravate the adverse financial and other impacts upon recipients of health care.

Therefore, the general assembly declares that such business practices are illegal and that violation thereof or the advertising thereof shall be grounds for disciplinary actions. The general assembly further declares that nothing contained in this section shall be construed to otherwise prohibit advertising by health care providers.

Except as otherwise provided in subsections (5), (6), and (8) of this section, if the effect is to eliminate the need for payment by the patient of any required deductible or copayment applicable in the patient's health benefit plan, a person who provides health care commits abuse of health insurance if the person knowingly:

Accepts from any third-party payor, as payment in full for services rendered, the amount the third-party payor covers; or

Submits a fee to a third-party payor which is higher than the fee he has agreed to accept from the insured patient with the understanding of waiving the required deductible or copayment.

Abuse of health insurance is a class 1 petty offense.

(a) Reimbursements made pursuant to articles 3 to 6 of title 25.5, C.R.S., federal medicare laws for inpatient hospitalization, and mental health services purchased in accordancewith article 66 of title 27, C.R.S., are exempt from the provisions of this section.

Health care services are exempt from the provisions of this section if such health care services are provided:

In accordance with a contract or agreement between an employer and an employee or employees and the contract includes, as a part of an employee's salary or employment benefits, terms that authorize a practice that would otherwise be prohibited by subsection (3) of this section; or

In accordance with a contract or agreement between a town, city, city and county, or municipality or a special health assurance district pursuant to section 31-15-302 (1), C.R.S., under terms that authorize a practice that would otherwise be prohibited by subsection (3) of this section.

(a) The waiver of any required deductible or copayment for charitable purposes is exempt from the provisions of subsection (3) of this section if:

The person who provides the health care determines that the services are necessary for the immediate health and welfare of the patient; and

The waiver is made on a case-by-case basis and the person who provides the health care determines that payment of the deductible or copayment would create a substantial financial hardship

for the patient; and

The waiver is not a regular business practice of the person who provides the health care.

(b) Any person who provides health care and who waives the deductible or copayment for more than one-fourth of his patients during any calendar year, excluding patients covered by subsection (5) of this section, or who advertises through newspapers, magazines, circulars, direct mail, directories, radio, television, or otherwise that he will accept from any third-party payor, as payment in full for services rendered, the amount the third-party payor covers shall be presumed to be engaged in waiving the deductible or copayment as a regular business practice.

Repealed.

The waiver of a required deductible or copayment for health care services provided by a school-based health center, as defined in section 25-20.5-502, C.R.S., is exempt from the provisions of this section.

**18-13-119.5. Abuse of property insurance.** (1) The general assembly hereby finds, determines, and declares that:

(I) Business practices that have the effect of reducing or eliminating the need for actual payment of required copayments and deductibles by an insured for property damages interfere with contractual obligations entered into by the insured and insurer relating to such payments;

(II) Interference described in subparagraph (I) of this paragraph (a) is not in the public interest because it has the effect of increasing insurance costs by removing the incentives that copayments and deductibles create in making the consumer a cost-conscious purchaser; and

(I) Business practices that have the effect of providing rebates or something of value to an insured to attract business relating to property damages when the costs of the rebate or thing of value is passed on to an insurer interfere with contractual obligations entered into by the insured and insurer relating to such property damages;

(II) Interference described in subparagraph (I) of this paragraph (b) is not in the public interest because it has the effect of increasing insurance costs by including items unrelated to the property damage in the costs paid by insurers; and

Advertising of practices described in paragraphs (a) and (b) of this subsection (1) may aggravate the impact of such practices.

(2) (a) The general assembly further declares that business practices described in subsection of this section are illegal and that such practices or the advertising thereof shall be grounds for disciplinary actions by any governmental body which

is responsible for licensing or regulating persons who engage in such practices.

(b) The general assembly further declares that this section shall create a private right of action in courts of the state of Colorado, including an action for injunctive relief.

Anyperson who provides repairs, goods, or services commits abuse of propertyinsurance if such person knowingly:

Submits a fee to an insurer which is higher than a fee estimate such person provided to the insured or which is higher than the fee such person has agreed to accept from the insured if the effect is to provide the insured a rebate or something of value to attract the insured to do business with such person and the cost of providing the rebate or thing of value is passed on to the insurer as

a part of the higher fee; or

Provides a rebate or a gift, cash, or thing of value to an insurance company or its representative, agent, employee, or others acting on behalf of the insurance company, in connection with any claim under an insurance policy which insures for property damage.

Any insurance company, or its agent, employee, representative, or other person acting on behalf of the insurance company, commits abuse of propertyinsurance if such company or person knowingly: Accepts a rebate or a gift, cash, or thing of value from any person who provides repairs, goods, or services in connection with any claim under an insurance policy which insures for property damage.

Abuse of property insurance is a class 2 misdemeanor.


18-13-120. Use, transportation, and storage of drip gasoline. (1) As used in this section, "drip gasoline" means a combustible hydrocarbon liquid formed as a product of condensation from either associated or nonassociated natural or casing-head gas which remains a liquid at the existing atmospheric temperature and pressure.

Every person, other than a producer, refiner, pipeline company, or owner or operator of a natural gas processing plant or their authorized agents, who transports or stores drip gasoline in this state shall have in his possession a written instrument issued and signed by a licensed seller of gasoline, stating the names and addresses of the seller and purchaser, the date of sale, and the amount sold and paid for such drip gasoline, or a copy of a contract authorizing the loading and transportation of the drip gasoline.

The use of drip gasoline in a motor vehicle operated on the highways of this state is prohibited.

Any person who violates subsection (2) or (3) of this section commits a class 2 misdemeanor.


18-13-121. Furnishing cigarettes, tobacco products, or nicotine products to minors. (1) (a) A person shall not give, sell, distribute, dispense, or offer for sale a cigarette, tobacco product, or nicotine product to any person who is under eighteen years of age.

Before giving, selling, distributing, dispensing, or offering to sell to an individual any cigarette, tobacco product, or nicotine product, a person shall request from the individual and examine a government-issued photographic identification that establishes that the individual is eighteen years of age or older; except that, in face-to-face transactions, this requirement is waived if the individual appears older than thirty years of age.

A person who violates paragraph (a) or (b) of this subsection (1) commits a class 2 petty offense and, upon conviction thereof, shall be punished by a fine of two hundred dollars.

It is an affirmative defense to a prosecution under paragraph (a) of this subsection (1) that the person furnishing the cigarette, tobacco product, or nicotine product was presented with and reasonably relied upon a document that identified the individual receiving the cigarette, tobacco product, or nicotine product as being eighteen years of age or older.

(a) A person who is under eighteen years of age and who purchases or attempts to purchase any cigarettes, tobacco products, or nicotine products commits a class 2 petty offense and, upon conviction thereof, shall be punished by a fine of one hundred dollars; except that, following a conviction or adjudication for a first offense under this subsection (2), the court in lieu of the fine may sentence the person to participate in a tobacco education program. The court may allow a person convicted under this subsection (2) to perform community service and be granted credit against the fine and court costs at the rate of five dollars for each hour of work performed for up to fifty percent of the fine and court costs.

(b) It is not an offense under paragraph (a) of this subsection (2) if the person under eighteen years of age was acting at the direction of an employee of a governmental agency authorized to enforce or ensure compliance with laws relating to the prohibition of the sale of cigarettes, tobacco products, or nicotine products to minors.

Nothing in this section prohibits a statutory or home-rule municipality from enacting an ordinance that prohibits a person under eighteen years of age from purchasing anycigarettes, tobacco products, or nicotine products or imposes requirements more stringent than provided in this section. (3.5) Nothing in this section affects federal laws concerning cigarettes, tobacco products, or

nicotine products, as they apply to military bases and Indian reservations within the state.

(Deleted by amendment, L. 98, p. 1185, 2, effective July 1, 1998.)

(a) As used in this section, "cigarette, tobacco product, or nicotine product" means:

A product that contains nicotine or tobacco or is derived from tobacco and is intended to be ingested or inhaled by or applied to the skin of an individual; or

Any device that can be used to deliver tobacco or nicotine to the person inhaling from the device, including an electronic cigarette, cigar, cigarillo, or pipe.

(b) Notwithstanding any provision of paragraph (a) of this subsection (5) to the contrary, "cigarette, tobacco product, or nicotine product" does not mean a product that the food and drug administration of the United States department of health and human services has approved as a tobacco use cessation product.


18-13-122. Illegal possession or consumption of ethyl alcohol or marijuana by an underage person - illegal possession of marijuana paraphernalia by an underage person - definitions - adolescent substance abuse prevention and treatment fund - legislative declaration. (1) (a) The general assembly finds and declares that it is necessary for the state of Colorado to educate Colorado youth about the dangers of early use of alcohol and marijuana, to actively promote programs that prevent the illegal use of alcohol and marijuana, and to teach Colorado youth about responsible use and the healthy choices available to an adult once he or she is able to legally consume alcohol or marijuana.

(b) The Colorado general assembly finds it is necessary for the state of Colorado to provide more adolescent substance abuse education and treatment in a developmentally, intellectually, and socially appropriate manner. Therefore, it is necessary to create the adolescent substance abuse prevention and treatment fund for that purpose.

As used in this section, unless the context otherwise requires:

"Establishment" means a business, firm, enterprise, service or fraternal organization, club, institution, entity, group, or residence; any real property, including buildings and improvements, connected therewith; and any members, employees, and occupants associated therewith.

"Ethyl alcohol" means any substance which is or contains ethyl alcohol.

"Marijuana" has the same meaning as in section 16 (2) (f) of article XVIII of the Colorado constitution.

"Marijuana paraphernalia" has the same meaning as marijuana accessories in section 16

(g) of article XVIII of the Colorado constitution.

"Possession of ethyl alcohol" means that a person has or holds any amount of ethyl alcohol anywhere on his or her person or that a person owns or has custody of ethyl alcohol or has ethyl alcohol within his or her immediate presence and control.

"Possession of marijuana" means that a person has or holds any amount of marijuana anywhere on his or her person or that a person owns or has custody of marijuana or has marijuana within his or her immediate presence and control.

"Private property" means any dwelling and its curtilage which is being used by a natural person or natural persons for habitation and which is not open to the public and privately owned real property which is not open to the public. "Private property" shall not include:

Any establishment which has or is required to have a license pursuant to article 46, 47, or 48 of title 12, C.R.S.;

Any establishment which sells ethyl alcohol or upon which ethyl alcohol is sold; or

Any establishment which leases, rents, or provides accommodations to members of the public generally.

(a) Except as described by section 18-1-711 and subsection (6) of this section, a person under twenty-one years of age who possesses or consumes ethyl alcohol anywhere in the state of Colorado commits illegal possession or consumption of ethyl alcohol by an underage person. Illegal possession or consumption of ethyl alcohol by an underage person is a strict liability offense.

Except as described by section 14 of article XVIII of the Colorado constitution and section 18-18-406.3, a person under twenty-one years of age who possesses one ounce or less of marijuana or consumes marijuana anywhere in the state of Colorado commits illegal possession or consumption of marijuana by an underage person. Illegal possession or consumption of marijuana by an underage person is a strict liability offense.

Except as described by section 14 of article XVIII of the Colorado constitution and section 18-18-406.3, a person under twenty-one years of age who possesses marijuana paraphernalia anywhere in the state of Colorado and knows or reasonably should know that the drug paraphernalia could be used in circumstances in violation of the laws of this state commits illegal possession of marijuana paraphernalia by an underage person. Illegal possession of marijuana paraphernalia by an underage person is a strict liability offense.

A violation of this subsection (3) is an unclassified petty offense.

(a) Upon conviction of a first offense of subsection (3) of this section, the court shall sentence the underage person to a fine of not more than one hundred dollars, or the court shall order that the underage person complete a substance abuse education program approved by the division of behavioral health in the department of human services, or both.

Upon conviction of a second offense of subsection (3) of this section, the court shall

sentence the underage person to a fine of not more than one hundred dollars, and the court shall order the underage person to:

Complete a substance abuse education program approved by the division of behavioral health in the department of human services;

If determined necessary and appropriate, submit to a substance abuse assessment approved by the division of behavioral health in the department of human services and complete any treatment recommended by the assessment; and

Perform up to twenty-four hours of useful public service, subject to the conditions and restrictions specified in section 18-1.3-507.

Upon conviction of a third or subsequent offense of subsection (3) of this section, the court shall sentence the defendant to a fine of up to two hundred fifty dollars, and the court shall order the underage person to:

Submit to a substance abuse assessment approved by the division of behavioral health in the department of human services and complete any treatment recommended by the assessment; and

Perform up to thirty-six hours of useful public service, subject to the conditions and restrictions specified in section 18-1.3-507.

Nothing in this section prohibits a prosecutor from entering into a diversion or deferred judgment agreement with any underage person for any offense under this section, and prosecutors are encouraged to enter into those agreements when they are consistent with the legislative declaration of this section and in the interests of justice.

A person convicted of a violation of this section is subject to an additional penalty surcharge of twenty-five dollars, which may be waived by the court upon a showing of indigency, that shall be transferred to the adolescent substance abuse prevention and treatment fund created pursuant to subsection (18) of this section.

It is an affirmative defense to the offense described in paragraph (a) of subsection (3) of this section that the ethyl alcohol was possessed or consumed by a person under twenty-one years of age under the following circumstances:

While such person was legally upon private property with the knowledge and consent of the owner or legal possessor of such private property and the ethyl alcohol was possessed or consumed with the consent of his or her parent or legal guardian who was present during such possession or consumption;

When the existence of ethyl alcohol in a person's body was due solely to the ingestion of a confectionery which contained ethyl alcohol within the limits prescribed by section 25-5-410

(i) (II), C.R.S.; or the ingestion of any substance which was manufactured, designed, or intended primarily for a purpose other than oral human ingestion; or the ingestion of any substance which was manufactured, designed, or intended solely for medicinal or hygienic purposes; or solely from the ingestion of a beverage which contained less than one-half of one percent of ethyl alcohol by weight; or

The person is a student who:

Tastes but does not imbibe an alcohol beverage only while under the direct supervision of an instructor who is at least twenty-one years of age and employed by a post-secondary school;

Is enrolled in a university or a post-secondary school accredited or certified by an agency

recognized by the United States department of education, a nationally recognized accrediting agency or association, or the "Private Occupational Education Act of 1981", article 59 of title 12, C.R.S.;

Is participating in a culinary arts, food service, or restaurant management degree program; and

Tastes but does not imbibe the alcohol beverage for instructional purposes as a part of a required course in which the alcohol beverage, except the portion the student tastes, remains under the control of the instructor.

The possession or consumption of ethyl alcohol or marijuana shall not constitute a violation of this section if such possession or consumption takes place for religious purposes protected by the first amendment to the United States constitution.

(a) An underage person is immune from arrest and prosecution under this section if he or she establishes the following:

The underage person called 911 and reported in good faith that another underage person was in need of medical assistance due to alcohol or marijuana consumption;

The underage person who called 911 provided his or her name to the 911 operator;

The underage person was the first person to make the 911 report; and

The underage person who made the 911 call remained on the scene with the underage person in need of medical assistance until assistance arrived and cooperated with medical assistance or law enforcement personnel on the scene.

(b) The immunity described in paragraph (a) of this subsection (7) also extends to the underage person who was in need of medical assistance due to alcohol or marijuana consumption if the conditions of said paragraph (a) are satisfied.

Prima facie evidence of a violation of subsection (3) of this section shall consist of:

Evidence that the defendant was under twenty-one years of age and possessed or consumed ethyl alcohol or marijuana or possessed marijuana paraphernalia anywhere in this state; or

Evidence that the defendant was under the age of twenty-one years and manifested any of the characteristics commonly associated with ethyl alcohol intoxication or impairment or marijuana impairment while present anywhere in this state.

During any trial for a violation of subsection (3) of this section, any bottle, can, or any other container with labeling indicating the contents of such bottle, can, or container shall be admissible into evidence, and the information contained on any label on such bottle, can, or other container shall be admissible into evidence and shall not constitute hearsay. A jury or a judge, whichever is appropriate, may consider the information upon such label in determining whether the contents of the bottle, can, or other container were composed in whole or in part of ethyl alcohol or marijuana. A label which identifies the contents of any bottle, can, or other container as "beer", "ale", "malt beverage", "fermented malt beverage", "malt liquor", "wine", "champagne", "whiskey" or "whisky", "gin", "vodka", "tequila", "schnapps", "brandy", "cognac", "liqueur", "cordial", "alcohol", or "liquor" shall constitute prima facie evidence that the contents of the bottle, can, or other container was composed in whole or in part of ethyl alcohol.

A parent or legal guardian of a person under twenty-one years of age or any natural person who has the permission of such parent or legal guardian may give or permit the possession and consumption of ethyl alcohol to or by a person under twenty-one years of age under the

conditions described in paragraph (a) of subsection (5) of this section. This subsection (10) shall not be construed to permit any establishment which is licensed or is required to be licensed pursuant to article 46, 47, or 48 of title 12, C.R.S., or any members, employees, or occupants of any such establishment to give, provide, make available, or sell ethyl alcohol to a person under twenty-one years of age.

Nothing in this section shall be construed to prohibit any statutory or home rule municipality from enacting any ordinance which prohibits persons under twenty-one years of age from possessing or consuming ethyl alcohol or marijuana or possessing marijuana paraphernalia, which ordinance is at least as restrictive or more restrictive than this section.

Nothing in this section shall be construed to limit or preclude prosecution for any offense pursuant to article 46, 47, or 48 of title 12, C.R.S., except as provided in such articles.

Sealing of record. (a) Upon dismissal of a case pursuant to this section after completion of a deferred judgment or diversion or any other action resulting in dismissal of the case or upon completion of the court-ordered substance abuse education and payment of any fine for a first conviction of subsection (3) of this section, the court shall immediately order the case sealed and provide to the underage person and the prosecutor a copy of the order sealing the case for distribution by the appropriate party to all law enforcement agencies in the case.

(b) Upon the expiration of one year from the date of a second or subsequent conviction for a violation of subsection (3) of this section, the underage person convicted of such violation may petition the court in which the conviction was assigned for an order sealing the record of the conviction. The petitioner shall submit a verified copy of his or her criminal history, current through at least the twentieth day prior to the date of the filing of the petition, along with the petition at the time of filing, but in no event later than the tenth day after the petition is filed. The petitioner shall be responsible for obtaining and paying for his or her criminal history record. The court shall grant the petition if the petitioner has not been arrested for, charged with, or convicted of any felony, misdemeanor, or petty offense during the period of one year following the date of the petitioner's conviction for a violation of subsection (3) of this section.

The qualitative result of an alcohol or marijuana test or tests shall be admissible at the trial of any person charged with a violation of subsection (3) of this section upon a showing that the device or devices used to conduct such test or tests have been approved as accurate in detecting alcohol or marijuana by the executive director of the department of public health and environment.

Official records of the department of public health and environment relating to the certification of breath test instruments, certification of operators and operator instructors of breath test instruments, certification of standard solutions, and certification of laboratories shall be official records of the state. Copies of such records, attested by the executive director of the department of public health and environment or his or her designee and accompanied by a certificate bearing the official seal for said department, which state that the executive director of the department has custody of such records, shall be admissible in all courts of record and shall constitute prima facie evidence of the information contained in such records. The official seal of the department described in this subsection (15) may consist of a watermark of the state seal within the document.

In any judicial proceeding in any court of this state concerning a charge under subsection (3) of this section, the court shall take judicial notice of methods of testing a person's blood, breath, saliva, or urine for the presence of alcohol or marijuana and of the design and

operation of devices certified by the department of public health and environment for testing a person's blood, breath, saliva, or urine for the presence of alcohol or marijuana. This subsection (16) shall not prevent the necessity of establishing during a trial that the testing devices were working properly and that such testing devices were properly operated. Nothing in this subsection (16) shall preclude a defendant from offering evidence concerning the accuracy of testing devices.

A law enforcement officer may not enter upon any private property to investigate any violation of this section without probable cause.

Cash fund. The surcharge collected pursuant to paragraph (e) of subsection (4) of this section must be transmitted to the state treasurer, who shall credit the same to the adolescent substance abuse prevention and treatment fund, which fund is created and referred to in this section as the "fund". The moneys in the fund are subject to annual appropriation by the general assembly to the unit in the department of human services that administers behavioral health programs and services, including those related to mental health and substance abuse, established in article 80 of title 27, C.R.S., for adolescent substance abuse prevention and treatment programs. The unit in the department of human services that administers behavioral health programs and services, including those related to mental health and substance abuse, is authorized to seek and accept gifts, grants, or donations from private or public sources for the purposes of this section. All private and public funds received through gifts, grants, or donations must be transmitted to the state treasurer, who shall credit the same to the fund. Any unexpended moneys in the fund may be invested by the state treasurer as provided by law. All interest and income derived from the investment and deposit of moneys in the fund must be credited to the fund. Any unexpended and unencumbered moneys remaining in the fund at the end of a fiscal year remain in the fund and shall not be credited or transferred to the general fund or another fund.

18-13-123. Unlawful administration of gamma hydroxybutyrate (GHB) or ketamine.

(1) and (2) (Deleted by amendment, L. 2001, p. 858, § 4, effective July 1, 2001.)

Except as otherwise provided in subsection (4) of this section, it shall be unlawful for any person to knowingly cause or attempt to cause any other person to unknowingly consume or receive the direct administration of gamma hydroxybutyrate (GHB) or ketamine or the immediate chemical precursors or chemical analogs for either of such substances.

(a) It shall not be a violation of this section if gamma hydroxybutyrate (GHB) or ketamine is distributed or dispensed for bona fide medical needs by or under the direction of a person licensed or authorized by law to prescribe, administer, or dispense such substances.

(b) It shall not be a violation of this section if ketamine is distributed or dispensed by or under the direction of such authorized person for use by a humane society that is duly registered with the secretary of state and has been in existence and in business for at least five years in this state as a nonprofit corporation or by an animal control agency that is operated by a unit of government to control animals and to euthanize injured, sick, homeless, or unwanted pets or animals if the humane society or animal control agency is registered pursuant to section 12-42.5-117 (12), C.R.S. Violation of the provisions of subsection (3) of this section is a class 3 felony; except that such violation is a class 2 felony if the violation is subsequent to a prior conviction for a violation of subsection (3) of this section or section 18-18-405 where the controlled substance was gamma

hydroxybutyrate (GHB) or ketamine or the immediate chemical precursors or chemical analogs for either of such substances.

18-13-124. Dissemination of false information to obtain hospital admittance or care. (1) Any person commits the offense of dissemination of false information to obtain hospital admittance or care where such person knowingly provides false identifying information for the purpose of either obtaining admittance to, or health services from, a hospital or evading an obligation by the person to make payment to the hospital for services provided at the person's request. For purposes of this section, "identifying information" includes, without limitation, a name, address, or telephone number, or health coverage information.

Any person who commits the offense of dissemination of false information to obtain hospital admittance or care commits a class 1 misdemeanor and, upon conviction thereof, shall be punished as provided in section 18-1.3-501.

18-13-125. Telephone records - sale or purchase. (1) A person commits unauthorized trading in telephone records if the person, without lawful authorization:

Knowingly procures or attempts to procure a telephone record;

Knowingly sells, buys, offers to sell, or offers to buy a telephone record;

Possesses a telephone record with the intent to use such record, or information contained in such record, to harm another person; or

Receives a telephone record of a resident of Colorado knowing that such record was obtained without lawful authorization or by fraud or deception.

For the purposes of this section:

"Lawful authorization" means authorization from the person or the agent of the person to whom the telephone number is assigned or from the person or the agent of the person who purchases the telephone service.

"Procure" means to obtain by any means, with or without consideration.

"Telecommunications provider" means a company and its affiliates that provide commercial telephone service to a customer, irrespective of the technology employed, including, without limitation, wired, wireless, cable, broadband, satellite, or voice-over-internet protocol.

(I) "Telephone record" means information retained by a telecommunications provider that relates to the number dialed by the customer or subscriber, to the number of a person who dialed the customer, or to other data that are typically contained on a customer's telephone bill for either wired or wireless telephone service, including, without limitation, the time a call was made, the duration of a call, or the charges for a call.

(II) "Telephone record" shall not include a directory listing or information collected and retained by customers utilizing caller identification technology or similar technology.

(a) This section shall not prohibit a peace officer, a law enforcement agency, or an employee or agent of a law enforcement agency from obtaining telephone records in the performance of their duties or as authorized by law.

This section shall not prohibit a telecommunications provider from obtaining, using,

disclosing, or permitting access to a telephone record when such access:

Is otherwise authorized by Colorado law, any other state law, or federal law, including, without limitation, the rules promulgated by the federal communications commission;

Is necessary to operations of the telecommunications provider, or to provide services or products, or to protect the rights and property of the telecommunications provider;

Protects users of the service and other telecommunications providers from fraudulent, abusive, or unlawful use of or subscription to such service;

Is made to a government entity if the telecommunications provider reasonably believes that an emergency involving immediate danger of serious physical injury to any person justifies disclosure of the information;

Is made to the national center for missing and exploited children or its successor entity and concerns a report submitted under 42 U.S.C. sec. 13032;

Is in connection with the sale, purchase, or transfer of all or part of a telecommunications provider's business; or

Is in connection with the migration of a customer from one telecommunications provider to another.

This section shall not be construed to imply that telephone records belong to a person other than the telecommunications provider that maintains them.

Unauthorized trading in telephone records is a class 1 misdemeanor.

This section shall not apply to a telecommunications provider or its agents or representatives who reasonably and in good faith act pursuant to Colorado law, any other state law, or federal law, including, without limitation, the rules promulgated by the federal communications commission, notwithstanding a later determination that the act was not authorized by such law.

18-13-126. Locating protected persons. (1) (a) Except as otherwise provided in paragraph

(b) of this subsection (1), a person shall not accept money or other form of compensation to assist a restrained person from discovering the location of a protected person when the person knows or reasonably should know that the restrained person is subject to a court order prohibiting contact with the protected person.

(b) The provisions of paragraph (a) of this subsection (1) shall not apply to a person who is working pursuant to an agreement with counsel for a restrained person or with the restrained person if he or she is representing himself or herself, if:

(A) The restrained person seeks discovery of the location of the protected person for a lawful purpose as specified in a written agreement between the person and the restrained person or his or her counsel; and

(B) The written agreement states that the location of the protected person shall not be disclosed by the person or by counsel for the restrained person to the restrained person unless the protected person has agreed to the disclosure in writing or the restrained person obtains court permission to obtain disclosure of the location for the stated lawful purpose; or

(A) The restrained person is a defendant in a criminal case or a party to a civil case, an action for dissolution of marriage, or other legal proceeding; and

(B) The agreement states that the lawful purpose for locating the protected person is to interview or issue a lawful subpoena or summons to the protected person or for any other lawful purpose relating to the proper investigation of the case.

A violation of subsection (1) of this section is a class 1 misdemeanor offense.

person:

It shall be an affirmative defense to a charge under subsection (1) of this section if the

Within seventy-two hours prior to disclosing the location of the protected person to the

restrained person, verified that there was not a protection order relating to the protected person; and

Prior to disclosing the location of the protected person to the restrained person, obtained from the restrained person a signed affidavit verifying that the restrained person was not aware of any protection order related to the protected person.

As used in this section, unless the context otherwise requires:

"Protected person" means the person or persons identified in a protection order as the person or persons for whose benefit the protection order was issued.

"Protection order" means an order as described in section 18-6-803.5 (1.5) (a.5) that prohibits a restrained person from contacting a protected person.

"Restrained person" means the person identified in the protection order as the person prohibited from doing the specified act or acts.


18-13-127. Trafficking in adults. (Repealed)


18-13-128. Smuggling of humans. (1) A person commits smuggling of humans if, for the purpose of assisting another person to enter, remain in, or travel through the United States or the state of Colorado in violation of immigration laws, he or she provides or agrees to provide transportation to that person in exchange for money or any other thing of value.

Smuggling of humans is a class 3 felony.

A person commits a separate offense for each person to whom he or she provides or agrees to provide transportation in violation of subsection (1) of this section.

Notwithstanding the provisions of section 18-1-202, smuggling of humans offenses may be tried in any county in the state where a person who is illegally present in the United States who is a subject of the action is found.


18-13-129. Coercion of involuntary servitude. (Repealed)


18-13-130. Bail bond - prohibited activities - penalties. (1) It is unlawful for any person who engages in the business of writing bail bonds to engage in any of the following activities related to a bail bond transaction:

Specify, suggest, or advise the employment of a particular attorney to represent the

licensee's principal;

Pay a fee or rebate or give or promise anything of value to a jailer, peace officer, clerk, deputy clerk, an employee of a court, district attorney or district attorney's employees, or any person who has power to arrest or to hold a person in custody;

Pay a fee or rebate or give anything of value to an attorney in bail bond matters, except in defense of any action on a bond or as counsel to represent the person who wrote or posted the bond or the person's representative or employees;

Pay a fee or rebate or give or promise to give anything of value to the person on whose bond the person is surety;

Accept anything of value from a person on whose bond the person in the business of writing bail bonds is surety or from others on behalf of the person except the fee or premium on the bond, but the producer or agent may accept collateral security or other indemnity if:

No collateral or security in tangible property is taken by pledge or debt instrument that allows retention, sale, or other disposition of the property upon default except in accordance with article 9 of title 4, C.R.S.;

No collateral or security interest in real property is taken by deed or any other instrument unless the interest in the property is limited to the amount of the bond and the interest is recorded in the name of the bail insurance company or insurance producer, cash-bonding agent, or professional cash-bail agent who posted the bond with the court;

The collateral or security is not pledged directly to any court as security for any appearance bond; and

The person from whom the collateral or security is taken is issued a receipt describing the condition of the collateral at the time it is taken into custody;

Coerce, suggest, aid and abet, offer promise of favor, or threaten any person on whose bail bond the person is surety or offers to become surety to induce that person to commit any crime;

Post a bail bond in any court of record in this state while the name of the person is on the board under section 16-4-114 (5) (e), C.R.S., or under any circumstance where the person has failed to pay a bail forfeiture judgment after all applicable stays of execution have expired and the bond has not been exonerated or discharged;

Except for the bond fee, to fail to return any nonforfeited collateral or security within fourteen days after receipt of a copy of the court order that results in a release of the bond by the court, or if the defendant fails to appear and the surety is exonerated, fails to return the collateral to the indemnitor upon request within fourteen days after the three-year period, unless:

The collateral also secures another obligation, premium payment plan, or bail recovery fee; or

The later of three years or, if the court grants an extension, six years have elapsed from the date the bond was posted.

Accept anything of value from a person on whose bond the person in the business of writing bail bonds is indemnitor or from another on behalf of the principal except the premium, except as authorized by title 10, C.R.S., or any rule of the division of insurance promulgated under title 10, C.R.S.;

Sign or countersign blank bail bonds;

To have more than one bond posted at one time in one case on behalf of one person;

Fail to issue to the person from whom collateral or security is taken a receipt that includes a description of the collateral or security when it is taken into custody.

(2) A person who violates subsection (1) of this section is guilty of an unclassified misdemeanor and, upon conviction thereof, shall be punished by a fine of not more than one thousand dollars, or by imprisonment in the county jail for not more than one year, or by both such fine and imprisonment. Any criminal penalty prescribed in this section for a violation of this article is in addition to, and not exclusive of, any other applicable penalty prescribed by law.

**ARTICLE 14   Hotel Facility Rates: Posting - Notice**

18-14-101. Definitions. "Hotel facility" means an establishment engaged in the business of furnishing overnight room accommodations primarily for transient persons.

18-14-102. Accommodations and rates posted. (1) There shall be displayed at each hotel facility in its office or place of guest registration, in a conspicuous place, a sign which includes, in letters and figures of the same size and prominence, the following information: The number of apartments, rooms, or units in the hotel facility and the rates charged for each; whether the rates quoted are for single or multiple occupancy where such fact affects the rates charged; and the dates during which rates are in effect.
(2) There shall be posted in a plainly legible fashion, in a conspicuous place in, or at, each room, unit, and apartment of every hotel facility, the rates at which such room or apartment is rented. Such posting shall be in the form of a sign showing the maximum amount charged for occupancy and the maximum amount per person if the rate varies with the number of occupants. The sign shall also show the amount charged for extra conveniences, more complete accommodations, or additional furnishings and shall show the dates during the year when such charges prevail.

18-14-103. Advertising prohibited - when. (1) No person shall display or cause to be displayed any sign which may be seen from a public highwayor street, which sign includes in dollars and cents a statement relating to the rates charged at a hotel facility unless accommodations are available at the rates quoted at all times such sign is posted.
No person shall publish or cause to be published an advertisement which includes in dollars and cents a statement relating to rates charged at a hotel facility unless such advertisement includes in letters or figures of similar size and prominence: The number of apartments or rooms in said hotel facility at the published rates; whether the rates quoted are for single or multiple occupancy where such fact affects the rates charged; the dates during which such rates are in effect;

and an indication as to whether there are other rates in effect in said hotel facility. Advertisements or listings in guides or directories which are published by nonprofit hotel, motel, motor court, or apartment organizations or similar associations are excepted from this subsection (2).
There shall not be published or displayed any sign with regard to any hotel facility which may be seen from a public highway or street and which contains any advertisement that contains false or misleading statements as to any matter whatsoever.

18-14-104. Violations - penalty. Any owner, agent, lessee, or manager of any hotel facility who violates, or causes to be violated, any of the provisions of this article commits a class 1 petty offense.

### ARTICLE 15 Offenses - Making, Financing, or Collection of Loans

18-15-101. Definitions. As used in this article, unless the context otherwise requires:
To "collect" an extension of credit means to induce in any way any person to make repayment thereof.
"Creditor" means any person who extends credit or any person claiming by, under, or through any such person.
"Debtor" means any person who receives an extension of credit or any person who guarantees the repayment of an extension of credit or in any manner undertakes to indemnify the creditor against loss resulting from the failure of any person who receives an extension of credit to repay the same.
To "extend credit" means to make or renew any loan or to enter into any agreement, express or implied, whereby the repayment or satisfaction of any debt or claim, whether acknowledged or disputed, valid or invalid, and however arising, may or will be deferred.
An "extortionate means" is any means which involves the use, or an express or implicit threat of use, of violence or other criminal means to cause harm to the person, reputation, or property of any person.
(a) "Loan finance charge" means the sum of all charges payable directly or indirectly by the debtor and imposed directly or indirectly by the lender as an incident to or as a condition of the extension of credit, whether paid or payable by the debtor, the lender, or any other person on behalf of the debtor to the lender or to a third party, including, but not limited to, any of the following types of charges that are applicable:
Interest or any amount payable under a point, discount, or other system of charges, however denominated;

Premium or other charge for any guarantee of insurance protecting the lender against the debtor's default or other credit loss;
Charges incurred for investigating the collateral or credit-worthiness of the debtor or for commissions or brokerage for obtaining the credit.
(b) The term does not include the charges as a result of additional charges as defined in section 5-2-202, C.R.S., delinquency charges as defined in section 5-2-203, C.R.S., deferral charges as defined in section 5-2-204, C.R.S., similar charges specifically authorized by law, or additional interest charges permitted by section 5-12-107 (3), C.R.S.
"Repayment" of an extension of credit includes the repayment, satisfaction, or discharge, in whole or in part, of any debt or claim, acknowledged or disputed, valid or invalid, resulting from or in connection with that extension of credit.

18-15-102. Extortionate extension of credit - penalty. Any person who makes any extension of credit in any amount regardless of the loan finance charge with respect to which it is the understanding of the creditor and the debtor at the time it is made that delay in making repayment or failure to make repayment will result in the use of extortionate means of collection is guilty of extortionate extension of credit, which is a class 4 felony.

18-15-103. Presumption that extension of credit is extortionate. (1) The provisions of this section are nonexclusive and in no way limit the effect or applicability of section 18-15-102.
In any prosecution under section 18-15-102, if it is shown that the factors enumerated in paragraphs (a), (b), and (c) of this subsection (2) were present in connection with the making of the extension of credit in question, there shall arise a presumption that the extension of credit was extortionate:
The extension of credit was made with a loan finance charge in excess of that established for criminal usury.
At the time credit was extended, the debtor reasonably believed that one or more extensions of credit by the creditor had been collected or attempted to be collected by extortionate means or the nonrepayment thereof had been punished by extortionate means.
Upon the making of the extension of credit, the total of the extensions of credit by the creditor to the debtor then outstanding, including any unpaid interest or similar charges, exceeded one hundred dollars.
In any prosecution under section 18-15-102, evidence of similar offenses tending to establish the existence of a plan, scheme, or design on the part of the defendant to produce a result of which the act charged is a part shall be admissible in evidence against the defendant. Such evidence of similar offenses, if known to the debtor, shall also be admissible in evidence for the purpose of establishing the reasonable belief of the debtor referred to in paragraph (b) of subsection

(2) of this section.

(4) Whether evidence introduced under the provisions of subsection (2) of this section giving rise to the presumption that the extension of credit was extortionate is sufficient to establish the guilt of the defendant beyond a reasonable doubt, if such evidence is not disputed, is a question to be

determined by the jury under proper instructions or by the court if no jury trial is had. Where there is evidence tending to show the innocence of the transaction, the issue of whether the extension of credit was extortionate shall be submitted to the jury, if trial is to a jury, unless the court is satisfied that the evidence as a whole clearly negates the presumed offense.

18-15-104. Engaging in criminal usury. (1) Any person who knowingly charges, takes, or receives any money or other property as a loan finance charge where the charge exceeds an annual percentage rate of forty-five percent or the equivalent for a longer or shorter period commits the crime of criminal usury, which is a class 6 felony.

It is an affirmative defense to criminal usury for a person, or his agent or assignee, who charges, takes, or receives money or property as a loan finance charge in excess of an annual percentage rate of forty-five percent in either of the following circumstances:

That at the time of making the loan finance charge it could not have been determined by a mathematical computation that the annual percentage rate would exceed an annual percentage rate of forty-five percent;

That the loan finance charge was not in excess of an annual percentage rate of forty-five percent when the rate of the finance charge was calculated on the unpaid balance of the debt on the assumption that the debt is to be paid according to its terms and is not paid before the end of the agreed term.

The affirmative defenses referred to in subsection (2) of this section shall only apply when the provisions relating to the loan finance charge are set forth in a written agreement signed by all the parties and such written agreement is submitted to the court and the district attorney at least ten days prior to trial.

This section shall not apply to:

Charges and fees permitted by articles 1 to 6 of title 5, C.R.S., or charges and fees that are similar to such charges and fees and are specifically authorized by law;

Credit card charges and fees not exceeding those permitted for consumer transactions under articles 1 to 6 of title 5, C.R.S., when imposed upon or collected from a person or in a transaction not subject to said provisions;

A reverse mortgage as defined in section 11-38-102, C.R.S.; and

Additional interest charges permitted by section 5-12-107 (3), C.R.S.

18-15-105. Financing extortionate extensions of credit. Any person who knowingly advances money or property, whether as a gift, a loan, or an investment, pursuant to a partnership or profit-sharing agreement, or otherwise, to any person, with reasonable grounds to believe that it is the intention of the person to whom the advance is made to use the money or property, directly or indirectly, for the purpose of making an extortionate extension of credit, commits financing extortionate extensions of credit, which is a class 5 felony.

18-15-106. Financing criminal usury. Any person who knowingly advances money or

property, whether as a gift, a loan, or an investment, pursuant to a partnership or profit-sharing agreement, or otherwise, to any person, with reasonable grounds to believe that it is the intention of the person to whom the advance is made to use the money or property, directly or indirectly, for the purpose of engaging in criminal usury, commits financing criminal usury, which is a class 6 felony.

18-15-107. Collection of extensions of credit by extortionate means. (1) It is unlawful for any person knowingly to participate in any way, or to conspire to do so, in the use of any extortionate means to collect or to attempt to collect any extension of credit or to punish any person for the nonrepayment of any extension of credit.

Any person who violates the provisions of subsection (1) of this section commits collection of extensions of credit by extortionate means, which is a class 4 felony.

In any prosecution under this section for the purpose of showing an implicit threat as a means of collection, evidence may be introduced tending to show that one or more extensions of credit by the creditor were, to the knowledge of the person against whom the implicit threat was alleged to have been made, collected or attempted to be collected by extortionate means or that the nonrepayment of an extension of credit was punished by extortionate means.

18-15-108. Possession or concealment of records of criminal usury. (1) Any person who possesses or conceals any writing, paper, instrument, or article used to record criminally usurious transactions, and who knows or has reasonable grounds to know that the contents have been used, are being used, or are intended to be used to conduct a criminally usurious transaction, or who possesses or conceals such instruments with intent to aid, assist, or facilitate criminal usury commits possession or concealment of records of criminal usury, which is a class 6 felony.

This section is not applicable to any person who may take possession of any such documents while acting on behalf of another as attorney or in a related capacity with respect to judicial proceedings already commenced.

18-15-109. Loan finder - definitions - prohibited fees. (1) As used in this section, unless the context otherwise requires:

"Borrower" means any person seeking to obtain a loan through the services of a loan finder.

"Loan" has the same meaning as set forth in section 5-1-301 (25), C.R.S.

"Loan finder" means any person who, directly or indirectly, serves or offers to serve as

a lender or as an agent to obtain a loan or who holds himself out as capable of obtaining a loan for any person; except that the following persons shall be exempt from the provisions of this section:

A supervised financial organization, as defined in section 5-1-301 (45), C.R.S., and its employees, when acting within the scope of their employment;

A person duly licensed to make supervised loans pursuant to part 3 of article 2 of title 5, C.R.S.;

A business development corporation, created pursuant to article 48 of title 7, C.R.S.;

A pawnbroker licensed pursuant to article 56 of title 12, C.R.S., acting as such;

Any governmental entity or employee thereof, acting in his official capacity;

A mortgage broker, as defined in paragraph (d) of this subsection (1), acting as such.

"Mortgage broker" means any person who, directly or indirectly, serves or offers to serve as an agent for any person to obtain a loan secured by a mortgage, deed of trust, or lien on real property.

A loan finder shall not charge or collect any fee from a borrower until a borrower actually receives the agreed-upon loan; except that nothing in this section shall preclude a borrower from paying for a credit check or for an appraisal of security for the loan where such payment is by check or money order made payable to a party independent of the loan finder.

In any proceeding brought pursuant to this section, the burden of production with respect to an exemption from its provisions shall be upon the person claiming the exemption, and said claim of exemption shall constitute an affirmative defense.

Any person who violates this section commits a class 1 misdemeanor. A violation of this section shall also constitute a class 1 public nuisance subject to the provisions of part 3 of article 13 of title 16, C.R.S.

### ARTICLE 16  Purchasers of Valuable Articles

18-16-101. Legislative declaration. The general assembly herebyfinds and determines that illicit traffic in stolen valuable articles is encouraged by the absence of any required record-keeping system by persons purchasing such valuable articles. The general assembly further finds that law enforcement officials are hindered in the identification and recovery of stolen valuable articles, and that law enforcement officials are hindered in the discovery and identification of persons selling stolen valuable articles due to the absence of such a required record-keeping system. Accordingly, it is the intent of the general assembly, by enacting this article, to aid law enforcement officials in the discovery and identification of sellers of stolen valuable articles and in the identification and recovery of stolen valuable articles by providing a mandatory record-keeping and reporting system by purchasers and by providing a holding period during which time such articles shall not be disposed of or altered in any manner. Local governments may adopt ordinances more strict than the provisions of this article.

18-16-102.  Definitions. As used in this article, unless the context otherwise requires:

"Local law enforcement agency" means any marshal's office, police department, or sheriff's office with jurisdiction in the locality in which the purchaser makes the purchase.

"Peace officer" means any undersheriff, deputy sheriff other than one appointed with

authority only to receive and serve summons and civil process, police officer, state patrol officer, town marshal, or investigator for a district attorney or the attorney general who is engaged in full- time employment by the state, a city, city and county, town, judicial district, or county within this state.

"Precious or semiprecious metals or stones" means such metals as, but not limited to, gold, silver, platinum, and pewter and such stones as, but not limited to, alexandrite, diamonds, emeralds, garnets, opals, rubies, sapphires, and topaz. For the purposes of this article, ivory, coral, pearls, jade, and such other minerals, stones, or gems as are customarily regarded as precious or semiprecious are deemed to be precious or semiprecious stones.

"Purchase" means giving money to acquire any valuable article, taking valuable articles in full or part satisfaction of a debt, taking valuable articles for resale for the purpose of full or part satisfaction of a debt, or taking valuable articles for sale on consignment.

"Purchaser" means any person holding himself out to the public as being engaged in the business of buying valuable articles or any person who purchases five or more valuable articles during any thirty-day period. "Purchaser" does not include a person purchasing valuable articles from an estate or from a retail or wholesale merchant.

"Seller" means any person offering a valuable article for money to any purchaser, offering a valuable article in full or part satisfaction of a debt, or offering a valuable article for resale for the purpose of full or part satisfaction of a debt.

(a) "Valuable article" means any tangible personal property consisting, in whole or in part, of precious or semiprecious metals or stones, whether solid, plated, or overlaid, including, but not limited to, household goods, jewelry, United States commemorative medals or tokens, and gold and silver bullion.

(b) "Valuable article" shall also include foreign currency when purchased for more than its face value or foreign currency exchange value.

18-16-103. Purchaser to identify seller. (1) No purchaser shall purchase any valuable article without first securing adequate identification from the seller. The type and kind of identification shall be limited to the following:

A valid Colorado driver's license;

An identification card issued in accordance with section 42-2-302, C.R.S.;

A valid driver's license, containing a picture, issued by another state;

A military identification card;

A valid passport;

An alien registration card; or

A nonpicture identification document issued by a state or federal government entity if the purchaser also obtains a clear imprint of the seller's right index finger.

18-16-104. Purchases prohibited. No purchaser shall purchase any valuable article from any person under the age of eighteen years.

18-16-105. Purchaser to maintain register and obtain declaration of seller's ownership. (1) Every purchaser of valuable articles shall keep a register, in a permanent, well- bound book, in which he shall record the following information: The name, address, and date of birth of the seller and his driver's license number or other I.D. number from any other allowed form of identification pursuant to section 18-16-103; the date, time, and place of the purchase; an accurate and detailed account and description of each valuable article being purchased, including, but not limited to, any trademark, identification number, serial number, model number, brand name, or other identifying marks on such articles and a description by weight and design of such articles. The purchaser shall also obtain a written declaration of the seller's ownership which shall state whether the valuable article is totally owned by the seller, how long the seller has owned the article, whether the seller or someone else found the article, and, if the article was found, the details of its finding.

The seller shall sign his name in such register and on the declaration of ownership.

Such register shall be made available to any peace officer for inspection at any reasonable time.

The purchaser shall keep each register for at least three years after the last date of purchase of valuable articles described therein.

18-16-106. Holding period. (1) Except as provided in subsection (2) of this section, a purchaser shall hold all valuable articles within the jurisdiction of purchase for a period of thirty days from the date of purchase, during which time the valuable articles shall be held separate and apart from any other transaction and shall not be changed in form or altered in any way. The purchaser shall permit any requesting law enforcement officer to inspect the valuable articles during the thirty- day period.

(2) Stamped and assayed gold and silver bullion and gold coins shall not be subject to the holding requirement imposed by subsection (1) of this section. In lieu of such requirement, the purchaser shall be required to record the identity of any person to whom he transfers any such bullion or coins and the date, time, and place of such transfer.

18-16-107. Reports required. (1) Every purchaser of valuable articles shall provide the local law enforcement agency, on a weekly basis, with two records, on a form to be provided by the local law enforcement agency, of all valuable articles purchased during the preceding week and one copy of the seller's declaration of ownership. The form for recording such purchases shall contain the information required to be recorded in the purchaser's register pursuant to section 18-16-105 and shall also include a physical description of the seller and the dollar amount of the purchase. Said form shall be signed, at the time of the purchase, by the seller and by the individual purchaser or his agent who participated in the purchase. The local law enforcement agency shall designate the day of the week on which the records and declarations shall be submitted.

A copy of such record and the seller's declaration of ownership shall also be forwarded to the local law enforcement agency having jurisdiction in the area where the seller resides.

The local law enforcement agency shall forward copies of such records and declarations

of sellers' ownership, upon request, to any other law enforcement agency.

18-16-108. Penalty. Any person who violates any of the provisions of this article commits a class 6 felony. Any person who knowingly gives false information with respect to the information required by sections 18-16-103 and 18-16-105 commits a class 6 felony.

18-16-109. Applicability. The provisions of this article shall not apply to private collectors purchasing collectors' items from other private collectors or businesses engaged in selling valuable articles exclusively as collectors' items, and who pay for such purchases by check, nor shall the provisions of sections 18-16-101 to 18-16-108 apply to valuable articles purchased exclusively in interstate commerce and paid for by check mailed to the seller in another state, if a record of the check by which payment was made and the name and address of the seller is maintained for a period of three years, or a retail merchant who, in a retail transaction involving the sale of a valuable article, receives another valuable article as a trade-in and credits the retail purchaser with the value thereof if the retail purchaser provides proof satisfactory to the retailer that the valuable article was originally purchased from that retailer. For the purpose of this section, a "private collector" is an individual, business, or corporation who purchases an item for a price based on the value of the article as a historical item rather than the prevailing market price of the item's metallic or stone composition; who has an interest in preserving the item in its unique or historical form and who does not alter the form of the article; and whose primary purpose is to keep the article in a collection or to sell to another collector.

18-16-110. Severability. If any provision of this article or the application thereof to any person or circumstances is held invalid, such invalidity shall not affect the other provisions of this article which may be given effect without the invalid provision or application, and, to this end, the provisions of this article are declared to be severable.

### ARTICLE 17  Colorado Organized Crime Control Act

18-17-101. Short title. This article shall be known and may be cited as the "Colorado Organized Crime Control Act".

18-17-102. Legislative declaration. The general assembly hereby finds that organized crime in the state of Colorado, as well as nationwide, is a highly sophisticated, diversified, and widespread activity that annually consumes millions of dollars locally and billions of dollars nationally from this state's and the nation's economy through unlawful conduct and the illegal use of force, fraud, and corruption. Organized crime derives a major portion of its power through money procured from such illegal endeavors as syndicated and organized gambling, loan-sharking, the theft of property and fencing of stolen property, the illegal importation, manufacture, and distribution of drugs and other controlled substances, and other forms of social exploitation. This money and power are increasingly being used to infiltrate and corrupt legitimate business and labor organizations and to subvert and corrupt our democratic processes. Organized crime activities within this state weaken the stability of this state's and the nation's economy, harm innocent investors and competing organizations, impede free competition, threaten the peace and health of the public, endanger the domestic security, and undermine the general welfare of the state and its citizens. The general assembly further finds that organized crime continues to grow and flourish because of defects in the evidence-gathering process of the law which inhibits the development and use of the legally admissible evidence necessary to bring criminal and other sanctions or remedies to bear on the unlawful activities of those engaged in organized crime and because the sanctions and remedies presently available to the state are unnecessarily limited in scope and impact. Therefore, the general assembly declares that it is the purpose of this article to seek the eradication of organized crime in this state by strengthening the legal tools in the evidence-gathering process, by establishing new penal prohibitions, and by providing enhanced sanctions and new remedies to deal with the unlawful activities of those engaged in organized crime.

18-17-103. Definitions. As used in this article, unless the context otherwise requires:

"Documentary material" means any book, paper, document, writing, drawing, graph, chart, photograph, phonorecord, magnetic tape, computer printout, other data compilation from which information can be obtained or from which information can be translated into usable form, or other functionally similar tangible item.

"Enterprise" means any individual, sole proprietorship, partnership, corporation, trust, or other legal entity or any chartered union, association, or group of individuals, associated in fact although not a legal entity, and shall include illicit as well as licit enterprises and governmental as well as other entities.

"Pattern of racketeering activity" means engaging in at least two acts of racketeering activity which are related to the conduct of the enterprise, if at least one of such acts occurred in this state after July 1, 1981, and if the last of such acts occurred within ten years (excluding any period of imprisonment) after a prior act of racketeering activity.

"Person" means any individual or entity holding or capable of holding a legal or beneficial interest in property.

"Racketeering activity" means to commit, to attempt to commit, to conspire to commit, or to solicit, coerce, or intimidate another person to commit:
Any conduct defined as "racketeering activity" under 18 U.S.C. 1961 (1) (A), (1) (B), (1) (C), and (1) (D); or

Any violation of the following provisions of the Colorado statutes or any criminal act committed in any jurisdiction of the United States which, if committed in this state, would be a crime under the following provisions of the Colorado statutes:
Offenses against the person, as defined in sections 18-3-102 (first degree murder), 18-3- 103 (second degree murder), 18-3-104 (manslaughter), 18-3-202 (first degree assault), 18-3-203 (second degree assault), 18-3-204 (third degree assault), 18-3-206 (menacing), 18-3-207 (criminal extortion), 18-3-301 (first degree kidnapping), 18-3-302 (second degree kidnapping), 18-3-503 (human trafficking for involuntaryservitude), and 18-3-504 (human trafficking for sexual servitude);
Offenses against property, as defined in sections 18-4-102 (first degree arson), 18-4-103 (second degree arson), 18-4-104 (third degree arson), 18-4-105 (fourth degree arson), 18-4-202 (first degree burglary), 18-4-203 (second degree burglary), 18-4-301 (robbery), 18-4-302 (aggravated robbery), 18-4-303 (aggravated robbery of controlled substances), 18-4-401 (theft), 18-4-409 (aggravated motor vehicle theft), and 18-4-501 (criminal mischief);
Offenses involving computer crime, as defined in article 5.5 of this title;
Offenses involving fraud, as defined in sections 18-5-102 (forgery), 18-5-104 (second degree forgery), 18-5-105 (criminal possession of forged instrument), 18-5-109 (criminal possession of forgery devices), 18-5-110.5 (trademark counterfeiting), 6-16-111, C.R.S., (felony charitable fraud), 18-5-206 (defrauding a secured creditor or debtor), 18- 5-309 (money laundering), 18-5-403 (bribery in sports), 18-5-113 (criminal impersonation), 18-5-114 (offering a false document for recording), 18-5-702 (unauthorized use of a financial transaction device), 18-5-705 (criminal possession or sale of a blank financial transaction device), 18-5-706 (criminal possession of forgery devices), 18-5-707 (unlawful manufacture of a financial transaction device), 18-5-902 (identity theft), 18-5-903 (criminal possession of a financial device), 18-5-903.5 (criminal possession of an identification document), 18-5-904 (gathering identity information by deception), and 18-5-905 (possession of identity theft tools);
Offenses involving the family relation, as defined in section 18-6-403 (sexual exploitation of children);
Offenses relating to morals, as defined in sections 18-7-102 (wholesale promotion of obscenity or promotion of obscenity), 18-7-203 (pandering), 18-7-206 (pimping), 18-7-402 (soliciting for child prostitution), 18-7-403 (pandering of a child), 18-7-404 (keeping a place of child prostitution), and 18-7-405 (pimping of a child);
Offenses involving governmental operations, as defined in sections 18-8-302 (bribery), 18-8-303 (compensation for past official behavior), 18-8-306 (attempt to influence a public servant), 18-8-402 (misuse of official information), 18-8-502 (first degree perjury), 18-8-503 (second degree perjury), 18-8-603 (bribe-receiving by a witness), 18-8-606 (bribing a juror), 18-8-608 (intimidating a juror), 18-8-609 (jury-tampering), 18-8-610 (tampering with physical evidence), 18-8-703 (bribing a witness or victim), 18-8-704 (intimidating a witness or victim), and 18-8-707 (tampering with a witness or victim);
Offenses against public peace, order, and decency, as defined in sections 18-9-303 (prohibited wiretapping) and 18-9-304 (prohibited eavesdropping);
Gambling, as defined in sections 18-10-103 (2) (professional gambling), 18-10-105 (possession of a gambling device or record), 18-10-106 (transmission of receipt of gambling information), and 18-10-107 (maintaining gambling premises);

Offenses relating to firearms and weapons, as defined in sections 18-12-102 (possessing an illegal weapon or a dangerous weapon), 18-12-107.5 (illegal discharge of a firearm), and 18-12-
109 (possession, use, or removal of explosives or incendiary devices or the possession of components thereof);
Offenses involving the making, financing, or collection of loans, as defined in sections 18-15-102 (extortionate extension of credit), 18-15-104 (engaging in criminal usury), 18-15-105 (financing extortionate extensions of credit), 18-15-106 (financing criminal usury), 18-15-107 (collection of extensions of credit byextortionate means), and 18-15-108 (possession or concealment of records of criminal usury);
Fraud upon the department of revenue, as defined in section 39-21-118, C.R.S.;
Securities offenses, as defined in sections 11-51-401 and 11-51-603 (registration of brokers and dealers), 11-51-301 and 11-51-603 (registration of securities), and 11-51-501 and 11-51- 603 (fraud and other prohibited practices), C.R.S.;
Offenses relating to controlled substances (part 1 of article 42.5 of title 12, C.R.S., part 2 of article 80 of title 27, C.R.S., and article 18 of this title);
Offenses relating to taxation, as defined in section 39-22-621, C.R.S.;
Offenses relating to limited gaming, as defined in article 47.1 of title 12, C.R.S., or article 20 of this title; and
Offenses relating to telecommunications crime as set forth in section 18-9-309.

"Unlawful debt" means a debt incurred or contracted in an illegal gambling activity or business or which is unenforceable under state or federal law in whole or in part as to principal or interest because of the law relating to usury.


18-17-104. Prohibited activities. (1) (a) It is unlawful for any person who knowingly has received any proceeds derived, directly or indirectly, from a pattern of racketeering activity or through the collection of an unlawful debt to use or invest, whether directly or indirectly, any part of such proceeds or the proceeds derived from the investment or use thereof in the acquisition of any title to, or any right, interest, or equity in, real property or in the establishment or operation of any enterprise.
(b) A purchase of securities on the open market for purposes of investment, and without the intention of controlling or participating in the control of the issuer, or of assisting another to do so, shall not be unlawful under this subsection (1) if the securities of the issuer held by the purchaser, the members of his immediate family, and his or their accomplices in any pattern of racketeering activity or the collection of an unlawful debt after such purchase do not amount in the aggregate to one percent of the outstanding securities of any one class and do not confer, either in law or in fact, the power to elect one or more directors of the issuer.
It is unlawful for any person, through a pattern of racketeering activity or through the collection of an unlawful debt, to knowingly acquire or

maintain, directly or indirectly, any interest in or control of any enterprise or real property.

It is unlawful for any person employed by, or associated with, any enterprise to knowingly conduct or participate, directly or indirectly, in such enterprise through a pattern of racketeering activity or the collection of an unlawful debt.

It is unlawful for any person to conspire or endeavor to violate any of the provisions of subsection (1), (2), or (3) of this section.

18-17-105. Criminal penalties. (1) Any person convicted of engaging in activity in violation of the provisions of section 18-17-104 commits a class 2 felony and, upon conviction thereof, shall, in addition to the penalty provided for in section 18-1.3-401:

Be fined not more than twenty-five thousand dollars; and

Forfeit to the state any interest, including proceeds, he has acquired or maintained in violation of section 18-17-104 and any interest in, security of, claim against, or property or contractual right of any kind affording a source of influence over any enterprise which has established, operated, controlled, conducted, or participated in the conduct of in violation of section 18-17-104.

In lieu of the fine authorized by paragraph (a) of subsection (1) of this section, any person convicted of engaging in conduct in violation of the provisions of section 18-17-104, through which he derived pecuniary value, or by which he caused personal injury or property damage or other loss, may be sentenced to pay a fine that does not exceed three times the gross value gained or three times the gross loss caused, whichever is the greater, plus court costs and the costs of investigation and prosecution, reasonably incurred.

The court shall hold a hearing to determine the amount of the fine authorized by subsection (2) of this section.

For the purposes of subsection (2) of this section, "pecuniary value" means:

Anything of value in the form of money, a negotiable instrument, or a commercial interest or anything else, the primary significance of which is economic advantage; or

Any other property or service that has a value in excess of one hundred dollars.

In any action brought under this section, the district court may, at any time, enter such injunctions, prohibitions, or restraining orders, or take such actions, including the acceptance of satisfactory performance bonds, in connection with any property or other interest subject to forfeiture under this section, as the court may deem proper.

Upon conviction of a person under this section, the district court shall authorize the district attorney or the attorney general to seize all property or other interest declared forfeited under this section upon such terms and conditions as the court shall deem proper. The state shall dispose of all property or other interest seized under this section as soon as feasible, making due provision for the rights of innocent persons. If a property right or other interest is not exercisable or transferable for value by the state, it shall expire and shall not revert to the convicted person. The disposition of seized property shall be as follows:

Any personal property which is required by law to be destroyed, or the possession of which is illegal, or which, in the opinion of the court is not properly the subject of a sale may be destroyed pursuant to a warrant for the destruction of personal property, issued by the district court, directed to the sheriff, and returned by the sheriff upon execution thereof. The district court shall stay the execution of any such warrant during the period in which the property is used as evidence in any pending criminal or civil proceeding.

Any personal property seized and forfeited under the provisions of this section shall be

sold by the sheriff in the manner provided for sales on execution. In lieu of ordering the sale of such property, the court may, if it finds that it can be used by a law enforcement agency, order it delivered to a law enforcement agency for such use.

As to any real property, the district court shall enter a permanent order of abatement. The order of abatement shall direct the sheriff to sell such building or place and the ground upon which it is situated, to the extent of the interest, direct or indirect, of such person convicted under this section, at public sale in the manner provided for sales of property upon execution.

The proceeds realized from such sales shall be applied as follows:

To the fees and costs of sale;

All costs and expenses of investigation and prosecution, including, but not limited to, costs of resources and manpower incurred in investigation and prosecution;

The balance, if any, to the general fund of the state.

18-17-106. Civil remedies. (1) Any district court may, after making due provision for the rights of innocent persons, enjoin violations of the provisions of section 18-17-104 by issuing appropriate orders and judgments, including, but not limited to:

Ordering any defendant to divest himself of any interest in any enterprise, including real property;

Imposing reasonable restrictions upon the future activities or investments of any defendant, including, but not limited to, prohibiting any defendant from engaging in the same type of endeavor as the enterprise in which he was engaged in violation of the provisions of section 18-17-104;

Ordering the dissolution or reorganization of any enterprise;

Ordering the suspension or revocation of a license, permit, or prior approval granted to any enterprise by any agency of the state;

Ordering the forfeiture of the charter of a corporation organized under the laws of this state or the revocation of a certificate authorizing a foreign corporation to conduct business within the state, upon finding that the board of directors or a managerial agent acting on behalf of the corporation, in conducting the affairs of the corporation, has authorized or engaged in conduct in violation of section 18-17-104 and that, for the prevention of future criminal activity, the public interest requires the charter of the corporation forfeited and the corporation dissolved or the certificate revoked.

All property, real or personal, including money, used in the course of, intended for use in the course of, derived from, or realized through conduct in violation of the provisions of section 18-17-104 is subject to civil forfeiture to the state. The state shall dispose of all forfeited property as soon as commercially feasible. If property is not exercisable or transferable for value by the state, it shall expire. All forfeitures or dispositions under this section shall be made with due provision for the rights of innocent persons. The disposition of seized property shall be as follows:

Any personal property which is required by law to be destroyed, or the possession of which is illegal, or which, in the opinion of the court is not properly the subject of a sale may be destroyed pursuant to a warrant for the destruction of personal property, issued by the district court, directed to the sheriff, and returned by the sheriff upon execution thereof. The district court shall

stay the execution of any such warrant during the period in which the property is used as evidence in any pending criminal or civil proceeding.

Any personal property seized and forfeited under the provisions of this section shall be sold by the sheriff in the manner provided for sales on execution.

As to any real property, the district court shall enter a permanent order of abatement. The order of abatement shall direct the sheriff to sell such building or place and the ground upon which it is situated, to the extent of the interest, direct or indirect, of such person found to be in violation of the provisions of section 18-17-104, at public sale in the manner provided for sales of property upon execution.

The proceeds realized from such sales shall be applied pursuant to section 16-13-311 (3) (a), C.R.S.

Property subject to forfeiture under this section may be seized by a law enforcement officer upon court process. Seizure without process may be made if:

The seizure is incident to a lawful arrest or search or an inspection under an administrative inspection warrant;

The property subject to seizure has been the subject of a prior judgment in favor of the state in a forfeiture proceeding based upon this section.

In the event of a seizure under subsection (3) of this section, a forfeiture proceeding shall be instituted promptly. Property taken or detained under this section shall not be subject to replevin but is deemed to be in the custody of the law enforcement officer making the seizure, subject only to the order of the court. When property is seized under this section, pending forfeiture and final disposition, the law enforcement officer may:

Place the property under seal;

Remove the property to a place designated by court;

Require another agency authorized by law to take custody of the property and remove it to an appropriate location.

The attorney general or district attorney may institute civil proceedings under this section. Any action instituted under this section shall conform to the procedures set forth in part 3 or part 5 of article 13 of title 16, C.R.S. In any action brought under this section, the district court shall proceed as soon as practicable to the hearing and determination. Pending final determination, the district court may, at any time, enter such injunctions, prohibitions, or restraining orders or take such actions, including the acceptance of satisfactory performance bonds, as the court may deem proper.

Any aggrieved person may institute a proceeding under subsection (1) of this section. In such proceeding, relief shall be granted in conformity with the principles that govern that granting of injunctive relief from threatened loss or damage in other civil cases; except that no showing of special or irreparable damage to the person shall have to be made. Upon the execution of proper bond against damages for an injunction improvidently granted and a showing of immediate danger of significant loss or damage, a temporary restraining order and a preliminary injunction may be issued in any such action before a final determination on the merits.

Any person injured by reason of any violation of the provisions of section 18-17-104 shall have a cause of action for threefold the actual damages sustained. Such person shall also recover attorney fees in the trial and appellate courts and costs of investigation and litigation

reasonably incurred; except that:

The defendant or any injured person may demand a trial by jury in any civil action brought pursuant to this section; and

Any injured person shall have a right or claim to forfeited property or to the proceeds derived therefrom superior to any right or claim the state has in the same property or proceeds.

A final judgment or decree rendered in favor of the people in any criminal proceeding under this article shall estop the defendant in any subsequent civil action or proceeding as to all matters as to which such judgment or decree would be an estoppel as between the parties.

The application of one civil remedy under any provision of this article shall not preclude the application of any other remedy, civil or criminal, under this article or any other provision of law. Civil remedies under this article are supplemental and not mutually exclusive.

Whenever it is established in an action brought pursuant to this section that a person has received proceeds derived from activities prohibited by section 18-17-104, the court shall, upon request, award to the plaintiff a money judgment of forfeiture for the amount of such proceeds. The person subjected to such a money judgment may claim a setoff in an amount equal to the fair market value of other property forfeited if he shows that said property is traceable to a pattern of racketeering activity.

The burden of proof in an action brought pursuant to this section shall be by clear and convincing evidence.

(Deleted by amendment, L. 2002, p. 931, § 14, effective July 1, 2002.)

18-17-107. Civil investigative demand. (1) Whenever the attorney general or the district attorney has reason to believe that any person or enterprise may be in possession, custody, or control of any documentary materials relevant to a racketeering investigation, he or she may, prior to the institution of a civil or criminal proceeding thereon, issue in writing, and cause to be served upon such person, a civil investigative demand requiring such person to produce such material for examination.

Each such demand shall:

State the nature of the conduct constituting the alleged racketeering violation which is under investigation and the provision of law applicable thereto;

Describe the class or classes of documentary material demanded thereunder with such definiteness and certainty as to permit such material to be fairly identified;

State that the demand is returnable forthwith or prescribe a return date which will provide a reasonable period of time within which the material so demanded may be assembled and made available for inspection and copying or reproduction;

Identify the custodian to whom such material shall be made available; and

State an advisement of rights, available under the provisions of this article, in addition to any appropriate constitutional rights advisement.

No such demand shall:

Contain any requirement which would be held to be unreasonable if contained in a subpoena duces tecum issued by a court of the state in aid of a grand jury investigation of such

alleged racketeering violation; or

Require the production of any documentary evidence which would be privileged from disclosure if demanded by a subpoena duces tecum issued by a court of the state in aid of a grand jury investigation of such alleged racketeering violation.

Service of such demand or any petition filed under this section may be made upon a person by:

Delivering a duly executed copy thereof to any partner, executive officer, managing agent, or general agent thereof, or to any agent thereof authorized by appointment or by law to receive service of process on behalf of such person or upon any individual person;

Delivering a duly executed copy thereof to the residence, principal office, or place of business of the person to be served; or

Depositing such copy in the United States mail, by registered or certified mail, duly addressed to such person at its residence, principal office, or place of business.

A verified return by the individual serving any such demand or petition setting forth the manner of such service shall be prima facie proof of such service. In the case of service by registered or certified mail, such return shall be accompanied by the return post-office receipt of delivery of such demand.

(a) The attorney general or district attorney shall designate an investigator to serve as racketeer document custodian and such racketeering investigators as he or she shall determine to be necessary to serve as deputies to such officer.

Any person upon whom any demand issued under this section has been duly served shall make such material available for inspection and copying or reproduction to the custodian designated therein at the principal place of such person, or at such other place as such custodian and such person thereafter may agree and prescribe in writing or as the court may direct, pursuant to this section, on the return date specified in such demand or on such later date as such custodian may prescribe in writing. Such person may, upon written agreement between such person and the custodian, substitute for copies of all or any part of such material originals thereof.

The custodian to whom any documentary material is so delivered shall take physical possession thereof and shall be responsible for the use made thereof and for the return thereof pursuant to this article. The custodian may cause the preparation of such copies of such documentary material as may be required for official use under regulations which shall be promulgated by the attorney general or the district attorney. Under such reasonable terms and conditions as the attorney general or district attorney shall prescribe, documentary material, while in the possession of the custodian, shall be available for examination by the person who produced such material or any duly authorized representatives of such person.

Whenever any attorney has been designated to appear on behalf of the state before any court or grand jury in any case or proceeding involving any alleged violation of this article, the custodian may deliver to such attorney such documentary material in the possession of the custodian as such attorney determines to be required for use in the presentation of such case or proceeding on behalf of the state. Upon the conclusion of any such case or proceeding, such attorney shall return to the custodian any documentary material so withdrawn which has not passed into the control of such court or grand jury through the introduction thereof into the record of such case or proceeding.

Upon the completion of the racketeering investigation for which any documentary

material was produced under this article or in any case or proceeding arising from such investigation, the custodian shall return to the person who produced such material all such material other than copies thereof made by the attorney general or the district attorney pursuant to this subsection (6) which has not passed into the control of any court or grand jury through the introduction thereof into the record of such case or proceeding.

When any documentary material has been produced by any person under this section for use in any racketeering investigation, and no such case or proceeding arising therefrom has been instituted within a reasonable time after completion of the examination and analysis of all evidence assembled in the course of such investigation, such person shall be entitled, upon written demand made upon the attorney general or district attorney, to the return of all documentary material other than copies thereof made pursuant to this subsection (6) so produced by such person.

In the event of the death, disability, or separation from service of the custodian of any documentary material produced under any demand issued under this section or the official relief of such custodian from responsibility for the custody and control of such material, the attorney general or district attorney shall promptly designate another racketeering investigator to serve as custodian thereof and transmit notice in writing to the person who produced such material as to the identity and address of the successor so designated. Any successor so designated shall have with regard to such materials all duties and responsibilities imposed by this section upon his predecessor in office with regard thereto; except that he shall not be held responsible for any default or dereliction which occurred before his designation as custodian.

Whenever any person fails to comply with any civil investigative demand duly served upon him under this section or whenever satisfactory copying or reproduction of any such material cannot be done and such person refuses to surrender such material, the attorney general or a district attorney may file, in the district court of the state for any judicial district in which such person resides, is found, or transacts business, and serve upon such person a petition for an order of such court for the enforcement of this section.

Within twenty-one days after the service of any such demand upon any person, or at any time before the return date specified in the demand, whichever period is shorter, such person may file, in the district court of the state for the judicial district within which such person resides, is found, or transacts business, and serve upon such custodian a petition for an order of such court modifying or setting aside such demand. The time allowed for compliance with the demand in whole or in part as deemed proper and ordered by the court shall not run during the pendency of such petition in the court. Such petition shall specify each ground upon which the petitioner relies in seeking such relief and may be based upon any failure of such demand to comply with the provisions of this section or upon any constitutional or other legal right or privilege of such person.

At any time during which any custodian is in custody or control of any documentary material delivered by any person in compliance with any such demand, such person may file, in the district court of the state for the judicial district within which the office of such custodian is situated, and serve upon such custodian a petition for an order of such court requiring the performance by such custodian of any duty imposed upon him by this section. Whenever any petition is filed in any district court of the state under this section, such court shall have jurisdiction to hear and determine the matter so presented and to enter such order or orders as may be required to carry into effect the provisions of this section.

18-17-108. Construction of article. To effectuate the intent and purpose of this article, the provisions of this article shall be liberally construed.

18-17-109. Severability. If any provision of this article or the application thereof to any person or circumstances is held invalid, such invalidity shall not affect other provisions of this article which may be given effect without the invalid provision or application, and, to this end, the provisions of this article are declared to be severable.

## ARTICLE 18   Uniform Controlled Substances Act of 2013

PART 1 DEFINITIONS

18-18-101. Short title. This article shall be known and may be cited as the "Uniform Controlled Substances Act of 2013".

18-18-102. Definitions. As used in this article:
"Administer", unless the context otherwise requires, means to apply a controlled substance, whether by injection, inhalation, ingestion, or any other means, directly to the body of a patient or research subject by:
A practitioner (or, in the practitioner's presence, by the practitioner's authorized agent);
or
The patient or research subject at the direction and in the presence of the practitioner.
"Agent" means an authorized person who acts on behalf of or at the direction of a person
licensed or otherwise authorized under this article or under part 2 of article 80 of title 27, C.R.S. "Agent" does not include a common or contract carrier, a public warehouseman, or an employee of a carrier or warehouseman.
(a) "Anabolic steroid" means any material, drug, hormonal compound, salt, isomer or salts of isomers of testosterone, or synthetic or natural derivatives of testosterone having pronounced anabolic properties which is used primarily to promote growth of muscle tissue, which includes, but is not limited to, any of the following:

Boldenone;
Chlorotestosterone;
Clostebol;
Dehydrochlormethyltestosterone;

Dihydrotestosterone;

Drostanolone;

Ethylestrenol;

Fluoxymesterone;

Formebulone;

Human chorionic gonadotropin;

Human growth hormone;

Mesterolone;

Methandienone;

Methandranone;

Methandriol;

Methandrostenolone;

Methenolone;

Methyltestosterone;

Mibolerone;

Nandrolone;

Norethandrolone;

Oxandrolone;

Oxymesterone;

Oxymetholone;

Stanolone;

Stanozolol;

Testolactone;

Testosterone;

Trenbolone;

Any salt, ester, or isomer of a drug or substance described or listed in this paragraph
if that salt, ester, or isomer promotes muscle growth.

(I) Except as provided in subparagraph (II) of this paragraph (b), such term does not include an anabolic steroid which is expressly intended for administration through implants to cattle or other nonhuman species and which has been approved by the secretary of health and human services for such administration.

(II) If any person prescribes, dispenses, or distributes a steroid described in subparagraph (I) of this paragraph (b) for human use, such person shall be considered to have prescribed, dispensed, or distributed an anabolic steroid within the meaning of paragraph (a) of this subsection (3).

(3.5) (a) "Cathinones" means any synthetic or natural material containing any quantity of a cathinone chemical structure, including any analogs, salts, isomers, or salts of isomers of any synthetic or natural material containing a cathinone chemical structure, including but not limited to the following substances and any analogs, salts, isomers, or salts of isomers of any of the following substances:

alpha-Phthalimidopropiophenone;

N, N-Dimethylcathinone (Metamfepramone);

N-Ethylcathinone (Ethcathinone);

alpha-Pyrrolidinopropiophenone (-PPP);

2-Methylamino-1-phenylbutan-1-one (Buphedrone);

alpha-Pyrrolidinobutiophenone (-PBP);

alpha-Pyrrolidinovalerophenone (-PVP, PVP);

4-Methylmethcathinone (4-MMC, Mephedrone);

4'-Methyl-alpha-pyrrolidinopropiophenone (MePPP);

4'-Methyl-alpha-pyrrolidinobutiophenone (MPBP);

4'-Methyl-alpha-pyrrolidinohexiophenone (MPHP);

4-Methoxymethcathinone (PMMC, Methedrone, bk-PMMA);

4'-Methoxy-alpha-pyrrolidinopropiophenone (MOPPP);

Fluoromethcathinone (4-FMC, Flephedrone, 3-FMC);

3,4-Methylenedioxymethcathinone (methylone, bk-MDMA);

3,4-Methylenedioxyethcathinone (Ethylone, bk-MDEA);

3',4'-Methylenedioxy-alpha-pyrrolidinopropiophenone (MDPPP);

2-Methylamino-1-(3,4-methylenedioxyphenyl)-1-butanone (Butylone, bk-MDBD);

3',4'-Methylenedioxy-alpha-pyrrolidinobutiophenone (MDPBP);

2-Methylamino-1-(3,4-methylenedioxyphenyl)-1-cpentanone (bk-MBDP);

3,4-Methylenedioxypyrovalerone (MDPV);

Naphthylpyrovalerone (Naphyrone);

2-(Methylamino)-1-phenyl-1-pentanone Pentedrone);

N-methylethcathinone (4-MEC); and

(S)-2-Amino-1-phenyl-1-propanone (cathinone).

"Cathinones" does not include diethylproprion or buproprion.

As used in this subsection (3.5), "analog" means any chemical that is substantiallysimilar in chemical structure to the chemical structure of any cathinones.

"Cocaine" means coca leaves, except coca leaves and extracts of coca leaves from which cocaine, ecgonine, and derivatives of ecgonine or their salts have been removed; cocaine, its salts, optical and geometric isomers, and salts of isomers; ecgonine, its derivatives, their salts, isomers, and salts of isomers; or any compound, mixture, or preparation which contains any quantity of any of the substances referred to in this subsection (4).

"Controlled substance" means a drug, substance, or immediate precursor included in schedules I through V of part 2 of this article, including cocaine, marijuana, marijuana concentrate, cathinones, any synthetic cannabinoid, and salvia divinorum.

(a) "Controlled substance analog" means a substance the chemical structure of which is substantially similar to the chemical structure of a controlled substance in or added to schedule I or II and:

Which has a stimulant, depressant, or hallucinogenic effect on the central nervous system substantially similar to the stimulant, depressant, or hallucinogenic effect on the central nervous system of a controlled substance included in schedule I or II; or

With respect to a particular individual, which the individual represents or intends to have a stimulant, depressant, or hallucinogenic effect on the central nervous system substantially similar to the stimulant, depressant, or hallucinogenic effect on the central nervous system of a controlled substance included in schedule I or II.

The term does not include:

A controlled substance;

A substance for which there is an approved drug application, so long as such substance is in its intended and unconverted form;

A substance with respect to which an exemption is in effect for investigational use by a particular person under section 505 of the "Federal Food, Drug, and Cosmetic Act", 21 U.S.C. sec. 355, to the extent conduct with respect to the substance is pursuant to the exemption; or

Any substance to the extent not intended for human consumption before an exemption takes effect with respect to the substance.

"Deliver" or "delivery", unless the context otherwise requires, means to transfer or attempt to transfer a substance, actually or constructively, from one person to another, whether or not there is an agency relationship.

"Department" means the department of human services.

"Dispense" means to deliver a controlled substance to an ultimate user, patient, or research subject by or pursuant to the lawful order of a practitioner, including the prescribing, administering, packaging, labeling, or compounding necessary to prepare the substance for that delivery.

"Dispenser" means a practitioner who dispenses.

"Distribute" means to deliver other than by administering or dispensing a controlled substance, with or without remuneration.

"Distributor" means a person who distributes.

(a) "Drug" means:

Substances recognized as drugs in the official United States pharmacopoeia, national formulary, or the official homeopathic pharmacopoeia of the United States, or any supplement to any of them;

Substances intended for use in the diagnosis, cure, mitigation, treatment, or prevention of disease in individuals or animals;

Substances (other than food) intended to affect the structure or any function of the body of individuals or animals; and

Substances intended for use as a component of any substance specified in subparagraph (I), (II), or (III) of this paragraph (a).

(b) The term does not include devices or their components, parts, or accessories.

"Drug enforcement administration" means the drug enforcement administration in the United States department of justice, or its successor agency.

(14.5) "Enclosed" means a permanent or semi-permanent area covered and surrounded on all sides. Temporary opening of windows or doors or the temporary removal of wall or ceiling panels does not convert the area into an unenclosed space.

"Immediate precursor" means a substance which is a principal compound commonly used or produced primarily for use, and which is an immediate chemical intermediary used, or likely to be used, in the manufacture of a controlled substance, the control of which is necessary to prevent,

curtail, or limit manufacture.

"Isomer" means an optical isomer, but in paragraph (e) of subsection (20) of this section and sections 18-18-203 (2) (a) (XII) and (2) (a) (XXXIV) and 18-18-204 (2) (a) (IV) the term includes a geometric isomer; in sections 18-18-203 (2) (a) (VIII) and (2) (a) (XLII) and 18-18-206

(c) the term includes a positional isomer; and in sections 18-18-206 (2) (b) (XXXV) and (2) (c) and 18-18-205 (2) (a) the term includes any positional or geometric isomer.

(16.5) "Locked space" means secured at all points of ingress or egress with a locking mechanism designed to limit access such as with a key or combination lock.

"Manufacture" means to produce, prepare, propagate, compound, convert, or process a controlled substance, directly or indirectly, by extraction from substances of natural origin, chemical synthesis, or a combination of extraction and chemical synthesis, and includes any packaging or repackaging of the substance or labeling or relabeling of its container. The term does not include the preparation, compounding, packaging, repackaging, labeling, or relabeling of a controlled substance:

By a practitioner as an incident to the practitioner's administering or dispensing of a controlled substance in the course of the practitioner's professional practice; or

By a practitioner, or by the practitioner's authorized agent under the practitioner's supervision, for the purpose of, or as an incident to, research, teaching, or chemical analysis and not for sale.

"Marijuana" means all parts of the plant cannabis sativa L., whether growing or not, the seeds thereof, the resin extracted from any part of the plant, and every compound, manufacture, salt, derivative, mixture, or preparation of the plant, its seeds, or its resin. It does not include fiber produced from the stalks, oil, or cake made from the seeds of the plant, or sterilized seed of the plant which is incapable of germination if these items exist apart from any other item defined as "marijuana" in this subsection (18). "Marijuana" does not include marijuana concentrate as defined in subsection (19) of this section.

"Marijuana concentrate" means hashish, tetrahydrocannabinols, or any alkaloid, salt, derivative, preparation, compound, or mixture, whether natural or synthesized, of tetrahydrocannabinols.

"Narcotic drug" means any of the following, however manufactured:

Opium, opium derivative, and any derivative of either including any salts, isomers, and salts of isomers of them that are theoretically possible within the specific chemical designation, but not isoquinoline alkaloids of opium;

Synthetic opiate and any derivative of synthetic opiate, including any isomers, esters, ethers, salts, and salts of isomers, esters, and ethers, of them that are theoretically possible within the specific chemical designation;

Poppy straw and concentrate of poppy straw;

Coca leaves, except coca leaves and extracts of coca leaves from which cocaine, ecgonine, and derivatives of ecgonine or their salts have been removed;

Cocaine, or any salt, isomer, or salt of isomer of cocaine;

Cocaine base;

Ecgonine, or any derivative, salt, isomer, or salt of isomer of ecgonine;

Any compound, mixture, or preparation containing any quantity of a substance listed in

this subsection (20).

"Opiate" means a substance having an addiction-forming or addiction-sustaining liability similar to morphine or being capable of conversion into a drug having addiction-forming or addiction-sustaining liability. The term includes opium, opium derivatives, and synthetic opiates. The term does not include, unless specifically scheduled as a controlled substance under section 18-18-201, the dextrorotatory isomer of 3-methoxy-n-methylmorphinan and its salts (dextromethorphan). The term includes the racemic and levorotatory forms of dextromethorphan.

"Opium poppy" means the plant of the species Papaver somniferum L., except its seeds.

"Order" means:

A prescription order which is any order, other than a chart order, authorizing the dispensing of drugs or devices that is written, mechanically produced, computer generated, transmitted electronically or by facsimile, or produced by other means of communication by a practitioner and that includes the name or identification of the patient, the date, the symptom or purpose for which the drug is being prescribed, if included by the practitioner at the patient's authorization, and sufficient information for compounding, dispensing, and labeling; or

A chart order which is an order for inpatient drugs or medications to be dispensed by a pharmacist, or pharmacy intern under the direct supervision of a pharmacist, which is to be administered by an authorized person only during the patient's stay in a hospital facility. It shall contain the name of the patient and of the medicine ordered and such directions as the practitioner may prescribe concerning strength, dosage, frequency, and route of administration.

"Peace officer" shall have the same meaning as set forth in section 16-2.5-101, C.R.S.

"Person" means an individual, corporation, business trust, estate, trust, partnership, association, joint venture, government or governmental subdivision or agency, or any other legal or commercial entity.

"Peyote" means all parts of the plant presently classified botanically as lophophora williamsii lemaire, whether growing or not, the seeds thereof, any extraction from any part of such plant, and every compound, manufacture, salt, derivative, mixture, or preparation of such plant or its seeds or extracts.

"Pharmacy" means a prescription drug outlet as defined in section 12-42.5-102 (35), C.R.S.

"Poppy straw" means all parts, except the seeds, of the opium poppy, after mowing.

"Practitioner" means a physician, podiatrist, dentist, optometrist, veterinarian, researcher, pharmacist, pharmacy, hospital, or other person licensed, registered, or otherwise permitted, by this state, to distribute, dispense, conduct research with respect to, administer, or to use in teaching or chemical analysis, a controlled substance in the course of professional practice or research.

"Production", unless the context otherwise requires, includes the manufacturing of a controlled substance and the planting, cultivating, growing, or harvesting of a plant from which a controlled substance is derived.

"Remuneration" means anything of value, including money, real property, tangible and intangible personal property, contract rights, choses in action, services, and any rights of use or employment or promises or agreements connected therewith.

"Researcher" means any person licensed by the department pursuant to this article to

experiment with, study, or test any controlled substance within this state and includes analytical laboratories.

"Sale" means a barter, an exchange, or a gift, or an offer therefor, and each such transaction made by any person, whether as the principal, proprietor, agent, servant, or employee. (33.5) "Salvia divinorum" means salvia divinorum, salvinorin A, and any part of the plant classified as salvia divinorum, whether growing or not, including the seeds thereof, any extract from any part of the plant, and any compound, manufacture, salts, derivative, mixture, or preparation of the plant, its seeds, or its extracts.

"State", unless the context otherwise requires, means a state of the United States, the District of Columbia, the Commonwealth of Puerto Rico, or a territory or insular possession subject to the jurisdiction of the United States.

(34.5) (a) "Synthetic cannabinoid" means any chemical compound that is chemically synthesized and either:

Has been demonstrated to have binding activity at one or more cannabinoid receptors; or

Is a chemical analog or isomer of a compound that has been demonstrated to have binding activity at one or more cannabinoid receptors.

"Synthetic cannabinoid" includes but is not limited to the following substances:

HU-210: (6aR, 10aR)-9-(hydroxymethyl)-6, 6-dimethyl-3-(2-methyloctan-2-yl)- 6a,7,10,10a-tetrahydrobenzo[c]chromen-1-ol;

HU-211: dexanabinol, (6aS, 10aS)-9-(hydroxymethyl)-6, 6-dimethyl-3-(2- methyloctan- 2-yl)-6a, 7, 10, 10a-tetrahydrobenzo[c]chromen-1-ol;

JWH-018: 1-pentyl-3-(1-naphthoyl)indole;

JWH-073: 1-butyl-3-(1-naphthoyl)indole;

JWH-081: 1-pentyl-3-(4-methoxy-1-napthoyl)indole, also known as 4- methoxynapthalen-1-yl-(1-pentylindol-3-yl)methanone;

JWH-200: 1-[2-(4-morpholinyl)ethyl]-3-(1-napthoyl)indole;

JWH-250: 1-pentyl-3-(2-methoxyphenylacetyl)indole, also known as 2-(2- methoxyphenyl)-1-(1- pentylindol-3-yl)ethanone; and

CP 47, 497, and homologues: 2-[(1R, 3S)-3-hydroxycyclohexyl]-5-(2- methyloctan-2- yl)phenol.

"Synthetic cannabinoid" does not mean:

Any tetrahydrocannabinols, as defined in subsection (35) of this section; or

Nabilone.

As used in this subsection (34.5), "analog" means any chemical that is substantially similar in chemical structure to a chemical compound that has been determined to have binding activity at one or more cannabinoid receptors.

(a) "Tetrahydrocannabinols" means synthetic equivalents of the substances contained in the plant, or in the resinous extractives of, cannabis, sp., or synthetic substances, derivatives, and their isomers with similar chemical structure and pharmacological activity, such as the following:

$\pi$Cis or trans tetrahydrocannabinol, and their optical isomers;

6Cis or trans tetrahydrocannabinol, and their optical isomers;

3,4Cis or trans tetrahydrocannabinol, and their optical isomers.

(b) Since the nomenclature of the substances listed in paragraph (a) of this subsection (35) is not internationally standardized, compounds of these structures, regardless of the numerical designation of atomic positions, are included in this definition.

"Ultimate user" means an individual who lawfully possesses a controlled substance for the individual's own use or for the use of a member of the individual's household or for administering to an animal owned by the individual or by a member of the individual's household.

18-18-103. Special definition - board. As used in parts 1 and 2 of this article, "board" means the state board of pharmacy. As used in parts 3, 4, 5, and 6 of this article, "board" means the respective licensing board responsible for licensing and registering practitioners or other persons who are subject to registration pursuant to part 3 of this article. For physicians the respective board is the Colorado medical board; for podiatrists the respective board is the Colorado podiatry board; for dentists the respective board is the Colorado dental board; for optometrists the respective board is the state board of optometry; for pharmacists and pharmacies the respective board is the state board of pharmacy; for veterinarians the respective board is the state board of veterinary medicine; and for manufacturers, distributors, and humane societies the respective board is the state board of pharmacy.

PART 2 STANDARDS AND SCHEDULES

18-18-201. Authority to control. The board shall administer this part 2 and the general assembly, by bill, may add substances to or delete or

236

reschedule substances listed in section 18-18- 203, 18-18-204, 18-18-205, 18-18-206, or 18-18-207.

18-18-202. Nomenclature. The controlled substances listed in or to be added to the schedules in sections 18-18-203, 18-18-204, 18-18-205, 18-18-206, and 18-18-207 are listed or added by any official, common, usual, chemical, or trade name used.

when:

and

18-18-203. Schedule I. (1) A substance shall be added to schedule I by the general assembly

The substance has high potential for abuse;
The substance has no currently accepted medical use in treatment in the United States;

The substance lacks accepted safety for use under medical supervision.
Unless specifically excepted by Colorado or federal law or Colorado or federal regulation
or more specifically included in another schedule, the following controlled substances are listed in

schedule I:
Any of the following synthetic opiates, including any isomers, esters, ethers, salts, and salts of isomers, esters, and ethers of them that are theoretically possible within the specific chemical designation:
Acetyl-alpha-methylfentanyl      (N-[1-(1-methyl-2-phenethyl)-4-piperidinyl ] -N- phenylacetamide);
Acetylmethadol;
Allylprodine;
Alphacetylmethadol;
Alphameprodine;
Alphamethadol;
Alpha-methylfentanyl (N-[1-(alpha-methyl-beta-phenyl)          ethyl-4-piperidyl] propionanilide; 1-(1-methyl-2-phenylethyl)- 4-(N-propanilido) piperidine);
Alpha-methylthiofentanyl (N-[1-methyl-2-(2-thienyl) ethyl-4-piperidinyl]-N- phenylpropanamide);
Benzethidine;
Betacetylmethadol;
Beta-hydroxyfentanyl (N-[1-(2-hydroxy-2-phenethyl)-4-          piperidinyl]-N- phenylpropanamide);
Beta-hydroxy-3-methylfentanyl (other name: N-[1-(2-hydroxy-2-phenethyl)-3-methyl- 4-piperidinyl-] N-phenylpropanamide);
Betameprodine;
Betamethadol;
Betaprodine;
Clonitazene;
Dextromoramide;
Diampromide;
Diethylthiambutene;
Difenoxin;
Dimenoxadol;
Dimepheptanol;
Dimethylthiambutene;
Dioxaphetyl butyrate;
Dipipanone;
Ethylmethylthiambutene;
Etonitazene;
Etoxeridine;
Furethidine;
Hydroxypethidine;
Ketobemidone;
Levomoramide;
Levophenacylmorphan;
3-methylfentanyl      (N-[3-methyl-1-(2-      phenylethyl)-4-piperidyl]-N-

phenylpropanamide);
3-methylthiofentanyl (N-[3-methyl-1-(2-      thienyl)ethyl-4-piperidinyl]-N- phenylpropanamide);
Morpheridine;
MPPP (1-methyl-4-phenyl-4-propionoxypiperidine);
Noracymethadol;
Norlevorphanol; (XL) Normethadone; (XLI) Norpipanone;
(XLII)      Para-fluorofentanyl (N-(4-fluorophenyl)-N- [1-(2-phenethyl) -4-piperidinyl]- propanamide);
(XLIII) PEPAP (1-(-2-phenethyl)-4-phenyl- 4-acetoxypiperidine); (XLIV) Phenadoxone;
(XLV) Phenampromide; (XLVI) Phenomorphan; (XLVII) Phenoperidine; (XLVIII) Piritramide; (XLIX) Proheptazine;
(L) Properidine; (LI) Propiram;
(LII) Racemoramide;
(LIII) Thiofentanyl (N-phenyl-N-[1-(2- thienyl) ethyl-4-piperidinyl]-propanamide); (LIV) Tilidine;
(LV) Trimeperidine.
Any of the following opium derivatives, including their salts, isomers, and salts of isomers of them that are theoretically possible within the specific chemical designation:
Acetorphine;
Acetyldihydrocodeine;
Benzylmorphine;
Codeine methylbromide;
Codeine-N-Oxide;
Cyprenorphine;
Desomorphine;
Dihydromorphine;
Drotebanol;
Etorphine, except hydrochloride salt;
Heroin;

Hydromorphinol;
Methyldesorphine;
Methyldihydromorphine;
Morphine methylbromide;
Morphine methylsulfonate;
Morphine-N-Oxide;

Myrophine;
Nicocodeine;
Nicomorphine;
Normorphine;
Pholcodine;
Thebacon.

Any material, compound, mixture, or preparation containing any quantity of the following hallucinogenic substances, including any salts, isomers, and salts of isomers of them that are theoretically possible within the specific chemical designation:

4-bromo-2, 5-dimethoxy-amphetamine (Some trade or other names: 4-bromo-2, 5- dimethoxy-alpha- methylphenethylamine; 4-bromo-2, 5-DMA.);
2,5-dimethoxyamphetamine (Some trade or other names: 2,5-dimethoxy-alpha- methylphenethylamine; 2,5-DMA.);
(II.5) 2,5-Dimethoxy-4-ethylamphetamine (DOET);
4-methoxyamphetamine (Some trade or other names: 4-methoxy-alpha- methylphenethylamine; paramethoxyamphetamine, PMA.);
5-methoxy-3,4-methylenedioxy amphetamine;
(IV.5) 5-methoxy-N, N-diisopropyltryptamine (5-MeO-DiPT);
4-methyl-2,5-dimethoxy-amphetamine (Some trade and other names: 4-methyl-2,5- dimethoxy-alpha- methylphenethylamine; DOM; and STP.);
3,4-methylenedioxy amphetamine;
3,4-methylenedioxymethamphetamine (MDMA);
3,4,5-trimethoxy amphetamine; (VIII.5) Alpha-methyltryptamine (AMT);
Bufotenine (Some trade and other names: 3-(beta-Dimethylaminoethyl)-5- hydroxyindole; 3-(2- dimethylaminoethyl)-5-indolol; N, N-dimethylserotonin; 5-hydroxy-N,N- dimethyltryptamine; mappine.);
Diethyltryptamine (Some trade or other names: N,N-Diethyltryptamine; DET.);
Dimethyltryptamine (Some trade or other names: DMT.);
Ibogaine (Some trade and other names: (7-Ethyl-6,6B,7,8,9,10,12,13-octahydro-2- methoxy-6,9-methano-5H-pyrido [1', 2':1,2] azepine [5,4- b] indole; Tabernanthe iboga.);
Lysergic acid diethylamide;
Mescaline;
Parahexyl (Some trade or other names: 3-Hexyl-1-hydroxy-7,8,9,10-tetrahydro-6,6,9- trimethyl-6H-dibenzo[b,d]pyran; Synhexyl.);
Peyote (Meaning all parts of the plant classified botanically as Lophophora williamsii Lemaire, whether growing or not, its seeds, any extract from any part of the plant, and every compound, salt, derivative, mixture, or preparation of the plant, or its seeds or extracts);
N-ethyl MDA;
N-ethyl-3-piperidyl benzilate;
N-hydroxy MDA;
N-methyl-3-piperidyl benzilate;
Psilocybin;

Psilocyn;
Tetrahydrocannabinols;
Ethylamine analog of phencyclidine (Some trade or other names: N-ethyl-1- phenylcyclohexylamine, (1-phenylcyclohexyl) ethylamine, N-(1-phenylcyclohexl) ethylamine, cyclohexamine, PCE.);
Pyrrolidine analog of phencyclidine (Some trade or other names: 1-(1- phenylcyclohexyl)- pyrrolidine, PCPy, PHP.);
Thiophene analog of phencyclidine (Some trade or other names: 1-]1-(2-thienyl)- cyclohexyl- piperidine, 2-thienyl analog of phencyclidine, TPCP, TCP.);
TCPy.

Any material, compound, mixture, or preparation containing any quantity of the following substances having a depressant effect on the central nervous system, including any salts, isomers, and salts of isomers of them that are theoretically possible within the specific chemical designation:
Mecloqualone;
Methaqualone.

Any material, compound, mixture, or preparation containing any quantity of the following substances having a stimulant effect on the central nervous system, including their salts, isomers, and salts of isomers:
Repealed.
Fenethylline;
Methcathinone;
N-ethylamphetamine;
(+) Cis-4-methylaminorex;
N,N-dimethylamphetamine.

Any material, compound, mixture, or preparation containing any quantity of gamma hydroxybutyrate [GHB], including its salts, isomers, and salts of isomers.

Any material, compound, mixture, or preparation which is a controlled substance analog, the chemical structure of which is substantially similar to the chemical structure of a controlled substance listed in this subsection (2) or that was specifically designed to produce an effect substantially similar to or greater than the effect of a controlled substance listed in this subsection (2), all or part of which is intended for human consumption.

Any material, compound, mixture, or preparation containing any quantity of N- benzylpiperazine (BZP), including its salts, isomers, and salts of isomers.

18-18-204. Schedule II. (1) A substance shall be added to schedule II by the general assembly when:
The substance has high potential for abuse;

239

The substance has currently accepted medical use in treatment in the United States, or currently accepted medical use with severe restrictions; and
The abuse of the substance may lead to severe psychological or physical dependence.
Unless specificallyexcepted by Colorado or federal law or Colorado or federal regulation

or more specifically included in another schedule, the following controlled substances are listed in schedule II:
Any of the following substances, however manufactured:
Opium and opium derivative, and anysalt, compound, derivative, or preparation of opium or opium derivative, excluding apomorphine, dextrorphan, nalbuphine, butorphanol, nalmefene, naloxone, and naltrexone, but including:
Raw opium;
Opium extracts;
Opium fluid;
Powdered opium;
Granulated opium;
Tincture of opium;
Codeine;
Ethylmorphine;
Etorphine hydrochloride;
Hydrocodone;
Hydromorphone;
Metopon;
Morphine;
Oxycodone;
Oxymorphone;
Thebaine.
Any salt, compound, derivative, or preparation that is chemically equivalent or identical with any of the substances listed in subparagraph (I) of this paragraph (a), but not isoquinoline alkaloids of opium;
Opium poppy and poppy straw;
Coca leaves and anysalt, compound, derivative, or preparation of coca leaves, including cocaine and ecgonine and their salts, isomers, derivatives, and salts of isomers and derivatives, and any salt, compound, derivative, or preparation that is chemically equivalent or identical with any of these substances, but not including decocainized coca leaves or extractions of coca leaves which do not contain cocaine or ecgonine;
Concentrate of poppy straw (the crude extract of poppy straw in either liquid, solid, or powder form which contains the phenanthrene alkaloids of the opium poppy).
Any of the following synthetic opiates, including any isomers, esters, ethers, salts, and salts of isomers, esters, and ethers of them that are theoretically possible within the specific chemical designation:
Alfentanil;
Alphaprodine;
Anileridine;
Benzitramide;
Carfentanal;
Dihydrocodeine;
Diphenoxylate;

acid;

.

Fentanyl;

Isomethadone;

(IX.5) Levo-alphacetylmethadol;

Levomethorphan;

Levorphanol;

Metazocine;

Methadone;

Methadone - Intermediate, 4-cyano-2- dimethylamino-4, 4-diphenyl butane;

Moramide - Intermediate, 2-methyl-3-morpholino-1, 1-diphenylpropane-carboxylic

Pethidine (meperidine);

Pethidine - Intermediate-A, 4-cyano-1- methyl-4-phenylpiperidine;

Pethidine - Intermediate-B, ethyl-4- phenylpiperidine-4-carboxylate;

Pethidine - Intermediate-C, 1-methyl- 4-phenylpiperidine-4-carboxylic acid;

Phenazocine;

Piminodine;

Propoxyphene (non-dosage forms);

Racemethorphan;

Racemorphan;

Sufentanil.

Any material, compound, mixture, or preparation containing any quantity of the

following substances, their salts, isomers, or salts of isomers, having a stimulant effect on the central nervous system:

Amphetamine;

Methamphetamine;

Phenmetrazine;

Methylphenidate.

Any material, compound, mixture, or preparation containing any quantity of the following substances having a depressant effect on the central nervous system, including any salts, isomers, and salts of isomers of them that are theoretically possible within the specific chemical designation:

Amobarbital;

Pentobarbital;

Phencyclidine;

Secobarbital;

Glutethimide.

(I) Repealed.

(II) Nabilone [Another name for nabilone: (+) trans-3-(1,1-demethylheptyl)-6,6a,7,8,10, 10a- hexahydro- 1-hydroxy-6,6-dimethyl-9Hdibenzo [b,d] pyran-9-one].

Anymaterial, compound, mixture, or preparation containing anyquantityof the following substances:

Immediate precursor to amphetamine and methamphetamine: phenylacetone (Some trade or other names: phenyl-2-propanone; P2P; benzyl methyl ketone; methyl benzyl ketone.), ephedrine,

alpha-phenylacetoacetonitrile, phenylacetic acid, and 1-phenyl-2-nitropropene;

Immediate precursors to phencyclidine:

1-phenylcyclohexylamine;

1-piperidinocyclohexanecarbonitrile (PCC);

Piperdine;

Morpholine;

Pyrrolidine;

Remifentanil hydrochloride.

Unless specifically excepted or unless listed in another schedule, any material, compound, mixture, or preparation which is a controlled substance analog, as defined in section 18- 18-102 (6), the chemical structure of which is substantially similar to the chemical structure of a controlled substance in schedule II of this part 2 or that was specifically designed to produce an effect substantially similar to or greater than the effect of a controlled substance in schedule II of this part 2, all or part of which is intended for human consumption, shall be treated for the purposes of this article as a controlled substance in schedule II of this part 2.

18-18-205. Schedule III. (1) A substance shall be added to schedule III by the general assembly when:

The substance has a potential for abuse less than the substances included in schedules I and II;

The substance has currently accepted medical use in treatment in the United States; and

The abuse of the substance may lead to moderate or low physical dependence or high psychological dependence.

Unless specifically excepted by Colorado or federal law, or Colorado or federal regulation, or more specifically included in another schedule, the following controlled substances are listed in schedule III:

Any material, compound, mixture, or preparation containing any quantity of the following substances having a stimulant effect on the central nervous system, including any salts, isomers, and salts of isomers of them that are theoretically possible within the specific chemical designation:

Any compound, mixture, or preparation in dosage unit form containing any stimulant substance included in schedule II and which was listed as an excepted compound on August 25, 1971, pursuant to the federal "Controlled Substances Act", and any other drug of the quantative composition shown in that list for those drugs or which is the same except for containing a lesser quantity of controlled substances;

Benzphetamine;

Chlorphentermine;

Clortermine;

Phendimetrazine.

Any material, compound, mixture, or preparation containing any quantity of the following substances having a depressant effect on the central nervous system:

Any compound, mixture, or preparation containing any of the following drugs or their salts and one or more other active medicinal ingredients not included in any schedule:

Amobarbital;

Secobarbital;

Pentobarbital;

Any of the following drugs, or their salts, in suppository dosage form, approved by the federal food and drug administration for marketing only as a suppository:

Amobarbital;

Secobarbital;

Pentobarbital;

Any substance containing any quantity of a derivative of barbituric acid, or any salt of a derivative of barbituric acid;

Chlorhexadol;

Lysergic acid;

Lysergic acid amide;

Methyprylon;

Sulfondiethylmethane;

Sulfonethylmethane;

Sulfonmethane;

Tiletamine and zolazepam or any of their salts (Some trade or other names for a tiletamine-zolazepam combination product: Telazol. Some trade or other names for tiletamine: 2- (ethylamino)-2-(2- thienyl)-cyclohexanone. Some trade or other names for zolazepam: 4-(2- fluorophenyl)-6,8-dihydro-1,3,8-trimethylpyrazolo-[3,4-e] [1,4]-diazepin-7(1H)-one. flupyrazapon.).

Nalorphine;

Any material, compound, mixture, or preparation containing any of the following narcotic drugs, or their salts calculated as the free anhydrous base or alkaloid, in limited quantities as follows:

Not more than 1.8 grams of codeine per 100 milliliters or not more than 90 milligrams per dosage unit, with an equal or greater quantity of an isoquinoline alkaloid of opium;

Not more than 1.8 grams of codeine per 100 milliliters or not more than 90 milligrams per dosage unit, with one or more active, nonnarcotic ingredients in recognized therapeutic amounts;

Not more than 300 milligrams of hydrocodone per 100 milliliters or not more than 15 milligrams per dosage unit, with a fourfold or greater quantity of an isoquinoline alkaloid of opium;

Not more than 300 milligrams of hydrocodone per 100 milliliters or not more than 15 milligrams per dosage unit, with one or more active, nonnarcotic ingredients in recognized therapeutic amounts;

Not more than 1.8 grams of dihydrocodeine per 100 milliliters or not more than 90 milligrams per dosage unit, with one or more active, nonnarcotic ingredients in recognized therapeutic amounts;

Not more than 300 milligrams of ethylmorphine per 100 milliliters or not more than 15 milligrams per dosage unit, with one or more active, nonnarcotic ingredients in recognized therapeutic amounts;

Not more than 500 milligrams of opium per 100 milliliters or per 100 grams, or not more than 25 milligrams per dosage unit, with one or more active, nonnarcotic ingredients in

recognized therapeutic amounts;

Not more than 50 milligrams of morphine per 100 milliliters or per 100 grams with one or more active, nonnarcotic ingredients in recognized therapeutic amounts.

Anabolic steroids.

Dronabinol (synthetic) in sesame oil and encapsulated in a soft gelatin capsule in a federal food and drug administration approved drug product [Other names for dronabinol: (6aR-trans)- 6a,7,8,10a- tetrahydro-6,6,9-trimethyl-3-pentyl-6H-dibenzo [b,d] pyran-1-ol, or (-)-delta-9-(trans)-tetrahydrocannabinol];

Ketamine, its salts, isomers, and salts of isomers [Other names for ketamine: (+)-2-(2- chlorophenyl)-2-(methylamino)-cyclohexanone].

The board may exempt by rule a compound, mixture, or preparation containing any stimulant or depressant substance listed in paragraph (a) or (b) of subsection (2) of this section from the application of all or part of this article if the compound, mixture, or preparation contains one or more active medicinal ingredients not having a stimulant or depressant effect on the central nervous system and if the admixtures are in combinations, quantity, proportion, or concentration that vitiate the potential for abuse of the substances having a stimulant or depressant effect on the central nervous system.


18-18-206. Schedule IV - repeal. (1) A substance shall be added to schedule IV by the general assembly when:

The substance has a low potential for abuse relative to substances included in schedule III;

The substance has currently accepted medical use in treatment in the United States; and

The abuse of the substance may lead to limited physical dependence or psychological dependence relative to the substances included in schedule III.

Unless specificallyexcepted by Colorado or federal law or Colorado or federal regulation or more specifically included in another schedule, the following controlled substances are listed in schedule IV:

Any material, compound, mixture, isomers or salts or isomers, or preparation containing any of the following narcotic drugs, or their salts calculated as the free anhydrous base or alkaloid, in limited quantities as follows:

Not more than 1 milligram of difenoxin and not less than 25 micrograms of atropine sulfate per dosage unit;

Propoxyphene (dosage forms);

Butorphanol;

Any material, compound, mixture, or preparation containing any quantity of the following substances having a depressant effect on the central nervous system, including any salts, isomers, and salts of isomers of them that are theoretically possible within the specific chemical designation:

Alprazolam;

Barbital;

Bromazepam;


Camazepam;

Chloral betaine;

Chloral hydrate;

Chlordiazepoxide;

Clobazam;

Clonazepam;

Clorazepate;

Clotiazepam;

Cloxazolam;

Delorazepam;

Diazepam;

Estazolam;

Ethchlorvynol;

Ethinamate;

Ethyl loflazepate;

Fludiazepam;

Flunitrazepam;

Flurazepam;

Halazepam;

Haloxazolam;

Ketazolam;

Loprazolam;

Lorazepam;

Lormetazepam;

Mebutamate;

Medazepam;

Meprobamate;

Methohexital;

Methylphenobarbital (mephobarbital);

Midazolam;

Nimetazepam;

Nitrazepam;

Nordiazepam;

Oxazepam;

Oxazolam;

Paraldehyde; (XL)  Petrichloral; (XLI) Phenobarbital; (XLII) Pinazepam; (XLIII) Prazepam; (XLIV) Quazepam; (XLV) Temazepam; (XLVI) Tetrazepam;


(XLVII) Triazolam; (XLVIII)  Zolpidem;

(I) Any material, compound, mixture, or preparation containing any quantity of the following substance, including any salts, isomers of it that are theoretically possible: Fenfluramine.

(II) This paragraph (c) is repealed upon removal of fenfluramine and its salts and isomers from schedule IV of the federal "Controlled Substances Act" (21 U.S.C. sec. 812; 21 CFR 1308.14).

Any material, compound, mixture, or preparation containing any quantity of the following substances having a stimulant effect on the central nervous system, including their salts, isomers, and salts of isomers:

Cathine;

Diethylpropion;

Fencamfamin;

Fenpropore;

Mazindol;

Pemoline (including organometallic complexes and chelates thereof);

Phentermine;

Pipradrol;

SPA ((-)-1-dimethylamino-1,2-diphenylethane);

Any material, compound, mixture, or preparation containing any quantity of the following substances, including their salts and isomers:

Modafinil;

Pentazocine;

Sibutramine;
Stadol (butorphanol tartrate);
Zaleplon.

The board may exempt by rule any compound, mixture, or preparation containing any depressant substance listed in paragraph (b) of subsection (2) of this section from the application of all or any part of this article if the compound, mixture, or preparation contains one or more active medicinal ingredients not having a depressant effect on the central nervous system, and if the admixtures are in combinations, quantity, proportion, or concentration that vitiate the potential for abuse of the substances having a depressant effect on the central nervous system.


18-18-207. Schedule V. (1) A substance shall be added to schedule V by the general assembly when:
The substance has a low potential for abuse relative to substances included in schedule
IV;

The substance has currently accepted medical use in treatment in the United States; and
The abuse of the substance may lead to limited physical dependence or psychological dependence relative to the substances included in schedule IV.
(2) Unless specifically excepted by Colorado or federal law or Colorado or federal regulation or more specifically included in another schedule, the following controlled substances are listed in schedule V:

Any material, compound, mixture, or preparation containing any of the following narcotic drug and its salts: Buprenorphine;
Any compound, mixture, or preparation containing any of the following narcotic drugs, or their salts calculated as the free anhydrous base or alkaloid, in limited quantities as set forth in this paragraph (b), which also contains one or more nonnarcotic active medicinal ingredients in sufficient proportion to confer upon the compound, mixture, or preparation valuable medicinal qualities other than those possessed by the narcotic drug alone:
Not more than 200 milligrams of codeine per 100 milliliters or per 100 grams;

Not more than 100 milligrams of dihydrocodeine per 100 milliliters or per 100 grams;
Not more than 100 milligrams of ethylmorphine per 100 milliliters or per 100 grams;
Not more than 2.5 milligrams of diphenoxylate and not less than 25 micrograms of atropine sulfate per dosage unit;
Not more than 100 milligrams of opium per 100 milliliters or per 100 grams;

Not more than 0.5 milligram of difenoxin and not less than 25 micrograms of atropine sulfate per dosage unit;
Any material, compound, mixture, or preparation containing any quantity of the following substances having a stimulant effect on the central nervous system, including their salts, isomers, and salts of isomers: Pyrovalerone.

PART 3

REGULATION OF MANUFACTURE, DISTRIBUTION, AND DISPENSING OF CONTROLLED SUBSTANCES

18-18-301. Rules. The board or the department may adopt rules and charge reasonable fees relating to the registration and control of the manufacture, distribution, and dispensing of controlled substances within this state.

18-18-302. Registration requirements - definitions. (1) Every person who manufactures, distributes, or dispenses any controlled substance within this state, or who proposes to engage in the manufacture, distribution, or dispensing of any controlled substance within this state, shall obtain annually or biannually, if applicable, a registration, issued by the respective licensing board or the department in accordance with rules adopted by such board or by the department. For purposes of this section and this article, "registration" or "registered" means the registering of manufacturers, pharmacists, pharmacies, and humane societies located in this state, and distributors located in or doing business in this state, by the state board of pharmacy as set forth in article 42.5 of title 12, C.R.S., the licensing of physicians by the Colorado medical board, as set forth in article 36 of title 12, C.R.S., the licensing of podiatrists by the Colorado podiatry board, as set forth in article 32 of title 12, C.R.S., the licensing of dentists by the Colorado dental board, as set forth in article 35 of

title 12, C.R.S., the licensing of optometrists by the state board of optometry, as set forth in article 40 of title 12, C.R.S., the licensing of veterinarians by the state board of veterinary medicine, as set forth in article 64 of title 12, C.R.S., and the licensing of researchers and addiction programs by the department of human services, as set forth in part 2 of article 80 of title 27, C.R.S.
A person registered by the board or the department under this part 3 to manufacture, distribute, dispense, or conduct research with controlled substances may possess, manufacture, distribute, dispense, or conduct research with those substances to the extent authorized by the registration and in conformity with this article and with article 42.5 of title 12, C.R.S.
The following persons need not register and may lawfully possess controlled substances under this article:
An agent or employee of any registered manufacturer, distributor, or dispenser of any controlled substance if the agent or employee is acting in the usual course of business or employment;
A common or contract carrier or warehouseman, or an employee thereof, whose possession of any controlled substance is in the usual course of business or employment;
An ultimate user or a person in possession of any controlled substance pursuant to a lawful order of a practitioner.
The board or department may waive by rule the requirement for registration of certain manufacturers, distributors, or dispensers upon finding it consistent with the public health and safety.
The board or department may inspect the establishment of a registrant or applicant for registration of those persons they are authorized to register under this part 3 in accordance with rules adopted by the board or department.

18-18-303. Registration. (1) The board or department shall register an applicant to manufacture or distribute substances included in schedules I through V unless the board or department determines that the issuance of that registration would be inconsistent with the public interest. In determining the public interest, the board or department shall consider the following factors:
Maintenance of effective controls against diversion of controlled substances into other than legitimate medical, scientific, research, or industrial channels;
Compliance with applicable state and local law;
Promotion of technical advances in the art of manufacturing controlled substances and the development of new substances;
Any convictions of the applicant under any laws of another country or federal or state laws relating to any controlled substance;
Past experience of the applicant in the manufacture or distribution of controlled substances, and the existence in the applicant's establishment of effective controls against diversion of controlled substances into other than legitimate medical, scientific, research, or industrial channels;
Furnishing by the applicant of false or fraudulent material in any application filed under this article;
Suspension or revocation of the applicant's federal registration or the applicant's

registration of another state to manufacture, distribute, or dispense controlled substances as authorized by federal law; and
Any other factors relevant to and consistent with the public health and safety.

Registration under subsection (1) of this section entitles a registrant to manufacture or distribute a substance included in schedule I or II only if it is specified in the registration.

A practitioner must be registered with the board or department before dispensing a controlled substance or conducting research with respect to a controlled substance included in schedules II through V. The department need not require separate registration under this article for practitioners engaging in research with nonnarcotic substances included in schedules II through V where the registrant is already registered under this article in another capacity. Practitioners registered under federal law to conduct research with substances included in schedule I may conduct research with substances included in schedule I within this state upon furnishing the department evidence of that federal registration.

A manufacturer or distributor registered under the federal "Controlled Substances Act", 21 U.S.C. sec. 801 et seq., may submit a copy of the federal application as an application for registration as a manufacturer or distributor under this section. The board may require a manufacturer or distributor to submit information in addition to the application for registration under the federal act.

Persons licensed or registered under article 42.5 of title 12, C.R.S., or article 32, 35, 36, 40, or 64 of title 12, C.R.S., need not be licensed separately to distribute or dispense controlled substances to the extent provided under law if they are registered or are exempt from registration by the federal drug enforcement administration, provided that such persons indicate on any initial application or renewal application the schedules of controlled substances that the persons are authorized to use under Public Law 91-513, known as the federal "Comprehensive Drug Abuse Prevention and Control Act of 1970".

18-18-304. Suspension or revocation of registration. (1) The board or department may suspend or revoke a registration under section 18-18-303 to manufacture, distribute, or dispense a controlled substance upon finding that the registrant has:
Furnished false or fraudulent material information in any application filed under this part 3;
Been convicted of a felony under any state or federal law relating to any controlled substance;
Had the registrant's federal registration suspended or revoked and is no longer authorized by federal law to manufacture, distribute, or dispense controlled substances; or
Committed acts that would render registration under section 18-18-303 inconsistent with the public interest as determined under that section.

The board or department may deny, suspend, revoke, or take other authorized disciplinary action to limit the authority of any registrant to prescribe, distribute, dispense, or administer controlled substances, or any classification thereof, within this state if grounds for denial, suspension, or revocation exist. These proceedings shall be conducted in accordance with the

provisions of article 4 of title 24, C.R.S.

If a registration is suspended or revoked, the board or department may place under seal all controlled substances owned or possessed by the registrant at the time of suspension or the effective date of the revocation order. No disposition may be made of substances under seal until the time for taking an appeal has elapsed or until all appeals have been concluded unless a court, upon application, orders the sale of perishable substances and the deposit of the proceeds of the sale with the court. When a revocation order becomes final, the court may order the controlled substances forfeited to the state.

The board or department may seize or place under seal any controlled substance owned or possessed by a registrant whose registration has expired or who has ceased to practice or do business in the manner contemplated by the registration. The controlled substance must be held for the benefit of the registrant or the registrant's successor in interest. The board or department shall notify a registrant, or the registrant's successor in interest, whose controlled substance is seized or placed under seal, of the procedures to be followed to secure the return of the controlled substance and the conditions under which it will be returned. The board or department may not dispose of any controlled substance seized or placed under seal under this subsection (4) until the expiration of one hundred eighty days after the controlled substance was seized or placed under seal. The costs incurred by the board or department in seizing, placing under seal, maintaining custody, and disposing of any controlled substance under this subsection (4) may be recovered from the registrant, any proceeds obtained from the disposition of the controlled substance, or from both. Any balance remaining after the costs have been recovered from the proceeds of any disposition must be delivered to the registrant or the registrant's successor in interest.

The board or department shall promptly notify the drug enforcement administration of all orders restricting, suspending, or revoking registration and all forfeitures of controlled substances.

18-18-305. Order to show cause. (1) Before denying, suspending, or revoking a registration, or refusing a renewal of registration, the board or department shall serve upon the applicant or registrant an order to show cause why registration should not be denied, revoked, or suspended, or the renewal refused. The order must state its grounds and direct the applicant or registrant to appear before the board or department at a specified time and place not less than thirty days after the date of service of the order. In case of a refusal to renew a registration, the order must be served not later than thirty days before the expiration of the registration. These proceedings must be conducted in accordance with section 24-4-105, C.R.S. The proceedings do not preclude any criminal prosecution or other proceeding. A proceeding to refuse to renew a registration does not affect the existing registration, which remains in effect until completion of the proceeding.

(2) The board or department may suspend, without an order to show cause, any registration simultaneously with the institution of proceedings under section 18-18-304, or where renewal of registration is refused, upon finding that there is an imminent danger to the public health or safety which warrants this action. The suspension continues in effect until the conclusion of the proceedings, including judicial review thereof, unless sooner withdrawn by the board or department or dissolved by a court of competent jurisdiction.

18-18-306. Records of registrants. Persons registered to manufacture, distribute, or dispense controlled substances under this part 3 shall keep records and maintain inventories in conformance with the record keeping and inventory requirements of federal law and with any additional rules adopted by the board or department.

18-18-307. Order forms. A substance included in schedule I or II may be distributed by a registrant to another registrant only pursuant to an order form. Compliance with the provisions of federal law respecting order forms constitutes compliance with this section.

18-18-308. Prescriptions. (1) As used in this section, "medical treatment" includes dispensing or administering a narcotic drug for pain, including intractable pain.
Except as provided in section 18-18-414, a person may dispense a controlled substance only as provided in this section.

246

(a) Except as provided in paragraph (b) of this subsection (3), a person shall not dispense a substance included in schedule II to an ultimate user of the substance without:

The written prescription of a practitioner; or

An electronic prescription drug order for a schedule II substance that is created and transmitted in accordance with 21 CFR 1311.

(b) A practitioner, other than a pharmacy, may dispense a schedule II substance directly to the ultimate user without a written prescription.

(a) Except as provided in paragraph (b) of this subsection (4), a person shall not dispense a substance included in schedule III, IV, or V to an ultimate user of the substance without:

A written or oral prescription order of a practitioner; or

An electronic prescription drug order for a schedule III, IV, or V substance that is created and transmitted in accordance with 21 CFR 1311.

A practitioner, other than a pharmacy, may dispense a schedule III, IV, or V substance directly to the ultimate user without a written prescription.

A prescription order for a schedule III, IV, or V substance must not be filled or refilled more than six months after the date of the order or be refilled more than five times.

A practitioner may dispense or deliver a controlled substance to or for an individual or animal only for medical treatment or authorized research in the ordinary course of that practitioner's profession.

No civil or criminal liability or administrative sanction may be imposed on a pharmacist for action taken in reliance on a reasonable belief that an order purporting to be a prescription was issued by a practitioner in the usual course of professional treatment or in authorized research.

18-18-309. Diversion prevention and control. (1) As used in this section, "diversion" means the transfer of any controlled substance from a licit to an illicit channel of distribution or use.

The department shall regularly prepare and make available to other state regulatory, licensing, and law enforcement agencies a report on the patterns and trends of actual distribution, diversion, and abuse of controlled substances.

The department shall enter into written agreements with local, state, and federal agencies for the purpose of improving identification of sources of diversion and to improve enforcement of and compliance with this article and other laws and regulations pertaining to unlawful conduct involving controlled substances. An agreement must specify the roles and responsibilities of each agency that has information or authority to identify, prevent, and control drug diversion and drug abuse. The department shall convene periodic meetings to coordinate a state diversion prevention and control program. The department shall arrange for cooperation and exchange of information among agencies and with neighboring states and the federal government.

The department shall annually report to the governor and to the president of the senate and the speaker of the house of representatives on the outcome of this program with respect to its effects on distribution and abuse of controlled substances, including recommendations for improving control and prevention of the diversion of controlled substances in this state.

PART 4 OFFENSES AND PENALTIES

18-18-401. Legislative declaration. (1) The general assembly hereby finds, determines, and declares that:

The regulation of controlled substances in this state is important and necessary for the preservation of public safety and public health;

Meeting the public safety and public health needs of our communities demands a collaborative effort involving primary health care, behavioral health, criminal justice, and social service systems;

Successful, community-based substance abuse treatment and education programs, in conjunction with mental health treatment as necessary, provide effective tools in the effort to reduce drug usage and enhance public safety by reducing the likelihood that drug users will have further contact with the criminal justice system. Therapeutic intervention and ongoing individualized treatment plans prepared through the use of meaningful and proven assessment tools and evaluations offer an effective alternative to incarceration in appropriate circumstances and should be utilized accordingly.

Savings recognized from reductions in incarceration rates should be dedicated toward funding community-based treatment options and other mechanisms that are accessible to all of the state's counties for the implementation and continuation of such programs;

The Colorado commission on criminal and juvenile justice submitted a report to the general assembly on December 15, 2012, after significant study of effective approaches to reduced drug abuse and use of criminal justice sanctions that recommends multiple changes to the criminal law relating to controlled substances. The commission continues work to develop a more effective

treatment system in Colorado and continues to collect data to measure the impact of the changes to this part 4 enacted in 2013.

18-18-402. Definitions - terms used. As used in this part 4, unless this part 4 otherwise provides or unless the context otherwise requires, terms used in this part 4 shall have the same meanings as those set forth in part 2 of this article.

18-18-403. Additional definition. As used in this part 4, unless the context otherwise requires:

"Sale" includes a barter, an exchange, or a gift, or an offer therefor, and each such transaction made by any person, whether as the principal, proprietor, agent, servant, or employee, with or without remuneration.

18-18-403.5. Unlawful possession of a controlled substance. (1) Except as authorized by part 1 or 3 of article 42.5 of title 12, C.R.S., part 2 of article 80 of title 27, C.R.S., section 18-1-711, section 18-18-428 (1) (b), or part 2 or 3 of this article, it is unlawful for a person knowingly to possess a controlled substance.

A person who violates subsection (1) of this section by possessing:

Any material, compound, mixture, or preparation that contains any quantity of flunitrazepam, ketamine, cathinones, or a controlled substance listed in schedule I or II of part 2 of this article commits a level 4 drug felony.

(Deleted by amendment, L. 2013.)

Any material, compound, mixture, or preparation that contains any quantity of a controlled substance listed in schedule III, IV, or V of part 2 of this article except flunitrazepam or ketamine commits a level 1 drug misdemeanor.

If the circumstances described in section 18-18-428 (1) (b) occur, the peace officer shall not arrest the person pursuant to this section for any minuscule, residual controlled substance that may be present in the used hypodermic needle or syringe, and the district attorney shall not charge or prosecute the person pursuant to this section for any minuscule, residual controlled substance that may be present in a used hypodermic needle or syringe. The circumstances described in section 18- 18-428 (1) (b) may be used as a factor in a probable cause or reasonable suspicion determination of any criminal offense if the original stop or search was lawful.

18-18-404. Unlawful use of a controlled substance. (1) (a) Except as is otherwise provided for offenses concerning marijuana and marijuana concentrate in sections 18-18-406 and 18-18-406.5, any person who uses any controlled substance, except when it is dispensed by or under the direction of a person licensed or authorized by law to prescribe, administer, or dispense the controlled substance for bona fide medical needs, commits a level 2 drug misdemeanor.

(b) Repealed. (1.1) Repealed.
(2) and (3) (Deleted by amendment, L. 2010, (HB 10-1352), ch. 259, p. 1163, § 2, effective August 11, 2010.)
(4) Repealed.

18-18-405. Unlawful distribution, manufacturing, dispensing, or sale. (1) (a) Except as authorized by part 1 of article 42.5 of title 12, C.R.S., part 2 of article 80 of title 27, C.R.S., or part 2 or 3 of this article, it is unlawful for any person knowingly to manufacture, dispense, sell, or distribute, or to possess with intent to manufacture, dispense, sell, or distribute, a controlled substance; or induce, attempt to induce, or conspire with one or more other persons, to manufacture, dispense, sell, distribute, or possess with intent to manufacture, dispense, sell, or distribute, a controlled substance; or possess one or more chemicals or supplies or equipment with intent to manufacture a controlled substance.
(b) As used in this subsection (1), "dispense" does not include labeling, as defined in section 12-42.5-102 (18), C.R.S.
(2) Except as otherwise provided for an offense concerning marijuana and marijuana concentrate in section 18-18-406 and for special offenders as provided in section 18-18-407, any person who violates any of the provisions of subsection (1) of this section:
Commits a level 1 drug felony and is subject to the mandatory sentencing provisions in section 18-1.3-401.5 (7) if:
The violation involves any material, compound, mixture, or preparation that weighs:
More than two hundred twenty-five grams and contains a schedule I or schedule II controlled substance; or
More than one hundred twelve grams and contains methamphetamine, heroin, ketamine, or cathinones; or
More than fifty milligrams and contains flunitrazepam; or
An adult sells, dispenses, distributes, or otherwise transfers any quantity of a schedule I or schedule II controlled substance or any material, compound, mixture, or preparation that contains any amount of a schedule I or schedule II controlled substance, other than marijuana or marijuana concentrate, to a minor and the adult is at least two years older than the minor;
Commits a level 2 drug felony if:
The violation involves any material, compound, mixture, or preparation that weighs:
More than fourteen grams, but not more than two hundred twenty-five grams, and contains a schedule I or schedule II controlled substance;
More than seven grams, but not more than one hundred twelve grams, and contains methamphetamine, heroin, ketamine, or cathinones; or
More than ten milligrams, but not more than fifty milligrams, and contains flunitrazepam;
An adult sells, dispenses, distributes, or otherwise transfers any quantity of a schedule III or schedule IV controlled substance or any material, compound, mixture, or preparation that contains any quantity of a schedule III or schedule IV controlled substance to a minor and the adult

is at least two years older than the minor;
Commits a level 3 drug felony if the violation involves any material, compound, mixture, or preparation that weighs:
Not more than fourteen grams and contains a schedule I or schedule II controlled substance;
Not more than seven grams and contains methamphetamine, heroin, ketamine, or cathinones;
Not more than ten milligrams and contains flunitrazepam; or
More than four grams and contains a schedule III or schedule IV controlled substance;
Commits a level 4 drug felony if:
The violation involves any material, compound, mixture, or preparation that weighs not more than four grams and contains a schedule III or schedule IV controlled substance; or
Notwithstanding the provisions of paragraph (c) of this subsection (2), the violation involves distribution or transfer of the controlled substance for the purpose of consuming all of the controlled substance with another person or persons at a time substantially contemporaneous with the transfer; except that this subparagraph (II) applies only if the distribution or transfer involves not more than four grams of a schedule I or II controlled substance or not more than two grams of methamphetamine, heroin, ketamine, or cathinones;
Commits a level 1 drug misdemeanor if the violation involves:
A schedule V controlled substance; or
A transfer with no remuneration of not more than four grams of a schedule III or schedule IV controlled substance.
(2.1) Repealed.
(2.3) (a) (Deleted by amendment, L. 2010, (HB 10-1352), ch. 259, p. 1163, § 3, effective August 11, 2010.)
(b) Repealed.
(2.5) to (4) Repealed.
When a person commits unlawful distribution, manufacture, dispensing, sale, or possession with intent to manufacture, dispense, sell, or distribute any schedule I or schedule II controlled substance, as listed in section 18-18-203 or 18-18-204, flunitrazepam, ketamine, or cathinones, or conspires with one or more persons to commit the offense, pursuant to subsection (1) of this section, twice or more within a period of six months, without having been placed in jeopardy for the prior offense or offenses, the aggregate amount of the schedule I or schedule II controlled substance, flunitrazepam, ketamine, or cathinones involved may be used to determine the level of drug offense.
and (7) Repealed.

18-18-406. Offenses relating to marijuana and marijuana concentrate. (1) (a) The sale, transfer, or dispensing of more than two and one-half pounds of marijuana or more than one pound of marijuana concentrate to a minor if the person is an adult and two years older than the minor is a level 1 drug felony subject to the mandatory sentencing provision in section 18-1.3-401.5 (7).
The sale, transfer, or dispensing of more than six ounces, but not more than two and one-

half pounds of marijuana or more than three ounces, but not more than one pound of marijuana concentrate to a minor if the person is an adult and two years older than the minor is a level 2 drug felony.

The sale, transfer, or dispensing of more than one ounce, but not more than six ounces of marijuana or more than one-half ounce, but not more than three ounces, of marijuana concentrate to a minor if the person is an adult and two years older than the minor is a level 3 drug felony.

The sale, transfer, or dispensing of not more than one ounce of marijuana or not more than one-half ounce of marijuana concentrate to a minor if the person is an adult and two years older than the minor is a level 4 drug felony.

(a) (I) It is unlawful for a person to knowingly process or manufacture any marijuana or marijuana concentrate or knowingly allow to be processed or manufactured on land owned, occupied, or controlled by him or her any marijuana or marijuana concentrate except as authorized pursuant to part 1 of article 42.5 of title 12, C.R.S., or part 2 of article 80 of title 27, C.R.S.

(II) A person who violates the provisions of subparagraph (I) of this paragraph (a) commits a level 3 drug felony.

(b) (I) Except as otherwise provided in subsection (7) of this section and except as authorized by part 1 of article 42.5 of title 12, C.R.S., part 2 of article 80 of title 27, C.R.S., or part 2 or 3 of this article, it is unlawful for a person to knowingly dispense, sell, distribute, or possess with intent to manufacture, dispense, sell, or distribute marijuana or marijuana concentrate; or attempt, induce, attempt to induce, or conspire with one or more other persons, to dispense, sell, distribute, or possess with intent to manufacture, dispense, sell, or distribute marijuana or marijuana concentrate.

As used in subparagraph (I) of this paragraph (b), "dispense" does not include labeling, as defined in section 12-42.5-102 (18), C.R.S.

A person who violates any of the provisions of subparagraph (I) of this paragraph (b) commits:

A level 1 drug felony and is subject to the mandatory sentencing provision in section 18- 1.3-401.5 (7) if the amount of marijuana is more than fifty pounds or the amount of marijuana concentrate is more than twenty-five pounds;

A level 2 drug felony if the amount of marijuana is more than five pounds but not more than fifty pounds or the amount of marijuana concentrate is more than two and one-half pounds but not more than twenty-five pounds;

A level 3 drug felony if the amount is more than twelve ounces but not more than five pounds of marijuana or more than six ounces but not more than two and one-half pounds of marijuana concentrate;

A level 4 drug felony if the amount is more than four ounces, but not more than twelve ounces of marijuana or more than two ounces but not more than six ounces of marijuana concentrate; or

A level 1 drug misdemeanor if the amount is not more than four ounces of marijuana or not more than two ounces of marijuana concentrate.

(a) It is unlawful for a person to knowingly cultivate, grow, or produce a marijuana plant or knowingly allow a marijuana plant to be cultivated, grown, or produced on land that the person owns, occupies, or controls. A person who violates the provisions of this subsection (3) commits:

A level 3 drug felony if the offense involves more than thirty plants;

A level 4 drug felony if the offense involves more than six but not more than thirty plants; or

A level 1 drug misdemeanor if the offense involves not more than six plants.

It is not a violation of this subsection (3) if:

The person is lawfully cultivating medical marijuana pursuant to the authority granted in section 14 of article XVIII of the state constitution in an enclosed and locked space.

The person is lawfully cultivating marijuana in an enclosed and locked space pursuant to the authority granted in section 16 of article XVIII of the state constitution; except that, if the cultivation area is located in a residence and:

A person under twenty-one years of age lives at the residence, the cultivation area itself must be enclosed and locked; and

If no person under twenty-one years of age lives at the residence, the external locks of the residence constitutes an enclosed and locked space. If a person under twenty-one years of age enters the residence, the person must ensure that access to the cultivation site is reasonably restricted for the duration of that person's presence in the residence.

(a) A person who possesses more than twelve ounces of marijuana or more than three ounces of marijuana concentrate commits a level 4 drug felony.

A person who possesses more than six ounces of marijuana but not more than twelve ounces of marijuana or not more than three ounces of marijuana concentrate commits a level 1 drug misdemeanor.

A person who possesses more than two ounces of marijuana but not more than six ounces of marijuana commits a level 2 drug misdemeanor.

(a) (I) Except as described in section 18-1-711, a person who possesses not more than two ounces of marijuana commits a drug petty offense and, upon conviction thereof, shall be punished by a fine of not more than one hundred dollars.

(II) Whenever a person is arrested or detained for a violation of subparagraph (I) of this paragraph (a), the arresting or detaining officer shall prepare a written notice or summons for the person to appear in court. The written notice or summons must contain the name and address of the arrested or detained person, the date, time, and place where such person shall appear, and a place for the signature of the person indicating the person's written promise to appear on the date and at the time and place indicated on the notice or summons. One copy of the notice or summons must be given to the person arrested or detained, one copy must be sent to the court where the arrested or detained person is to appear, and such other copies as may be required by the law enforcement agencyemploying the arresting or detaining officer must be sent to the places designated by such law enforcement agency. The date specified in the notice or summons to appear must be at least seven days after the arrest or detention unless the person arrested or detained demands an earlier hearing. The place specified in the notice or summons to appear must be before a judge having jurisdiction of the drug petty offense within the county in which the drug petty offense charged is alleged to have been committed. The arrested or detained person, in order to secure release from arrest or detention, must promise in writing to appear in court by signing the notice or summons prepared by the arresting or detaining officer. Any person who does not honor the written promise to appear commits

a class 3 misdemeanor.

(I) Except as described in section 18-1-711, a person who openly and publicly displays, consumes, or uses two ounces or less of marijuana commits a drug petty offense and, upon conviction thereof, shall be punished by a fine of up to one hundred dollars and up to twenty-four hours of community service.

Open and public display, consumption, or use of more than two ounces of marijuana or any amount of marijuana concentrate is deemed possession thereof, and violations shall be punished as provided for in subsection (4) of this section.

Except as otherwise provided for in subparagraph (I) of this paragraph (b), consumption or use of marijuana or marijuana concentrate is deemed possession thereof, and violations must be punished as provided for in paragraph (a) of this subsection (5) and subsection (4) of this section.

Transferring or dispensing not more than two ounces of marijuana from one person to another for no consideration is a drug petty offense and is not deemed dispensing or sale thereof.

(5.5) (a) It is unlawful for a person to transfer marijuana or marijuana concentrate at no cost to a person if the transfer is in any way related to remuneration for any other service or product.

(b) A violation of this subsection (5.5) is a level 1 drug misdemeanor.

The provisions of this section do not apply to any person who possesses, uses, prescribes, dispenses, or administers any drug classified under group C guidelines of the national cancer institute, as amended, approved by the federal food and drug administration.

The provisions of this section do not apply to any person who possesses, uses, prescribes, dispenses, or administers dronabinol (synthetic) in sesame oil and encapsulated in a soft gelatin capsule in a federal food and drug administration approved drug product, pursuant to part 1 of article 42.5 of title 12, C.R.S., or part 2 of article 80 of title 27, C.R.S.

18-18-406.1. Unlawful use or possession of synthetic cannabinoids or salvia divinorum. (1) On and after January 1, 2012, it is unlawful for any person to use or possess any amount of any synthetic cannabinoid or salvia divinorum.
A person who violates any provision of subsection (1) of this section commits a level 2 drug misdemeanor.

18-18-406.2. Unlawful distribution, manufacturing, dispensing, sale, or cultivation of synthetic cannabinoids or salvia divinorum. (1) It is unlawful for any person knowingly to:
Manufacture, dispense, sell, or distribute, or to possess with intent to manufacture, dispense, sell, or distribute, any amount of any synthetic cannabinoid or salvia divinorum;
Induce, attempt to induce, or conspire with one or more other persons, to manufacture, dispense, sell, distribute, or possess with intent to manufacture, dispense, sell, or distribute, any amount of any synthetic cannabinoid or salvia divinorum; or
Cultivate salvia divinorum with intent to dispense, sell, or distribute any amount of the salvia divinorum.
A person who violates any provision of subsection (1) of this section commits a level 3 drug felony.

Notwithstanding the provisions of subsection (2) of this section, a person who violates any provision of subsection (1) of this section by dispensing, selling, or distributing any amount of any synthetic cannabinoid or salvia divinorum commits a level 2 drug felony if the person:
Dispenses, sells, or distributes the synthetic cannabinoid or salvia divinorum to a minor who is less than eighteen years of age; and
Is at least eighteen years of age and at least two years older than said minor.
As used in this section, "dispense" does not include labeling, as defined in section 12- 42.5-102 (18), C.R.S.

18-18-406.3. Medical use of marijuana by persons diagnosed with debilitating medical conditions - unlawful acts - penalty - medical marijuana program cash fund. (1) The general assembly hereby finds and declares that:
Section 14 of article XVIII of the state constitution was approved by the registered electors of this state at the 2000 general election;
Section 14 of article XVIII of the state constitution creates limited exceptions to the criminal laws of this state for patients, primary care givers, and physicians concerning the medical use of marijuana by a patient to alleviate an appropriately diagnosed debilitating medical condition;
Section 14 of article XVIII of the state constitution requires a state health agency designated by the governor to establish and maintain a confidential registry of patients authorized to engage in the medical use of marijuana;
The governor, in accordance with paragraph (h) of subsection (1) of section 14 of article XVIII of the state constitution, has designated the department of public health and environment, referred to in this section as the department, to be the state health agency responsible for the administration of the medical marijuana program;
Section 14 of article XVIII of the state constitution requires the department to process the applications of patients who wish to qualify for and be placed on the confidential registry for the medical use of marijuana, and to issue registry identification cards to patients who qualify for placement on the registry;
Section 14 of article XVIII of the state constitution sets forth the lawful limits on the medical use of marijuana;
Section 14 of article XVIII of the state constitution requires the general assembly to determine and enact criminal penalties for specific acts described in the constitutional provision;
In interpreting the provisions of section 14 of article XVIII of the state constitution, the general assembly has applied the definitions contained in subsection (1) of the constitutional provision and has attempted to give the remaining words of the constitutional provision their plain meaning;
This section reflects the considered judgment of the general assembly regarding the meaning and implementation of the provisions of section 14 of article XVIII of the state constitution.
(a) Any person who fraudulently represents a medical condition to a physician, the department, or a state or local law enforcement official for the purpose of falsely obtaining a marijuana registry identification card from the department, or for the purpose of avoiding arrest and prosecution for a marijuana-related offense, commits a class 1 misdemeanor.

(b) If an officer or employee of the department receives information that causes such officer or employee reasonably to believe that fraudulent representation, as described in paragraph (a) of this subsection (2), has occurred, such officer or employee shall report the information to either the district attorney of the county in which the applicant for the marijuana registry identification card resides, or to the attorney general.
The fraudulent use or theft of any person's marijuana registry identification card, including, but not limited to, any card that is required to be returned to the department pursuant to section 14 of article XVIII of the state constitution, is a class 1 misdemeanor.
The fraudulent production or counterfeiting of, or tampering with, one or more marijuana registry identification cards is a class 1 misdemeanor.
Any person including, but not limited to, any officer, employee, or agent of the department, or any officer, employee, or agent of any state or local law enforcement agency, who releases or makes public any confidential record or any confidential information contained in any such record that is provided to or by the marijuana registry or primary caregiver registry of the department without the written authorization of the marijuana registry patient commits a class 1 misdemeanor.
The use, possession, manufacturing, dispensing, selling, or distribution of a synthetic cannabinoid, as defined in section 18-18-102 (34.5), shall not be considered an exception to the criminal laws of this state for the purposes of this section or of section 14 of article XVIII of the state constitution.
An owner, officer, or employee of a business licensed pursuant to article 43.3 of title 12, C.R.S., or an employee of the state medical marijuana licensing authority, a local medical marijuana licensing authority, or the department of public health and environment, who releases or makes public a patient's medical record or any confidential information contained in any such record that is provided to or by the business licensed pursuant to article 43.3 of title 12, C.R.S., without the written authorization of the patient commits a class 1 misdemeanor; except that the owner, officer, or employee shall release the records or information upon request by the state or local medical marijuana licensing authority. The records or information produced for review by the state or local licensing authority shall not become public records by virtue of the disclosure and may be used only for a purpose authorized by article 43.3 of title 12, C.R.S., or for another state or local law enforcement purpose. The records or information shall constitute medical data as defined by section 24-72-204 (3) (a) (I), C.R.S. The state or local medical marijuana licensing authority may disclose any records or information so obtained only to those persons directly involved with any investigation or proceeding authorized by article 43.3 of title 12, C.R.S., or for any state or local law enforcement purpose.

18-18-406.5. Unlawful use of marijuana in a detention facility. (1) A person confined in a detention facility in this state who possesses or uses marijuana commits a level 1 drug misdemeanor.
Repealed.
For purposes of this section, "detention facility" means anybuilding, structure, enclosure, vehicle, institution, or place, whether permanent or temporary, fixed or mobile, where persons are

or may be lawfully held in custody or confinement under the authority of the state of Colorado or any political subdivision of the state of Colorado.


18-18-406.6. Extraction of marijuana concentrate - definitions. (1) It shall be unlawful for any person who is not licensed pursuant to article 43.3 or 43.4 of title 12, C.R.S., to knowingly manufacture marijuana concentrate using an inherently hazardous substance.
It shall be unlawful for any person who is not licensed pursuant to article 43.3 or 43.4 of title 12, C.R.S., who owns, manages, operates, or otherwise controls the use of any premises to knowingly allow marijuana concentrate to be manufactured on the premises using an inherently hazardous substance.
A person who violates this section commits a level 2 drug felony.
As used in this section, unless the context otherwise requires, "inherently hazardous substance" means any liquid chemical, compressed gas, or commercial product that has a flash point at or lower than thirty-eight degrees celsius or one hundred degrees fahrenheit, including butane, propane, and diethyl ether and excluding all forms of alcohol and ethanol.


18-18-406.7. Unlawful possession of cathinones. (Repealed)


18-18-406.8. Unlawful distribution, manufacturing, dispensing, or sale of cathinones. (Repealed)


18-18-407. Special offender - definitions. (1) A person who commits a felony offense under this part 4 under any one or more of the following aggravating circumstances commits a level 1 drug felony and is a special offender:
The defendant committed the violation as part of a pattern of manufacturing, sale, dispensing, or distributing controlled substances, which violation is a felony under applicable laws of Colorado, which constituted a substantial source of that person's income, and in which that person manifested special skill or expertise;
The defendant committed the violation in the course of, or in furtherance of, a conspiracy with one or more persons to engage in a pattern of manufacturing, sale, dispensing, or distributing a controlled substance, which offense is a felony under applicable laws of Colorado, and the defendant did, or agreed that he or she would, initiate, organize, plan, finance, direct, manage, or supervise all or part of such conspiracy or manufacture, sale, dispensing, or distributing, or give or receive a bribe, or use force in connection with such manufacture, sale, dispensing, or distribution;
The defendant committed the violation and in the course of that violation, introduced or imported into the state of Colorado more than fourteen grams of any schedule I or II controlled substance listed in part 2 of this article or more than seven grams of methamphetamine, heroin, ketamine, or cathinones, or ten milligrams of flunitrazepam;
(I) The defendant used, displayed, or possessed on his or her person or within his or her

immediate reach, a deadly weapon as defined in section 18-1-901 (3) (e) at the time of the commission of a violation; or
(II) The defendant or a confederate of the defendant possessed a firearm, as defined in section 18-1-901 (3) (h), to which the defendant or confederate had access in a manner that posed a risk to others or in a vehicle the defendant was occupying at the time of the commission of the violation;
The defendant solicited, induced, encouraged, intimidated, employed, hired, or procured a child, as defined in section 19-1-103 (18), C.R.S., to act as his or her agent to assist in the unlawful distribution, manufacturing, dispensing, sale, or possession for the purposes of sale of anycontrolled substance at the time of the commission of the violation. It shall not be a defense under this paragraph (e) that the defendant did not know the age of any such child.
(I) The defendant engaged in a continuing criminal enterprise by violating any felony provision; and
(II) The violation is a part of a continuing series of two or more violations of this part 4 on separate occasions:
Which are undertaken by that person in concert with five or more other persons with respect to whom that person occupies a position of organizer, supervisor, or any other position of management; and
From which that person obtained substantial income or resources.
(I) The defendant is convicted of selling, distributing, possessing with intent to distribute, manufacturing, or attempting to manufacture any controlled substance either within or upon the grounds of any public or private elementary school, middle school, junior high school, or high school, vocational school, or public housing development; within one thousand feet of the perimeter of any such school or public housing development grounds on any street, alley, parkway, sidewalk, public park, playground, or other area or premises that is accessible to the public; within any private dwelling that is accessible to the public for the purpose of the sale, distribution, use, exchange, manufacture, or attempted manufacture of controlled substances in violation of this article; or in any school vehicle, as defined in section 42-1-102 (88.5), C.R.S., while such school vehicle is engaged in the transportation of persons who are students.
The department of education may cooperate with local boards of education and the officials of public housing developments and make recommendations regarding the uniform implementation and furnishing of notice of the provisions of this paragraph (g). Such recommendations may include, but need not be limited to, the uniform use of signs and other methods of notification that may be used to implement this paragraph (g).
For the purposes of this section, the term "public housing development" means any low- income housing project of any state, county, municipal, or other governmental entity or public body owned and operated by a public housing authority that has an on-site manager. "Public housing development"does not include single-familydispersed housing or small or large clusters of dispersed housing having no on-site manager.
(2) (a) In support of the findings under paragraph (a) of subsection (1) of this section, it may be shown that the defendant has had in his or her own name or under his or her control income or property not explained as derived from a source other than such manufacture, sale, dispensing, or distribution of controlled substances.

For the purposes of paragraph (a) of subsection (1) of this section only, a "substantial source of that person's income" means a source of income which, for any period of one year or more, exceeds the minimum wage, determined on the basis of a forty-hour week and fifty-week year, or which, for the same period, exceeds fifty percent of the defendant's declared adjusted gross income under Colorado or any other state law or under federal law, whichever adjusted gross income is less.
For the purposes of paragraph (a) of subsection (1) of this section, "special skill or expertise" in such manufacture, sale, dispensing, or distribution

includes any unusual knowledge, judgment, or ability, including manual dexterity, facilitating the initiation, organizing, planning, financing, directing, managing, supervising, executing, or concealing of such manufacture, sale, dispensing, or distributing, the enlistment of accomplices in such manufacture, sale, dispensing, or distribution, the escape from detection or apprehension for such manufacture, sale, dispensing, or distribution, or the disposition of the fruits or proceeds of such manufacture, sale, dispensing, or distribution.

For the purposes of paragraphs (a) and (b) of subsection (1) of this section, such manufacture, sale, dispensing, or distribution forms a pattern if it embraces criminal acts which have the same or similar purposes, results, participants, victims, or methods of commission or otherwise are interrelated by distinguishing characteristics and are not isolated events.

(4) and (5)  (Deleted by amendment, L. 2013.)


18-18-408.  Money laundering - illegal investments - penalty. (Repealed)


18-18-409. Reduction or suspension of sentence for providing substantial assistance. Notwithstanding any other provision of this article, the district attorney may request the sentencing court to reduce or suspend the sentence of any individual who is convicted of a violation of section 18-18-405 or 18-18-407 (1) (e) and who provides substantial assistance in the identification, arrest, or conviction of any person for a violation of this article. Upon good cause shown, the request may be filed and heard in camera. The judge hearing the motion may reduce or suspend the sentence if the judge finds that the assistance rendered was substantial.


18-18-410. Declaration of class 1 public nuisance. Any store, shop, warehouse, dwelling house, building, vehicle, boat, or aircraft or any place whatsoever which is frequented by controlled substance addicts for the unlawful use of controlled substances or which is used for the unlawful storage, manufacture, sale, or distribution of controlled substances is declared to be a class 1 public nuisance and subject to the provisions of section 16-13-303, C.R.S. Any real or personal property which is seized or confiscated as a result of an action to abate a public nuisance shall be disposed of pursuant to part 7 of article 13 of title 16, C.R.S.


18-18-411. Keeping, maintaining, controlling, renting, or making available property for unlawful distribution or manufacture of controlled substances. (1) It is unlawful for any

person knowingly or intentionally to keep, maintain, control, rent, lease, or make available for use any store, shop, warehouse, dwelling, building, vehicle, vessel, aircraft, room, enclosure, or other structure or place, which that person knows is resorted to for the purpose of keeping for distribution, transporting for distribution, or distributing controlled substances in violation of this article.

Except as authorized by this article, it is unlawful for any person to:

Knowingly or intentionally open or maintain any place which that person knows is resorted to for the purpose of unlawfully manufacturing a controlled substance; or

Manage or control any building, room, or enclosure, either as an owner, lessee, agent, employee, or mortgagee, and knowingly or intentionally rent, lease, or make available for use, with or without compensation, the building, room, or enclosure which that person knows is resorted to for the purpose of unlawfully manufacturing a controlled substance.

A person does not violate subsection (2) of this section:

By reason of any act committed by another person while that other person is unlawfully on or in the structure or place, if the person lacked knowledge of the unlawful presence of that other person; or

If the person has notified a law enforcement agency with jurisdiction to make an arrest for the illegal conduct.

A person who violates this section commits a level 1 drug misdemeanor.


18-18-412. Abusing toxic vapors - prohibited. (1) No person shall knowingly smell or inhale the fumes of toxic vapors for the purpose of causing a condition of euphoria, excitement, exhilaration, stupefaction, or dulled senses of the nervous system. No person shall knowingly possess, buy, or use any such substance for the purposes described in this subsection (1), nor shall any person knowingly aid any other person to use any such substance for the purposes described in this subsection (1). This subsection (1) shall not apply to the inhalation of anesthesia or other substances for medical or dental purposes.

A person who knowingly violates the provisions of subsection (1) of this section commits the offense of abusing toxic vapors. Abusing toxic vapors is a level 2 drug misdemeanor; except that a person shall not receive a sentence to confinement in jail for being convicted of a first offense pursuant to this subsection (2). A person convicted of a second or subsequent offense pursuant to this subsection (2) may receive a sentence to confinement in jail.

For the purposes of this section, the term "toxic vapors" means the following substances or products containing such substances:

Alcohols, including methyl, isopropyl, propyl, or butyl;

Aliphatic acetates, including ethyl, methyl, propyl, or methyl cellosolve acetate;

Acetone;

Benzene;

Carbon tetrachloride;

Cyclohexane;

Freons, including freon 11 and freon 12;

Hexane;

Methyl ethyl ketone;

Methyl isobutyl ketone;

Naphtha;

Perchlorethylene;

Toluene;

Trichloroethane; or

Xylene.

In a prosecution for a violation of this section, evidence that a container lists one or more of the substances described in subsection (3) of this section as one of its ingredients shall be prima facie evidence that the substance in such container contains toxic vapors and emits the fumes thereof.

Any juvenile charged with an offense pursuant to this section shall be subject to the jurisdiction of the juvenile court pursuant to section 19-2-104,

C.R.S.

18-18-412.5. Unlawful possession of materials to make methamphetamine and amphetamine - penalty. (1) The general assembly finds and declares that persons are manufacturing methamphetamine and amphetamine using nonprescription drugs that are readily and legally available. The general assembly further finds that it is necessary to make illegal the possession of such nonprescription drugs with the intent to use them as immediate precursors in manufacturing any controlled substance.

Notwithstanding any other provision of law to the contrary, no person shall possess ephedrine, pseudoephedrine, or phenylpropanolamine, or their salts, isomers, or salts of isomers, with the intent to use such product as an immediate precursor in the manufacture of any controlled substance.

A person who violates the provisions of this section commits a level 2 drug felony.

18-18-412.7. Sale or distribution of materials to manufacture controlled substances. (1) A person who sells or distributes chemicals, supplies, or equipment, and who knows or reasonably should know or believes that a person intends to use the chemicals, supplies, or equipment to illegally manufacture a controlled substance violates this section.

(2) A violation of this section is a level 2 drug felony.

18-18-412.8. Retail sale of methamphetamine precursor drugs - unlawful acts - penalty.

(Deleted by amendment, L. 2006, p. 1705, § 3, effective July 1, 2006.)

(a) A person may not knowingly deliver in or from a store to the same individual during any twenty-four-hour period more than three and six-tenths grams of a methamphetamine precursor drug or a combination of two or more methamphetamine precursor drugs.

A person may not purchase more than three and six-tenths grams of a methamphetamine precursor drug or a combination of two or more methamphetamine precursor drugs during any twenty-four-hour period.

It is unlawful for a methamphetamine precursor drug that is offered for retail sale in or

from a store to be offered for sale or stored or displayed prior to sale in an area of the store to which the public is allowed access.

(2.5) (a) A person may not deliver in a retail sale in or from a store a methamphetamine precursor drug to a minor under eighteen years of age.

(b) It shall be an affirmative defense to a prosecution under this subsection (2.5) that the person performing the retail sale was presented with and reasonably relied upon a document that identified the person receiving the methamphetamine precursor drug as being eighteen years of age or older.

(a) A person who knowingly violates a provision of this section commits a level 2 drug misdemeanor and, upon conviction, shall be punished as provided in section 18-1.3-501.

A person who is an owner, operator, manager, or supervisor at a store in which, or from which, a retail sale of a methamphetamine precursor drug in violation of this section is made shall not be liable under this section if he or she:

Did not have knowledge of the sale; and

Did not participate in the sale; and

Did not knowingly direct the person making the sale to commit a violation of this section.

For purposes of this section:

(I) Except as otherwise provided in subparagraph (II) of this paragraph (a), "methamphetamine precursor drug" means ephedrine, pseudoephedrine, or phenylpropanolamine or their salts, isomers, or salts of isomers.

(II) "Methamphetamine precursor drug" does not include a substance contained in any package or container that is labeled by the manufacturer as intended for pediatric use.

"Person" means an individual who owns, operates, is employed by, or is an agent of a store.

"Store" means any establishment primarily engaged in the sale of goods at retail.

Nothing in this section shall be construed to restrict the discretion of a district attorney

to bring charges under this section against a person who also is charged with violating section 18-18- 412.7.

18-18-413. Authorized possession of controlled substances. A person to whom or for whose use any controlled substance has been prescribed or dispensed by a practitioner may lawfully possess it, but only in the container in which it was delivered to him unless he is able to show that he is the legal owner or a person acting at the direction of the legal owner of the controlled substance. Any person convicted of violating this section commits a drug petty offense, and the court shall impose a fine of not more than one hundred dollars.

18-18-414. Unlawful acts - licenses - penalties. (1) Except as otherwise provided in this article or in article 42.5 of title 12, C.R.S., the following acts are unlawful:

The dispensing or possession of a schedule I controlled substance except by a researcher who is registered under federal law to conduct research with that schedule I controlled substance;

Except as provided in subsection (2) of this section, the dispensing of any schedule II controlled substance unless such substance is dispensed:

From a pharmacy pursuant to a written order or an order electronically transmitted in accordance with 21 CFR 1311; or

By any practitioner in the course of his or her professional practice;

The dispensing of any schedule III, IV, or V controlled substance unless such controlled substance is dispensed from a pharmacy pursuant to a written, oral, mechanically produced, computer generated, electronically transmitted, or facsimile transmitted order or is dispensed by any practitioner in the course of his or her professional practice;

The dispensing of any marijuana or marijuana concentrate;

To refill any schedule III, IV, or V controlled substance more than six months after the date on which such prescription was issued or more than five times;

The failure of a pharmacy to file and retain the prescription as required in section 12- 42.5-131, C.R.S.;

The failure of a hospital to record and maintain a record of such dispensing as provided in section 12-42.5-131 or 27-80-210, C.R.S.;

The refusal to make available for inspection and to accord full opportunity to check any record or file as required by this article, part 1 of article 42.5 of title 12, C.R.S., or part 2 of article 80 of title 27, C.R.S.;

The failure to keep records as required by this article, part 1 of article 42.5 of title 12, C.R.S., or part 2 of article 80 of title 27, C.R.S.;

The failure to obtain a license or registration as required by this article, part 1 of article

42.5 of title 12, C.R.S., or part 2 of article 80 of title 27, C.R.S.;

Except when controlled substances are dispensed by a practitioner for direct administration in the course of his practice or are dispensed for administration to hospital inpatients, the failure to affix to the immediate container a label stating:

The name and address of the person from whom such controlled substance was dispensed;

The date on which such controlled substance was dispensed;

The number of such prescription as filed in the prescription files of the pharmacy which dispensed such prescription;

The name of the prescribing practitioner;

The directions for use of the controlled substance as contained in the prescription; and

The name of the patient and, if for an animal, the name of the owner;

The failure of a practitioner, in dispensing a controlled substance other than by direct administration in the course of his practice, to affix to the immediate container a label bearing directions for use of the controlled substance, his name and registry number, the name of the patient, the date, and, if for an animal, the name of the owner;

The administration of a controlled substance other than to the patient for whom prescribed;

The possession, by any practitioner, of a controlled substance which was not obtained from a pharmacy and which was received from a person who is not licensed as a manufacturer, distributor, or practitioner. It is also unlawful for a pharmacy to have possession of a controlled

substance which is received from any person who is not licensed as a manufacturer or distributor; except that a pharmacy may buy controlled substances from another pharmacy.

Knowingly transferring drug precursors to any person who uses them for an unlawful activity;

(Deleted by amendment, L. 96, p. 149, § 5, effective April 8, 1996.)

Knowingly acquiring or obtaining, or attempting to acquire or obtain, possession of a drug precursor by misrepresentation, fraud, forgery, deception, or subterfuge;

Knowingly furnishing false or fraudulent material information in, or omitting any material information from, any application, report, or other document required to be kept or filed under this article, part 1 of article 42.5 of title 12, C.R.S., or part 2 of article 80 of title 27, C.R.S., or any record required to be kept by this article, part 1 of article 42.5 of title 12, C.R.S., or part 2 of article 80 of title 27, C.R.S.;

(Deleted by amendment, L. 96, p. 149, § 5, effective April 8, 1996.)

The refusal of entry into any premises for any inspection authorized by this article, part 1 of article 42.5 of title 12, C.R.S., or part 2 of article 80 of title 27, C.R.S.

(a) A pharmacist in an emergency situation, in lieu of a written or electronically transmitted prescription order, in good faith, may dispense up to a seventy-two-hour supply of any controlled substance listed in schedule II of part 2 of this article without a written or electronically transmitted prescription order. An "emergency situation", as used in this paragraph (a), means a situation in which the prescribing practitioner determines:

That immediate dispensing of the controlled substance is necessary for proper treatment of the intended ultimate user;

That no alternative prescription drug is available, including drugs that are not controlled substances under schedule II of part 2 of this article;

That it is not reasonably possible for the prescribing practitioner to provide a written prescription order to be presented to the person dispensing the controlled substance, or to electronically transmit a prescription order to the dispenser, prior to such dispensing.

(I) Upon receiving an emergency oral prescription order from the practitioner, the pharmacist shall immediately reduce the prescription order to writing or an electronic format and shall write or otherwise ensure that the following language and information is recorded in the prescription record: "Authorization for emergency dispensing" and the date and time of dispensing of the oral prescription.

The prescribing practitioner shall reduce the prescription order to writing or an electronic format and shall deliver the prescription order to the pharmacist in person, by facsimile transmission as provided in paragraph (c) of this subsection (2), by mail, or by electronic transmission within seventy-two hours after prescribing the schedule II controlled substance. If delivered by mail, the envelope must be postmarked within seventy-two hours after prescribing. Upon receipt of the prescription order, the pharmacist shall maintain the prescription order with the oral prescription order that has been reduced to writing or an electronic format.

The pharmacist shall notify the board if the prescribing practitioner fails to deliver the written or electronic prescription order to the pharmacist.

(I) A prescription for a controlled substance listed in schedule II of part 2 of this article may be transmitted via facsimile equipment, so long as the original written, signed prescription is

presented to the pharmacist for review prior to the actual dispensing of the controlled substance, except as provided in subparagraph (II) of this paragraph (c).

A prescription written for a schedule II controlled substance for a hospice patient or for a resident of a long-term care facility or for the direct home administration to a patient by parenteral, intravenous, intramuscular, subcutaneous, or intraspinal infusion (infusion drug therapy) may be transmitted by the practitioner or the practitioner's agent to the dispensing pharmacy or pharmacist by facsimile transmission. The practitioner or the practitioner's agent shall note on the prescription that the patient is a hospice patient or a resident in a long-term care facility or a patient receiving infusion drug therapy. The facsimile serves as the original written prescription for purposes of this section and shall be maintained as specified by the board.

For the purposes of this paragraph (c):

"Hospice patient" means an individual who is receiving hospice care from an entity licensed and regulated by the department of public health and environment pursuant to sections 25- 1.5-103 (1) (a) (I) and 25-3-101, C.R.S.

"Long-term care facility" means a facility that is licensed and regulated as a skilled nursing facility or nursing care facility by the department of public health and environment pursuant to sections 25-1.5-103 (1) (a) (I) and 25-3-101, C.R.S.

A person who violates paragraph (a), (b), (c), or (d) of subsection (1) of this section commits a level 4 drug felony.

A person who violates paragraph (e), (f), (g), (h), (i), (j), (k), (l), (m), or (n) of subsection
(1) of this section or subsection (2) of this section or any other provision of this part 4 for which a penalty is not specified is guilty of a level 2 drug misdemeanor.

(5) A person who violates paragraph (o), (q), (r), or (t) of subsection (1) of this section commits a level 3 drug felony.


18-18-415. Fraud and deceit. (1) (a) No person shall obtain a controlled substance or procure the administration of a controlled substance by fraud, deceit, misrepresentation, or subterfuge; or by the forgery or alteration of an order; or by the concealment of a material fact; or by the use of a false name or the giving of a false address.

Information communicated to a practitioner in an effort to procure a controlled substance other than for legitimate treatment purposes or unlawfully to procure the administration of any such controlled substance shall not be deemed a privileged communication.

No person shall willfully make a false statement in any order, report, or record required by this article.

No person, for the purpose of obtaining a controlled substance, shall falsely assume the title of, or represent himself to be, a manufacturer, distributor, practitioner, or other person authorized by law to obtain a controlled substance.

No person shall make or utter any false or forged order.

No person shall affix any false or forged label to a package or receptacle containing a controlled substance.

Any person who violates any provision of this section commits:

A level 4 drug felony and shall be punished as provided in section 18-1.3-401.5.

(Deleted by amendment, L. 2010, (HB 10-1352), ch. 259, p. 1170, § 8, effective August 11, 2010.)


18-18-416. Controlled substances - inducing consumption by fraudulent means. (1) It is unlawful for any person, surreptitiously or by means of fraud, misrepresentation, suppression of truth, deception, or subterfuge, to cause any other person to unknowingly consume or receive the direct administration of any controlled substance, as defined in section 18-18-102 (5); except that nothing in this section shall diminish the scope of health care authorized by law.

A person who violates the provisions of this section commits a level 3 drug felony.


18-18-417. Notice of conviction. Upon the conviction of any person for a violation of any provision of this part 4, a copy of the judgment, sentence, and opinion, if any, of the court shall be sent by the clerk of the court to the state board of pharmacy or the department of public health and environment or officer, if any, by whom the convicted defendant has been licensed or registered to practice his profession or to carry on his business.


18-18-418. Exemptions. (1) The provisions of section 18-18-414 shall not apply to:

Agents of persons licensed under part 2 of article 80 of title 27, C.R.S., or under part 3 of this article, acting within the provisions of their licenses; or

Officers or employees of appropriate agencies of federal, state, or local governments acting pursuant to their official duties; or

A student who is in possession of an immediate precursor who is enrolled in a chemistry class for credit at an institution of higher education, or a work study student, a teaching assistant, a graduate assistant, or a laboratory assistant, if such student's or technician's use of the immediate precursor is for a bona fide educational purpose or research purpose and if the chemistry department of the institution of higher education otherwise possesses all the necessary licenses required by the department.

All combination drugs that are exempted by regulation of the attorney general of the United States department of justice, pursuant to section 1006 (b) of Public Law 91-513 (84 Stat. 1236), known as the "Comprehensive Drug Abuse Prevention and Control Act of 1970", on or after July 1, 1981, are exempted from the provisions of part 1 of article 42.5 of title 12, C.R.S., part 2 of article 80 of title 27, C.R.S., and part 3 of this article.

The provisions of this part 4 do not apply to peyote if said controlled substance is used in religious ceremonies of any bona fide religious organization.

The provisions of section 12-42.5-131 and 27-80-210, C.R.S., shall not apply to a practitioner authorized to prescribe with respect to any controlled substance that is listed in schedule III, IV, or V of part 2 of this article and that is manufactured, received, or dispensed by the practitioner in the course of his or her professional practice unless he or she dispenses, other than by direct administration, any such controlled substance to patients and they are charged therefor either separately or together with charges for other professional services or unless the practitioner

regularly engages in dispensing any such controlled substance to his or her patients.

The exemptions set forth in this section shall be available as a defense to any person accused of violating the provisions of section 18-18-414.

It shall not be necessary for the state to negate any exemption or exception in this part 4, part 1 of article 42.5 of title 12, C.R.S., part 2 of article 80 of title 27, C.R.S., or part 3 of this article in any complaint, information, indictment, or other pleading or in any trial, hearing, or other proceeding under this part 4. The burden of proof of any such exemption or exception is upon the person claiming it.

18-18-419. Imitation and counterfeit controlled substances act. Sections 18-18-419 to 18-18-424 shall be known and may be cited as the "Imitation and Counterfeit Controlled Substances Act".

18-18-420. Imitation controlled substances - definitions. As used in sections 18-18-419 to 18-18-424, unless the context otherwise requires:
"Controlled substance" shall have the same meaning as set forth in section 18-18-102 (5).
"Distribute" means the actual, constructive, or attempted transfer, delivery, or dispensing to another of an imitation controlled substance, with or without remuneration.
"Imitation controlled substance" means a substance that is not the controlled substance that it is purported to be but which, by appearance, including color, shape, size, and markings, by representations made, and by consideration of all relevant factors as set forth in section 18-18-421, would lead a reasonable person to believe that the substance is the controlled substance that it is purported to be.
"Manufacture" means the production, preparation, compounding, processing, encapsulating, packaging or repackaging, or labeling or relabeling of an imitation controlled substance.

18-18-421. Imitation controlled substances - determination - considerations. (1) In determining whether a substance is an imitation controlled substance, the trier of fact may consider, in addition to all other relevant factors, the following:
Statements by an owner or by anyone in control of the substance concerning the nature of the substance or its use or effect;
Statements made to the recipient that the substance may be resold for inordinate profit which is more than the normal markup charged by legal retailers of similar pharmaceutical products;
Whether the substance is packaged in a manner normally used for illicit controlled substances;
Evasive tactics or actions utilized by the owner or person in control of the substance to avoid detection by law enforcement authorities;
The proximity of the imitation controlled substance to any controlled substances when conduct purported to be illegal under this article is observed.

18-18-422. Imitation controlled substances - violations - penalties. (1) (a) Except as provided in section 18-18-424, it is unlawful for a person to manufacture, distribute, or possess with intent to distribute an imitation controlled substance.
A person who violates the provisions of paragraph (a) of this subsection (1) commits:
A level 4 drug felony.
(Deleted by amendment, L. 2013.)
(a) If an adult distributes an imitation controlled substance to a minor and the adult is at least two years older than the minor, the adult commits a level 3 drug felony.
(b) (Deleted by amendment, L. 2013.)
(a) It is unlawful for a person to place in a newspaper, magazine, handbill, or other publication or to post or distribute in a public place an advertisement or solicitation that the person knows will promote the distribution of imitation controlled substances.
(b) A person who violates the provisions of paragraph (a) of this subsection (3) commits a level 1 drug misdemeanor.
It is not a defense to a violation of this section that the defendant believed that the imitation controlled substance was a genuine controlled substance.

18-18-423. Counterfeit substances prohibited - penalty. (1) It is unlawful for any person knowingly or intentionally to manufacture, deliver, or possess with intent to manufacture or deliver, a controlled substance which, or the container or labeling of which, without authorization, bears the trademark, trade name, or other identifying mark, imprint, number, or device, or anylikeness thereof, of a manufacturer, distributor, or dispenser, other than the person who in fact manufactured, distributed, or dispensed the substance.
It is unlawful for any person knowingly or intentionally to make, distribute, or possess a punch, die, plate, stone, or other thing designed to print, imprint, or reproduce the trademark, trade name, or other identifying mark, imprint, or device of another or any likeness of any of the foregoing upon any drug or container or labeling thereof.
A person who violates this section commits a level 3 drug felony.

18-18-424. Imitation controlled substances - exceptions. The provisions of sections 18-18- 419 to 18-18-424 shall not apply to practitioners licensed, registered, or otherwise authorized under the laws of this state to possess, administer, dispense, or distribute a controlled substance, if the distribution, possession, dispensing, or administering of the imitation controlled substance is done in the lawful course of his professional practice.

18-18-425. Drug paraphernalia - legislative declaration. (1) The general assemblyhereby finds and declares that the possession, sale, manufacture, delivery, or advertisement of drug paraphernalia results in the legitimization and encouragement of the illegal use of controlled

substances by making the drug culture more visible and enticing and that the ready availability of drug paraphernalia tends to promote, suggest, or increase the public acceptability of the illegal use of controlled substances. Therefore, the purposes of the provisions controlling drug paraphernalia are:
To protect and promote the public peace, health, safety, and welfare by prohibiting the possession, sale, manufacture, and delivery, or advertisement, of drug paraphernalia; and
To deter the use of controlled substances bycontrolling the drug paraphernalia associated with their use.

18-18-426. Drug paraphernalia - definitions. As used in sections 18-18-425 to 18-18-430, unless the context otherwise requires:
"Drug paraphernalia" means all equipment, products, and materials of any kind which are used, intended for use, or designed for use in planting, propagating, cultivating, growing, harvesting, manufacturing, compounding, converting, producing, processing, preparing, testing, analyzing, packaging, repackaging, storing, containing, concealing, injecting, ingesting, inhaling, or otherwise introducing into the human body a controlled substance in violation of the laws of this state. "Drug paraphernalia" includes, but is not limited to:
Testing equipment used, intended for use, or designed for use in identifying or in analyzing the strength, effectiveness, or purity of controlled substances under circumstances in violation of the laws of this state;

Scales and balances used, intended for use, or designed for use in weighing or measuring controlled substances;

Separation gins and sifters used, intended for use, or designed for use in removing twigs and seeds from or in otherwise cleaning or refining marijuana;

Blenders, bowls, containers, spoons, and mixing devices used, intended for use, or designed for use in compounding controlled substances;

Capsules, balloons, envelopes, and other containers used, intended for use, or designed for use in packaging small quantities of controlled substances;

Containers and other objects used, intended for use, or designed for use in storing or concealing controlled substances; or

Objects used, intended for use, or designed for use in ingesting, inhaling, or otherwise introducing marijuana, cocaine, hashish, or hashish oil into the human body, such as:

Metal, wooden, acrylic, glass, stone, plastic, or ceramic pipes with or without screens, permanent screens, hashish heads, or punctured metal bowls;

Water pipes;

Carburetion tubes and devices;

Smoking and carburetion masks;

Roach clips, meaning objects used to hold burning material, such as a marijuana cigarette that has become too small or too short to be held in the hand;

Miniature cocaine spoons and cocaine vials;

Chamber pipes;

Carburetor pipes;

Electric pipes;

Air-driven pipes;

Chillums;

Bongs; or

Ice pipes or chillers.

"Drug paraphernalia" does not include any marijuana accessories as defined in section 16 (2) (g) of article XVIII of the state constitution.


18-18-427. Drug paraphernalia - determination - considerations. (1) In determining whether an object is drug paraphernalia, a court, in its discretion, may consider, in addition to all other relevant factors, the following:

Statements by an owner or by anyone in control of the object concerning its use;

The proximity of the object to controlled substances;

The existence of any residue of controlled substances on the object;

Direct or circumstantial evidence of the knowledge of an owner, or of anyone in control of the object, or evidence that such person reasonably should know, that it will be delivered to persons who he knows or reasonably should know, could use the object to facilitate a violation of sections 18-18-425 to 18-18-430;

Instructions, oral or written, provided with the object concerning its use;

Descriptive materials accompanying the object which explain or depict its use;

National or local advertising concerning its use;

The manner in which the object is displayed for sale;

Whether the owner, or anyone in control of the object, is a supplier of like or related items to the community for legal purposes, such as an authorized distributor or dealer of tobacco products;

The existence and scope of legal uses for the object in the community;

Expert testimony concerning its use.

(2) In the event a case brought pursuant to sections 18-18-425 to 18-18-430 is tried before a jury, the court shall hold an evidentiary hearing on issues raised pursuant to this section. Such hearing shall be conducted in camera.


18-18-428. Possession of drug paraphernalia - penalty. (1) (a) Except as described in section 18-1-711 and paragraph (b) of this subsection (1), a person commits possession of drug paraphernalia if he or she possesses drug paraphernalia and knows or reasonably should know that the drug paraphernalia could be used under circumstances in violation of the laws of this state.

(b) (I) Prior to searching a person, a person's premises, or a person's vehicle, a peace officer may ask the person whether the person is in possession of a hypodermic needle or syringe that may cut or puncture the officer or whether such a hypodermic needle or syringe is on the premises or in the vehicle to be searched. If a hypodermic needle or syringe is on the person, on the person's premises, or in the person's vehicle and the person, either in response to the officer's question or

voluntarily, alerts the officer of that fact prior to the search, assessment, or treatment, the peace officer shall not arrest or cite the person pursuant to this section for the hypodermic needle or syringe or section 18-18-403.5 for any minuscule, residual controlled substance that may be present in a used hypodermic needle or syringe, and the district attorney shall not charge or prosecute the person pursuant to this section for the hypodermic needle or syringe or section 18-18-403.5 for any minuscule, residual controlled substance that may be present in a used hypodermic needle or syringe. The circumstances described in this paragraph (b) may be used as a factor in a probable cause or reasonable suspicion determination of any criminal offense if the original stop or search was lawful.

(II) Prior to assessing or treating a person, an emergency medical technician or other first responder may ask the person whether the person is in possession of a hypodermic needle or syringe that may cut or puncture the technician or first responder. If a hypodermic needle or syringe is on the person, and the person, either in response to the question or voluntarily, alerts the technician or first responder of that fact, a peace officer shall not arrest or cite the person pursuant to this section for the hypodermic needle or syringe or section 18-18-403.5 for any minuscule, residual controlled substance that may be present in a used hypodermic needle or syringe, and the district attorney shall not charge or prosecute the person pursuant to this section for the hypodermic needle or syringe or section 18-18-403.5 for any minuscule, residual controlled substance that may be present in a used hypodermic needle or syringe.

Any person who commits possession of drug paraphernalia commits a drug petty offense and, upon conviction thereof, shall be punished by a fine of not more than one hundred dollars.


18-18-429. Manufacture, sale, or delivery of drug paraphernalia - penalty. Any person who sells or delivers, possesses with intent to sell or deliver, or manufactures with intent to sell or deliver equipment, products, or materials knowing, or under circumstances where one reasonably should know, that such equipment, products, or materials could be used as drug paraphernalia commits a level 2 drug misdemeanor.

18-18-430. Advertisement of drug paraphernalia - penalty. Any person who places an advertisement in a newspaper, magazine, handbill, or other publication and who intends thereby to promote the sale in this state of equipment, products, or materials designed and intended for use as drug paraphernalia commits a level 2 drug misdemeanor.

18-18-430.5. Drug paraphernalia - exemption. A person shall be exempt from the provisions of sections 18-18-425 to 18-18-430 if he or she is participating as an employee, volunteer, or participant in an approved syringe exchange program created pursuant to section 25-1-520, C.R.S.

18-18-431. Defenses. The common law defense known as the "procuring agent defense" is not a defense to any crime in this title.

18-18-432. Drug offender public service and rehabilitation program. (1) As used in this section, unless the context otherwise requires:
"Convicted" and "conviction" mean a plea of guilty, including a plea of guilty entered pursuant to a deferred sentence under section 18-1.3-102, or a verdict of guilty by a judge or jury, and includes a plea of no contest accepted by the court.
"Drug offender" means any person convicted of any offense under this article.

"Useful public service" means any work which is beneficial to the public and which involves a minimum of direct supervision or other public cost. "Useful public service" does not include any work which would endanger the health or safety of a drug offender.
(2) (a) Upon conviction, each drug offender, other than an offender sentenced to the department of corrections or an offender sentenced directly to a communitycorrections facility, shall be sentenced by the court to pay for and complete, at a minimum, forty-eight hours of useful public service for any felony, twenty-four hours of useful public service for any misdemeanor, and sixteen hours of useful public service for any petty offense. Such useful public service shall be in addition to, and not in lieu of, any other sentence received by the drug offender. The court shall not suspend any portion of the minimum number of useful public service hours ordered. If any drug offender is sentenced to probation, whether supervised by the court or by a probation officer, the order to pay for and complete the useful public service hours shall be made a condition of probation.
The provisions of this subsection (2) relating to the performance of useful public service are also applicable to any drug offender who receives a diversion in accordance with section 18-1.3- 101 or who receives a deferred sentence in accordance with section 18-1.3-102 and the completion of any stipulated amount of useful public service hours to be completed by the drug offender shall be ordered by the court in accordance with the conditions of such deferred prosecution or deferred sentence as stipulated to by the prosecution and the drug offender.
If not already established pursuant to law, there may be established in each judicial district in the state a useful public service program under the direction of the chief judge of the judicial district. It shall be the purpose of the useful public service program to identify and seek the cooperation of governmental entities and political subdivisions thereof and corporations organized not for profit or charitable trusts for the purpose of providing useful public service jobs; to interview and assign persons who have been ordered by the court to perform useful public service to suitable useful public service jobs; and to monitor compliance or noncompliance of such persons in performing useful public service assignments as specified in paragraph (a) of this subsection (2).

Any general public liability insurance policy obtained pursuant to this subsection (2) shall be in a sum of not less than the current limit on government liability under the "Colorado Governmental Immunity Act", article 10 of title 24, C.R.S.
For the purposes of the "Colorado Governmental Immunity Act", article 10 of title 24, C.R.S., "public employee" does not include any person who is sentenced pursuant to this subsection
to participate in any type of useful public service.
No governmental entity shall be liable under the "Workers' Compensation Act of Colorado", articles 40 to 47 of title 8, C.R.S., or under the "Colorado Employment Security Act",

articles 70 to 82 of title 8, C.R.S., for any benefits on account of any person who is sentenced pursuant to this section to participate in any type of useful public service, but nothing in this subsection (2) shall prohibit a governmental entity from electing to accept the provisions of the "Workers' Compensation Act of Colorado" by purchasing and keeping in force a policy of workers' compensation insurance covering such person.
Upon a plea of guilty, including a plea of guilty entered pursuant to a deferred sentence under section 18-1.3-102 or a verdict of guilty by the court or a jury, to any offense under this article, or upon entry of a diversion pursuant to section 18-1.3-101 for any offense under this article, the court shall order the drug offender to immediately report to the sheriff's department in the county where the drug offender was charged, at which time the drug offender's fingerprints and photographs shall be taken and returned to the court, which fingerprints and photographs shall become a part of the court's official documents and records pertaining to the charges against the drug offender and the drug offender's identification in association with such charges. On any trial for a violation of any criminal law of this state, a duly authenticated copy of the record of former convictions and judgments of any court of record for any of said crimes against the drug offender named in said convictions and judgments shall be prima facie evidence of such convictions and may be used in evidence against the drug offender. Identification photographs and fingerprints that are part of the record of such former convictions and judgments of any court of record or which are part of the record at the place of the drug offender's incarceration after sentencing for any of such former convictions and judgments shall be prima facie evidence of the identity of the drug offender and may be used in evidence against such drug offender. Any drug offender who fails to immediately comply with the court's order to report to the sheriff's department, to furnish fingerprints, or to have photographs taken may be held in contempt of court.

18-18-433. Constitutional provisions. The provisions of this part 4 do not apply to a person twenty-one years of age or older acting in conformance with section 16 of article XVIII of the state constitution and do not apply to a person acting in conformance with section 14 of article XVIII of the state constitution.
PART 5 ENFORCEMENT AND
ADMINISTRATIVE PROCEDURES

18-18-501. Administrative inspections and warrants. (1) As used in this section, "controlled premises" means:
Places where persons registered or exempted from registration requirements under this article are required to keep records; and

Places including factories, warehouses, establishments, and conveyances in which persons registered or exempted from registration requirements under this article are permitted to hold, manufacture, compound, process, sell, deliver, or otherwise dispose of any controlled

substance.

The procedure for issuance and execution of administrative inspection warrants is as follows:

A judge of a state court of record within the judge's jurisdiction, and upon proper oath or affirmation showing probable cause, may issue warrants for the purpose of conducting administrative inspections of controlled premises as authorized by this article or rules adopted under this article, and seizures of property appropriate to the inspections. For purposes of the issuance of administrative inspection warrants, probable cause exists upon showing a reasonable belief that this article or the rules adopted therein have been violated, sufficient to justify administrative inspection of the area, premises, building, or conveyance in the circumstances specified in the application for the warrant.

A warrant may issue only upon an affidavit of a designated officer or employee having knowledge of the facts alleged, sworn to before the judge and establishing the grounds for issuing the warrant. If the judge is satisfied that grounds for the application exist or that there is probable cause to believe they exist, the judge shall issue a warrant identifying the area, premises, building, or conveyance to be inspected, the purpose of the inspection, and, if appropriate, the type of property to be inspected, if any. The warrant must:

State the grounds for its issuance and the name of each individual whose affidavit has been taken in support thereof;

Be directed to an individual authorized under Colorado law to execute it;

Command the individual to whom it is directed to inspect the area, premises, building, or conveyance identified for the purpose specified and, if appropriate, direct the seizure of the property specified;

Identify the item or types of property to be seized, if any; and

Direct that it be served during normal business hours and designate the court to which it must be returned.

A warrant issued pursuant to this section must be executed and returned within fourteen days after its date unless, upon a showing of a need for additional time, the court orders otherwise. If property is seized pursuant to a warrant, a copy must be given to the person from whom or from whose premises the property is taken, together with a receipt for the property taken. The return of the warrant must be made promptly, accompanied by a written inventory of any property taken. The inventory must be made in the presence of the individual executing the warrant and of the person from whose possession or premises the property was taken, if present, or in the presence of at least one credible individual other than the individual executing the warrant. A copy of the inventory must be delivered to the person from whom or from whose premises the property was taken and to the applicant for the warrant.

The judge or court who has issued a warrant shall attach to the warrant a copy of the return and all papers returnable in connection therewith and file them with the clerk of the appropriate state court for the judicial district in which the inspection was made.

The board or department may make administrative inspections of controlled premises of those persons they are authorized to register under this article in accordance with the following provisions:

If authorized by an administrative inspection warrant issued pursuant to subsection (2)

of this section, an officer or employee designated by the board or department, upon presenting the warrant and appropriate credentials to the owner, operator, or agent in charge, may enter controlled premises for the purpose of conducting an administrative inspection.

If authorized by an administrative inspection warrant, an officer or employee designated by the board or department may:

Inspect and copy records required by this article to be kept;

Inspect, within reasonable limits and in a reasonable manner, controlled premises and all pertinent equipment, finished and unfinished material, containers and labeling found therein, and, except as provided in paragraph (d) of this subsection (3), all other things therein, including records, files, papers, processes, controls, and facilities bearing on violation of this article; and

Inventory any stock of any controlled substance therein and obtain samples thereof.

This section does not prevent the inspection without a warrant of books and records pursuant to an administrative subpoena issued in accordance with section 24-4-105, C.R.S., nor does it prevent entries and administrative inspections, including seizures of property, without a warrant:

If the owner, operator, or agent in charge of the controlled premises consents;

In situations involving inspection of conveyances if there is reasonable cause to believe that the mobility of the conveyance makes it impracticable to obtain a warrant;

In any other exceptional or emergency circumstance where time or opportunity to apply for a warrant is lacking; or

In all other situations in which a warrant is not constitutionally required.

An inspection authorized by this section may not extend to financial data, sales data, other than shipment data, or pricing data unless the owner, operator, or agent in charge of the controlled premises consents in writing.


18-18-502. Injunctions. (1) The district courts of this state have jurisdiction to restrain or enjoin violations of this article.

The defendant may demand trial by jury for an alleged violation of an injunction or restraining order under this section. Nothing in this section shall preclude any person from applying for injunctive relief from administrative inspections and warrants conducted under this article or for the immediate return of property seized under this article.


18-18-503. Cooperative arrangements and confidentiality. (1) The board and the department shall cooperate with federal and other state agencies in discharging the board's and the department's responsibilities concerning controlled substances and in controlling the abuse of controlled substances. To this end, the department may:

Arrange for the exchange of information among governmental officials concerning the use and abuse of controlled substances;

Coordinate and cooperate in training programs concerning controlled substance law enforcement at local and state levels;

Cooperate with the drug enforcement administration by establishing a centralized unit to accept, catalog, file, and collect statistics, including records of drug dependent persons and other

controlled substance law offenders within this state, and make the information available for federal, state, and local law enforcement purposes, but may not furnish the name or identity of a patient or research subject whose identity could not be obtained under subsection (3) of this section; and

Conduct programs of eradication aimed at destroying wild or illicit growth of plant species from which controlled substances may be extracted.

Results, information, and evidence received from the drug enforcement administration relating to the regulatory functions of this article, including results of inspections conducted by it, may be relied and acted upon by the board or department in the exercise of the regulatory functions under this article.

A practitioner engaged in medical practice or research is not required or compelled to furnish the name or identity of a patient or research subject to the board or department, nor may the practitioner be compelled in any state or local civil, criminal, administrative, legislative, or other proceedings to furnish the name or identity of an individual that the practitioner is obligated to keep confidential.

18-18-504. Pleadings - presumptions - liabilities. (1) It is not necessary for the state to negate any exemption or exception in this article in any complaint, information, indictment, or other pleading or in any trial, hearing, or other proceeding under this article.

No person is presumed to be the holder of an appropriate registration or order form issued under this article.

No civil or criminal liability is imposed by this article upon any authorized state, county, or municipal officer, engaged in the lawful administration or enforcement of this article.

18-18-505. Judicial review. All final determinations, findings, and conclusions of the board or department under this article are subject to judicial review pursuant to section 24-4-106, C.R.S.

18-18-506. Education and research. (1) The department shall carry out educational programs designed to prevent and deter misuse and abuse of controlled substances. In connection with these programs, the department may:

Promote better recognition of the problems of misuse and abuse of controlled substances within the regulated industry and among interested groups and organizations;

Assist the regulated industry and interested groups and organizations in contributing to the reduction of misuse and abuse of controlled substances;

Consult with interested groups and organizations to aid them in solving administrative and organizational problems;

Evaluate procedures, projects, techniques, and controls conducted or proposed as part of educational programs on misuse and abuse of controlled substances;

Disseminate the results of research on misuse and abuse of controlled substances to promote a better public understanding of what problems exist and what can be done to alleviate them; and

Assist in the education and training of state and local law enforcement officials in their efforts to control misuse and abuse of controlled substances. The department shall encourage research on misuse and abuse of controlled substances. In connection with the research, and in furtherance of the enforcement of this article, the department may:

Establish methods to assess accurately the effects of controlled substances and identify and characterize those with potential for abuse;

Make studies and undertake programs of research to:

Develop new or improved approaches, techniques, systems, equipment, and devices to strengthen the enforcement of this article;

Determine patterns of misuse and abuse of controlled substances and the social effects thereof; and

Improve methods for preventing, predicting, understanding, and dealing with the misuse and abuse of controlled substances; and

Enter into contracts with public institutions of higher education and private organizations or individuals for the purpose of conducting research, demonstrations, or special projects which bear directly on misuse and abuse of controlled substances.

The department may enter into contracts for educational and research activities.

The department may authorize persons engaged in research on the use and effects of controlled substances to withhold the names and other identifying characteristics of individuals who are the subjects of the research. Persons who obtain this authorization are not compelled in any civil, criminal, administrative, legislative, or other proceeding to identify the individuals who are the subjects of research for which the authorization was obtained.

The department may authorize the possession and distribution of controlled substances by persons engaged in research. Persons who obtain this authorization are exempt from state prosecution for possession and distribution of controlled substances to the extent of the authorization.

PART 6 MISCELLANEOUS

18-18-601. Pending proceedings - applicability. (1) This article does not affect or abate a prosecution for a violation of law occurring before July 1, 1992. If the offense being prosecuted is similar to one set out in part 4 of this article, the penalties under said part 4 apply if they are less than those under prior law.

This article does not affect a civil seizure, forfeiture, or injunctive proceeding commenced before July 1, 1992.

All administrative proceedings pending under previous laws that are superseded by this article must be continued and brought to a final determination in accord with the laws and rules in effect before July 1, 1992. Any substance controlled under prior law but which is not listed in section 18-18-203, 18-18-204, 18-18-205, 18-18-206, or 18-18-207 is automatically controlled without

further proceedings and must be included in the appropriate schedule.

The board or department shall initially permit persons to register who own or operate any establishment engaged in the manufacture, distribution, or dispensing of any controlled substance prior to July 1, 1992, and who are registered or licensed by the state.

18-18-602. Continuation of rules - application to existing relationships. Any orders and rules adopted under any law affected by this article and in effect on July 1, 1992, and not in conflict with this article continue in effect until modified, superseded, or repealed. Rights and duties that matured, penalties that were incurred, and proceedings that were begun prior to July 1, 1992, are not affected by the enactment of the "Uniform Controlled Substances Act of 2013" or the corresponding repeal of provisions in article 42.5 of title 12, C.R.S., and part 6 of article 5 of this title.

18-18-603. Statutes of limitations. A civil action under this article must be commenced within seven years after the claim for relief became known or should have become known, excluding any time during which a party is out of the state or in confinement or during which criminal proceedings relating to a party are in progress.

18-18-604. Uniformity of interpretation. To the extent that this article is uniform, the judiciary may look to decisions regarding the "Uniform Controlled Substances Act of 2013" among states enacting it, subject to rights and obligations provided under other Colorado statutes and the state constitution.

18-18-605. Severability. If any provision of this article or the application thereof to any person or circumstance is held invalid, the invalidity does not affect other provisions or applications of the article which can be given effect without the invalid provision or application, and to this end the provisions of this article are severable.

18-18-606. Drug case data collection. (1) The division of criminal justice in the department of public safety shall collect the data specified in subsection (2) of this section for the period between October 1, 2013, and September 30, 2016, and issue a report by December 31, 2016, on the impact of Senate Bill 13-250, enacted in 2013.
The data must include, but is not limited to:
The total number of drug cases diverted from prosecution prior to filing through referral to law enforcement or district attorney diversion programs;
The total number of drug cases filed statewide by jurisdiction;
All demographic information and relevant background information on the defendants for which a drug case has been filed or diverted including prior criminal history; and

For all cases filed, the nature of the charges by statutory citation and the outcome or disposition information on all the cases filed, which shall include but not be limited to:
Dismissal without prosecution;
Dismissal as a result of a plea bargain;
Deferred judgment to the original charge or a lesser charge;
Any plea bargain that reduces the original charge or charges filed;
Any sentence bargain including, but not limited to, a stipulation to a certain sentence or a limit on the amount of jail or department of corrections imposed;
Any plea bargain that involves multiple cases;
Any sentence bargain that involves concurrent or consecutive time in the custody of the department of corrections;
Any probation or deferred judgment revocation filed and the result of any revocation;
Any successful completion of probation or a deferred judgment; and
Any successful completion of supervision resulting in conversion of the felony to a misdemeanor pursuant to the provisions of section 18-1.3-103.5 (2).

ARTICLE 18.5

Methamphetamine Abuse Prevention, Intervention, and Treatment and the Response of the Criminal Justice System

18-18.5-101. Legislative declaration. (1) The general assembly finds that:
Each year Colorado spends significant amounts of money related to untreated substance abuse. The magnitude of public funds spent on the direct and indirect consequences of substance use and abuse is staggering, and dozens of Colorado public agencies play a part in controlling substance use or dealing with its consequences.
Deaths in Colorado related to the abuse of prescription opioids, such as oxycodone, hydrocodone, and fentanyl, nearly doubled from one hundred eighty in 2000 to three hundred forty- three in 2010;
Children whose parents abuse alcohol or drugs are three times more likely to be verbally, physically, or sexually abused and four times more likely than other children to be neglected. Additionally, research indicates that children in families affected bysubstance use are at an increased risk for substance use and mental health issues in adolescence. The health, safety, and future success of drug-endangered children are pressing issues in Colorado.
Substance use by youth is detrimental to brain maturation, impacting brain structure, functioning, and neurocognition;
Substance use during pregnancyplaces children at direct risk for complications, including premature delivery, altered neonatal behavior patterns such as abnormal reflexes and extreme irritability, congenital deformities, low birth weight, attention deficit disorder, and prenatal and

postnatal neglect, many of which cause lifelong defects; and
Each year Colorado spends significant moneys related to untreated substance abuse.
The general assembly further finds that substance abuse, including that related to illicit drugs, prescription drugs, underage marijuana use, and methamphetamine labs and abuse, harms citizens of Colorado. Responses to substance abuse should be supported in the criminal justice system, the public health system, mental health services, social services, child welfare and youth services, community task forces, and with treatment for parents who abuse drugs and prevention and treatment for children affected by substance abuse and nonfederally regulated pharmaceutical drug production and distribution, and other systems affected by substance abuse.
The general assembly, therefore, determines and declares that it is necessary to change the state methamphetamine task force into a substance abuse trend and response task force to:
Examine drug trends and the most effective models and practices for:
The prevention of and intervention into substance abuse;
The prevention of unintended harmful exposures due to nonfederal-drug-administration- regulated pharmaceutical drug production and distribution;
The prevention of potential negative public health impacts due to improper dispensing, management, and disposal of drugs; and
The treatment of children and adults affected by drug addiction;
Formulate a response to current and emerging substance abuse problems from the criminal justice, prevention, and treatment sectors; and
Make recommendations to the general assembly for the development of statewide strategies and legislative proposals related to these issues. The recommendations made to the general assembly shall be made in coordination with the task force and the department of human services, the agency responsible for the administration of behavioral health programs and services.

18-18.5-102. Definitions. As used in this article, unless the context otherwise requires:

"Task force" means the state substance abuse trend and response task force established pursuant to section 18-18.5-103.

18-18.5-103. State substance abuse trend and response task force - creation - membership - duties. (1) There is hereby created the state substance abuse trend and response task force.

The task force shall consist of the following members:

(I) The attorney general or his or her designee, who shall serve as the chair;

An expert in the field of substance abuse prevention, who shall be appointed by the president of the senate and serve as a vice-chair;

An expert in the field of substance abuse treatment, who shall be appointed by the speaker of the house of representatives and serve as a vice-chair;

A representative of the criminal justice system, who shall be appointed by the governor and serve as a vice-chair;

The president of the senate or his or her designee;

The minority leader of the senate or his or her designee;

The speaker of the house of representatives or his or her designee;

The minority leader of the house of representatives or his or her designee;

(a.5) The terms of the members appointed by the speaker of the house of representatives and the president of the senate and who are serving on March 22, 2007, shall be extended to and expire on or shall terminate on the convening date of the first regular session of the sixty-seventh general assembly. As soon as practicable after such convening date, the speaker and the president shall each appoint or reappoint one member in the same manner as provided in subparagraphs (II) and (III) of paragraph (a) of this subsection (2). Thereafter, the terms of members appointed or reappointed by the speaker and the president shall expire on the convening date of the first regular session of each general assembly, and all subsequent appointments and reappointments by the speaker and the president shall be made as soon as practicable after such convening date. The person making the original appointment or reappointment shall fill any vacancy by appointment for the remainder of an unexpired term. Members appointed or reappointed by the speaker and the president shall serve at the pleasure of the appointing authority and shall continue in office until the member's successor is appointed.

Twenty-two members appointed by the task force chair and vice-chairs as follows:

A representative of a local child and family service provider;

A representative of a major health facility that focuses on the treatment of children;

A representative of a human services agency with experience in child welfare issues;

A representative of the criminal defense bar;

A representative of a behavioral health treatment provider that is an expert in substance abuse treatment procedures;

A representative of the department of education, who is familiar with the department's drug prevention initiatives;

A representative of the Colorado district attorneys council;

A representative of a Colorado sheriffs' organization;

A representative of a Colorado police chiefs' organization;

A county commissioner from a rural county;

A representative of an organization that provides information, advocacy, and support services to municipalities located in rural counties;

A licensed pharmacist;

A representative of the department of public safety;

A representative of the office of the child's representative;

A representative of the division of adult parole of the department of corrections;

A representative of the Colorado drug investigators association;

A youth representative;

A representative of a substance abuse recovery organization;

An expert in environmental protection;

A representative of a community prevention coalition;

A representative of the Colorado department of public health and environment;

A representative of the office of behavioral health in the Colorado department of

human services.

Two members appointed by the chief justice of the Colorado supreme court who represent the judicial department, one of whom is a district court judge experienced in handling cases involving substance abuse and one of whom represents the division of probation within the judicial department;

A member appointed by the governor who represents the governor's policy staff.

A vacancy occurring in a position shall be filled as soon as possible by the appropriate appointing authority designated in subsection (2) of this section.

The task force, in collaboration with state agencies charged with prevention, intervention, or treatment of substance abuse, shall:

Assist local communities in implementing the most effective models and practices for substance abuse prevention, intervention, and treatment and in developing the responses by the criminal justice system;

Review model programs that have shown the best results in Colorado and across the United States and provide information on the programs to local communities and local drug task forces;

Assist and augment local drug task forces without supplanting them;

Investigate collaborative models on protecting children and other victims of substance abuse and nonfederal- drug-administration-regulated pharmaceutical drug production and distribution;

Measure and evaluate the progress of the state and local jurisdictions in preventing substance abuse and nonfederal-drug-administration-regulated pharmaceutical drug production and distribution and in prosecuting persons engaging in these acts;

Evaluate and promote approaches to increase public awareness of current and emerging substance abuse problems and strategies for addressing those problems;

Assist local communities with implementation of the most effective practices to respond to current and emerging substance abuse problems and nonfederal-drug- administration-regulated pharmaceutical drug production and distribution;

Consider any other issues concerning substance abuse problems and nonfederal-drug- administration- regulated pharmaceutical drug production and distribution that arise during the course of the task force study;

Develop a definition of a "drug-endangered child" to be used in the context of the definition of "child abuse or neglect" as set forth in section 19-1-103 (1), C.R.S., and include the definition in its January 1, 2014, report to the judiciary committees of the senate and the house of representatives, or any successor committees.

All state and local agencies shall cooperate with the task force and provide such data and other information as the task force may require in carrying out its duties under this section. Any state or local agency or organization that is represented on the task force may provide staff assistance to the task force, subject to the discretion of the chair. Any staff assistance provided to the task force pursuant to this subsection (5) shall be without compensation.

In addition, the task force shall:

Meet at least four times each year from the date of the first meeting until January 1, 2018, or more often as directed by the chair of the task force;

Communicate with and obtain input from groups throughout the state affected by the issues identified in subsection (4) of this section;

Create subcommittees as needed to carry out the duties of the task force. The subcommittees may consist, in part, of persons who are not members of the task force. Such persons may vote on issues before the subcommittee but shall not be entitled to a vote at meetings of the task force.

Submit a written report to the judiciary committees, or any successor committees, of the senate and the house of representatives of the general assembly by January 1, 2014, and by each January 1 thereafter through January 1, 2018, at a minimum specifying the following:

Issues to be studied in upcoming task force meetings and a prioritization of those issues;

Findings and recommendations regarding issues of prior consideration by the task force;

Legislative proposals of the task force that identify the policy issues involved, the agencies responsible for the implementation of the changes, and the funding sources required for such implementation.

(a) Except as otherwise provided in section 2-2-326, C.R.S., members of the task force shall serve without compensation.

(b) (Deleted by amendment, L. 2014.)


18-18.5-104. Task force funding. (1) The division of criminal justice in the department of public safety, on behalf of the task force, is authorized to receive and expend contributions, grants, services, and in-kind donations from any public or private entity for any direct or indirect costs associated with the duties and functions of the task force set forth in this article.

The task force shall, no later than August 1, 2006, identify all funding sources described in subsection (1) of this section that the task force intends to utilize for its operation through August 1, 2008.

Subject to available moneys, the task force may approve grants to recipients. In selecting grant recipients, the task force, to the extent possible, shall ensure that grants are awarded to law enforcement agencies or other applicants in a variety of geographic areas of the state.


18-18.5-105. Cash fund - created. (1) (a) All private and public funds received by the task force or the division of criminal justice in the department of public safety, on behalf of the task force, through grants, contributions, and donations pursuant to this article shall be transmitted to the state treasurer, who shall credit the same to the substance abuse prevention, intervention, and treatment cash fund, which fund is hereby created and referred to in this section as the "fund". The moneys in the fund shall be subject to annual appropriation by the general assembly for the direct and indirect costs associated with the implementation of this article. All moneys in the fund not expended for the purpose of this article may be invested by the state treasurer as provided by law. All interest and income derived from the investment and deposit of moneys in the fund shall be credited to the fund. Any unexpended and unencumbered moneys remaining in the fund at the end of a fiscal year shall remain in the fund and shall not be credited or transferred to the general fund or another fund. All unexpended and unencumbered moneys remaining in the fund as of July 1, 2018, shall be transferred

to the general fund.

(b) It is the intent of the general assembly that the task force and the division of criminal justice of the department of public safety, on behalf of the task force, shall not be required to solicit gifts, grants, or donations from any source and that the task force shall operate in accordance with the provisions of this article, independently of the balance in the fund.

(2) Compensation as provided in section 18-18.5-103 (7) (b) for legislative members of the task force shall be approved by the chair of the legislative council and paid by vouchers and warrants drawn as provided by law from moneys appropriated for such purpose and allocated to the legislative council from the fund.


18-18.5-106. Repeal of article. This article is repealed, effective July 1, 2018.

### ARTICLE 19   Drug Offender Surcharge

18-19-101. Legislative declaration. The general assembly hereby finds, determines, and declares that the use of controlled substances exacts an unacceptable toll on the fiscal resources of both state and local government and thereby increases the fiscal burden on the taxpayers of this state. It is the intent of the general assembly in enacting this article to shift the costs of controlled substance use to those persons who unlawfully traffic, possess, or use controlled substances.

18-19-102. Definitions. As used in this article, unless the context otherwise requires:

"Alcohol- or drug-related offender" means a person convicted of any of the following offenses or of attempt to commit any of the following offenses:

Violation of a protection order as described in section 18-1-1001 (4), if the protection order prohibited the possession or consumption of alcohol or controlled substances and the violation related to such provisions;

Vehicular homicide as described in section 18-3-106 (1) (b);

Vehicular assault as described in section 18-3-205 (1) (b);

Bringing alcohol beverages into the major league stadium as described in section 18-9- 123 (1) (a) (I); or

Illegal possession or consumption of ethyl alcohol or marijuana by an underage person or illegal possession of marijuana paraphernalia by an underage person, as described in section 18- 13-122.

(1.5) "Convicted" and "conviction" means a plea of guilty, including a plea of guilty entered pursuant to a deferred sentence under section 18-1.3-102, or a verdict of guilty by a judge or jury,

and includes a plea of no contest accepted by the court.

"Drug offender" means any person convicted of any offense under article 18 of this title or an attempt to commit such offense as provided by article 2 of this title.


18-19-103. Source of revenues - allocation of moneys. (1) For offenses committed on and after July 1, 1996, each drug offender who is convicted, or receives a deferred sentence pursuant to section 18-1.3-102, shall be required to pay a surcharge to the clerk of the court in the county in which the conviction occurs or in which the deferred sentence is entered. Such surcharge shall be in the following amounts:

For each class 2 felony or level 1 drug felony of which a person is convicted, four thousand five hundred dollars;

For each class 3 felony or level 2 drug felony of which a person is convicted, three thousand dollars;

For each class 4 felony or level 3 drug felony of which a person is convicted, two thousand dollars;

For each class 5 felony or level 4 drug felony of which a person is convicted, one thousand five hundred dollars;

For each class 6 felony of which a person is convicted, one thousand two hundred fifty dollars;

For each class 1 misdemeanor or level 1 drug misdemeanor of which a person is convicted, one thousand dollars;

For each class 2 misdemeanor of which a person is convicted, six hundred dollars;

For each class 3 misdemeanor or level 2 drug misdemeanor of which a person is convicted, three hundred dollars.

Each drug offender convicted of a violation of section 18-18-406 (5) (a) (I), or who receives a deferred sentence pursuant to section 18-1.3-102 for a violation of section 18-18-406 (5)

(a) (I), shall be assessed a surcharge of two hundred dollars.

The clerk of the court shall disburse the surcharge required by subsection (1) of this section as follows:

Five percent shall be retained by the clerk for purposes of administering the disbursal of the surcharge pursuant to this subsection (3).

Four percent shall be disbursed to the investigating agency to cover the costs of fingerprinting and photographing offenders pursuant to section 16-21-104 (1), C.R.S.

One percent shall be disbursed to the sheriff of the county in which the conviction or deferred sentence is entered, to cover the costs of fingerprinting and photographing offenders pursuant to section 18-18-432 (3).

Ninety percent shall be disbursed to the state treasurer who shall credit the same to the correctional treatment cash fund created pursuant to subsection (4) of this section.

(3.5) (a) Repealed.

The general assembly shall appropriate to the correctional treatment cash fund created pursuant to subsection (4) of this section at least seven million six hundred fifty-six thousand two hundred dollars in fiscal year 2012-13 from the general fund, at least nine million five hundred

thousand dollars in fiscal year 2013-14 from the general fund, and each year thereafter generated from estimated savings from House Bill 10-1352, enacted in 2010.

The general assembly shall appropriate to the correctional treatment cash fund created pursuant to subsection (4) of this section at least three million five hundred thousand dollars in fiscal year 2014-15 from the general fund generated from estimated savings from Senate Bill 13-250, enacted in 2013.

(a) There is hereby created in the state treasury the correctional treatment cash fund, referred to in this paragraph (a) as the "fund", which consists of moneys appropriated pursuant to section 39-28.8-501, C.R.S., moneys received by the state treasurer pursuant to paragraph (d) of subsection (3) of this section and subsection (3.5) of this section, and, in addition, each year, the general assembly shall appropriate at least two million two hundred thousand dollars generated from estimated savings from the enactment of Senate Bill 03-318, enacted in 2003, to the fund. The moneys in the fund shall be used for the purposes described in paragraph (c) of subsection (5) of this section. All interest derived from the deposit and investment of moneys in the fund shall be credited to the fund. Any moneys not appropriated by the general assembly shall remain in the fund and shall not be transferred or revert to the general fund of the state at the end of any fiscal year.

(a.5) Repealed.

Notwithstanding any provision of paragraph (a) of this subsection (4) to the contrary, on April 20, 2009, the state treasurer shall deduct one hundred fifty-one thousand three hundred forty- one dollars from the drug offender surcharge fund and transfer such sum to the general fund.

Notwithstanding any provision of paragraph (a) of this subsection (4) to the contrary, on July 1, 2009, the state treasurer shall deduct one million three hundred sixty thousand dollars from the drug offender surcharge fund and transfer such sum to the general fund.

(a) The correctional treatment board, hereby created and referred to in this subsection (5) as the "board", shall prepare an annual treatment funding plan that includes a fair and reasonable allocation of resources for programs throughout the state. The judicial department shall include the annual treatment funding plan in its annual presentation to the joint budget committee.

The board consists of:

The executive director of the department of corrections or his or her designee;

The director of the division of probation services in the judicial department or his or her designee;

The executive director of the department of public safety or his or her designee;

The executive director of the department of human services or his or her designee. If the executive director appoints a designee, the executive director is encouraged to select someone with expertise in addiction counseling and substance abuse issues;

The state public defender or his or her designee;

The president of the statewide association representing district attorneys or his or her designee; and

The president of the statewide association representing county sheriffs or his or her designee.

The board may direct that moneys in the correctional treatment cash fund may be used for the following purposes:

Alcohol and drug screening, assessment, and evaluation;

Alcohol and drug testing;

Substance abuse education and training;

An annual statewide conference regarding substance abuse treatment;

Treatment for assessed substance abuse and co-occurring disorders;

Recovery support services; and

Administrative support to the correctional treatment board including, but not limited to, facilitating and coordinating data collection, conducting data analysis, developing contracts, preparing reports, scheduling and staffing board and subcommittee meetings, and engaging in budget planning and analysis.

Moneys from the correctional treatment cash fund may be used to serve the following populations:

Adults and juveniles on diversion for a state offense and adults and juveniles under supervision in a pretrial diversion program for a state offense;

Adults and juveniles serving a probation sentence for a state offense, including Denver county;

Adults and juveniles on parole;

Offenders sentenced or transitioned to a community corrections program;

Offenders serving a sentence in a county jail, on a work-release program supervised by

the county jail, or receiving after-care treatment following release from jail if the offender participated in a jail treatment program; and

Offenders on bond or on summons, with a pending criminal case in a pre-trial treatment program.

Before adopting the annual treatment fund plan, the board shall review the information specified in paragraph (f) of this subsection (5) and shall consider proposals from the drug offender treatment boards created in section 18-19-104 for funding local assessed treatment needs.

The board shall determine the scope, method, and frequency of the data collection and the parties responsible for data collection, analysis, and reporting. The data shall be organized by judicial district and shall include, at a minimum, the following from each treatment program:

Name and location of the program, including the county and judicial district;

The referring criminal agency;

Demographic information including gender and ethnicity;

Level of treatment delivered;

Actual length of time in treatment for each client;

Discharge status and, if the status is negative, the reason for the negative discharge; and

Any special licenses held by the treatment program. (5.5) Repealed.

(a) The court may not waive any portion of the surcharge required by this section unless the court first finds that the drug offender is financially unable to pay any portion of said surcharge.

The finding required by paragraph (a) of this subsection (6) shall only be made after a hearing at which the drug offender shall have the burden of presenting clear and convincing evidence that he is financially unable to pay any portion of the surcharge.

The court shall waive only that portion of the surcharge which the court has found the drug offender is financially unable to pay.

18-19-103.5. Rural alcohol and substance abuse surcharge - repeal. (1) In addition to the surcharges established in section 18-19-103, each drug offender and each alcohol- or drug-related offender who is convicted, or receives a deferred sentence pursuant to section 18-1.3-102, shall be required to pay a surcharge to the clerk of the court in the county in which the conviction occurs or in which the deferred sentence is entered. The surcharge shall be in an amount determined by the judge but shall be not less than one dollar nor more than ten dollars.

The clerk of the court shall disburse the surcharge required by subsection (1) of this section as follows:

Five percent shall be retained by the clerk for purposes of administering the disbursal of the surcharge pursuant to this subsection (2);

Ninety-five percent shall be disbursed to the state treasurer who shall credit the same to the rural alcohol and substance abuse cash fund created in section 27-80-117 (3), C.R.S.

The minimum penalty surcharge shall be mandatory, and the court shall have no discretion to suspend or waive the surcharge; except that the court may suspend or waive the surcharge for a defendant determined by the court to be indigent.

This section is repealed, effective July 1, 2016, unless the general assembly extends the repeal of the rural alcohol and substance abuse prevention and treatment program created in section 27-80-117, C.R.S.

18-19-104. Judicial district drug offender treatment boards. (1) Each judicial district shall create a drug offender treatment board, whose membership is knowledgeable about adult criminal and juvenile justice matters, consisting of:

The district attorney serving the judicial district or his or her designee;

The chief public defender serving the judicial district or his or her designee;

The chair of the local community corrections board or his or her designee;

A parole officer working in the judicial district chosen by the director of the department of corrections or his or her designee;

A sheriff that serves the judicial district chosen by the chief judge of the judicial district;

A representative of a drug court or similar problem-solving court if such a court exists in the judicial district chosen by the chief judge of the judicial district;

A person with expertise in juvenile matters chosen by the chief judge of the judicial district; and

A probation officer working in the judicial district chosen by the chief judge of the judicial district.

The board shall give priority to drug court funding if the jurisdiction operates a drug court and the drug court operates with best evidence-based or promising practices. Each drug offender treatment board shall annually make recommendations to the correctional treatment board

for funding local assessed treatment needs.

Each judicial district's drug offender treatment board may adopt rules and guidelines as necessary to perform the functions of the board.

and (5) Repealed.

### ARTICLE 20 Offenses Related to Limited Gaming

18-20-101. Legislative declaration. The general assembly hereby finds, determines, and declares that the strict control of limited gaming in this state is necessary for the immediate and future preservation of the public peace, health, and safety.

18-20-102. Definitions - terms used. (1) As used in this article, unless this article otherwise provides or unless the context otherwise requires, terms used in this article shall have the same meanings as those set forth in article 47.1 of title 12, C.R.S.

The term "repeating gambling offender" means anyperson who is convicted of an offense under section 18-10-103 (2), sections 18-10-105 to 18-10-107, or sections 18-20-103 to 18-20-114 or sections 12-47.1-809 to 12-47.1-811 or 12-47.1-818 to 12-47.1-832 or 12-47.1-839, C.R.S., within five years after a previous misdemeanor conviction under said sections or under a former statute prohibiting gambling activities or at any time after a previous felony conviction under any of said sections. A conviction in any jurisdiction of the United States of an offense which, if committed in this state, would be professional gambling shall constitute a previous conviction for purposes of a prosecution in this state as a repeating gambling offender.

18-20-103. Violations of taxation provisions - penalties. (1) Any person who:

Makes any false or fraudulent return in attempting to defeat or evade the tax imposed by article 47.1 of title 12, C.R.S., commits a class 5 felony;

Fails to pay tax due under article 47.1 of title 12, C.R.S., within thirty days after the date the tax becomes due commits a class 1 misdemeanor;

Fails to file a return required by article 47.1 of title 12, C.R.S., within thirty days after the date the return is due commits a class 1 misdemeanor;

Violates section 12-47.1-603 (1) (b) or (1) (c), C.R.S., two or more times in any twelve- month period commits a class 5 felony;

Willfully aids or assists in, or procures, counsels, or advises the preparation or presentation under or in connection with any matter arising under any title administered by the commission or a return, affidavit, claim, or other document which is fraudulent or is false as to any

material fact, whether or not such falsity or fraud is with the knowledge or consent of the person authorized or required to present such return, affidavit, claim, or document commits a class 5 felony.

(2) For purposes of this section, "person" includes corporate officers having control or supervision of, or responsibility for, completing tax returns or making payments pursuant to article

47.1 of title 12, C.R.S.


**18-20-104. False statement on application - violations of rules or provisions of article**

47.1 of title 12, C.R.S., as felony. Any person who knowingly makes a false statement in any application for a license or in any statement attached to the application, or who provides any false or misleading information to the commission or the division, or who fails to keep books and records to substantiate the receipts, expenses, or uses resulting from limited gaming conducted under article

47.1 of title 12, C.R.S., as prescribed in rules or regulations promulgated by the commission, or who falsifies any books or records which relate to any transaction connected with the holding, operating, and conducting of any limited card games or slot machines, or who knowingly violates any of the provisions of article 47.1 of title 12, C.R.S., or any rule or regulation adopted by the commission or any terms of any license granted under said article 47.1, commits a class 5 felony.


**18-20-105. Slot machines - shipping notices.** (1) Any slot machine manufacturer or distributor shipping or importing a slot machine into the state of Colorado shall provide to the Colorado limited gaming control commission created in section 12-47.1-301, C.R.S., at the time of shipment a copy of the shipping invoice which shall include, at a minimum, the destination, the serial number of each machine, and a description of each machine. Any person within the state of Colorado receiving a slot machine shall, upon receipt of the machine, provide to the Colorado limited gaming control commission upon a form available from the commission information showing at a minimum the location of each machine, its serial number, and description. Such report shall be provided regardless of whether the machine is received from a manufacturer or any other person. Anymachine licensed pursuant to section 12-47.1-803, C.R.S., shall be licensed for a specific location, and movement of the machine from that location shall be reported to said commission within the time period set out in rules promulgated pursuant to section 12-47.1-803 (1) (d), C.R.S. Any person violating any provision of section 12-47.1-803, C.R.S., commits a class 5 felony. Any slot machine which is not in compliance with article 47.1 of title 12, C.R.S., is declared contraband and may be summarily seized and destroyed after notice and hearing.

Slot machines which because of age and condition bear no manufacturer serial number shall be assigned a serial number by a remanufacturer of slot machines. Such new serial number shall be duly recorded as required by federal regulations.

The director of the division of gaming appointed pursuant to section 12-47.1-201, C.R.S., may approve a change to the registration of a slot machine under circumstances constituting an emergency. If said director approves such an emergency change, the registration of the slot machine shall not be suspended pending the filing of a supplemental application.


**18-20-106. Cheating.** (1) It is unlawful for any person, whether he is an owner or employee of, or a player in, an establishment, to cheat at any limited gaming activity.

For purposes of article 47.1 of title 12, C.R.S., "cheating" means to alter the selection of criteria which determine:

The result of a game; or

The amount or frequency of payment in a game.

Any person issued a license pursuant to article 47.1 of title 12, C.R.S., violating any provision of this section commits a class 6 felony, and any other person violating any provision of this section commits a class 1 misdemeanor. If the person is a repeating gambling offender, the person commits a class 5 felony.


**18-20-107. Fraudulent acts.** (1) It is unlawful for any person:

To alter or misrepresent the outcome of a game or other event on which wagers have been made after the outcome is made sure but before it is revealed to the players;

To place, increase, or decrease a bet or to determine the course of play after acquiring knowledge, not available to all players, of the outcome of the game or any event that affects the outcome of the game or which is the subject of the bet or to aid anyone in acquiring such knowledge for the purpose of placing, increasing, or decreasing a bet or determining the course of play contingent upon that event or outcome;

To claim, collect, or take, or attempt to claim, collect, or take, money or anything of value in or from a limited gaming activity with intent to defraud and without having made a wager contingent thereon, or to claim, collect, or take an amount greater than the amount won;

Knowingly to entice or induce another to go to any place where limited gaming is being conducted or operated in violation of the provisions of article 47.1 of title 12, C.R.S., with the intent that the other person play or participate in that limited gaming activity;

To place or increase a bet after acquiring knowledge of the outcome of the game or other event which is the subject of the bet, including past-posting and pressing bets;

To reduce the amount wagered or to cancel a bet after acquiring knowledge of the outcome of the game or other event which is the subject of the bet, including pinching bets;

To manipulate, with the intent to cheat, any component of a gaming device in a manner contrary to the designed and normal operational purpose for the component, including, but not limited to, varying the pull of the handle of a slot machine, with knowledge that the manipulation affects the outcome of the game or with knowledge of any event that affects the outcome of the game;

To, by any trick or sleight of hand performance, or by fraud or fraudulent scheme, cards, or device, for himself or another, win or attempt to win money or property or a representative of either or reduce a losing wager or attempt to reduce a losing wager in connection with limited gaming;

To conduct any limited gaming operation without a valid license;

To conduct any limited gaming operation on an unlicensed premises;

To permit any limited gaming game or slot machine to be conducted, operated, dealt, or carried on in any limited gaming premises by a person other than a person licensed for such premises pursuant to article 47.1 of title 12, C.R.S.;

To place any limited gaming games or slot machines into play or display such games or slot machines without the authorization of the Colorado limited gaming control commission;

To employ or continue to employ any person in a limited gaming operation who is not duly licensed or registered in a position whose duties require a license or registration pursuant to article 47.1 of title 12, C.R.S.; or

To, without first obtaining the requisite license or registration pursuant to article 47.1 of title 12, C.R.S., be employed, work, or otherwise act in a position whose duties would require licensing or registration pursuant to said article.

Any person issued a license pursuant to article 47.1 of title 12, C.R.S., violating any provision of this section commits a class 6 felony, and any other person violating any provision of this section commits a class 1 misdemeanor. If the person is a repeating gambling offender, the person commits a class 5 felony.


18-20-108. Use of device for calculating probabilities. (1) It is unlawful for any person at a licensed gaming establishment to use, or possess with the intent to use, any device to assist:

In projecting the outcome of the game;

In keeping track of the cards played;

In analyzing the probability of the occurrence of an event relating to the game; or

In analyzing the strategy for playing or betting to be used in the game, except as permitted by the Colorado limited gaming control commission.

(2) Any person issued a license pursuant to article 47.1 of title 12, C.R.S., violating any provision of this section commits a class 6 felony and any other person violating any provision of this section commits a class 1 misdemeanor. If the person is a repeating gambling offender, the person commits a class 5 felony.


18-20-109. Use of counterfeit or unapproved chips or tokens or unlawful coins or devices - possession of certain unlawful devices, equipment, products, or materials. (1) It is unlawful for any licensee, employee, or other person to use counterfeit chips in any limited gaming activity.

It is unlawful for any person, in playing or using any limited gaming activity designed to be played with, to receive, or to be operated by chips or tokens approved by the Colorado limited gaming control commission or by lawful coin of the United States of America:

Knowingly to use anything other than chips or tokens approved by the Colorado limited gaming control commission or lawful coin, legal tender of the United States of America, or to use coin not of the same denomination as the coin intended to be used in that limited gaming activity; or

To use any device or means to violate the provisions of article 47.1 of title 12, C.R.S.

It is unlawful for any person to possess any device, equipment, or material which he knows has been manufactured, distributed, sold, tampered with, or serviced in violation of the provisions of article 47.1 of title 12, C.R.S.

It is unlawful for any person, not a duly authorized employee of a licensee acting in furtherance of his or her employment within an establishment, to have on his or her person or in his or her possession any device intended to be used to violate the provisions of article 47.1 of title 12, C.R.S.

It is unlawful for any person, not a duly authorized employee of a licensee acting in furtherance of his or her employment within an establishment, to have on his or her person or in his or her possession while on the premises of any licensed gaming establishment any key or device known to have been designed for the purpose of and suitable for opening, entering, or affecting the operation of any limited gaming activity, drop box, or electronic or mechanical device connected thereto, or for removing money or other contents therefrom.

Possession of more than one of the devices, equipment, products, or materials described in this section shall give rise to a rebuttable presumption that the possessor intended to use them for cheating.

It is unlawful for any person to use or possess while on the premises any cheating or thieving device, including but not limited to, tools, drills, wires, coins, or tokens attached to strings or wires or electronic or magnetic devices, to facilitate the alignment of any winning combination or to facilitate removing from any slot machine any money or contents thereof, unless the person is a duly authorized gaming employee acting in the furtherance of his or her employment.

Any person violating any provision of this section commits a class 6 felony; except that, if the person is a repeating gambling offender, the person commits a class 5 felony.


18-20-110. Cheating game and devices. (1) It is unlawful for any person playing any licensed game in licensed gaming premises to:

Knowingly conduct, carry on, operate, or deal or allow to be conducted, carried on, operated, or dealt any cheating or thieving game or device; or

Knowinglydeal, conduct, carryon, operate, or expose for play any game or games played with cards or any mechanical device, or any combination of games or devices, which have in any manner been marked or tampered with or placed in a condition or operated in a manner the result of which tends to deceive the public or tends to alter the normal random selection of characteristics or the normal chance of the game which could determine or alter the result of the game.

(2) Any person violating any provision of this section commits a class 6 felony; except that, if the person is a repeating gambling offender, the person commits a class 5 felony.


18-20-111. Unlawful manufacture, sale, distribution, marking, altering, or modification of equipment and devices related to limited gaming - unlawful instruction. (1) It is unlawful to manufacture, sell, or distribute any cards, chips, dice, game, or device which is intended to be used to violate any provision of article 47.1 of title 12, C.R.S.

It is unlawful to mark, alter, or otherwise modify related equipment or a limited gaming device in a manner that:

Affects the result of a wager by determining win or loss; or

Alters the normal criteria of random selection, which affects the operation of a game or

which determines the outcome of a game.

It is unlawful for any person to instruct another in cheating or in the use of any device for that purpose, with the knowledge or intent that the information or use so conveyed may be employed to violate any provision of article 47.1 of title 12, C.R.S.

Any person issued a license pursuant to article 47.1 of title 12, C.R.S., violating any provision of this section commits a class 6 felony, and any other person violating any provision of this section commits a class 1 misdemeanor. If the person is a repeating gambling offender, the person commits a class 5 felony.

18-20-112. Unlawful entry by excluded and ejected persons. (1) It is unlawful for any person whose name is on the list promulgated by the Colorado limited gaming control commission pursuant to section 12-47.1-1001 or 12-47.1-1002, C.R.S., to enter the licensed premises of a limited gaming licensee.

It is unlawful for any person whose name is on the list promulgated by the Colorado limited gaming control commission pursuant to section 12-47.1-1001 or 12-47.1-1002, C.R.S., to have any personal pecuniary interest, direct or indirect, in any limited gaming licensee, licensed premises, establishment, or business involved in or with limited gaming or in the shares in any corporation, association, or firm licensed pursuant to article 47.1 of title 12, C.R.S.

Any person violating the provisions of this section commits a class 5 felony.

18-20-113. Personal pecuniary gain or conflict of interest. (1) It is unlawful for any person to issue, suspend, revoke, or renew any license pursuant to article 47.1 of title 12, C.R.S., for any personal pecuniary gain or any thing of value, as defined in section 18-1-901 (3) (r), or for any person to violate any of the provisions of part 4 of article 47.1 of title 12, C.R.S.

(2) Any person violating any of the provisions of this section commits a class 3 felony.

18-20-114. False or misleading information - unlawful. (1) It is unlawful for any person to provide any false or misleading information under the provisions of article 47.1 of title 12, C.R.S.

(2) Any person violating any of the provisions of this section commits a class 5 felony.

18-20-115. Exceptions. Nothing contained in this article shall be construed to modify, amend, or otherwise affect the validity of any provisions contained in article 10 of this title.

### ARTICLE 21  Sex Offender Surcharge

18-21-101. Legislative declaration. The general assembly hereby finds, determines, and declares that the commission of sex offenses exacts an unacceptable toll on the fiscal resources of both state and local government and thereby increases the fiscal burden upon the taxpayers of this state. It is the intent of the general assembly in enacting this article to require, as much as possible, that persons convicted of a sex offense pay for the cost of the evaluation, identification, and treatment and continuing monitoring to protect victims and potential victims as described in article of title 16, C.R.S.

18-21-102. Definitions. As used in this article, unless the context otherwise requires:
"Convicted" and "conviction" means a plea of guilty, including a plea of guilty entered pursuant to a deferred sentence under section 18-1.3-102 or a verdict of guilty by a judge or jury, and includes a plea of no contest accepted by the court.
"Sex offense" has the same meaning as defined in section 16-11.7-102 (3), C.R.S.

18-21-103. Source of revenues - allocation of moneys - sex offender surcharge fund - creation. (1) On and after July 1, 1992, each person who is convicted of a sex offense, or receives for such offense a deferred sentence pursuant to section 18-1.3-102, shall be required to pay a surcharge to the clerk of the court in which the conviction occurs or in which the deferred sentence is entered. Such surcharge shall be in the following amounts:
For each class 2 felony of which a person is convicted, three thousand dollars;

For each class 3 felony of which a person is convicted, two thousand dollars;
For each class 4 felony of which a person is convicted, one thousand dollars;
For each class 5 felony of which a person is convicted, seven hundred fifty dollars;
For each class 6 felony of which a person is convicted, five hundred dollars;
For each class 1 misdemeanor of which a person is convicted, four hundred dollars;
For each class 2 misdemeanor of which a person is convicted, three hundred dollars;
For each class 3 misdemeanor of which a person is convicted, one hundred fifty dollars. (1.5) On and after July 1, 2000, each juvenile who is adjudicated for commission of an offense that would constitute a sex offense if committed by an adult or who receives for such offense a deferred adjudication shall be required to pay a surcharge to the clerk of the court in which the adjudication occurs or in which the deferred adjudication is entered. The amount of such surcharge shall be half the amount that would have been assessed against an adult offender pursuant to subsection (1) of this section for commission of the offense.
The clerk of the court shall allocate the surcharge required by subsection (1) of this section as follows:
Five percent shall be retained by the clerk for administrative costs incurred pursuant to this subsection (2). Such amount retained shall be transmitted to the state treasurer, who shall credit the same to the general fund, and such amount shall be subject to appropriation by the general

assembly for the costs of such administration.
Ninety-five percent shall be transferred to the state treasurer who shall credit the same to the sex offender surcharge fund created pursuant to subsection (3) of this section.
There is hereby created in the state treasury a sex offender surcharge fund which shall consist of moneys received by the state treasurer pursuant to paragraph (b) of subsection (2) of this section. The state treasurer may invest any moneys in the fund not expended for the purpose of this section as provided by law. The state treasurer shall credit all interest and income derived from the investment and deposit of moneys in the fund to the fund. Any moneys not appropriated by the general assembly shall remain in the sex offender surcharge fund and shall not be transferred or revert to the general fund of the state at the end of any fiscal year. All moneys in the fund shall be subject to annual appropriation by the general assembly to the judicial department, the department of corrections, the division of criminal justice of the department of public safety, and the department of human services, after consideration of the plan developed pursuant to section 16-11.7-103 (4) (c), C.R.S., to cover the direct and indirect costs associated with the evaluation, identification, and treatment and the continued monitoring of sex offenders.
The court may waive all or any portion of the surcharge required by this section if the court finds that a person convicted of a sex offense is indigent or financially unable to pay all or any portion of such surcharge. The court shall waive only that portion of the surcharge which the court has found that the person convicted of a sex offense is financially unable to pay.

### ARTICLE 22    Juvenile Offender Surcharge

18-22-101. Legislative declaration. The general assembly hereby finds, determines, and declares that the commission of violent crimes by juveniles exacts an unacceptable toll on the fiscal resources of both state and local government and thereby increases the financial burden upon the taxpayers of this state. It is the intent of the general assembly in enacting this article to require, as much as possible, that juveniles convicted as adults of violent crimes pay for the cost of the rehabilitation, education, and treatment of juveniles sentenced to the youthful offender system or committed to the department of human services.

18-22-102. Definitions. As used in this article, unless the context otherwise requires:
"Convicted" and "conviction" means a plea of guilty, including a plea of guilty entered pursuant to a deferred sentence under section 18-1.3-102 or a verdict of guilty by a judge or jury, and includes a plea of no contest accepted by the court.
"Juvenile" means a person under the age of eighteen years.
"Violent crime" means a felony enumerated as a crime of violence pursuant to section 18-1.3-406 or a felony involving a weapon or firearm.

18-22-103. Source of revenues - allocation of moneys. (1) Each juvenile who is convicted as an adult of a violent crime shall be required to pay a surcharge to the clerk of the court in which the conviction occurs in an amount equal to any fine imposed by such court.
The clerk of the court shall allocate the surcharge required by subsection (1) of this section as follows:
(I) Five percent shall be retained by the clerk for administrative costs incurred pursuant to this section. Such amount retained shall be transmitted to the state treasurer, who shall credit the same to the general fund, and such amount shall be subject to appropriation by the general assembly for the costs of such administration.
(II) Notwithstanding the provisions of subparagraph (I) of this paragraph (a), on and after July 1, 2008, the portion of the surcharge that is retained under this paragraph (a) shall be transmitted to the state treasurer for deposit in the judicial stabilization cash fund created in section 13-32-101 (6), C.R.S.
Ninety-five percent shall be transferred to the state treasurer who shall credit the same to the youthful offender system surcharge fund created pursuant to subsection (3) of this section.
There is hereby created in the state treasury a youthful offender system surcharge fund which shall consist of moneys received by the state treasurer pursuant to paragraph (b) of subsection
of this section. In accordancewith section 24-36-114, C.R.S., all interest derived from the deposit and investment of this fund shall be credited to the general fund. Any moneys not appropriated by the general assembly shall remain in the youthful offender system surcharge fund and shall not be transferred or revert to the general fund of the state at the end of any fiscal year. All moneys in the fund shall be subject to annual appropriation by the general assembly to the department of corrections to cover the direct and indirect costs associated with the rehabilitation, education, and treatment of youthful offenders sentenced to a youthful offender system.
(4) A surcharge assessed by the court pursuant to this section may be collected in the same manner as a judgment in a civil action and the court shall order the district attorney to institute proceedings to collect such surcharge if the court finds that a juvenile convicted as an adult of a violent crime is financially unable to pay all or any portion of such surcharge at the time of sentencing.

## ARTICLE 23   Gang Recruitment Act

18-23-101. Definitions. As used in this article, unless the context otherwise requires:
"Criminal street gang" means any ongoing organization, association, or group of three
or more persons, whether formal or informal:
Which has as one of its primary objectives or activities the commission of one or more predicate criminal acts; and
Whose members individually or collectively engage in or have engaged in a pattern of criminal gang activity.
"Pattern of criminal gang activity" means the commission, attempt, conspiracy, or solicitation of two or more predicate criminal acts which are committed on separate occasions or by two or more persons.
"Predicate criminal acts" means the commission of or attempt, conspiracy, or solicitation to commit any of the following:
Any conduct defined as racketeering activity in section 18-17-103 (5);
Any violation of section 18-8-706 or any criminal act committed in any jurisdiction of the United States which, if committed in this state, would violate section 18-8-706.

18-23-102. Recruitment of juveniles for a criminal street gang. (1) A person commits recruitment of a juvenile for a criminal street gang if he or she is eighteen years of age or older and:
Knowingly solicits, invites, recruits, encourages, coerces, or otherwise causes a person younger than eighteen years of age to actively participate in or become a member of a criminal street gang; or
By use of force, threat, or intimidation directed at any person, or by the infliction of bodily injury upon any person, knowingly prevents a person younger than eighteen years of age from leaving a criminal street gang.
Recruitment of a juvenile for a criminal street gang is a class 1 misdemeanor.

Nothing in this section shall affect the ability to charge criminal offenses under article 17 of this title.

## ARTICLE 24   Crimes Against Children Surcharge

18-24-101. Definitions. As used in this article, unless the context otherwise requires:
"Convicted" and "conviction" mean a plea of guilty accepted by the court, including a plea of guilty entered pursuant to a deferred sentence under section 18-1.3-102, a verdict of guilty by a judge or jury, or a plea of no contest accepted by the court.
"Crime against a child" means anyoffense listed in section 18-3-411, or criminal attempt, conspiracy, or solicitation to commit any of those offenses, and any of the following offenses, or criminal attempt, conspiracy, or solicitation to commit any of the following offenses:
Incest, in violation of section 18-6-301;
Child abuse, in violation of section 18-6-401;
Contributing to the delinquency of a minor, in violation of section 18-6-701;
Internet luring of a child, in violation of section 18-3-306;
Sexual assault on a client by a psychotherapist, in violation of section 18-3-405.5, when the victim is a child;
Invasion of privacy for sexual gratification, in violation of section 18-3-405.6, when the victim is a child; or
Human trafficking of a minor for involuntary servitude, in violation of section 18-3-503.

18-24-102. Surcharge. (1) Each person who is convicted of a crime against a child shall be required to pay a surcharge to the clerk of the court for the judicial district in which the conviction occurs.

Surcharges pursuant to subsection (1) of this section shall be in the following amounts:

For each class 2 felony of which a person is convicted, one thousand five hundred dollars;

For each class 3 felony of which a person is convicted, one thousand dollars;

For each class 4 felony of which a person is convicted, five hundred dollars;

For each class 5 felony of which a person is convicted, three hundred seventy-five dollars;

For each class 6 felony of which a person is convicted, two hundred fifty dollars;

For each class 1 misdemeanor of which a person is convicted, two hundred dollars;

For each class 2 misdemeanor of which a person is convicted, one hundred fifty dollars; and

For each class 3 misdemeanor of which a person is convicted, seventy-five dollars.

18-24-103. Collection and distribution of funds - child abuse investigation surcharge fund - creation. (1) The clerk of the court shall allocate the surcharge required by section 18-24-102 as follows:

Five percent shall be retained by the clerk of the court for administrative costs incurred pursuant to this subsection (1). Such amount retained shall be transmitted to the state treasurer for deposit in the judicial stabilization cash fund created in section 13-32-101 (6), C.R.S.

Ninety-five percent shall be transferred to the state treasurer, who shall credit the same to the child abuse investigation surcharge fund created pursuant to subsection (2) of this section.

(a) There is hereby created in the state treasury the child abuse investigation surcharge fund that shall consist of moneys received by the state treasurer pursuant to this section. The moneys in the fund shall be subject to annual appropriation by the general assembly to the division of criminal justice in the department of public safety for distribution to the state chapter of a nonprofit or not-for-profit organization that coordinates programs that offer a multidisciplinary team response for child sexual abuse intervention in child-friendly, child-appropriate facilities, referred to in this section as the "state chapter".

(a.1) The division of criminal justice in the department of public safety shall establish guidelines for the distribution of the moneys from the fund, including but not limited to:

Procedures for programs to use in applying to the state chapter for moneys from the fund;

Procedures for the state chapter to use in reporting to the division pursuant to paragraph (a.7) of this subsection (2); and

Accountability and performance standards for programs that receive moneys from the fund.

(a.3) The state chapter may use a portion of the moneys that it receives pursuant to paragraph of this subsection (2) for training and technical assistance to facilitate the coordination of programs that offer a multidisciplinary team response for child sexual abuse intervention in child- friendly, child-appropriate facilities. The state chapter shall distribute the remainder of the moneys directly to the programs.

(a.5) Each program that receives moneys from the fund shall:

Include in the services provided forensic interviews, therapeutic intervention, medical evaluations, victim advocacy, case tracking, and case review;

Have a signed interagency agreement and protocol with the law enforcement agencies, the district attorney's office, and the county department of social services in the jurisdiction where the program is operating;

Meet the national performance standards of a national accrediting body that requires programs to satisfy the criteria described in subparagraphs (I) and (II) of this paragraph (a.5); and

Satisfy the accountability and performance standards established by the division pursuant to subparagraph (III) of paragraph (a.1) of this subsection (2).

(a.7) The state chapter shall report to the division of criminal justice in the department of public safety on a regular basis to be specified by the division of criminal justice. The report shall include, but need not be limited to:

A list of all programs that received moneys from the fund in the preceding fiscal year;

A description of how each program that received moneys from the fund in the preceding fiscal year used those moneys;

Documentation demonstrating that each program that received moneys from the fund in the preceding fiscal year satisfied all of the criteria specified in paragraph (a.5) of this subsection (2); and

Documentation demonstrating that each program that received moneys from the fund in the preceding fiscal year satisfied all of the accountability and performance standards established by the division pursuant to subparagraph (III) of paragraph (a.1) of this subsection (2).

The division of criminal justice shall not expend any moneys until the fund has enough money to pay the expenses necessary to administer the fund. All interest derived from the deposit and investment of moneys in the fund shall be credited to the fund. Any moneys not appropriated by the general assembly shall remain in the fund and shall not be transferred or revert to the general fund of the state at the end of any fiscal year.

The court may waive all or any portion of the surcharge required by section 18-24-102 if the court finds that a person convicted of a crime against a child is indigent or financially unable to pay all or any portion of the surcharge. The court may waive only that portion of the surcharge that the court finds that the person convicted of a crime against a child is financially unable to pay.

### ARTICLE 25    Restorative Justice Surcharge

18-25-101. Restorative justice surcharge - definitions. (1) Each person who is convicted of a crime and each juvenile adjudicated of a crime shall be required to pay a ten-dollar surcharge to the clerk of the court for the judicial district in which the conviction occurs.

The clerk of the court shall allocate the surcharge required by subsection (1) of this section as follows:

Five percent shall be retained by the clerk of the court for administrative costs incurred pursuant to this subsection (1). Such amount retained shall be transmitted to the state treasurer for deposit in the judicial stabilization cash fund created in section 13-32-101 (6), C.R.S.

Ninety-five percent shall be transferred to the state treasurer, who shall credit the same to the restorative justice surcharge fund created pursuant to subsection (3) of this section.

(a) There is created in the state treasury the restorative justice surcharge fund that consists of moneys received by the state treasurer pursuant to this section and section 19-2-213 (4.5),

C.R.S. The moneys in the fund are subject to annual appropriation by the general assembly to the judicial department for distribution to judicial districts that offer restorative justice programs and to the restorative justice coordinating council for administrative expenses.

The judicial department shall establish guidelines for the distribution of the moneys from the fund to assist in defraying the costs of restorative justice programs, including but not limited to procedures for programs to use in applying to the judicial department for moneys from the fund.

The judicial department shall not expend any moneys until the fund has enough money to pay the expenses necessary to administer the fund.

All interest derived from the deposit and investment of moneys in the fund must be credited to the fund. Any moneys not appropriated by the general assembly must remain in the fund and may not be transferred or revert to the general fund of the state at the end of any fiscal year.

The court may waive all or any portion of the surcharge required by subsection (1) of this section if the court finds that a person or juvenile is indigent or financially unable to pay all or any portion of the surcharge. The court may waive only that portion of the surcharge that the court finds that the person or juvenile is financially unable to pay.

As used in this section, "convicted" and "conviction" mean a plea of guilty accepted by the court, including a plea of guilty entered pursuant to a deferred sentence under section 18-1.3-102, a verdict of guilty by a judge or jury, or a plea of no contest accepted by the court.

### ARTICLE 26  Statewide Discovery Sharing System Surcharge

18-26-101. Statewide discovery sharing system surcharge. (1) Each person who is represented by private counsel or appears pro se and is convicted of a felony, misdemeanor, drug felony, or drug misdemeanor shall be required to pay a surcharge to the clerk of the court for the judicial district in which the conviction occurs.

Surcharges pursuant to subsection (1) of this section are in the following amounts:

For each felony or drug felony of which a person is convicted, ten dollars; and

For each misdemeanor or drug misdemeanor of which a person is convicted, five dollars.

The court may waive all or any portion of the surcharge required by this section if the court finds that a person convicted of a crime is indigent or financially unable to pay all or any portion of the surcharge. The court may waive only that portion of the surcharge that the court finds that the person convicted of a crime is financially unable to pay.

Repealed.


18-26-102. Collection and distribution of funds - statewide discovery sharing system surcharge fund - creation. (1) The clerk of the court shall allocate the surcharge required by section 18-26-101 as follows:

Five percent shall be retained by the clerk of the court for administrative costs incurred pursuant to this subsection (1). The amount retained shall be transmitted to the state treasurer for deposit in the judicial stabilization cash fund created in section 13-32-101 (6), C.R.S.

Ninety-five percent shall be transferred to the state treasurer, who shall credit the same to the statewide discovery sharing system surcharge fund created pursuant to subsection (2) of this section.

(2) (a) There is created in the state treasury the statewide discovery sharing surcharge fund that consists of moneys received by the state treasurer pursuant to this section. The moneys in the fund are subject to annual appropriation by the general assembly to the judicial department for distribution to the Colorado district attorneys' council for development, continuing enhancement, and maintenance of the statewide discoverysharing system under section 16-9-702, C.R.S. These moneys are in addition to general fund moneys appropriated to the judicial department for distribution to the Colorado district attorneys' council for development, continuing enhancement, and maintenance of the statewide discovery sharing system under section 16-9-702, C.R.S.

(b) The state treasurer shall credit all interest derived from the deposit and investment of moneys in the fund to the fund. Any moneys not appropriated by the general assembly must remain in the fund and shall not be transferred or revert to the general fund of the state at the end of any fiscal year.

Made in the USA
Middletown, DE
14 September 2024